Handbook of
Wage and Salary
Administration

Second Edition

Handbook of Wage and Salary Administration

Milton L. Rock *editor-in-chief*
MANAGING PARTNER, THE HAY GROUP

McGraw-Hill Book Company

New York   St. Louis   San Francisco   Auckland
Bogotá   Hamburg   Johannesburg   London
Madrid   Mexico   Montreal   New Delhi
Panama   Paris   São Paulo   Singapore
Sydney   Tokyo   Toronto

Library of Congress Cataloging in Publication Data

Main entry under title:
Handbook of wage and salary administration.

    Includes index.
    1. Compensation management—Handbooks, manuals,
etc.   I. Rock, Milton L.
HF5549.5.C67H36 1983   658.3'2   82-22876
ISBN 0-07-053349-0

    5 6 7 8 9   VBVB   898

ISBN 0-07-053349-0

The coordinating editor for this book was David L. Hewitt,
the editors were William F. Newton, Bonnie Binkert, and Chet Gottfried,
the designer was Naomi Auerbach, and the production
supervisor was Thomas G. Kowalczyk. It was set in Melior
by University Graphics, Inc.

*To the next generation, especially Liza Herzog
and William and Thomas Rock. May their contribution
fulfill this generation's aspirations for them.*

Contents

Part K. Trends and Issues

Part L. Total Remuneration

Dr. Milton L. Rock's professional life has been devoted to management consulting. He joined Hay Associates in 1949 and directed the firm's growth to its current standing as the largest human resources consulting firm in the world. Today the enterprises and activities of the Hay Group are carried forward by a network of more than 90 offices in 28 countries. Dr. Rock served as Managing Partner of the Hay Group until it was acquired by Saatchi & Saatchi Company PLC of London in December 1984, at which time he became Chairman and CEO of Hay Group, Inc. In October 1985, he relinquished chairmanship of Hay Group, Inc., and became Chairman of Saatchi & Saatchi Consulting (UK) Limited. In 1986, Dr. Rock retired from an active role in the consulting business and became Chairman Emeritus of Saatchi & Saatchi. He is also Chairman of MLR Publishing Company and Publisher of *Mergers and Acquisitions* and *Directors and Boards.*

Dr. Rock holds a B.A. and M.A. from Temple University and a Ph.D. in psychology from the University of Rochester. He is a Fellow and Diplomat, American Psychological Association, Industrial Psychology; past President of the Association of Management Consultants (ACME); and a founding member of the institute of Management Consultants, Inc.

His fields of specialization in management consulting include general management, organization, manpower development and compensation, and business strategy. He has written extensively in both professional and business publications, is the author of psychological instruments, is coauthor of *The Executive Perceptanalytic Scale* and *Development of Bank Management Personnel,* and is editor of *The Mergers and Acquisitions Handbook.*

Dr. Rock served on the President's National Commission for Manpower Policy from September 1974 until August 1977, and in September 1974 he became a member of the Board of Governors of Temple University Hospital, for which he currently serves as Chairman. In 1979, he became a Trustee of Temple University. In 1981 he joined the Advisory Council of the J. L. Kellogg Graduate School of Management at Northwestern University; he also became a member of the Philadelphia Orchestra Board. In 1983, he became a member of the boards of the Curtis Institute of Music and of the Pennsylvania Ballet. He joined the board of the Philadelphia Museum of Art in 1986.

Contributors

JAROLD G. ABBOTT *Professor of Management, College of Business and Public Administration, Florida Atlantic University, Boca Raton, Fla.* (CHAPTER 21)

R. C. ALBRIGHT *Director, Human Resources, Student Loan Marketing Association, Washington, D.C.* (CHAPTER 23)

LOIS H. BARKER *Partner, The Hay Group, Philadelphia, Pa.* (CHAPTER 40)

MARSH W. BATES *Partner, The Hay Group, Chicago, Ill.* (CHAPTER 65)

ALVIN O. BELLAK *General Partner, The Hay Group, Philadelphia, Pa.* (CHAPTER 15)

EUGENE J. BENGE *Boca Raton, Fla.* (CHAPTER 12)

ROGER L. BOBERTZ *Director, Corporate Compensation Department, Union Carbide Corporation, Danbury, Conn.* (CHAPTER 49)

PHYLLIS K. BONFIELD *Administrative Management Society, Willow Grove, Pa.* (CHAPTER 37)

ALFRED R. BRANDT *Senior Wage Practices Specialist (Retired), Western Electric Company, Inc., Greensboro, N.C.* (CHAPTER 2)

PHILIP S. BRAUN *Compensation Consultant, General Electric Company, Fairfield, Conn.* (CHAPTER 18)

JOHN H. BURNETT *Principal, The Hay Group, Chicago, Ill.* (CHAPTER 7)

JESSE T. CANTRILL *Principal, The Hay Group, Philadelphia, Pa.* (CHAPTER 5)

MICHAEL F. CARTER *Vice President, Hay/Huggins, Philadelphia, Pa.* (CHAPTER 44)

JOHN T. CHANDLER *Manager of Compensation and Benefits, Cox Cable Communications, Atlanta, Ga.* (CHAPTER 54)

CHARLES J. COGILL *Professor, Graduate School of Business, University of Witwatersrand, Johannesburg, South Africa* (CHAPTER 10)

HERBERT F. CREHAN *Partner, The Hay Group, Boston, Mass.* (CHAPTER 43)

C. S. DADAKIS *Manager, Compensation, Howmet Aluminum Corporation, Greenwich, Conn.* (CHAPTER 49)

ROBERT J. DAVENPORT, JR. *Principal, The Hay Group, Chicago, Ill.* (CHAPTER 29)

JAMES H. DAVIS   *General Manager, Compensation, Aluminum Company of America, Pittsburgh, Pa.* (CHAPTERS 1, 56, *and* 59)

ROY DELIZIA   *Senior Principal, The Hay Group, Philadelphia, Pa.* (CHAPTER 27)

CHARLES R. DRAUGHON, JR.   *Senior Staff Advisor, Compensation, Exxon Company, U.S.A., Houston, Tex.* (CHAPTER 35)

J. R. ENGEL   *Director, Executive Compensation Service, Inc., New York, N.Y.* (CHAPTER 38)

T. MICHAEL FAIN   *Manager, Wage and Salary Administration, Duke Power Company, Charlotte, N.C.* (CHAPTER 32)

GLENN T. FISCHBACH   *Director Emeritus of Engineering Services, American Association of Industrial Management, Willow Grove, Pa.* (CHAPTER 13)

KENNETH E. FOSTER   *Director, Compensation Planning, Towers, Perrin, Forster & Crosby, New York, N.Y.* (CHAPTER 42)

RICHARD C. FREMON   *Past Chairman, Engineering Manpower Commission, New York, N.Y.* (CHAPTER 58)

WILLIAM GOMBERG   *Professor of Industrial Relations and Management, Wharton School, University of Pennsylvania, Philadelphia, Pa.* (CHAPTER 17)

DORIS M. GRAFF   *Manager of Surveys, Administrative Management Society, Willow Grove, Pa.* (CHAPTER 37)

HAROLD B. GUERCI   *Director, Salary Administration, Bell Telephone Laboratories, Murray Hill, N.J.* (CHAPTER 53)

W. T. HAIGH   *Manager, Corporate Compensation, General Foods Corporation, White Plains, N.Y.* (CHAPTER 33)

HEIDI I. HARTMANN   *Associate Executive Director, Commission on Behavioral and Social Sciences and Education, National Academy of Sciences, Washington, D.C.* (CHAPTER 63)

ALLAN T. HAUSER   *Manager, Corporate Compensation Planning, Merrill Lynch & Co., Inc., New York, N.Y.* (CHAPTER 26)

RICHARD I. HENDERSON   *Professor, Department of Management, Georgia State University, Atlanta, Ga.* (CHAPTER 54)

R. E. HOLLERBACH   *Management Consultant, Retired Personnel Director, Parke Davis & Co., Detroit, Mich.* (CHAPTER 16)

WILLIAM H. HRABAK   *Director, Compensation and Benefits, Bankers Life and Casualty Company, Chicago, Ill.* (CHAPTER 25)

R. W. HUDOCK   *Staff Vice President, Compensation and Benefits, Scott Paper Company, Philadelphia, Pa.* (CHAPTER 3)

VICTOR P. IANNUZZI   *Vice President, Citibank, N.A., New York, N.Y.* (CHAPTER 30)

BERNARD INGSTER   *Consultant in Human Resources Management, Philadelphia, Pa.* (CHAPTER 22)

R. G. JAMISON   *Corporate Director of Compensation, Rockwell International Corporation, Pittsburgh, Pa.* (CHAPTER 52)

HARRY L. JUDD   *Vice President, Personnel, United States Gypsum Company, Chicago, Ill.* (CHAPTER 24)

CHRISTY KARR   *General Manager, American Association of Industrial Management, Willow Grove, Pa.* (CHAPTER 13)

PAUL A. KATZ   *Assistant Director, U.S. Office of Personnel Management, Washington, D.C.* (CHAPTER 14)

IRA T. KAY   *Senior Principal, The Hay Group, Philadelphia, Pa.*   (CHAPTER 4)

ALAN LANGER   *Former Consultant, The Hay Group, Boston, Mass.*   (CHAPTER 51)

JAMES E. McELWAIN   *Assistant Vice President of Compensation and Benefits, NCR Corporation, Dayton, Ohio*   (CHAPTER 57)

DAVID J. McLAUGHLIN   *National Director and General Manager, Strategic Compensation Services, The Hay Group, Philadelphia, Pa.*   (CHAPTER 46)

JAMES R. McMAHON   *Consultant, Management Compensation Services, Scottsdale, Ariz.*   (CHAPTER 41)

GEORGE E. MELLGARD   *Principal, The Hay Group, Pittsburgh, Pa.*   (CHAPTER 34)

GEORGE T. MILKOVICH   *Professor, Department of Personnel and Human Resource Studies, New York School of Industrial and Labor Relations, Cornell University, Ithaca, N.Y.*   (CHAPTER 10)

LAWRENCE W. MUTH   *Director, Corporate Economic Research and Statistical Reporting, Johnson & Johnson, New Brunswick, N.J.*   (CHAPTER 50)

ROBERT C. OCHSNER   *Partner and Regional Director, Strategic Compensation Services, The Hay Group, Philadelphia, Pa.*   (CHAPTER 61)

LESTER N. ODAMS, JR.   *Compensation Consultant, General Electric Company, Fairfield, Conn.*   (CHAPTER 18)

JOHN R. ROARK   *Partner, The Hay Group, Philadelphia, Pa.*   (CHAPTER 7)

ROBERT H. ROCK   *Partner, The Hay Group, Philadelphia, Pa.*   (CHAPTER 31)

ARMANDO M. RODRIGUEZ   *Commissioner, Equal Employment Opportunity Commission, Washington, D.C.*   (CHAPTER 62)

JOHN S. ROGERS   *Partner, The Hay Group, Pittsburgh, Pa.*   (CHAPTER 29)

JOHN M. ROSENFELD   *Partner, The Hay Group, Pittsburgh, Pa.*   (CHAPTER 59)

THOMAS S. ROY, JR.   *Director, Salaried Compensation, Armstrong World Industries, Lancaster, Pa.*   (CHAPTER 6)

HENRY A. SARGENT   *Principal, The Hay Group, Philadelphia, Pa.*   (CHAPTER 11)

FRED E. SCHUSTER   *Professor of Management, College of Business and Public Administration, Florida Atlantic University, Boca Raton, Fla.*   (CHAPTER 21)

ROBERT H. SELLES   *Consulting Actuary, The Hay Group, San Francisco, Calif.*   (CHAPTER 45)

ERVIN SELTZER   *Senior Consultant, The Hay Group, Philadelphia, Pa.*   (CHAPTER 28)

KENNETH P. SHAPIRO   *Partner, The Hay Group, and General Manager, Hay/Huggins, Philadelphia, Pa.*   (CHAPTER 44)

EDWARD B. SHILS   *Professor of Entrepreneurial Studies, Wharton School, University of Pennsylvania, Philadelphia, Pa.*   (CHAPTER 8)

DONALD R. SIMPSON   *Partner, The Hay Group, Philadelphia, Pa.*   (CHAPTER 47)

GEORGE L. STELLUTO   *Associate Commissioner, Wages and Industrial Relations, Bureau of Labor Statistics, U.S. Department of Labor, Washington, D.C.*   (CHAPTER 39)

DANIEL L. STIX   *General Partner, The Hay Group, Philadelphia, Pa.*   (CHAPTER 66)

C. IAN SYM-SMITH   *General Partner, The Hay Group, Philadelphia, Pa.*   (CHAPTER 55)

PAUL THOMPSON, II   *Director, Executive Financial Planning, The Hay Group, Philadelphia, Pa.*   (CHAPTER 48)

DONALD J. TREIMAN   *Professor, Department of Sociology, University of California, Los Angeles, Calif.*   (CHAPTER 63)

HARRIETT(A. WEISS   *Partner, The Hay Group, New York, N.Y.   (CHAPTER 51)*

MARK S. WHITE, JR.   *Director of International Compensation, The Hay Group, Philadelphia, Pa.   (CHAPTER 55)*

GEORGE P. WHITTINGTON   *Manager, Exempt Job Evaluation, The Dow Chemical Company, Midland, Mich.   (CHAPTER 19)*

RICHARD E. WING   *Former Director, Corporate Compensation Department, Eastman Kodak Company, Rochester, N.Y.   (CHAPTERS 9 and 64)*

MARTIN G. WOLF   *Senior Principal, The Hay Group, Philadelphia, Pa.   (CHAPTER 20)*

LARRY L. WYATT   *Manager, Human Resource Planning, Aluminum Company of America, Pittsburgh, Pa.   (CHAPTER 59)*

JOHN YURKUTAT   *Manager, Survey Programs, The Hay Group, Philadelphia, Pa.   (CHAPTER 36)*

LEONARD ZIMMERMAN   *Partner, Communications, The Hay Group, Philadelphia, Pa.   (CHAPTER 60)*

Preface

The *Handbook of Wage and Salary Administration* offers the compensation executive both a practical and a theoretical view of the problems he or she faces, together with hands-on advice on how to solve them. Over 75 experts have contributed to this volume.

The 12 new chapters in this second edition, together with over 50 updated chapters, reflect the social, political, economic, and technological changes of the last decade and position the reader to address the compensation issues of the 1980s and 1990s.

The most significant new *emphasis* is on the interaction of compensation policy with all elements of corporate planning. The most significant *development*, which is reflected throughout this volume, is the unprecedented entry and reentry of women into the work force. Other characteristics of our time, which translate themselves into compensation problems and their solutions, are the size and persistence of inflation, the uses and complexities of benefit programs, and the impact of governmental policies. This handbook is an up-to-date manual dealing with the basics of compensation policy in our current environment.

I am grateful for the professional contribution of the coordinating editor, David Hewitt. And to Betty McHugh, my deep appreciation for valuable administrative assistance and support. My thanks to all who participated.

MILTON L. ROCK
Editor-in-Chief

Note from the Editor-in-Chief

Management's challenge is to create an environment which stimulates people in their jobs and fosters company growth, and a key aspect of the environment is compensation. Its dramatic impact is felt not only in the area of costs but also in the area of individual motivation. Motivation, in turn, is an essential prerequisite to top corporate as well as individual performance. A company's reward system and its application demonstrate just how highly a person and his or her contributions are valued. The attributes and visible accomplishments of the individuals who are recognized with larger and more frequent pay and promotional increases tangibly communicate to employees at large what kind of behavior is needed and desired.

Viewed from this perspective, compensation is more than pay. It is a total reward system involving incentives and noncash benefits, performance appraisal, and work force development as well as base wages and salaries. Thus, in addition to providing for material needs, the compensation administrator must consider the employee's need for self-realization—the need to feel that he or she is having a real impact on the organization. While money, in one form or another, is a major source of satisfaction and motivation, other factors can be equally important to employee morale. These include the nature of the work, the organizational environment and style of management, and the company's past performance and its outlook for the future.

As a total package, compensation is an integral part of the art and science of management. It involves people, job design, organization design, and corporate effectiveness. Compensation policies must therefore accurately reflect the organization's style and philosophy as well as attract the type of people suited to that style and philosophy.

The *Handbook of Wage and Salary Administration* has been written to help managers create a compensation process which meets these needs. Intended as a practical reference work for managers who want to improve their effectiveness, the handbook sets forth the concepts, techniques, and processes which are basic to good wage and salary administration. These include the work, products, ideas, services, and end results for which jobs are created, leading inevitably to the *people* who fill the jobs. People, not jobs, get rewarded for their contributions to the organization. Therefore, a company that cares about its employees needs a systematic, organized vehicle for wage and salary administration which will minimize subjectivity and be equitable to all.

Our underlying belief in planning this handbook has been that no element of the pay system stands alone; each is a part of the whole, and all are affected by the design and administration of the others. In keeping with this fundamental idea, the handbook is organized to guide the reader through the compensation process, showing how the principles and procedures are coordinated to build a solid foundation for an *integrated total compensation program*.

To get the best thinking on this entire process, we have brought together a group of authors who are experts in wage and salary administration. These professionals represent a number of the major corporations and financial institutions of the United States as well as influential universities, trade associations, and the government. Despite their varying backgrounds and environments, they share the objectives common to wage and salary administration: that the system of pay be equitable, sufficient to attract and retain the talents and capabilities a company needs, and motivating to employees.

The concept of equity is multidimensional. Our feeling is that, in most cases, equity is best established and maintained by calculating pay according to job content—that is, according to the job's functions and accountabilities and its relative importance to the organization. The job content approach is based on the idea that the job's importance and impact are inherent in its content, and, therefore, the job can be evaluated in terms of content.

We also recognize, however, that for some jobs the job content approach by itself is not sufficient. Although the experience and education required to fill the job can be specified, the job's potential contribution and value to the organization are harder to define. For example, one research chemist may do a perfectly acceptable job for years, while the person in the next lab may discover nylon. Their relative value to the organization is inherent not in the content of the job but in their performance, which cannot be predicted very precisely because the range of possibilities is so wide. Hence, pay for these jobs cannot be based solely on job content.

In addition, many professionals see a trend toward broader definitions of jobs. They believe people will have roles, rather than jobs, in an integrated process aimed at specific end results. These roles will change continuously as goals are achieved and individuals move on to new projects; and pay will be related to performance and contribution in these varying roles.

Recognizing the diverse needs a total compensation program must satisfy, we have designed the handbook to provide a conceptual and practical basis for dealing with compensation issues related to all kinds of jobs in all kinds of situations. Also, we feel that the material in the handbook is applicable in all economic situations. It is our firm belief, after years of experience in this field, that a wage and salary program that is inherently sound and flexible will provide a strong foundation from which management can respond to the difficulties of an economic downturn, inflation, price and wage controls, etc. As a matter of fact, even in good times, a company cannot administer compensation effectively without a formal, flexible, and fair program.

Looking at the future, we recognize that American society is changing rapidly and that industry, commerce, and government structures must at least accommodate themselves to these changes, if not lead them. Many younger workers view companies and jobs in the broad context of society's needs. Moreover, having grown up in relative affluence, they tend to be less concerned with money and security than their elders and more concerned with self-expression. It appears to us that this pattern is widespread and not, as some would have it, confined to disaffected and politically radical young people. Among those who enter business, the trend will manifest itself in their desire to make an immediate and visible contribution to any endeavor in which they are engaged.

Thoughtful managers have always known that involving people in something—giving them the sense that they are making a real impact—is the key to motivating them. The difference now is that people are less willing to serve long apprenticeships before they can make their presence felt. Hence, jobs will have to be redesigned to allow incumbents more autonomy in choosing how they carry out their responsibilities, and new relationships will have to be established among jobs within an organization so that employees have an opportunity to influence results on a broader plane. In addition, a career path development factor will be built into more jobs: few will stand alone, unrelated to any other jobs. Instead, a job's design will recognize preconceived extensions or relationships both with surrounding jobs and with jobs that may logically lie ahead of each employee. Second, more and more professionals will come to recognize compensation as a total, integrated system rather than a bundle of discrete elements. It is no longer news that noncash compensation is growing in importance and in proportion to total payroll expense (for the company) and total income (for the employee). The reasons for this are well documented and include inflation, tax laws, union activities, and a number of changes in the thinking of the general public about how it wants to be paid. One aspect of this trend will be the growing emphasis on the cafeteria style in employee compensation, in which the individual is given a choice among various forms of payment. An outgrowth of the cafeteria style will be a real need for expert financial counseling for executives to assist them in selecting the compensation alternatives best suited to their unique needs.

Third, wage and salary administration will be woven even more tightly into the general management process. This means more stress on performance standards, performance measurement, and accountability management and a drive for greater efficiency through interrelating functions and accountabilities. Organizations will devote greater effort to appraising the potential of employees in the light of future organizational needs, and they will follow up by developing employees on a career basis to fill those needs. Furthermore, there will be a heightened awareness of the subtle implications of management style coupled with a more sophisticated use of internal communications to foster employee understanding of and commitment to the corporation's philosophy and goals.

Fourth, wage earners are going to demand that the modern techniques developed for salary administration be applied in determining their pay structures. Wage inequities resulting from poor evaluation techniques or procedures will have to be corrected. Wage earners and unions will place greater emphasis on the total compensation package, as have their salaried counterparts. We find more interest in individual and group incentives. The benefits package will expand and take in many new areas.

Finally, when all is said and done, base salary or wages in the form of cash will continue to be the core of the compensation package. We've already conceded that cash equivalents—pensions, health and life insurance, disability income, etc.—will grow in importance and that higher-paid executives will give increasing attention to incentive plans and tax-minimizing measures. But cash will continue to be the largest single compensation element, as well as the element that sets the tone for the entire package. It is not likely that this will change during the time that people refer to this handbook.

Handbook of
Wage and Salary
Administration

Job Content

chapter 1

Designing Jobs

James H. Davis

GENERAL MANAGER, COMPENSATION, ALUMINUM
COMPANY OF AMERICA, PITTSBURGH, PENNSYLVANIA

WHY JOB DESIGN?

To ask why managers should concern themselves with job design is really to ask whether they should concern themselves with how things get done in the organization and who does them. In any organization, be it the neighborhood hardware store or an international corporation, jobs must be designed in some manner or other, with or without the attention of the manager. In other words, job content will be fixed by some means. The process may be elementary, for example, hiring another salesperson; or it may be extremely complex, involving a wide range of organization restructuring and performance implications. A job's design may evolve from the myriad influences in and on the organization. Or conversely, it may be the product of caprice or expediency and therefore relatively insensitive to circumstances with which it should be reconciled.

So the question really is not whether jobs will be designed or not. If jobs exist, they will be designed in some way—even if the design process appears to be more of a "happening" than anything else. The question to be decided, then, is the extent to which managers should involve themselves in this inevitable process. To what extent and how should they endorse, influence, and direct the process?

Few would quarrel with the manager's responsibility to make the best and most productive use of all resources, including materials, intangibles, and workers. In many industries, the people portion of the manager's resources represents the major cost area. In most industries, it is at least a very significant cost area. Thus the manager who is to fulfill the total responsibility must be interested in any management technique that promises better utilization of people resources and contributes to making each job as productive and meaningful as possible. An active, conscious effort to analyze and design jobs is just such a technique.

DESIGN OR DESCRIBE?

Webster defines the word "design" in these terms: "To contrive, to project with an end in view, to decide upon and outline the main feature of; to plan." That's quite a different thing from "describe," which is defined: "To tell or write about, to picture in words." The main difference is the element of planning that is integral to the design process. Planning is generally accepted as a sine qua non of the management process. By the same token, it is the very essence of job design.

Active designing must be an analytical and creative process. For example, a decision to increase the sales force by one hardly taxes the analytical skills of the manager. It does, nevertheless, represent the result of a decision-making process that gave at least fleeting attention to such questions as whether an added person is really needed, at what location, selling what products, and whether the job is to be similar in all respects to the jobs of other salespeople already on the payroll. To that extent, some designing took place but not necessarily the kind that truly warrants the label of a specific management technique. If managers are to use job design as a significant tool for utilizing human resources, a seat-of-the-pants approach will not suffice. By comparison, most managers deal with questions of major capital expenditures in the most probing and analytical manner. These are questions of the allocation of money resources. The alternatives can be quantified. Further, the validity of the choice is frequently measurable within a specific time period.

Likewise, a prudent manager will allocate and control the organization's people resources in the same probing and analytical manner, although, unlike the capital expenditure, people often elude precise quantification. This is particularly true when it comes to those whom Peter Drucker calls the "knowledge workers." They simply cannot be assigned to work or their duties defined in the same way as assembly line workers. In short, people are complex resources, difficult to deal with, and, what's more, their complexity is ever-changing—often in unpredictable ways.

Many good managers possess a charisma or leadership style that truly inspires people to unusual achievement. But they know that inspiration will not, of itself, consistently produce results—especially over the long pull of managing a successful enterprise. Planning is required. If workers are inspired or well motivated, the manager has accomplished a great deal. But it will go for naught if the workers lack a sense of individual direction and an appreciation of their individual roles in the larger scheme of things. They will find it difficult to succeed if they do not know what constitutes success. And the manager will have to devote a great deal of time to the short-range direction of their efforts.

Thus good job design should be looked upon as a critical ingredient of the management process at all levels of the organization. It can forestall the need for constant or excessive supervision and free the supervisor to pursue broader, long-range accountabilities. The justification for management time and effort spent in designing jobs, therefore, is not different from the justification for any other kind of planning. The fact that job design deals with the complexities of human behavior simply places it in a distinct category of planning and one requiring specialized techniques.

PERSPECTIVE ON JOB DESIGN

Job design has existed as long as humankind. Even the lone hunter set himself a task and then, on the basis of his experience, modified the way he performed it each time. And, to those to whom the word "job" connotes a specific task-oriented relationship between two or more people, the history of job design is every bit as ancient.

The basic circumstance of some people performing tasks in response to the direction of others has never really changed. What is continually changing is the nature of the tasks, the manner in which they are performed, and the relationship between subordinate and superior. This is not to say that these changes have occurred to the same degree and in the same manner in all facets of our society. For example, military organizations still insist on rigid obedience within a fixed hierarchy of command. But goals and objectives have changed markedly, as have the kinds of duty assignments made to military personnel.

It was the industrial revolution that engendered the sort of division of labor we think of today as designed jobs. For years prior to the industrial revolution, work activity was specialized to a degree. The farmer, the craftsperson, and the merchant all went about their affairs in their own ways. But it was the marriage of technology and money in mideighteenth-century England that brought numbers of workers together under one roof.

The factory—the place where a single source of mechanical energy could be put to use—was not simply a collection of craftspeople. It became, especially between 1760 and 1790, a production system requiring coordination of specialized work by both people and machines.

The industrial revolution produced a dramatic change in our view of work. The interdependence of their labors increased sharply when people became factory employees instead of independent producers. The machine emerged as the center of attention. No longer was it a curiosity of the inventor—it was an immensely productive and profitable device. And, by its nature, the machine required a highly specialized but repetitive function from each of its parts. So it was with the worker who tended the machine. It is not surprising that job design in this context was almost as mechanistic in approach as machine design.

The cost of labor may have been modest in the beginnings of the industrial revolution, but it increased steadily over the years and commanded more and more of management's attention. World War I, with its attendant inflation and worker shortage, forced industrial management to look in earnest for better ways to manage the cost of labor. Thus the work of Frederick Taylor and others became quite pertinent. In their work was the beginning of industrial engineering concepts, especially time and motion study, standardization of tasks, and highly structured jobs. Scientific management was the byword, promising a truly analytical approach to the human element in the productive process.

The adoption of scientific management filled a real need, and today's industrial engineering discipline owes a great deal to the concept. Half a century later, however, the original approach appears to many observers to be too mechanistic and too prone to ignore worker psychological factors not directly related to such basic elements as heat, light, and fatigue. So while scientific management was far more sophisticated than the techniques used by the factory bosses of eighteenth-century England, the resulting job design tended toward the mechanistic specialization of tasks.

TODAY'S JOB DESIGN ENVIRONMENT

Today, a growing number of behavioral scientists, management consultants, and commentators find the mechanistic or overspecialized approach to job design at cross purposes with the goals of the organization. Much has been written about the effect of impersonal and standardized work situations on the worker's attitude and, in turn, the effect of the worker's attitude on productivity. In fact, the whole broad area of worker motivation and how it is influenced by job and organization design and leadership style has received considerable attention from such authors as Chris Argyris, Rensis Likert, Frederick Herzberg, and Douglas McGregor.

Concepts of job design which feature job enlargement and increased latitude for the employee are presented as desirable alternatives to the traditional approach of maximum specialization. This is not to say that the ultimate goal is a jack-of-all-trades assignment for everyone. Good, solid expertise in specialized fields is more in demand today than ever before. But jobs which are designed to utilize expertise need not necessarily restrict their incumbents to the practice of that expertise alone. Moreover, the rate of technological change and the evolutionary growth of most organizations can make the specialist obsolete with little warning. So today's manager is cautioned to seek out an approach to job design that broadens the worker's horizon rather than limits it.

There is another reason, in addition to productivity, for designing jobs so that they satisfy the worker as well as utilize him or her. It is a simple reason: workers want it that way and have learned how to get what they want.

Perhaps it would be more accurate to speak of society's wants instead of just the workers'. Certainly, the events of the past two decades have demonstrated that industry can no longer confine itself to the profit motive. Protests, both active and passive, by important segments of the citizenry are quite explicit about their concern for broad quality-of-life issues. Their message carries authority, and industry is well aware of this. So regardless of what any individual manager may feel about the importance of job meaningfulness to the individual versus the enterprise, there is little choice but to listen and respond. The plain fact is that today's corporate recruiters frequently encounter a skepticism about business among the very people industry needs for its own sustenance.

THE DESIGN PROCESS

The actual process of designing jobs is not necessarily a fixed sequence. There are, however, two basic activities that must take place. The first is identifying the need to either design a new job or redesign an old one. Once it has been established that the need is real, the second activity must be undertaken: job content must be developed.

Identifying the Need to Design a New Job   When a new activity or function is introduced into some part of the organization, the manager must make a judgment as to whether or not conditions suggest that a new or revised job should be designed. This is the point where job analysis can be most valuable, so, in making this decision, the manager can consider some of the questions discussed below.

Is the need current and valid?   Normally, there is a sense of permanency in the business of establishing and filling new jobs—at least, the incumbent tends to view it that way. A new job assignment, and especially a promotion, is usually not undone painlessly. Without being an obstructionist, the manager can be a stabilizing influence and insist that the proposal for a new job in fact represent a valid need.

Are the job specifications realistic?   One excellent technique to determine whether a valid need exists is to state the job's duties or objectives in writing. Better yet, have the supervisor who is requesting the new job write the statement. This need not be a complete description; an informal list of duties will suffice. If the proposed job function is only a hazy idea, the supervisor will have considerable difficulty setting down that list of duties. Experience has demonstrated that a job that cannot be described usually cannot be performed. The very least this technique contributes to the process of job design is to force the concerned parties to be analytical rather than expedient, thus avoiding costly errors.

What about permanency?   Thus far, job design has been discussed in terms of relatively permanent functions in the organization. However, there are many occasions, such as during peak work loads or vacation periods or when specialized technical help is required, when a critical but temporary function needs to be performed.

Several avenues are open to the manager in filling temporary needs. Temporary personnel may be hired from an agency specializing in this field, or the function may be contracted to another firm. Also, the function may be assigned temporarily to an existing employee within the organization. The project-oriented task force often used in larger organizations is a good example of this alternative. Existing employees are assigned full- or part-time to a specific critical but temporary project. One advantage of this method is that, as permanent employees, task force members are particularly well motivated to accomplish the objective—a motivation that might be lacking in an outside group.

The important point is that temporary jobs be identified as such and not treated as new permanent assignments. To do otherwise is to create conditions that become untenable.

Where should the job be placed?   The tendency toward empire building can be quite innocent, especially in a large organization. A department head who perceives the need for an accountant or engineer may really be thinking in terms of an accountant or engineer within the department. The proposed job may pass with flying colors the test of having its duties set out in writing. There may be no question of the need for the function to be performed. The real question may be, "Where?"

Here again, the manager's duty is to take the overall organizational viewpoint. Perhaps an accountant or an engineer performing an identical function but with a meager work load already exists in another part of the organization. The possibilities for shopping within the organization for help should not be overlooked.

If it's only work load. . . .   When the need for a new job is based on work load alone, and the increased work load has all the appearances of permanency, the solution seems evident: hire another for whatever job is in short supply of help! It may not be quite that simple. And, equally important, circumstances may present an opportunity for some organizational creativity.

For example, a growth situation requiring frequent hiring and assigning of more of the same kinds of jobs will eventually reach the point where all the "sames" can no longer be properly supervised by the existing boss. At this point (or in anticipation of this point), the organizational structure should be examined for job design possibilities such as the creation of "working supervisors." An alert management will seek such opportunities for organizational structure change and job design in a growth situation not only to maintain a smoothly functioning organization but also to provide sound promotional routes.

The incumbent's judgment.   Designers of jobs should keep in mind that their designs inevitably are judged by an astute critic—the incumbent. The ultimate test of a job's viability is whether it can be performed by a qualified incumbent. He or she will know whether it passes the test soon after being assigned to it, and this judgment should be considered a significant contribution to the design process. If job design problems are not corrected as they are discovered, their cost to the organization, both monetary and intangible, could become substantial. Avoidance of this damage is the real reward for thoughtful attention to good job design.

Developing Job Content   The second basic activity in job design is developing job content. Once the need for a new job has been identified, the manager can address himself or herself specifically to its content. Consideration of the checkpoints and guidelines discussed below may be helpful to the manager.

Sources of design information.   One important source of design information is the person who wants the job designed. This is often the person who will supervise the work to be performed. A skillful interviewer will be alert to the particular strengths and weaknesses of information provided by the job's creator. That person may be able to express the job specifications without precisely identifying how the job contributes to the organization's objectives or, in contrast, may have the need for the job clearly in mind and not be able to express the job's specifications.

Industry sources, salary surveys, reference material, and articles about the performance of certain functions provide excellent guidelines for the design of jobs that fit into certain recognized patterns. Jobs of similar content within the organization are another source of design information. The job candidate may provide a particular insight into the design of a job that is not available from any other source. Involving the proposed incumbent in the construction of job content is, in itself, important not only to achieve the objectives of the organization but to assure a strong commitment by the incumbent.

Compatibility.   Compare the goal of the job to be designed and the goal of the organization. It is easy to concentrate so completely on design information that a job could be designed which is not compatible with the goals of the parent organization. The manager should consider whether the position being designed will meet the test of compatibility.

Realistic objectives. The objectives of the designed job must be attainable and realistic. The manager should avoid the frustration that comes from proposing objectives which simply cannot be achieved. For example, to require a safety director to achieve a zero injury goal would present a virtually impossible task in most industrial and commercial situations. Job design provides the opportunity to identify realistic objectives.

Can the job be filled or refilled? In some cases, the first incumbent is on hand when the job is being designed. Even in these circumstances, the question of whether the job can be filled should be answered if there is a likelihood of turnover in the job. Generally, jobs should be built with a sensitivity to the traditional disciplines in the industry or business where the job is found. The requirement for bizarre or unusual combinations of skills or duties should be avoided if the job must be refilled routinely.

Combinations of several disciplines or skills reduce dramatically the candidates for a job. For example, if typing is the principal skill required, the job might be filled by a large number of applicants; if typing and shorthand both are required, the number shrinks significantly; and if typing, shorthand, and the ability to read a particular foreign language are all requirements, the number of available candidates would be limited.

Legal implications. Certain positions are identified by their titles or organizational placements with stated legal responsibilities. For example, the general duties of the secretary and the treasurer of a corporation are often included in the bylaws. It is important that job design not usurp or compromise the legal responsibilities vested in those jobs.

Contractual agreements. Job content can be the subject of union agreement. In certain industries, jobs are designed, and their content approved, by both management and the bargaining union. In this situation, it is important to distinguish between the type of work covered under the bargaining agreement and that which is excluded from it. With this precaution, jobs will be designed so that they do not cross the line between bargained and nonbargained work, thereby forestalling the possibilities of union grievance or incorporation into the bargaining unit of work that had previously been excluded.

Judgment. The range of discretion, judgment, or original thinking to be exercised in a job should be clearly understood by the designer of the job. It is essential that these elements of job content be compatible with and supported by the job's required level of know-how or experience.

Management style. Consider the management style prevalent in the hierarchy over the job. For example, if the style is typically participative, a job designed to be most effective in an autocratic environment might be literally unperformable.

Clarity. Avoid stereotypes and cliches. Confine the description to meaningful words and rigorously exclude excessive language which tends to describe the general environment but does not clarify the situation in which the job is performed.

The job and the incumbent. It is appropriate, in certain circumstances, to design the job around the incumbent. This is a useful technique to make the best use of some specialized expertise or available talent. The job may be built around a particular person whom the supervisor hopes to attract to the job, and the design may take in some of that person's particular interests as an incentive to make the job look attractive.

Designing a job around the incumbent is a most effective device for solving certain personnel problems, such as those resulting from health or performance deficiencies. It provides an opportunity to assure that each incumbent can fill his or her job with dignity and that the position is not a burden but rather an asset to the rest of the organization.

Some jobs are designed specifically to develop or train the incumbent. This specification is most appropriate when the time available for training is limited and the job must establish a particular training environment. Most managers agree, however, that given enough time, the best design is one that includes definite accountabilities beyond "being trained."

Prototypes.   The prototype is a generalized description that is useful for positions held by large numbers of people, usually performing rather similar tasks. A prototype often selects gradient language to describe a series of levels in a hierarchy of skills. Words like "simple," "routine," "difficult," and "complex" appear in prototypes to create the band of job levels that covers a range of skills or other characteristics which are difficult to describe precisely.

Prototypes are valuable in describing points along a continuum, and generally they simplify the administrative process that attends job descriptions, job evaluation, and salary administration. They are, however, subject to abuse. There is a tendency for employees to become misclassified in prototypes either because supervisors, not recognizing the speed at which subordinates attain proficiency, fail to upgrade them promptly or because supervisors are reluctant to discuss a subordinate's limitations frankly and therefore advance him or her to a position along the continuum beyond actual performance or ability.

Titles.   Titles are often regarded as the frosting on the cake of job substance, but it is sometimes difficult to recognize the cake without the frosting. The title given to a position represents one more opportunity for an organization to display its management style. If it prefers vague or imprecise job descriptions, it would probably prefer imprecise titles. In an organization where the descriptions of jobs tend to be very precise, the titles are usually more descriptive. In addition, the title's status implications, both inside and outside the organization, must be considered.

MAINTENANCE AND REDESIGN

In most organizations, the elements that affect job design are subject to change. For example, a company's business objectives, its organization structure, the level of technology, and the general economy all change and bring different emphases to the design of jobs. Accordingly, jobs must be reviewed constantly and changed if they are to be kept current.

Redesign is usually initiated in the same way as new design; that is, the need is identified and the job content is established. Redesign can be initiated by reviewing the evaluations or the descriptions of jobs that are in place. Sometimes it is a chain reaction: the impact from the design or redesign of related or similar jobs triggers an examination of other jobs. The guidelines for redesign and the elements of concern are the same as those for original job design.

As with most activities that merit the manager's attention, maintaining a current job design program requires constant effort. The program's usefulness rests not only on the technique employed at its inception but equally on its being kept up to date. With a sound introduction and a conscientious maintenance effort, the job design program can be one of the manager's indispensable tools.

BIBLIOGRAPHY

Argyris, Chris: *Personality and Organization*, Harper & Row Publishers, Incorporated, New York, 1957.

Dale, Ernest: *Planning and Developing the Company Organization Structure*, American Management Association, New York, 1952. (Contributions by F. W. Taylor.)

Drucker, Peter F.: *Management: Tasks, Responsibilities, Practices*, Harper & Row Publishers, Incorporated, New York, 1974.

Likert, Rensis: *New Patterns of Management*, McGraw-Hill Book Company, New York, 1961.

McGregor, Douglas: *The Human Side of Enterprise*, McGraw-Hill Book Company, New York, 1960.

Miglione, R. Henry: *MBO: Blue Collar to Top Executive*, The Bureau of National Affairs, Inc., Washington, D.C., 1977.

Odiorne, George S.: *Management by Objectives*, Pitman Publishing Corporation, New York, 1965. (Contributions by Rensis Likert and Douglas McGregor.)

Sutermeister, Robert A.: *People and Productivity*, 2d ed., McGraw-Hill Book Company, New York, 1963. (Contributions by Chris Argyris, Frederick Herzberg, Douglas McGregor, and Rensis Likert.)

chapter 2

Describing Hourly Jobs

Alfred R. Brandt

SENIOR WAGE PRACTICES SPECIALIST (RETIRED),
WESTERN ELECTRIC COMPANY, INC., GREENSBORO,
NORTH CAROLINA

USES OF HOURLY JOB DESCRIPTIONS

No single instrument is as important to effective wage and salary administration as the job description. Yet, at least until recently, it has received far less attention than it requires to assure either that it is properly understood or directed. Now, with growing numbers of equal opportunity cases and increasing interest in the issue of "equal pay for equal work," companies are coming to recognize the need for a document that is a legally defensible basis for staffing actions, job administration, and compensation determinations.

To begin with, there is considerable confusion as to what a description really is. In literature relevant to management practices, a variety of terms are used for this particular instrument—"job analysis," "job specification," "job evaluation sheet," etc. To provide a firm foundation for this discussion, some definitions would seem to be in order. L. B. Michael defines a job as "a recognized, normal, recurring set of duties and responsibilities, assigned to a particular employee or to a number of employees as their part in the whole work or service function."[1] A job description, then, is simply a narrative statement or listing of these duties and responsibilities (sometimes referred to as "functions"). In actual practice, the job description format generally includes for identifica-

---

[1] L. B. Michael, *Wage and Salary Fundamentals and Procedures*, McGraw-Hill Book Company, New York, 1950, p. 52.

tion purposes a job title and, usually, some sort of code number. Depending on its use, this may be the limit of information involved, or the description may be incorporated into a more comprehensive document called a "job specification" (or "job grade specification"). Typically included in job specifications is information about tools, equipment, products, or processes involved, amount of supervision provided, responsibility for directing efforts of other employees, job conditions, and occasionally such items as the identity of the organization and job supervisor and the number of employees covered by the specification. If used in connection with job evaluation, the specification may include, either on the same or a separate page, evaluation-supporting information under the heading of "substantiating data sheet" or "job evaluation sheet."

The job description, when properly developed to meet specific needs, has vast potential for a wide variety of administrative applications.

1. *Training:* as a guide to new job incumbents and job supervisors in explaining functions, sequence of actions, and nature of overall work load, and in planning training programs

2. *Hiring:* as a guide in assessing qualifications of applicants and explaining jobs to them

3. *Placement (Promotion, Demotion, or Lateral Transfer):* for matching qualifications of individuals to specific jobs, planning of force adjustments, development of employee movement systems, and posting of job openings (usually in compliance with the union contract)

4. *Test Development:* for information about job content and requirements in devising tests of aptitude and proficiency

5. *Personnel Statistics:* for various management planning and control purposes and work force usage reports to the government

6. *Engineering Planning:* in preparing job layouts, specifying labor requirements, automating operations, improving methods, and making wage incentive applications

7. *Health and Safety:* in identification of hazardous operations and development of protective equipment and preventive measures

8. *Labor Relations:* in resolving questions of job overlap, pay treatment, and proper recognition of responsibilities

9. *Performance Rating:* for performance appraisals and establishment of performance standards and objectives

10. *Organization Planning:* for alignment of functions, determination of work force requirements, proper utilization of skills, job enrichment, and development of personnel tables or tables of organization

11. *Accounting Effort:* in establishing expense ratios, cost estimating, and budget control

12. *Miscellaneous Personnel Concerns:* for employee morale (explanation of job changes), equal employment opportunity planning and control, and counseling

While extensive, this list is not all-inclusive. Past studies have shown that, aside from hiring and placement, most companies made little use of job descriptions for other than wage administration. A possible explanation of this may lie in two factors: (1) the language and format of most job descriptions tend to be tailored to wage administration needs, thus limiting their value for other applications, and (2) a general failure to instruct and encourage supervisors and management specialists in the use of this tool.

The latter problem can be solved by education and a conviction by upper management as to its potential uses. Altering language and format, however, will be accomplished only when companies choose to take a broader systems approach to job analysis and conduct much more comprehensive studies to answer a wide variety of questions about work.

The job description's role in the wage determination process varies from company to company. In companies which do not have a formal job evaluation program, the description is most commonly used to rank jobs internally, as a basis for comparison in an industry or area wage survey or as the basis for bargaining job rates with the union. Usually such descriptions are rather brief and general. Sometimes they are little more than a title definition as found in the *Dictionary of Occupational Titles* prepared by the U.S. Employment Service.

In more sophisticated applications, the job description usually becomes a part of the job grade specification. These descriptions tend to be more comprehensive, more delineative of differences in jobs, and supportive of evaluation statements. In some cases, the description is the basis or backbone of the evaluation. In others, both the evaluation and the description are developed from more detailed information contained in a job analysis booklet or a job study folder. Since job descriptions of this type are used more extensively for comparisons in the job evaluation procedure and for job administration by line supervisors, it is essential that they be prepared by individuals who are properly selected and trained for this activity.

SELECTING AND TRAINING JOB ANALYSTS

Since very few companies employ persons for the sole purpose of writing descriptions, the observations that follow apply to the occupation most commonly identified as *job analyst*—also variously known as "job evaluation engineer," "job grader," "compensation specialist," etc. Generally speaking, these titles reflect primary responsibilities, such as job evaluation, wage surveys, and work force planning in various combinations. This is important when one considers the qualifications and training required for these jobs.

Criteria for Selecting Job Analysts   Major factors to be considered in choosing people to act as analysts are formal education, previous work experience, and personal qualifications. Specific requirements in these areas are discussed in the following paragraphs.

Education and experience.   Ideally, analysts should have taken college-level courses concerned with industrial or commercial operations, i.e., any discipline that would provide the desired background in industrial measurement and control theories and techiques. This should be supplemented by a broad exposure to varied kinds of work. Lack of the formal education mentioned is not a major obstacle if an individual has an analytical mind and sufficient pertinent work experience. Any educational deficiency would, of course, dictate some modifications of the training process.

The knowledge/experience requirement is important in providing the analyst with an appreciation of how jobs are designed and how work is organized—for example, that some work by its very nature is repetitive or sporadic, short or long cycle, etc. It also contributes to an understanding of the terminology of the field of work—both legitimate technical terms and the accepted language of the shop (so-called trade jargon). Finally, it facilitates comprehending the significance and *relative* importance of facts picked up in the job study.

In addition, this background is important in fulfilling the analyst's major responsibilities:

1. Planning the job study or investigation, conducting interviews and any preliminary or corroborative research, observing operations, and obtaining supportive information and exhibit material
2. Evaluating the job on the basis of the evaluation plan and comparisons with what one knows about other jobs and other kinds of work
3. Writing the description to assure that functions are given their proper emphasis
4. Where applicable, assisting or advising in the design of jobs and alignment or assignment of functions and responsibilities

Personal qualifications.   Personal qualifications are of vital importance, since analyst jobs involve extensive contacts with all types of people, at all levels in the company, and in a wide variety of circumstances and situations. Most job information is gleaned through observation and interview, so that the analyst should possess tact, empathy, and a liking for people in order to frame questions that will not irritate or arouse unwarranted suspicions. Emotions must not be permitted to interfere with objectivity. Finally, the analyst must be able to demonstrate to supervisors, employees, and union representatives an ability to be objective, fair, and thorough and to comprehend the significance of information obtained in the job study.

Writing ability.   Analysts should be able to prepare a narrative statement of job functions that is clear, concise, and free from redundancy. Furthermore, because the description is used to compare a particular job with others, writers should be able to use modifiers and delineative phrases that will facilitate such comparisons. Style is not a consideration, since description preparation by design tends to follow a stereotyped form.

Training Job Analysts   Methods of training analysts will vary considerably according to specific job requirements and the emphasis that a company gives to this effort. Indoctrination in the mechanics of job analysis, evaluation, and description writing generally begins by having the new analyst study the company's evaluation plan and the procedures of its application. Familiarization with the plan and how it has been used on some selected jobs ordinarily requires a relatively short time. If a union is involved, this study period should include familiarization with the applicable portions of the union contract. Finally—and the importance of this cannot be overstated—the analyst should be thoroughly instructed in company policies and organizational structure. It is essential to know what departments make what products or perform what services. Another requirement is knowledge of the company philosophy on job enrichment versus job simplification, at what level and by what procedure functional conflicts are resolved, and how to handle problems which may arise—for example, finding that a supervisor's design of a particular job is not in the best interests of the company. This understanding of the company is a vital ingredient in the broad systems approach to job analysis that was mentioned earlier.

Following familiarization with the company and the evaluation plan, the trainee is teamed with an experienced analyst for the second phase of training. This phase usually involves:

1. Accompanying the experienced analyst in conducting a job study. In this phase, the experienced person explains actions taken during the interview and the job observation and provides an analysis of the resulting evaluation and job description.

2. A joint study effort in which the experienced analyst conducts the interview and the trainee takes notes, records observations, and prepares an evaluation and job description independently, all of which is followed by a comparison with the findings and conclusions of the experienced analyst and discussion of results.

3. A job study performed by the trainee with the experienced analyst observing, analyzing, and commenting on the results.

Any of these steps should be repeated as often as necessitated by the progress of the new analyst.

After being judged capable of performing without close guidance, the new analyst should be reviewed closely for six to twelve months, primarily for assuring consistency of his or her efforts with existing job grade descriptions. It is this period which is the most significant part of the training program.

Since the application of the analyst's knowledge to the description and evaluation of jobs takes place in a comparative context, the mastery of the required skills can be achieved only through exposure to a wide variety of jobs. It is obvious that, except under most unusual circumstances, this learning process will take considerable time.

KINDS OF JOB DESCRIPTIONS

Job descriptions in current use vary widely, ranging from very brief (no more than an occupational title definition) to extremely lengthy and detailed with much supplementary information. Past studies have determined that there is little or no apparent correlation between the character of the description and its intended use or the size or type of company involved. In fact, it has been found that in some companies differences prevail between plants or divisions in both the type and the use of descriptions.

Length or detail in descriptions depends on the type of job involved. Jobs involving functions, tasks, or operations which are familiar to everybody concerned and/or which do not entail any significant variation or range of difficulty can be described briefly with a minimum of embellishment. Where some of the same terminology might be used for a number of different job situations, so that a condition of ambiguity could evolve, or where there is a definite range of difficulty, then more descriptive or delineative language will be required to bring out the distinctive features of the job for evaluation or comparison purposes. Companies are beginning to refine their descriptions to avoid equal opportunity challenges of unsupportable language that could have an adverse effect on staffing or compensation.

Aside from differences in length and detail, job descriptions may be classified generally as specific or individual, standard or general. As the name implies, the *specific or individual description* is a statement of *all* the duties and responsibilities assigned to one or more individuals in the job. The specific description is usually rather detailed and comprehensive, providing good support for evaluation and serving as a useful document in comparing the relative requirements of jobs. On the other hand, because of its exactness, this type of description demands a through job study, considerable care in preparation, and active effort in maintaining the description. Consequently, while this is probably the soundest type of job description to use, it is also likely to be the most costly. Figures 1, 2, and 3 are examples of good, specific descriptions for low-, intermediate-, and higher-level jobs.

Standard and *general* descriptions both apply to varying job situations and are designed to permit more flexibility in application and to be less sensitive to changes in duties and responsibilities. The *standard description* is usually a rather brief, very broadly written listing of functions. It is designed to cover

---

FIGURE 1   Specific Description for a Low-Level Job

JOB GRADE SPECIFICATION
(SHOP-TYPE JOB)

JOB TITLE: Assembler

JOB FUNCTION: Assemble spacers and select bars to crossbar switches. Work is performed from detailed directions and part is positioned in positive locating fixture.

JOB DUTIES AND PROCEDURES: Obtain switch from hold or staging area and place switch on bench with contact side down. Assemble and set spacers using proper hand tool. Place switch in holding fixture, obtain appropriate number of select bars, lubricate with proper oil, and assemble the select bars to the crossbar switch frame.

Remove the switch carrier from the switch and position check fixture on switch. Align bearing blocks, run in pivot screws on both sides of switch, and tighten lock nuts on right side of switch. Remove the checking fixture, replace the switch carrier, and place switch on conveyor.

Detail switches for select bar lubrication, as required.

Perform related material handling, when required.

Notify supervisor or other designated personnel when unusual conditions occur.

Post record of daily output.

TYPICAL PRODUCTS INVOLVED: Crossbar switches, spacers, and select bars.

MACHINES AND EQUIPMENT: HOW USED	Operate	Change Tools	Adjust	Set Up
Switch carriers	x			
Select bar positioning fixture	x			
Oil containers	x			
Holding fixtures	x			

TOOLS AND GAGES USED: Oil, spin wrench, and other general-purpose hand tools.

SOURCE OF METHODS AUTHORITY: Detailed verbal instructions.

FIGURE 2   Specific Description for an Intermediate-Level Job

---

JOB GRADE SPECIFICATION

(SHOP-TYPE JOB)

JOB TITLE: Saw Operator (Power Equipment)

JOB FUNCTION: Set up and operate table saws and special cutting machines to cut panels, piece parts, and details from rod, bar, and sheet stock.

JOB DUTIES AND PROCEDURES: Read and interpret drawings, cutting tickets, layouts, and shop orders to determine requirements such as size of material, equipment to be used, and number of parts and details to be cut.

Lay out and scribe material for proper size and notching so that waste is held to a minimum.

Set up and operate machines to cut and notch metal stock and to cut and bevel composition panels. Involves setting stops, making adjustments to maintain setups, and changing saw blades and cutting and beveling wheels.

Wash off composition panels after cutting and clean drainage outlet tank. Perform hand cutting operations such as sawing cutouts in composition panels and removing burrs and rough edges by filing.

Keep records of parts and details cut. Perform associated handling of material, using hand truck as necessary.

TYPICAL PRODUCTS INVOLVED: Various-size composition panels and metal stock used in the manufacture of power equipment.

MACHINES AND EQUIPMENT: HOW USED	Operate	Change Tools	Adjust	Set Up
Cochrane-Bly Semiautomatic Power Saw	x	x	x	x
Patch Wagner Cutting Machine	x	x	x	x
Oliver Table Saws	x	x	x	x
Hand Trucks	x			
Water Hose	x			
Hand and Electric Hoists	x			

TOOLS AND GAGES USED: Hacksaw, scale, files, square.

SOURCE OF METHODS AUTHORITY: Verbal instructions; simple piece part drawings, cutting tickets, and shop orders.

ACCURACY REQUIREMENTS AND DIFFICULTY OF MEETING THEM: Tolerances of normally $\frac{1}{32}''$ on composition panels and $\frac{1}{64}''$ on metal details are not difficult to maintain.

---

multiple applications of essentially the same functional combinations which would be evaluated at the same level. When properly written, it should be based on a fairly thorough study of several job situations. All too often such studies are omitted. Problems are then compounded by making only a superficial analysis of the tours of duty to which the description is subsequently applied.

Most commonly, the standard description omits references to specific product codes, model numbers of equipment, details about procedures, or modifying words or phrases which pin down difficulty or complexity. It is the easiest,

---

FIGURE 3   Specific Description for a Higher-Level Job

JOB GRADE SPECIFICATION
(SHOP-TYPE JOB)

JOB TITLE: Machine Setter (Wire-forming and Cutting Machines)

JOB FUNCTION: Set up and operate wire-cutting and forming machines, and collaborate with engineers and supervisors in overcoming operational difficulties to produce a large variety of metal piece parts.

JOB DUTIES AND PROCEDURES: Obtain, read, and understand manufacturing information to determine requirements and procedures involved in setting up and operating wire-cutting and forming machines for producing small, delicate, metal piece parts to close tolerances.

Set up and adjust wire-cutting and forming machines for production of metal piece parts to close tolerances by performing operations such as changing camming surfaces, referring replacement of cams to machine repair organization, mounting and making multiple, accurate, interrelated adjustments to forming tools, mandrels, strippers, feed rate, cutoff position, and wire straightener. Collaborate with product engineers and toolmakers in the setup and prove-in of new and repaired tools and discuss problems concerning their operating characteristics and acceptability. Remove and sharpen cutoff tool as required. Make trial runs and check quality of piece parts with the aid of a microscope, optical comparator, go–no-go gages, vernier calipers, dial indicator gage, micrometer, and scale.

Diagnose and clear job difficulties such as failure of product to meet close tolerances or frequent jamming of machine. Devise mucket arrangements as necessary to clear difficulties. Clean and lubricate machines and equipment as required. Report unusual conditions to supervisor and maintenance organization. Record production and quality obtained and compute and post information on control charts. Receive work orders and schedule work as required to meet demands. Order, obtain, and maintain the necessary supply of wire and ribbon. Instruct machine operators in the setup and operation of the equipment involved.

TYPICAL PRODUCTS, PROCESSES, AND CHARACTERISTICS INVOLVED: Cut and form wire and ribbon piece parts such as base tabs, clips, folded armatures, pole pieces, heater connectors, springs, slugs. *This tour is limited to not more than one employee per shift.*

MACHINES AND EQUIPMENT: HOW USED	Operate	Change Tools	Adjust	Set Up
"Bundgens" Wire Cutoff Machine, "Nilson" Multi-Slide Press #S2F, "Nilson" 4-Slide Press #0 and #00	x	x	x	x
Stacking Machine	x		x	
Pedestal Grinder	x			

TOOLS AND GAGES USED: Vernier calipers, go–no-go gages, micrometer, dial indicator gage, metal scales, weighcount scales, toolmakers' microscope, optical comparator, and associated gage charts and common-use hand tools.

SOURCE OF METHODS AUTHORITY: Verbal instructions; layouts, piece part drawings.

ACCURACY REQUIREMENTS AND DIFFICULTY OF MEETING THEM: Considerable accuracy required to set up and adjust wire-cutting and forming machines to produce small, delicate, metal piece parts to tolerances of 0.0005″.

quickest, and least costly description to apply, gives the supervisor the greatest amount of administrative latitude, and is least demanding in terms of maintenance effort. At the same time, its use assumes a knowledge in depth by the analyst (not always true) of each application situation, and it provides the weakest support for evaluations, lends itself most readily to misadministration, and is most vulnerable to union challenge. See Chapter 4 for further information on standard descriptions.

The *general description* is a compromise between standard and specific descriptions. It covers a basic combination of functions and responsibilities common to several jobs and requires a thorough study of each job involved. It is written broadly enough to allow for some variations in product, equipment, or procedure as long as the evaluation is not affected. Also, the general description might include some functions performed by one or more of the jobs but not necessarily all of them, a fact which imposes constraints on its preparation and use. Because these descriptions are broadly written and allow for different combinations of functions, their language must be properly qualified to forestall misleading information as to specific individuals.

The general description can be a useful tool, but it is not as good as the specific description for making comparisons. Furthermore, experience has shown that it can generate administrative problems and union grievances if not properly written in the first place or if a supervisor chooses to ignore the limitations built into the description. Although the time required to make a job study (per job) for a general description is nearly the same as it is for a specific description, and although description writing time may actually be a little longer, the per-job cost of coverage should be lower, since it will be spread over several jobs. Finally, it takes more care and skill to prepare a good general description than any other kind. Figure 4 is an example of a good general description for a low-grade-level job.

PREPARATION OF DESCRIPTIONS

Description writers are advised to strive for brevity, since excessive detail makes a description unwieldy. Certainly, a description is unnecessarily cluttered with such phrasing as "it is the duty of _____," "a _____ should be able to _____," and "a _____ must be thoroughly familiar with _____." Also, a description should not be regarded as a manufacturing layout specifying "how to" for every task.

On the other hand, the description should contain enough detail to assure its effectiveness as an instrument of wage administration. The aim should be both to reflect the intent of the job (the reason for its existence) and to delineate its content in such a way as to support the evaluation of the job, facilitate comparisons with other jobs, and minimize the supervisor's job administration problems. Because of legal considerations, it is important that statements made in the description (whether applicable to job duties or conditions or to qualification requirements for incumbents) be accurate and provable. The following sections discuss the description format, arrangement, and style which best help achieve these aims.

Format Except for the very brief descriptions, it is common for descriptions to have two parts. The first, frequently designated the "job function" or "job sum-

FIGURE 4   General Description for a Low-Level Job

JOB GRADE SPECIFICATION
(SHOP-TYPE JOB)

JOB TITLE: Material Handler (General)

JOB FUNCTION: Handle and transport piece parts, assemblies, equipment, tools, and miscellaneous materials and supplies between storerooms, storage areas, work positions, inspection, and other designated areas. Maintain quantities of supplies on hand and perform associated handling, stacking, sorting, packing, and counting duties.

JOB DUTIES AND PROCEDURES: Refer to tab cards, delivery tickets, packing and stock lists, identification tags, and similar information in order to identify and verify quantities of items required for transport.

Transport various items between storerooms, storage areas, and work positions. Maintain levels of stock consistent with needs of individual work positions and available storage space. Increase or decrease quantities provided as instructed by responsible personnel. Requisition items as required.

Supply individual work positions with necessary parts, materials, supplies, and containers. Remove completed work from work positions and transport to subsequent work, inspection, or storage areas. Store items on multiple-tiered racks using hi-lift truck. Assist operators in loading, unloading, and handling materials and parts.

Perform associated duties, such as sorting and arranging items in storage area; weighing, counting, packing, unpacking, stamping, loading, and unloading parts and materials; cleaning parts in solutions; and removing burrs from parts. Perform stock selecting and bench and degreasing operations where instructions and demonstrations are provided by designated personnel. Post records of stock on hand and in process. Take inventory of items in stockrooms and storage areas on a periodic basis. Record quantities of items on hand, using a programmed teletype machine and keep punched teletype tape and printout for disposition by others.

Maintain storage areas in a clean and orderly condition. Dispose of empty cartons, boxes, scrap, and similar items.

MACHINES AND EQUIPMENT: HOW USED	*Operate*
Walkie-type hi-lift fork truck and hand transporter	x
Hydraulic hand-lift truck, tea carts, floor-controlled electric bridge crane, shelf trucks, and similar material-handling equipment, steel strapper and tape dispenser, storage racks, cargotainers, containers, trays, skids and weight scales	x
Blakeslee degreaser, vacuum cleaner, and teletype machine	x

TOOLS AND GAGES USED: Pliers, screwdriver, wrenches, files, band and wire cutters, tapers, brushes, brooms, and similar items.

SOURCE OF METHODS AUTHORITY: Detailed verbal instructions; identification tags, packing and stock lists, material requisitions, scrap tickets, delivery tickets, tab cards, and similar information.

mary," is a concise summation in one or two sentences of the job's main functions, intended to reflect the purpose of the job. The second is a more detailed series of statements about the functions, labeled "major job duties" or "work performed" or something similar. In some formats, this section will include the products, equipment, and sources of instruction as an integral part of the description. In others, separate sections will be set aside for this information.

Arrangement Functions are most commonly arranged in one of the following sequences:

1. In order of importance, i.e., the main reasons for the existence of the job regardless of the amount of time involved or the effect on evaluation
2. Chronologically, i.e., the sequence in which the functions are performed
3. For their significance to the evaluation of the job, i.e., highlighting those functions which have greatest impact on main evaluation factors
4. According to the proportion of time spent out of the full tour

Occasionally these sequences may coincide, but when they do not, evaluation significance is the preferred arrangement. However, it is often impossible to determine the significance of a particular function. When this is the case, proportion of time is usually preferred, although order of importance is equally acceptable.

Style Comments on style found in various texts generally recommend terse or concise sentences built around action verbs. One company goes a bit further in its instruction manual by providing word lists wherein those grouped in list 1 are relatively clear as to meaning, while those grouped in list 2 are somewhat ambiguous and require supplementary explanation. To facilitate understanding, every effort should be made to quantify the description. Where it is necessary to use such words as "large" or "complex," the terms should be defined by concrete examples. Writers should avoid negative language and, wherever possible, such terms as "simple" and "minor importance," which would demean the job in the mind of the incumbent.

EMPLOYEE'S ROLE IN WRITING AND MAINTAINING JOB DESCRIPTIONS

The role of the employee in description writing is almost universally kept to a minimum. In those few companies where incumbents have been involved, it has always been in collaboration with either the job supervisor or the analyst. This is understandable, since description writing for wage administration application requires skill in using meaningful language and in organizing descriptions for effective comparisons. Attempts have been made to involve the employee through the use of questionnaires and a rather elaborate set of instructions. However, experience has shown that results from the questionnaire approach are generally unsatisfactory. In most instances, the job description is the logical follow-up of a job analysis by a specialist. To bring the analyst into the picture at some later point would either impair the effectiveness of the effort or result in a wasteful duplication.

Of course, this does not preclude employee involvement in the job study as an interviewee, but in companies with a wage incentive plan, some unions have ruled out even this kind of participation as an interference with the employee's earning process.

In the area of job description maintenance, employee participation is almost always a matter of self-interest. For example, when changes occur in their own jobs or nearby jobs, employees may question either the job supervisor or the union representative about the adequacy of their job descriptions (and grade levels).

PROCEDURES FOR APPROVALS OF JOB DESCRIPTIONS

Approval procedures vary according to the kind of responsibility vested in job supervisors and wage administrators, the extent to which a company uses administrative controls, the extent to which job descriptions are used for other purposes, and the terms of union contracts relative to approvals.

Since it is a management responsibility to organize work and design jobs, incumbents are seldom involved in the approval process. An exception to this may occur where there is an inexperienced supervisor and job study information has been obtained from the employee. In such cases, confirmation is obtained as to the accuracy and completeness of the write-up of job study information, but approval of the job description itself is not sought.

Depending on the authority given, the supervisor may have approval over the entire job grade specification or be limited to approval of the job description alone or of the write-up of job study information. In some cases, while lacking approval authority per se, the supervisor may have the right to challenge the accuracy of the job grade specification within a given time.

Because the design of jobs occasionally involves questions of functional alignment and delegation of responsibility, most companies require the approval of upper-level supervision of the line organization. Approval by upper-level supervision in the wage administration sector is also generally required with regard to the acceptability of the job description and evaluation.

Except where the job description is actually used in bargaining a grade level or pay rate, union involvement generally consists of challenging the accuracy of the job grade specification within a given time.

An ideal arrangement would involve the following aspects:

1. Job supervisor's agreement that the job analysis write-up is a comprehensive, error-free representation of the job
2. Job supervisor's agreement that the job description is complete, accurate, and a usable administrative document
3. Upper-level line supervision's agreement as to functional alignment and responsibility delegations
4. Wage administration supervision's agreement as to the acceptability of the job description and evaluation
5. Where several plants use the same job evaluation plan and grade structure, corporate wage administration approval as to consistency of plan application
6. If applicable, union review and approval as to completeness and accuracy of job grade specification

SEPARATING THE PERSON FROM THE JOB

In most hourly jobs, the procedure or technique employed by the operator is rather rigidly prescribed, with little opportunity to personalize the job. Designing jobs to get maximum use of the talents of a particular employee is not too uncommon in more complicated jobs which require the employee to solve problems—for example, to identify causes of defects and to propose remedial measures or to improvise tooling or methods for accomplishing tasks.

It takes experience and judgment on the part of the job analyst to ascertain the extent to which the skill of the operator makes functions appear easier or more difficult than they really are. This calls for an appreciation of both the relative requirements of a wide variety of jobs and what constitutes normal operator proficiency on various kinds of tasks, as well as some knowledge of the things employees can do and sometimes do to distort the appearance of what the job really entails.

THE IMPORTANCE OF UPDATING JOB DESCRIPTIONS

If job descriptions are of any significance to a company's wage and salary administration or to any other area of management control, then it is essential that they be kept up to date. Changes in jobs take many forms and occur for a variety of reasons. For example:

1. A change in physical facilities or surroundings might affect the comfort, fatigue, or hazard factors of a job, creating or eliminating the need for protective garments or equipment and/or altering the way in which functions are performed.

2. A technological change either in the product itself or in the process or equipment used to manufacture, test, transport, or pack the product could affect the environmental factors mentioned above. It might make the job easier or more difficult to perform. It might create or eliminate a need for special knowledge. It might also affect the time needed to perform a particular function, so that the employee would be required to operate several machines or perform several procedures instead of one, or the function might now be combined with other functions in order to fill out the job tour.

3. A change in supervisors might result in a realignment of several jobs into completely new combinations of functions which could entail an increase or decrease of difficulty and/or responsibility of any given job. Some of this restructuring might be a reflection of current interest in job enrichment or of a companywide drive for more efficient use of personnel. The same consequences might result from changes in the corporate structure, product lines, or volume of business.

Some changes are abrupt and quite marked, clearly calling for a review of the job and a revision of the description. Others are more gradual or more subtle and frequently go unnoticed. Also, it is sometimes difficult to decide when a change in a job has enough significance to merit the time and effort involved in rewriting a job description. Minor changes are often ignored. Occasionally, however, even though the change may only be a minor one, pressure from job supervision or the union may force a description rewrite. Some companies cope with minor changes by issuing a supplement sheet noting the changes. Another method is to reissue the job description, noting the change and coding the sheet as a revision. Sometimes the change is merely noted in the study folder with nothing being done to the job description until a major change occurs. Any of these approaches is adequate; the important point is that the change has been recognized and recorded.

The issue of job description maintenance entails several questions of urgency, importance, and responsibility. What are they and how should they be handled?

The need for prompt action in description maintenance relates to the nature of the change. Anything affecting the rate of pay (labor cost) of a job or requiring the movement of personnel should be dealt with as soon as possible. Experience has shown that when updating action is put off for an extended period after a change, job descriptions tend to lose their effectiveness as a management tool. Moreover, if the change affects the employee's rate of pay adversely and a union is involved, it is almost impossible to regrade the job.

Changes which have no effect on the evaluation or location of the job can be processed on an as-time-permits basis, but even these should not be unduly postponed.

What are the potential effects of a change? Paycheck and placement considerations have already been mentioned. Very closely related to these are employee morale and motivation. The change and/or a failure to recognize it might generate complaints or claims from employees on other jobs. Where a union is involved, the change could offer the union a means of demonstrating to employees that it is guarding their interests. It could also be the basis for unwanted militancy and might provide an item of leverage in negotiating contracts. From the company's standpoint, aside from labor costs and preservation of employee morale, changes affect the planning of schedules, functional alignments, organization structures, personnel movements, training and hiring needs, etc.

It is obvious then that description maintenance is everybody's concern. But what about the responsibility for initiating action? Since it is management's responsibility to organize work, it follows that the job supervisor should arrange for a review of the job. All too often, though, the supervisor is ignorant of this responsibility—or may be inclined to put self-interest before company interest, hoping to avoid an unpleasant personnel situation, the need to train a replacement at a lower level, or the creation of a high-turnover job. Naturally, if there is something to be gained by the review, it is quite likely that the supervisor will take prompt action. Also, it is certain that employees and the union will be quick to call attention to changes that could result in increased pay for the job.

What can be done to assure that everybody's interest is protected when changes occur? Basic to everything is executive-level support of the company's wage administration program. Next, and almost as important, is education. Supervisors, employees, and the union must all understand the importance the company attaches to description maintenance. In particular, supervisors should know they will be held accountable for any undesirable consequences of inaction. Two other protective measures can be taken by the wage administration organization: (1) a program of periodic audits should be designed not only to ascertain if any unrecorded changes have occurred but also to detect any breaches of supervisory responsibility in wage administration and (2) where feasible, job analysts should have a close working relationship with the line organization so that they are aware of changes taking place and, if necessary, can remind the supervisor of his or her responsibility. Various other ways might be explored, such as requiring product planning or manufacturing engineers to keep the wage administration organization informed of anticipated technological changes. Regardless of the techniques employed, the important point is that everybody should be functioning as a team to preserve the integrity of the wage administration program.

chapter 3

Describing Salaried Jobs

A. W. Hudock

**STAFF VICE PRESIDENT, COMPENSATION AND BENEFITS,
SCOTT PAPER COMPANY, PHILADELPHIA,
PENNSYLVANIA**

Although in the past descriptions of salaried jobs were typically summarizations of job duties, used primarily for job evaluation, this is no longer the case. The art and science of management have become more complex, and as a result, a simple list of responsibilities is no longer sufficient to describe realistically the content of management jobs. Further, management has recognized that job descriptions can be useful in meeting a variety of organizational needs beyond the traditional job evaluation applications.

Today the job description format recognizes that management jobs exist not to perform a prescribed set of duties but to play a part in managing the total enterprise by being accountable for the accomplishment—either personally, through the supervision of others, or through the managing of functions—of some objectives of the enterprise.

A marketing vice president, for example, is accountable for moving goods profitably from the factory floor into the hands of the consumer. A plant manager is accountable for the timely production of a given volume of goods which meet prescribed quality standards at a budgeted cost while maintaining the equipment properly. Each is accountable for the safety, development, and motivation of his or her work force.

The environment within which management jobs operate will vary from company to company, depending upon the degree of delegation or centralization of authority and to some extent on individual incumbents, but the basic reason for a mangement job to be on the payroll—to accomplish some desired end result—is the same.

PURPOSES AND USES OF JOB DESCRIPTIONS

Considering the breadth of responsibility of management jobs, the descriptions of these jobs can serve as a vital management tool not only in job evaluation but also in:

1. *Organization Analysis.* Job descriptions provide a solid foundation for examining job relationships, exposing overlaps and omissions in accountabilities, and highlighting the critical aspects and needs of each job.

2. *Performance Appraisal.* The job description's list of accountabilities (end results) can be used to develop short-term objectives, against which individual performance can be measured.

3. *Selection and Training.* Whether it be for hiring or promotion, a good job description provides the essential requirements of a job, against which the applicant's qualifications can be measured. Once an individual has been selected, the job description provides him or her with an overall charter of the position.

4. *Management Development.* By focusing attention on the know-how and problem-solving elements of a job, management can determine the development needs of present and potential job incumbents. Job descriptions, together with a management audit, followed up by a training or recruitment program, are the prime ingredients of a management continuity program.

5. *Career Planning.* Job descriptions, together with job evaluation, form the basis for a planned career development program, including a promotional path through successive levels of job accountability and exposure to various management functions.

To serve these multiple functions, as well as to provide the basic information needed for job evaluation, the description must specify:

1. *Why the Job Exists:* its general function and primary objective. In addition, the description should list the important end results (accountabilities) which the incumbent must achieve to fulfill his or her mission and attain the primary objective of the job.

2. *The Kind of Job It Is:* the general framework and environment in which it operates; its role in the organizational scheme; its relationship with and dependence upon other functions and jobs; its important external relationships; and the basic challenges of the job. Additionally, the description must bring out the general nature of technical, managerial, problem-solving, and human relations skills required by the job.

3. *The Job's Freedom to Act:* the nature and source of controls limiting the incumbent's ability to make final decisions and take action.

4. *The Job's Impact:* how the primary objective of the job affects major corporate objectives; how significant the impact of the job is.

5. *The Magnitude of the Job:* the general dollar size of the area most clearly affected by the job. A distinction should be made here between dynamic dol-

lars (sales quota, budget expenditure, etc.) and static dollars (assets, money managed, etc.). Usually, manufacturing organizations are concerned with dynamic dollars, while financial institutions are involved with static dollars.

6. *The Supporting Staff:* the size, scope, and nature of each major function reporting to the job.

SELECTING JOB ANALYSTS

It is apparent that the job assigned the accountability to develop management job descriptions itself requires considerable management skills. The job analyst must be of management caliber, with enough managerial know-how to understand how the various parts of the enterprise function and interact. He or she must be sufficiently familiar with management's philosophy and the organization's climate and objectives to be able to extract the essence and ignore the frills of management jobs. The analyst must be perceptive enough to distinguish between why a job exists and how it operates and to identify the content of the job as distinct from a particular individual's handling of it. The job analyst must be a persistent but tactful interviewer, always keeping in mind that he or she is dealing with a sensitive area, which ultimately is associated with compensation level. The job analyst must have analytical ability and the integrity to use it, coupled with the ability to write with clarity and precision.

CONDUCTING THE INTERVIEW

Preparing a job description requires a high order of integrity and objective thinking by the job analyst, both in interviewing the job incumbent and in writing the description. The job analyst should always keep in mind that he or she is concerned with the job and what it is intended to accomplish, and not with the person in the job.

This is not easy. Some persons will aggressively overstate the roles they perform, while others will depreciate the roles of their jobs. The job analyst can best avoid either extreme by being prepared with a checklist of questions which will keep the interview focused on facts.

During the interview, the job analyst should give the incumbent full attention, since this is the incumbent's "day in court." Detailed notes should be taken, but not in a fashion which disrupts the incumbent's chain of thought. The interview can be kept on track by following an outline prepared beforehand; for example:

1. Please give me a brief description of your overall function.
2. What is the overall end result expected from your job?
3. What annual dollar dimensions (budgets, sales, payroll, etc.) does your job impact upon?
4. Sketch briefly for me your departmental organization, showing the functions and persons reporting to you and the person and function to whom you report.
5. Describe briefly the types of policies you initiate, interpret, or work within.
6. Give me some examples of the types of procedures you initiate, interpret, or work within.

7. Give me some examples of the planning you do to carry out your job. Do these plans include other functional areas?

8. Tell me the makes or breaks (principal accountabilities) of your job. What are the end results which your boss expects you to accomplish? Which of these do you do yourself and which are delegated to subordinates?

9. What accountability do you have for establishing, approving, or recommending budgets, quotas, work performance standards, etc.?

10. What maximum dollar approval authority do you have?

11. Describe the type of guidance, direction, or supervision you receive.

12. What do you feel is needed in the way of formal education and/or experience to do your job in an acceptable manner?

13. What human relations skills does your job require? Describe for me some typical people relationships in your job—with subordinates, with other departments, with people outside the company.

WRITING THE JOB DESCRIPTION

The written job description should help the reader grasp the essential and significant facts—"the guts"—of the position. Extraneous details should be avoided.

The description should be written on the basis of how the job is being done *now*, not how the incumbent thinks it should be done, nor how it was done in the past, nor how it might be done in the future. In the vast majority of cases, the truly significant facts concerning any job can be recorded in no more than two pages. In fact, establishing two pages as the maximum length for a management job description forces precise and clear thinking as to what facts are truly relevant and encourages crisp, concise writing. The usefulness of the job description is also enhanced by the adoption of a uniform format and writing style.

The analyst's job is to record significant facts, not to reach conclusions concerning them. For example, a statement such as, "This position requires a high degree of aptitude in dealing with people," is an opinion and should be avoided. Instead, state factually *just what is involved in dealing with people*. Similarly, if a need for a knowledge of electronics is claimed, indicate why the need exists.

Use figures whenever possible instead of less precise phrases such as "few," "many," "very large," "very small," etc. Where the amount fluctuates, show the range. Let the reader decide whether 20 or 2000 is "a few," "many," or "a large amount."

In summary, in writing a job description, the job analyst should:

1. Focus on important, significant facts, stated in objective terms.
2. Follow a uniform outline.
3. Write in clear, concise language, using a uniform style.
4. Avoid repetition and trivia.

JOB DESCRIPTION FORMAT

After a standard heading that would include job title, name of incumbent, department or division in which the job is located, date, and the name of the job analyst, a good job description should begin with a capsule statement which in two or three sentences tells why the job is on the payroll. This section should give the reader a quick grasp of the specific end results the job is intended to accomplish. Other sections normally included in a written job description are described below.

Dimensions   This section should summarize in broad terms all statistics pertinent to the job, giving the reader a clear picture of the magnitude of the end results affected by the job. Magnitude is measured in terms of money on an annual basis, whether operating budget, sales volume, cost of wages and salaries, assets or funds managed, or other aspects significant to the job. To provide additional perspective, pertinent items other than money, e.g., number of subordinates, unit volumes, number of plants, etc., should be included.

Nature and Scope   This section is the real heart of a job description. It should be written in narrative fashion and should tell the reader what the job is all about. This section should describe the following facets of the job:

1. How the job fits into the organization, including reference to significant internal and external relationships.

2. The general composition of supporting staff, including a short summary of each function supervised, if any.

3. The general nature of technical, managerial, and human relations know-how required. If this is a marketing job, for example, the narrative should describe what is sold, how it is sold, the nature of the distribution, what promotional techniques are used, the nature of the competition, and the other major challenges of the job.

4. The nature of the problem solving required. The narrative should describe the key problems that accrue to the job, including problems which are dealt with by the incumbent and problems which are referred to higher authority.

5. The nature and source of controls on the incumbent's freedom to solve problems and take action. Controls on freedom to act will exist to some degree in the form of established policy and procedures in supervisory relationships or inherently in the job itself. A cost accountant in a manufacturing operation, for example, may analyze and pinpoint the reason for a variance in production costs but is not free to take corrective action. Even the chief executive officer of a company has constraints imposed by the board of directors, shareholders, federal and state laws, etc.

Principal Accountabilities   This section is a listing of the important end results which the job exists to achieve. These will vary in number from perhaps four to as many as eight or ten. Each statement should be a concise "do" statement, accompanied by a "why" statement or clause. Each statement should pinpoint an accountability against which some measure of performance can be applied. The following checklist will help ensure complete coverage of the broad managerial areas for which a job might possibly be held accountable:

1. *Organization.* What accountability, if any, does the job incumbent have for (1) planning the structure of the organization; (2) staffing the organization; and (3) developing and motivating the organization, including selection, training, appraisal, wage and salary administration, hiring and firing, etc.?

2. *Strategic Planning.* What accountability, if any, does the job have for long-range planning? Does the job have an accountability to establish policy objectives, set long-range goals and targets, or establish quality standards of people, equipment, and product? Usually, only top-level jobs have an accountability for long-range planning.

3. *Tactical Planning, Execution, and Directing the Attainment of Objectives.* What accountability does the job have for managing, supervising, or performing activities on a day-to-day basis in order to carry out assigned functions effectively?

4. *Review and Control.* What accountability does the job have for assessing the effectiveness of the organization in achieving its objectives? What key controls are available to the job to give warning signals when things go wrong? If there are none, should there be?

It is worth reemphasizing here that an accountability is an end result or objective which the job exists to achieve. In contrast, a duty or responsibility is the means by which end results are achieved. Management job descriptions should concern themselves with the former, not the latter. Whether a sales manager keeps the sales force effective and enthusiastic by means of group meetings, memos, or personal visits to the field is immaterial; one of the end results expected of a sales manager is to maintain an effective and enthusiastic sales force.

Thus the total job description should tell the reader in two typewritten pages or less:

1. *Why* the job is on the payroll
2. *What* there is to do
3. *How* and *under what conditions* these things are done

Sample job descriptions for exempt and nonexempt salaried jobs are shown as Figures 1 and 2.

JOB DESCRIPTION APPROVAL

The foregoing discussion assumes that information about each job has been obtained by means of an interview conducted by the job analyst with the job incumbent. This is without doubt the best method, although it is time-consuming. Alternatively, the job incumbent may be given a set of instructions and asked to write his or her own job description subject to clarification and editorial revision by the job analyst, or the incumbent may be asked to complete a questionnaire, the responses to which are used by the job analyst to develop a job description.

In any event, once the job description has been developed by the job analyst, it should be reviewed with the incumbent and approved by at least the immediate supervisor. Differences of opinion as to how the job is perceived are ironed out, and the final description is prepared.

Here, too, the job analyst must function as an analyst and not as a mere recorder of opinion. If two persons have laid claim to the same accountability, for example, the analyst should point out the overlap to the supervisor and resolve the matter. Frequently the overlap of accountabilities involves more

FIGURE 1   Sample Job Description—Exempt

JOB TITLE: Manager of Compensation   DATE:
            and Benefits
INFORMATION PROVIDED BY:
JOB ANALYST:
DIVISION/PLANT:
DEPARTMENT:
REVIEWED BY:

Accountability Objectives

Plans and directs the development and implementation and audits the administration of programs in salaried job evaluation, salary administration, incentive compensation, and employee benefits which enable the company to attract, motivate, and retain high-caliber employees within the bounds of competitive costs.

Dimensions

Total Salary Payroll	$_____
Retirement Plan Costs	$_____
Group Insurance Costs	$_____
Stock Plans Costs	$_____
Budget	$_____
Persons Supervised	_____ exempt
	_____ nonexempt

Nature and Scope of Position

This position reports to the Vice President–Industrial Relations. This position is expected to keep informed of developments in compensation and benefits among leading companies in the national industrial community and to develop total compensation programs tailored to the needs of the company which will enable it to attract, retain, and motivate high-caliber employees. The incumbent directs and personally performs research in salary administration, management bonus plans, stock option plans, group insurance plans, pension plans, stock purchase plans, etc., and works with consultants, actuaries, and insurance carriers to develop new programs or changes to existing programs as well as internal policies and procedures to keep the company at a competitive level in total compensation. Detailed recommendations, including costs, are reviewed by the Vice President–Industrial Relations prior to presentation to the Chief Executive Officer. Once programs have been approved, the incumbent directs their implementation through the various divisional personnel organizations.

The incumbent serves as a consultant in compensation and benefits to all divisions and audits their ongoing administration of compensation and benefits programs. The incumbent secures all required Internal Revenue Service approvals and directs the filing of annual Form 5500 and related reports and the maintenance of corporatewide salary records. The incumbent serves as Secretary of the Retirement Board and works closely with the Vice President–Industrial Relations and the Executive Compensation Committee in the administration of such programs as the Management Incentive Plan, the Stock Option Plan, and executive salary reviews. The incumbent participates in labor negotiations as an employee benefits expert as required.

This position maintains close working relationships with the Law, Controller, Treasurer, and Tax Departments. Outside contacts are maintained with actuaries, insurance consultants, and compensation consultants. This position maintains membership and participates in associations of professional compensation and benefits administrators.

The principal challenge of this position is to develop and recommend programs of com-

---

FIGURE 1   Sample Job Description—Exempt (Continued)

---

pensation and benefits, appropriately balanced between direct and indirect compensation, which will maintain a total compensation climate at a sufficiently competitive level to enable the company to develop and maintain a highly talented and motivated managerial staff and a skilled and company-oriented work force and to minimize the cost of such programs by the use of effective funding methods and by the avoidance of duplication and errors in administration, both internally and with insurance carriers and actuaries.

Reporting to this position are:

Employee Benefits Analyst. This position performs research and develops recommendations for changes in all employee benefit programs—group insurance, pension plans, and stock purchase plans. The incumbent serves as a consultant to the operating divisions of the administration of these programs corporatewide and audits the effectiveness of the programs and their administration.

Compensation Analyst. This position conducts salary surveys and performs research in other forms of direct compensation and develops recommendations. The incumbent audits the administration of the salaried job evaluation program corporatewide.

Principal Accountabilities

1. Directs the development of compensation and benefits policy and programs which will enable the company to attract, retain, and motivate high-caliber employees within the bounds of competitive cost.

2. Keeps informed, through research and participation in professional associations, of current trends and levels in compensation and benefits to assure that the company's programs are maintained at competitive levels.

3. Serves all profit centers as a consultant in compensation and benefits to assure accurate and equitable administration.

4. Participates in labor negotiations as a pension and insurance expert as required to assure that the required expertise on these matters is available to the management bargaining team.

5. Directs the development of booklets, brochures, and other communications devices to communicate the company's compensation and benefits programs to all employees.

6. Keeps informed on laws and Internal Revenue regulations dealing with compensation and benefits matters to assure that all programs achieve maximum effectiveness within federal, state, and local regulations.

7. Selects, trains, and develops department personnel to ensure excellent current performance and the opportunity for future growth and development.

---

than one department. For example, the accountability for new-product development may well be claimed as a primary role by the sales department, the market planning department, and the research department. In such an instance, the job analyst can play a major role in organizational clarity by having the matter resolved by top management.

KEEPING JOB DESCRIPTIONS CURRENT

After a job evaluation system is installed, a procedure for maintaining current job descriptions and evaluations must be established. Since the job description focuses on end results and not duties, there is no need to revise the job description and reevaluate the job unless significant job changes occur. Nonetheless, departmental, divisional, and corporate reorganizations do occur. New jobs are

---

FIGURE 2   Sample Job Description—Nonexempt

JOB TITLE: Salary Records Clerk   DATE:
INFORMATION PROVIDED BY:
WRITTEN BY:
DIVISION/PLANT:
DEPARTMENT:
REVIEWED BY:

Accountability Objectives

Maintains and updates companywide salary records and compiles salary information for the preparation of surveys and special studies.

Nature and Scope of Position

This position reports to the Compensation Analyst.

The Salary Records Clerk is responsible for maintaining salary records for all exempt salaried employees. This is accomplished by inputting data from personnel status forms received from all divisions to computer-maintained records. Such records are updated weekly. Accuracy is vital, for these records are the central storehouse of salary information.

The Salary Records Clerk extracts information from salary records for the preparation of surveys and special studies. These surveys and special studies require some arithmetical calculations, such as percentages and averages. These studies require approximately half the incumbent's time.

In addition, the incumbent prepares monthly stock distribution award lists and major employment anniversary lists; collects data for periodic reports of salary administration activity; and assists with the general typing work load in the department.

This position requires clerical and typing skills and some familiarity with computers and CRTs. Accuracy in record keeping and arithmetical calculation is important in preparing reports and studies.

This incumbent is in contact with staff and plant personnel departments, department heads, and executives concerning salary information.

Principal Accountabilities

1. Maintains salary records for all exempt salaried employees. Prepares maturity study and salary review data.
2. Gathers data for salary surveys and special studies and performs necessary arithmetical calculations.
3. Assists with general typing work load.

---

created and existing jobs are combined with others. Additionally, minor changes take place which cumulatively amount to a significant change over time.

Whenever a new job is created, preferably *before* the job is filled, a job description should be written for it. Frequently, there is resistance to writing a job description at this juncture, based on the assumption that the job won't jell until it has been operative for a few months. Balderdash! If the need for a new job is perceived so clearly that management has authorized the expenditure of additional payroll dollars to have that perceived end result accomplished, the job can be reduced to a written job description. The day that a new job incumbent appears on the scene, someone must know enough about what he or she is to do to get started. If that much is known, the job can be described in a job description.

In fact, the intellectual exercise of developing a description for a new job frequently results in a much better understanding of how the new job is to function and what it really is intended to accomplish. The existence of a written job description is a valuable aid to the new incumbent, giving quick understanding of the role to be played and reducing the wheel spinning and frustration to a minimum. Finally, since the job will ultimately be evaluated, and a salary range established in any event, it is far better to have these facts in hand before the job is filled rather than after the incumbent is placed in it and a salary level agreed upon. The job may change somewhat after it has been operative for a time, and if this happens, the job description and evaluation can be revised accordingly.

Whenever a major change occurs in an existing job, the job should be reanalyzed and a new description written. In a large organization, jobs are restructured rather frequently as employees are promoted or retire and managers rearrange accountabilities to fit the talents of the work force. Periodically, major reorganizations occur to meet new or changed conditions within or outside the organization. In each case, the changed jobs should be reanalyzed and described and a new evaluation made.

Additionally, all job descriptions should be reviewed periodically, perhaps at two- or three-year intervals, to take into account minor changes which may have occurred. The "dimension" portion of the job description is particularly likely to change over time. The job description should be updated as required and a judgment made as to whether the change is significant enough to warrant reevaluation.

In all cases of new jobs or restructured jobs, the job analyst can and should play a significant management role by being alert to duplication and overlap of accountabilities and by assuring that the problem is resolved at the appropriate management level. In most cases, duplication of accountabilities occurs not as a result of any deliberate attempt at empire building on the part of individual managers but simply because an individual manager perceives a need to be met and develops a capability to meet it. At the same time, another manager perceives the same need and develops a capability in that department to meet it. The job analyst is in a unique position to detect such overlaps and to call them to the attention of top management for clarification as to where in the organization the accountability should be placed.

NONEXEMPT SALARIED JOBS

Nonexempt salaried jobs are those which, because of their routine nature, fail to meet the test for exemption from the overtime requirements of the Fair Labor Standards Act. Typically, such jobs perform secretarial, clerical, or technician functions.

While nonexempt salaried jobs are more limited in scope and freedom to act than are exempt jobs, the format of the job description can be essentially the same. The emphasis, however, is on duties and skills rather than on broad accountability for end results.

chapter 4

Standard Descriptions

Ira T. Kay

SENIOR PRINCIPAL, THE HAY GROUP, PHILADELPHIA,
PENNSYLVANIA

A *standard* job description is a job analysis report that emphasizes the common characteristics of the work performed by many different employees in one or more employment situations. It is useful where (1) a large number of employees in one or more companies perform similar work and (2) the description is for general purposes rather than specific application to an individual employee. Standard descriptions are used best for nonexempt or lower-level exempt positions. A standard description is suited for advertising employment opportunities, for multiemployee selection, for organization design, for work process improvement, or for job matching in compensation comparisons. On the other hand, to attract a particular individual, conduct specific performance improvement efforts, build a sense of individual importance within the organization, or maintain records of detailed activities, more specific and unique descriptions are required.

JOB TITLE ALONE

The shortest and most general form of standard job description is a job title. If a job is relatively simple and widely known, such as "telephone operator," and particularly if the total job is defined by observable physical events and surroundings, such as "ditch digger," the title alone may provide a solid basis for communication among people who need to understand the work. In some cases, expanded statements of work elements, tasks, activities, duties, results, qualifications, and specifications may even be more confusing than clarifying.

On the other hand, a job title alone may not be very informative. Reconsider "telephone operator." The Office of Employment Statistics of the Bureau of Labor Statistics, Department of Labor, *Survey Dictionary,* in 1980, included both:

61430: CENTRAL OFFICE OPERATOR: Operates telephone switchboard to establish, or assist customers in establishing, local or long-distance telephone connections.

61377: SWITCHBOARD OPERATOR-RECEPTIONIST: In addition to performing duties of switchboard operator, acts as receptionist and may also type or perform routine clerical work as part of regular duties. The typing or clerical work may take part of this worker's time while at the switchboard.

The *Dictionary of Occupational Titles* (4th ed., 1977) of the Employment and Training Administration of the U.S. Department of Labor includes thirteen specific listings of telephone operator.

JOB COMPONENTS

Beyond job titles, standard job descriptions may cover some or all of the following hierarchical work components:

Element. The basic component of a work process that may include initiating, performing, and terminating units of work. Elements are the smallest individual units of identifiable and definable physical and mental work that produce an output.

Task. A coordinated series of work elements, used to produce an identifiable and definable output that can be independently consumed or used.

Activity. A group of tasks that form part of an employee's job requirements.

Duty. One or more activities performed in carrying out a job responsibility.

Responsibility. One or a group of duties that identifies and describes a major purpose or reason for the existence of a job.

Result. The intended outcome of work performance, from the perspective of a purposeful enterprise.

JOB REQUIREMENTS AND CHARACTERISTICS

Other items that might be included in standard job descriptions, to be even more complete and to cover more complex kinds of work, are:

Qualifications. Specific personal characteristics that are associated with the probability of success in performance in a job. Qualification must be defined relative to a standard for success, such as completion of training, minimum acceptable performance (placement), performance required by organizational achievement standards (proficiency), or exceptional performance.

Specifications. Personal characteristics and experiences that are likely to be associated with particular levels of qualification and, therefore, indirectly associated with the probability of success in performing a job. (In some usages "specifications" incorporates or is synonymous with "qualifications.")

Dimensions. Quantitative statements of performance standards and of context variables that define the scope within which performance must occur and the related level of proficiency.

A STANDARD DESCRIPTION

The above range of components and characteristics can be drawn upon selectively in communicating the job. The following example highlights these concepts:

Title. Driver, automobile.

Activity. Drives standard passenger car.

Duty. Transport visitors by car between the main gate and specified buildings within the facility.

Result. Timely, safe, secure, unobtrusive transportation for visitors while at the facility.

Qualification. Must hold a valid driver's license in the Commonwealth of Pennsylvania.

Dimensions. Approximately 25 visitors per day. Approximately 50 miles per day.

ADVANTAGES

The principal advantages of standard job descriptions, in situations where they are appropriate, are lower costs and easier maintenance than custom descriptions. They represent a compromise in validity—highly accurate regarding the covered jobs in general but limited accuracy with regard to the work of any particular employee. Where standard (or generic) descriptions are used, they usually must be supplemented by work station procedures in order to be useful for a particular firm.

Standard job descriptions are helpful because they can summarize and minimize distinctions that may not be important. While there is a loss of some information, it can be appropriate under certain circumstances.

chapter 5

Collecting Job Content Information through Questionnaires

Jesse T. Cantrill

PRINCIPAL, THE HAY GROUP, PHILADELPHIA,
PENNSYLVANIA

An effective salary administration program depends on a thorough understanding of the content and requirements of jobs. This information is used as a basis for job measurement, for comparison with other jobs in the labor marketplace, and for performance appraisal. A variety of methods exists to collect such information, including observation of the incumbent at work, interviews, and the use of questionnaires. Each method, alone or in combination with others, is appropriate in certain circumstances, and each method has its benefits and costs. This chapter focuses on the use of questionnaires to obtain job content information, explaining how to design and administer a questionnaire most effectively.

DECIDING TO USE A QUESTIONNAIRE

The primary source of information about a job is usually the incumbent, the person who performs the work. Normally, the job holder is able to explain or demonstrate what he or she does and is trying to achieve. Although some incumbents have difficulty articulating their roles, and a few are tempted to overstate the importance of their jobs, most people take great care to explain their jobs with accuracy and balance.

Problems in the use of a questionnaire are formidable, and they must be considered in any decision to employ this method of gathering information. A common criticism of the questionnaire is that respondents have difficulty providing a complete account of their work: they do not fully understand the questions or they have difficulty explaining themselves in writing. Other concerns are that the job holder will exaggerate the role or that the explanations will be incomprehensible to the job analyst who does not understand the technical language. These are legitimate problems and require care to overcome.

Another serious problem associated with the use of questionnaires is related to employee anxiety about the purpose of the study. In contrast to an interview or personal observation, the questionnaire reduces the contact between incumbent and analyst and limits opportunities for the job holder to query the analyst or defend the importance of the job. Many employees are suspicious, to some degree, of any study about their jobs; they fear that standards will be changed or that their jobs will be eliminated. They worry that their own contributions will be minimized, their pay reduced. The use of a questionnaire heightens this anxiety, particularly when the incumbent feels weak in organizing written thoughts.

Sound reasons exist for use of a questionnaire. Among them is the desire to reduce the cost and time of individual interviews or observations by an analyst. Another is the desire to collect similar information about each job, uninfluenced by the various differences among interviewers participating in a large project. A third reason to use a questionnaire is the desire to allow every employee to participate in the project rather than selecting and interviewing a representative smaller group.

At its best, the questionnaire is similar to a structured interview, with the important exception that the analyst is unable to explain questions or follow up on incomplete answers. While a questionnaire cannot substitute for the richness of a good interview, sufficient information about most jobs can be obtained from most incumbents if the questionnaire is carefully prepared and properly administered. Observing a few simple rules makes use of a questionnaire both efficient and effective.

DESIGNING THE QUESTIONNAIRE

The analyst must create a document which is easy for the job holder to read, understand, and answer. The questions should elicit sufficient information about the job to meet the specific purpose of the study. Although this seems simple enough, the design of a good questionnaire can be time-consuming and frustrating.

At the Hay Group, the "Position Information Questionnaire" is prepared on letter-size, white bond paper. This format is chosen because our questionnaires are often photocopied for use by a job evaluation committee. The multipage document includes instructions, a set of questions, and adequate space for typical responses.

Writing the questions is the essential task of the job analyst and requires judgment appropriate to the intended use of the information. If the study will emphasize organizational relationships or work flow and control procedures, questions must be designed to learn about those aspects of jobs. If the study is designed to elicit information about the training needs of job holders, other questions will be asked. We commonly use questionnaires to provide information for job evaluation, so our questions pertain to the job factors which we measure.

Our questionnaire is composed of four distinct sections:

- Heading
- Dimensional data
- Instructions
- Job content questions

Figure 1 illustrates the cover page of a typical questionnaire. It includes the first three of the above four items.

The heading corresponds to the identifying information found on a job description and should be consistent with the language used by the organization. Space for the signatures of reviewing officials is important if you want to assure that the document represents an approved account of the job.

FIGURE 1   Position Information Questionnaire

Position Title: _____   Date Prepared: _____

Incumbent: _____   Reviewed by: _____
                      (name)   (signature of
                                                                                                     supervisor)

Reports to: _____   _____
                                                                             (signature of
                                                                              department
                                                                              manager)

Department: _____

DIMENSIONAL DATA:

EMPLOYEES:		BUDGETS:	
Exempt	_____	Payroll	_____
Nonexempt	_____	Total Expenses	_____
		Sales Revenue	_____

Instructions:

The information which you provide on this questionnaire about your job will be used by a committee of organization managers to evaluate your job. The information will also be used by the Personnel Department to prepare a formal job description. Your care in completing the questionnaire fully and accurately is very important.

Please answer all the questions which apply to your job. Try to use specific examples to illustrate your ideas, remembering that many people who will read the questionnaire do not understand technical language which is familiar to you.

You do not need to type your responses, but try to write clearly so they can be read easily. If you need more space, please add extra sheets of paper. Do not write on the back of any pages, because we plan to make photocopies and might miss part of your answer.

Call [name and telephone number of project coordinator] if you have any questions. Please forward your completed questionnaire through your supervisor to [office and date when due]. Thank you for your assistance.

Dimensional data are used in the evaluation of jobs in order to understand the size of the organizational unit which is impacted by the job. Where we find that accurate information about budgets is more easily obtained by the job analyst from the official records of the organization or from senior managers than from each job holder, we may indicate that the incumbent need not complete this section.

The instructions request each job holder to take care in completing the document, explaining its purpose and use. We ask that additional pages be attached if more space is needed, provide the telephone number of a person who can provide assistance, and request that the completed document be routed through the supervisor to a central collection point. We usually ask that the document be completed within two weeks, knowing that we will need to follow up on those which are late.

The questions we ask are similar to those asked by the job analyst in a structured interview and are intended to provide the information needed to prepare a comprehensive job description or to evaluate the job using the "Hay Guide Chart-Profile Method." We are trying to learn about the know-how and problem-solving requirements of the job and to understand the magnitude and nature of its impact on the end results of the organization. Figure 2 illustrates a set of questions prepared for use by a nonprofit service organization.

There is much discussion about the need to prepare different questions for different groups of employees. Our view is that the questions illustrated in Figure 2 are appropriate to all groups, nonexempt and hourly employees as well as technical and professional groups. Others disagree and prefer to administer different questionnaires for each group. Each analyst must write questions to suit particular purposes of the study, selecting and modifying questions as appropriate for the target audience. Think about the information you need, and write questions to obtain that information.

ADMINISTERING THE QUESTIONNAIRE

Preparation and distribution of a questionnaire is a straightforward process, but adherence to a few simple guidelines will contribute to the collection of good quality information from job holders.

1. Pretest the questions.   Ask a friend or colleague to fill out the questionnaire; find out in advance which questions are obscure. Try to write a job description or evaluate the job from the completed document, and determine what other information needs to be learned.

Eliminate unnecessary or repetitious questions. There is a great temptation to ask more questions than are necessary for a sound understanding of the job, but it is also discouraging to miss one or more vital pieces of information for failure to include a question.

2. Type and duplicate the document with care.   This sounds too obvious, but precision in spelling and punctuation, as well as attention to layout and reproduction, indicates to the respondent that the project is important and worthy of care in answering the questions.

3. Meet with the employees who are being asked to complete the questionnaire.   This step is often neglected, but it is important if you desire complete information about each job. Answering the questionnaire requires several

FIGURE 2   Job Content Questions

SUMMARY OF POSITION
1. Briefly, why does your job exist? (State the primary purpose of your job, in one or two sentences.)

NATURE OF WORK
2. What kind of work do you perform most of the time? What are typical activities or projects assigned to you? If you have subordinates, how do you organize and direct their work? (Please try to give some specific examples which illustrate the nature of your work.)
3. If other employees report to you, what is each position title and what is the basic purpose of each job?

Position Title: _____
Basic Purpose of Job:

Position Title: _____
Basic Purpose of Job:

JOB ENVIRONMENT
4. How do you get work assignments?
5. What kind of guidance is available to help you solve problems?
6. What are typical decisions which you are authorized to make after you have studied a problem or situation, and what are those decisions which must be referred to others before you can take action?
7. How is your work reviewed or checked? What kinds of controls exist to assure that you achieve the objectives of the job?

CHALLENGES
8. What is the most difficult or complex part of your work? (Please describe a specific example to illustrate the kinds of problems you try to solve.)

JOB REQUIREMENTS
9. If you were to be transferred or promoted, what kinds of experience or training should you expect in the person who replaced you? What special skills are required to do your job?
10. What equipment do you operate or maintain? What unusual working conditions do you normally experience?

PRINCIPAL ACCOUNTABILITIES
11. What specific end results are expected from your job?
(1)
(2)
(3)
(4)
(5)
(6)

ADDITIONAL INFORMATION
12. What other information can you provide to help us to understand the unique requirements of your job?

hours of time and, for most people, represents a laborious task. Some job holders work on the project at home, others fit it in during slack time on the job. The analyst is asking job holders to provide information which the analyst would otherwise have to record.

Employees should be told how the information will be used. Not only is it important to reduce anxiety about the purpose of the project, but job holders are able to provide more helpful information if they understand why it is being collected. Meeting with groups of employees to describe the project and review the questions does not fully overcome the impersonal characteristics of a questionnaire, but it does allow job holders to understand what the analyst is asking.

4. *Assure incumbents that they are not being measured by their writing skills.* This is the most pervasive fear of job holders whenever a job content questionnaire is administered: many people believe that their own jobs will be minimized unless they can express themselves well in writing. We take great pains to explain how our job evaluation method measures the requirements of jobs in order to assure people that we are not judging their writing style.

5. *Identify someone who will answer employees' questions.* Be sure that the instructions on the questionnaire provide a name and telephone number in order to make it easy for the job holder to get assistance. If an outside consultant is administering the questionnaire, designate a representative from the organization's own personnel department or other office to answer routine inquiries.

6. *Assure that the incumbent's supervisor reviews the completed form.* Obviously, the supervisor lends a very important perspective to the job, particularly about its relationship to other jobs in the unit and the incumbent's authority to make decisions and take action. We ask incumbents to forward their completed questionnaires through their supervisors to a central collection point, and we keep a master list to record both receipt of the document and supervisory approval.

Occasionally, we are asked how to resolve differing views of a job; this question usually comes from an incumbent who believes that he or she is performing a different job from that originally assigned. We study the content of jobs as they are now being performed, but we cannot, as analysts or outside consultants, reconcile differences between employees and supervisors about the design of a job. We ask the two parties to come to agreement about the job before the questionnaire is submitted for our use, and we accept the supervisor's signature as indicating concurrence with the content described in the questionnaire.

7. *Edit the questionnaires when they are received.* Be sure to allow sufficient time to review and clarify the incumbent's responses. This may usually be done by telephone but could require a visit by the analyst to look at the equipment or materials described by the job holder. Remember that use of a questionnaire does not eliminate personal contact with job holders; it only reduces the time which must be spent by the analyst to document routine information. Complex jobs are still complex, and they require careful study by the analyst if they are to be properly understood.

8. *Prepare the completed questionnaires for use.* In many of our projects, the completed questionnaires are used by a job evaluation committee before formal job descriptions are prepared by the organization. When this occurs, it is very helpful to the committee to have the questionnaire in typed form. Be sure to make sufficient copies for each member of the committee and to save the original for the official file.

USING OTHER DOCUMENTS TO OBTAIN INFORMATION

In many organizations, some information about jobs is already available to an analyst. Often there has been a previous effort to describe jobs, even if this is only a list of duties or a brief summary of each position. Other useful references include such standard descriptions as those found in the *Dictionary of Occupational Titles* or in many salary surveys. Job specifications used by the employment department are also helpful.

None of these sources provides enough information to permit thorough analysis of a job, but each is useful as a preliminary view. The analyst can design the questionnaire to supplement this existing information and avoid collecting the same material a second time. This is particularly important if the original job descriptions were prepared with assistance from job holders who remember their earlier exertions.

SUMMARY

We find the questionnaire to be a most effective method of gathering information about jobs. Our experience has been that job holders at all levels in the organization make a serious effort to describe their work accurately. As a basis for the preparation of a job description or for the measurement of job content, the questionnaire is very useful when prepared and administered with care.

chapter 6

Collecting Data through Interviews and Observations

Thomas S. Roy, Jr.

**DIRECTOR, SALARIED COMPENSATION, ARMSTRONG
WORLD INDUSTRIES, LANCASTER, PENNSYLVANIA**

The preceding chapters discussed the collection of data on job content through the use of standard descriptions and questionnaires. These are probably the least expensive and most expeditious techniques that can be employed for this purpose. They do, however, have severe limitations. A complete review of a total operation, division, or company requires a broad range of descriptions and questionnaires. Moreover, using questionnaires with hourly factory workers is generally impractical, as many of them simply are not able to adequately describe and place proper emphasis in writing the duties involved in their work. Even supervisors are often unfamiliar with the duties of subordinates. Further, these approaches to the collection of data may be too impersonal and mechanized and presume considerable knowledge and understanding of the jobs being studied.

Generally, the interview and the observation, used in combination, are the best means of gathering complete information to develop a job description. These techniques are time-consuming and costly, but the quality of the data generated usually justifies the additional investment of time and money.

The observation technique is best-suited to factory jobs. The observation is usually carried out by an industrial engineer as part of more general responsibilities, and the observation is often the primary—even the sole—source of information used in developing the job description. Interviews are used for higher-level jobs, and they are conducted by interviewer-analysts specially selected and trained to fill this function. Interviews may serve as the exclusive source of job information, or they may be buttressed by additional study—for example, of the job's position in the organization structure.

OBSERVATION

Observation is the gathering of information by physically watching workers as they perform their tasks. Its major advantage is that information is gathered firsthand, thereby eliminating omissions and permitting a thorough understanding of the work. The analyst is thus familiarized with the working conditions, process flow, required skills, and equipment and materials involved.

This method is widely used in the factory for hourly jobs and is also successful for certain clerical jobs—those which are repetitious and require relatively little skill. It is applied best where the cycle of work is brief enough to permit the analyst to observe the entire job in a relatively short time. Observation of administrative or managerial jobs is considered impractical; its use for clerical jobs having a variety of duties is tedious and lengthy, and it is therefore often restricted to studies of clerical systems and procedures.

The steps involved in preparing for and carrying out an observation include the following:

1. Communicate purpose of observation. The beginning point for any procedure requiring personal contact is to gain the cooperation of the people involved and to remove any suspicions. It is important to review the purpose of the study with the supervisory personnel, so they may understand what information is required and why, and to communicate the purpose to the workers being observed. Often a departmental meeting is held for this purpose.

2. Gain overall picture. By means of prior study of available materials and through discussions with appropriate department heads, the observer should gain a general knowledge of the process flow, reporting relationships, and other pertinent information to obtain an overall view of the operations.

3. Determine observation points. To profitably observe the workers and to understand the task performed, key vantage points should be selected with the aid of the supervisor. Such posts should be relatively unobtrusive but still permit a clear view of the work. If possible, the sequence of observation points should follow the flow of work.

4. Begin observation. The actual observation should begin at the work station with the analyst visually studying the worker performing the job and carefully determining the overall nature and purpose of the assignment.

5. Observe in depth. Continued observations are made, through a complete work cycle if possible, with the analyst attempting to organize the pattern of work into a logical sequence. A successful analyst will be alert and attentive throughout the observation period. The analyst should seek an understanding of the important elements of the job and the task performed, to gain insight into the skills, abilities, and qualifications required.

6. Conclude the observation. After the observation has been completed, the analyst should immediately review the notes taken and fill in or expand on the various items noted. If areas are unclear or further elaboration is required, questions are noted for further clarification with the worker and/or supervisor.

For hourly rated or relatively routine clerical jobs, a skilled observer normally will be able to obtain sufficient information for practical job evaluations through the techniques described. For other salaried positions, particularly at the administrative and management levels, it is desirable that information on job content be obtained by means of a skilled interview. This is usually the most complete and accurate means of compiling needed data and gaining a thorough understanding of the job.

THE ROLE OF THE INTERVIEWER

Interviewing, for the purpose of this chapter, is defined as the process of obtaining information for job analysis by skilled, professional questioning of the people most directly involved with the job being analyzed. The interviewer is defined as the analyst charged with the responsibility of conducting the interview and, on the basis of the information obtained, analyzing and evaluating the position reviewed. While it is conceivable that the interviewer and the analyst could be different persons, as a practical matter—to ensure probing, analytical questions eliciting the responses required for effective analyses—the interviewer and analyst are normally one person.

Selecting Interviewers Since the interviewer's abilities largely determine the success of the interviews and the quality of the job evaluation program, interviewers must be selected with great care. Among some pertinent questions to be considered when staffing the organization for this purpose are:

1. Are people available within the company with the necessary skills and personal characteristics to be good interviewers?
2. From what departments will the interviewers be drawn?
3. Should experienced interviewers be employed from the outside?
4. What is the external job market situation for such people?
5. Who will conduct the training of interviewers, and what will it cost?
6. How will a job as interviewer-analyst fit into a career path?
7. How will the interviewers be received within the organization?

In addition to the organizational considerations involved in selecting interviewers, other criteria relating to personal traits and characteristics must also be considered. Although the specific requirements for an interviewer will vary from company to company, depending on the company's internal environment and management style, some requirements are shared by practically all companies, and these are discussed below.

1. *Communication skills.* The ability to speak, write, and understand the language of the employee is absolutely essential. It is not necessary for the respondent to feel the interviewer is a "person like myself" but rather that the interviewer is a person who can "understand me"; thus the language of the interview must conform to a shared vocabulary, and the interviewer must show the capability of understanding. The interviewer will deal with people of differing backgrounds, skills, and abilities, and so must have the varied communication skills required to intelligently discuss job content with all.

2. *Extensive business knowledge.* The interviewer must possess considerable knowledge of business and industry and of the varied operations and positions likely to be analyzed. A wide acquaintance with jobs in general is required in order to understand better any particular position being analyzed by comparing or contrasting it with other jobs. Imagine, for example, the varied knowledge and ability required to interview and analyze effectively such diverse positions as an accounting clerk, a physicist, a structural engineer, and a vice president of finance. The interviewer must, in short, be conversant with many fields and disciplines. While such knowledge can be acquired through extensive experience, formal education in the business disciplines is desirable. Those having such formal training normally would also possess the broadening outlook and poise essential for an effective interview.

3. *Analytical abilities.* Information-gathering interviews and job evaluation require good judgment and an analytical mind. The interviewer must be able to probe, question, verify, and comprehend during the interview; to gain necessary facts and eliminate the unnecessary (or untruthful); to place all in its proper perspective; and then to make sound judgments based on the information obtained.

4. *Knowledge of behavioral science.* Any profession which requires considerable human interaction calls for an understanding of personality and behavior. Interviews to collect job data in particular require a mature understanding of human behavior, since an analytic rather than an impressionistic approach is emphasized. The quality of the interview and the type of interaction achieved depend strongly on the ability of the interviewer to motivate the respondent to participate in the interview and to communicate fully. The interviewer must develop rapport and gain cooperation, guarding against suspicions, hostility, or embarrassment.

5. *Objectivity.* Those who are objective and have the ability to think critically and independently are most likely to be successful interviewers. Simply stated, there is no room for preconceived notions, biases, or persons likely to give extreme opinions.

Other favorable personality traits include an even temperament, sincerity, integrity, and the ability to get along with others. Particular note should be made of this last point. It is essential for an effective interview, and, for that matter, for a successful evaluation program, that those most closely associated with it be able to develop a rapport with the respondents and all levels of management.

An interviewer who is unable to obtain sufficient or accurate job information or evaluate properly the information obtained undermines the reliability of the job evaluation program. One who creates hostility or suspicion or who leaves poor impressions damages the reputation of the wage and salary program and of those who administer it and can foster serious employee relations problems. On the other hand, an interviewer who is a true professional will make contributions to the company that extend beyond the collection of data on job content.

Training Interviewers Despite the complexity of interviewing and its importance to the job evaluation program, newly selected interviewers often begin their jobs without any previous formal training in this field. New interviewers must be thoroughly trained—both in a formal training program and continually on the job.

The formal training program will vary according to the background and experience of the new interviewer and the particular requirements of the company.

An effective course of study, conducted by a capable individual and supplemented by available readings, should cover, at a minimum, the following subjects:

1. Interviewing objectives
2. Preparing for the interview
3. Opening the interview
4. Conducting the interview
5. The art of questioning
6. Observing the respondent
7. Importance of objectivity
8. Closing the interview

These subjects will be elaborated in subsequent portions of this chapter.

The interviewer-trainee must also gain exposure to the job evaluation technique utilized by the company to enable a probing for information essential to evaluation. Obviously, if the interviewer also analyzes the job, then extensive study in job evaluation is mandatory as part of the training program.

A thorough and well-implemented study program of the areas indicated above will provide considerable knowledge about interviewing. However, basic knowledge alone does not make a good interviewer, because interviewing is a skill developed through practice and experience.

As part of the formal training, various techniques can be employed to develop this skill. An important technique is role playing, in which one member plays the part of the interviewer, another the part of a respondent, and others in the group serve as observers. At the conclusion of the role-playing session, the group, led by the trainer, discusses the strengths and weaknesses of the interview. This technique is more readily used when a large number of interviewers are being trained.

Observation of actual interviews conducted by an experienced interviewer is also a useful and highly recommended technique for training interviewers. The new interviewer does not actively participate in the interview other than to take brief notes and observe. The actual interviewer and the observer then analyze the interview after its conclusion. It is desirable, if the situation permits, to have the trainee observe interviews conducted by several different interviewers so as to gain from their diverse experience and varying techniques. In a more sophisticated training program, the trainer can use audiovisual aids to demonstrate the principles and techniques of interviewing and to provide actual interview examples, and the trainee can listen, watch himself or herself in action, and analyze the conduct of the interview.

The length of the formal training program depends upon the varying background and skills of the new interviewer, the abilities of those conducting the training programs, and company requirements. It need not be of great length; however, the development of basic interviewing skills requires considerable practice.

With the completion of the formal training program, the second stage of the training process begins, with the interviewer refining the skills and ability to interact with others through actual experience. One who learns from mistakes, builds on experience, engages in critical self-examination, and strives for improvement will acquire the skill and reputation of a professional interviewer.

THE INTERVIEW PROCESS

Let us turn our attention now to the interview process itself. In the sections that follow, we will consider, in sequence, the steps involved in carrying out an interview.

Preparing for the Interview   Adequate preparation is essential to a successful interview. Before a position can be intelligently reviewed, the interviewer must possess considerable knowledge of the industry, the company, and the job. The interviewer must be able to talk in a common language with the respondents and thus be familiar with the jargon and technical terms of the positions being reviewed. Some of this knowledge is attained through formal education, but most is a result of experience and specific advance preparation.

To acquire this knowledge, it is recommended that the interviewer consult technical literature pertaining to industry processes and techniques, company history and financial data, company publications, including annual reports, product literature, and recruiting aids, and advertising materials. For specific jobs, organization charts should be studied to review reporting relationships, job titles, and the interaction between line and staff departments. Consultations should be held with management and supervisory personnel prior to the interviews to obtain guidance on the current organization and specific data on the interpretation of job content. Job information may also be obtained from existing job descriptions for the positions being reviewed, similar positions in other areas of the company (or other companies), and other positions in the same department, which will provide the interviewer with an overall view of the various interactions of jobs. The interviewer should use caution in relying on existing position descriptions. They may introduce biases which could hinder factual information gathering.

Advance formulation of questions is also recommended in the preparation stage. An interview that has little or no continuity, or in which the interviewer searches aimlessly for questions, is likely to be incomplete and perhaps even damaging. The interviewer who is well prepared with previously thought-out and carefully formulated questions is more likely to communicate effectively and obtain the full information required from the respondent.

The value of an on-site inspection, such as a tour of plant operations before the interview, is surprisingly debated, with one school of thought holding that such tours are needlessly time-consuming or tend to introduce a bias or at least reduce the detachment required for impartial analysis. Most people, however, believe that a "picture is worth a thousand words" and therefore that the actual viewing of the concerned operations prior to the interviews provides a clearer understanding of the total picture and the specifics of the processes. A skilled observer may identify aspects of the job that ordinarily would not be discovered in the course of the interview.

As part of the preparation, an interviewer must gain the close cooperation of the management most directly involved. Interviewers and job analysts may be looked upon with disdain or suspicion, and this is especially noticeable if they are outsiders. Unless the analyst gains management's cooperation, the task is considerably more difficult and, in fact, could lead to incomplete information gathering or biased evaluation. As a first priority, the analyst should secure proper authorization for the study and inform appropriate personnel in advance that the interviews are to take place. Further, such personnel must understand and concur with the purposes and objectives of the study and the procedures to be followed.

One further point, significant and yet easily overlooked, concerning preparation for interviewing: A respondent's reaction to the interviewer (and thus the interview, the job evaluation program, and the company) can be strongly influenced by the physical appearance and manner of the interviewer and the degree to which the interviewer fulfills the role envisioned by the respondent. Matters such as the dress, personal appearance, and demeanor of the interviewer are notably important and demand careful attention and consideration prior to the interview.

Setting for the Interview   It is difficult to generalize on the proper setting for an interview, because of the varying conditions encountered and differences in job levels. It is often desirable to secure information directly at the work place and thus actually see the work in progress, the files or records kept, and the machines or equipment operated. This permits details to be uncovered that might otherwise be overlooked and permits questions to be answered firsthand, perhaps even by demonstration.

On the other hand, even though such on-site discussions are desirable, they are distracting and preclude privacy. It is generally agreed that the interview is so important to the collection of job data for evaluation purposes it deserves the undivided attention, to the extent feasible, of both the interviewer and the respondent. Thus unless interruptions are necessary or particularly helpful, interviews should be conducted under circumstances wherein distractions are kept to a minimum and sufficient privacy is afforded to facilitate full communication.

To gain the benefits of both an on-site visit and a private interview, it is quite common to use both methods to gather data. For most administrative and middle- and upper-level management positions, this is academic, of course, since on-site inspections are generally of little value.

The office or room used for the interview should afford privacy and be pleasant and comfortable enough to put the parties at ease. As indicated, telephone calls or other interruptions should be eliminated or kept to a minimum, and for this reason, even though the respondent may have a private office, the interview should be scheduled in a room reserved for interviewing purposes.

The Opening   The first five to ten minutes of an interview are considered crucial to the success of the interview. During this period, the initial and most influential impressions are created and the prevailing climate of the interview and the rapport between the interviewer and respondent are established.

The necessity for rapport requires special emphasis. An interview is an act of personal communication, an exchange of information, and a sharing of perceptions. This series of interactions occurs to the maximum mutual advantage only when the respondent sees the interviewer as one who is sincerely interested and likely to understand and accept what he or she has to say. When such a basis has been established, conversation is freer and a more revealing and objective dialogue emerges.

Most employees approach an interview with apprehension, so the interviewer should begin by putting the respondent at ease through a few minutes of small talk, commenting on things that may be of mutual interest. The interviewer should be friendly and unhurried and show genuine care. Since the respondent is also usually not sure of the role expected, the interviewer should introduce himself or herself by name and explain the purpose of the interview, the interview's structure, and how the information obtained will be used. Beginning questions should be those the respondent can handle with ease and assurance.

With the proper opening, the setting is established for proceeding with an in-depth information-gathering interview.

Conducting the Interview   It must be recognized at the outset that because of the human factor in interviewing, people conduct, participate in, and react to interviews in countless different ways. The methods and techniques should therefore vary with individual situations.

Motivating the Respondent   In order to obtain complete information, the interviewer must motivate the respondent to communicate readily and fully. This means the burden is upon the interviewer to make the interview meaningful and rewarding to the respondent and to create an atmosphere of sincerity, understanding, and acceptance. Obviously the human relations skills of the interviewer, as emphasized in the selection process, are of particular importance if the respondent is to be properly and effectively motivated.

Techniques of Interviewing   The skillful interview is vastly different from a simple question-and-answer session. In-depth and complete job information is acquired by the skilled interviewer through the use of varied interviewing techniques, examples of which include:

1. *Implication.* Without actually asking a question directly, the interviewer "implies" the question. This can be accomplished in several ways—for example, making a brief comment such as "I see" or "Oh, yes"; repeating a portion of a previous statement, thus implying that additional information is sought; and nodding and using various facial expressions. The major value of an implied question when used effectively is that it encourages continued response with little or no thought interruption on the part of the respondent.

2. *Pause.* A brief pause on the part of the interviewer, used at the right time, prompts additional and often more revealing responses. It makes the respondent feel the interviewer wants the response to continue and is interested in what is being said.

3. *Listening.* Not to be confused with the pause, listening is another important technique. When the interviewer is talking, information is not being gained from the respondent. The vast majority, perhaps 75 percent or more, of the talking in the information-gathering interview should be done by the interviewee.

But listening is not a passive thing. To listen intelligently and with comprehension, the good listener must pay close attention and remember what is said.

4. Observation. Unlike on-site inspections of processes, machinery, records, or files, such as were referred to earlier, observation in this context is the attention to detail and notably to the behavior of the interviewee, thus gaining facts by inference and impression.

5. Probe. Not a question or even a series of questions per se, the probe is a technique to stimulate additional and more revealing information. It is a carefully tailored in-depth question which seeks to translate an inadequate response to one that meets specific objectives.

6. Artful Questioning. While this may seem obvious, it cannot be taken for granted. Skilled interrogation requires carefully phrased questions and the proper use of gestures, tone of voice, and facial expressions to overcome resistance, encourage participation, and impel the person interviewed to reveal the information needed.

Formulating and Posing Questions Not only is a skilled interview not a simple question-and-answer session, but the questions are not mere impulsive queries. The questions posed during a skilled interview are the product of careful forethought and attention to specific objectives. They should encourage participation and elicit the information needed.

The questions must be worded so as to be meaningful and appropriate. If they are irrelevant to the subject at hand, they can lead to skepticism or distrust. They must be posed in a context familiar to the respondent. To generate proper responses, questions must not be embarrassing or threatening, contain elements of bias, or lead the respondent to the "proper answer."

Not only should questions be well thought out and carefully worded, but the manner in which the questioning itself is handled by the interviewer is of significance. Listed below are several suggestions for proper questioning:

1. Ask only one question at a time.
2. The voice and manner used in asking questions may be as important as the question itself, so use them to advantage.
3. Remain flexible and take advantage of openings suggested by answers of the respondent.
4. Be completely objective so that interview biases do not influence the respondent.
5. Encourage the interviewee to do the talking.

Control of the Interview A major task of the interviewer is to focus and control the interaction between the parties so as to meet the interview objectives. This requires careful attention to the organization of the interview and consciousness of the time element. The interview cannot proceed helter-skelter; instead, the interview should:

1. Be conducted in a logical and orderly manner. However, for a more stimulating session, every once in a while the sequence of questions may be changed, particularly if they have fallen into a repetitive pattern.
2. Ensure adequate coverage of each area. All important areas should be explored, but a new topic should be started only when the current one is completed.

3. Be properly balanced. Subject areas should be given an amount of time commensurate with their importance. Problems will result if 90 percent of the interview is devoted to 10 percent of the job content.

4. Penetrate into the most important job duties so as to ensure the full and complete understanding of the critical elements of the job.

5. Efficiently utilize the time available. Rushing an interview or conveying impatience to the respondent is certain to lead to interview failure. On the other hand, the element of time is, of course, important, and the skilled interviewer will tactfully guide the respondent away from irrelevant discussions, let it be known when a question or a topic has been sufficiently answered, and generally control the pace of the interview.

Control of the interview is the task of the interviewer, and how well it is controlled depends primarily on skill. Interviewers often use prepared interview guides to ensure control and thorough coverage. Samples of such guides are provided in Figures 1, 2, and 3.

Ending the Interview   Many interviewers are uncertain how to end the interview. When the interviewer feels all the job information has been obtained, the respondent should be asked if there are any questions or additional information to add, and then the interview should be terminated. To the extent manageable, the interview should be ended promptly, particularly if a predetermined time allotment has been specified.

To close the interview, a simple statement will suffice, such as, "Thank you for coming to talk with me today. I'm glad we had this chance to explore your job together." At this point the interviewer simply rises (maybe extending a hand for a handshake) and walks toward the door.

FIGURE 1   Interview Guide (Nonexempt)

Date: _____

Position Title: _____   Department: _____

Incumbent: _____

1. FUNCTION of position.

2. PRINCIPAL ACTIVITIES, and to what or to whom they relate. Type, calculate, post—what? Take dictation or answer phone for whom? Test what materials for what characteristics?

3. Where accuracy of your work is important, how is it checked?

4. What is most difficult or complicated about your job? What makes it so?

5. What kinds of problems or questions do you refer to your immediate superior?

6. What kinds of contacts do you have with others and with whom?

7. Do you instruct or follow up on the work of anyone else?

8. Other comments.

9. Approximate breakdown of time.

FIGURE 2   Interview Guide (Line Management)

Date: _____

Position Title: _____   Department: _____

Incumbent: _____

1. ACCOUNTABILITY OBJECTIVE
   Reports to
   Accountable for

2. DIMENSIONS (appropriate statistics)
   Volumes
   Products
   Formulations (no.)

3. ORGANIZATION (supervision)
   Total people
   Salaried
   Hourly
   Crews
   Fluctuations
   Union
   Seniority groups

4. PRINCIPAL ACTIVITIES (what you do)
   Assignments
   Instruction
   Follow-up
   Discipline
   Complaints
   Grievances
   Contract interpretation
   Policy interpretation
   Selection
   Training
   Performance evaluation and recognition
   Investigating operational problems
   Expedite correction
   Follow through
   Schedule
   Cost reduction
   Reports
   Other

5. Most important OPERATING JUDGMENTS AND ACTIONS within your authority

6. Important OPERATING RECOMMENDATIONS made, for approval by others

7. Approximate breakdown of time

Immediately after the interview, the interviewer should try to relax and think about the pertinent facts of the interview, making further notes as appropriate. If consecutive interviews are scheduled, a short break is recommended for this purpose and also to allow the interviewer an opportunity to organize for the next session.

FIGURE 3   Interview Guide (Staff Management)

Date: _____

Position Title: _____   Department: _____

Incumbent: _____

1. ACCOUNTABILITY OBJECTIVE
   Reports to
   Accountable for

2. SCOPE OF POSITION'S CONCERN—products—processes—equipment—operations—materials—people or their activities. Get statistics.

3. NATURE OF SERVICES RENDERED—controls developed or exercised

4. PROJECT EXAMPLES

5. MOST FREQUENT CONTACTS—with whom—why
   Inside
   Outside

6. ORGANIZATION SUPERVISED

7. PRINCIPAL ACTIVITIES—(what you do)

8. Approximate breakdown of time

The interviewer's job is far from complete when the interview session is over. The information has been gathered for some specific purpose—in this case, for job evaluation—and thus the interviewer must carefully review and analyze what has been gathered and answer two critical questions: "Is the information complete, and is the information accurate?"

The completeness of the information is strongly dependent upon such interviewer-controlled factors as adequate preparation for the interview; organization of the interview; the use of carefully formulated and penetrating questions; and the interviewer's ability to conduct the interview in a manner which obtains complete information.

Concerning the accuracy of the interview, there is, of course, the possibility that a person may unwittingly give wrong information or make statements which it is thought must be made for one reason or another, even if they are wrong. But again the interviewer is responsible for accuracy and must, therefore, be able to distinguish facts from inaccurate statements. The skilled interviewer will verify information through questioning and, on the basis of experience, identify erroneous statements or inferences. However, to the extent that information needs to be verified beyond the interview, or that questions remain unanswered, the interviewer should follow up by recourse to additional and, if practical, independent sources.

In conclusion, the interview as an information-gathering technique is not infallible and is subject to errors and biases. However, although possibilities for inaccuracy exist, a skillfully conducted interview is still considered the best information-gathering technique available.

chapter 7

Objective Methods of Job Analysis

John R. Roark

PARTNER, THE HAY GROUP, PHILADELPHIA,
PENNSYLVANIA

John H. Burnett

PRINCIPAL, THE HAY GROUP, CHICAGO, ILLINOIS

Management has often been described as the art of getting things done through people. Human resource management attempts to bring some science to this art by providing mechanisms to support both ongoing administrative activities (i.e., orientation, appraisal, compensation, etc.) and those helping the organization respond to change (i.e., selection, development, job design). One of the fundamental supports of this whole effort is job analysis, a process that links the needs of the organization with the talent resources of its employees. This chapter considers the uses and limitations of job analysis as an ongoing and key part of your management information system.

THE RATIONALE FOR JOB ANALYSIS

There are many sound reasons for undertaking a job analysis program, but perhaps the best is that it is simply good management. It is an old business axiom that good management depends upon good information, and an effective job analysis system will provide you with a reliable information base about your organization, your jobs, and your employees.

On a more pragmatic level, it is readily apparent that a clear understanding of job responsibilities and required skills and attributes is essential to the design and operation of selection, appraisal, development, and compensation programs. Each is intimately linked to the other through the job definition and the information it provides on worker behavior, standards of performance, selection criteria, and the contribution of the job to the mission of the organization.

Federal regulations against discriminatory employment practices now require employers to validate their actions in these areas with accurate job and employment information. Meeting the requirements of the Fair Labor Standards Act on exempt/nonexempt classifications requires supporting job analysis information. And the recent rise of comparable-worth issues and similar equal-pay controversies can only be resolved with accurate job documentation.

Job analysis information can also prove invaluable in bargaining unit negotiations on duties, responsibilities, and wage rates as well as in clarifying the roles and responsibilities of supervisory personnel. The latter point carries over into professional and staff positions where accountabilities are often ill-defined and selection, compensation, and appraisal decisions are particularly difficult to make. Indeed, one of the principal benefits of the entire job analysis process is the dialogue it produces between managers and employees about their jobs.

Factors Critical to Success   Job analysis can provide the key for efficiently integrating a variety of personnel functions through a common information base, but this does not happen automatically or without problems. Many managers and employees view job analysis as a casual activity, loosely associated with the development of job descriptions, and may be unwilling to commit the time or resources required to collect accurate information. Others may see the process as an opportunity to advance their personal or organizational status, authority, or pay levels and may seek to manipulate it.

The benefits you achieve in your job analysis program are directly related to the care taken in overcoming resistance, manipulative tactics, and competition for resources. The overall success of your job analysis program will depend to a great degree on the following three critical factors:

- Proper planning
- Management commitment
- Effective communications

Proper planning for a job analysis program begins with a careful definition of the goals of the program and the specific uses planned for the information. Different functions, e.g., selection, compensation, etc., require different types of information. This has a strong impact on data collection and analysis methods. Each separate personnel function which will utilize the job analysis information should have an opportunity to describe its specific needs and recommend process and format changes. Careful thought should also be given to updating, storage and access methods, and requirements for clerical and data processing support. Finally, a formal training program in the use of the data should be developed for managers and supervisors at all levels of the company.

A strong commitment by such managers and supervisors is needed to ensure that accurate information is initially collected. Their support is also required to maintain and update the information. However, the most important commitment required of them is to use the information as an integral part of their decision making.

Effective employee communications is another critical, and often overlooked, part of the job analysis process. Much of the success of the data collection effort depends on the cooperation of job holders to supply information. That cooperation is best achieved when employees have a clear understanding of the goals of the program, the benefits they can expect, and an opportunity to review as well as provide job information.

Figure 1 abridges the above concepts for the reader.

The key point to remember in the design and implementation of any job analysis program is that its effectiveness is measured in the utility of the information rather than in its specific content, format, or collection method.

Job Analysis: A Systems Approach   Strange as it may seem, a good job analysis study does not begin with a study of jobs. Rather, the analysis must begin and be guided by a full understanding of the nature of the organization itself, its overall enterprise philosophy, and the strategic role of each major unit.

The reason is that job analysis is more than simply the compilation of job-related information. It is an analytical effort directed toward synethesizing data about the organization, the job, and incumbents into a document that is useful in decision making. Job analysis, like the jobs it describes, should not exist simply as an activity, but should contribute to the organization's achievement of its goals. Thus the nature and scope of the job analysis program should be determined by the intended use of the information. Figure 2 shows the relationship between various personnel functions, job analysis information, and results areas.

Planning for a job analysis program should include the following questions:

- What objectives are you trying to achieve?
- What information is required?
- What analysis method is most likely to capture and synthesize the information effectively?
- What resources will be required to implement it?
- What administrative procedures must be developed to maintain and maximize the use of the information?

FIGURE 1   Job Analysis Factors

PROPER PLANNING	MANAGEMENT COMMITMENT	EFFECTIVE COMMUNICATION
PROGRAM GOALS	DATA COLLECTION	PROGRAM GOALS
FUNCTIONAL NEEDS	ACCURACY	DATA REQUIRED
ANALYSIS METHODS	UPDATING	
ACCESS AND USE	USE IN DECISIONS	BENEFITS

FIGURE 2   Relationship between Personnel Functions, Job Analysis Information, and Results Areas

FUNCTION	INFORMATION		RESULT
Recruitment and selection	Required attributes	→ →	Selection criteria
Training and development	Worker behavior	→ →	Training programs
Appraisal and counseling	Standards of performance	→ →	Appraisal and counseling
Job design and organization development	Mission and accountabilities	→ →	Continuity and flexibility
Job evaluation and compensation	Compensable factors	→ →	Equitable pay decisions

The objectives you set determine the type of information you will need and the suitability of any given job analysis method. The common and often fatal temptation to avoid is designing your analysis program around the features of some particular analytic method. On the other hand, do not overlook the fact that many job analysis methods can provide you with information that can help you with many different personnel decisions. The key is to admire the bells and whistles only after you have made certain the train is stopping at your station.

The circle diagram in Figure 3 shows the general planning flow for a job analysis program from key objectives to ongoing use. Beginning with key program objectives, planning proceeds in a clockwise direction around the circle although the elements may interact with each other.

For example, a specific job analysis methodology may have to be rejected even though it provides the information needed, because the resources it requires are not available or because the output it provides cannot be readily

FIGURE 3   General Planning Flow for a Job Analysis Program

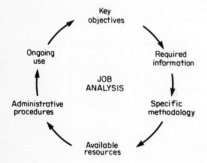

used in ongoing management decisions. On the other hand, a specific methodology may make additional information available which will allow new objectives to be addressed.

Let us assume that you decide to implement a job analysis program to assist you in job evaluation, compensation, and performance appraisal. Your primary information needs will revolve around the compensable factors contained in the job evaluation and appraisal systems. If both of the latter systems utilize job functions and accountabilities, it may be possible to integrate data collection, communication, and training methodologies. If the two utilize different factors—e.g., worker behaviors for job evaluation and compensation, and job responsibilities for performance appraisal—different data collection and communications methods may be required.

Also, let the scope of the programs you wish to impact, i.e., compensation, selection, training, etc., define the employee population to be studied, but remember that somewhat different emphases may be required for nonexempt, exempt, professional, and managerial groups.

The desired end result is a job analysis system which achieves your key objectives yet allows the greatest efficiency and integration of collection, communication, and training efforts.

The Nature and Scope of Job Analysis   Job analysis is the ongoing systematic collection and synthesis of information about organizational functions, work activities, and required incumbent attributes presented in a standardized format that aids management decisions. The organization, the job, the incumbent, and the job requirements are part of an interconnected whole. Figure 4 shows this relationship.

In essence, the organization's goals are translated into unit or departmental objectives and further refined into functional areas. It is at this point that jobs are actually defined in terms of desired end results achieved through the performance of certain functions. The end results are called "principal accountabilities," and they define the expected outcome of competent performance of the major job functions.

Functions describe in broad terms the major activity areas of the job. The

FIGURE 4   Relationship between Organization, Job, Incumbent, and Job Requirements

WHAT NEEDS TO BE DONE	Organization mission
	Unit objectives
	Functional areas
	Accountabilities
HOW IT IS BEING DONE	Job functions
	Tasks
	Work elements
	Required competencies

nature and scope of these depend on the accountability they support rather than on their underlying subtasks, so one may see functions which remain unchanged even though specific subtasks change. Or conversely, one may find new functions being created from a previously existing series of tasks.

Tasks are organized sequences of actions or thought processes which produce a definable product or service. Tasks are composed of work elements. These are the smallest practical subdivision of the work one can arrive at without describing individual motions or thought processes.

The required competencies are the skills and abilities needed to perform the various tasks and work elements. These are usually defined in terms of performance standards and training and experience requirements. Particular care should be exercised in this area to avoid making them too generic or tied into academic credentials or so specific that they apply only to the incumbent currently holding the job.

The following example shows some of these different levels for a director of compensation at a consumer products company:

WHAT NEEDS TO BE DONE

ENTERPRISE MISSION:	Produce high-quality consumer goods at the lowest production cost.
DIVISIONAL OBJECTIVE:	*Human Resources Division:* Contribute to the effective management of the company in the areas of organizational development, industrial relations, and compensation and benefits.
FUNCTIONAL AREA GOAL:	*Compensation and Benefits:* Contribute to the control of labor cost in compensation and benefits.
SPECIFIC JOB:	*Director of Compensation:* Accountable for compensation practices and policies which enhance the attraction and retention of desired employees and the control of labor costs.
1 PRINCIPAL ACCOUNTABILITY:	Avoid attraction and retention problems and enhance productivity and performance through effective reward management.

HOW IS IT BEING DONE

MAJOR FUNCTION:	Develop, implement, monitor, and adjust internally equitable and externally competitive compensation policies and practices.
1 TASK:	Review survey and current practice data to determine an appropriate base-salary position for the coming fiscal year.
1 WORK ELEMENT:	Calculate actual salary practice line for current company exempt employees using computerized statistical programs.
1 REQUIRED COMPETENCY:	Working knowledge of basic regression statistics as applied to compensation and familiarity with computer printouts of the data.

Each level is best understood in terms of its contribution to the preceding one and its impact on the one below it. Without this perspective, jobs tend to be viewed in terms of their activities and requirements and can assume a functional autonomy that ensures their continuance long after their usefulness is gone. Job analysis should thus answer the "why" of a job as well as the "how."

As different objectives and applications are addressed (i.e., selection, compensation, training and development, etc.), the focus of the job analysis effort shifts between macro and micro. What should not change is the emphasis on understanding each aspect as part of a decision-making process.

POSITION ANALYSIS QUESTIONNAIRE (PAQ)

PAQ[1] is a job documentation and analysis technique used by some 400 organizations covering 80,000 positions. Aside from several items which relate to descriptions of the job incumbent and his or her compensation, the remainder of the 187 questionnaire items score the requirement of worker behaviors and the existence of environmental or contextual factors surrounding the job. The questionnaire may be applied to any and all jobs since it is only concerned with the activities the worker performs and not with the purposes or outcomes of the activities, the occupational field in which the worker is trained, or considerations that have historically required explosion of the relevant worker behaviors into thousands of possible job activity or task statements.

The questionnaire forms are normally completed by analysts through relatively structured interviews with job incumbents or their supervisors although, on occasion, the questionnaire forms have been completed directly by incumbents or supervisors. The preferred method is to use multiple analysts for each job, which permits the calculation of relatively high analyst reliability coefficients (McCormick, 1976).

The questionnaire form is machine-readable through optical scanning. It is a structured and quantifiable job content document and, as such, is seen as replacing conventional prose job descriptions or free-response, custom-tailored job content questionnaires within which interviewer and/or job incumbent biases may operate. Because it is quantifiable, it is amenable to direct statistical analysis, which is one of its principal advantages.

PAQ, by collecting responses to the 187 items, identifies major unique requirements or worker behaviors included in a job. As the technique evolved, factor analyses were applied to determine whether a smaller number of variables could be used effectively. Emerging from these analyses were 45 job dimensions clustered into the following groupings: information input (6 items); mental processes (2 items); work output (8 items); relationships with others (5 items); job context (3 items); other job characteristics (8 items); and overall dimensions (13 items).

A job is scored on these dimensions, permitting the development of a job profile. Two jobs having the same or very similar profiles and scored at the same level of dimension intensity have equal requirements, regardless of title, occupational grouping, or organization. If jobs have the same profiles but at

---

[1]PAQ materials are copyrighted by the Purdue Research Foundation and distributed by the Purdue University Bookstore or by PAQ Services Inc. Computer support for analysis of PAQ materials is provided by PAQ Services Inc. which uses computer facilities located in Logan, Utah. Marketing and installation support consulting services for the PAQ are provided by PAQ Services Inc. The principals of PAQ Services Inc. are E. J. McCormick, P. R. Jeanneret, and R. C. Mecham, who have Ph.D.s in industrial psychology.

different levels, the higher one is seen as an advanced form of the other. Job families can be identified through the relative similarity of job profiles within a sample. In addition, an organization can match its job profiles with the *Dictionary of Occupational Titles (DOT)* code profiles to determine whether it identifies jobs in conformity with *DOT* practice.

PAQ Services found that many critical behaviors of professionals and managers were not covered completely enough or with sufficient sensitivity by PAQ so they have recently developed a comparison inventory called the Professional and Managerial Position Questionnaire (PMPQ). It is being subjected to the same rigorous research that eventuated in PAQ. Preliminary results have identified 10 dimensions from PMPQ as follows:

- Personal job requirements
- Planning and decision making
- Complex analysis
- Technical activities
- Processing information/ideas
- Relevant experience
- Interpersonal activities
- Special training
- Communicating/instructing
- Second language usage

PAQ appears better suited for analyzing jobs found in operating, craft, clerical, and basic supervisory job families.

The PAQ analysis may be used for the same purposes as any other job analysis document serves.

If general job requirements related to worker behaviors can be identified, it would be possible to validate currently established tests of aptitude or achievement or to construct and validate new assessment techniques against these identified job requirements. The PAQ authors have produced research results using the General Aptitude Test Battery as well as commercially available tests that are persuasive although not technically conclusive. They are currently developing a full set of tests of worker behaviors, the Occupational Aptitude and Ability Test Series, that relates to distinct job dimensions. An analysis option is available from them that identifies tests with "cutting" scores which would likely prove valid for a given job and identify proficient or trainable candidates.

Existence of general job requirements identified through PAQ and related aptitude measures should make it possible to match worker preferences and aptitudes with job requirements for career development purposes. The Job Activity Preference Questionnaire (JAPQ) has been developed by the PAQ authors to be directly compatible with PAQ. Through job aptitude and interest matching, career counseling efforts can be supported.

PAQ lends itself to performance appraisal and identifies behavioral training requirements of jobs although, since it does not identify purposes or outcomes of behaviors, it is weaker than conventional task analysis for identifying specific results and action patterns related to specific job content.

PAQ has also been used to measure and price jobs for compensation purposes. Through multiple regression, it is possible to identify a pattern for weighting job dimension scores in a way to match market prices or results from other job measurement processes. An analysis option identifies job value points that arise from incumbent current compensation and model all-industry, all-functions, or all-region market-pricing patterns.

The major strengths for the PAQ family of techniques include:

1. It was developed through carefully conducted research by industrial psychologists whose competence encompasses job analysis, human effectiveness, statistical analysis, and automated data processing fields.

2. It is efficient. While analyst training and data collection time is comparable to those of conventional job analysis processes, no time is required for prose formatting and approvals. Since a computer is used rather than a committee, virtually no time is required to produce point, grade, or pricing output.

3. It is objective. The same questions are answered about every job. Judgments can be checked statistically for reliability. Judgments about jobs rely on models developed through empirical research and statistical techniques and not on individual or committee judgments.

4. Conceptually and, to some extent, in fact, it is an integrated, computer-supported, human resource management process based on required worker behavior.

Some of the issues involved in the use of PAQ are:

1. In order to achieve generality, PAQ techniques ignore specific products, results, and consequences of jobs. It is hard to convince most workers and managers that those are not important distinctions between jobs. Behaviorally, the job of a surgeon may have a lot in common with butchers, barbers, plumbers, tailors, druggists, and teachers, but the differences in outcomes are far more important than the similarities.

2. When workers and supervisors see all the PAQ items, they tend to think that many of the items are irrelevant. Factually, it is as important to identify "what is not" as "what is," but most people are interested only in the positive distinctions.

3. Statistical indices of rater reliability in testing the use of PAQ are artificially high because of the number of "does not exist" ratings among 187 items for any job. This can be misleading.

4. Use of standardized methods, computers, and statistical analyses to replace human judgment can be mistaken for management when realistically it is an imitation which may or may not respond to the needs of a particular organization. The PAQ family of techniques has that risk by using "black-box" methods to the detriment of proper human judgments.

COMPREHENSIVE OCCUPATIONAL DATA ANALYSIS PROGRAMS (CODAP)

CODAP is a collection of some 36 or 50 software products (depending upon whether IBM or Univac programs are used) designed to analyze and report occupational information collected through task inventories. It has been in development over the past 22 years by the Personnel Research Division of the U.S. Air Force Human Resources Laboratory. Within the military, the research has had, as its objectives, the development of methodologies for job analysis (the collection, analysis, and reporting of information performed by personnel); job evaluation (for grade, pay, and skill levels): job structuring (including job engineering, work organization, and occupational classification); job requirements identification (for identifying aptitudes, training, and work experience needs); career development; personnel utilization; and job satisfaction assessment, particularly related to retention (Christal, 1974).

CODAP output defines the realm of work actually performed by a population of workers. Beyond fairly broad application within the military, variations of CODAP are to be found in a number of municipal and county governments and in a sprinkling of private industry environments.

Taking advantage of computer storage of task information, the system can generate reports in a variety of ways to facilitate decision making in the areas of job classification, recruitment and selection, career planning, increased productivity, performance evaluation, and training. Within the military, the emphasis has been on identifying task elements that facilitate the development of training programs. In other words, it identifies when tasks tend to be assigned to an occupational grouping and, therefore, when training workers to perform these tasks becomes timely.

Other programs can be used to generate job descriptions, including the amount of time each worker spends on a given set of tasks. Additionally, CODAP can be used to compute the difficulty level or grade requirements for each job. The system uses task-level data, develops job factor scores for each job, and generates a hierarchy of evaluations among the jobs within an occupational family.

The job incumbent questionnaire designed to generate the basic information for CODAP can take a variety of forms but normally includes background information on incumbent education and training; major items of equipment, tools, and materials used in the job; the inventory of task items—constructed through inputs from job analysis experts, knowledgeable incumbent employees, management, and, if appropriate to the situation, labor representatives; and an incumbent self-generated assessment of necessary skills and abilities to perform in the job.

The primary and most important step in the process is to produce a listing of tasks that appropriately represent a job family. This must be accomplished for each job family that is to be submitted to analysis. An essential first step before embarking upon the construction of task inventories is that of establishing the purpose(s) to be served by the resulting output, whether they be job evaluation, recruitment, training, performance evaluation, or what have you. This step requires an analysis of organizational needs by human resources function, so that the investment in such a process can be explained and understood by those in management as well as by the work group providing the basic information on the task inventory.

The next step in developing the inventory is that of defining the job families to be studied, followed by researching appropriate source materials, such as the *DOT*, documents available on job families from other task inventory installations, classification specifications or standards, existing job descriptions, training manuals, or performance appraisal audits. Task item definitions should be refined by "subject matter" experts. Before commitment to producing the final product, the inventory should be tested in the field through interviews with job incumbents and supervisors as well as through a final review by the subject matter experts. Inventory formalization and administration follow.

The task inventory requires each job incumbent to rate whether a task is or is not part of his or her job, the degree of importance the task plays in the performance of the job, and the time spent performing the task during an identified time frame. After inputting the results to the computer, programs can iterate comparisons of individual job records, one to another, and group them on the basis of similarity of relative time spent at each task, eventuating in a number of outputs. Possibilities include definition of the overlap between all individual jobs, followed by clustering into a hierarchy within the job family under study. There is also a program that will produce a diagram flow chart of how the clusters found in the overlap/group process relate one to the other relative to the family hierarchy.

While there are reported attempts to develop task inventories for professional and managerial jobs, the effort is a difficult one. This is mainly because much of what managers and professionals do in their work is ideational, and consequently manifestations of such activities are not observable. Additionally, because of the cognitive nature of these kinds of jobs, it becomes more difficult to develop task statements that are time-ratable. It is likely to require the development of many more task statements to effectively cover the content of such jobs. Managers and professionals analyze, create, evaluate, organize, control, plan, and so on. For example, a controller may be required to perform essentially the same financial analysis tasks as a subordinate tax accountant. However, the controller carries a higher authority for decision making or administration. A task analysis process must assure that the distinctions are articulated between the two positions.

To build a task analysis process from ground zero requires important consideration of staffing and time commitments to see the process launched and successfully completed. In a study for Prince Georges County, Maryland, Gambordella and Alvord (1980) describe the human resources used to install a CODAP process. They included a full-time project director who combined good management and communications skills with a broad personnel background, knowledge of the "work domain," and knowledge of computer processing and data management principles and three to seven job analysts supported by a system analyst skillful with the operating language appropriate to the available hardware. For completing one task inventory, an inexperienced project staff required 44 weeks to move from the first steps of defining the scope of the inventory and identifying job family membership to the final stage of producing management reports. Obviously, such an effort requires considerable investment in time and money. (Milkovich and Cogill in Chapter 10 also comment on the costs and time requirement for installing a quantitative job analysis program in another work environment.)

The attractions of the CODAP system are twofold. First, the Air Force will provide the CODAP programs at no cost to not-for-profit organizations. Second, CODAP seems to provide a more objective way of classifying jobs, and computer-generated job descriptions and analyses seem quite appropriate when contemplating the emerging efforts to establish comparable worth as the touchstone for proper compensation for all classes of workers. However, when considering the advantages of free software, the point can be made that the various programs are relatively old and inflexible, and they lack state-of-the-art report generation and graphing capabilities. This suggests a formidable maintenance and modification effort for in-house programming. Even though CODAP may provide a more objective, defensible approach to job analysis, there is still the potential for considerable subjectivity and even bias to enter into the development of the task lists by job experts. Just because a job description is computer-generated does not mean that the population of task statements produced is above reproach.

Other weaknesses in the Air Force's CODAP system include the limited data reduction capabilities of the programs, the importance of the relative-time-spent variable, and the limitations of its applications to a focus on nonexempt-like jobs.

The future applicability of the CODAP process centers on two necessary efforts. First, the software requires modernizing and updating with a concomitant increase in the flexibility of its report generation and graphics. Second, the need for exhaustive task lists which are job family specific must be reduced, and more generic task definitions developed. Control Data Corporation through its subsidiary, Control Data Business Advisors, has undertaken the job of attempting both these efforts. A description of those follows.

POSITION DESCRIPTION QUESTIONNAIRE (PDQ) AND THE FLEXIBLE OCCUPATIONAL ANALYSIS SYSTEM (FOCAS)

A team of researchers and consultants from the University of Minnesota and Control Data Corporation have undertaken the job of making questionnaire-type job analysis systems become user compatible. Their primary concern is to develop a system that integrates a quantitative means of assessing job content with computer technology. Emerging from this effort is the Flexible Occupational Analysis System (FOCAS), a job analysis methodology which uses CODAP as a software tool. Thus FOCAS is a task analysis approach to job analysis.

Their studies have resulted in two approaches to inventorying job content. One, the Position Description Questionnaire (PDQ), is designed to analyze management/professional positions. The other is the Occupational Analysis Questionnaire which appears to be responsive to analyzing nonexempt and technical positions. Whereas the PDQ is a multidimensional effort to elicit, analyze, describe, and classify management jobs, the Occupational Analysis Questionnaire, using FOCAS as a methodology, develops information on tasks within job families of nonexempt and technical positions. To date, Control Data Business Advisors Inc. (CDBAI) have developed seven occupational analysis questionnaires covering as many job families. They project a total of 16 separate questionnaires by 1983 and have, as a goal, the description, analysis, and evaluation of all nonmanagerial positions (some 50,000 in number) in Control Data by the end of 1983.

In a to-be-published article, Gomez-Mejia et al. (1982) compare traditional and statistical job evaluation approaches, point out that computer scoring methods which weight and combine items based on purely statistical considerations work almost as well as methods that weight and combine items based on expert judgments. Also, simple statistical methods worked as well as or better than very complex statistical methods. They also found that practicing compensation managers find the purely statistical approach difficult to understand because of its complexity. The results appear difficult to explain and defend. An automated method which combines and weights job information items on a statistical basis within compensable factors defined by expert judgments for given grades, and also provides explanatory information relating to compensable factors and to job information, worked well compared with other methods and was highly acceptable to compensation managers. "Therefore, it appears that questionnaire-based job evaluation information, without supplemental information, is insufficient for stand-alone grading decisions" (page 30 of prepublication draft).

CDBAI has endeavored to overcome management's objection to the computer manipulation or CODAP part of the technology in two ways. First, they view it as highly important to communicate the nature of FOCAS to users through the publication and dissemination of informational pieces describing the method's capabilities and results. Second, they have developed enhancements to CODAP which make the outputs less intimidating and more understandable. Formats have been altered to enhance readability, and users may access job or incumbent information through CRTs. FOCAS products include individual position descriptions, composite job descriptions, and comparison reports that isolate key similarities and differences among pairs and groups of composite job descriptions.

Two studies (Tornow and Pinto, 1976; Gomez-Mejia et al., 1979) describe the evolution of PDQ.

The first study (Tornow and Pinto, 1976) endeavored to identify the key behaviors that managers engage in. A 197-item questionnaire was given to 489 managers (212 executives, 172 middle managers, and 105 first-line managers) split into groups of 433 and 56, the latter being held out for cross validation. A factor analysis of the item responses revealed 13 independent job factors, including:

- Product marketing and financial strategy planning (long-range thinking and planning)
- Coordination of other organizational units and personnel who are not directly controlled
- Internal business control (review and control allocation of resources)
- Products and services responsibility (planning, scheduling, monitoring products, services, quality, and costs)
- Public and customer relations (promoting products, services, and goodwill)
- Advanced consulting (applying advanced principles, theories, and concepts)
- Autonomy of action (freedom to act)
- Approval of financial commitments (committing the company)
- Staff service (provided to others)
- Supervision of others
- Complexity and stress (operating under pressure)
- Advanced financial responsibility (assets preservation, investment decisions)
- Broad personnel responsibility (managing human resources)

A fairly high level (73 percent) of agreement as to which salary grade and function the 56 held-out managers belonged in was demonstrated.

The second study (Gomez-Mejia et al., 1979) started with a base of thousands of items gleaned from the literature and developed with experts through workshops. It first reduced this number to about 500 items, relating to different aspects of managerial jobs. The resulting questionnaire ("comprehensive, behavior-based and easily scored by computer") was administered to a large pool of executives and managers. The responses were fine-tuned through item analysis to capture the more discriminating items, resulting in a self-administered questionnaire that takes about one and a half hours to administer.

The next step was to identify and develop a list of compensable factors. A panel of experts was convened (some 26 top personnel officials) and asked to name compensable factors and weight each independently as to value, on a scale of 1 to 100 points. The averages and standard deviations of the weights for each item were fed back at a second meeting, resulting in further refinement to identify the principal compensable factors. Eight factors emerged as follows:

- Internal contacts
- Human resource responsibility
- Know-how/problem solving
- Decision making
- Planning
- Impact
- Supervising
- Representing

The questionnaire items were then classified by factor, through meetings with compensation specialists, personnel managers, and line managers. This resulted in identifying about seven items per factor without loss of the evaluative power of the factors. The next step was to readminister the questionnaire to a stratified benchmark sample (executives, managers, and supervisors) to develop norms which permit identification of the position with the pay grade structure (18 grades) used by Control Data to classify managers. The results permit grade classification of other management jobs based on the similarities or differences in the factor weights identified with each grade level.

Both studies produced and described weighted quantitative measures of work elements or compensable factors which most traditional methods of management job analysis and evaluation take into account. If there are weaknesses, they reside in the fact that experts' opinions about what is important to identify as compensable served as the basis for item construction and that an established grade-salary structure served as the validating criterion for the predictable utility of the PDQ.

COMPUTER-ASSESSED HUMAN RESOURCES MANAGEMENT (COMPTECH)

Comptech is a job analysis methodology designed by Hay Associates. It can be used for identifying, defining, classifying, and evaluating professional or technical jobs typically filled by incumbents who, prior to entering such jobs, have received professional or technical training of some extent or depth. Examples include engineering positions, computer-related positions, natural science positions (chemists, physicists, biologists, physicians), economists, and others. The driving force behind the development of Comptech was the recognition of the need to develop a human resources management model capable of linking traditional and evolving human resource systems within an operational environment epitomized by accelerated technological change so that management decisions impacting upon the organization and people would be optimized. The end result is a plan to better allocate, utilize, and develop the human resources in support of short- and long-term organizational needs. The job analysis process operates to describe, classify, and interrelate patterns of work activity related to jobs directly or indirectly associated with the professions or technologies named above.

The operational model of Comptech was established through the study of computer and computer-related positions within a large technologically oriented company. Five phases were identified for the final model: planning; design of the data collection instrument; data collection; data analysis; and user model development.

Planning. A team of the company's human resources and computer professionals participated with Hay in formulating and designing the project. (Involvement of company people later facilitated communication with incumbents in computer-related positions.) Since job content information was designed for incumbents in all computer-related positions in the company, a standardized data collection questionnaire was required. The project team interviewed some 200 computer professionals as a first step. Out of the comprehensive view of computer-related work throughout the company, developed from the interviews, two major findings were forthcoming which enabled the team to develop the questionnaire. First, computer-related positions can be described by seven critical work activity areas arising from generalizations of major phases of a standard computer project. These are problem definition, description of the solution, detailed system design, development of the solution/system, start-up, maintenance, and project leadership.

Instrument design and data collection. A machine-scoreable questionnaire was developed based on the findings of the first phase. It focused on specific, project-oriented work and elicited the incumbent's assessment of the degree of importance (on a five-point rating scale) each work element possessed for the job performance. Additionally, a wide range of demographic information was requested, so that a set of external relationships could be related to the pattern of work activities (i.e., education, training, sex, pay, budget, subordinates, organizational level, and so on). The questionnaire required 172 answers for managers and fewer for project leaders and individual contributors.

Analysis. Software was developed to analyze the data from 8000 questionnaires. It operated in three phases. First, the computer calculated the mean of the ratings provided by the incumbents on the important work elements in the seven critical work activity areas. Second, the computer analyzed all job content data to identify which jobs had similar work activity patterns. Third, the computer grouped or clustered jobs into a series of "job families" based on similarity of work activity patterns. Nine job families emerged from this final computer stage, and a position description was developed for each position within each job family. A point-factor job evaluation method (Hay Guide Chart-Profile System) was used to measure and "size" each position for job content.

At the conclusion of job analysis and evaluations, the following capabilities were available:

- Position any computer-related job within a job family.
- Establish whether a job was wholly or partially computer-related.
- Define relative size of the job (in relation to other representative jobs within other job families).
- Determine the knowledge, skills, problem-solving, and action style requirements of families and positions.
- Establish the basis for accessing competitive information on compensation opportunities for incumbents filling various positions.

User model development. Out of the software process described above, a users' reference manual was developed that, in effect, operationalized for individual jobs what the computer accomplished for a myriad of jobs. Users (human resource or line management people) are more able to classify any position into one of the nine clearly defined job families; assess each position against specific representative positions in the respective families relative to skills, knowledge, problem solving, and so on; and establish the relative size and market value of each job in the population.

Reference back to the software package was available where questions of demographics became relevant.

Comptech positioned the company to describe, organize, and plan its computer-oriented work force. Further, it was now possible to examine the technological environment along a variety of dimensions regarding essential work elements and, thereby, contribute a substantive information base to its human resource, technological, and organizational growth.

The methodology of Comptech provides a number of applications. It allows:

- Matching experienced and inexperienced applicants to appropriate job families, directing their applications toward vocations having compatible families and positions
- Determining internal equity (job size to pay size across the participant company) within all business components
- Determining appropriate career pathing across business components or functional areas, allowing an optimal decision process for the right people in the right jobs at the right time, again to reinforce each individual's capabilities and experience along with the attainment of organizational objectives
- Forecasting job families and positions required to achieve organizational alternatives and identifying position requirements for project positions and likely candidates
- Identifying individuals who are protected against discrimination by the law and responding positively by establishing avenues of advancement for such individuals

The emergent process of job analysis supported by advancement in handling job content and demographic information enables any organization with a high concentration of professional and/or technical jobs to respond effectively with "tried and true" human resource management processes or systems in optimizing return on the investment in people filling these positions.

CONCLUSION

As described in this chapter, a plethora of objective job analysis techniques exist. Most are receiving further investigation from both private and public organizations. In all likelihood, such investments of time and money will eventuate into a generalized process of objective job analysis that makes available critical information essential to proper decisions about people, jobs, and organizations. It necessitates all who are accountable for investment in human resources to remain curious, if not investigatory, over the next decade to assure themselves and their organizations of a readiness to capitalize on emerging technologies in the field of job analysis.

REFERENCES

Christal, R. E.: The United States Air Force Occupational Research Project (AFHRL-PR-73-75). Lackland Air Force Base, Tex.: Air Force Human Resources Laboratory, Occupational Research Division, January 1974.

Gambardella, J. J. N., and W. G. Alvord: "Ti-CODAP: A Computerized Method of Job Analysis for Personnel Management," Prince Georges County, Maryland, April 1980.

Gomez-Mejia, L. R., R. C. Page, and W. W. Tornow: "Development and Implementation of a Computerized Job Evaluation System," *The Personnel Administrator*, February 1979.

Gomez-Mejia, L. R., R. C. Page, and W. W. Tornow: "Comparison of the Practical Utility of Traditional, Statistical and Hybrid Job Evaluation Approaches," *Academy of Management Journal*, September 1982.

McCormick, E. J.: "Job and Task Analysis" in M. D. Dunnette (ed.), *Handbook of Industrial and Organizational Psychology*, Rand McNally & Company, Chicago, 1976.

Tornow, W. W., and P. R. Pinto: "The Development of a Managerial Job Taxonomy: A System for Describing, Classifying and Evaluating Executive Positions," *Journal of Applied Psychology*, vol. 61, no. 4, 1976.

Job Measurement

chapter 8

A Perspective on Job Measurement

Edward B. Shils

GEORGE W. TAYLOR PROFESSOR OF ENTREPRENEURIAL
STUDIES AND DIRECTOR, WHARTON ENTREPRENEURIAL
CENTER, UNIVERSITY OF PENNSYLVANIA,
PHILADELPHIA, PENNSYLVANIA

The objective of the employer who sets up a job evaluation system is to provide a consistent measure of job worth which can be understood by everyone who is involved. In addition, a rationalization program can help in job training, personnel selection and recruitment, safety, work simplification, and other important areas.

One of the weightiest criticisms of job evaluation is that it is so rigid that it cannot adjust to changes in the job or in the marketplace. Critics oversimplify what they see as the prime function of job evaluation; namely, to determine salaries. Clearer thinking on the part of these critics would help them understand that the principal function of job evaluation is to set up a hierarchy of jobs to help in solving the problems of wage structure—not to solve the problem of wage levels.

Formal job evaluation grew out of management thinking, while union wage scales emerged from collective bargaining. Both systems aimed to measure job worth and could be used together to improve understanding of what one pays wages for.

NOTE: Dr. Shils acknowledges the contributions of Eugenie Marie Steele in researching and preparing this chapter.

Today, almost all job evaluation programs are based upon job content analysis, the basic document being the job description, which defines the job's scope, difficulty, and end result if the job is performed adequately. Job evaluation begins with job analysis. On a basis of the job analysis by a trained evaluator, job descriptions and job specifications (attributes needed to fulfill the demands of the job) are developed. On a basis of this job information, each job is rated or evaluated. Job values or ratings provided by job evaluation may then be translated into wage rates, or jobs may be grouped to provide a series of grades, with rate ranges for each grade.

PRINCIPAL JOB EVALUATION SYSTEMS

The four major methods of job evaluation in use among American companies and in the public service are job ranking, job classification, the point system, and the factor comparison system. The ranking and classification methods are relatively simple, since no attempt is made to obtain quantitative measures of job value. These plans are generally described as the "nonquantitative" plans. The factor comparison and point methods are rather complex and are referred to as "quantitative" plans because of their use of points or monetary units in totaling the values of each factor included in each job.

The classification plan has been used widely in federal, state, and local governmental agencies as well as in smaller companies, since it is relatively inexpensive to install. However, most American companies that use job measurement techniques employ the quantitative plans.

This frequency of use may indicate that quantitative systems are well suited to many industrial companies, but it does not indicate that such systems are any better in the abstract than any other evaluation systems. A 1948 study by David J. Chesler showed an average correlation of .94 between point, factor comparison, and ranking systems in use. The Chesler analysis stimulated other investigations which produced the conclusion that less complex systems tend to lead to results which are just as good as those contributed by the sophisticated quantitative plans. Many quantitative systems are finally converted to classification plans by ranging point spreads between jobs.This leads to better administration in the pricing of jobs.

Job Ranking Method   The ranking system of job evaluation is the simplest of the four methods and the easiest to explain. Jobs in the organization are ranked from the highest to the lowest. Rather than worry about several compensable factors, the job is ranked as a whole.

Job descriptions in this plan are generally very brief and similar to the length of such descriptions in the *Dictionary of Occupational Titles* issued by the U.S. Labor Department. In the procedure, a job evaluation committee studies descriptions of the jobs to be evaluated. Each member then ranks the job with a numerical value, "1" being the highest-rated job, "2" the second highest, and so on. The average for each job is its new ranking.

The system's major disadvantage is that it is employed without actually securing job facts; hence it becomes somewhat subjective. Staff specialists or supervisors who know the organization generally do the job, and often the results reflect their biases. The raters undoubtedly are influenced by the present pay of the job, the incumbent, or the prestige value of the job. It might be possible to instruct raters to follow certain compensable factors rather than to regard the job as a whole, but if this is done, the plan would lose some of its basic simplicity.

In the ranking method, jobs are generally considered by department, which reduces the value of the method for large companies in which interdepartmental ratings are necessary. Raters generally set up a deck of cards for the department and then use the card-sorting methods or the "paired comparison" method. The cards have the job title and description written on them. Each job is compared with every other job on which ratings are required. Then departmental rankings must be combined into interdepartmental rankings. It becomes a problem to do this. To secure the services of one person who knows the ins and outs of all departments is difficult, so a committee made up of department heads is often used. Grades can be established for the entire firm by collating the number of rankings in a department and in the total organization. If this is done, the ranking system will actually operate as a job classification system.

Job Classification Method   The job classification method involves defining a number of classes or grades and fitting jobs into the classes provided. The job classification method may be compared to a bookcase which includes a series of carefully labeled shelves. The vertical arrangement defines a number of classes or grades, each of which can then be considered as one of the shelves. The toughest job is to describe each class or grade so that it will be possible to fit any of the jobs in the organization into a proper niche or shelf. The written grade descriptions permit the rater to evaluate the particular job and then to fit it into the proper class.

This method has a strong advantage inasmuch as in most organizations employees tend mentally to classify jobs in a shelf order in the job hierarchy. Managers tend to be stimulated by thinking of jobs as belonging to classes, and thus the problems of wage and salary administration become simpler.

In private industry this plan is often set up into job series, such as the engineering series, sales, etc. The number of classes or grades in each series need not necessarily be uniform among the series. The classification method is used by many small firms, which find that it provides a less awesome approach to job evaluation and reduces resistance on the part of employees and the union.

One weakness in the system is the difficulty of writing good grade descriptions. Most of these grade descriptions are based on duties and responsibilities rather than on compensable factors. The grade description must be so general that it will permit the classification of many different types of jobs, some administrative and some technical, unless there are many series or clusters created. When grade descriptions are written generally in terms of duties and responsibilities, it encourages supervisors and employees to aggrandize the description of their own duties in their job statements, which later are evaluated by job analysts, who compare them with job and grade descriptions before final classification.

Another weakness of this system is that many jobs have duties which tend to fall in a higher grade while there are other duties in the same job which would fall in a lower grade. This forces the rater to average out the duties, thus putting the entire job into one grade. This weakness is eliminated by the use of the quantitative systems, which provide a weight for each factor evaluated in a numerical or monetary way.

The "Point" System   The point system is the method most widely used at the present time. It is one of the two quantitative systems, the other being the factor comparison system. In the quantitative system, separate judgments are made on each of the selected factors and hence numerical values are attached to each factor. The value of the entire job is the sum of the factors.

The point method is somewhat similar to the classification method because both systems involve comparing jobs indirectly with a written scale. In the classification system the grade scale is vertical, while in the point system the degrees of each factor are described horizontally. For a detailed description of the mechanics of point plans, see Chapter 11.

The point plan is sophisticated and expensive to install. However, a valuable result of its employment is the development of a job evaluation manual which consolidates the factor and degree definitions as well as point values. These yardsticks can be used for many years without changes, even though the jobs themselves may change as a result of new technology, job dilution, or modification in the allocation of responsibility. Once the manual is complete, job rating can be initiated. The scales in the manual are used to evaluate jobs.

The popularity of the point plan is attributed to its wide use by trade associations and consultants who work with large enterprises. The most widely used of all the standard or ready-made point plans is the one developed for factory jobs by the National Electric Manufacturers Association and the National Metal Trades Association [now the American Association of Industrial Management (AAIM)]. The AAIM plan is described in detail in Chapter 13.

The major advantage of the point plan is the longevity and stability of the rating scales. Point plans may increase in accuracy and consistency with use. The use of graphic rating scales and checklists reduces rating error and limits the influence of bias. In view of the fact that points for each job may vary from 100 to, say, 500, with many jobs carrying weights of 333, 335, 336, 337, etc., plans often provide for ultimate conversion into job classes. Arbitrary point ranges then have to be decided upon.

Point plans, however, may be difficult to develop without outside consultants and internal committee members who have the time to worry about the details of factor selection and definition. Degrees of each factor must be worked out and weights allocated to factors with minute care. A point plan takes time to install, involves considerable clerical work, and is not easy to explain to workers and to the union. It very definitely will require centralized administration and appears more appropriate for use by larger companies.

Factor Comparison   Under the factor comparison method of job evaluation, one finds job-to-job comparisons similar to those made in the ranking system used in small enterprises. This differs from the point and job classification methods, where jobs are compared with scales.

Generally, the same five factors are used in all factor comparison plans, namely, mental requirements, skills, physical requirements, responsibilities, and working conditions. This factor rigidity may limit the technique's usefulness for particular organizations. "Key" jobs, which have the five factors in varying proportions, are selected and then compared with all other jobs, one factor at a time. For a detailed discussion of how factor comparison methods work, see Chapter 12.

It is quite possible that the major advantage of the system, namely, its simplicity in using the current hourly pay for each key job and applying a monetary unit to price each factor, might also be its major disadvantage, inasmuch as the use of the monetary unit can result in bias and subjectivity.

Another possible weakness in this plan is that to utilize the concept of key or anchor jobs, the wage rate must first be correct in terms of both internal and external alignment. Since these are anchor jobs, their usefulness will depend upon the validity of the anchor points represented by the jobs. Jobs, however, change slowly and imperceptibly. If the anchor jobs were to change over time, unnoticed and without correction of the scale, users would be making decisions on the basis of warped standards.

A still futher disadvantage, especially to a small company, is the number of complicated steps necessary to build the job comparison scale from the key jobs.

Other Evaluation Systems   There are other evaluation processes that are based upon elements other than job content. They are not as widely used or as well understood. It might be useful to review one of them before proceeding.

Elliott Jaques developed the time-span method to measure the level of work in a job and to serve as the basis of an equitable salary structure. The concepts and mechanics of his system are explained in his *Time-Span Handbook*.[1] Jaques measures jobs in terms of their span of discretion, i.e., the longest span of directly applied time, continuous or intermittent, involved in the performance of a task under the incumbent's own discretion. This period ends when the task is reviewed by the superior. "Equitable payment" is defined as the common norm of payment held by individuals of the same time span, when asked confidentially what they would consider fair pay.

Like other major systems, the time-span approach seeks to measure job content. This, in engineering terms, corresponds to weight. The principal difference between Jaques's system and other systems is that Jaques used the calendar as a criterion of weight, while the more traditional systems consider size and density. In effect, then, the time space of discretion starts out with its end result—a total value based upon opinions of people asked in confidence how much the job is worth. Then the process proceeds to search for time units which can be arranged in a scale to reproduce the end results identified at the outset.

The time-span approach is an interesting development in the field of job evaluation, and research on it is continuing. However, most job evaluation systems today still rely on job descriptions.

---

[1]Elliot Jaques, *Time-Span Handbook*, Heinemann Educational Books, Ltd., London, 1964. An application of Jaques's principles of job measurement can be found in his book, *Measurement of Responsibility*, Halsted Press, New York, 1972.

HISTORY AND DEVELOPMENT OF JOB CLASSIFICATION

The Federal Classification Act of 1923 was the pioneer legislation in job classification. By developing this rationalized system early, the government was able to persist in its theory of being accountable for the pay of several million federal employees under civil service. There had to be a doctrine of internal equity for the government to document and justify its accountability under the law.

The need for a classification of positions by duties and the gearing of salaries thereto was recognized in the federal government over 140 years ago. On the insistence of a number of government clerks urging "equal pay for equal work" in 1838, the U.S. Senate was moved to pass a resolution instructing department heads to prepare a "classification of the clerks . . . in reference to the character of the labor to be performed, the care and responsibility imposed, the qualifications required, and the relative value to the public of the services of each class as compared with the others."[2]

It was in 1923 that the federal government finally prepared the comprehensive program first demanded of it in 1838. Nevertheless, other governmental jurisdictions were in the field as early as 1912, when the city of Chicago adopted its first classification plan. This was followed by Pittsburgh (1915), New York City (1917), Detroit (1925), and Los Angeles and San Francisco in 1930 and 1931, respectively.

The classification movement in government fitted admirably into the idea of a merit system and also into the wider aims of the efficiency and economy program. Hiring requirements in the federal civil service were to stem from job descriptions and job specifications after 1923. New principles of centralized financial control also demanded classification if the full possibility of better government was to be realized. Uniform accounting required a uniform job terminology in place of the hodgepodge of nondescript and conflicting titles.

Significant improvements in pay scales and in other provisions of the Federal Classification Act took place in 1928, 1930, 1941, 1942, 1945, 1946, and 1948. Finally, the old act was completely replaced by the Classification Act of 1949. For the first time, it made a clear distinction between the establishment of job evaluation standards (a task assigned to the Civil Service Commission) and classification of individual positions (a function left to the departments and agencies, subject to the Commission's power of postaudit and power to correct misclassifications). It also eliminated the former occupational services by setting up just two schedules (clusters) of grades, one for crafts and protective and custodial jobs and another, called the "general schedule" (consisting of 18 grades), for all other classes of employment.

The development of job evaluation in the private sector can be traced in great part to national wage and price controls during World War II. Wage and salary boards were not overly permissive in permitting compensation increases even when they were negotiated by employers and unions. The main drive was

---

[2]Sen. Res. 25th Cong., 2nd Sess., March 5, 1838, reported in Mosher, Kingsley, and Stahl, *Public Personnel Administration*, 3d ed., Harper & Brothers, New York, 1950, p. 208.

to hold the line except for catching up with increases in the consumer price index.

However, the War Labor Board in World War II did relax the "freeze" to permit periodic merit increases under some type of previously installed job classification plan. The government recognized the justification for an employee moving up through his or her grade range on the basis of merit and length of time in the grade. Upward pay adjustments were also allowed when the aim was elimination of internal inequities. When a systematic job measurement analysis showed an individual to be in a lower grade or pay status than that justified by comparison with other employees, the government permitted the adjustment, provided a rational job evaluation plan was in effect.

Also recognized as a criterion for upward pay adjustments was external inequity. The Bureau of Labor Statistics (BLS) provided monthly data which showed area or national hourly earnings in such specific crafts as tool and die makers, carpenters, welders, etc. The employer—or in the case of a unionized firm, both the company and the union—would present a petition to demonstrate that a negotiated pay increase for a given group of employees was necessary. If the BLS survey disclosed the wages to be less than the market, its data were used to justify the raises.

In order to correctly apply BLS market data or even private market survey data accumulated by a company or union, it was necessary to make certain that the data covered comparable job content. The government was not receptive to granting raises simply on the basis of comparative job titles which were not supported by comparisons of job content. Company officials who raised their own wages or the wages of others without authorization by the War Labor Board could be fined and sent to prison. Therefore, it was very important to present a rationalized plan showing proper job measurement to governmental representatives.

In World War II, millions of employees were working in defense industries and were "frozen" in their jobs. This meant that they could not leave to seek work elsewhere without notifying their draft boards. Those without dependents who changed jobs without permission were in danger of being drafted. Since these employees were often being held in jobs in which earnings were frozen, the pastures always looked greener elsewhere. Hence employers, unions, and government were very happy to have a pay rationalization plan to justify wage levels.

Because there were not many pay plans prior to World War II, the War Manpower Commission developed the *Dictionary of Occupational Titles (DOT)* early in the war. This compendium was of great value to those involved in personnel matters, since it provided 21,000 short job descriptions, each with a code number. These books were made available to unions and firms and soon became the basis for moving forward into further rationalized pay plans.

The U.S. Department of Labor has continued to publish the *DOT,* and it now contains many thousands of additional short job descriptions. It serves as a bible for those who use it. When personnel directors or compensation specialists develop their own company custom-tailored pay plans, they are often not able to relate either a point total or a standard title to similar jobs in all companies. Therefore, when the job being analyzed in the company plan can be identified in the *Dictionary of Occupational Titles*, the dictionary title code should be entered in the company's personnel records. This can be done, however, only when the job under analysis is in all significant respects identical with the job defined in the dictionary.

During the Korean war, prices and wages were again frozen. The U.S. Wage Stabilization Board and the U.S. Salary Stabilization Board were then set up to follow procedures virtually identical to those employed during World War II. While workers in defense industries were not frozen in their jobs, their willingness to stay in defense work was predicated on both internal and external pay equity. The government once more honored the criteria it had set up in World War II for relaxing the pay freeze. It permitted many adjustments to firms with rationalized pay and classification plans. By this time, pay rationalization had arrived.

In 1980, the Civil Service Reform Bill revamped the federal employment system. The existing Civil Service Commission was replaced by two agencies. The Office of Personnel Management (OPM) supervises personnel management functions and the Merit Systems Protection Board (MSPB) directs the board of appeals for employee grievances. The reorganization of the Civil Service Commission separated the agency's conflicting duties of managing a personnel system for the government and acting as an unbiased appeals board for employees.

The Civil Service Reform Bill also addressed the comparability of federal wages with private sector wages for both blue- and white-collar government positions. The pay reforms were based on the issues of comparability and the parallelism of federal wages to private wages in a given region.

While the Civil Service Reform Bill maintained the general schedule of 18 grades (GS-1 through GS-18), the bill did add flexibility to the compensation of upper-level federal executives. Executives of grades 16, 17, 18 were designated to be of the senior executive service (SES). These career bureaucrats were eligible for "supergrade" bonuses and salary increases of three types. First, the wage compression in the upper ranks was eased by expansion of the pay scale. Second, members of the SES were eligible for a bonus of up to 20 percent of their base salaries. Third, special stipends were established, with awards of $20,000 to those with "distinguished" executive service and $10,000 to those with "meritorious" executive service.

The adjustments which the government has made in determining the wage structure for executives mirror the problems that the private sector has had developing job evaluations for its managerial employees.

While many front-line supervisory jobs are covered by job evaluation plans, managerial, sales, and professional positions are seldom formally evaluated.

Why is it that a company which has a good job evaluation plan for the clerical staff does not have an equally valid plan for its managerial group? Some of the reasons for the difficulty in applying job evaluation plans to managerial jobs are given below:

1. Higher-level jobs range more broadly in duties and responsibilities than do manual or clerical jobs. This worries executives—they do not see how job evaluation can cope with this problem.

2. There is a widespread feeling that at the higher level the person makes the job.

3. Higher-level jobs are politically sensitive, and unless strongly supported by top management, the evaluation of these positions is not likely to be pressed by staff people.

4. Failures of job evaluation plans for higher-level management continue to exert a restraining influence on their adoption. Generally, the failures are due to an inept approach to the problem. The common mistake has been to stretch clerical or manual plans upward.

The evaluation of exempt jobs is still in its infancy as compared with job evaluation at the manual and clerical level. As a result, the base salaries of exempt employees have tended to increase more slowly than those in the manual and clerical classifications.

JOB EVALUATION ISSUES RAISED BY UNIONS AND EMPLOYEES

Union efforts toward a more rational internal pay structure have aimed at establishing wage scales by collective bargaining; setting pay rates for particular jobs; and attempting to put a floor under wages through advocacy of minimum wage legislation. While industrial unions have tended to push for increases in the entire structure, craft unions have fought for increases in the few selective occupations with which their members were concerned. These differing approaches are not as significant as they once were because interjob differentials measured in percentage terms have decreased, and both industrial and craft unions have bargained for wage scales that eliminate formal differentials based on race or sex. Area differentials still remain, with craft unions seeking their continuation, while industrial unions in nationwide contracts seek to eliminate them.

The official union position on job evaluation, with only a few exceptions— e.g., the United Steelworkers of America—has been one of the strong opposition. The opposition has been theoretical rather than pragmatic. Most union officials approve job rationalization techniques when they are faced with the issue and determine that job measurement can be helpful to their cause.

Unions might officially frown on management-engineered job evaluation plans but have long used the principles of simple ranking and job classification in negotiations. Moreover, unions have never opposed job evaluation as long as it is not the sole determinant of wages and is not substituted for collective bargaining. When faced with the need for a yardstick to resolve intraunion disputes on relative job content, unions have welcomed job measurement techniques. But if other criteria were available to ascertain relative job content, they often ignored job evaluation.

Charges have been levied by unions and employees that management-initiated evaluation plans are unnecessarily cumbersome, hard to administer, and difficult to understand. Unions want to know why simpler plans, like the classification and ranking systems, cannot be used instead of the point or factor comparison systems. Unions point out that for years before management initiated the sophisticated plans, the ranking or classification approach had been employed by unions on an informal basis as part of collective bargaining. Demands for craft minima have had this basis.

Another prime objection to job evaluation is a fear that supply and demand will not be considered in pricing the jobs. Many local unions lack professional staff who understand that jobs are evaluated first and then a study is made of wage levels for each key position. The average wage of the entire job hierarchy must be considered in terms of supply and demand, and where the union is involved, there will always be the protection of collective bargaining to temper the structure and provide modest adjustments.

Workers appear to be more concerned with their relative pay than with absolute wages, and hence they welcome rationalization which corrects internal injustice. Union leaders may not support formal job evaluation systems, but they do approve of job descriptions when used on a more informal basis. Furthermore, job rates are more honored by unionists than personal rates; unions, too, believe in paying for the job rather than for the individual.

While management often shows a rigid posture with respect to job content as the controlling factor in determining wages, union leaders more realistically point to other factors which in today's industrial scene have a more direct influence on pay. Included are the shortage of workers in certain skills, the traditional sequence of jobs in the job hierarchy, seasonality of employment, promotional sequence, etc.

Another major issue between unions and management is that unions press for national wage levels and want to get away from the constraints of area wage surveys. Many employers—concerned with local living costs—want to compare rates within the area in which their plants are located. Unions want to bargain rates within the industry in which they represent workers, and look at wages as a national pattern, industry by industry. They tend to reject arguments that living costs vary.

Unions and employees in nonunion firms fear skill dilution. Job statements and formal job descriptions permit job evaluation to be employed in work planning and work improvement. For example, if the employer finds that eight employees are spending one hour each on the same responsibility, this work might be assigned to one full-time employee. The deleted duty might require a skill higher on the average than those remaining in each employee's package of duties. The net result might be a reduction in classification or "points" for the job. There is no doubt that changing technology is bound to influence job content and could result in reorganization and job displacement. However, even without wage rationalization programs, employers would still be interested in work improvement. As employers introduce new technologies, they will seek to fund the new capital costs by increased employee productivity. This could result in displacement or the need to retrain employees for transfer to other jobs.

The effects of technology on job structure have aroused much speculation. Will the new technologies result in massive downgrading of job content? Should job classifications be broadened? Will new job descriptions for machine operators more closely resemble those of supervisors or technicians? Will automated jobs generally be worth less than conventional jobs? These and similar questions about the job structure are thorny issues demanding the attention of both management and unions.

Knowledgeable executives believe that current methods of job pricing are inappropriate to new machine-tending jobs. They believe the job description format needs more emphasis on mental activities and less on manual. The idea that automation leads to wholesale downgrading of jobs has not been supported by most executives.

A proper maintenance program is necessary to avoid slippage in a new job evaluation system. Staff and line must work together on job audits, to minimize the fears and personal concerns of reviewed employees.

Employees and unions continue to be disturbed by changes in traditional job relationships resulting from job evaluations. As one psychologist said about morale, "It's not that the worker is right or wrong about an issue, it's what's in his mind that must be considered." If a company hopes to improve performance through the application of job measurement, the techniques and procedures should reduce conflict, not increase it.

How do workers feel about distinctions between two positions which appear to the job analyst to have the same skill content? The analyst may see the job demands as being the same, while the employee sees one job as a dead end and the other as a step toward promotion and upward mobility in the organization.

A similar puzzle may be found when two jobs have similar content but one is characteristic of many firms in the community, while the other is found only in the firm under study. It could be contended that one should receive higher pay than the other because displacement in it would result in the worker requiring considerable retraining in order to qualify for a new position in another firm.

These complaints by employees or unions can be solved without trauma if the job measurement system builds in compensable factors to take care of these requirements. Also, where the plant is unionized, fears can be reduced by the collective-bargaining pact.

Union reluctance to accept a company plan stems from its fear and from traditional distrust of any kind of "industrial or human engineering." All too often, management's compensation specialists claim that their methods are scientific and therefore infallible. Union leaders and employees in nonunion establishments argue, however, that even the most scientific system requires numerous judgments. Some managements have followed the advice of their consultants or internal committees blindly and have laid themselves open to charges of being closed-minded. While a statistical or quantified answer may get a nonunionized manager off the hook, a union business agent would be accused of playing "sweetheart" with the company by accepting the new system.

IMPLICATIONS FOR THE FUTURE

The usefulness of job evaluation systems depends on their ability to establish equitable wage structures. The recent application of "comparable worth" in evaluating women's wages as compared to those of men may cast present job evaluation systems in doubt. If it is proven that men's and women's jobs of comparable worth are not paid equivalently, then the job evaluation system is biased.

Government personnel service may again be at the forefront of changes in the job evaluation system. Municipal workers have gone on strike over the issue of comparable worth; some states have incorporated the concept of comparable worth in their job evaluation systems. The Equal Employment Opportunity Commission, responsible for enforcing Title VII, is studying the effectiveness of present systems in evaluating job worth.

Job evaluation systems must also be monitored for racial bias. Most job evaluation systems are implemented through some type of work measurement. However, work measurement systems can operate as selection systems. For example, intelligence tests or academic requirements have been used to determine an individual's suitability for a job. Some of these selection systems have been shown to be racially discriminatory, requiring preparation that minorities would not have had and demanding skills that are not part of the job. Therefore, it is important that job evaluation systems use work measurements which are precise in their measurement while being broad in their application.

The present relevance of comparable worth has arisen because job evaluation systems, as implemented in corporations and governments, reflect the social biases of the time that they were established. Job evaluation systems can be used to justify and externalize the invisible hierarchies that exist in corporations. However, when the social hierarchies or work structures change, the job evaluation system must be adjusted to reflect new definitions of internal equity in wage structures.

chapter 9

Achieving Internal Equity through Job Measurement

Richard E. Wing

**FORMER DIRECTOR, CORPORATE COMPENSATION
DEPARTMENT, EASTMAN KODAK COMPANY, ROCHESTER,
NEW YORK**

This is a peculiar time in which to describe job measurement and equity and their relationship to the administration of wages and salaries. Twenty years ago, it was generally agreed that equity in compensation could be achieved through careful job measurement; the untested assumptions implicit in most wage and salary administration practices were accepted without question. D. W. Belcher's book of 1955 outlined rather well some existing methods of job evaluation.[1]

These systematic practices had hardly been put to work, however, when theorists began to question their theoretical underpinnings. In a 1969 *California Management Review* article, Belcher himself reviewed the implications of recent work in psychology, sociology, and management science for compensation administration and concluded that existing practices were based on "untested assumptions—assumptions about the relationship between money and motivation; assumptions about how employees perceive equity and how this compares with employer concepts of equity; and assumptions about the relationship between perceived equity and motivation."[2]

---

[1]David W. Belcher, *Wage and Salary Administration*, Prentice-Hall, Inc., Englewood Cliffs, N.J., 1955.

[2]David W. Belcher, The Changing Nature of Compensation Administration," *California Management Review*, vol. XI, no. 4, 1969, pp. 89 ff.

Now in this decade comes the strongest, or noisiest, criticism ever leveled at the entire pay administration process—the demand for an equal worth standard for judging pay discrimination. On one hand, recognizing certain deficiencies of job evaluation processes, proponents for equal worth see job evaluation as the method for ultimately establishing equal job worth. Still other critics, such as Ruth Blumrosen, condemn job evaluation and insist that occupational segregation of females and minorities is of itself prima facie evidence of pay discrimination aided and abetted by job evaluation plans which rationalize as appropriate the pay for segregated jobs.[3]

The following material comes from the synthesis of ideas exchanged informally between compensation administrators in industry and government and consultants faced with the immediate task of designing and implementing workable pay programs. Research is always welcomed. It may ultimately place some of this practical work on a firmer base, and it may likely reject and replace parts of this work with better concepts. This is progress.

EQUITY DEFINED

What is equity? Are there many types? Internal, external? Perceptions of those who determine salaries? Perceptions of those whose salaries are determined?

Equity is a perceived sense of rewards balancing outputs—pay proportionate to achievement—a parent's praise and criticism balanced with a child's perception of his or her behavior compared with the rewards and behavior of a brother or sister. Some might accept the notion that equity relates closely to fairness, but fairness is equally hard to define. The philosopher might say that equity, like beauty, is in the eye of the beholder.

Certainly there are many perceptive points from which pay equity can be viewed or felt.

If the foregoing descriptions of equity are confusing, try then to present a solid, tested, acceptable definition to the many managers of a large organization employing a variety of staff and professional specialists. Current practice *assumes* that the more important individual perceptions of compensation equity are derived within the organization in which a person works. Perceptions of equity may be influenced more forcefully by factors close to the person's actual work environment. One can hypothesize that an individual may derive equity perceptions from sources which may be ranked in descending order of importance somewhat as shown below:

1. Within the smallest work unit: department or task group
2. Within the next larger organization unit: department, laboratory, or division
3. Among peers doing similar work
4. Among peers doing dissimilar work
5. Within the plant
6. Within the union, within the profession, or among managers having similar responsibility
7. Between plants within the company

---

[3]Ruth G. Blumrosen, "Wage Discrimination, Job Segregation, and Title VII of the Civil Rights Act of 1964," *Journal of Law Reform*, vol. 12, no. 3, 1979.

8. Within the company as a whole
9. With outside companies

Probably the order of importance varies according to the type of job an individual has—i.e., a salesperson's perception would probably differ from a factory worker's. *Presumably,* the broader the exposure of the individual to practices outside an individual work unit, the greater the number of considerations leading to perceptions of equity or lack of equity.

Several conclusions are suggested by this analysis of equity perceptions:

1. Executive perceptions of equity may be derived from sources far different from those influencing the majority of people in the organization. For example, one executive expressed great concern because a staff person suggested a specific pay action for factory people at one location based on community practice but recommended the action be withheld from other locations under the administration of the executive. The executive's perception of equity encompassed all locations; the staff person rated the local situation as more important.

2. It is probable that individual concepts of compensation equity are strongly influenced by the existing reward system in an organization and the way the reward system is administered. Thus an organization that works hard to develop sound job measurement practices, promotes on the basis of ability and achievement, and awards salary increases for observable results will probably create an environment in which internal equity is perceived by many. Management reinforces its desire for achievement by rewarding those who achieve. Conversely, every time a salary increase is awarded to a nonperformer, equity perception among employees may be damaged. Poor promotion decisions are even more discernible.

3. Perceptions of equity, or standards of work value, are so variable and changing among people, among professions, and among various organizations that a single organization must develop its own set of value standards and sustain those standards over a period of time if they are to have meaning and are to influence perceptions of equity. Thus the organization should use caution in attacking or changing a long-established set of job relationships, regardless of the source of the equity perceptions which originally generated the relationships. In the long run, internal relationships between job values (internal equity) are far more important than external relationships with other companies (external equity). There are some high-morale, effective organizations which pay wages and salaries that are modest by comparison with other organizations having similar work. Frequently these organizations have given great care to developing firm standards of internal job measurement. Therefore, pay distinctions are generally perceived as internally equitable.

It has been suggested that equity, or inequity, exists as an individual perception and that these perceptions are influenced by a variety of factors. Actually, psychologists have developed a theory of equity and continue to explore the relationships of equity to motivation. J. S. Adams[4] defined inequity as follows:

> Inequity exists for Person whenever he perceives that the ratio of his *outcomes* to *inputs* and the ratio of Other's outcomes to Other's inputs are unequal. This

---

[4]J. S. Adams, "Toward an Understanding of Inequity," *Journal of Abnormal Psychology,* 67, 1963, pp. 422 ff.

may happen either (a) when he and Other are in a direct exchange relationship or (b) when both are in an exchange relationship with a third party and Person compares himself to Other.

The general observations previously made on the subject of equity are consistent with Adams's definition. However, it should be emphasized that when people weigh their *outcomes* and *inputs* relative to their job and the jobs of others, they will consider many nonfinancial elements as well as financial rewards. Traditional restraints imposed on compensation administration, however, confine its actions to evaluating jobs and determining only financial rewards. Hence this chapter should technically be titled "Achieving *Pay* Equity through Job Measurement." The concerned manager should always consider the fact that individuals paid well for the job they are doing may still feel a sense of gross inequity from a variety of nonfinancial factors which overwhelm the pay rewards. Such factors include lack of recognition, failure to achieve promotion, and inherent job dissatisfaction as "Person" compares his or her education, achievements, and interests with those of others.

PURSUING EQUITY

Two extremely different approaches can be taken to establish job values in an organization:

1. Derive value and price concurrently from measures outside the organization: *market value approach.*
2. Develop internal standards of comparison and measure relative job values within the organization: *job evaluation approach.*

Market Value Approach   The market value approach—using salary survey data to determine the price to be paid for various jobs—appears the easiest to pursue. It is frequently the expedient approach for some public, nonprofit institutions—situations requiring acceptance by employees, taxpayers, and political leaders. It is difficult to quarrel with salaries determined exclusively by market survey information.

For most business organizations, however, the market value approach is less desirable because it may invite comparison between jobs that are not truly comparable. It tends to ignore internal considerations and can produce inequities noticed by employees and executives. Wage and salary surveys—even among companies within the same industry—are of questionable value if used for anything more specific than an overall reference point from which to price a company's salary structure. Casually acquired survey information is no substitute for solid analysis of the relationships among the jobs designed to meet specific company objectives.

However, even if one assumes the data collected are sound and are a well-balanced representation of the marketplace, does it necessarily follow that internal decisions of relative job worth should be based on the average prevailing statistical accident in society?

Staff and managerial jobs typically vary from company to company. A sound salary program, therefore, demands careful analysis of jobs and their interrelationships based on the intrinsic value of the jobs to a specific company.

Job Evaluation Approach   The objective of job evaluation is to develop a set of value standards for establishing the *relative* worth of each job to a specific organization. Job evaluation is *not* intended to provide absolute answers in terms of current dollar values. (The absolute assignment of dollar values based upon surveys and pricing decisions is a separate problem discussed in Parts C and G.) The job evaluation process can be designed to group jobs into clusters having similar internal worth. The process can further develop a relationship between and among all clusters. The net result is to establish an internal structure of jobs. However, it is *not* essential to produce job clusters and assign them salary grade numbers; the process can be designed to produce continuous job values without forcing jobs into clusters. A soundly conceived and administered job evaluation plan offers many advantages to any organization:

1. *It permits top management to influence the standards against which jobs are evaluated without getting involved in the detail of job description.*   Since no set of standards will apply to jobs in all companies, management participation in the determination of these standards must be an integral part of the job evaluation plan.

After all jobs are evaluated, key jobs should be selected to illustrate the full spectrum of relative values established for each activity. The key jobs for each major activity in an organization—e.g., finance, marketing, research, and administration—should be charted to present the relative values horizontally between the activities as well as vertically within each. Executive management can carefully examine the relative job value relationships between and within activities in order to appraise the results of the evaluation process and to determine whether evaluation guidelines are producing desired end results. This process can be repeated periodically to keep management up to date with the program.

2. *It serves as an aid to work force management.*   The involvement of operating managers in the job evaluation process allows them to relate organization plans, job design, and work force planning to their total objective. Jobs are characterized; value-determining elements of jobs are delineated. Selecting people with appropriate experience and abilities to meet job requirements becomes a more precise process.

3. *It can help improve employee perceptions of pay equity.*   With sound job evaluation, presumably employees will perceive that their pay is related fairly to the value of the work they are asked to do.

Weakness in application of job evaluation principles, however, may retard complete acceptance of job evaluation as an important management tool, particularly in medium- to large-size companies and as applied to exempt jobs. Such weaknesses may arise from:

1. *Overemphasis on technique.*   Some wage and salary staff personnel have taken a rather mediocre evaluation plan and presented it to managers as a scientific measuring device as reliable as a physicist's measurement of atomic weights. Using carefully chosen adjectives and point evaluation scales, some people have attempted to define relative values with precision, in some cases with only limited knowledge of the jobs to which the evaluation techniques were applied. Thoughtful managers tend to rebel against such "expert" staff assistance, and they question the ability of a few staff people to judge the intrinsic value of jobs.

2. Inappropriate use of evaluation plans. A few evaluation plans that have been highly successful in relating hourly and clerical job values have been extrapolated to professional, administrative, and executive jobs. Few plans are equally effective throughout the entire range of job content from janitor to company president. In the exempt salary area, the ranking technique has also contributed to poor acceptance of evaluation plans. With the ranking technique every manager and staff person is immediately expert in evaluation. Each may develop personal rules of thumb, and each can select particular jobs to produce desired results. Also, ranking plans may tend to encourage managers to develop and defend high job values in their activities.

3. Poor analysis of jobs. All too frequently, job content has not been analyzed adequately. Even with a good evaluation plan, poor job analysis will yield poor evaluation results.

4. Staff failures. Good evaluation demands a breadth of perspective and a keen insight into the management process and into the nature of a wide variety of jobs in a company. The ideal evaluation expert is the executive with the broadest company experience. Such a person is always too burdened with responsibilities to spend hours each week carefully collecting data and analyzing job values. In choosing wage and salary administrators to supervise the data gathering, analysis, and surveys and to guide the evaluation process, managers have not always selected people with sufficient breadth and perspective to devise, maintain, and improve an evaluation program.

Understanding some factors that impair the acceptance of job evaluation helps to define the conditions under which sound internal value relationships can be developed and maintained.

There is no single panacea. The best evaluation plans can fail. A staff with heavy authority and executive support can fail. The development of sound internal job relationships within a company requires a full set of balanced conditions, much as a high-performance engine requires excellent materials, machining to close tolerances, and a precision balancing of the assembled pistons, connecting rods, and drive shaft.

The best evaluation work within an organization requires a self-imposed total discipline. Managers must thoroughly understand and accept the objectives of internal evaluation. They must impose the discipline upon themselves because of the favorable objectives they perceive and want to achieve.

CHOOSING AN EVALUATION PLAN

An evaluation plan should be relatively straightforward in design. It should apply to a wide range of highly specialized managerial and staff jobs, or specifically to nonexempt jobs. The plan should emphasize the major elements of job value and ignore the trivial or irrelevant. Above all, the plan should be applied with sensitivity and understanding. Most evaluation plans are improved if they are first applied to an array of key jobs which serve to calibrate the evaluation factors.

The plan should be carefully developed and thoroughly tested. Frequently the experience of qualified consultants is helpful in developing and implementing a program. The better consultants will thoroughly involve responsible management and appropriate staff people in the design and testing of a plan.

No long-term useful result is achieved by having a consultant actually evaluate all jobs, review the results with a few key executives, install the plan, and leave. Such an approach fails to develop the staff involvement necessary for continued application of the plan: the person appointed by management to administer the program would be forced to apply the plan by rote, not having been exposed to the subtle philosophy and experience on which the plan was based.

Job evaluation requires extensive use of disciplined human judgment. No existing plan applied by inexperienced staff people can produce creditable results. A major part of the disciplined judgment comes about by involvement in the design and testing of the plan. Some may feel that the existence of the judgmental element and the requirement of experience would indicate that evaluation plans are of little value. Are the tools of a skilled cabinetmaker poor or useless because an inexperienced worker fails in an attempt to build a complicated piece of furniture?

IMPLEMENTING THE PLAN

A member of the wage and salary staff should analyze jobs in considerable detail. He or she should discuss the jobs with incumbents and, with their supervisors or managers, should identify and define the reporting relationships surrounding a job and define the broad purpose for which the job is intended. Value-determining factors within the job should be identified on the basis of the major duties and job responsibilities. A summary of the major features of the job should be committed to writing and submitted to the responsible manager for approval.

Job analysis has always been guided by one basic rule: *define and measure the job and not the individual.* This important guiding principle applies to all job levels. Perhaps it is worthwhile to add one other precaution in evaluating exempt jobs—namely, consider only those aspects of the job that are currently being performed and are currently delegated. Responsibilities that are expected to unfold at some future date should *not* be considered unless the manager is in the actual process of redesigning a job. Incumbents do influence jobs; evaluation decisions need not be permanent; and a job can be reevaluated if a significant increase or decrease in responsibility is reported.

Roles of Staff and Management   Proper evaluation of jobs should be the responsibility of line management, with each level of management accountable to the next level for evaluation results. However, there is a definite role for qualified staff to perform in the process. Their role should be recognized, supported, and utilized if equitable job values are to be attained. It is essential that managers avoid reaching agreement with subordinate members about job values through a casual discussion of factors and without a prior review by a competent staff person. Only by exercising considerable care in this regard can the impact of neutral and experienced staff analysis become meaningful.

Within a large organization a systematic approach to job evaluation provides the framework within which final approval or authorization of recommended job values can be delegated to various levels of management. It also provides a framework within which both central and decentralized staff work can be conducted with recognition, respect, and cooperation between staffs. The charters of responsibility for central and decentralized staff in the evaluation process should be clearly defined.

Review and Approval   Details of an appropriate review and approval process must be related to the size and complexity of an organization. Nevertheless, there are some general principles worthy of consideration.

The final authorization of job values should be delegated to some degree and should not be retained in total as a chief executive function. For example, in a large company having at least six broad levels of management, final authorization of job values might be delegated as shown in Table 1.

The generalized scheme shown in Table 1 suggests that no managers, except the top executive group, authorize job values for people reporting directly to them. The term "authorize" is used in the context of a final decision, with no further executive review.

Before authorization, there should be an approval and recommendation routing for all job value changes or for the introduction of new job values. This vital sequence helps guarantee independent staff analysis. A typical sequence of preliminary approval and recommendation could be as follows:

Approval	→	*Review and Approval*	→	*Review and Approval*	→	*Authorization*
Recommending Manager		Wage and Salary Admin. Staff (Staff of Oper. Executive)		Wage and Salary Admin. Staff (Corporate)		Appropriate Level of Management

Suggested approval and authorization schemes vary widely, depending on the size of an organization and the degree of centralization. However, some principles are always applicable:

1. Managers should not authorize values for jobs reporting directly to them.
2. Final authorization of job values should be a line management responsibility.

TABLE 1   Proposed Delegation of Authority for Job Values

Level number	Job level	Authorization for
	Board of directors	Top executives
6	Top executives	All operating executives and fourth-level management jobs
5	Operating executives	All third-level managements jobs and any corresponding level of staff jobs
4	Activity managers	Two levels of management jobs and corresponding levels of staff jobs
3	Third-level management	All nonexempt jobs
2	Second-level management	
1	Foremen	

3. Independent staff analysis will be guaranteed by the approval sequence if the sequence is followed rigorously.

4. Dissenting viewpoints should be reconciled at each step in the approval and authorization process.

5. Any changes made along the approval route should be communicated promptly to the originating manager. Variations in the staff approval plan may exclude one of the staff approvals but should not exclude both.

What are the benefits of following a systematic job evaluation program as outlined in this chapter?

1. Managers are completely involved in job design and evaluation judgments. They are then in the best position to relate organization plans and work force development considerations to the total process of managing people.

2. An orderly relationship of job values evolves. Key jobs can be abstracted and surveyed to price the entire structure of jobs.

3. Valid external comparisons can be made. Evaluation principles are useful in sampling representative jobs in outside companies and pinpointing their place in the internal salary structure.

4. Results may be supported by social science research:

(a) *Learning theory.* Individuals find reinforcement of a company's stated policy that pay is determined on the basis of work performed.

(b) *Training.* A systematic body of knowledge, as opposed to personal whims and hunches, can be transferred between executives and between and among responsible staff personnel.

(c) *Communications.* A well-defined approach lends itself to forthright communications to all whose pay is affected by evaluation decisions.

(d) *Credibility.* The application of common evaluation principles to all jobs from the chief executive to entry-level jobs for inexperienced people avoids gaps in understanding and communications. Similar messages flow up and down the organization levels. People gradually perceive the fact that achievement is the biggest factor in pay determination.

(e) *Motivation.* Many demotivating or negative attitudes among employees are avoided by good internal evaluation of jobs.

A well-delineated approach lends itself to future improvement and change in an orderly fashion as social research and experience suggest practical improvements.

At this point it should be obvious that developing and maintaining internal equity through job evaluation requires work—constant work on the part of many people, both management and staff. Is it worth all the time required? Cannot the process be simplified? Managers have heavy work loads. How can they be expected to spend so much time on job evaluation? Job evaluation should play an important role in the total management of human resources. If a company expects to manage these resources successfully, and if the cost of total compensation is considered, developing and maintaining a sound evaluation program are well worth both time and effort.

Job evaluation is not a science. Guiding, training, and sharpening judgmental processes cannot be done by a computer. Every effort should be made to keep the evaluation process as simple as possible. Nevertheless, there is no shortcut for the initial and recurring individual involvement that managers should give to the program.

Finding the time within a busy work schedule is perhaps really a question of being convinced that the problem is significant and that results achieved bring a favorable return to the manager and to the company.

BALANCING INTERNAL AND EXTERNAL EQUITY

After the internal job relationships have been established, and after the job structure has been priced in some policy relationship to prevailing wages and salaries, there are other important variables to identify, analyze, and control.

Specific to job evaluation is the problem of reconciling decisions about internal equity with pay competition from external sources. During the past ten years, managers responsible for specialized functions have been constantly plagued by the tension existing between internal equity of job values and outside pay competition. At one time or another an imbalance between supply and demand has created special pay problems for a variety of specialists, such as scientists and engineers, mathematicians, data processing personnel, machinists, technicians, and patent attorneys. The future will bring other tensions which tend to distort internal equity of job evaluation. To maintain job evaluation integrity, important administrative actions must be taken periodically. Even without the tensions created by imbalances between supply and demand for certain skills, dynamic dimensions for salary administration must be identified and directed by policy.

The dollar values assigned to the salary structure must be adjusted periodically and by a sufficient amount to maintain a prescribed policy relationship to some defined external pattern of pay. The failure to adjust the price of a salary structure adequately accounts for much of the tension many organizations consider to be unusual external market pressures. First one group of specialists and then another begins to complain about external pay relationships. A more insidious problem for job evaluation is this: if structure repricing is inadequate, a slow "slippage" or "creep" of job values takes place. Faced with the need to pay competitive salaries, managers react to external pressure by rationalizing higher job values for their people. The upgrading of jobs does not take place uniformly. Some managers are more aggressive than others in promoting the upgrading; some functions do not have personnel with the kinds of specialized backgrounds that make such personnel susceptible to external pressure. Nevertheless, such jobs and output may be just as significant to an organization as the jobs subject to external pay pressure.

Failure to maintain a constant price structure relative to a defined external pattern of pay will ultimately result in the total disruption of internal job relationships. Even with a properly maintained salary structure, there will be pressures to upgrade jobs without justification. The evaluation program should define the criteria for determining whether a job has changed in value. In establishing these criteria, one should recognize that many changes in a job may not contribute to an increase in its intrinsic value, but may represent changes in emphasis caused by differing business conditions. Reasonably firm standards for upgrading can be justified on the basis that a company moving the price of its wage and salary structure properly is providing increases in real income in the long term. Some of this increase in real income adequately recognizes minor growth in job content accruing to many jobs.

If an organization has a policy of updating its pay structure, and if it has reasonable criteria for upgrading jobs, unique market pressure on pay for some jobs is probably a real fact and not the result of aberrations in salary program management.

There is no one best solution to unusual outside pressure on a few jobs. Many purists, in their support of internal equity, argue that the proper solution is to retain the established values for such jobs (keep internal equity) while providing special salary ranges that meet external pay pressure. The objective behind this solution is to maintain proper job values and to accept a temporary internal pay inequity; if the unique external pay pressure subsides, the salary ranges can be brought into line with those for other jobs having similar value. This is the only general solution worthy of detailed comment. If the problem is *clearly* one of external salary pressure, this approach is certainly to be preferred over other solutions.

Unfortunately, it has been this writer's experience that there are relatively few *real* serious market aberrations. The extent to which these aberrations exist and can be identified is related to how generously an organization's overall salary structure is priced compared with those of outside companies. Often a manager of a special activity reports inadequate pay for some specialty, but a detailed review of the problem indicates something quite different from pay competition. At one time or another, these have been the findings of practicing salary administrators:

1. A manager is quoting some information that relates to the *highest* salaries available for the specialty.

2. The pay competition reflects greater intrinsic job opportunity in some other companies. For example, one would expect that the internal value of specialists in the field of industrial design (design devoted to appearance and customer appeal) might be greater in automotive companies than in companies manufacturing industrial machine tools.

3. The internal evaluation program of a company is too rigid. For example, many companies have complained about the special market pressure on data processing jobs. Some of these companies failed to analyze and appreciate the impact of some of the systems design jobs. In other instances, the organization did not require (or sense the need for) sophisticated data processing that was necessary to other companies. No doubt, the supervisor of a small data processing operation chartered to do little more than an extension of key punch and tabulating work has problems in attracting and retaining specialists in systems design and programming. However, this problem is not one that can be solved with special salary treatment; the problem instead represents a situation in which more intrinsic job opportunity exists in other establishments.

4. A manager rightly identifies special pay competition, but all of it comes from establishments that are not included in the organization's general appraisal of external salaries.

It is always possible to find some evidence somewhere in society that practically any job is underpaid or overpaid. Pay administrators should resist reacting to salary competition that comes from companies or organizations that are not included in salary surveys influencing the price of a company's entire pay structure.

Considerable space has been devoted to the subject of maintaining internal equity in the face of seemingly inequitable external pay relationships. There is always some degree of conflict between internal and external pay equity. The position taken by most salary administrators is that internal relationships should be given *first* priority, and external pay relationships for certain jobs must be compromised on occasion.

chapter 10

Measurement as an Issue in Analysis and Evaluation of Jobs

George T. Milkovich

PROFESSOR, NEW YORK STATE SCHOOL OF INDUSTRIAL
AND LABOR RELATIONS, CORNELL UNIVERSITY, ITHACA,
NEW YORK

Charles J. Cogill

PROFESSOR, GRADUATE SCHOOL OF BUSINESS,
UNIVERSITY OF THE WITWATERSRAND, JOHANNESBURG,
SOUTH AFRICA

Work is a coat of many colors. As any compensation professional knows, work is varied and diverse, with different tasks and duties required to be performed; with different types and degrees of knowledge, skills, and abilities required to perform them; and with different rewards and returns offered.

Work is vital to all of us. It affects the nation's productivity and economic vitality. As employees, the work we perform and the returns we receive influence our psychological and physical as well as economic well-being. It influences our feelings of self-worth, lifestyle, health, friendships, and relations. Profits, the ability to compete, and the very makeup and essence of organizations are all influenced by the design and performance of work.

Yet despite this diversity and importance, there is often in contemporary compensation practices only the slightest suggestion that understanding what employees do (work) is at all salient. Further, it is probably a safe bet that the majority of practices which do systematically attempt to describe work were designed and implemented at least 10 to 20 years ago. While some wines improve with age, many compensation practices were not designed to capture the changing nature of the work, the changing expectations of employees with respect to work, and the changing regulatory and legal climate that we observe in society today. Consequently, they run the risk of obsolescence.

This chapter was motivated by the belief that many of the traditional compensation practices are in need of reexamination and, where necessary, redesign. This belief is based in part on the changing conditions mentioned above and the need to respond to the challenges to current practices. Some of these challenges are clear, such as the pressures surrounding male-female wage differentials and comparable worth. Others come from the users of the system: operating managers and employees who question the logic of pay decisions. Other pressures, less evident, are emerging from the advancing state of research and development related to compensation decision making. All these pressures combine to make this a period of ferment in compensation management, and it seems safe to predict that pressures for reexamination will increase during the foreseeable future.

The purpose of this chapter is to examine critically one component of contemporary compensation systems, work measurement. By doing so, we hope to encourage compensation professionals to reexamine their approaches to work measurement and hopefully to help ensure the work relatedness of their decisions.

WORK MEASUREMENT: A CRITICAL LINK

The measurement of work, through such practices as job analysis, job description, and job evaluation, plays a critical role in compensation decision making. Just as human resources planning helps ensure that human resources decisions are linked to the organization's strategic and operational plans, the process of work measurement should help ensure that compensation decisions are linked to what employees do—the work itself. Without the critical link to the work, the likelihood of achieving the objectives of any compensation system, be they performance improvement, cost effectiveness and containment, legal compliance, or some other goals, seems slight.

Simply stated, work measurement involves the systematic assignment of numerals or symbols to the properties of work. In job evaluation, for example, we attempt to "measure" the *worth* of work to the organization in terms of properties such as problem solving, know-how, accountability, skill, effort, responsibility, or working conditions. In job analysis such as functional job analysis or the Position Analysis Questionnaire (PAQ), the *content* of the work is represented in terms of properties such as information input, mental processes, work output, relationship with others, and job content.

A key question in measurement is what is actually meant by the assignment of numbers to properties of work. Part of the answer lies in the measurement scales used. Figure 1 describes the four basic scales—nominal, ordinal, interval, and ratio—lists their properties, and illustrates them. While distinctions between these four scales may seem academic compared to the daily problems

FIGURE 1   Levels of Measurement Scaling

Levels	Description	Examples
Nominal	Each numeral represents a group or class; all elements in a class are equal.	Race/sex designations
Ordinal	Each numeral stands in some ordered relationship (greater, equal, less) to the others.	Rankings and job evaluation classification levels in the organization; performance rankings
Interval	Possesses all the properties above, plus the distance between the numerals are of a known and common unit; e.g., the distance between 230 and 231 points equals that between 3 and 4 points.	Assumed in point job evaluation and performance ratings
Ratio	Possesses all the properties above, plus the existence of a zero point in reality.	Wage rates

facing professionals in this field, these distinctions take on importance because they limit the interpretation and meaning that can be ascribed to the results of job analysis and job evaluation. For example, using ordinal scales permits one to measure the rank order of the properties of two jobs: job A may have greater stress or higher experience requirements than job B. But it does not permit interpretation about "how much" or how many units more. To answer that question requires interval scaling.

The critical advantages of work measurement are that end results are objective, documentable, and quantified. Such data can be analyzed in a more rigorous manner with greater precision. These attributes become doubly important when we consider the importance of ensuring and demonstrating that pay decisions are, at least in part, based upon the work performed.

Yet the very objectivity and documentation afforded by work measurement permit the results to be scrutinized by any and all who may obtain them. Such scrutiny comes from many sources, such as an employee whose job has been measured, managers who want a subordinate's job slotted into higher ranges, or experts during litigation. For the results of work measurement to withstand such analysis, four thorny standards must be met.

FOUR STANDARDS FOR WORK MEASUREMENT

Four standards for evaluating any process of measuring work are accuracy, reliability, acceptance, and efficiency. We will briefly examine each and then evaluate the current state of work measurement against them.

Accuracy   Accuracy is the validity of the results obtained. It is quite possible for two analysts using the same method to agree completely—and for both to be wrong. The error could be the result of *contamination* in the method used, such as biased interpretation by the analysts, or it could result from deficiencies in the *comprehensiveness* of the measurement. The measuring of an administrative secretary in terms of the skills demanded in shorthand, typing, filing, etc., may be true as far as it goes but not comprehensive because it does not include answering the telephone, interacting with the public, or accepting and relaying messages.

Reliability   Reliability is the consistency of the results obtained. Do the results vary depending on who does the measurement and what methods are used? How consistent are perceptions of importance and difficulty of work? To what extent do different work measurement methods give different results? Are there differences in the way operating managers, compensation analysts, consultants, members of protected groups, or employees perceive the job?

Efficiency   Efficiency reflects costs relative to benefits obtained. Is the process the most efficient and feasible under the circumstances?

Acceptability   Both the process and the results of job measurement must be accepted by the parties involved and must comply with prevailing regulatory and legal requirements. While no process of work measurement will be acceptable to all the parties, at least the critical players—managers and employees—must accept it. Certainly, understanding the process should aid in gaining acceptance.

Turning to an examination of current work measurement processes against these standards, we next consider procedures for collecting the needed information.

ANALYSIS OF CONTENT

Job analysis is a systematic process for collecting work-related information. When considering job analysis as a process of measurement, it is useful to distinguish between conventional and quantitative approaches. All compensation professionals are familiar with the conventional approach, even though specific details vary among users. Best described in the *Handbook for Analyzing Jobs*[1] and exemplified by functional job analysis,[2] it typically involves an analyst using a questionnaire to conduct interviews with job incumbents and supervisors. The results are essay descriptions of the work, agreed to by incumbents and supervisors. They typically include five properties of the work: (1) function, (2) area of application, (3) equipment used, (4) materials worked on, subject matter, or clients, and (5) worker traits.

---

[1] *Handbook for Analyzing Jobs*, U.S. Department of Labor, Washington, D.C.: U.S. Superintendent of Documents, no. 2900-0131, 1972.

[2] S. A. Fine and A. W. Wiley, "An Introduction to Functional Job Analysis" (Monograph no. 4), Upjohn Institute for Employment Research, Kalamazoo, Mich., 1971.

FIGURE 2   Methods of Job Analysis Rated Against Standards of Work Measurement

	Analysis Methods	
Standards	Conventional	Quantitative
Reliability	Largely unknown	Favorable
Accuracy	Largely unknown	Largely unknown
Acceptability	Questionable	Acceptable/unknown
Efficiency	Largely unknown	Questionable

At the outset, we acknowledge the positive contributions of conventional approaches, recognizing the importance of any work-related data to personnel decision making. Yet those of us who think back to our first-entry analyst positions will recall that vague, queasy feeling of floundering in semantic confusion. Ramras said it best: "We all know the classic procedures. One [person] watched and noted the actions of another [person] at work on [the] job. The actions of both are biased, and the resulting information varied with the wind, especially the political wind."[3]

As a process of measurement, conventional job analysis approaches simply do not meet the standards. This conclusion, illustrated in Figure 2, is based on the fact that it is largely unknown whether the results obtained from conventional approaches are reliable, accurate, acceptable, and efficient. The reason for this lack of knowledge is that most of the effort in this area has been devoted to design and implementation and none to evaluating the process or results. A strict interpretation would argue that such a conclusion cannot be drawn because of the absence of evaluative results. So a more "correct" evaluation is that it is largely unknown if conventional approaches yield results that are accurate, reliable, acceptable, and efficient.

Inventories are the heart of quantitative job analysis (QJA). Inventories, illustrated in Figures 3 and 4, are questionnaires in which the work tasks and worker traits relevant for the work are listed. Note the scales in the inventory: a task is assessed, usually by both the job incumbent and the supervisor, in terms of time spent, importance, and/or learning time. The knowledge, skills, and abilities required to perform the work may be measured in degrees of importance and education equivalency or experience required. Several QJA plans are available. The most publicized are the Position Analysis Questionnaire (PAQ),[4] Position Description Questionnaire (PDQ),[5] the Personnel Deci-

---

[3] E. M. Ramras, "Discussion," in *Proceedings of the 77th Annual American Psychological Association*, 1969, pp. 75–76.

[4] E. J. McCormick, "Job and Task Analysis," in M. D. Dunnette (ed.), *Handbook of Industrial and Organizational Psychology*, Rand McNally & Company, Chicago, 1976.

[5] L. R. Gomez-Mejia, R. C. Page, and W. Tornow, "A Comparison of the Practical Utility of Traditional, Statistical and Hybrid Job Evaluation Approaches," *Personnel Research Report* #169–79, Control Data Corporation.

FIGURE 3 Example of Task- or Activity-Oriented Job Checklist*

	TIME SPENT					IMPORTANCE					LEARNING TIME					
THIS IS A PART OF MY JOB	MUCH LESS TIME Than Other Activities	LESS TIME Than Other Activities	ABOUT THE SAME Amount of Time as Other Activities	MORE TIME Than Other Activities	MUCH MORE TIME Than Other Activities	UNIMPORTANT	Minor Importance	IMPORTANT	Very Important	CRUCIAL	1 Day or Less	2 or 3 Days	4 or 5 Days	Up to a Month	1–3 Months	More than 3 Months
	[1]	[2]	[3]	[4]	[5]	[1]	[2]	[3]	[4]	[5]	[1]	[2]	[3]	[4]	[5]	[6]
153. Plan special sales promotions and see that they are carried out according to plan.																
154. Keep track of and follow up on the activities of subordinates.																
155. Transcribe from dictating machine records or tapes.																

156. Schedule dates or times for appointments, meetings, etc., or delivery, pick-up, and repair of merchandise by checking with those involved for time and place.															
157. Perform routine preventive mechanical maintenance on machines or equipment.															
158. Look up, search for, or locate information in readily available sources such as files, parts lists, records, manuals, tables, catalogs, etc.															
159. Set objectives for a department or unit of the company.															
	(1)	(2)	(3)	(4)	(5)	(1)	(2)	(3)	(4)	(5)	(1)	(2)	(3)	(4)	(5) (6)

SOURCE: L. M. Hough. *Job Activities Questionnaire for Retail Employees*, Personnel Decisions Research Institute, Minneapolis, 1977.

FIGURE 4   Example of Supervision- and Control-Oriented Job Checklist

SUPERVISING & CONTROLLING

This part addresses activities directed toward the supervision and control of subordinates in your organization. It is recognized that many of these activities are not required in consultant positions.

DIRECTIONS:

STEP 1

Indicate how significant a part of your position each item represents by entering a number between 0 and 4 in the column next to it. (Remember to consider both its **importance** in light of all the other position activities and **frequency** of occurrence.)

0—**Definitely not** a part of the position.
1—A **minor** part of the position.
2—A **moderate** part of the position.
3—A **substantial** part of the position.
4—A **crucial** and **most significant** part of the position.

STEP 2

Use this space to clarify or comment on any aspects of the SUPERVISING & CONTROLLING function that you feel were not adequately covered by the preceding questions.

SOURCE: Control Data Corporation, Minneapolis, Minn. Reprinted by permission.

AN INDIVIDUAL IN MY POSITION WOULD:

113___ 1. Make use of administrative staff consultants.

114___ 2. Define areas of responsibility for managerial personnel.

115___ 3. Analyze operating performance reports.

116___ 4. Delegate to subordinates or others when a course of action is decided.

117___ 5. Interact face-to-face with subordinates on an almost daily basis.

118___ 6. Assign priorities for others on no less than a quarterly basis.

119___ 7. Develop subordinates for improved job performance and future responsibility.

120___ 8. Develop executive level management talent.

121___ 9. Monitor closely the progress of specific projects.

122___ 10. Review subordinates' work almost continually.

123___ 11. Analyze at least monthly the effectiveness of operations.

124___ 12. Review subordinates' work methods for possible increases in productivity.

125___ 13. Motivate subordinates to change or improve performance.

126___ 14. Analyze subordinates' weaknesses and training needs.

127___ 15. Conduct regular performance reviews with subordinates.

128___ 16. Guide subordinates on technical matters.

129___ 17. Disseminate complete information to subordinates.

130___ 18. Monitor my unit's progress toward its objectives and adjust activities as necessary to reach them.

131___ 19. Provide complete instructions to subordinates when giving assignments.

132___ 20. Maintain a smooth working relationship among various individuals who need to work cooperatively.

133___ 21. Monitor the progress of geographically separate units toward their objectives and adjust activities as necessary to reach them.

→ **COMMENTS**

134 _____

_____

_____

_____

_____

_____

_____

_____

_____

_____

sions Research Institute (PDRI) approach,[6] the Air Force Inventory, and Krzystofiak, Newman, and Anderson's applications.[7] See Chapter 7.

As Figure 2 suggests, considerable effort has been devoted to appraising QJA as a measurement process. Developers of QJA typically report reliability results, and they tend to be favorable. Thus different analysts using the same QJA on the same jobs tend to get the same results. Little work has been reported using the same analyst over time, but McCormick reports favorable reliability over time with the PAQ.

Some disquieting results have been reported by O'Reilly, who found that "One's frame of reference, as represented by factors such as past experiences, present jobs, expectations, may result in different perceptions and definitions of the same work."[8] For example, some employees who have been on the job a long time may change the job by adopting shortcuts and new routines. The point here is that the employees' and supervisors' backgrounds may influence the results of QJA.

The validity of the QJA process and of the results obtained are largely unknown. Consistent job information does not necessarily mean it is accurate, comprehensive, and uncontaminated. Research on how to estimate the validity of job analysis is difficult, since there is almost no way of showing statistically the extent to which results are accurate portraits of the work. The most promising approach is to examine the extent of convergence among multiple sources (analysts, incumbents, supervisors) and multiple methods. Such multimethod, multisource research has yet to be conducted.

The acceptability of QJA approaches is mixed. McCormick,[9] Dunnette,[10] and Krzystofiak et al.[11] all report success in gaining acceptance by the employees and managers involved. However, Gomez-Mejia, in a project at Control Data Corporation, and Christal's work in the Air Force describe experiences in which managers refused to accept the results of QJA.[12] Gomez-Mejia suggests that the statistical methods used in QJA may be difficult for some managers to understand; consequently, they could not adequately explain the process or results to employees affected by the system.

Finally, the efficiency of QJA is relatively unexplored. Krzystofiak et al. report that an application at Northern States Power Company in 1978 required one year of development and administration of the QJA, at least one personnel

---

[6] M. D. Dunnette, L. M. Hough, and R. L. Rosse, "Task and Job Taxonomies," *Human Resources Planning*, vol. 2, no. 1, 1979.

[7] F. Krzystofiak, J. Newman, and G. Anderson, "A Quantified Approach to Measurement of Job Content," *Personnel Psychology*, vol. 32, no. 2, 1979.

[8] C. A. O'Reilly, G. N. Parlette, and J. R. Bloom, "Perceptual Measures of Task Characteristics: The Biasing Effects of Different Frames of Reference and Job Attitudes," *Academy of Management Journal*, 1980, pp. 118–131.

[9] McCormick, op. cit.

[10] Dunnette et al., op. cit.

[11] Krzystofiak et al., op. cit.

[12] Gomez-Mejia et al., op. cit; R. E. Christal, *U.S. Air Force Occupational Research Project*, National Technical Information Service, U.S. Dept. of Commerce, Jan. 1974.

professional, and direct costs between $10,000 and $20,000 for computing and consulting. Further, they counsel that QJA approaches seem most appropriate in moderate to large organizations (over 1000 employees). The practical utility of QJA, with its relatively complex procedures and analysis, remains in doubt for many organizations. However, this may suggest that marketing or packaging skills are required to increase its practical utility and acceptance.

Reflecting upon Figure 2, it is clear that QJA approaches to the collection of work-related information fare better than conventional analysis as a measurement process. Work-related data obtained through QJA are more likely to be reliable and perhaps acceptable. Considering the importance placed on ensuring the work relatedness of data used in personnel decision making, it remains disturbing that more resources have not been devoted to evaluating conventional approaches relative to QJA. This is even more disturbing considering that pay decisions may in the future have to be demonstrably embedded in work-related logic.

EVALUATION

Job evaluation is a systematic process designed to aid in establishing pay differences among jobs. It does so by helping to identify the differential worth of jobs. Jobs worth more are paid more. Differential worth of jobs, in turn, depends on the use to which they are put and the exchange that their output can bring. The interactions of a variety of forces may influence job worth. These include market forces, bargaining among employers and unions, economic conditions, the wage policies of employers, and norms and customs (including discrimination) in the work place. Job evaluation is one of a variety of components (including job analysis, market surveys, and wage policies) that constitute contemporary compensation systems.

Before examining job evaluation as a process of measurement, it is worth noting that job evaluation has a dual nature. It is also an administrative procedure. As such, it combines aspects of measurement as well as "the rules of the game" by which the differential worth of work is established. The process includes the give-and-take—the higgling among the players—within the framework established by the compensable factors. In this light, job evaluation can be viewed as a process to gain agreement on a wage structure.

For the purpose of examining job evaluation as a measurement process, it is useful to consider two basic approaches to evaluation: policy capturing and a priori. Under the policy-capturing approach, compensable factors are identified through job analysis. Next, these factors are correlated with an agreed-upon wage structure of selected benchmark jobs. The wage structure for the benchmarks defines the value of the work. This structure, while not necessarily mirroring the rates in the market, does include them. It also reflects other factors such as bargaining among the parties, mentioned above. The compensable factors, derived from the work content and the managers' judgments about the work, are appropriately weighted to predict the agreed-upon wage structure. This approach, called "policy capturing" because it captures the work factors that explain the agreed-upon wage structure, was used to aid in the design of many of the original job evaluation plans. The steel industry plan, NMTA, and specific organization plans such as AT&T's management job evaluation plan are examples. More recently, the policy-capturing approach has been used with quantitative job analysis by McCormick (PAQ),[13] and Gomez-Mejia et al. (PDQ).[14].

The best example of the a priori approach to job evaluation is the Hay Guide Charts. Rather than attempting to capture an agreed-upon structure of rates, the Guide Charts reflect factors (problem solving, know-how, and accountability) and degrees (units of job content) that were derived from early studies reported by Edward Hay and Dale Purves.[15] "A priori" means derived by reasoning from self-evident propositions presupposed by experience. Therefore, the Guide Charts are a priori (based upon earlier experience and applications) measures of the units of job content and are treated by many (especially advocates of comparable worth) as units of value of job content.

Considerable effort has been devoted to the examination of job evaluation as a measurement process. Figure 5 reflects a summary of the reported work. Reliability in job evaluation is concerned with the extent to which the results of different job evaluation procedures are consistent among different evaluators. The evidence is mixed; while consistency for the total points assigned to a job is high, it still can show disagreement among evaluators.[16] Evidence has also been reported on the influence that the evaluators' background, experience, and training may have on reliability. Surprisingly, there is some indication that experience as an evaluator, per se, has little effect on reliability, though familiarity with the job does increase the degree of agreement among raters. There is even evidence suggesting that an evaluator's affiliation with unions or management has little effect on the consistency of the ratings. Finally, evidence suggests that pooled evaluation results from groups of five evaluators are acceptably reliable.[17] Note in Figure 5 that all this evidence pertains mainly to the policy-capturing approach. While it may generalize to a priori approaches, such evidence has not been publicly reported.

The standard of validity or accuracy has been examined in terms of whether alternative systems yield similar results. Strictly considered, however, convergence of this sort only suggests that the measurement is consistent across plans; it still may lack accuracy. Several studies have been reported on the convergence of alternative evaluation plans. The overall results suggest that the more

---

[13] McCormick, op. cit.

[14] Gomez-Mejia et al., op. cit.

[15] E. N. Hay and Dale Purves, "The Profile Method of High Level Job Evaluation," *Personnel*, vol. 28, no. 2, 1951, pp. 162–170. E. N. Hay and Dale Purves, "A New Method of Job Evaluation," *Personnel*, vol. 31, no. 1, 1954, pp. 72–80.

[16] J. M. Madden, "The Effect of Varying the Degree of Rater Familiarity in Job Evaluation," *Personnel Administrator* 25, 1962, pp. 42–45; J. M. Madden, "A Further Note on the Familiarity Effect in Job Evaluation," *Personnel Administrator* 26, 1963, pp. 52–54.

[17] See, for example, C. H. Lawshe, Jr., and P. C. Farbo, "Studies in Job Evaluation: 8. The Reliability of an Abbreviated Job Evaluation System," *Journal of Applied Psychology* 33, 1949, pp. 158–166; C. H. Lawshe, Jr., and R. F. Wilson, "Studies in Job Evaluation: 6. The Reliability of Two Point Rating Systems," *Journal of Applied Psychology* 31, 1947, pp. 355–365; Philip Ash, "The Reliability of Job Evaluation Rankings," *Journal of Applied Psychology* 32, 1948, pp. 313–320.

FIGURE 5   Methods of Job Evaluation Rated Against Standards of Work Measurement

	Evaluation Methods	
Standards	A Priori	Policy Capturing
Reliability	Largely unreported	Favorable
Accuracy	Largely unknown	Mixed
Acceptability	Favorable/under challenge	Favorable/under challenge
Efficiency	Largely unknown	Largely unknown

similar the type of plan employed, the more similar the results.[18] Results obtained from different point plans have more similarity, for example, than results obtained from point versus ranking or classification plans. Unfortunately, much of the evidence on the consistency and convergence of results obtained through job evaluation is drawn from studies conducted over 20 years ago. Only a few studies have been reported in the past decade.

Little effort has been devoted to studying the acceptability of policy-capturing and a priori approaches. However, the fact that over 3000 employers use some version of the Hay Guide Charts attests to their acceptability, and the widespread use of policy-capturing plans tailored to the uniqueness of various organizations also reflects their acceptability. Yet the acceptability of these plans to regulatory agencies, in light of the emerging definition of wage discrimination under Title VII, remains an open question.

It is clear to us, however, that as a process of measurement, job evaluation, both policy capturing and a priori, ought to yield similar results among evaluators and be free from bias.

CONCLUSIONS

This chapter gives job analysis and job evaluation, viewed as processes for the *measurement* of work content and value, mixed reviews. Considering that both have been part of wage systems for at least two decades it is disturbing that so little effort has been devoted to evaluating the reliability, accuracy, acceptability, and efficiency of these two fundamentals of compensation practices.

Yet anyone who has designed and implemented job analysis and evaluation plans knows the difficulties. First there is the matter of priorities—and reex-

---

[18] T. Atchison and W. French, "Pay Systems for Scientists and Engineers," *Industrial Relations 7*, 1967, pp. 44–56; David J. Chesler, "Reliability and Comparability of Different Job Evaluation Systems," *Journal of Applied Psychology 32*, 1948, pp. 465–475; Randall B. Dunham, "Job Evaluation: Two Instruments and Sources of Pay Satisfaction" (paper presented to the American Psychological Association, Toronto, 1978); David D. Robinson and Owen W. Wahlstrom, "Comparison of Job Evaluation Methods: A 'Policy-Capturing' Approach Using the Position Analysis Questionnaire," *Journal of Applied Psychology 59*, no. 5, 1974, pp. 633–637.

amining the job analysis and evaluation plans does not seem to rate too high. Second there is the dual nature of these plans. Both are administrative procedures, designed to gain acceptance of the resulting wage structure. The procedures are often tuned to aid in achieving that acceptance. So how well job analysis and job evaluation meet standards of a measurement process is a secondary issue to many.

Compensation decision making must be based upon work-related data that are both reliable and accurate and collected in as acceptable and efficient a manner as possible. With such data, decision makers are more likely to achieve their objectives and, we believe, stand a greater likelihood of withstanding challenges, be they from inside or outside the organization.

chapter 11

Specific Job Evaluation Systems: The Point Method

Henry A. Sargent

PRINCIPAL, THE HAY GROUP, PHILADELPHIA,
PENNSYLVANIA

In a broad sense, the point method includes any method of job measurement (or job evaluation, which is the more common term) in which jobs are measured quantitatively in terms of abstract numbers (usually referred to as "points"), which determine pay relationships but do not show the pay amounts. Some such methods, however, possess additional characteristics, and these are discussed further in Chapters 13, 14, and 15. This chapter is concerned with the point method in its basic form, which may be described as follows:

1. The objective is to measure the *content* of each job (i.e., the requirements, responsibilities, and conditions which distinguish that job from others and determine its relative worth) and thus establish equitable pay *relationships* between all the jobs under consideration.

2. The job is evaluated by *factors* (i.e., determinants of job content and relative worth) instead of as a whole.

3. Although different point evaluation systems use different factors and different numbers of factors, under a given point system each factor carries its own scale of point values.

4. Each job is measured independently by each factor scale, thus determining individual factor point values, the total of which constitutes that job's evaluation.

5. These measurements are based on the job's requirements, responsibilities,

and conditions when occupied by a fully qualified incumbent performing at the normal rate, i.e., a rate which is neither abnormally high nor abnormally low, but acceptable. It follows that pay relationships determined by evaluation are base-rate relationships and do not reflect pay for length of service, premium for superior performance, etc.

6. Evaluations, once established, remain unchanged as long as the jobs remain the same. From time to time, however, jobs change or are eliminated and new jobs are created, thus requiring reevaluation of changed jobs and evaluation of new jobs by the same criteria to perserve equitable relationships.

HOW POINT SYSTEMS WORK

The validity of the set of factors and factor scales used in a point evaluation system can be judged only by the validity of the job relationships resulting from their application. Consequently, factors are selected and weighted on the basis of past experience. Criteria for choosing factors typically include (1) common sense combined with understanding of the jobs, (2) acceptability to interested parties (company line and staff employees and the union, where one is involved), (3) prevailing pay relationships in the company and the labor market, coupled with analysis of the reasons for deviating from existing patterns (such as where qualified personnel to fill certain jobs are scarce and in high demand, thus artifically inflating going rates), and (4) satisfactory experience with like factors and factor scales used in other companies with similar operations and jobs. More important than the specific factors and factor scales used, however, are the skill and consistency with which they are applied. Experience has shown that a questionable system properly administered produces much better results than a fine system which is poorly administered.

The Factors   The factors represent the significant requirements, responsibilities, circumstances, and conditions which determine the content of the particular jobs to be evaluated, and should be selected with the following considerations in mind:

1. *Acceptability* to the parties of interest (top, middle, and lower levels of management, the employees, and the union if it is involved), since the factors are the basis of the evaluations, and the objective is to establish equitable relationships which will be accepted with confidence.

2. *Applicability* to the group of jobs to be evaluated. Each factor should contribute to the evaluation of at least one job (and preferably more).

3. *Ratability*, i.e., jobs to be evaluated, should carry different degrees of the factors by which they are evaluated. It is useless and confusing to use a factor which applies equally to all jobs.

4. *Distinctive nature.* Each factor should represent a separate element of job content, without overlapping another. It follows that each factor must be defined clearly.

5. *Number of factors.* It might seem that the greater this number, the greater the refinement of evaluations. This may be true, but only up to an optimum number, beyond which the danger of overlapping increases and the evaluation process becomes more complex, thereby increasing time and cost of application and the likelihood of inconsistency, differences in judgment, and controversy.

A balance must be struck, and opinion and practice vary widely as to the optimum number. In the majority of cases, between 10 and 15 factors are used.

6. *Ease and economy of administration* tend to vary inversely with the number of factors. Reduction can be carried too far, however. Where very few (hence, very broad) factors are used, it becomes difficult to define clearly and comprehensively the ground covered by each factor and, therefore, to assure accurate and consistent application of factor scales. Resulting increases in time and cost of achieving a consensus of evaluators and management and of gaining employee and union acceptance may outweigh economies in administration.

Different sets of factors are ordinarily used in evaluating different types of jobs unless the evaluation system is to be applied to more than one job category. For example, factors for evaluating hourly paid factory jobs might include:

1. Requirements:
   Education
   Experience
   Mechanical ability
   Job complexity
   Physical skill and complexity
2. Responsibility for:
   Materials and equipment
   Effect on subsequent operations
   Alertness and attention to orders
   Teamwork
   Safety of others
3. Working conditions:
   Repetitiveness and monotony
   Physical requirements (position, strength)
   Surroundings
   Exposure to hazard

On the other hand, a somewhat different set of factors might be used to evaluate nonexempt office jobs:

1. Factors of responsibility for materials and equipment, safety of others, surroundings, and exposure to hazard might be dropped because they apply to all jobs in the same degree and are of minor importance.

2. Mechanical ability might be replaced by one or more factors reflecting technical competence, analytical ability, etc.

3. Responsibility factors might be added for monetary effect, contact with others, etc.

4. Factor scales would probably be different in that maximum point values would be lower or higher, reflecting differences in the effect of the factors in determining job content.

For evaluating supervisory, managerial, technical, and professional jobs, a still different set of factors might be used, the nature of which depends in part on how far up the organizational ladder the evaluation system is to be applied:

1. Factors for working conditions would be dropped (or, where used, their maximum point values would be quite low) because they would have little or no influence on job content.

2. Factors for job requirements would not include physical or manual skills (for the same reason) but would include factors for managerial, motivational, and persuasive skills; and scales would probably be carried to substantially higher point value maximums.

3. Responsibility factors would be completely different, covering such considerations as responsibility for planning, execution, control, effect on costs and/or profit, etc.; and factor scales would also be carried to substantially higher point value maximums.

In practice, some point evaluation systems use fewer factors than those referred to, combining two or more into one factor and identifying each factor appropriately. In other point systems, a larger number of factors are used, each of which is usually an element of one of the factors referred to and carries its own name.

Factor Weight   Experience has shown that except by rare coincidence each factor carries a different force (or weight) in determining job content. Consequently, each factor scale has a different point value, although the maximum for two or more factors seldom applies to the same job. Respective factor weights (or maximum point values) are usually determined through (1) pooled judgment of the relative importance of each factor as a determinant of job content and (2) correlation of results of these judgments with prevailing relevant pay patterns.

Where few jobs are involved and little difficulty is expected in gaining acceptance, the procedure can be relatively simple. Typically, (1) each of several knowledgeable people ranks the factors according to their importance, judgments are compared, and a tentative consensus is reached; (2) after factor scales have been tentatively determined, a representative sample of jobs is tentatively evaluated and the evaluations are plotted against rates of pay. If the line of central tendency is smooth (whether straight or curved) and there are few—if any—divergent cases, and if there is an acceptable explanation for each such case, the tentative factor weightings and scales can be adopted. If not, they are reexamined (together with the tentative evaluations), sources of trouble are identified, and the procedure is repeated.

Where a large number of jobs are involved or acceptance poses more of a problem, the procedure may be more complex. The sample of jobs tentatively evaluated should be larger, and sophisticated mathematical analyses may be required to cope with the volume in reasonable time and at minimum cost. The essential nature of the work performed is the same, however.

Factor Scales   The upper end of each factor scale is usually the maximum point value reflecting the factor's weight. In some systems a higher point value is shown to accomodate future developments, but this has the disadvantage of inviting its unjustified use. The lower end of the scale is either zero points (sometimes designated as "base" to make it more acceptable) or a specific minimum number of points commensurate with factor weight.

Most jobs are evaluated between maximum and minimum, and the scales therefore include intermediate point values, each of which must be identified clearly to guide evaluators in determining accurately and consistently the number of points to be assigned to each job. In a well-conceived system this is done by incorporating in the scale, for each point value shown, both written definitions of that factor level and judiciously selected illustrative examples of jobs evaluated at that factor level.

Two types of scale may be used, either one of which is acceptable, but only one type may be used in a given point evaluation system:

1. In one type, point value progresses arithmetically (i.e., intervals between point values are equal), so that when total evaluation points are plotted against pay rates they result in a curved line.

2. In the other type, the progression is geometric (i.e., intervals increase by a fixed percentage), and the resulting line is straight.

There are wide differences between point evaluation systems as to the absolute level of maximum and minimum point values. In some cases maximum is in the general order of 10, and in others it is substantially higher (even in the general order of 100 or more). Such differences are of no consequence insofar as job relationships within the scope of the particular system are concerned, since, irrespective of their absolute level, the evaluations express only relationships between jobs.

Benchmark Jobs   Evaluations of a selected group of representative (benchmark) jobs supplement and clarify the intent of factor scales, establish a framework within which other jobs can be evaluated, provide the basis for forecasting the system's effect on existing pay relationships, and provide one of the elements needed to determine the pay scale by which the evaluation program is put into effect. Where an evaluation system is developed from scratch, time and cost are minimized by using such a sample of the jobs to be covered. To serve these purposes, the benchmark jobs must be:

1. *Noncontroversial* as to rates of pay and other significant factors, to assure acceptance

2. *Definable,* thus excluding jobs with unclear and/or varying assignments, responsibilities, etc., to minimize opportunities for inconsistency, error, and controversy

3. *Representative* of the jobs to be evaluated, i.e., including jobs at low, intermediate, and high levels in major functional areas

Since the validity of benchmark evaluations and the pattern of job relationships which they establish are critically important, they should be examined from as many standpoints as possible to assure they are reasonable and acceptable to (1) the evaluators before releasing their evaluations and (2) individuals responsible for the decision to adopt the system. Benchmark jobs and their evaluations should then be listed in the sequence of evaluation points. Such a list would help evaluators by highlighting questionable evaluations and keeping overall relationships in full view while the former are investigated and resolved. Where departmental management is involved in benchmark evaluations, a single list by total points for jobs in the particular department is adequate. For senior managers with interdepartmental perspective and executives responsible for approval of the system, a single list of all benchmark jobs by total points is appropriate, and its usefulness is enhanced by tabulating jobs in each major functional area in separate columns and placing jobs up and down the page at levels corresponding to total point values.

When there are benchmark jobs of the same character, as may be the case when a system is applied at several locations, job family tabulations—e.g., for crane operator, typist-clerk, machine shop foreman, plant manager, etc.—may be useful. These are most effective when they display the jobs and their respective evaluations under each factor and in total, arranged in the sequence of total points.

Evaluation Manual   Good practice requires that evaluation criteria be consolidated, recorded, and placed in the hands of personnel concerned with evaluation work. This material constitutes the company's evaluation manual for the system and is the basic evaluation tool.

A manual's length and degree of detail are determined by the needs of the situation. Where relatively few jobs are covered by the system, where few individuals are involved in the evaluation process, and where acceptance is not a major problem, the manual may consist of only a statement of the factors and factor scales, their definitions, and selected benchmark illustrations; additional criteria may be provided by the complete file of benchmark evaluations. In more complex situations, the manual may also incorporate (1) detailed procedures, (2) statements of purposes for which evaluations are (and/or are not) to be used, and (3) a list of benchmark jobs, or even the descriptions and detailed evaluations of selected or all benchmark jobs.

Initial Evaluation of Nonbenchmark Jobs   Jobs are evaluated one at a time, usually by functional area to preserve perspective. Criteria are (1) the factors, factor scale, and their definitions and (2) the factor-by-factor evaluations of benchmark jobs. As evaluations are established for nonbenchmark jobs, these supplement the basic criteria. Accuracy, consistency, and impartiality are achieved through familiarity with evaluation criteria and techniques, clear understanding of each job, mature and well-informed judgment, cross-checking of independent evaluations, and validation of relationships, such as by reference to lists of the type previously described. Descriptions, specifications, and factor-by-factor evaluations of benchmark and nonbenchmark jobs are referred to frequently; consequently, these should be filed systematically and kept readily available.

Maintenance of the System   Once the system is installed, it must be maintained thereafter to preserve its integrity. This involves reevaluating changed jobs and evaluating new jobs to keep pace with inevitable changes in products, processes, organization structure, etc. Too often over the course of time there comes a tendency to neglect this crucially important work, as a result of which pay relationships get out of line and the program becomes less useful and acceptable. Many sound programs have been permitted to deteriorate until time-consuming and costly wholesale revision or complete replacement were required, at needless expense and with considerable loss in employee confidence. Management's commitment to maintenance of an evaluation program should be a prerequisite to its adoption.

New and changed jobs are evaluated by the same criteria as in an initial application, but there evaluations are also guided by the detailed evaluations of jobs already covered by the system. After the system has been in effect for a reasonable period, it is better understood by supervisors, managers, employees, and union representatives, and acceptance of new and changed evaluations is usually easier to gain. Jobs to be evaluated at a given time usually come singly or in small batches from different functional areas, tending to make the evaluation and approval process less time-consuming than when interdepartmental patterns are being established. Even so, thorough grounding in evaluation, clear understanding of each job, mature and well-informed judgment, and cross-checking of independent evaluations remain as basic requirements.

PERSONNEL INVOLVED AND THEIR ROLES

The equity of pay relationships, although it can be evaluated by established criteria, is finally a matter of judgment. Similarly, the appropriateness and effectiveness of the criteria depend on the soundness of judgment used in determining them. Seldom, if ever, is a single individual possessed of sufficient maturity, knowledge, perspective, and unquestionable impartiality to assure validity of his or her judgment alone in development and/or application of the criteria. Consequently, it is practically always essential that actions in each phase of the evaluation program be based on a consensus of several appropriately selected individuals. Different types of experience and different degrees of maturity and perspective are required in different phases, thus making it possible to vary participants from phase to phase. The participants and their roles in each phase are outlined in the following paragraphs.

Top management should sponsor the program from its inception to establish clearly that it is adopted as a matter of policy and constitutes an important tool of management. Top management should also assure that the system's design and projected effect on pay relationships are appropriate for the company and the jobs involved and that it is implemented and maintained properly.

A standing group of senior executives, such as the corporate compensation committee or a senior evaluation committee created for the purpose, usually is assigned responsibility for evaluation activities. Where membership does not include a senior executive who is well grounded in evaluation, the nonvoting secretary usually is the company official in charge of the program and thoroughly qualified in the subject. The committee's role is to provide perspective, broad guidance, and control, and usually involves:

1. In the *development phase;* (a) assuring timely and economical design of a workable and economical system appropriate for the operations and jobs to be covered, (b) assuring reasonable equity of resulting pay relationships and probability of acceptance, and (c) approving the system for adoption or recommending its approval

2. In the *initial application phase:* (a) assuring timely and economical evaluation of nonbenchmark jobs in accordance with established criteria and procedures and (b) resolving differences not settled at a lower level

3. In the *maintenance phase:* (a) assuring prompt and economical reevaluation of changed jobs and evaluation of new jobs in accordance with established criteria and procedures, (b) resolving differences not settled at a lower level, and (c) approving all changed and new evaluations

In large companies some of these functions are frequently delegated to divisional committees or to a subordinate company official. In small companies it is not unusual for a single senior executive (preferably assisted by an evaluation specialist) to perform these functions. These senior executive groups (or individuals) are normally also concerned with determining or recommending pay scales and adjustment thereof, approving individual pay adjustments within rate ranges where this is discretionary with management, etc.

Company evaluation specialists are almost always involved in all phases of the program and combine internal knowledge and perspective with evaluation know-how. In most cases they are also involved in related activities, such as job description and specification writing, salary administration, etc. These activites should constitute their exclusive assignments unless the volume of work is so small that they can also carry other unrelated duties. Their place in the organization structure should be such as to assure their impartiality and independence of judgment. More often than not when an evaluation program is undertaken, the company lacks qualified specialists, and they must either be hired or developed internally under an outside consultant. The latter course is usually preferable since acceptable candidates can ordinarily be found who are already well oriented internally and can be trained relatively quickly. The roles of company specialists usually involve:

1. In the *development phase,* under direction and guidance of the senior executives in charge of the program (and of the outside consultant, where used), performing detail work and participating in developing recommendations as to: (a) selecting and defining factors, (b) weighting of factors, (c) determining and defining factor scales, (d) selecting and evaluating benchmark jobs, and (e) keeping related records. Where union agreement is required, they may also participate in supporting and explaining the company's position.

2. In the *initial application phase,* under direction and guidance of the senior executives (and of the consultant, where used): (a) evaluating nonbenchmark jobs, (b) recommending these for approval, and (c) keeping related records. Where union acceptance is desirable or agreement is required, they also participate in explaining and supporting the company position.

3. In the *maintenance phase:* (a) reevaluating changed jobs and evaluating new jobs, (b) communicating these evaluations to managers in the organizational units involved, (c) recommending mutually agreed-upon evaluations for approval at a higher level, (d) reconciling differences with departmental management where possible and referring unreconciled differences to a higher level, and (e) keeping related records. Where union acceptance is customary or required, company specialists also explain and support the company's position.

Good practice requires that at least two specialists develop the evaluation of each job independently and that their evaluations be compared and reconciled before release outside the evaluation unit. In the maintenance phase this is frequently accomplished by having a qualified specialist determine a proposed evaluation, which is reviewed and approved by the senior specialist.

Departmental management has an interest in the evaluations of jobs under its direction and is in a position to contribute valuable insight to determination of pay relationships in its particular area of responsibility. On the other hand, it frequently lacks interdepartmental perspective and can be suspected of bias. Consequently its role:

1. In the *development phase,* usually consists of furnishing and clarifying facts, although upon occasion opinions may be called for.

2. In the *initial application phase,* is usually about the same, although departmental opinions may be called for more often and carry more weight.

3. In the *maintenance phase,* usually assumes a different character, in that departmental management has a definite voice in determining evaluations of new and changed jobs within its jurisdiction. Departmental approval is normally required, and if there is disagreement with evaluation specialists, differences are referred to senior management for adjudication. Good practice also requires that departmental management be charged with responsibility to notify evaluation specialists promptly when jobs within its jurisdiction are changed or eliminated and new jobs are created.

The outside consultant, when one is used, plays a widely varying role, depending on the degree of expertise possessed by company personnel. If the company has competent evaluation specialists, the consultant's role may be limited to providing broad independent judgment relative to the appropriateness and adequacy of the program and its administration, resolving particularly troublesome problems, etc. If qualified company personnel are lacking at the outset of the program, the consultant usually carries the major burden and trains company personnel as the work progresses. In the latter case, typically:

1. In the *development phase,* the consultant's role, subject to approval of senior management, is (a) to determine whether a new system should be developed from scratch or whether a system used and tested elsewhere should be adopted (perhaps with modifications) and (b) to direct activities of assigned company personnel (and sometimes members of the consultant's staff as well) in designing the new system where one is to be developed, or selecting and evaluating benchmark jobs where an existing system is adopted. Although the amount of consultant time used in this phase may tend to decrease as company personnel become more proficient, the consultant usually continues in charge, presents the system to senior and top management, and in some situations plays an important part in gaining union acceptance.

2. In the *inital application phase,* the consultant's role is determined by the progress of company specialists in mastering evaluation principles and practice. It can vary from direction and participation in evaluation of nonbenchmark jobs to occasionally reviewing progress and evaluation patterns and resolving problem cases. His or her involvement in this phase should decrease markedly as work moves toward completion, since company specialists are expected to become better and better qualified during the course of application.

3. In the *maintenance phase,* the consultant's role, if any, is usually one of occasional review and audit and contributing an outside view where appropriate.

Once the evaluation program is approved, the consultant usually plays an important role in applying evaluation results to compensation questions— determining pay scales, policies, and practices.

Union representatives are important participants if union acceptance is customary or required. Their function may include broad surveillance of pay relationships and amounts determined by management, pressure to change those with which employees or the union are dissatisfied, and direct participation in designing, applying, and maintaining the system. Typically, when the evaluation program is a contractual matter:

1. In the *development phase*, the union becomes involved after the company has developed a complete system and submits it as a proposal. Union representatives in this phase are usually either empowered to execute an agreement or responsible for negotiating an acceptable package and recommending its adoption. They make such counterproposals as they deem appropriate and negotiate with company representatives until agreement is reached. The package usually includes not only the evaluation system but also provisions governing its initial application and maintenance, the pay scale, etc.

2. In the *initial application phase*, union representatives familiar with the system (frequently below the contracting level) keep in touch with local union officials and members, investigate complaints, and confer as necessary with appropriate company personnel to protect union and employee interests.

3. In the *maintenance phase*, new and changed job descriptions and specifications (usually prepared by company specialists) are submitted through appropriate channels to designated local union officials for review and signature. They may negotiate changes or disagree and refer the case to agreed-upon procedures for resolution of differences.

Union participation restricts the company's freedom of action, may bring into play bias and inexperience in evaluation, and adds to the burden of developing, applying, and administering the program. It also provides advantages. Some union officials (such as staff representatives) are competent in the evaluation field through experience or training elsewhere, or become so as the system is developed and applied in the company. Some local union officials also become familiar with the system through experience when their tenure is long enough. Their participation provides an additional check on evaluation judgments and tends to assure policing in the maintenance phase. More importantly, union agreement on pay relationships and amounts, criteria for their determination, and provisions for resolution of differences provides an outlet for claims of inequity, which otherwise could lead to major problems and serious cost consequences, and substantially enhances employee confidence and acceptance.

FEASIBILITY OF THE POINT METHOD

When a company is considering adopting a job evaluation program, the first step should be to analyze the purposes to be served and the conditions under which the program is to be applied. If the purpose is unilateral determination of internally equitable pay relationships for a small number of jobs, and if employee acceptance is not a problem, a simple and inexpensive system such as overall job ranking may be adequate. Such a system, however, may present difficulties in assuring consistent application in the maintenance phase. If a large number of jobs is to be evaluated unilaterally, a more systematic and detailed approach is needed to assure impartiality and consistency.

When employee and/or union acceptance is a major consideration, a systematic approach is necessary to enable management to demonstrate the validity of its position and defend it in the event of controversy.

When the job evaluation program is intended to determine the external competitiveness of the company's pay structure as well as its internal equity, a systematic approach is required. Furthermore, the system chosen must be compatible with systems used by other companies with which the company wants to make comparisions.

The point evaluation method meets the needs for determining internal equity and can be applied in whatever detail may be required, at commensurate cost. It is probably more widely used in industry and business than any other single method, particularly for evaluating blue-collar and white-collar jobs. It has also been used successfully in evaluating supervisory, managerial, technical, and professional jobs, usually through the adoption of systems developed by consultants (or adaptation of such systems), since development of an acceptable system is time-consuming and costly. There are a few point systems which are used widely enough to provide valid information on competitive pay levels, although characteristically their use is confined to a few types of industry.

The decision to adopt the point evaluation method and the determination of the particulars of the system should be based on the facts in the case, balancing advantages against disadvantages and taking into account available variations in application of the method. In selecting a specific system, it is useful to remember that although the details (number and names of factors, factor weights, and absolute point values) of individual point evaluation systems may vary, they normally yield similar job relationships when they are competently administered.

The advantages of the point method may be summarized as follows:

1. Appraisal of the relative worth of each job from more than one standpoint (i.e., through independent measurement by different yardsticks, one for each factor) provides greater assurance of accuracy and consistency than a single appraisal of the job as a whole.

2. Since relationships are stated in numerical terms, direct comparisons between jobs are easily made and quickly understood.

3. Equitable evaluations in terms of points are readily translated into equitable pay scales, and the latter can be adjusted from time to time while preserving equitable pay relationships. Hence the point method presents great advantages from the standpoint of long-term applicability.

4. Evaluations in terms of points make it possible to accommodate the need for either (a) fine distinctions between jobs by establishing an individual rate of pay for each number of total points or (b) pay grades of any desired breadth by grouping jobs within specified point ranges.

5. Appropriate and clearly defined factors and factor scales for the type of jobs involved and an adequate framework of benchmark evaluations minimize the chance for error, inconsistency, bias, manipulation, differences in judgment, and controversy.

6. Skill, accuracy, and consistency in evaluation improve with the use of the system.

7. Experienced and well-informed evaluators (whether they represent the company, the employees, or the union) in most cases agree on evaluations or resolve differences quickly.

8. With proper initial application of the system, an adequate evaluation manual, and a systematic and accessible file of descriptions and evaluations for all jobs covered by the system, means are provided for assuring its continuing integrity through effective maintenance.

9. Adequate coverage in union agreements (where applicable) of subjects essential to initial application and continuing maintenance facilitates employee acceptance and establishes criteria and procedures for resolving controversies.

10. Management, employee, and union acceptance is facilitated by the system's flexibility in such matters as selecting factors, determining and defining factor scales, and selecting and evaluating benchmark jobs.

The disadvantages of the point method may be summarized as follows:

1. Development of an acceptable point evaluation method from scratch is time-consuming and costly and requires expert guidance. Consequently, the company should consider carefully whether a tailor-made system is needed. In most cases, an existing system can be adopted or modified with commensurate savings.

2. The point method's seemingly arbitrary and complex use of a variety of factors, differing factor weights, abstract point values, pricing of evaluation points, etc., is confusing to individuals unacquainted with the subject (supervisors, managers, employees, and union representatives) and tends to arouse suspicion. Consequently, time, effort, patience, and perseverance are required to gain understanding and acceptance of the reasons for using such an approach and of the validity of results.

3. The point method entails the time and cost of competent evaluation specialists to assure validity, consistency, and impartiality of evaluations.

4. Considerable time and attention of senior management are required in the development and initial application phases to assure that the system and its results are appropriate, and to a lesser extent in the maintenance phase to assure proper administration, to resolve differences, to approve new and changed evaluations, and periodically to review and adjust pay scales. Departmental management time and attention are also required in the maintenance phase for review and approval of new and changed evaluations.

5. Considerable clerical time and expense are required in the continuing process of typing, filing, etc., of job descriptions and specifications, evaluation records, and other material involved in administration of the program.

chapter 12

Specific Job Evaluation Systems: The Factor Method

Eugene J. Benge
BOCA RATON, FLORIDA

The factor comparison system of job evaluation was originated in 1926 when the writer was employed by the Philadelphia Rapid Transit Company to install an hourly wage rate evaluation plan. At that time, a few large and well-known companies had set up job evaluation systems. Attempts to apply one of these— a point system—failed, largely because of the great diversity of jobs included and the wide range of abilities and training required.

During World War I, Dr. Walter Dill Scott had developed a "man-to-man" merit rating system in which officers being considered for promotion were compared with known officers as to various attributes. We adapted this idea to evaluate selected key jobs and soon discovered that knowledgeable people, whether executives or union representatives, came up with virtually the same job evaluation once a key scale, with anchor points, had been established.

The system was later used and expanded by Samuel L. H. Burk and Edward N. Hay, and ultimately the three of us coauthored one of the early books on job evaluation.

The key scale is one basic difference between a point system and the factor comparison system. Once this measuring stick has been set up, evaluation becomes a simple process. Moreover, this measuring scale can be used for many years thereafter. Judgments on a given job are made against the key scale, one factor at a time.

Before job evaluation can actually begin, it is necessary to:

1. Gain approval of the study by management or by management and the union, if there is to be union participation.

2. Appoint a chief job analyst, with the necessary assistants.

3. Appoint a job evaluation committee to program the initial study, construct the key scale, evaluate jobs, and develop a wage and salary administration plan. A minimum of five members is desirable.

4. Designate adequate space for housing the analyst and for meetings of the committee. A large blackboard, 4 by 8 feet, will prove helpful in committee deliberations.

5. Inform employees and supervisors of the purposes and procedures of the entire effort, through either a series of meetings or a detailed letter to employees.

THE FACTORS

Five basic factors should be considered in evaluating hourly jobs:

1. Mental requirements
2. Skill requirements
3. Physical requirements
4. Responsibilities
5. Working conditions

When supervisory, technical, or clerical jobs are being evaluated, these factors become:

1. Mental requirements
2. Skill requirements, wherein skill is largely equated with experience rather than with muscular coordination
3. Physical factors, a combination of physical requirements and working conditions
4. Responsibility for supervision
5. Other responsibilities

As ever-higher jobs are being evaluated, the meaning of the five factors will change. This situation is illustrated in Figure 1, which suggests varying content of the five factors at eight job levels.

Since the specific characteristics of the factors are not absolutes, each company's job evaluation committee should define the five factors' content to best suit the purposes of the company's job evaluation program. The following sections describe factor content as established by a committee that evaluated salaried jobs in a railroad.

Mental Requirements   This factor considers the intellectual and educational level required to do the job, including:

1. Education—general level
2. Additional specialized education
3. Solutions to complex problems
4. Goal setting
5. Level of mathematics used
6. Analyzing cost or statistical data

FIGURE 1 Changing Scope of Factors

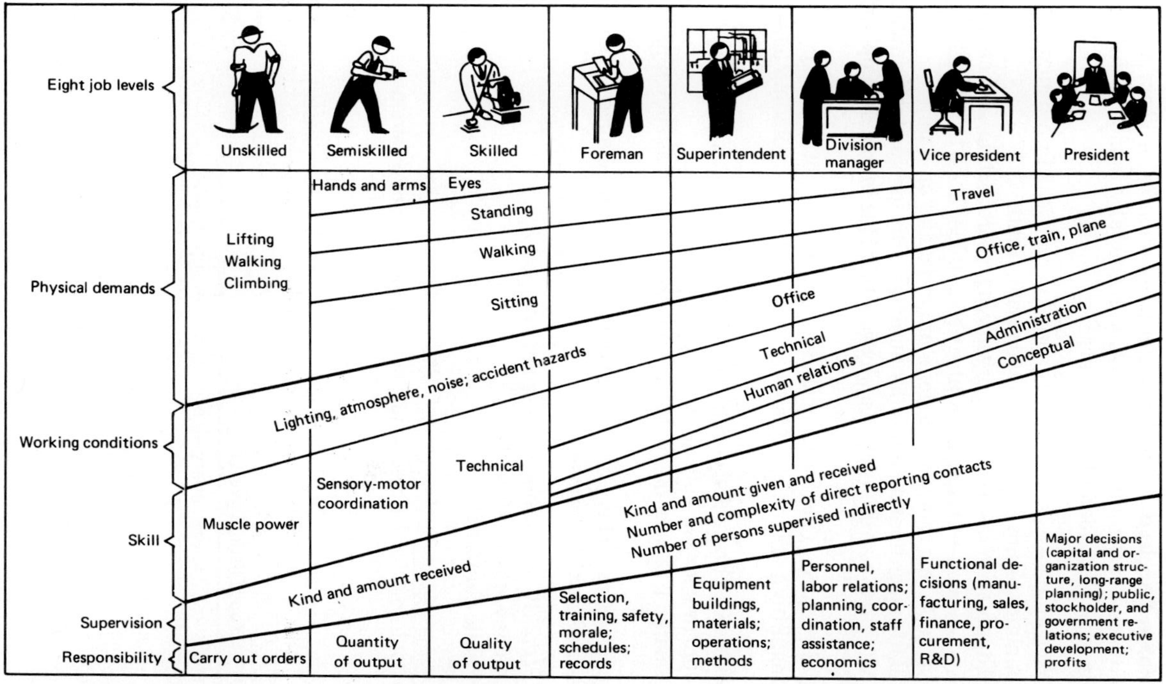

	Unskilled	Semiskilled	Skilled	Foreman	Superintendent	Division manager	Vice president	President
Eight job levels	Unskilled	Semiskilled	Skilled	Foreman	Superintendent	Division manager	Vice president	President
Physical demands	Lifting Walking Climbing	Hands and arms	Eyes Standing Walking Sitting				Travel	Office, train, plane
Working conditions	Lighting, atmosphere, noise; accident hazards							
Skill	Muscle power	Sensory-motor coordination	Technical			Technical	Administration	Conceptual
						Human relations		
Supervision	Kind and amount received			Selection, training, safety, morale; schedules; records	Equipment buildings, materials; operations; methods	Personnel, labor relations; planning, coordination, staff assistance; economics	Functional decisions (manufacturing, sales, finance, procurement, R&D)	
				Kind and amount given and received — Number and complexity of direct reporting contacts — Number of persons supervised indirectly				
Responsibility	Carry out orders	Quantity of output	Quality of output					Major decisions (capital and organization structure, long-range planning); public, stockholder, and government relations; executive development; profits

12/3

7. Writing reports
8. Public speaking and persuasive presentations
9. Creativity

Experience Required This factor considers months or years on the same or lower types of jobs. Five skill levels are generally found; each level assumes facility or experience in lower levels:

1. Conceptual—converting conceptual to practical; forecasting consequences of economic, social, industry, and company trends
2. Administrative—planning, organizing, coordinating, and controlling
3. Supervisory—carrying out plans and procedures; telling who to do what, and when; seeing that work is done properly, and on time
4. Skill—coordinating muscular activites with specific job knowledge[1]
5. Muscular coordination, usually repetitive (as in machine operation)[2]

Physical Factors This factor considers expenditure of muscular energy, as in walking, lifting, travel, etc. Also working conditions, including hazards.

Supervision This factor considers the importance and complexity of supervision and/or counsel, both given and received.

Normally, it is possible to differentiate nine levels, as shown in Table 1.

Responsibilities This factor considers the consequences if the employee makes a mistake in terms of:

1. Property or equipment—capital invested
2. Money, costs, or profits
3. Public contact

---

[1]May not be needed for present job, but may be desirable experience.
[2]Ibid.

TABLE 1   Supervisory Levels

Job level	Gives supervision	Receives supervision
1	Much	Little
2	Much	Some
3a	Much	Much
3b	Some	Little (gives counsel)
4	Some	Some
5a	Some	Much
5b	None*	Little (gives counsel)
6	None*	Some
7	None*	Much

*Has no subordinates.
3b may be more important than 3a.
5b may be more important than 5a.

4. Methods, systems, procedures, or records
5. Safety of employees or public
6. Meeting emergencies

GUIDELINES FOR WRITING JOB SPECIFICATIONS

The job evaluation committee should instruct the job analysts on how job specifications should be prepared. Following are the instructions one committee developed:

1. Your primary interest is in the work as it is now being done.

2. Confine your attention to the job you are analyzing, and do not be influenced by the ability, or lack of it, of the employee on the job.

3. Avoid any preconception as to the importance of any job you are analyzing. Describe the job as you find it.

4. Use a single paragraph to express the duties which revolve around one phase of the work.

5. Use the active and not the passive voice: Do not say, "Typing is done by typist" but "Types reports."

6. Omit the subject of a sentence when the subject has been used once and is identical with the title of the job being described.

7. Omit articles like *a, an,* and *the* where they are unnecessary to the meaning.

8. Do not use technical terms without explanation. The explanation may be made on the specification form or, if a somewhat lengthy explanation is required, use an attached paper.

9. Arrange the contents of the duties description in some logical order—e.g., in the sequence of a work cycle.

10. Where there are varied duties, list the important duties first.

11. State the duties as duties, not as qualifications. Do not say, "Should be able to operate machines," but "Operates machine."

12. State nothing but duties in the "Duties" section. Do not state requirements.

13. Avoid generalization. Specify exact activities incident to the task.

14. Indicate reporting line. For example, say, "Under supervision of *(position)*, directs *(position)*."

15. Quantify wherever possible. State number of units, or percentage of total time devoted to a particular activity, or weights and distances involved.

16. Use action verbs to eliminate misunderstandings of the meaning or scope of the action described. At times, broad terms, such as *handles, supervises,* or *prepares,* can be used only when the terms are expanded and the action broken down.

17. There are three criteria for determining the accuracy of the specification:

(a) *Is it correct?* Does it express the correct activities, requirements, and conditions of work?

(b) *Is it comprehensive?* Does it cover all the important and normal duties of a job?

(c) *Is it specific?* Are the various items on the job specification so specific that they permit differential comparisons with other jobs?

Figure 2 presents a completed job specification, ready for use by the job evaluation committee.

PROCEDURE

After the organizing activities are completed, the job evaluation committee:

1. Selects and analyzes key jobs.
2. Constructs a key scale.
3. Evaluates nonkey jobs.
4. Evaluates key jobs.
5. Plots a scatter diagram.
6. Assigns jobs to grades.

Selecting and Analyzing Key Jobs   Much of the success of the program lies in the care with which the key jobs are selected and analyzed. These jobs provide the framework into which all other jobs are integrated.

It is common practice to select from 24 to 30 tentative key jobs. These should sample all levels of the organization vertically and all departments horizontally. Thus if there were 10 major departments, it might be desirable to select recognized high, medium, and low jobs from each department. The jobs des-

---

FIGURE 2   Job Specification

JOB SPECIFICATION

Date _3/10/81_

Job title _ASSISTANT CONTROLLER_   Dept. _CONTROLLER_   Employee(s) Interviewed _EDWARD VOIGT_

Duties (continue on other side if necessary) _UNDER SUPERVISION OF CONTROLLER, RECONCILES VARIOUS CONTROLS WITH SUBSIDIARY AND DETAIL RECORDS. ASSISTS IN PREPARATION OF FINANCIAL REPORTS FOR USE OF MANAGEMENT. ANALYZES GENERAL LEDGER ACCOUNTS TO VERIFY ACCURACY (PAYROLL, PENSION, SALES TAX RETURNS, ETC) HELPS COMPILE ANNUAL FINANCIAL REPORT. OCCASIONALLY MAKES SPECIAL STUDIES AS ASSIGNED BY CONTROLLER._

Mental requirements	Skill requirements	Physical factors	Responsibilities	Supervision
C-4 Years education	Kind: _SCHEDULE AND COORDINATE CLERICAL EFFORT, DICTATION._	___Sitting _95%_ ___Standing _5%_ ___Walking	Equipment _ADDING MACHINE_	Supervises _5_ Persons
XX Add and subtract XX Multiply and divide XX Fractions and decimals		_X_ Eyesight ___Endurance	Materials	Analysis:
XX Accounting ___Shorthand ___Grammar ___Other	Desirable prior experience: _ACCOUNTING BACKGROUND, SYSTEMATIZING_	___Lifting	Records – _CLERICAL AND ACCOUNTING_ Methods – _SUGGESTS CHANGES_	RECEIVES None Some Much
Job instructions: _GRADUATE OF ACCOUNTING COURSE_	Time to develop average performance: _4-6 MOS_ Prerequisite jobs: _ACCOUNTANT_	_X_ Indoor ___Outdoor ___Unlocalized _X_ Desk ___Machine ___Counter	Money _PREPARES CASH REQUISITION SLIPS_ Savings	Receives supervision from: _CONTROLLER_ Plans _WORK OF CLERKS_
___Meet distractions ___Meet emergencies ___Stand monotony _X_ Make decisions _XX_ Analyze		Illumination: _EXCELLENT_	Public contact Confidential matters _PAYROLL, FINANCIAL STATEMENTS_	Instructs _SUBORDINATES_ Approves _STATIONERY REQUISITIONS_ Control devices:
___Patience ___Tact _X_ Superior memory	___Repetitive _X_ Varied Sensory training ___Sight ___Hearing _OPERATES ADDING MACHINE & CALCULATOR_	Atmosphere: _EXCELLENT_ Hazards:	Other	Highest job under: _CHIEF ACCOUNTANT_ ___Written instructions _X_ Plans own time _WITH SUPERVISION BY CONTROLLER_

GIVES: Much 3 2 1 / Some 6 5 4 / None 9 8 7

Symbols: Use X to indicate; XX to stress, P—preferred; R—required; or show amount or %

Prepared by _____J.R.B._____   Approved by _____T.W._____

ignated should be stable and representative of usual tasks in the industry. Any jobs whose current compensation is in dispute or for which there is a wide variation in rates should be excluded.

In addition, the purpose of the program should be fully explained to employees interviewed.

At the outset, it is desirable that the chief job analyst work painstakingly with an analyst in preparing the first few job specifications. In this way the analyst learns how to translate rough notes into concise statements on the specification.

We shall here carry through a simple example, using only 20 jobs to be evaluated, with 10 of them selected as tentative key jobs. Let us designate the jobs by letters:

A	F	K	P	The 10 under-
B	$\overline{G}$	L	$\underline{Q}$	lined jobs are
C	H	$\overline{M}$	$\overline{R}$	selected as
$\overline{D}$	$\overline{I}$	N	S	tentative key
$\overline{E}$	$\underline{J}$	$\underline{O}$	$\overline{T}$	jobs.

In the example we are following, we first analyze the 10 tentative key jobs and then prepare specifications for them. While the committee is studying these jobs to prepare the key scale, the analysts continue preparing nonkey specifications for evaluation by the committee.

Ranking Key Jobs   The first step in preparing the key scale is to rank the tentative key jobs in importance, one factor at a time.

Each member of the general committee is supplied with a set of specifications for the tentative key jobs. There are only 10 of these in our example, but normally there are at least 24 of them. It would be possible for each committee member to rank the specification forms themselves according to the mental requirements. However, this practice would require that each member have a work surface capable of providing room for 24 specifications.

Usually it is better to give each member a set of cards (3 by 2½ inches), one for each of the tentative key jobs. The committee member will have the 24 specifications in a three-ring binder and will make constant reference to them while ranking the 24 cards in mental requirements.

Each committee member will also have a data sheet on which are listed the tentative key jobs in alphabetical order. After having sorted the cards to satisfaction, each committee member will enter on the data sheet in the Mental Requirements column the rank order he or she has assigned to the 24 jobs.

The chief analyst will then summarize the mental rankings chosen by the five members on a large blackboard. The blackboard will show the 24 jobs listed alphabetically at the left; following that will be five columns, one column for each member of the committee. The members record their rankings on their data sheets, and the rankings are then transferred to the blackboard. When all five members have recorded their rankings on the blackboard, it becomes possible to compare the mental ranking which each person has assigned to a given job with the rankings given it by the other four members of the committee.

Usually there will be considerable agreement, even at the outset. The objective of the blackboard work is to bring out the marked disagreements. These disagreements should be debated to clarify how each member has interpreted the mental requirements factor. As a result of the discussion, it is usual for committee members to wish to change some of their ranks. Each one should do this by reranking his or her cards and *not* merely by changing the numbers on the blackboard. After the cards are reranked, they should enter their final rankings on the data sheets.

The same process should be followed, a factor at a time, for the other four factors. This is a tedious task which usually requires about five hours of a committee's time.

After this step, the data sheets should be collected and summarized by averaging the five members' rankings as to each factor on each job. This averaging should be carried out to one decimal place only, and these figures in turn reranked from 1 to 24 in each factor.

The final ranks are considered the stable judgment of the committee. A final importance rank can be changed only if a majority of the committee votes that it should be changed and the entire committee reranks the factor or factors involved.

Table 2 shows the 10 key jobs as ranked by the committee in our simplified example.

Preparing the Key Scale   Since the tentative key jobs represent a good sample of all jobs, their present wage or salary rates presumably provide a good sampling of the pay scale.

If committee members evaluate in terms of dollars, experience shows that they may, consciously or otherwise, manipulate figures to achieve some fixed notion as to the monetary value of certain jobs. To defeat this possibility, we multiply present (or average) rates of the tentative key jobs by some arbitrary number, such as 1.7 or 2.3, to yield "units." Thus a job paying $300 per week might be allotted 510 units.

The next step in preparing the key scale is to distribute present unit values of each tentative key job horizontally over the five factors. Thus if the first of the key jobs now receives 420 units, each member of the committee must ask how many of those units should be allocated to the mental requirements, to

TABLE 2   Importance Ranks Assigned by Committee

Job			Factors		
	MR	E/S	PF	S	R
C	1	2	9	1	2
D	8	9	2	9	8
F	3	4	8	4	3
H	2	1	7	2	1
J	6	6	5	6	5
L	5	5	6	5	6
N	4	3	10	3	4
O	9	8	3	8	9
Q	7	7	4	6	7
S	10	6	1	10	10

MR = mental requirements; E/S = experience/skill; PF = physical factors; S = supervision; R = responsibilities

experience, to the physical factors, to supervision, and to other responsibilities. Having made the decision about one job, he or she goes on to the next.

The votes of all members are then posted on the large blackboard and discussions about discrepancies ensue. In this case it is possible for members to change their entries on the board provided their figures always add up to the present unit value. That is, if they take five units off one factor, they must add that amount to one or more of the other factors of the same job.

When committee members are satisfied with the distribution shown on the blackboard, the figures are totaled, averaged, and checked mathematically.

Next, the units' rankings for each factor are determined *vertically*—e.g., the job receiving the largest number of units in the Mental Requirements column is ranked first and the job receiving the smallest number is ranked lowest.

The importance ranks are then compared with the units' ranks on a summary sheet in which the importance rank, units allocated, and units rank of each factor of each job are designated. Table 3 shows the summary sheet for the jobs in our simplified example.

Inspection of the tabulation in Table 3 reveals that:

1. The importance ranks of jobs J and O in all five columns are poorer than the units' ranks (indicating that there were too many units for distribution, relative to the other eight jobs).

2. The five importance ranks of job F are consistently better than the units' ranks (indicating that we did not have enough units to distribute).

Hence jobs J, O, and F must be eliminated as key jobs. Note that in job H, if six points were transferred from Supervision to Other Responsibilities, the units' ranks would then match the importance ranks for that job and for job C. This transferring of units may be necessary with a number of jobs to bring about reconciliation of ranks.

Justification for this arbitrary balancing lies in the proven fact that the distributed units are not stable figures. If the committee were to repeat the distri-

TABLE 3   Summary of Importance Ranks Assigned Units

Units	Job	Mental			Experience			Physical Factors			Supervision			Other Responsibilities		
		IR	U	UR	IR	U	UR	IR	U	UR	IR	U	UR	IR	U	UR
331	C	1	91	1	2	76	2	9	7	8	1	61	2	2	96	1
132	D	8	32	9	9	21	10	2	19	25	9	21	9	8	39	9
222	F	3	60	6	4	50	5	8	6	9	4	40	5.5	3	66	6
323	H	2	77	2	1	78	1	7	11	7	2	66	1	1	91	2
234	J	6	67	3.5	10	40	8	5	18	4.5	6	40	5.5	5	69	4.5
244	L	5	66	5	5	54	4	6	14	6	5	41	4	6	69	4.5
270	N	4	67	3.5	3	63	3	10	4	10	3	53	3	4	83	3
180	O	9	39	8	8	49	6.5	3	19	2.5	8	33	7	9	40	8
194	Q	7	48	7	7	38	9	4	18	4.5	6	32	8	7	58	7
140	S	10	22	10	10	49	6.5	1	22	1	10	20	10	10	27	10

IR = importance rank
U = units allocated
UR = units rank

butions a week later, many of the figures would change, which means that there is a large personal error in the units' allocations.

We have now *priced the ranks*, by:

1. Eliminating jobs J, O, and F where the (fixed) importance ranks are consistently better, or poorer, than the (variable) units' ranks.

2. Transferring units within each job from one factor to another to achieve a correspondence of ranks.

The resulting tabulation is shown in Table 4.

When the figures in Table 4 are reranked from 1 to 7, they fall into perfect correspondence, as shown in Table 5.

Table 5 gives us a price, in units, for each factor of each of the seven final key jobs. In an actual installation we might expect to salvage 15 or 20 of an originally selected 24 to 30 tentative key jobs.

From Table 5 we can prepare a key scale, with seven "anchor points" in each factor column. Thus in the Mental Requirements column, job C would be shown at position 91, job H at 77, job N at 67, etc. Job titles, and not mere letters, would be inserted, as in Figure 3.

Evaluating Nonkey Jobs   The evaluation of nonkey jobs begins with the selection of six or more jobs from one department. Starting with the mental requirements factor, each member of the committee:

1. Ranks the *specifications* (or their small proxy cards) according to mental requirements.

2. Beginning with the highest in mental requirements, refers to the Mental Requirements column of the key scale to find a job there for which the mental requirements are approximately equal to those of the job under consideration. Sometimes the location falls between two jobs on the key scale.

3. Enters the units' value of the key scale level on the data sheet.

4. Proceeds similarly with the lowest job, entering its units' value on the data sheet.

5. Selects values for jobs between the highest and lowest, entering the values

TABLE 4   Seven Final Key Jobs

Units	Job	Mental IR	Mental U	Mental UR	Experience IR	Experience U	Experience UR	Physical Factors IR	Physical Factors U	Physical Factors UR	Supervision IR	Supervision U	Supervision UR	Other Responsibilities IR	Other Responsibilities U	Other Responsibilities UR
331	C	1	91	1	2	76	2	9	7	8	1	61	1	2	96	2
132	D	8	32	9	9	21	10	2	19	2.5	9	21	9	8	39	9
323	H	2	77	2	1	78	1	7	11	7	2	60	2	1	97	1
244	L	5	66	5	5	54	4	6	14	6	5	41	4	6	69	4.5
270	N	4	67	3.5	3	63	3	10	4	10	3	53	3	4	83	3
194	Q	7	48	7	7	38	9	4	18	4.5	6	32	8	7	58	7
140	S	10	22	10	6	49	6.5	1	22	1	10	20	10	10	27	10

IR = importance rank
U = units allocated
UR = units' rank

TABLE 5   Final Key Jobs (Reranked)

Units	Job	Mental			Experience			Physical Factors			Supervision			Other Responsibilities		
		IR	U	UR	IR	U	UR	IR	U	UR	IR	U	UR	IR	U	UR
331	C	1	91	1	2	76	2	6	7	6	1	61	1	2	96	2
132	D̄	6	32	6	7	21	7	2	19	2	6	21	6	6	39	6
323	H̄	2	77	2	1	78	1	5	11	5	2	60	2	1	97	1
244	L̄	4	66	4	4	54	4	4	14	4	4	41	4	4	69	4
270	N̄	3	67	3	3	63	3	7	4	7	3	53	3	3	83	3
194	Q̄	5	48	5	6	38	6	3	18	3	5	32	5	5	58	5
140	S̄	7	22	7	5	49	5	1	22	1	7	20	7	7	27	7

IR = importance rank
U = units allocated
UR = units' rank

FIGURE 3   Portions of a Key Scale

Units	Mental	Skill	Physical	Responsibilities	Working Conditions	Units
201						201
200						200
~						~
181						181
180						180
179						179
178				Office manager		178
177						177
176						176
175						175
174						174
173						173
172	Office manager					172
171						171
170						170
169						169
168	Tax accountant			Tax accountant		168
167						167
166	Cost accountant	Estimator				166
165				Cost accountant		165
~						~
96		Multilith operator	Shipping clerk		Shipping clerk	96
95	Typist	Shipping clerk	Estimator			95
94				Shipping clerk		94
93					Estimator	93
92	Multilith operator					92
91				Multilith operator		91
90			Typist	Typist		90
89						89
88				File clerk		88
87			File clerk		Cost accountant	87
86					Typist	86
85					File clerk	85
84	File clerk		Office manager			84
83		File clerk				83
82			Cost accountant		Office manager	82
81			Tax accountant		Tax accountant	81
80						80

on a data sheet. The jobs have been subjected to *factor comparisons*, from which process the name of the system is derived.

6. Reranks the cards according to experience, using the same procedure to place the entries in the proper column of the data sheet, proceeding then to physical factors, supervision, and other responsibilities.

The "votes" of all members are then recorded on a blackboard, wide discrepancies ironed out, changes, if any, made on the data sheets, and data sheets turned in to the job analyst for summarization and averaging. The total units accorded a job constitute its evaluation.

Experience shows that it requires about half an hour for a job evaluation committee to cover one job. Thus, eight jobs might be thoroughly studied and evaluated in a four-hour sitting of the committee. Most committees believe that the importance of the subject with which they are dealing warrants this expenditure of time.

After a group of jobs has been evaluated, it is customary to enter their values in the scale. If the original key scale had 22 jobs, and 8 jobs of a certain department were evaluated against that scale, there would be a total of 30 jobs in each column of the key scale. So the process of adding jobs to the key scale continues until all nonkey jobs have been evaluated.

Evaluating the Original Key Jobs   Employees holding key jobs could justifiably claim that their job rates were frozen into the system, for the assumption was made that their relative rates were about right. The reconciliation process (importance ranks against units' ranks) has certainly substantiated considerable relativity. However, it is well to evaluate the key jobs in the same manner as nonkey jobs.

To do this, remove the key jobs from the enlarged key scale, leaving only nonkey jobs to serve as a scale. The key jobs themselves are then treated as a group, much as a departmental grouping was treated. They are ranked in each factor, the highest and lowest ranks "pinned" to the nonkey scale being used, and intermediate jobs fitted in. When all five factors have been assigned values, the values are added to get a total unit value for each key job.

The chances are high that the new unit values will not differ greatly from the originals. Nonetheless, to ensure that the original key jobs are placed properly in the hierarchy for each factor, they must be reevaluated. This step completes the evaluation proper.

Having total units' values for all jobs, we are in a position to:

1. Translate unit dollar values by means of a scatter diagram.
2. Set up grades, by dividing the continuum of units into levels.

APPLICATION OF JOB EVALUATION RESULTS

To convert units to money, a scatter diagram is plotted (see Figure 4) on graph paper, with money on the vertical axis and evaluation in units on the horizontal. A point is plotted for each job at the intersection of its two values, i.e., its present (or average) rate and its evaluated units. This procedure yields a path of dots running from the lower left to the upper right of the chart.

The wage (or salary) line is calculated by dividing the horizontal scale into

FIGURE 4   Scatter Diagram

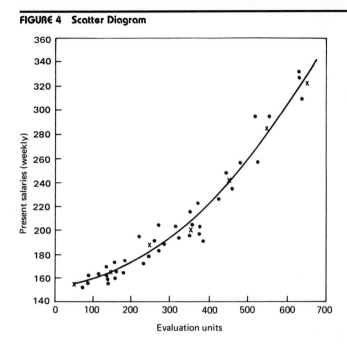

six or more (seven, in this case) equal columns. The money values of the dots plotted in each column are averaged and this average value shown as an "X" in the center of each column. The line is drawn through these averages so that the distances above the drawn line approximately equal those below it. More refined mathematical methods are available.

The wage line provides the means for converting evaluated units (horizontal scale) to equivalent money value (vertical scale). For example, 500 units equal $260 and 600 units, $304.

Some companies pay the indicated job value, regardless of length of service; others use this value as a base rate for incentive pay. Usually, however, grades—having minimum and maximum rates—are established. In the next section we discuss two methods of setting up grades.

Grades   One way to establish grades is to divide the units into progressively larger fractions, as shown in Table 6.

TABLE 6   Unit Values Assigned to Grades

Grade	Units
1	0–99
2	100–124
3	125–157
4	158–200
5	201–257
etc.	etc.

Thus all jobs valued between 0 and 99 would be assigned to grade 1, and minimum and maximum rates selected for this grade, above and below the wage line.

A second way is to establish the pay grades *first*, determining how much overlap there will be, as shown in Tables 7 and 8.

Plan A, shown in Table 7, is characteristic of static organizations; plan B, shown in Table 8, is typical of rapidly expanding organizations with high profits.

To determine the units' limits of grades, the middle area (in dollars) is first computed, as shown in Table 9.

The scatter diagram in Figure 4 relates these money values to job values, thereby allowing grade minimums and maximums to be established, as shown in Table 10.

Unit limits (minimum and maximum) of grades can be retained for many years, even though money values may change. The simplest way to effect a general salary (or wage) increase is to drop step 1 of each grade and add a step to the existing maximum. All (or most) employees then receive the next step rate above the present. In plan A, Table 7, this method would approximate a 6 percent payroll increase; in plan B, Table 8, an 8 percent increase.

Before a final application of findings is made, it is customary to make a survey of rates being paid elsewhere for comparable jobs. For low-level jobs, this survey may cover the nearby community, but for technical and middle-management jobs a wide geographic area is usually necessary.

Payroll   The effect of job evaluation on each employee must be worked out by filling out a summary sheet with the following column headings:

Department   Grade minimum
Name of employee   Grade maximum
Job Title   Present salary
Evaluated units   Proposed salary
Grade   Date effective

Usually jobs being paid below the minimum of their respective grades are immediately, or rapidly, brought up to the minimum.

Job rates above the maximum are not cut, but incumbents do not receive increases until the salary level catches up to them.

Employees within a grade are adjusted to the established step rates over a 12-month period, taking into account job performance.

TABLE 7   Plan A—Weekly; Slow Progression with Large Overlap of Grades

Grade	Min. step	Step 2	Step 3	Step 4	Max. step 5	Step Increases 1 to 2	2 to 3	3 to 4	4 to 5
1	$160	$170	$180	$192	$204	$10	$10	$12	$12
2	170	180	192	204	218	10	12	12	14
3	180	192	204	218	232	12	12	14	14
4	192	204	218	232	248	12	14	14	16
5	204	218	232	248	264	14	14	16	16

TABLE 8   Plan B—Monthly; Rapid Progression with Less Overlap of Grades

Grades	Min. step 1	Step 2	Step 3	Step 4	Max. step 5	Step Increases 1 to 2	2 to 3	3 to 4	4 to 5
1	$ 800	$ 860	$ 930	$1010	$1100	$ 60	$ 70	$ 80	$ 90
2	930	1010	1100	1200	1310	80	90	100	110
3	1100	1200	1310	1430	1560	100	110	120	130
4	1310	1430	1560	1700	1850	120	130	140	150
5	1560	1700	1850	2010	2180	140	150	160	170

TABLE 9   Middle Range of Pay Grades

Grade	Plan A	Plan B
1	Up to $184	Up to $1009
2	$185 to 196	$1010 to 1199
3	$197 to 210	$1200 to 1429
4	$211 to 224	$1430 to 1699
5	$225 to 238	$1700 to 2009

TABLE 10   Grade Limits

Grade	Plan A Minimum	Maximum
1	—	259 units
2	260 units	309 units
3	310 units	356 units
4	357 units	400 units
5	401 units	439 units

Wage and Salary Administration   Not infrequently, the job evaluation committee becomes a wage and salary committee. Likewise, the chief job analyst may become wage and salary administrator.

The committee and the administrator develop policies on performance rating, salary increases, promotions, transfers, area rate surveys, reevaluations, evaluations of new jobs, etc.

As a result, the wage and salary plan becomes a valuable management procedure to control the complex problem of wages and salaries.

chapter 13

Specific Job Evaluation Systems: American Association of Industrial Management

Christy Karr

GENERAL MANAGER, AMERICAN ASSOCIATION OF
INDUSTRIAL MANAGEMENT, WILLOW GROVE,
PENNSYLVANIA

Glenn T. Fischbach

DIRECTOR EMERITUS OF ENGINEERING SERVICES,
AMERICAN ASSOCIATION OF INDUSTRIAL MANAGEMENT,
WILLOW GROVE, PENNSYLVANIA

THE AAIM JOB EVALUATION PLANS

The American Association of Industrial Management (AAIM; formerly the National Metal Trades Association, or NMTA) believes that the use of job evaluation will promote good employer-employee relations in any organization. The data developed in the course of the rating process will provide a factual basis for discussion of pay differentials between jobs. Moreover, the adoption of a uniform job evaluation plan by a large number of companies, institutions, and organizations provides the basis for dependable, informative compensation surveys. Jobs of a generally comparable nature or type will have been classified according to the same criteria and using the same method.

The Association has offered its member organizations three basic job evaluation plans. These plans are practical, easily understood, and thoroughly tested.

The AAIM plan covering production, maintenance, and service occupations (also referred to as the NMTA Point Factor Job Evaluation Plan) is comprised of 11 factors applicable to the skill, effort, responsibility, and job conditions that are considered in the evaluation process. The factors and point values of each degree under this plan are shown in Table 1. The appropriate point values are added to determine the resulting score.

The AAIM plan covering clerical, technical, administrative, and supervisory positions generally paid on a nonexempt and exempt salary basis is comprised of nine factors common to all occupations in this category plus two additional factors for those positions involving the supervision of others. These factors are applicable to the training, initiative, responsibility, job conditions, and supervisory requirements that are considered in the evaluation process. The factors and point values of each degree under this plan are shown in Table 2.

The AAIM plan covering upper-middle and top management positions referred to as the Executive Rating Plan is comprised of four factors applicable to knowledge and background, initiative and creativeness, functional responsibilities, and managerial responsibility. The factors and the point values applicable to the breadth and depth of each factor under this plan are shown in Table 3.

TABLE 1   Points Assigned to Factor Degrees and Score Ranges for Grades   (Production, Maintenance, and Service Occupations)

Factors	1st degree	2d degree	3d degree	4th degree	5th degree
Skill					
1. Education	14	28	42	56	70
2. Experience	22	44	66	88	110
3. Initiative and ingenuity	14	28	42	56	70
Effort					
4. Physical demand	10	20	30	40	50
5. Mental or visual demand	5	10	15	20	25
Responsibility					
6. Equipment or process	5	10	15	20	25
7. Material or product	5	10	15	20	25
8. Safety of others	5	10	15	20	25
9. Work of others	5	10	15	20	25
Job conditions					
10. Working conditions	10	20	30	40	50
11. Hazards	5	10	15	20	25

Score range	Grade	Score range	Grade
139	12	250–271	6
140–161	11	272–293	5
162–183	10	294–315	4
184–205	9	316–337	3
206–227	8	338–359	2
228–249	7	360–381	1

TABLE 2   Points Assigned to Factor Degrees and Score Ranges for
Grades   (Clerical, Technical, Administrative, and Supervisory Positions)

Factors	1st degree	2d degree	3d degree	4th degree	5th degree	6th degree	7th degree
Training							
1. Education	15	30	45	60	75	100	
2. Experience	20	40	60	80	100	125	150
Initiative							
3. Complexity of duties	15	30	45	60	75		
4. Supervision received	5	10	20	40	60		
Responsibility							
5. Errors	5	10	20	40	60		
6. Contacts with others	5	10	20	40	60		
7. Confidential data	5	10	15	20	25		
Job conditions							
8. Mental or visual demand	5	10	15	20	25		
9. Working conditions	5	10	15	20	25		
Supervision							
10. Character of supervision	5	10	20	40	60		
11. Scope of supervision	5	10	20	40	60		

Score range	Grade	Score range	Grade
100 and under	1	311–340	9
101–130	2	341–370	10
131–160	3	371–400	11
161–190	4	401–430	12
191–220	5	431–460	13
221–250	6	461–490	14
251–280	7	491–520	15
281–310	8	521–550	16

In each of the aforementioned job or position evaluation plans, the first step in the process is to prepare an adequate description of the duties and responsibilities. If this is done in a proper manner, the primary function or purpose of the occupation will be emphasized with enough detail of the duties and responsibilities to make it easily identifiable by the incumbent, his or her supervisor, and others familiar with the job environment.

The description for production, maintenance, and service occupations is based on observation of the work place, including operations, materials, tools, equipment, methods, surroundings, and other distinguishing characteristics and discussion with the immediate supervisor with respect to assignment, workload, operations, and quality requirements (Figure 1).

The description for clerical, technical, administrative, and supervisory positions is based upon a questionnaire or questionnaires filled out by all incumbents along with appropriate interviews of the incumbents. The questionnaire and description are reviewed and approved by the immediate supervisor to ensure completeness and agreement (Figure 3).

Once the supervisor has approved the job description, the person assigned the responsibility of job evaluation will provide adequate explanation on the

TABLE 3 American Association of Industrial Management Executive Position Evaluation Chart

	Factors															
	1 Training and Background*			2 Initiative and Creativeness†				3 Functional Responsibilities‡			4 Managerial Responsibility§					
	A	B	C	A	B	C	D	A	B	C	A	B	C	D	E	F
1	280	310	360	200				200	210		120					
2	320	350	400	230	270			240	250		160	200				
3	370	400	450	280	320	360		280	290	300	200	240	280			
4	420	450	500		370	410	450	320	330	340	240	280	320	360		
5	470	500	550			480	520		370	380		320	360	400	450	
6	520	550	600				600						410	450	500	550
7	570	600	650											500	550	600
8															600	650
9																700
10																750

*Factor 1: This factor measures the overall training requirements of the position and includes education, experience, and any special skills needed for a normal person possessed of the necessary mental capacity to become competent in the position being surveyed and analyzed.

†Factor 2: This factor measures the amount of resourcefulness and decision making in the determination and planning of broad company or divisional objectives, the amount of creative effort involved in original engineering applications, scientific discoveries, new procedures, policies, and programs. It also includes the latitude inherent in the position in installation of and controlling the formulated plans and decisions in operation.

‡Factor 3: This factor measures the accountability for results and the impact incorrect planning, decisions, and failure to take proper action may have on the present and future operation of the business. Consideration is given relative to the extent reports, records, plans, and programs are available; the meeting, dealing with and influencing others, and the proper utilization of assets involving new equipment, new or expanded facilities, mergers, investment, surplus funds, etc.

§Factor 4: This factor measures the managerial responsibility for achieving results through people. Consideration is given to the location of the position on the organization chart, the extent to which accountability for these results is vested, and the number of people reporting to and indirectly reporting through subordinate supervisors.

FIGURE 1 Job Rating Specifications (Shop)

JOB RATING SPECIFICATIONS
(SHOP)

CODE NO. ______

DEPT ______

______

GRADE 3

JOB NAME N/C TURRET LATHES, PROGRAMMER/OPERATOR CLASS ______

JOB DESCRIPTION:

Plan, lay out and perform machine programming, setup and operation of numerical controlled turret lathes to perform a normal range of rough and finish turning, facing, boring, drilling, reaming, tapping, threading, forming and similar machining operations. Set up and operate machine to prove out program tapes. Incorporate various changes and corrections to tape, as necessary, to meet drawing and quality requirements. Perform the job of N/C Turret Lathe Operator in its entirety as assigned.

Receive direction from Supervisor and work from work orders, detailed machine parts drawings, programming manuals, specifications, tool charts, and instructions relative to work assignment.

Interpret drawings to develop sequence of operations and tools required for the machining of a variety of ferrous, nonferrous, and alloy pump parts such as suction cases and bells, impellers, discharge cases, packing boxes and bearing retainers, etc. Prepare and otherwise compile reference materials such as tool charts for use in preparing setup sheets and program tapes.

Prepare setup sheets, prescribe operations, specify tools and document in accordance with programming procedures manual. Make applicable mathematical calculations for a variety of machining dimensions, tool advance and clearance; and determine feeds and speeds in accordance with machinability of material. Monitor and document all approved changes made by other operators during production runs and make applicable changes, as required for on-going production requirements. Collaborate with operators from other shifts to transmit and exchange information pertinent to new and existing programs.

Detect and report faulty operation, defective material and equipment, drawing discrepancies and other unusual conditions to proper Supervisor. Oil and grease machine, replenish coolant, and replace cutting inserts as required.

Maintain workplace area in neat and orderly condition. Make out time and production reports or enter the prescribed information into a designated data input terminal.

Observe all safety regulations.

REVISED	
BY	DATE

DATE ______

THE ABOVE DESCRIPTION COVERS THE MOST SIGNIFICANT DUTIES PERFORMED BUT DOES NOT EXCLUDE OTHER OCCASIONAL WORK ASSIGNMENTS NOT MENTIONED, THE INCLUSION OF WHICH WOULD BE IN CONFORMITY WITH THE FACTOR DEGREES ASSIGNED TO THIS JOB.

FIGURE 2 **Analysis of Job Rating Specifications (Shop)**

CODE NO._____

DEPT._____
_____

JOB RATING SPECIFICATIONS
(SHOP)

GRADE_____ 3 _____

JOB NAME___N/C TURRET LATHES, PROGRAMMER/OPERATOR___ CLASS_____ TOTAL POINTS___321___

FACTORS	SUBSTANTIATING DATA	DEG.	PTS.
EDUCATION	Use shop mathematics. Work from work orders, detail parts drawings, programming manuals, specifications, tool charts and instructions. Use various precision measuring instruments and gauges. Requires knowledge of machine programming, machine operations, tools and cutting qualities of metals. Equivalent to 2 to 3 years applied trades training.	3	42
EXPERIENCE	Over 4 years up to and including 5 years.	4	88
INITIATIVE AND INGENUITY	Plan, lay out and perform machine programming, sequence of operations, setup and operation of numerically controlled turret lathes. Requires considerable judgment to program and make exacting setups, prove out computer tape, make appropriate offset adjustments and operate equipment to produce acceptable quality on a wide range of pump parts.	4	56
PHYSICAL DEMAND	Light physical effort required to perform assigned work. Equivalent to occasionally lifting or moving average weight material.	2	20
MENTAL OR VISUAL DEMAND	Concentrated mental and visual attention required to perform assigned work.	4	20
RESPONSIBILITY FOR EQUIPMENT * OR PROCESS	Careless, negligent or improper performance of work may cause damage to tools and equipment. Probable damage over $250 but seldom over $1000.	4	20
RESPONSIBILITY FOR MATERIAL * OR PRODUCT	Careless, negligent or improper performance of work may cause losses in rejections, rework, or scrap. Probable loss over $100 but seldom over $250.	3	15
RESPONSIBILITY FOR SAFETY OF OTHERS	Improper performance of work or equipment operation may cause lost time to others due to hand, foot or eye injuries.	3	15
RESPONSIBILITY FOR WORK OF OTHERS	Responsible for 1 or 2 persons 50% or more of the time.	2	10
WORKING CONDITIONS	Good working conditions. Exposed to office and shop conditions that are not disagreeable.	2	20
HAZARDS	Accidents may result in loss of time due to hand, foot or eye injuries.	3	15
REMARKS	*Always stated in terms of 1935-1939 price levels. Current prices adjusted to that level by use of B.L.S. index. 1982 prices are over 7.2 times the Manual base figure.		

FIGURE 3   Job Rating Specifications (Clerical, Technical, Supervisory)

CODE NO._____

JOB RATING SPECIFICATIONS
(CLERICAL. TECHNICAL. SUPERVISORY)

DEPT._____

_____

GRADE____ 11 ____

JOB NAME ____ MANAGER, ACCOUNTING ____ CLASS _____

JOB DESCRIPTION:

Responsible for the direction and supervision of personnel employed in the financial accounting office, the maintenance of fiscal records and the preparation of various financial reports under the general direction of the Controller.

Plan, schedule and direct, the personnel performing various accounting office services that include general and cost accounting, accounts payable, payroll, accounts receivable, credit and collection, data processing, courier and receptionist activities.

Monitor the work of those supervised, including source documents, the posting of various journals, the computer data sheets, computer printouts and the preparation of various financial reports to insure that the established practices and procedures are adhered to and that financial data, records and reports are compiled in an accurate, realistic and timely manner.

Prepare a consolidated monthly and year end financial statement that includes remote Distribution Centers.

Prepare various pro forma reports that may be required or requested.

Review for approval all purchase orders and respective invoices prior to release for payment.

Prepare local, state and federal tax returns, concerned with payroll, real estate, excise, sales and use taxes.

Consult with outside auditors and actively participate in the supervision of the taking of physical inventories. Balance physical to book values, in accordance with established procedures.

Direct payroll and cash disbursements activities following established policies and directives.

Collaborate with all department supervisors to insure compliance with established procedures and effect accuracy of source data.

Assume the administrative direction of the department in the absence of the Controller.

Direct, assist, and train personnel in the proper performance of their work. Conduct merit reviews and maintain positive employee relations. Appraise work performance, make recommendations on wage and salary, new hires, transfers, promotions, discipline, and termination as required.

Perform other related functions in support of the Controller and associated with the responsibility.

REVISED	
BY	DATE

DATE_____

various factors and degrees so that the two working together may determine the degree of each factor that accurately reflects the duties performed and described. The degrees, corresponding point values, and substantiating data are entered on the job specification sheet, the points totaled, and applicable labor grade recorded (Figures 2 and 4).

In any job evaluation process, it is important to prepare a departmental sum-

FIGURE 4   Analysis of Job Rating Specifications (Clerical, Technical, Supervisory)

CODE NO. _____

JOB RATING SPECIFICATIONS

(CLERICAL, TECHNICAL, SUPERVISORY)

DEPT _____

GRADE ___11___

JOB NAME _____ MANAGER, ACCOUNTING _____ CLASS _____ TOTAL POINTS ___395___

FACTORS	SUBSTANTIATING DATA	DEG.	PTS.
EDUCATION	Broad knowledge of accounting theory, practices and procedures that include tax accounting, credit and collection, cost accounting, preparation of operating statements, financial reports and related budgetary control reporting. Equivalent to a complete college education.	4	60
EXPERIENCE	Over 4 years up to and including 5 years.	4	80
COMPLEXITY OF DUTIES	Direct and supervise the financial accounting office, maintain all fiscal records, and prepare financial reports. Considerable judgment is required to work independently, devise new or modify existing procedures and make decisions guided by precedent and within limits of established policies.	4	60
SUPERVISION RECEIVED	Under general direction working from policies and general objectives with little functional guidance.	4	40
ERRORS	Considerable accuracy and responsibility is required in the maintenance of fiscal records and preparing financial reports. Improper performance would have adverse effect on financial reports.	4	40
CONTACTS WITH OTHERS	Contacts involve dealing with persons of higher rank on matters requiring explanation and obtaining approvals. Considerable tact required.	4	40
CONFIDENTIAL DATA	Regularly work with confidential financial data, disclosure of which might be detrimental to the company's interests.	4	20
MENTAL OR VISUAL DEMAND	Character of duties involve normal mental and visual attention.	2	10
WORKING CONDITIONS	Usual office working conditions.	1	5

FOR SUPERVISORY POSITIONS ONLY

CHARACTER OF SUPERVISION	Direct supervision of the Accounting and Office Services function with responsibility for costs, methods and personnel.	3	20
SCOPE OF SUPERVISION	Responsible for supervising 10 to 13 persons.	3	20
REMARKS			

mary of each factor in order to eliminate any inconsistencies should they exist. After all departments are completed, each job and its respective factor rating is posted to a master summary by labor grade for the organization as a whole for a final review and elimination of any inconsistencies that may still exist. This will ensure that the evaluations are consistent with the manual and all other jobs or positions in the organization. Another test that may be applied is to compare the evaluation with other evaluations of similar jobs in other plants that have been evaluated by this plan. The AAIM/NMTA job evaluation plans afford this opportunity since they have been installed in so many organizations over the past 40 years.

Job descriptions and evaluations concerned with the upper echelons of management are heavily dependent on the interview of the incumbent executives and the top governing authority of the organization. There is a point in the management structure at which descriptions are tailored to the long-range planning of the chief executive or functional head. A thorough knowledge and understanding of the organization—its facilities, products or services, size, and operating level—is necessary to perform this important phase of job evaluation. This task is definitely not a do-it-yourself type of exercise. The Association recommends that a trained staff professional be engaged to perform top management staff evaluations in collaboration with top management authority (Figures 5 and 6).

FIGURE 5   Executive Position Specifications

CODE NO. _____

EXECUTIVE POSITION SPECIFICATIONS   LOCATION _____

GRADE ____ E 8 ____

POSITION ____ DIRECTOR, FINANCIAL ADMINISTRATION ____

DESCRIPTION:

Responsible for overall planning and administration of the accounting and financial function of the Company under the direction of the Executive Vice President. Responsibilities include financial planning, provisions for capital requirements, administration of funds, accounting and control, protection of assets, tax administration, and consultation with and advice to other members of the executive staff on financial policy and objectives.

Develop, coordinate, and administer long and short range financial planning that includes budgeting for capital expenditures, profit and loss evaluation, economic appraisal and analysis of acquisitions and divestments.

Establish and execute programs for the provision of capital requirements.

Administer the management of cash, banking arrangements, credit and collection, pension funds, and investments.

Establish accounting policies, the development and reporting of accounting data, cost standards, auditing, accounting procedures, government reporting, reports on operating results, and interpretations to top management.

Assure protection of business assets, loss prevention and provide for insurance coverage as required.

Establish and administer tax policies and procedures.

Collaborate with Manager, Data Processing, in the development and use of electronic data processing facilities to implement computerized financial management system and procedures.

Perform other related functions that may be assigned or dictated by responsibility.

FIGURE 6   Analysis of Executive Position Specifications

EXECUTIVE POSITION SPECIFICATIONS

CODE NO. _____

LOCATION _____

GRADE _____ E8 _____

POSITION NAME _____ DIRECTOR, FINANCIAL ADMINISTRATION _____   TOTAL POINTS _____ 1350 _____

FACTORS	SUBSTANTIATING DATA	POINTS
KNOWLEDGE AND BACKGROUND	Broad knowledge of financial administration in a manufacturing environment that includes financial planning, administration of funds, accounting and control, tax administration and provisions for capital requirements. Equivalent to a masters degree in finance and business administration with a background of over 10 years up to and including 13 years.	450
INITIATIVE AND CREATIVENESS	Responsible for the overall planning and administration of the accounting and financial functions of the Company. Under direction of the Chief Executive Officer, effectively participate in the formulation and implementation of Company financial policies. Direct and coordinate the work of the Controller in attainment of financial objectives.	360
FUNCTIONAL RESPONSIBILITIES	Responsible for making recommendations and decisions involving major expenditures for capital investments. A high degree of diplomacy, judgment and the ability to deal with and influence people in all levels is required.	340
SPAN OF SUPERVISION	Direct and coordinate the operation of the accounting and financial function that is comprised of approximately 10 to 12 persons.	200

REPORTS TO:

Executive Vice President

REPORTING POSITIONS:

Controller
Assistant Controller
Accounting Manager

DATE: _____

REMARKS:

	REVISED	
	BY	DATE

ESTABLISHMENT OF WAGE AND SALARY STRUCTURES

The wage and salary structure should be calculated with the objective of distributing the available payroll money in a manner consistent with the grades established through the job evaluations. In other words, pay progress from grade to grade should be consistent, in terms of either money (straight-line structure) or percentages (curved-line structure), whether a single rate or a range is applied to each grade. The Association recommends the use of ranges overlapping approximately half a grade with a percentage progression where AAIM rating plans are installed, but contractual obligations or other considerations may preclude this in some instances. Figure 7 illustrates graphically the recommended type of structure. A wage structure would be in terms of hourly rates but structured in the same manner.

FIGURE 7   Sample Salary Structure

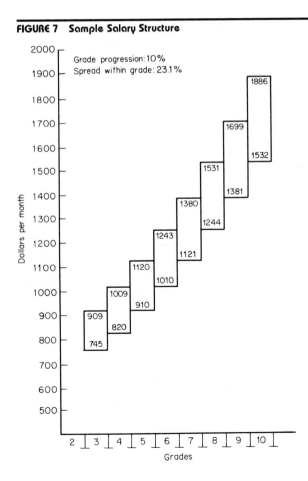

CONCLUSION

The American Association of Industrial Management job evaluation plans have been developed to consider factors of importance to both the employer and the employee. The plans are simple and understandable. Their soundness has been validated by more than 40 years of installations in manufacturing companies, banks and financial institutions, hospitals, universities, and town and city governments. Their broad coverage enables users to participate in meaningful surveys of wage and salary rates.

When used in conjunction with a sound employee appraisal program, these plans provide the basis for a fair and equitable compensation policy, which in turn is the keystone of good industrial relations.

chapter 14

Specific Job Evaluation Systems: White-Collar Jobs in the Federal Civil Service

Paul A. Katz

ASSISTANT DIRECTOR, U.S. OFFICE OF PERSONNEL
MANAGEMENT, WASHINGTON, D.C.

The decade of the 1970s saw unprecedented change in the white-collar job evaluation and pay system of the federal government. An entirely new job evaluation system was developed and installed. Pay comparability with private enterprise became a permanent fixture in law for annually adjusting pay rates. Merit pay in lieu of automatic step increases was legislated and partially installed for 75,000 higher-level supervisors. Finally, the federal government's 7000 senior civil servants at grades GS-16 and above ("supergrades") were organized, by statute, into a single, gradeless structure called the "Senior Executive Service" (SES). Under this system pay increases, except for infrequent general adjustments, are achieved by nonaccumulating bonuses payable annually to no more than 20 percent of the SES.

As we enter the 1980s with decreasing government employment and expectations, further changes are being considered. Among them are modification of the single national pay schedule to allow for geographic adjustments, fine tuning of occupational pay to better meet labor market conditions, general lowering of pay increase expectations, and consideration of pay and benefits simultaneously in determining overall compensation levels.

COVERAGE OF COMPENSATION SYSTEMS

Although the General Schedule (GS) is correctly known as the federal government's basic pay system, it is but one part of a multitude of related and unrelated pay systems.

The General Schedule covers over 1 million white-collar civilian civil servants in virtually every one of the executive branch's more than 60 agencies. Similarly, the Federal Wage System (FWS) covers another half a million blue-collar employees in trades and laboring occupations. These two systems, administered by the U.S. Office of Personnel Management (formerly the U.S. Civil Service Commission), have one principal difference. FWS pay levels are set differentially in 187 local wage areas. The General Schedule has but one national pay schedule. (Although both systems utilize job evaluation and a hierarchy of grades, the FWS utilizes a whole-job evaluation technique, while the GS utilizes a factor-point system.)

Leading the pack of more than 50 separate compensation systems is the U.S. Postal Service, with more than half a million employees. Until 1972, when the U.S. Post Office Department became the semi-independent U.S. Postal Service, its job evaluation and pay systems were statutorily linked to the GS and the FWS. Today, these are as separate and different from GS and FWS as is any private sector system. Two other major and separate federal systems are still linked to the General Schedule: the Foreign Service system of the U.S. Department of State and the Department of Medicine and Surgery system of the U.S. Veterans Administration. Interestingly, both systems (covering a total of 50,000 employees) utilize a rank-in-person (qualifications) methodology rather than the rank-in-job (classification) methodology, the latter being typical of government compensation philosophies. Nevertheless, the 100,000 other employees of these two agencies are covered by the same GS and FWS systems that apply to the rest of the federal civil service.

For example, though major portions of the legislative and judicial branches are clearly exempt from the GS and FWS, their managers have decided to adopt or adapt elements of these basic systems. This is also true for job evaluation and pay systems in exempt executive branch agencies as intriguing as the Central Intelligence Agency. In summary, virtually all civilian white-collar federal employees are effectively covered by the single General Schedule.

To complete this tour of the federal government, there are 2 million uniformed military personnel who are graded under the rank-in-person concept. Here again, Department of Defense managers and others have developed semiofficial links between their ranks and the GS and FWS. Did you know that a full colonel or navy captain is "equivalent" to a GS-15 and that generals and admirals are equivalent to the Senior Executive Service?

HISTORY AND RATIONALE OF THE FEDERAL SYSTEM

The history of and need for detailed, documented job evaluation and pay systems in the federal government parallels experience in private industry. In the 1800s federal government "clerks" continually petitioned Congress to equalize their pay with similar jobs in other agencies that were more highly paid. At that time there was no unified, governmentwide pay system. The head of each agency had independent authority to grade and pay its own jobs within congressionally set limits. In the private sector, the new unions presented similar equalization requests across company lines. Significant action was not taken in either sector, perhaps for two reasons. First, government agencies, as well as business organizations, regarded themselves as clearly separate administrative entities; second, a simple fact, accepted job evaluation techniques were not yet available. At the turn of the century, however, the scientific management movement took hold. As a result, job evaluation plans were developed in large organizations, in corporations as well as in state and local governments. That growth finally prompted the federal government to develop the 1923 forerunner to the General Schedule and institute centralized job evaluation practices.

Grades and Pay   The 1923 Classification Act (which is conceptually repeated in the still-current 1949 Classification Act) clearly placed emphasis on internal equity. Grades were first established and defined in terms such as "difficulty," "responsibility," and "qualifications required." These grades were thought to be so central to the system that they and their short definitions were established in law. Interpretation of the grades and implementation of the system were, however, left to administrators in the executive branch. All the government's various white-collar jobs were then analyzed and evaluated in terms of those measures and placed (or "classified") into grades. Only then was pay attached to the grades, yielding a pay rate for an employee in a job classified to that grade. Thus diverse jobs, in diverse occupations, in diverse agencies, but with the same intrinsic value to the government (as defined in law) found their way into the same single grade, whose incumbents were then paid the same rate. While the placement of a job in a grade was the executive branch's province, the pay attached to that grade was almost entirely the province of the legislative branch—the Congress. These 1923 basic system elements, except for pay, continue today.

Pay Comparability   In the depression years of the 1930s no need was felt for a system to determine the pay rates for the various grades. The war and postwar years of the 1940s and nationwide wage and price controls similarly prevented the development of a rationalized system for pay-rate determination. However, the 1950s saw task forces trying to develop such policies and practices. In 1959–1960 the first pay survey of private enterprise white-collar jobs similar to General Schedule jobs was taken by the U.S. Bureau of Labor Statistics (BLS). Congress directly used that survey in establishing the 1962 GS pay rates. In succeeding years Congress placed greater emphasis on the BLS pay survey and formally involved the executive branch in making pay analyses and determinations. In 1969 full pay comparability with the private sector was reached. In 1970, with 10 successful years of experience behind it, Congress statutorily established the comparability survey process as the standard methodology for determining pay rates for GS grades. The following decade however, saw increasing use of a special provision of the Pay Comparability Act. That provision gave the President authority to limit pay increases to less than comparability in times of economic or other national emergencies. Thus most pay increases in the 1970s and into the 1980s were limited to about half of what they would have been. This provided the impetus for the establishment of new task forces and proposals to replace or adjust the 1970 Pay Comparability Act. A second and very important impetus for reviewing the 1970 act is a growing feeling that its survey methodology does not provide a fair evaluation of comparable salaries in the private sector.

Multiple and Single Schedules   Although the 1923 Classification Act established five different job evaluation (or pay) services, they were conceptually (though not officially) interrelated. The services were P for professional and scientific; CAF for clerical, administrative, and fiscal; SP for subprofessional; CU for custodial; and CM for clerical-mechanical.

By 1949 only the first three services were in extensive use for white-collar jobs. However, all during the 1923–1949 period certain grades in the P and CAF services always had the same pay rates. The principal link between these separate services was the equating of grade P-1 (beginning college graduate or professional) with CAF-5 (full-performance secretary, accounting technician, or personnel assistant). Apparently, this resulted from the belief that a four-year (i.e., 36-month) college education was equivalent to three years of progressively responsible experience in a demanding office or technical job. Thus when the two major schedules were merged into one, P-1 and CAF-5 became the single grade of GS-5. The 10-graded CAF system became the first 10 grades of the new GS system and (with a several-grade overlap—GS-5 through GS-10) the eight-graded P system became the GS system's last eight grades (GS-5, GS-7, GS-9, and GS-11 through GS-15). Among other reasons, this merger became necessary to eliminate unwinnable arguments such as whether a job's duties were more typical of the upper end of the CAF system or the lower end of the P system. (This issue is equally pronounced today in multiple-schedule compensation plans.) Also considered were the increasing educational requirements for "A" (administrative) and "F" (fiscal) jobs (e.g., personnel and budget jobs), making them more like professional than clerical jobs. Finally, the 400 jobs above GS-15 (but below the handful of single-rate political appointee jobs) were placed into the new supergrade levels of GS-16, GS-17, and GS-18.

This is basically the system that exists today. One General Schedule for virtually all white-collar jobs in the civilian federal civil service, characterized by grade levels defined in statute, diverse but equally valued jobs in the same grade levels, and pay rates attached to grades via a statutory comparability survey process. All this because employees in the 1800s noticed that jobs similar to theirs were being paid a variety of rates by a variety of agencies in the single employer organization known as the federal government.

THE GENERAL SCHEDULE

Each of the 18 grades in the General Schedule established by the 1949 act is defined, by law, in about 150 words. Conceptually, the definitions are even shorter since each definition allows for a variety of value measures. Many of these alternative measures are, in fact, drawn intact from the earlier 1923 multiple and overlapping schedules. GS-5, the key overlap point, is defined, in part, as (1) difficult and responsible office work, (2) subordinate technical work, or (3) elementary professional work. Over the years these GS-5 definitions have applied to senior secretary, full technician, and first-level professional. The related minimum qualification requirements are a high school diploma plus three years (36 months) of progressively responsible experience or an academic four-year (36-month) baccalaureate degree, or a combination of the two.

Other key grades have also been given shortened, though not technically accurate, definitions. GS-1, for which there is no minimum educational requirement, is known as the messenger grade; GS-2 is a beginning clerk or typist, just out of high school; GS-5 is a new college graduate or experienced senior clerk; GS-7 is related to a one-year masters degree, GS-9 to a two-year masters, and GS-11 to a Ph.D. More often than not GS-11 is also the full-performance level of professional and administrative jobs. Of course, the minimum qualification requirements of each grade level must be related to the duties of the job. Thus a person holding a masters degree can often start at GS-5, if all the entry-level job requires is a baccalaureate degree. Similarly, very few GS-11s entered as new Ph.D.s; most were promoted to that level after about four years, having entered with a baccalaureate at GS-5. Finally, as with any system covering thousands of employees in a multitude of jobs and agencies, exceptions abound.

Jobs above GS-11 and approaching GS-15 are, more often than not, supervisory. Most such supervisory jobs begin at GS-13, the level at which there is a clear falloff of nonsupervisory positions. (There are, of course, clerical supervisory jobs at grades GS-5 through GS-10.) The GS-16, GS-17, and GS-18 supergrades developed in 1949 are almost a relic of the past; jobs in these grades have fallen off to about 1000. Such jobs are nonsupervisory and are typically the most senior technical advisers (e.g., scientists and attorneys) to government officials at the highest levels. For all intents and purposes, the Civil Service Reform Act of 1978 replaced the supergrades with the Senior Executive Service.

The above semiofficial definition of the grades in the GS is borne out by the distribution of the 1,400,000 GS and equivalent employees among the 18 grades. The two most heavily populated grades are GS-5 (full-performance clerical) and GS-11 (full-performance professional and administrative) with approximately 12 percent each. The bimodal nature of this distribution is further strengthened with 2 percent or less, each, at grades GS-1, GS-8, and GS-15. Capping the General Schedule are the SES and supergrades. These two groups amount to about 8000 jobs, or ½ of 1 percent of the General Schedule. These positions also supervise the government's half a million blue-collar workers.

SENIOR EXECUTIVE SERVICE

The Senior Executive Service is a separate personnel system at the top levels of government. It covers managerial and supervisory jobs equivalent to GS-16, GS-17, GS-18, and Executive Levels V and IV in ascending order. (Executive Levels III, II, and I combined contain only about 100 positions in the executive branch of government. Executive Level I essentially contains the cabinet secretaries. Executive Level II is the level at which members of Congress and others are compensated. Finally, Executive Level III covers administrators of smaller agencies, undersecretaries, and the like.) Supreme Court justices are equivalent to—but somewhat higher than—Executive Level I.

Agencies are allotted a finite number of SES "spaces" by the U.S. Office of

Personnel Management (OPM) depending on, for example, the size, scope, and complexity of the agency's programs. OPM, by statute, may not allot more than about 10,000 spaces. (Since the advent of the supergrades in 1949, Congress has closely controlled and limited the number of such positions.) Agencies then determine which of their senior positions and people to place in the SES. That placement is not necessarily by classical job evaluation techniques with strong OPM oversight, as was the case with the supergrades. Under SES, agencies independently establish their own SES positions, within their total SES allocation, subject to OPM postaudit. This concept under SES is a reflection of a basic tenet of the 1978 Civil Service Reform Act: let management manage.

Other tenets under SES include management's flexibility to reassign SES members on short notice, SES members' ability to hold appointed positions and subsequently return to career status, and, finally, a reward system based heavily on performance, not position classification. Basic pay, however, is set by statute, adjusted from time to time, and forms a continuum with pay rates in the General Schedule.

There are six basic pay rates in the SES. Management determines which rate each SES member is paid. Among the bases for such determinations are performance, duties, or change to a more expensive location. At the time of conversion to SES, virtually all supergraders were placed in the upper three rates, rate four being most typical. New appointees to the SES are typically placed in rate one or two. Finally, up to 20 percent of the SES corps may receive a lump-sum bonus of up to 20 percent of basic pay, if their performance is at least fully successful. These performance awards are highly valued, considering that several years often pass between general increases in the SES basic pay schedule.

MERIT PAY (GS-13 TO GS-15 SUPERVISORS)

Another major accomplishment of the 1978 Civil Service Reform Act was the elimination of the semiautomatic step-increase system for certain supervisors and the establishment of a merit pay system. This system covers approximately 75,000 employees who are supervisors or management officials in grades GS-13 to GS-15. At the time of adoption, it was thought to be a test ground for merit pay for all GS employees, considering that the 1978 act requires all employees to have specific performance standards and be evaluated against them each year.

Each October, when all nonmerit pay personnel are receiving their annual pay comparability adjustment (a general increase), all merit pay personnel are evaluated against their detailed performance standards. These evaluations determine the extent to which these supervisors will share in the merit pay pool. That pool is comprised of one-half of the general increase plus very small amounts from other sources. (It should be noted that merit pay personnel no longer receive step increases and that the first half of the comparability adjustment is granted automatically.) Experience under this merit pay system has been good, particularly with the performance standards and performance appraisal portions. Some agencies were able to significantly vary pay increases; using the example of a 9 percent general increase, the spread could be from a minimum of 4.5 percent to a maximum of over 15 percent (general and merit increase combined).

THE FACTOR EVALUATION SYSTEM

During the entire history of the federal government's personnel system, the classic technique of whole-job evaluation had basically been used for placing jobs into grades. By the late 1950s, and particularly during a 1970s study, it was recommended that this system be eliminated. In its place a factor-point and benchmark methodology was developed. Two principal objectives were to be served by such a massive change: (1) that a single quantifiable measuring system could be developed which would reconfirm the previous system's internal equity requirements and (2) that all the administrative elements of the new system would utilize the same formats and processes. For example, the format for writing job descriptions, evaluating jobs, and issuing job evaluation policy and guidance would be the same. The *Factor Evaluation System of Classification for Nonsupervisory Positions GS-1 through GS-15* (FES), now more than 50 percent implemented, has easily met these goals as well as the additional one of significantly reducing arguments over grade levels, because of its finite specificity. When fully implemented, FES will cover about 1 million nonsupervisory employees. (Supervisory positions are evaluated by a guide utilizing over 20 weighted factors, which has rarely been criticized. In practice, most first-line supervisory positions—immediately over nonsupervisory personnel—are one full GS grade higher than the grade of the full-performance work they supervise.)

FES Criteria   FES has 9 factors and a total of 46 factor levels. The factors and factor levels are weighted among and between each other. Weighting was accomplished by an iterative process designed to yield the same grades as would have been produced by the application of the grade-level definitions in the statute as well as those produced by the job evaluation methodology which FES replaced. A sample of over 4000 jobs was used to perform the weighting and to develop the factor-level definitions. Performing the evaluations were Civil Service Commission experts, agency classifiers, and some managers and employees.

The FES factors, along with their number of factor levels and point ranges, are:

Factor 1: Knowledge required by the position (9 levels, 50 to 1850 points)
Factor 2: Supervisory controls (5 levels, 25 to 650 points)
Factor 3: Guidelines (6 levels, 25 to 650 points)—nature of guidelines to perform the job and judgment needed to apply or develop them
Factor 4: Complexity (6 levels, 25 to 450 points)
Factor 5: Scope and effect (6 levels, 25 to 450 points)
Factor 6: Personal contacts (4 levels, 10 to 110 points)
Factor 7: Purpose of contacts (4 levels, 20 to 220 points)
Factor 8: Physical demands (3 levels, 5 to 50 points)
Factor 9: Work environment (3 levels, 5 to 50 points)

In utilizing FES, positions are point-rated by level within each factor, the points are added together, and the following list is used to convert a position's total point score to a GS grade.

GS Grade	Range
1	190–250
2	255–450
3	455–650
4	655–850
5	855–1100
6	1105–1350
7	1355–1600
8	1605–1850
9	1855–2100
10	2105–2350
11	2355–2750
12	2755–3150
13	3155–3600
14	3605–4050
15	4055 and over

Factors Each of the 46 factor levels in this 9-factor system is defined in the Primary Standard by a short, discrete paragraph. An example of such a paragraph follows: the fifth level of Knowledge, 750 points. This factor level is often found, though not exclusively, in GS-5 positions whether they are beginning professionals, advanced technicals, or middle clericals.

LEVEL 1-5   750 points

Knowledge (such as would be acquired through a pertinent baccalaureate educational program or its equivalent in experience, training, or independent study) of basic principles, concepts, and methodology of a professional or administrative occupation, and skill in applying this knowledge in carrying out elementary assignments, operations, or procedures;

or

In addition to the practical knowledge of standard procedures in Level 1-4, practical knowledge of technical methods to perform assignments such as carrying out limited projects which involves use of specialized, complicated techniques;

or

Equivalent knowledge and skill

Since the federal government operates a highly decentralized classification system, it can be seen that a factor-level definition by Primary Standard would not be specific enough to ensure accurate grading. (There are about 2000 position classification specialists, worldwide, who utilize the system to evaluate 1.5 million positions in hundreds of organizational locations.) Thus the U.S. Office of Personnel Management, as directed by statute, interprets the Primary Standard's factor levels by describing them in specific occupational terms. These descriptions, along with other guidance, are found in individual published *standards* for each of the federal government's major occupations. (There are about 300 occupational standards for the government's 425 occupations. The remaining 125 occupations are evaluated by cross-reference to related occupations.) An example of how the above level 1-5 is restated in the specific occupational terms of mechanical engineering follows:

LEVEL 1-5   MECHANICAL ENGINEER   750 points

A basic foundation of the concepts and principles of mechanical engineering including thermodynamics, mechanics and other physical, mathematical, and engineering sciences concerned with the production, transmission, measurement, and use of energy, especially heat and mechanical power. These knowledges would typically be acquired through a bachelor's degree program in mechanical engineering.

Benchmarks   In each occupational standard there are also *benchmark* position descriptions. Benchmarks are prototype position descriptions which are officially classified by the Office of Personnel Management. The GS-830, Mechanical Engineering Series Position Classification Standard, has a total of 18 benchmarks, from grades GS-5 through GS-14. Each benchmark contains a summary duty statement and a further interpretation of each of the FES factors. Continuing with the level 1-5 example, the following is drawn from the OPM, GS-5 Mechanical Engineer benchmark description.

LEVEL 1-5   GS-5 MECHANICAL ENGINEER BENCHMARK   750 points

Professional knowledge of mechanical engineering concepts and principles as would typically be acquired through a bachelor's degree program in mechanical engineering and would enable the engineer to perform trainee-level duties.

Thus while OPM occupationally interprets the position classification statute and the FES Primary Standard, agencies evaluate their positions by either (1) factor-point analysis using the occupations' published factor-level descriptions or (2) whole-job comparison using the benchmarks which contain the most highly refined and specific descriptions of factor levels.

All these parts—statute, Primary Standard, occupational factor-level descriptions, occupational benchmarks, and factor format position descriptions—comprise an interlocking job evaluation system that helps assure accurate grading of jobs whether done by different analysts, in different agencies, or in different geographic locations. Such an integrated system also helps assure employee understanding and management support and facilitates OPM compliance reviews.

Standards   A special and detailed mention should also be made about the OPM-issued occupational "standards." Position classification standards are, in operation, the heart of the government's job evaluation system. They are often regarded by management, employees, and the courts as the final word. Standards contain the highly specific measures which agencies are required to apply in grading their positions. Included in standards are the occupationally based factor-level descriptions which interpret an appropriate number of the Primary Standard's factor levels, benchmarks covering from 3 to 20 positions depending on the occupation's complexity and diversity, and a host of other guidance materials.

Each occupational standard covers from 20 to 100 pages and takes about one year to complete. (Also produced, at the same time, are the occupation's qualification requirements.) Involved is extensive nationwide (or worldwide) on-site fact-finding, meetings, analyses, and a public comment period often resulting in withering critique of the published draft standard. Comments typically come from agency personnel and subject matter experts, unions, professional associations, individual employees, OPM officials, members of Congress, and agency executives. From this a final standard emerges, and thousands of copies are distributed to personnel offices, associations, unions, libraries, and hundreds of individual subscribers.

SUMMARY

The federal government's job evaluation system is regarded as the conceptual foundation to the entire personnel system. It establishes the grades of jobs and the pay of employees and, through the related qualification standards, determines who qualifies for entry or promotion. Thus both great care and expense are accorded to job evaluation. Similarly, great pressures are placed on it. In consideration, our legislators have protected the system's basic tenets in statute and have reaffirmed them when quick-fix changes were lobbied for. The only significant change made since 1949 was to establish, in the 1978 Civil Service Reform Act, that there should be equal pay for work of equal value. Finally, Presidents and administrators of the system have pledged their support of the system and directed that it be scrupulously followed.

chapter 15

Specific Job Evaluation Systems: The Hay Guide Chart–Profile Method

Alvin O. Bellak

GENERAL PARTNER, THE HAY GROUP, PHILADELPHIA, PENNSYLVANIA

The Guide Chart–Profile Method of Job Evaluation was conceived by the Hay Group in the early 1950s. Its roots are in factor comparison methods in which Edward N. Hay was a pioneer. In its evolved form, it has become the most widely used single process for the evaluation of management, professional, and technical jobs in existence. It is used by more than 4000 profit and nonprofit organizations in some 30 countries.

The Hay organization was founded in 1943. While job evaluation processes of various kinds had existed for many years prior to that date, they were applied for the most part to factory and clerical positions. "Edward N. Hay and Associates," the founding organization, thought it not only had a better "mousetrap," its own factor comparison method, but that the method could be applied effectively to exempt as well as nonexempt jobs. This was quite audacious at a time when few managers thought their jobs could be described in written form, let alone evaluated.

The Guide Charts were created in 1951 in a client situation. The consultants had led a corporate committee in its application of the Hay Factor Comparison Method. A review board was pleased with the results but mystified as to the reasons which equated jobs in different functions with each other. As one member put it, "Tell me again on what precise premises this sales job was equated with that manufacturing job." It became apparent that to repeat end-lessly an explanation of factor comparison processes would be hopeless. What was needed was a record for present and future use which would show exactly the descriptive considerations and their quantitative measures which entered into each evaluation. This forced a search for the basic reasons, arranged in some kind of rational order, on a scale. Thus the Guide Charts came into being. It is important to note that the creation came through an inductive process in a real situation. It required a deep understanding of jobs and organizations as well as scaling techniques. The creators of the Guide Chart–Profile Method made four critically important observations:

1. While there were many factors one could consider (indeed, some methods had dozens), the most significant could be grouped as representing the knowl-edge required to do a job, the kind of thinking needed to solve the problems commonly faced, and the responsibilities assigned.

2. Jobs could be ranked not only in the order of importance within the struc-ture of an organization, but the distances between the ranks could be determined.

3. The factors appeared in certain kinds of patterns that seemed to be inher-ent to certain kinds of jobs.

4. The focus of the process of job evaluation must be on the nature and requirements of the *job* itself, *not* on the skills or background or characteristics or pay of the *job holder*.

THE GUIDE CHART–PROFILE METHOD

What evolved was a three-factor codification with a total of eight elements (see Figure 1):

Know-How The sum total of every kind of capability or skill, however acquired, needed for acceptable job performance. Its three dimensions are requirements for:

- Practical procedures, specialized techniques and knowledge within occu-pational fields, commercial functions, and professional or scientific disciplines.
- Integrating and harmonizing simultaneous achievement of diversified functions within managerial situations occurring in operating, technical, sup-port, or administrative fields. This involves, in some combination, skills in plan-ning, organizing, executing, controlling, and evaluating and may be exercised consultatively (about management) as well as executively.
- Active, practicing person-to-person skills in work with other people.

Problem Solving The original, self-starting use of the *know-how* required by the job, to identify, define, and resolve problems. "You think with what you know." This is true of even the most creative work. The raw material of any thinking is knowledge of facts, principles, and means. For that reason, *problem solving* is treated as a percentage of *know-how*.

Problem solving has two dimensions:

- The environment in which thinking takes place
- The challenge presented by the thinking to be done

FIGURE 1a Hay Guide Chart of Know-How

| | ●●BREADTH OF MANAGEMENT KNOW-HOW | | | | | | | | |
| | I. NONE OR MINIMAL Performance or supervision of an activity (or activities) highly specific as to objective and content, with appropriate awareness of related activities. | | | II. RELATED Operational or conceptual integration or coordination of activities which are relatively homogeneous in nature and objective. | | | III. DIVERSE Operational or conceptual integration or coordination of activities which are diverse in nature and objectives, in an important management area. | | |
●●●Human Relations Skills ▶	1	2	3	1	2	3	1	2	3
A. BASIC Basic work routines plus work indoctrination.	50	57	66	66	76	87	87	100	115
	57	66	76	76	87	100	100	115	132
	66	76	87	87	100	115	115	132	152
B. ELEMENTARY VOCATIONAL Familiarization in uninvolved, standardized work routines and/or use of simple equipment and machines.	66	76	87	87	100	115	115	132	152
	76	87	100	100	115	132	132	152	175
	87	100	115	115	132	152	152	175	200
C. VOCATIONAL Procedural or systematic proficiency, which may involve a facility in the use of specialized equipment.	87	100	115	115	132	152	152	175	200
	100	115	132	132	152	175	175	200	230
	115	132	152	152	175	200	200	230	264
D. ADVANCED VOCATIONAL Some specialized (generally nontechnical) skill(s), however acquired, giving additional breadth or depth to a generally single functional element.	115	132	152	152	175	200	200	230	264
	132	152	175	175	200	230	230	264	304
	152	175	200	200	230	264	264	304	350
E. BASIC TECHNICAL - SPECIALIZED Sufficiency in a technique which requires a grasp either of involved practices and precedents; or of scientific theory and principles; or both.	152	175	200	200	230	264	264	304	350
	175	200	230	230	264	304	304	350	400
	200	230	264	264	304	350	350	400	460
F. SEASONED TECHNICAL - SPECIALIZED Proficiency, gained through wide exposure or experiences in a specialized or technical field, in a technique which combines a broad grasp either of involved practices and precedents or of scientific theory and principles; or both.	200	230	264	264	304	350	350	400	460
	230	264	304	304	350	400	400	460	528
	264	304	350	350	400	460	460	528	608
G. TECHNICAL - SPECIALIZED MASTERY Determinative mastery of techniques, practices and theories gained through wide seasoning and/or special development.	264	304	350	350	400	460	460	528	608
				400	460	528		608	700

Copyright 1981 Hay Associates.

FIGURE 1b Hay Guide Chart of Problem Solving

| | ●●THINKING CHALLENGE | | | |
Thinking guided or circumscribed by:	1. REPETITIVE Identical situations requiring solution by simple choice of learned things.	2. PATTERNED Similar situations requiring solution by discriminating choice of learned things.	3. INTERPOLATIVE Differing situations requiring search for solutions within area of learned things.	4. ADAPTIVE Variable situations requiring analytical, interpretive, evaluative and/or constructive thinking.
A. STRICT ROUTINE Simple rules and detailed instructions.	10% — 12%	14% — 16%	19% — 22%	25% — 29%
B. ROUTINE Established routines and standing instructions.	12% — 14%	16% — 19%	22% — 25%	29% — 33%
C. SEMI-ROUTINE Somewhat diversified procedures and precedents.	14% — 16%	19% — 22%	25% — 29%	33% — 38%
D. STANDARDIZED Substantially diversified procedures and specialized standards.	16% — 19%	22% — 25%	29% — 33%	38% — 43%
E. CLEARLY DEFINED Clearly defined policies and principles.	19% — 22%	25% — 29%	33% — 38%	43% — 50%
F. BROADLY DEFINED Broad policies and specific objectives.	22% — 25%	29% — 33%	38% — 43%	50% — 57%
G. GENERALLY DEFINED General policies and ultimate goals.	25% — 29%	33% — 38%	43% — 50%	57% — 66%
H. ABSTRACTLY DEFINED	29%	38%	50%	66%

THINKING ENVIRONMENT

Copyright 1981 Hay Associates.

FIGURE 1c   Hay Guide Chart of Accountability

● ● IMPACT OF JOB ON END RESULTS

INDIRECT
REMOTE: Informational, recording, or incidental services for use by others in relation to some important end result.

CONTRIBUTORY: Interpretive, advisory, or facilitating services for use by others in taking action.

DIRECT
SHARED: Participating with others (except own subordinates and superiors), within or outside the organizational unit, in taking action.

PRIMARY: Controlling impact on end results, where shared accountability of others is subordinate.

● ● ● MAGNITUDE ➤

AMI for use with _1980_ dollars is _245_ .   — AMI EQUIVALENT ➤

● ● IMPACT ➤

		(1) VERY SMALL OR INDETERMINATE Under $100M				(2) SMALL $100M - $1MM				(3) MEDIUM $1MM - $10MM		
		R	C	S	P	R	C	S	P	R	C	S
A. PRESCRIBED These jobs are subject to: Direct and detailed instructions Close supervision		10	14	19	25	14	19	25	33	19	25	33
		12	16	22	29	16	22	29	38	22	29	38
		14	19	25	33	19	25	33	43	25	33	43
B. CONTROLLED These jobs are subject to: Instructions and established work routines Close supervision		16	22	29	38	22	29	38	50	29	38	50
		19	25	33	43	25	33	43	57	33	43	57
		22	29	38	50	29	38	50	66	38	50	66
C. STANDARDIZED These jobs are subject, wholly or in part, to: Standardized practices and procedures General work instructions Supervision of progress and results		25	33	43	57	33	43	57	76	43	57	76
		29	38	50	66	38	50	66	87	50	66	87
		33	43	57	76	43	57	76	100	57	76	100
D. GENERALLY REGULATED These jobs are subject, wholly or in part, to: Practices and procedures covered by precedents or well-defined policy Supervisory review		38	50	66	87	50	66	87	115	66	87	115
		43	57	76	100	57	76	100	132	76	100	132
		50	66	87	115	66	87	115	152	87	115	152
E. DIRECTED These jobs, by their nature or size, are subject to: Broad practice and procedures covered by functional precedents and policies Achievement of a circumscribed operational activity Managerial direction		57	76	100	132	76	100	132	175	100	132	175
		66	87	115	152	87	115	152	200	115	152	200
		76	100	132	175	100	132	175	230	132	175	230
F. ORIENTED DIRECTION These jobs, by their nature or size, are broadly subject to: Functional policies and goals General managerial direction		87	115	152	200	115	152	200	264	152	200	264
		100	132	175	230	132	175	230	304	175	230	304
		115	152	200	264	152	200	264	350	200	264	350
G. BROAD GUIDANCE These jobs are inherently subject only to broad policy and general management guidance.		132	175	230	304	175	230	304	400	230	304	400
		152	200	264	350	200	264	350	460	264	350	460
		175	230	304	400	230	304	400	528	304	400	528
H. STRATEGIC GUIDANCE These jobs, by reason of their size, independent complexity and high degree of effect on Company results, are subject only to guidance from top-most management.		200	264	350	460	264	350	460	608	350	460	608
		230	304	400	528	304	400	528	700	400	528	700
		264	350	460	608	350	460	608	800	460	608	800
		304	400	528			528	700	920	528	700	920

(Left side vertical label: A C T I O N   T O   F R E E D O M)

Copyright 1981 Hay Associates.

Accountability The answerability for action and for the consequences thereof. It is the measured effect of the job on end results of the organization. It has three dimensions in the following order of importance:

- *Freedom to Act.* The extent of personal, procedural, or systematic guidance or control of actions in relation to the primary emphasis of the job.
- *Job Impact on End Results.* The extent to which the job can directly affect actions necessary to produce results within its primary emphasis.
- *Magnitude.* The portion of the total organization encompassed by the primary emphasis of the job. This is usually, but not necessarily, reflected by the annual revenue or expense dollars associated with the area in which the job has its primary emphasis.

A fourth factor, *working conditions,* is used, as appropriate, for those jobs where hazards, an unpleasant environment, and/or particular physical demands are significant elements.

It is to be noted that the Equal Pay Act of 1963 reference to job-to-job comparisons based upon "skill, effort, and responsibility" relates remarkably to the
1951 Hay Guide Chart factors. Both, of course, were derived from the same
large body of knowledge as to what is common and measurable in job content.

Within the definitional structure, each Guide Chart has semantic scales
which reflect degrees of presence of each element. Each scale, except for *problem solving*, is expandable to reflect the size and complexity of the organization
to which it is applied. The language of the scales, carefully evolved over many
years and applied to literally many hundreds of thousands of jobs of every kind,
has remained fairly constant in recent years but is modified, as appropriate, to
reflect the unique nature, character, and structure of any given organization.

For each factor, the judgment of value is reflected in a single number. At a
later point, the size of the number is significant, but for the moment, it is the
sequence of the numbers which is important. The numbers (except for the very
lowest ones) increase at a rounded 15 percent rate. This conforms to a general
principle of psychometric scaling derived from Weber's Law:[1] "In comparing
objects, we perceive not the absolute difference between them, but the ratio of
this difference to the magnitude of the two objects compared." Further, for each
type of perceived physical difference, the extent of difference required in order
to be noticeable tends to be a specific constant percentage. The concept of "just
noticeable difference" was adopted for the Guide Chart scales and set at 15
percent. Specifically, it was found that a job evaluation committee, when comparing two similar jobs on any single factor, had to perceive at least a 15 percent
difference in order to come to a group agreement that job A was larger than
job B.

Again, for the moment, the *relationship* between the numbering scales on the
three charts is more significant than the absolute numbers themselves. Before
there were Guide Charts, it was observed that jobs had characteristic shapes.
Furthermore, these shapes were, in fact, known to managers and could be ver-
balized easily by them if they had a useful language for expression. Grouping
job content elements under the rubrics of *know-how, problem solving,* and
accountability gave them this language. Job shapes were characterized as:

- "Up-hill," where *accountability* exceeds *problem solving*
- "Flat," where these factors are exactly equal
- "Down-hill," where *accountability* is less than *problem solving*

While all jobs, by definition, must have some of each factor, however much
or little, relative amounts of each can be vastly different. Therefore, one of the
three shapes not only had to appear but also had to have a believable reality of
its own.

Thus an up-hill job was one where results to be achieved were a *relatively*
more important feature than intensive thinking, i.e., a "do" job. A down-hill
job was one where heightened use of knowledge through thinking was featured
more than answerability for consequent results, i.e., a "think" job. A flat job
was one with both "thinking" and "doing" in balance.

---

[1]See H. E. Garrett, *Great Experiments in Psychology,* Century Company, New York, 1930,
pp. 268–274, and Edward N. Hay, "Characteristics of Factor Comparison Job Evaluation,"
Personnel, 1946, pp. 370–375.

For example, in the context of a total business organization, a sales or direct production position would be a typical up-hill, "do" job where the emphasis is clearly and strongly upon performance against very specific, often quite measurable targets or budgets. A chemist doing basic research or a market analyst studying the eating habits of teenagers would be a typical down-hill, or "think," job, where the emphasis is more on collecting and analyzing information than on taking or authorizing action based on the results. A personnel or accounting manager would be a typical flat job characterized both by the requirement to develop information for use by others (recommend a new pension plan or a means of handling foreign currency transactions) and to answer for results (the accuracy of the payroll or the timely production of books of account).

The concept of typical job shape is the "Profile" in the "Guide Chart–Profile Method" that controls the relative calibration of the three Guide Charts. That is, the numbering patterns on the Guide Charts are set such that proper use produces points for the factors which, when arrayed for a given job, produce credible profiles.

It is very important to note that the Guide Chart–Profile Method gives an evaluation committee, or review board, quite uniquely, *two* means of assessing the accuracy of its evaluation for any given job. First, it can look at the points determined for a given job, relative to similar jobs and to jobs that are clearly larger or smaller. Second, by relying on its understanding of job shapes, it can assess the job's array on the three factors and make an independent judgment as to the probable validity of the evaluation. Relative point value and profile both must make sense for an evaluation to be accepted.

The final early observation that led to the creation of the Guide Chart–Profile Method was that jobs were to be measured *independently* of the job holders. This was not only correct but prescient, as it turns out. There was never, ever, any consideration of the talent, education, etc., of the job holder let alone the job holder's sex, age, ethnic origin, physical condition, or any other now-banned personal attribute. The further stricture, also present from the beginning, was that the pay of the job holder and the market for such positions were both irrelevant to job evaluation. Judgments were to be made only for the purpose of rank-ordering jobs and delineating the distances between ranks, i.e., to establish the relative importance of positions, top to bottom, within an organization structure.

Over the years since 1951, the fundamental principles of the Guide Chart–Profile Method have remained intact although there have been many refinements in language and application. Investigation of compensable job content elements continues, and there are refinements still to come. For example, is "concentration" a discrete, measurable element? Is working with many others in a vast, windowless office room an environmental unpleasantry comparable to the noxious quality of some factory environments? Should managers, as well as blue-collar workers, get *working conditions* points for spending time in dangerous, underground coal mines? or for frequent travel?

If one reflects on the material presented thus far—specifically, (a) Guide Chart "sizing" (adjusting the length of the scales to each particular organization), (b) modifying the scale language to reflect the character and structure of the organization, and (c) absorbing new information on job content-related requirements—then it becomes very clear that the Guide Chart–Profile Method is a *process*, not a fixed instrument like a physical measuring device. Further, it is a *relative* measurement process, not an *absolute* one. The theses of the Guide Chart–Profile Method thus become:

1. Every job that exists in an organizational context requires some amount of *know-how, problem solving,* and *accountability.*

2. Semantic scales reflecting degrees of these factors can be developed and applied, with consistency and with collective agreement, by any group of knowledgeable organization members after a modest amount of training.

3. The Guide Chart–Profile Method will produce a relative rank order, and a measure of the distances between ranks, for all jobs—which the organization will accept as reflective of its own perception of their relative importance.

4. The measurement principles are timeless and will hold until there is a fundamental change in the nature of jobs and in the interrelationship of jobs that make up organizations' structures.

5. As a process guided and controlled by principles rather than by immutable rules and scales, the Guide Chart–Profile Method is adaptable to the unique character of diverse jobs and organizations in changing environments.

Were these theses not correct, the Guide Chart–Profile Method would not be in the situation of increasing use in a broadly changing world after more than 30 years. A very substantial number of organizations have relied on the process in excess of 10 years and ranging up to over 25 years. They have applied the methodology through many reorganizations and to totally new product and service divisions during long periods of enormous growth and in an environment of great social change and legal challenge to the previously established order. While the Guide Chart–Profile Method was developed for business, industrial, and financial organizations, the theses have been proved to hold for nearly any organization. Among the long-term users are nonprofit trade, professional, charitable, and cultural organizations; federal government departments; states; municipalities; schools and universities; and hospitals within the United States and abroad. While the application is most common for exempt positions, there is widespread use for nonexempt clerical and office positions and growing use for blue-collar positions.

INSTALLATION OF THE GUIDE CHART–PROFILE METHOD

The objective is to place all the jobs in an organization in a sequence which represents the order and extent of their difficulty and importance within the organization.

A typical installation of the Guide Chart–Profile Method would proceed as follows:

1. After study of the organization, a set of Guide Charts is selected and sized, and appropriate language changes are made, as the initial step.

2. A benchmark sample of positions is selected to cover all organization levels, functions, and units where jobs are to be evaluated.

3. Position descriptions are prepared, and accepted for evaluation when approved by the job holder and one higher level of authority.

4. A job evaluation committee is selected to evaluate the benchmark sample. The usual criteria for committee selection are that its members should (a) be from diverse line and staff organizations; (b) be of roughly equivalent level within the organization; (c) hold positions somewhat higher than those to be evaluated (i.e., high enough up to have perspective but not so high as to be out of touch); and (d) be sufficiently familiar with the total organization to understand not only its purposes and structure but also its values. A member of the personnel department participates either as a formal committeeperson or ex officio. Where significant numbers of job holders are among the "protected classes,"[2] it is especially desirable to have a member or members from such classes on the committee. While in-house compensation experts would be the most technically proficient group to use for installing a job evaluation program, it has proved to be more beneficial to use a group of nonexperts for the benchmark effort. Since the benchmark committee is building the foundation and framework for all subsequent evaluations, it is important that it be built to reflect the values of the total organization. This can be done best by the people who work in, and know, the departments and divisions and who will have to live with the results. A committee selected from the finance, engineering, and manufacturing departments (among others) having to agree, for example, on the relative internal value of a financial analyst, a project engineer, and a production supervisor is of incalculable importance in achieving credibility for the job evaluation program.

5. The benchmark evaluation committee is led by a Hay consultant who acts as a combination teacher and coach. Initially, the consultant teaches the methodology in a learn-by-doing framework, then fades back as coach as the committee develops proficiency.

6. The committee evaluates each job for which it accepts the job description as a fair and clear statement that it finds believable. (Descriptions not meeting these criteria are sent back to the preparer for improvement.)

7. The instructions to the committee are clear and specific: (a) They must make judgments within the context of the total organization, not their own unit. (b) If they accept the description, they must evaluate it as it stands, without regard to any knowledge they may have of the current job holder's ability, performance, potential, or pay, or the market value of such a position. (c) They must achieve a common understanding and application of the semantic scales within the principles of the Guide Chart–Profile Method. (As the committee proceeds and gains competence, aspects of the preliminary Guide Charts that were problematic are resolved.) (d) No job in the benchmark sample is finally evaluated until they are *all* finally evaluated; i.e., any evaluation can be changed as the committee proceeds in its learning and becomes a coherent team. (e) The committee has completed its work when all agree that the total list of evaluations makes sense even though each member may have some reservations about an evaluation here and there.

8. In most cases, there is a review process of some kind, either done by a formal review board at a higher level of authority or through one-on-one

---

[2]The term "protected classes," as used by the EEOC, refers to various groups, such as females, blacks, hispanics, and the physically handicapped.

reviews with department and division heads. New information on job content, challenges, etc., is processed by the committee, to its own satisfaction and the reviewer's satisfaction, thus completing the benchmark project.

9. All other positions are then evaluated. Depending on the size, complexity, and culture of the organization, there are a number of ways this can be done, among which are (a) the original benchmark evaluation committee can do it all, (b) multiple committees can be appointed, with their output reconciled by the benchmark committee cum control committee, or (c) several single job evaluation experts (or very small teams) can be appointed to do the evaluations in batches subject to department and division head review followed by committee reconciliation. Any means which sustains the credibility of the evaluation process within the organization's culture is acceptable.

USE OF EVALUATIONS IN COMPENSATION ANALYSIS

Given the final, agreed evaluations, their most common application is to serve as a basis for studies of salary practices. (Other uses will be mentioned later.)

Internal Analysis If we plot the pay for each job holder against the sum of *know-how*, *problem solving*, and *accountability* points for his or her job, it will result in a scattergram, as in Figure 2; i.e., each dot represents one person's job points and pay. This can be done in consecutive scattergrams for actual current salary, salary midpoint assigned to the job held by the incumbent, and actual total cash compensation (i.e., salary plus cash bonus or incentive). For this explanation, we will use actual current salary only.

Through the scattergram we then draw a line of central tendency,[3] which

---

[3]One, or more, straight lines, drawn by sight or calculated by the least squares method, is appropriate and has proved to be practical and meaningful, since both axes are geometric scales. It has already been mentioned that the points on the Guide Charts increase on a compounded 15 percent incremental scale. Salary is also best thought of as a percentage incremental scale since one awards, for example, an 8 percent raise which amounts to, say, $2400, rather than vice versa.

FIGURE 2

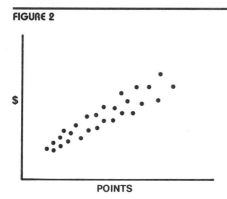

POINTS

FIGURE 3

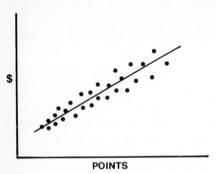

$

POINTS

becomes the "salary practice line," as in Figure 3. To the extent that the population is fairly homogeneous, the dispersion on the scattergram will be moderate, and a single straight line will be satisfactory representation of the median relationship between job size (expressed in points) and pay for the population as a whole.

To the extent that the dispersion is great, a scattergram as in Figure 4 will result. While one can nonetheless develop a line of central tendency, the existence of excessive dispersion suggests that the population is heterogeneous and further analysis is pursued.

By successive hypotheses, one searches out the reason for this dispersion. If we proceed to code the plottings, say, "x" for jobs in high-tech Division A and "o" for jobs in dull, old commodity product Division B, things become clear: hidden within the whole, there are multiple pay structures, as would be summarized in Figure 5. That is, if we plotted *separate* scattergrams for Division A and Division B, we would find that they have different salary practice lines. In other words, the salaries paid in Division A are greater than in Division B for jobs with the same points. Is this differential deliberate? Is it the result of generosity, or lack thereof, on the part of the division heads? Is it the result of inadequately managed or unmanageable salary systems?

FIGURE 4

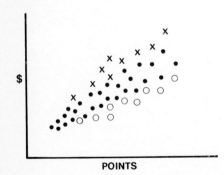

$

POINTS

FIGURE 5

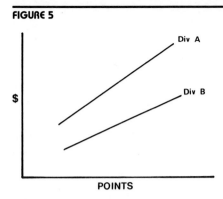

If the plottings were by sex and division, the x's would still be jobs in Division A but the o's could turn out to be not Division B but women throughout the whole organization. Since the job evaluations were made without regard to pay, sex, divisions, or anything other than job content, the dependent variable is pay. Higher dollars for the x's might be deliberate and appropriate for Division A, but what is the explanation for the o's? Depending on the facts, they *might* indicate an unacceptable, and perhaps illegal, practice.

The essence of this type of analytic exercise is to demonstrate that there is a means of searching out pay patterns that are not otherwise observable. Given an understanding of what might be buried in the data mass, management can be thoughtful in its understanding of what exists and in the development of the pay strategy it wants to follow. While it isn't likely to choose pay discrimination against women, there might well be good reason for having, or not having, multiple pay lines for various divisions.

Figure 6 illustrates a line of central tendency with a "dogleg" up, i.e, the higher-level jobs having a higher dollar rate of increment per point. This is a different kind of heterogeneity that might reflect different pay practices for the nonexempt versus the exempt populations, or it could be the entire exempt population but with a higher pay structure for the executive group.

FIGURE 6

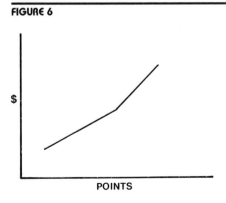

Figure 7 illustrates a dogleg down, i.e., the jobs with higher points having a *lower* rate of increment per point. The juncture of the two salary practice lines could be the job level where a management incentive plan kicks in. If this hypothesis is correct, then Figure 8 might be what would result if we plotted total cash compensation. The lower-level group gets salary only; i.e., salary equals total cash. The addition of incentive awards to the top management group causes both a discontinuity and a higher practice line for management.

Proper application of the Guide Chart–Profile Method provides a unique tool for analyzing the degree of internal consistency in the existing pay program and the validity and appropriateness of disparate pay practices. While it might seem at first glance that perfect internal consistency is the goal of equitable salary administration, one should keep in mind Ralph Waldo Emerson's admonishment, "Foolish consistency is the hobgoblin of small minds." Internal equity, or simple fairness, requires that pay and internal job value be consistent only for *homogeneous* populations—however desirable it might be for *all* jobs, functions, and divisions in *all* locations. Simple logic dictates that, for example, the same clerical job, with the same points, will most probably be paid on a different dollar scale at different geographic locations in view of the sometimes extreme cost-of-living differences we have in the United States. The existence of an incentive plan for only the management group will break the continuity of what might have otherwise been a perfectly consistent salary program for the total exempt population. Disparate markets periodically appear for individual jobs, whole functions, and whole lines of business. These realities must be recognized and dealt with when they appear.

The thesis, then, for the development of an effective and controllable pay structure is that one must *always* know the difference between *internal* job value and *external* markets for people. As in any complex phenomenon, whether a pay structure or a chemical compound, one must be able to identify the components in order to understand and manage the whole with intelligence. Given a firm baseline, i.e., carefully assigned points reflecting internal job value, the organization can knowledgeably and with strategic intent create pay structures which are rational, competitive, controllable, cost-effective, and motivational.

FIGURE 7

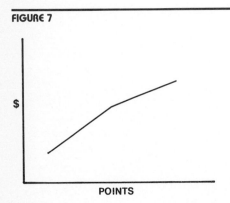

$

POINTS

FIGURE 8

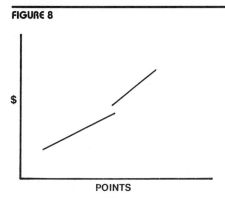

POINTS

External Comparison   To compare one's pay line(s) with those of external organizations, job evaluation points must first be converted to a standard scale. The
conversion process, conducted very carefully by highly specialized consultants,
is straightforward and serves its purpose as long as the organization has not
violated the basic evaluation principles and has been consistent in its application of the methodology to all units and functions.

Given a standard scale, compensation lines are *directly* comparable from one
organization to another. Hay facilitates this process by publishing annually the
actual salary, midpoint salary, and total cash compensation lines of subscribers
to the Hay Compensation Comparison (coded and arrayed in a manner that
protects the confidentiality of each subscriber).

Thus in the same way that an organization can compare pay practices among
segments *within* its structure, it can compare with segments or totalities of *outside* organizations. The Hay Compensation Comparisons will be addressed
briefly here but at length elsewhere in this handbook (Chapter 40).

To compare its salary practice lines with those of others who use the Guide
Chart–Profile Method, the organization would look to an array as in Figure 9.
This figure shows the distribution of salary practice lines, for the comparator

FIGURE 9

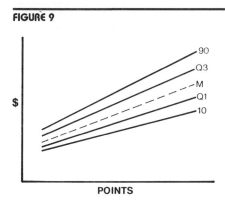

POINTS

organizations, in percentiles. Thus "M" is the median, or 50th percentile. The 10th and 90th percentiles are also shown, as are the third and first quartile lines (i.e., the 75th and 25th percentiles). An organization need only superimpose its own line on the distribution to determine, at a glance, its position in the market, as in Figure 10.

As the number of users of the Guide Chart–Profile Method has grown, so has the market data base, that is, the point-to-dollar practice lines that can be arrayed. They now exist for thousands of organizations and can be broken out by industry, line of business, function, location, and individual positions. They exist in some 30 countries for nationals in local currencies.

After making as many external comparisons as are useful—e.g., for salary practice, for total cash compensation practice, for segments, for functions, and so forth—the organization can position itself strategically in the market(s) for people. The selected position, represented by a line (or lines) drawn onto the comparison charts, is then, by simple calculation, turned into a set of midpoints and merit ranges. Thus (a) *internal equity* is achieved (the salary midpoints will relate exactly to job evaluation points), as is (b) *external competitiveness* (the organization will have positioned itself, i.e., priced its pay structure, in its best judgment, against the appropriate market or markets).

THE BOTTOM LINE: EMPLOYEE MOTIVATION

One of the "in" concepts in contemporary management thinking is "system," as in "information system" or "compensation system." Simplified, it means the assemblage of parts into an integrated, comprehensive whole to support a larger purpose. In this sense, a compensation system requires the parts dwelled upon in this section, namely, a process for establishing internal job value and internal pay equity and a means to access and appraise the marketplace for people. However, to become a complete system, there are more parts to be assembled. For example, there must be administrative procedures, a performance appraisal and merit award plan, a communications plan, the development and integration of benefits and extra pay elements (e.g., incentives), and so forth. All must thoughtfully be put together and managed to support the organization's human resources strategy, which in turn supports the achievement of the organization's ultimate goals.

FIGURE 10

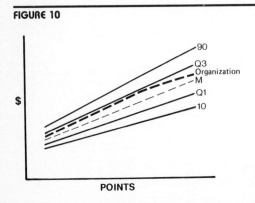

However, while assembling the compensation system to support the grand design, one must be sure not to overlook the less grandiose sounding, and very basic purpose, viz, employee motivation. Without it, the great goals will not be achieved.

Employee motivation is a very specific result to be sought from the compensation system. It is a truism that people work best when they know what is expected of them. After all, a job can be thought of as the interaction between the employer's expectations and the employee's intentions and actions. A well-written job description defines the context in which the job exists and spells out its accountabilities, i.e., the end results to be achieved. Job evaluation identifies and defines its place in the spectrum. The competitive midpoint salary assigned, the merit range, and the additional incentives to reward individual achievement link the critical three "P's" in a compensation system: "position, performance, and pay."

OTHER APPLICATIONS OF THE GUIDE CHART–PROFILE METHOD

EEO Compliance   This has become important in the United States, and similar requirements exist in a number of other countries. The Guide Chart–Profile Method, properly used, provides several specific tools to aid in achieving compliance with such laws and their objectives. Its uses can be summarized in three major areas:

Progress monitoring.   Job measurement enables an employer to identify the high-content, high-value jobs within the work force into which protected classes must be moved if meaningful progress toward compliance is to be made. With a demonstrable and reliable job measurement system, periodic monitoring of the relative and absolute progress of persons in terms of the value of jobs they hold (as distinguished from the number of jobs they hold) becomes possible.

Job requirement validation.   With Guide Chart methodology, an employer is able to define job requirements and accurately measure and compare job content and pay differences to prevent discrimination. Such validation efforts by employers are specifically required by some compliance agency regulations. The reason is to ensure that job requirements are not inflated with the consequence that protected classes are excluded or otherwise adversely affected.

Discrimination defense.   In addition to its importance in employer compliance efforts, a rational, systematic, and professionally maintained job measurement program can provide a defense against charges of discrimination. The books can be opened, the methodology explained, and the defense mounted.

Hay methodology has been successfully used in court proceedings, administrative hearings, and labor arbitration cases to determine the extent of internal equity of compensation. In addition, the Guide Charts have been used as a basis for determining minimum qualification requirements in recruitment and selection where corrective actions are required.

Organization Analysis and Planning   This is the discipline of defining an organization's jobs and the job clusters into sections, departments, and divisions and detailing how these are related to each other. The thoroughness and objectivity of the Hay job evaluation process brings out the nature and extent of those relationships and helps to reveal such things as work duplication, over-lapping of authority, and accountability vacuums. As part of assessing future strategic options, job measurement can be used to identify and make explicit the changes in organization structure which would be required.

Human Resource Appraisal, Planning, and Development   These aspects can be supported by assessing current and future requirements of jobs *and* existing and potential capabilities of people within the same measurement framework. This is possible because jobs can only exist in human terms. Differences between current capabilities and current job requirements identify immediate needs for specific training, career development, and recruiting. Differences between future job requirements and potential capabilities of current people facilitate human resource planning vis-à-vis long-term strategic organization plans, goals, and structures.

CONCLUSION

The Guide Chart-Profile Method has been tested and proved by continuing and expanding application. Organizations of all kinds in all major economies, and their employees, have found that it provides an accurate and clear reflection of the relative requirements they see in jobs, because:

1. It is based on concrete, practical concepts and principles that are easy to define and use.
2. It narrows matters of opinion to a minimum and brings sharp judgments to bear from more than one independent angle. It does not rely on single judgments, no matter how good they might be.
3. By providing a framework within which measurement decisions must be made, it does away with endless committee discussions, which frequently stall on the most basic issues.
4. It forces disciplined and orderly thinking about job content, quickly highlighting vague, poorly conceived or designed jobs.
5. It provides a clear, understandable basis for interrelating requirements of all kinds of jobs at all levels—top executives, middle managers, hourly workers, clerical workers, scientists, technical personnel, sales personnel, and professional people such as industrial physicians and lawyers. It considers the core content that is common to all jobs and can easily be adapted to reflect special determinants that affect some jobs in some organizations.

The Guide Chart-Profile Method is far more useful than ad hoc formulations which fit only singular work contexts and then only for limited periods of time. It is also far more useful than the "policy-capturing" job structures which are developed to mirror or model market practices. Guide Chart measurements are independent of the market and encourage rational determination of the basis for the pricing of job content rather than automatic reactions to the forces that drove pay in the past. The Guide Chart-Profile Method works because it is a dynamic process that people apply and adapt in ways that meet needs and solve problems in the situations that they face.

Wage and Salary Structure

chapter 16

Determining Wage and Salary Policy

R. E. Hollerbach

MANAGEMENT CONSULTANT, RETIRED PERSONNEL
DIRECTOR, PARKE DAVIS & CO., DETROIT, MICHIGAN

Formulating wage and salary policy is one of the most important activities within the *employee relations* function. Properly conceived and implemented, it will simultaneously satisfy the financial objectives of the company and its employees. Conversely, if poorly designed or implemented, it becomes a waste of expensive management time and company funds.

"Pay" cannot have the limited connotation of money in the paycheck but must be defined as the combined value of actual earnings plus benefit provisions. If pay takes a disproportionate share of profits, employees may be content with their gains temporarily, but the imbalance can lead to the failure of the company. Similarly, low pay rates allow higher company profits temporarily, but they do not attract or retain competent personnel. The result is performance mediocrity and its possible consequence, company instability and deterioration.

The compensation executive must be well informed about company objectives and employee viewpoints so as to develop policies that are mutually acceptable and beneficial. A sound compensation plan provides the employee with earnings and benefits which are highly competitive but not excessive within a local as well as a national comparative context. Pay policies must systematically and objectively identify job assignments of unlike complexity requiring different skills so that pay rates and pay scales reflect these variations. In addition, individual accomplishments must be properly rewarded and length of service appropriately recognized.

Conventional salary and wage administration techniques—writing job descriptions, evaluating jobs, providing for pay increases, conducting performance appraisals, and the like—are well-known tools to personnel executives. However, their effectiveness will be adversely affected if they are administered rigidly and fail to identify changes in the work place. New, more flexible approaches are necessary in the presence of quality circles and job enrichment programs which cross typical job assignment lines. They also encourage team action, intended to improve efficiency and job satisfaction, as well as potential for personal growth.

Above all, employees must perceive these policies to be highly competitive with those at other companies. Information about pay practices and benefit provisions elsewhere is readily available to that cadre of investigative persons in any organization who are able to extract such information from friends or neighbors employed at other companies. Personnel managment must freely admit that the company does not have identical benefits in every respect and should emphasize that it is highly competitive in the aggregate. When employees are encouraged to explore practices at other companies and to discuss them with appropriate management personnel to ensure accuracy, credibility of management increases significantly. This frank communication promotes the trust of employees and the feeling that programs are fairly administered while reducing inaccurate rumors. Without explicit proof of management's common sense and attitude of concern for employees, there will in all likelihood be problems of low morale which can result in excessive turnover, reduced productivity, and escalating costs due to the loss of the more competent employees. The highly probable consequence is increased employment demands and new employee training expenses as well as third-party involvement in the company.

The compensation executive bases management policy on the principle that career objectives of employees are not constant or alike for all, but differ from group to group and from individual to individual. Generally speaking, occupational groups can be classified along types of activities such as these:

- Plant personnel, such as production labor, service labor, skilled trades, etc.
- Clerical, stenographic, or semitechnical employees
- Professional personnel engaged as technical and administrative employees
- Management personnel who are first-line supervisors, middle managers, or top executives.

PRODUCTION, MAINTENANCE, AND SERVICE EMPLOYEES

This group is usually divided into three categories: general, semiskilled, and skilled workers.

General group. The general group is sometimes referred to as "unskilled" because previous experience is not required, on-the-job training is either unnecessary or minimal, and the employee has little, if any, opportunity to exercise judgment in carrying out the job. Typical work assignments are janitorial services, routine material handling, and repetitive production-line operations. This group consists of employees with limited service who have not yet been able to qualify for more skilled work or employees with long service who are well satisfied to remain on these jobs. The short-service unskilled employees know that any adverse business condition which necessitates a reduction in the work force is apt to affect them first. If they have dependents to support, a sharp curtailment of income is disastrous to them.

Pay policy for employees in this group should consider these factors:

1. These employees do not have skills which make it possible for them to gain other employment readily, and minimal skills result in relatively low income and in financial insecurity.

2. The rate of pay for all in the unskilled group should be about the same because their duties offer little or no opportunity to demonstrate skills uniquely suited to a function.

3. Rate increases should be based on length of service rather than performance, and job rate should be reached within 12 months of employment.

4. The personnel policy for this group should emphasize review and evaluation of such performance characteristics as punctuality, attendance, and adherence to instructions.

5. Benefit plans should offer immediate financial protection by providing layoff allowances, recall rights, and outplacement assistance, as well as training programs for those interested in developing skills.

Semiskilled group.   Semiskilled employees utilize manual and/or intellectual processes; have some opportunity to control the flow of work on responsible jobs such as shipping, receiving, and stock control; assemble units produced by less skilled employees into complex components or products; and operate production tools and equipment. Their effectiveness can be documented somewhat more precisely because the technique they use, through speed, accuracy and efficiency, results in greater or lesser output.

These employees share some of the need for security of their unskilled coworkers, but the reality of achievement has given a broader perspective to their needs. While immediate income security is still important, confidence and reliance on skills contribute to stronger personal security. Skills have developed to the point where they may be in demand by other companies. Furthermore, they can fill other less demanding jobs with ease, so that the probability of unemployment is reduced for them.

Assuming that pay scales are commensurate with their job responsibilities, personnel policy should recognize that:

1. Pay rates for the semiskilled should be predicated on individual levels of productivity and/or quality of work. Differences in rates paid can be defended on a relatively objective basis since performance expectations can be established.

2. As long as base pay is reasonably competitive and offers some personal recognition, emphasis on long-range benefit provisions such as pensions is apt to supersede the need for protection against unemployment.

3. Employee interest in training and development programs in preparation for more skilled occupations will be greater and should be satisfied.

Skilled group. The skilled group demonstrates some elements of professional knowledge and skill. These employees are able to determine the reason for mechanical breakdown and make an independent decision to institute corrective action which might include fabrication of special parts. If assigned to production processes, they exercise critical, timely judgment about process continuation based on weighing variables such as temperature, viscosity, and appearance, and may have the authority to stop the production of nonstandard items. Assembly of complex elements into a working unit—and its testing—may be a component of job responsibility. Individual competence is apparent through high volume, high quality, low scrap rate, and the low frequency of rework required.

As success is measured in the hourly group, the skilled employees have reached a pinnacle. Because they can perform a variety of jobs, including the most complex, they enjoy the deep sense of security peculiar to people who are in high demand at most companies. They do not fear lack of employment from any cause other than a general business recession. They are willing to take the risks of a move from one company to another for more pay or better benefits.

1. Pay scales and pay structures must recognize their assets and provide for individual contribution because they are the problem solvers of the hourly group and, frequently enough, the advisers to management as to the practicality of new or revised programs.

2. Their in-depth knowledge of equipment and processes enables them to initiate constructive, cost-reduction suggestions which must be rewarded by public acknowledgment and by a share of the savings resulting from their ideas.

3. Their loyalties can be stimulated by a company wise enough to ensure that their personal desires to contribute creatively cannot be better satisfied by other companies. They expect and must be provided not only a high rate of pay but one combined with liberal benefits in all areas such as extended vacations, tuition aid to enhance their skills, hospital-medical plans, life insurance, and pensions.

SALARIED EMPLOYEES

This group is usually separated into two groups for pay policy:

- Nonexempt-salaried employees entitled to overtime premium pay by law
- Exempt-salaried employees who are excluded from this legislation and do not typically receive overtime pay

The Nonexempt Group The nonexempt group includes clerical personnel engaged in maintenance of records and preparation of reports; typists, stenographers, secretaries; and duplicating machine operators. Length of employment and varying degrees of job skill lead to grouping these employees according to categories as beginners, intermediates, or seniors in each occupational group.

Beginner group. The beginner group is heavily populated by chronologically young employees who are not more than a few years past high school graduation. They have the basic education required for higher-level positions, but because of their lack of experience, they get the most routine assignments. They are predominantly women, who may or may not aspire to a business career.

Turnover will be high through rapid promotions or job shopping. These employees change employers for a variety of reasons and rarely have to be concerned about dependents and personal commitments.

Company policy should recognize that:

1. Long lunch hours and convenient shopping areas can take precedence over higher pay.

2. Frequent increases and higher pay will take precedence over the long-range security of retirement plans, life insurance, and the like.

3. The opportunity to demonstrate individual competence by assignment to more difficult tasks can act as an inducement in prolonging employment.

Intermediate group. The intermediate group consists of "graduates" from the beginner group. These employees have worked a sufficient length of time to demonstrate both competence and dependability. They not only are expected to know company policies and procedures applicable to their jobs but to perform more complex tasks, requiring individual judgment. They have demonstrated their reliability through consistently accurate work.

In length of service these employees can vary from relatively short- to long-service employees, to those who quit, raise a family, and then reenter the business world. Employee needs will thus differ, and policies should recognize that:

1. Some are as interested in base pay, shopping convenience, and so on, as is the beginner.

2. Immediate personal financial security available through benefits such as medical-surgical plans is as important to some as pay scales are to others.

3. Long-range security of retirement plans is also a major consideration for the older employee.

4. Training programs to sharpen skills and to qualify these employees for senior positions are essential.

Senior level. The senior level of employees are those with highly valued knowledge gained through experience or specialized training. Jobs for this group can be tailored to the individual's capabilities, personal interests, experience, and training. For the most part, these employees are career-minded, permanent members of the public and private sector. Deep loyalty to the company or to management members of the company is typically in evidence in these employees. However, since their skills are usually in high demand, they may receive attractive offers from other companies.

Job shopping can be minimized by:

1. A pay structure which is flexible enough to reward distinguished performance as well as length of service

2. A broad range of benefits related to long service, such as extended salary continuance in the event of illness, extra weeks of vacation corresponding to years of service, and leniency regarding paid personal time off

3. Opportunity through training and/or educational assistance to develop professional skills so that they may qualify for jobs with exempt status

The Exempt Group   Exempt employees are those not automatically entitled to overtime pay by law, who perform the most complicated and responsible professional or managerial duties.

Professional group.   Professional employees as a group are stratified in much the same way as the nonexempt-salaried group, according to beginning, intermediate, and senior levels. Most of these employees are career-minded people who have expended considerable time, effort, and money at school to obtain expertise in their chosen fields.

Recent college graduates appear in this group as beginners who are highly educated but lack experience. Movement to the intermediate group depends largely on demonstrated ability to blend theory with practical application in reaching solutions to problems in their fields. Senior status is reserved for the most creative, original thinkers who can solve the most complicated problems, reach new and different workable solutions, provide leadership to the less skilled, and maintain current knowledge in their chosen professions.

These employees take competitive salary and benefit plans for granted because they can find employment readily at companies that offer adequate financial provisions. Throughout their careers, a primary interest is an environment wherein they can function with a greater degree of independence and utilize their knowledge in the broadest, most uninhibited sense, that is, with considerable autonomy.

In addition to sound salary and basic benefit policies, they seek provisions for:

1. Financial assistance to permit study toward acquiring an advanced degree
2. Financial assistance for continuing education to keep up with current scientific developments, new business methods, legislation, and so on
3. The opportunity to attend conferences where recognized experts present papers on subjects of interest or where they can exchange viewpoints with their peers from other companies
4. Participation in the success of the company, resulting from their efforts, through special cash awards or stock ownership

The pay structure for these professional employees must have a high degree of flexibility. Slavish adherence to age, length of service, or similar norms will fail to recognize the employee who is on a "fast track" and may occasion the loss of his or her expertise to a more progressive company. Thus policy must be sensitive to the subtle changes in job content—typical of this group—which become apparent as theoretical knowledge and practical skills are better-integrated. Employees then assume or receive more complex problems on a highly individualized basis.

Management group.   The management group consists of supervisors, middle managers, and top executives and represents a variety of skills and educational levels. The nature of the company's product line is a determining factor in the weight that is given to experience and education. This is particularly true at the first level of supervision. For example, the education and experience required to supervise employees engaged in routine, repetitive operations will differ significantly from the skills required for supervision of complicated processes. Consequently, first-line supervisory positions may be held by either experienced employees who have been promoted from nonexempt jobs or relatively inexperienced employees who have specialized knowledge obtained through advanced education.

Supervisors. Supervisors have specialized needs since some are in a new role and a new environment. Being at the bottom of the management hierarchy, they feel the need to prove themselves to further their careers. The recent graduate has the professional credentials but has not had the opportunity to demonstrate his or her skills. The supervisor who was promoted from the nonexempt ranks must supervise employees who were formerly peers and is, in addition, competing with more experienced supervisors or highly educated younger people. In some ways this situation is analogous to the short-service, unskilled employee who is considered to have potential and has yet to demonstrate capacity.

Company policy should provide:

1. A grace or trial period during which these supervisors can assess for themselves their job satisfaction and return to their prior occupations without prejudice to their good standing in the company should they be inept as supervisors or should they find supervisory work distasteful. Similarly, the recent graduate should have the opportunity to transfer into nonsupervisory professional functions.

2. Comprehensive training programs designed to help the supervisor improve in the art of management of people, which is to say, delegating responsibility, providing guidance and control, and motivating to improve skills and identification with the company. Training programs also enable the supervisor to understand production standards and the techniques to be applied to meet quality and quantity requirements.

3. Clearly established parameters of responsibility and exact definitions of accountability within which authority can be independently exercised.

4. An adequate pay differential over the pay of subordinates so that it is not eliminated by overtime pay or off-shift premium pay.

5. Recognition of skills which result in higher group efficiency and better product quality, through tangible and intangible awards, for example, shares of company stock and reserved parking privileges or other perquisites.

6. Earnings for this group which are comparable to the earnings of employees with similar competence, experience, and education who conduct research, quality control, engineering, and other professional nonsupervisory activities.

Middle management. Middle-management needs are essentially the same except that the newly appointed middle-management member is "farther out on the limb" and more in the spotlight. Success or failure can be pinpointed more exactly.

Middle management usually contains the most successful and best-paid employees promoted from the first-line supervisory group, and their earnings are usually adequate. However, policies which fail to reward the excellence of individual contribution through high base salary and supplemental programs can make these employees easy prey for executive search agencies, enticing advertising, and contacts made while attending business conferences.

Special inducements include the following:

1. Status symbols, such as a private office, club membership, and a reserved parking space

2. Training and development programs designed to improve and broaden knowledge of other activities

3. Contingent compensation, such as bonus plans which dramatically improve earnings in any given year because they recognize unusual achievement

Top executives.   Top executives direct major functions, frequently are officers of the company, and affect most directly the profitability of the company. The members of this select group have had highly successful careers, which usually result in high income levels. Formalized salary structure and related benefits continue to be as important at the top executive level as with the middle-management group. However, although competitive salary structures, individualized salary increases, and status symbols are important, "aftertax" earnings take on greater significance.

Maximum flexibility is required, and programs should be designed to identify and reward individual achievement accurately as well as permit variations suitable to personal needs. Some of the items to consider are:

1. Executive bonus awards directly related to achievement and substantial enough to provide real incentive
2. The option to defer awards to a time which better suits the individual's financial- or tax-planning needs, such as after retirement
3. Perquisites such as a car at company expense, paid travel expenses for the spouse, and services such as investment and legal advice
4. The right to select the type and size of benefits preferred from within the company's overall benefit package

The Sales Group   In addition to the foregoing, another large group of employees may have to be considered. Companies with their own distribution systems may have sales employees in each of these exempt groups. While their personal and financial needs are essentially the same, a significant difference lies in the method of their payment and the isolation inherent in their jobs.

The highly individualized nature of a sales job leads many companies away from the base-salary method of compensation to plans wherein earnings are substantially or totally related to sales volume. Sales quotas and sales incentives are widely used for sales compensation on the assumption that the typical "sales type" prefers it that way. Given modest base salaries or drawing accounts, personnel in sales supposedly view the total earnings potential of their jobs as unlimited and subject only to their own personal ability.

Whether this is in fact the case is debatable as is the desirability of such a policy. The nature of the company's products, corporate actions, and the normal peaks and valleys in typical years are among the items that affect their ability to sell. Evaluation of these three influencing factors is essential in determining the appropriate compensation plan. Compensation executives should appreciate the fact that sales personnel are members of the company and entitled to the same opportunities for development and the same measures of security as are provided other employees.

EXTERNAL FORCES

The state of the job market and competitor employment practices at the local and national level condition employee attitudes and the wage and salary structure.

Peak Employment Periods   When companies are running at top capacity, employees at all levels of skill are difficult to recruit. Employees become aware of this, their expectations inflate accordingly, and the labor market becomes a "seller's market" in which employers bid against each other in their efforts to attract competent personnel.

There is a natural tendency to hold onto existing structures in the hope that "things will get better"—that is, revert to lower pay rates. For a short period of time, this procedure has merit. It avoids precipitous action which increases payroll costs. Payroll costs are difficult to reduce if the work force shortage proves to be temporary. During pressures of this type, maximum coordination is essential between the compensation executive and related departments of employment and work force planning. If the shortage continues to the point where the number of open jobs is excessive and the forecasted long-range needs of the company are jeopardized, the compensation executive must institute changes in pay policy.

A number of options are available as starting rates are increased. Some of these are:

1. *Maintain internal parity.* In a rising economy, if productivity is improving and if profits are adequate, salary and hourly rate structures can move upward as starting rates climb. Of all options, this modification is the easiest to administer because the earnings of all employees can be maintained in the proper relationship to the rates being paid new personnel.

2. *Modify increase policies.* When certain employees must be hired at a higher starting rate, subsequent increases in pay can be made less frequently to avoid excessive costs. For example, if eligibility for increases had been every six months, the policy can be extended to nine months; twelve-month intervals can be lengthened by three to six months; and so on. In addition, or instead, the size of increases can be reduced.

3. *Reduce range spread.* This method is particularly applicable if the spread from minimum to maximum of ranges was wide originally. By raising the range minimums without changing maximums, more attractive starting rates become available without a substantial increase in overall labor costs. Employees may reach the maximum in a shorter period of time, and the pay differential between new and long-service employees may be reduced, but the net effect on operating costs will not be altered significantly.

4. *Job enrichment or enlargement.* Frequently an analysis of internal work force requirements will reveal areas where imperceptible changes in workload demands over a period of time result in the availability of time on the part of some employees for additional assignments. Employees usually welcome more comprehensive assignments since they will likely result in greater job satisfaction, a larger income, and preparation for even more responsible duties. The company gains in several ways: it no longer has to seek hard to find candidates for unfilled jobs, and it experiences reduced costs due to the elimination of salary and benefit expenditures whenever employees are not replaced.

5. *Eliminate ranges.* Traditional progressions within rate ranges based on length of service or merit may have to be abandoned. While giving recognition to an individual employee via increases within a range is a highly desirable policy, it can become a prohibitive expense when starting rates are unreasonably high. This is the least desirable option and should be utilized only when profit margins are unacceptable.

Shortage of Specialized Skills   When candidates for specific jobs requiring specialized skills become scarce and starting rates begin to rise, there is a tendency to abort good job evaluation practice. On the surface there seems to be little hazard in artificially reclassifying these jobs upward so that a competitive rate range can be offered. Unfortunately, this solution fails to consider two significant administrative problems almost sure to occur in due time:

1. When the supply of candidates becomes more adequate and when more realistic starting rates can be applied, it is virtually impossible to reduce the job from its artificial classification to a rate range in keeping with the true dimensions of the job.

2. Overrated jobs are likely to become "benchmarks" and to exert pressure for the reclassification of other jobs with equivalent responsibilities but not subject to the pressure of work force shortage.

To avoid these situations, it is much more advisable to pay high in the properly evaluated rate range and, if necessary, to exceed the maximum—to prevent a skewed job evaluation system.

The compensation executive can usually exert better control of problems arising from a limited labor supply when the shortage applies to jobs which have been in existence for some time. His control is reduced when the source of the problem is a new technology.

A case in point might be electronic data processing. The advantages of the computer became obvious to many companies in a brief period of time. The demand for programmers and operators soared overnight, and their opportunity for higher earnings rose concurrently. Pressures for larger salaries increased at a time when it was very difficult to get a "handle" on these jobs from a job evaluation point of view.

Under such circumstances, there are advantages to be gained by ignoring existing rate ranges and conventional evaluation techniques. In a new, untried field, the true dimensions of relevant jobs are rarely identifiable until the company and industry have lived with them for some time.

To avoid precedents which will be difficult to break when supply catches up with demand and when more logical job analysis is possible, a "special" range can be set as an expedient, tentative provision. This special range can ignore typical company rate structures and can be designed with a broad spread from minimum to maximum which might overlap two or three conventional ranges. By its extreme breadth, the special range affords the opportunity to attract and retain competent personnel while avoiding the misuse of the company's official structure.

Ultimately, a "job family" should emerge from this broad category. As pressures diminish and objective evaluation becomes possible, several levels of skill, responsibility, etc., will be identifiable. At this time, the special range can be abandoned and the appropriate number of job levels integrated into the regular rate structure.

In some industries, however, such as aerospace, periodic shortages and overages can be a way of life because work loads depend upon the type and volume of signed order contracts. A large order requiring the design and implementation skills of engineers can cause an immediate shortage which reverses when the contract is completed. Such companies typically offer very attractive start-ing salaries, generally in excess of those at companies with a more stable work load and employment need.

Inflated wage patterns to meet special needs can carry over into an excessive pay policy. The compensation executive must not let these practices influence pay policy generally but must be willing to address the issue with employees. The remedy and explanation are not easily found, but emphasis on how the short-term advantages of high pay together with the disadvantages of an uncer-tain future are offset by more realistic policies and more job security usually resolves this issue.

Pay Practices of Competitors   At one time employers competing for the same employees were usually a few companies in the same small geographic area. A company on one side of a large city could ignore companies on the other side because employees tended to work close to their homes. As the work force became more mobile, competition for talent spread to include a 10- or 50-mile radius from the work site. At the present time it is not unusual to recruit on a national basis for certain skills. Competing for employees in the expanded hori-zon of the work force has affected not only pay rates but the hidden compen-sation offered through the benefit package. This total package has to be designed to provide favorable comparison with local industries and with national trends. A company at odds with local or national total compensation programs will have limited success in its recruiting efforts.

A company with different plant sites may have basic corporate policies to which it is committed, but these are subject to partial modifications in line with prevailing practices at any location. For example, increases on a merit basis may be corporate policy, but some localities or some employee groups will be allowed length-of-service adjustments in keeping with local practices. Six or seven holidays may be the corporate minimum, but ten or twelve can be autho-rized for some areas.

Whatever the variation, it must be based on facts which can be clearly explained to the employee candidates who have become well informed on compensation and benefits available at other companies.

To be able to show the advantages of company policy, the compensation executive cannot limit his or her attention to data generated from routine sur-veys of wages and salaries. In addition to comparison of basic income, the com-pensation executive must know the following specifics of the practices of other employers:

1. Frequency and size of increases.
2. Reasons for granting increases: Are they based on service or merit? Are they related to the rise in cost of living? Are they across-the-board sharing in the company's improved productivity?
3. Ratio of employee benefits to individual earnings: What life insurance is provided at various income levels? What retirement income accrues for various years of service and earnings?
4. Continuation of earnings: What holidays are recognized? What are the vacation schedules? What is the income protection for illness or injury?
5. Funding of the benefit package: What is the employee's share in the cost

of life insurance, medical coverage for self and dependents, retirement, etc.? Are supplemental provisions available at employee expense?

If all those provisions are taken into account, wage and salary policies can be designed to provide moderate earnings combined with liberal benefits, liberal earnings but moderate benefits, or any other variation.

CORPORATE CONCEPTS

Basic to the operation of almost every company is the need to make a profit. Nonprofit institutions exist but are in the minority, and even these usually try to earn enough to meet most of their expenses.

Because management wants to operate on a least-cost basis in every way, it has to develop techniques which assure that payroll dollars are expended in the most effective way. The degree of sophistication required in these techniques varies widely from company to company. Size and type of business, as well as growth opportunity, influence the variations in corporate attitudes toward pay and pay policies.

The well-established firm.   It can be very easy for the well-established firm to fall into a conservative approach to compensation. The company name is well known and attracts employees. Its years of success convey a sense of security to employees and candidates because adverse business conditions have been weathered successfully in the past. Stable employment exists because employees have accumulated too much service to leave for modest improvements in earnings.

The other side of this coin—the new candidates' viewpoint of the firm—cannot be overlooked in this atmosphere. Young, competent candidates can afford a few risks early in life, and consequently a "well-established firm" is not necessarily as meaningful to them as actual income. They may feel that promotional lines in older companies will be clogged with long-service candidates, thereby reducing the newer employees' opportunities. An additional obstacle may exist because policies and procedures are so deeply entrenched that creativity and innovation will be stifled.

Well-established companies, therefore, must modernize pay and benefit policies as assiduously as they do equipment and facilities for improved profit. One can stipulate that failure to do so will result in:

1. The loss of the most competent employees to more progressive firms
2. The inability to hire experienced or inexperienced replacements because their salary requirements exceed "par for the course" at the conservative firm
3. A drift toward mediocrity and the subsequent reduction in profit and growth

The new firm.   The new firm can err in the other direction just as easily. In its anxiety to "get up and go," it may:

1. Pay whatever a candidate asks just to get the talent
2. Pay a cadre of employees far above market price to assure their retention
3. Adjust salaries and wages too often and too liberally, to indicate that it is a live-wire outfit
4. Share profits with employees without regard to the company's long-range financial needs

In due time, the new firm establishes itself and stabilizes. More realistic pay structures and pay policies develop, but earlier freewheeling practices have resulted in exorbitant payroll costs which are not easily reduced. Employee resentments may grow as a result of the problems caused by the earlier free-wheeling practices. Among these will be:

1. Employees at or above the maximum rate for their jobs due to the high starting salaries of the past
2. Limited room in the rate range for additional increases as a result of size and frequency of adjustments previously authorized
3. Indefensible differences in pay as new employees are hired at realistic pay rates
4. New-employee resentment because of a slower, more selective approach to rate increases

Rise or fall of profits.   The rise or fall of profits tends to relax or constrict wage and salary policies. Any change has an effect on employees and consequently on one of the largest single cost items of a company—its payroll. Despite employee attitudes or competitor practices, the fundamental question facing the company is, How much should it cost to attract and retain the kind of employees we need?

In good times, when profits provide adequately for dividends and for broad corporate programs, approval of liberal pay ranges and pay increase programs can be obtained from top management more easily. Sharing the wealth with employees is less likely to be criticized because they are perceived as significant contributors to the company's unusual success. However, despite this freedom for the compensation executive to devise a more liberal wage and salary policy, normal base levels should be retained during high-profit periods. Dramatic increases in wages and salaries, which elevate them beyond the acceptable level for normal-profit years, should be avoided. Employee participation in the company's earnings is more logically accomplished through special periodic payments which take the form of profit sharing programs, Christmas bonuses, or similar plans. These are predicated on high profits and automatically disappear when profits fall.

When profits are below par, "tightening of the belt" in terms of wages and salaries is a natural tendency. At the same time pressure increases for greater production from every employee. Financial rewards for outstanding efforts may become so small they lose their significance as incentives. The work force may be cut and normal wage and salary increase policies may be suspended during adverse business conditions even though top management recognizes that the recovery of the company may depend on the continuation of good compensation techniques. These short-range and stopgap solutions should be avoided. If salaries and wages fall below a competitive level, the most capable employees will quit the company, leaving a preponderance of mediocrity to resolve the company's problems. Good replacement personnel will not be attracted to a low-paying company, with the result that recovery becomes impossible.

Maintenance of an adequate compensation plan through good and bad times depends on utilizing well-designed, logically constructed procedures and controls consistently.

CONCLUSION

The success of any technique or group of techniques at one company does not ensure success at another company. To develop an effective program with compensation and benefits intelligently integrated, the compensation executive must appraise each technique carefully, determining its desirability for the company and its employees.

The basic ingredients of a sound wage and salary policy include provisions which recognize the need for a fair wage and the opportunity for employees to progress. Less apparent but equally important are the provisions for the employee's more personalized concerns and requirements. Wage and salary policies based upon pure statistical reference to competitive wages and salaries are conceived in the dark. Unless they give credence to ancillary programs such as training and development and assure the employee that he or she is a highly regarded member of the team, they will not be persuasive in the attraction of new employees to the company or in the retention of the company's current employees.

Foresighted compensation executives thus must not only employ the most effectual techniques known at any given time but must continually search for improved methods and for higher ideals which will assure employees and employers of an equitable relationship. Personnel management tools designed to meet the requirements of a given time, and arising out of prevailing economic conditions, have the propensity for becoming obsolete, in need of replacement to meet new conditions. The task of replacement is analogous to that of a toolmaker who adjusts or remakes a tool to meet requirements of restyling, engineering changes, and the like. The tool in use may not be worn out but simply no longer effective.

This factor of "timeliness" of pay policy and personnel administration also needs to take into account the entry into today's work force of the younger employees who may be better-educated than their predecessors, more questioning and challenging of status quo practices, and less likely to accept policies which do not have a sound and contemporary perspective.

Management attitudes as perceived by employees can negate the best compensation program if deemed to be self-serving and indifferent to individual employee needs or current events. Management failure to recognize that exceptions to policy are necessitated by legitimate reasons, and refusal to authorize deviations from policy when required, will suggest that management rules are for the sake of rules and not guidelines to be administered wisely.

Periodically an external agency should conduct opinion or attitude surveys of employees to provide another avenue of communication between management and subordinates. The external agency can ensure anonymity so that employees need not fear reprisal if they make adverse comments regarding policy or give negative responses to audit questions. The external agency utilizes the audit to analyze employee viewpoints and summarize the findings. Meetings are held with employees by personnel and line management to review the results of the audit, stimulate open discussion, and secure feedback concerning misunderstandings and incipient problems. These meetings should be conducted by a level of management that has the authority to revise policy where justified or correct adverse situations and relationships. This process should not be invoked unless company management is open-minded and willing to demonstrate its receptiveness by taking corrective action where change is indicated.

Leadership in the field of compensation will require executives who are willing to face the challenge of policies which go beyond routine statistical indexes and may be construed as idealistic. Undue emphasis on economic values without a humanistic approach will lead to an impoverished program. Industry practices, employee viewpoints, and the problems that management faces must be communicated coherently. The efficacy of a good compensation program depends on clear communication between those who administer it and those who are affected by it. The rationale of the plan—why it is designed as it is and what it consists of—must be communicated widely. Unless communication is open and uncomplicated, misunderstandings, confusion, and resentment follow.

chapter 17

Establishing the Hourly Pay Structure

William Gomberg

WHARTON SCHOOL, UNIVERSITY OF PENNSYLVANIA,
PHILADELPHIA, PENNSYLVANIA

It used to be that employers hired and paid employees to do a specific job; the link between what was made and what was paid for was deceptively simple. The growth of industry, the bureaucratization of the labor organization, the breakdown of manufacturing into myriad processes, and the addition to the organization of a complex distribution mechanism have increased the complexity of the relationship between what a worker is paid and what a product is worth.

The relationship has become so remote at times that some people have recommended a guaranteed annual income, an idea incorporated in the 1970 welfare proposals of President Nixon. Thus money may be paid for a whole range of purposes with immediate production results at one pole and the welfare of the commonwealth at the other.

The assignment which we wish to cover, however, restricts itself to the hourly wage, the oldest method of paying people and now generally associated with blue-collar work.

We might also point out, however, that a number of large, progressive firms have abandoned the hourly wage for blue-collar workers and have instead put these workers on an annual salary—for example, IBM. In a sense, IBM has decided to treat blue-collar labor as a capital cost, paying for labor on the same basis it pays for capital equipment. Thus payment is made irrespective of the degree of use of the instrument or the amount of its production.

This may be possible for organizations in rapidly growing industries, but for most manufacturers, labor is so important a cost in their product that they are loath to take this kind of risk.

FORMULATING WAGE POLICY

Any wage structure must flow from a policy, and this policy must be consistent despite the often conflicting demands of internal equity and external competitiveness. In terms of external competitiveness, the primary aim, of course, is to establish wage levels high enough to attract and retain the skills necessary to operate the business, but not so high that labor costs drive up production costs to the point where the company is unable to compete in the product marketplace. Depending on its specific situation, a company may formulate its wage policy to compete with:

1. Community wages. The company may choose to pay the going rate in the community or higher than the going rate or, if it can make economical use of marginal workers, lower than the going rate.
2. National rates, as in the railroad industry.
3. Regional rates, as in the brewing industry.

In defining the work force marketplace in which it will compete, the company must consider how its workers and the labor market in general will react to its choice.

Some possible sources of information in determining wage policy are (1) other existing wage agreements, (2) government regulations, (3) union-management agreements, and (4) union policies and influences, especially regarding which payment plans and means of administering them will be considered acceptable.

In addition to expressing a company's competitive pay position, wage policy must be committed to preventing the "accordion effect."

The accordion effect, or wage compression, comes about when increases are given in fixed monetary increments across the board. What happens is that when general wage increases are expressed in so many cents per hour, over a period of time the cents-per-hour settlements will narrow the gap between unskilled and highly skilled workers, thereby destroying the internal pay relationships. To avoid the accordion effect and preserve existing relationships, wage increases may be expressed in percentages.

This phenomenon of compressing the wage rate has caused serious problems in the automotive industry, for both management and the union. Matters became so serious that the skilled workers were threatening to break away from the UAW and organize their own union. They were reconciled only when the UAW pledged to sign no agreement unless the skilled workers approved it as an independent voting unit.

DETERMINING ACTUAL WAGES

The problem of setting relative wages is subject to two contradictory forces:

1. *The equity sense of the job classification engineer.* The job classification engineer erects an internal value structure based upon a number of job vari-

ables applicable to the organization and then defines an equitable wage in accordance with the consistent treatment of these variables.

2. *The job market structure as viewed by the economist.* The economist is interested only in how many dollars the market is ready to pay for any wage. If tool and die workers are in excess supply, it will not trouble the economist that foundry hands who are in short supply may be momentarily receiving a higher wage than toolmakers. Obviously, we have exaggerated for emphasis. But nevertheless, from the market point of view, the important consideration is what the market commands rather than what engineering rationality demands.

The employer very often finds itself torn between these two considerations. The net result is that we may define five kinds of equity:

1. The job evaluation rate based on relative job content
2. The comparative rate for the same job in other industries in the same area
3. The comparative rate for the same job in the same industry in the same area—the local industrial labor rate
4. The comparative rate for the same job in the same industry in other areas—the cosmopolitan industry labor market rate
5. The comparative rate for the same job in other industries in other areas—the cosmopolitan craft labor market rate

As an example, let us take a machinist and see the way the rate could vary. Suppose the rate for a machinist in the X automobile factory in Speedunk is $10.25, whereas the rate for a machinist in the Y textile machinery works in Speedunk is only $9.85. Again, the machinist's rate in the rival Z automobile factory in Speedunk is $10.40, whereas the machinist's rate in the M textile works in Podunk is $10.30. Thus for the single job of machinist, we have several different rates, any one of which can be justified according to some concept of equity. Collective bargaining is the common method used to satisfy both labor and management that there has been equitable consideration of both the going rate for the job on the outside and its evaluated position in the internal job hierarchy.

External Consideration   Survey information can be helpful in establishing a fair and equitable measure for paying comparable wages for comparable work on the local level. A company may collect data by conducting its own survey, or it may wish to use data collected through:

1. The Bureau of Labor Statistics (Bureau of Labor Statistics Annual Regional Wage Data)
2. National and local trade associations set up to collect these types of data (e.g., local survey groups, chamber of commerce, and/or other trade association groups)
3. Other government agencies, such as state labor departments
4. Research agencies, such as the Conference Board
5. Union agreements and/or union surveys

Since the work content of jobs with the same title will vary considerably from company to company, it is best to build a survey around task groupings, or functions—for example, the paint shop or the machine shop—and compare similar jobs within the task groupings. (See Figure 1.)

FIGURE 1   Task Groupings

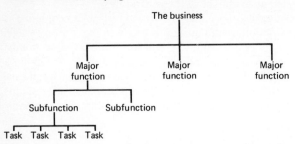

In conducting a survey, management must first decide which task groupings or jobs are key occupations in its particular labor market. These jobs are also called "benchmark jobs" and are defined as jobs that have stable content and skill requirements (also educational, training, or apprenticeship requirements, etc.) wherever they are found in industry. Some examples of benchmark jobs are tool and die maker, electrician, and janitor. A benchmark job generally should represent a significant number of employees. All other jobs are slotted into an internal hierarchy between the top- and bottom-rated key jobs. Methods for doing this are discussed later.

The going rate for any particular job can now be found by collecting data on applicable jobs (task summaries) by one of the survey methods mentioned earlier. The spread between the top and bottom of the remaining rates gathered from the various employers can then be considered sound and tested and can become the maximum and minimum of a bracket for a particular job in your area.

A good rule of thumb is to utilize only the middle 50 percent of the reported data. Therefore, a large enough sample must be used. The final outcome must be an intelligible and well-balanced wage schedule which is related to a carefully defined job classification. To derive this kind of classification, it is necessary to consider those factors which could influence the data, such as the reported base rate and its method of calculation, working conditions, personnel policies, fringe benefits, seniority of workers and their efficiency, and how closely the job description fits the factory under observation. Job descriptions that do not match up at least 75 percent should not be used. (See Figure 2.)

FIGURE 2   Determining the Going Rate

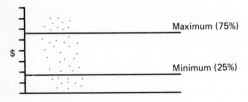

Job A

Note: *Dots represent reported wages for Job A.*

After the data have been collected, they should be classified and organized for analysis and comparison with internal personnel data.

Brackets are then established (1) by a weighted-average method in which the maximum and minimum are a fixed percentage above and below the weighted average, respectively, (2) where the rates actually paid cluster, (3) where the minimum rates cluster if the reporting companies have a bracket system already, or (4) some combination of the above.

There are several precautions of which to be mindful in using the survey method to establish hourly job rates:

1. The data must come from the local labor market area.
2. Only key or benchmark jobs can be compared directly.
3. In evaluating the data, one must consider the number and type of reporting companies and the number of employees doing the job in each reporting company.
4. The survey rates should be compared with the local factory rates with caution, since job content varies within the job title.

Internal Considerations   Job evaluation is a systematic method of appraising the value of each job in relation to other jobs in the organization. When applied consistently, it orders jobs into a hierarchy according to their relative contribution and provides a mutually agreeable payment for each job commensurate with its agreed-upon position in the hierarchy, regardless of the individual performing that particular job. The payment plan is based upon the theory that the more difficult the job, the more wage value the job comprises. It is important to recognize that jobs change over time, and that reevaluation may become necessary.

To evaluate jobs, the following steps must be taken:

1. Gather information about each job—identify the job, describe its duties and responsibilities, and specify the minimum qualifications necessary for a worker to hold the job. Optimally, tasks are grouped into logical packages which become the jobs under consideration.
2. Decide which factors are important in distinguishing the relative value of a job in relation to any other job (i.e., the "compensable factors"). The compensable factors should be present in all jobs in varying amounts, they should be important in the performance of the job, and they should be mutually exclusive.
3. Impose a logical value system on the jobs that forces them into a hierarchy according to the degree of compensable factors they possess. There are several widely used plans to determine the relative value of jobs—for example, the American Association of Industrial Management (formerly the National Metal Trades Association) plan, which considers 11 factors. (See Chapter 13 for a discussion of the AAIM system of job evaluation.) Eugene Benge and his coworkers developed a factor comparison plan with as few as five factors, which is discussed in Chapter 12. Other commonly used methods of job evaluation are ranking and job classification, covered fully in Chapter 8, and point systems, discussed in Chapter 11.

In determining relative job payments, other factors besides job evaluation will be influential:

1. Stability and duration of employment
2. Career aspects of the job; i.e., how high does the promotional sequence climb?
3. Market supply or demand for specific occupations
4. Traditional wage and factory social relationships
5. Working conditions, which are considered more important today than they used to be
6. Critical role of the job as a bottleneck

Influence of factors other than job evaluation is seen in many situations. For example, the increasing wage demands of sanitation workers in some cities have led to increased demands from teachers. Sanitation workers' wages were exceeding those of beginning teachers. The sanitation workers felt their demands were justified by the unpleasantness of their work and the critical need for the work to be done on time. It does not take long for a city to be buried in filth and threatened with disease when garbage remains uncollected. On the other hand, the results of a poor education for youngsters may not become apparent until years later when they are adults. Then again, teachers may look forward to a career as a principal or a superintendent. The sanitation worker is unlikely to go anywhere. In short, though a teacher must have at least four years of college, the sanitation workers insisted they were worth as much as beginning teachers because of the severity of their working conditions and the critical nature of the jobs they performed.

Another example of the influence of nonjob evaluation factors is in the building trades. Here, workers justify their high rates largely on the casual and seasonal nature of their employment. In addition, their union control over the size of the labor market through apprenticeship requirements enables them to take advantage of the law of supply and demand by restricting the supply of skilled workers.

PAYMENT

Payments of wages may be keyed to time alone or to expected production per time unit. The method for payment must be chosen early. Needs must be evaluated and the method that will work best for the establishment adopted. This is especially true in highly competitive enterprises where only a small difference in relative wages can destroy an otherwise advantageous market position.

Straight Time Payment   Wages may be keyed to time alone after a hierarchy of jobs within the plant has been established by job evaluation. The hierarchy may be developed simply by drawing a line from the top rate to the bottom rate and fitting all other jobs in between; alternatively, benchmark jobs can be picked and a trend line drawn on which to slot all the other jobs. (See Figure 3.)

The jobs may be covered by a single rate or a rate range.

Under a single-rate structure, each job or class of jobs in the hierarchy has one particular wage. Its advantages are that it is simple to understand and is

FIGURE 3   Establishing a Trend Line

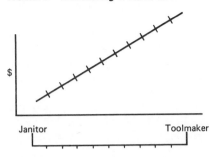

cheaply and easily administered. It works well for highly repetitive jobs having few skill requirements. It has the further advantage of limiting the possibility of supervisors playing favorites among the workers.

The principal disadvantage of single rates is that individual differences are lost, especially in highly repetitive operations, so that outstanding performance cannot be recognized. Also, because of this characteristic, nonmonetary motivators become necessary to increase output.

An example of a single-rate structure is shown in Table 1. Note that the relationship from job to job is determined by a varying increment that slowly increases as the structure climbs to rate 14, then increases more rapidly until

TABLE 1   Single-Rate Structure

Job or job class	Hourly pay	Percent increase between program steps
3	$4.655	
4	4.74	1.8
5	4.805	1.4
6	4.89	1.8
7	4.993	2.1
8	5.088	1.9
9	5.184	1.9
10	5.278	1.8
11	5.409	2.5
12	5.545	2.5
13	5.717	3.1
14	5.888	3.0
15	6.059	2.9
16	6.325	4.4
17	6.64	5.0
18	7.053	6.2
19	7.322	3.8
20	7.702	5.2
21	7.99	3.8
22	8.30	3.8
23	8.53	2.8
24	8.86	3.8
25	9.09	2.6

rate 20, when it slowly tapers off. This is only one example, and increments can be designed to fit every kind of taste, purpose, and union pressure.

A *rate range structure* can be either open-ended, i.e., $4.05 to $4.95 per hour, for example, or in steps, i.e., $4.05, $4.20, $4.35, . . . , $4.95 per hour. It is usually built around an appropriate single rate, e.g., $4.50 ± 10 percent. The spread depends on company policy or collective bargaining, and it can be expressed as a fixed dollar amount or as a percentage. Sometimes the bottom is what the job is allegedly worth. Payments above that represent performance, longevity, or a combination of both. Most often, however, the alleged value of the job is set at the midpoint. Everyone on that job can get to the midpoint, but above that, performance, longevity, union rule, or some combination determines the amount of compensation over time.

Just as single rates are consistently related, so are the midpoints of rate ranges. Movements within the range are governed by merit, seniority, or union rule, or some combination of all three. Unless the administration of the system is very sophisticated, all workers within a given range will be at the top of the rate over time. Furthermore, movement within the range is often subject to personal rate discrimination and is sensitive to differences in evaluators, supervisory or union, whose decisions as to work performance determine workers' wages. (See Figure 4.)

Sometimes a probationary rate is used. It is the minimum wage for a specific period of time after hiring or until work is satisfactory, after which time the incumbent receives the appropriate job rate.

Wage Incentive Payment   The incentive wage system presents essentially the same problem as does the time work wage system, and that is, How do you determine a base wage?

Determining the base wage for the wage incentive payment plan involves the same steps and problems that have been examined for the basic wage of the straight time system. Wage incentive payment plans in their application, however, do present certain problems.

First and foremost, if a union is in the picture, there is a subtle difference in philosophy of approach which if not explicitly expressed will be implicitly pursued. The original philosophy behind the wage incentive plan when it was developed by management was somewhat the following: The base time wage

FIGURE 4   The Rate Range

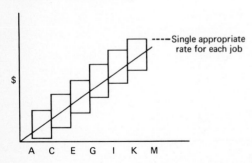

represents the payment of a fair day's wage for a fair day's work. Any excess work produced above this fair time standard is paid a bonus. Thus there is a subtle difference between the worker's involvement in the basic wage and the increment above the basic wage. This basic wage is paid to him or her as a matter of right; the increment above the basic wage, as a matter of performance.

This line of thinking will be rejected by the union. They will argue that wages can be paid either on the basis of the time that is spent or on the basis of the production that is achieved. If the choice is to pay workers in accordance with their productivity, then let the system be called "productivity wages" instead of a "wage incentive" payment plan. An implicit contract is entered into between the management and the worker, establishing a management obligation to furnish the opportunity for the workers to make a specified hourly wage at a normal working pace. The workers in turn obligate themselves to meet the production standard that is set.

Although the details of wage incentive payment plans are as various as the engineering authorities who use them, most plans will fit into one of three basic categories. In discussing these categories, it is assumed that the basic time for the 100 percent point is the same for the three systems.

First, there is the system which pays a worker less per unit for each unit turned out above the 100 percent point. Thus the worker receives less for the production above the 100 percent point than for the production below the 100 percent point. These plans will generally be rejected by the union. Or if the union is not in the picture, such a plan will probably serve as an excellent rallying point for any union that anticipates entering the plant.

In the second system, the worker receives more for production above the 100 percent point than for production up to 100 percent. These plans are to management's advantage when the overhead costs are heavy compared with the direct labor costs; the incremental cost of labor above the 100 percent point is more than compensated for by the savings in overhead. Usually, no union will object to this system. If there are any arguments, it will be over where the 100 percent production standard should be placed.

Then there is the straight piecework plan that pays a constant increment up to the 100 percent point and the same increment above the 100 percent point, and it is these plans that are most common.

In general, wage incentive plans are most useful in industries where individual workers exercise individual control over production speed. They do not make too much sense in factories where the worker tends an automatic process or where his or her speed is controlled by an assembly line. Here the worker's time is fixed by the speed of the line and the length of the work station.

Most of these plans are based upon standards which assume that a fully skilled operator is in the middle of working on a part with which he or she is familiar. If, as often happens in industries like the needle trades, runs of work change as often as two and three times a day, wide variation in performance over the entire workday is found. The reason for this may be time taken for learning a new part or, as the industry expression goes, time for getting your hand into the work.

It is not so much a matter of learning the work as it is a problem of regaining one's momentum as one shifts from old work to new work which, though done before, requires refamiliarization. In other words, the pace changes with every change of the psychological set.

Wage Increments   In addition to their basic wages—regardless of whether they are based on straight time or incentive methods—hourly workers generally receive extra compensation in circumstances specified below:

1. Overtime—usually time and one-half—paid for any hours worked beyond the standard day or week, and often double time on special holidays or Sunday
2. Late-shift differential—premium pay for hours worked on any shift other than the normal "day" shift
3. Call-back pay—guaranteed pay for a certain minimum number of hours if called back to work after completing a regularly assigned shift
4. Call-in pay—guaranteed pay for a certain minimum number of hours if called to work on a day one would not ordinarily work
5. Reporting pay—guaranteed pay for a certain minimum number of hours if the worker reports at the usual time but finds no work available

CONSIDERATIONS OTHER THAN BASIC WAGE

Fringe benefits—payments for old-age retirement, sickness, holidays and vacations, etc.—have become important for blue-collar workers since World War II. The principal item to remember in assessing the wage impact of fringe benefits is that their cost must be calculated in increments to the basic hourly rate.

Also to be considered in figuring wage costs are governmental constraints. For one thing, there is the federal wage and hour law, which provides a basic minimum wage. Revisions of the Fair Labor Standards Act, the Davis-Bacon Act for the building trades, and the Public Contracts Law develop various formulas for the payment of prevailing wages for work done for the federal government. These are basics which have not appeared from nowhere but are the results of organized labor's lobbying activities in the national and state legislatures. They are nonetheless important because the provisions may have great impact on hourly wages in both union and nonunion situations.

Finally to be considered is union influence. Administration of a wage program does not call so much for the mastery of endless technique as it does for the ability to live with tension. This tension governs whether a plant is union or nonunion. It has been said that the union seems to influence the nonunion plant even more strongly than the union plant. Wage administrators in unionized plants know exactly what their plans are after they are through negotiating with the union. Administrators in nonunion plants have to be able to anticipate that their particular formula will keep the union outside, and it happens quite often that it costs more to keep unions out than to let them in.

chapter 18

Establishing the Clerical Pay Structure

Lester N. Odams, Jr.

COMPENSATION CONSULTANT, GENERAL ELECTRIC
COMPANY, FAIRFIELD, CONNECTICUT

Philip S. Braun

COMPENSATION CONSULTANT, GENERAL ELECTRIC
COMPANY, FAIRFIELD, CONNECTICUT

A well-designed, symmetrical clerical salary structure must complement the job evaluation system being used if a successful program of salary administration is to be assured. A badly conceived structure, or faulty administration, will void the results obtained from the best job evaluation techniques. Many decisions are required during the construction of the structure, and the form of the final product should reflect the philosophy of salary administration of the organization's management.

The basic methodology utilized to establish a clerical salary structure is essentially the same as that used to establish hourly or professional salary structures. However, the nature of work performed by clerical employees determines the particular factors to be considered, and their weighting, so that the clerical pay structure itself may differ substantially from the structures for hourly or professional employees.

THE CLERICAL JOB HIERARCHY

Without some form of minimal job evaluation program, establishment of an equitable clerical salary structure is difficult, if not impossible. Without job evaluation, the structure would probably be merely a reaction to the market-place and individual managerial value judgments, with no protection from the internal salary inequities that would certainly occur.

A number of elements, other than those of a technical nature, have to be considered when designing the salary structure. The only real measures of the soundness of the clerical structure are, Will it meet the compensation needs of the clerical employees and the company and can it be economically adminis-tered, not only initially but also in the future? In other words, a cost-benefit analysis must indicate a preponderance of positive over negative factors if a given form of the structure is to be considered satisfactory.

Recognizing that individual managers and supervisors of clerical people will actually be administering the pay plan, of which the clerical structure is inte-gral, are these people knowledgeable enough to do so in an equitable, economic manner? No salary plan, no salary structure is any better than the manager's ability to administer it. Therefore, education of supervisors to sharpen salary administration skills may be desirable to maximize the operating integrity of the clerical plan.

Job Classification   In small organizations each clerical job may be different enough from other jobs to warrant separate pricing of the jobs. However, most firms have discovered that their clerical jobs may be conveniently grouped into levels of responsibility, difficulty, or other criteria. These levels are known as "job classes." Grouping jobs into classes reduces the number of pay rates which must be used for administering clerical salaries. This in turn reduces the administrative and economic burden of maintaining the salary structure.

Classifying jobs requires a decision as to the number of job classifications which will be established. Past practices of the company, number and types of jobs, and types of salary increases which the company gives will influence the number of classes in the job hierarchy. For example, if the hierarchy is extended to all levels of jobs—clerical, hourly, professional, etc.—the company would be required to construct more classes than would be necessary if only the clerical jobs were included. Having too few classes means that one classi-fication may be required to encompass several levels of difficulty and respon-sibility, whereas having too many classes makes it difficult to distinguish the jobs in one class from those in adjacent classes.

Union Considerations   A company will wish to consider the implications of a current, or potential, unionized clerical force in developing the structure. If sal-ary increases are contemplated using one of the varieties of merit—the concept of pay for performance—then the question of the extent and degree of union participation, current and eventual, is important. As a representative of employees, the union has a legitimate interest in the introduction of a new or revised clerical salary structure. It should also be recognized that the union can influence productivity either positively or negatively, depending upon the degree to which it supports the pay plan. Therefore, it is highly desirable that the management work with the union in the development, introduction, and administration of the clerical structure. Understanding and agreement con-cerning management's rights to determine the timing and amount of merit increases under the structure must be clear at the onset of the program, however.

Legislation Construction and application of the clerical salary structure are also impacted by both federal and state legislation—particularly the Fair Labor Standards Act, which set minimum wages, established overtime provisions, and included standards for exemption from the act. Title VII, of the Civil Rights Act, and the Equal Pay Act virtually mandate the need for a well-designed, clearly nondiscriminatory clerical structure as opposed to the random pay arrangements which may have preceded them. Specific application of these statutes to the job hierarchy means that jobs involving equal duties and responsibilities must be evaluated similarly without discrimination due to race, color, age, sex, religion, national origin, handicap, or veteran status.

The relatively recent concept of comparable worth, although still a theory and as yet undefined, will also receive consideration in both the design and administration of any clerical structure. While the primary impact of this concept is in the area of job evaluation, should it come to pass, there will obviously be a secondary effect on the hierarchy of jobs.

Maintaining the Job Hierarchy Once a job hierarchy has been designed, it is necessary to classify accurately all the employees who fall within it. After the hierarchy has been installed and employees classified, periodic checks should be made to ensure that each employee's job classification is appropriate to the work he or she is doing. A hierarchy is valid and effective only as long as employees are properly classified. Having a great number of improperly classified employees severely limits the usefulness of the hierarchy and may even cause a morale problem.

PRICING THE STRUCTURE

When the ultimate form of the job hierarchy has been established and, through the process of some type of job evaluation, the jobs have been grouped into pay grades or ranges that stand in an equitable relationship, one with another, it is necessary to examine the relationship between current rates and those of the labor market.

The Labor Market and Salary Survey The labor market for clerical salary jobs differs both in nature and extent from the market for either hourly production and maintenance workers or jobs of a managerial or professional nature, the latter ordinarily being of national scope. Many clerical jobs cannot be adequately related to a local labor market because of their nature: they may be almost unique to a given organization and thus be precluded from community comparisons. The clerical market rate survey must include only those jobs for which reasonably similar counterparts are known to exist in other organizations.

A rate survey based only upon like or similar titles existing in other organizations is almost certain to be faulty. Also, the greater the technical, as opposed to the routine, clerical content of any job, the more difficult it is to relate properly to other jobs in the community. The job content, education and training background needed, and, frequently, the job's position in the organizational hierarchy must be addressed for all jobs in the survey if valid comparisons are to be made. Obtaining and correlating this information can be very time-consuming but necessary if the survey is to be a reliable measurement.

Fortunately, it is not always necessary to undertake the task of designing and conducting a survey. A number of regularly conducted, usually well-designed, area surveys of clerical rate data exist and provide reliable information; among them are the Administrative Management Society surveys as well as the Standard Metropolitan Statistical Area (SMSA) surveys of the Bureau of Labor Statistics. Use of these, as well as of surveys made by other employers in the area, may eliminate the need of a company to conduct its own survey, but the cautionary points made above relative to matching job content should be observed even then.

Using Survey Data   Survey rate data should be compared with internal rate data. The importance to the organization of deviation from market rates must be weighed carefully. How much deviation is permissible before the organization experiences major attraction, retention, and morale problems if its current structure is on the low side? At what point does it become too costly and economically unsound if it should be on the high side? The problem of attraction and retention of qualified clerical employees is not the same for all jobs, and common sense would seem to dictate that the entire structure need not be redefined because of minor conflicts between the organization rates and those paid by other employers in the marketplace. Adjustment to individual job evaluations that are in full accord with the job evaluation plan simply because the evaluated rates are somewhat higher or lower than those paid elsewhere in the community may invite later trouble.

Accommodating Differences   How may a situation be resolved wherein the evaluation of a particular job, or job cluster, is felt to be sound, yet the resultant rate is such that qualified people cannot be attracted or retained? Some job evaluation plans contain a factor, variously titled, that will accommodate this situation by allowing added points as necessary to move the job or jobs higher in the hierarchy so that qualified applicants may be attracted. This approach, which obviously dilutes the equity of the overall evaluation plan, generally is not recommended as it has two major failings: the attraction-retention problem may not be permanent and it is difficult to limit the approach to those jobs for which it may be genuinely needed; there will always be pressure to include other less worthy jobs in this "points-plus" grouping.

A better approach would seem to be to exclude altogether certain jobs, or job clusters, from the evaluation and conversion to range. While their individual point values, arrived at under each factor of the evaluation plan, may continue to be used as guides in the evaluation or revaluation of other jobs, it should be conceded that their market value simply exceeds the salary structure value into which they would normally be placed. If the attraction-retention situation should change, this concession may later be withdrawn.

Management Philosophy   Management's approach to salary administration will largely determine the relationship between the company's clerical salary levels and the clerical salary market. This approach could be called management's "salary philosophy." Specifically, a clerical pay structure must attract and retain the caliber of employee desired at minimum expense to the company. The expense aspect of salaries will influence the perspective from which management evaluates the many factors which determine clerical salary levels.

The caliber of the employee desired will influence the level at which a company places its clerical salaries. If the organization seeks to recruit employees with better-than-average qualifications, it may have to sustain higher salary levels than would be necessary if it were willing to accept employees with average capabilities. Some companies have determined that for the lower-level clerical jobs which require little investment in training, a higher turnover rate is more financially advantageous than are the higher salaries necessary to prevent rapid turnover. This does not argue for a total structure which has rates substantially below those paid by other employers in the community. It does suggest that "key" people, people whose work effort is essential to the health of the business, will generally be found in the upper ranges of any salary structure.

Management must also consider the availability of the clerical employees whom it desires to hire. Higher clerical salary levels may be required to compete in an area where the potential supply is not equal to the demand. In areas where there is a surplus, overall salary levels might be set lower.

The preceding is representative of considerations needed by management to establish clerical salary levels suited to the company's own situation. At any particular time, social, political, and economic conditions may cause changes in the relative importance of one consideration over another and may introduce others. However, the salary levels ultimately established will be a direct result of managerial priorities in meeting the needs of the business.

MAINTAINING THE CLERICAL STRUCTURE

The structure which has been established and priced may be affected by one or more different occurrences: automatic cost-of-living adjustment (COLA) increases, general increases achieved by collective bargaining, a decision by management to increase (or decrease) the structure rates based upon its assessment of labor market conditions, the current economic status of the company, or other factors. COLA payments may be included in the structure rates, or they may be allowed to "float." In the latter case, those benefits which are based upon the structure rate would not automatically rise with each COLA payment.

If the original shape and symmetry of the structure are to be maintained, it is necessary that structure adjustments be made by percentage application rather than in flat dollar amounts. Adjusting the structure at all levels by the same dollar amount would eventually lead to serious compression between the lower and the higher portions of the structure. This would require "special" adjustments to the higher end in order to restore appropriate rate differentials. Unfortunately, the need for these special adjustments usually becomes evident only after serious attraction-retention problems develop and employee morale may have been damaged.

INDIVIDUAL PAY RATES

Once management has established the job hierarchy and determined at what levels the company will place its clerical salaries, it has the foundation of a clerical pay structure. However, it must now consider the manner in which rates will be determined within the structure.

Single Rates   This is the one-rate system where everyone on the same classification who has attained job proficiency receives the same rate. It is the simplest, least time-consuming method of all and is basic to most hourly pay industrial plans. The system is valid but cannot reward individual differences in performance. It is therefore limited to clerical jobs of a lower level where there is ordinarily little room for individual performance variation.

Rate Ranges   If some recognition of individual differences in contribution is desired, a salary rate range will be necessary. The rate range will establish a minimum and a maximum salary rate to be paid each evaluated classification with a job rate which may, or may not, correspond to the range maximum. In the rate range an employee in a given classification moves from the minimum rate for the range through intermediate steps toward the maximum rate. If the job rate has been selected as the range maximum, achievement will usually depend upon sustained, fully satisfactory performance. If additional steps beyond the job rate up to the maximum rate of the job have been designated, they will ordinarily be reached only by varying degrees of sustained superior performance.

Progression Increases   As opposed to the concept of merit increases, progression increases are usually automatic and scheduled at predetermined intervals, ordinarily one-month, three-month, six-month, or annual ones or some combination of these intervals. This is only a slight variation of the single-rate system wherein all individuals who remain in the particular classification would reach the job rate, or the range maximum, over a given time span. Although increases under this system are usually automatic, provisions may exist for withholding increases to those individuals who are not progressing satisfactorily and for speeding up increases to those achieving earlier proficiency. To the extent that this is done, the progression increase system becomes a modified merit plan. If time variation is extensively practiced, it could possibly be criticized by employees as only a pseudo-automatic increase plan without the capacity of a real merit plan to recognize and pay for superior performance.

Merit Increases   In principle, the merit system of granting increases cannot be faulted. It is really the only way in which individual differences in performance can be recognized and either rewarded or punished. Virtually all professional salary plans are merit plans, or contain strong elements of the merit principle. In the clerical salary area it is also the most equitable manner of compensating employees, but here it has certain administrative limitations that should not be ignored when contemplating its installation. Many managers are inclined to make small discriminations in salary treatment among individuals, regardless of perceived differences in performance. Their salary decision recommendations seem to be based on elements that should not intrude: length of service, employee future potential, and the like. There is some evidence that managers of clerical-secretarial employees are more prone to do this than managers of the more professional groups. Clerical employees perceiving such disparate treatment may find it difficult to relate pay to performance, and their motivation may be lowered. Also, it is axiomatic that the greater the payout against any COLA arrangement, the less enticement or justification there is for a company to adopt a merit pay plan. There are just so many dollars available for distribution, and if all employees receive a COLA payout, then the remaining dollars available for rewarding differing degrees of contribution will be reduced accordingly. These points are made, however, only to advise discretion. A full-merit plan, soundly administered, and supported by the employees involved, can be the most equitable method of granting salary increases.

Progression plus Merit   A salary payment plan may also combine the elements of an automatic, predetermined interval plan and the elements of a full-merit plan. Usually, this would involve automatic adjustments up to the job rate of the range (the fully satisfactory performance level) and merit increases beyond that up to the range maximum. With the need for careful managerial discrimination somewhat reduced because of the time-progression factor in this approach, the limitations discussed under merit increases would not completely apply here. Another, less popular approach is to grant automatic increases to employees in the lower classifications and merit increases only to employees in the upper classifications.

Step Rates or Open Ranges?   This question sometimes arises in the instance of a merit plan. Should a series of pay points within any given range be defined by fixed step rates, or should they be undefined, thus allowing for variation in amount of increase? An open-range plan would obviously facilitate granting differing amounts of increase to individuals in the same range or classification. The nature of the work covered by the structure will be a major factor in the decision. If the majority of individual classifications included are of an advanced clerical nature, closely approaching professional jobs in content, then an open-range approach may be appropriate and manageable. If, however, there are a large number of lower-skilled classifications, then the step-rate approach might be indicated. It is indeed an intrepid supervisor who will attempt to explain a difference of $3 a week to the lesser paid of two secretaries, both of whom have been on the job about the same length of time and have received almost identical performance appraisals!

SYMMETRY IN THE SALARY STRUCTURE

In the construction of any salary structure, proportion is important, and there are a number of individual, interrelated aspects to be balanced in the overall mathematical pattern. The rates within the structure must have a designed relationship to achieve balance.

Number of Ranges   The number of ranges in the overall structure will depend upon the percentage difference between the minimum and maximum rate in each range, the differential between ranges, and the total differential desired between the lowest and the highest classifications in the structure. Too few ranges will result in jobs with overly great evaluation differences grouped into a single range. If there are too many ranges, the salary administrator will constantly be called upon to show why a given job should not be included with those ranked one range higher or lower.

Generally, 8 to 12 separate ranges will be satisfactory on balance, but a basic rule is that the value of the jobs in each range must be distinguishable from those in adjacent ranges.

Range Spread   The width of the range may, or may not, be the same for each of the ranges making up the structure. In the instance of plans that contain merit elements and provide for payment above a normal job rate for superior performance, the nature of this superior performance must be examined. While the opportunity for top performance may be as great for jobs in the lowest-evaluated ranges, the resultant impact on the organization of superior performance could well be much less than in the higher-evaluated jobs. Many successfully applied clerical salary structures use a constant percentage spread for each of the ranges in the structure, usually 25 to about 40 percent between the minimum and the maximum of the range, depending upon the general work content involved. Other administrators have found that a series of ranges with gradually ascending percentage spreads have better met their needs in rewarding superior performance in the higher-evaluated levels.

There is an additional advantage to a structure of salary ranges with gradually increasing percentages: if a company frequently follows a practice of promoting from the higher ranges of the clerical structure into lower exempt professional or managerial levels, the transition from one structure to the other is facilitated. In other words, the upper ranges of the clerical structure could be integrated with and become a downward extension of the professional structure.

Normal Performance Point in the Range   Most salary range plans that provide for some form of payment above job rate for superior performance establish the approximate middle of the range as the normal, fully satisfactory performance point of payment. This is the rate which could be used for survey purposes as a basis of comparison with the rates of other employers of similar skills in the local labor market. In the plan, less-than-satisfactory performers, or performers still in the learning mode, would be paid below this point. The upper half of the range would then be used only to reward the various degrees of more meritorious performance.

Dollar Differentials   To avoid eventual range compression resulting in the possible need for special adjustments at the upper end of the salary structure, two elements must be considered. The difference between the normal point in contiguous ranges (the vertical factor of the structure) and individual range spread increments (the horizontal factor of the structure) should be designed to rise on a percentage basis rather than by uniform dollar amounts.

Two basic factors support the geometric principle in constructing the salary structure. The first involves sound pay principles: in progressing through a range, the same dollar amount differential between each step and the next successive step in the range would of course result in a series of decreasing percentage increases. This is inconsistent with the idea of increasing reward for increasing worth. Also, employee perception of the fairness of any plan is essential if it is to succeed. If the dollar amount of increase granted a messenger and an executive secretary were to be about equal, confidence in the equity of the plan could be expected to erode rapidly.

Acceptable Percentages   The number of incremental steps within each range and the width of the range will affect the difference between successive steps in the range. From an employee perspective, some studies have suggested that incremental increases below 5 percent seldom are satisfactory or motivative. On the other hand, percentage differentials greater than that, which may be necessary for motivational purposes, could result in overpayment for performance at each stage of the employee's progression through the range. This situation would generate to the company a significant cost that could have been avoided.

Range Overlap   Most salary structures provide range overlap. This means that a superior performer in a given range can be paid more than a newer or less effective performer in the next higher range, or even the one above that. This is a completely sound and acceptable practice, although it may require explanation to those employees paid under the structure who may only be familiar with the single-rate concept of salary administration.

The degree to which each range overlaps the next higher range, and is overlapped by the range immediately below, will primarily depend upon the percentage of spread in each range, the number of ranges in the structure, and the spread between the bottom and top of the structure. In those structures where the midpoint of the range is designated as the job rate, or point of normal satisfactory performance, and ranges are of equal width, 50 percent overlap is common. That is, the job rate of any given range would be equal to the minimum, or entry-level, rate of the next higher range. If there is to be a relatively large number of ranges in the structure, the overlap may have to be even greater.

Relating Job Evaluation Results   The type of job evaluation plan employed is not really material to the shape or form of the clerical salary structure. However, use of a quantitative method resulting in values expressed in points can be suggestive of the number of ranges appropriate for the structure.

Using the common scattergram, where dollar values are represented on the vertical scale and total point values on the horizontal, there seems to be a tendency for evaluated jobs to group themselves in rather narrow total point values as they move from the left (lowest point totals) to the right (highest point totals) across the scale. The dispersion and number of these groupings may provide some indication of the number of ranges that will be required in the completed structure. Usually a number of these scattergrams will have to be prepared and compared before optimum results are attained.

FURTHER CONSIDERATIONS

Pay Delivery   If the rates of a structure are adjusted, for reasons other than a COLA increase, and if no collective-bargaining agreement exists, management must also decide whether the new rate will be concurrently passed on or whether the new rate for each employee will commence at his or her next scheduled increase. Usually, if the ranges of the structure are made of step rates, the adjustment will be passed on to the employees concurrent with the structure change. In an open-range merit structure such an adjustment may or may not be immediately passed on, depending upon management philosophy. Some companies prefer to apply the merit principle and allow the structure increase to be earned through performance. This approach can only be successful, however, if employees understand that sustained good performance will gain them not only the amount of the structure adjustment but an additional increment as well.

Salary Planning   Many companies, who are extremely diligent in annual salary planning for employees paid under their exempt structure and who closely control labor costs through careful administration of their hourly structure, seem to regard the clerical structure as just another item of overhead akin to rent or the cost of office supplies. Today, with the significant rise in the relative numbers of clerical people and the resultant increase in cost of the clerical payroll, not giving the same attention to clerical salary planning as is given planning in the professional area is a mistake. There are significant cost-benefit advantages to the company in maintaining the controls imposed by salary planning for the clerical group, but such planning is very difficult in the absence of a soundly designed and administered clerical pay structure.

Auditing   Sometimes overlooked in the administration of the clerical structure is the need for a continuing audit program that will assure compliance with managerial objectives in compensating clerical people. In addition to periodic examination of the structure itself to determine if the salary rates are in a desired relationship to the local labor market, the audit should also examine current and actual job content vis-à-vis the content as previously evaluated. Jobs do change over time, with major elements of responsibilities increasing or decreasing in value, and these changes should be reflected in revaluation upward or downward.

There is often an unnecessary expenditure of many payroll dollars simply because the level of work currently performed differs from what the evaluated position description originally represented it to be. A company obviously should not be paying for a higher level of work than is actually being done. Not only is this costly, but employee morale may be involved. Employees are aware of the work that is being done by other employees and are quick to spot evaluation and pay discrepancies.

Faulty evaluation combined with poor administration of the best-designed structure can easily result in a company running afoul of current federal or state labor legislation. A well-designed and administered audit program will identify potential problems.

Managerial Understanding   It is not overstating the case to say that the supervisor or manager who will be using the clerical structure in administering employee compensation may well be the key to the success or failure of the plan. The manager of a clerical plan containing merit elements should understand that he or she must take the same impartial, pay-for-performance approach essential to the administration of the exempt pay plan. The quality of this administration could very well be a factor in the measurement of his or her own job performance.

COMMUNICATION

The need for effective communication before, during, and after the development and implementation of the clerical structure cannot be overstressed. Initially, management philosophy must be made clear in order that the design of the structure and its administration may completely reflect the overall compensation policy of the company. Altering original intentions once implementation of the structure is underway can vitiate subsequent administration.

Once the structure is designed and its administrative procedures established and clarified, the managers using it and the employees covered by it must be equally informed concerning its operation. It is at this point that most communication failures occur. If either the managers or the employees do not understand how the structure is designed, or how it will operate, installation should be postponed until complete understanding can be assured. If a spirit of nonacceptance is prevalent, this must be overcome, or the program altered to accommodate the objections, before introduction. A perception that the company is simply imposing the structure on managers and employees alike will create resistance that would inhibit the successful administration of the pay plan.

Internal publications, bulletin boards, handbooks, and group meetings with individual supervisors are all of value in the communication effort. Questions raised by employees or their managers should be immediately and factually answered.

All communication outlets should be utilized to inform clerical employees and their managers that the company has a salary structure and administrative approach which is not only competitive in the market but will permit individual employees to achieve their full potential. The communication must be factual and designed to avoid unrealistic expectations in the employees' minds. Future disenchantment could invalidate much good work that was devoted to formulating the structure. Sell the program—but don't oversell it.

SUMMARY

A well-designed, intelligently administered clerical pay structure may take many forms—merit, timed progression, and various combinations of these—and still be successful. Central to its success, however, is the understanding of how it works and what it will and will not accomplish. Both managers and employees need this understanding, which can only be provided by a continuing program of communication, upward as well as downward. The individual employee must understand what is expected of him or her to produce movement horizontally through a given range or vertically from one range to another, by promotion to higher-valued jobs. The structure should stimulate the employee toward superior performance.

A prudent management will recognize that it is much easier to develop and install a new clerical structure than it is to get rid of one that has not lived up to its expectations. They will develop a comprehensive compensation philosophy and will then carefully measure each aspect of any proposed structure against this philosophy to attain the complete spectrum of compensation objectives.

BIBLIOGRAPHY

Belcher, David W.: *Compensation Administration*, Prentice-Hall, Inc., Englewood Cliffs, N.J., 1974.

Henderson, Richard I.: *Compensation Management*, Reston Publishing Company, Inc., a Prentice-Hall Company, Reston, Va., 1976.

Kennedy, Dennis S., and H. Paul Abbott: "Establishing the Clerical Pay Structure," in M. Rock (ed.), *Handbook of Wage and Salary Administration*, 1st ed., McGraw-Hill Book Company, New York, 1972.

chapter 19

Establishing the Exempt and Management Pay Structure

George P. Whittington

MANAGER, EXEMPT JOB EVALUATION, THE DOW
CHEMICAL COMPANY, MIDLAND, MICHIGAN

Preceding chapters have covered the collection of necessary data to understand jobs and the subsequent process of measuring jobs in relation to one another. There has been discussion about obtaining and using information derived from surveys. Chapters 16 through 18 provided information on determining wage and salary policies, which are necessary before a pay structure can be established, and on establishing hourly and clerical structures. This chapter continues the discussion of pay structures and focuses on the development of structures for exempt and management personnel.

We will review the considerations basic to establishing the structure, cover the mechanics of establishing the structure, discuss maintaining the structure, and mention some important aspects related to exempt and management pay structures.

CONSIDERATIONS BASIC TO ESTABLISHING THE STRUCTURE

Several decisions must be reached before exempt and management pay structures can be designed. These include pay policy, the number of structures, and whether a pay line or salary grade structure is to be used. Another consideration is the relationship of the exempt and management structure to the nonexempt structures.

Salary Pay Policy   In the area of the exempt and management pay structures we have one of the same concerns that was discussed for production, maintenance, services, and office jobs. That concern is for pay policy. Anyone constructing a pay structure must know how management wants salaries to compare with those of competing companies. The answer must also delineate which employers are considered to be competition.

Number of Pay Structures   The question of number of exempt and management structures relates to the degree to which an organization is diverse geographically, internationally, and in lines of business. Management philosophy is also a determinant. An organization which operates in one geographic area and in one line of business will find the answer relatively easy. However, in international companies and in the case of mergers or acquisitions involving other businesses or other industries, the need for multiple structures must receive more attention.

There are more reasons for adopting one unified structure in the exempt and managerial areas than in the area of nonexempt jobs. The nonexempt jobs are generally oriented to the local labor market. Exempt and managerial jobs are oriented to a national labor market. College recruiting for professional talent tends to be national in scope, and hiring rates for a particular discipline are relatively uniform throughout the country. Professional and managerial search firms look for candidates on a broad geographic basis. Exempt and managerial employees are comparatively mobile, and some are willing to relocate for an advanced position or a similar job with an increase in compensation.

When an organization operates internationally, it almost certainly means increasing the number of structures. It is expected that there will be the necessity for a separate structure for each country. Then it is likely that it will be desirable to have a salary structure for the nationals in each country and a different one for expatriates to maintain their compensation in line with their home base.

Suffice it to say at this point that the question of the number of pay structures cannot be taken lightly. Research and discussion with other compensation people who are operating in the same businesses or countries will provide background helpful to the decision.

Type of Structure to Be Used   There are two types of pay structures in general use today for exempt and managerial jobs. We will refer to one as a salary pay line structure and the other as a salary grade structure. Their concepts have been described in earlier chapters (though perhaps by different names), but we will review them briefly. The pay line structure is a continuous structure. If two jobs have evaluations with only a one-point difference, each will have a different salary range minimum and maximum. With the salary grade structure, ranges of job points are grouped together, and all jobs falling within a particular range of points have the same salary range minimum and salary range maximum. There are two schools of thought on which of these approaches provides the best type of pay structure for exempt and managerial jobs. It is believed that both types can be administered well and provide excellent results.

We will discuss some aspects of each approach. With the salary pay line structure, it is necessary to establish the change in job points that constitutes a promotion (qualification for considering a promotional salary increase). Is it an increase in job points of 5, 10, 15, or what percent? Once the percent point change to warrant promotion is established, another area must be watched.

The job evaluator or job evaluation committee must guard against real or imagined pressures from supervisors or managers or against subjective tendencies when reevaluating jobs. There will be many cases where a few less points would mean that a promotion for the incumbent would not be considered. There will be as many other instances where a few more points would mean that a promotion could be granted the job incumbent.

Advocates of a salary grade structure (which is based on a job evaluation system) believe that evaluations are judgmental and not as precise as a single point value placed on a job would seem to indicate. Thus if you group jobs by ranges of points into salary grades, you may have a more equitable pay structure than with the salary pay line structure. In any event, the situation with regard to job evaluation and promotions is similar to that discussed under the salary pay line structure. With salary grades it is usually the practice to consider a promotion when an incumbent's job points change enough to place the individual in a higher salary grade. Now, you might have, as an example, the situation where 350 points is the top of the range of points for Grade 10, and 351 points is the bottom of the point range for grade 11. One point in the evaluation of the job determines whether or not there is a promotion.

Whichever type of structure is chosen, it is necessary to set down administrative practices and to live by these practices for the sake of equity.

Relationship to Other Structures   There is another consideration that deserves mention. The design of an exempt and managerial pay structure must relate appropriately to wage and nonexempt salary structures in the organization. Also, in doing this the impact of overtime paid to the hourly or nonexempt jobs must be taken into account. In most organizations there are some exempt jobs where candidates are promoted from the wage or nonexempt salaried groups.

MECHANICS OF ESTABLISHING THE STRUCTURE

A method of constructing the exempt and managerial pay structure will now be discussed. Computer design of the structure is included in the discussion. Then an approach to building a pay-for-performance system into the pay structure will be described.

Developing the Pay Structure   Probably the most accepted method of designing the pay structure is to plot a scattergram. Job evaluation points for each job are plotted against actual salaries paid to incumbents of each of the jobs. A line can then be drawn on the plot to depict the line of best fit. This line can be developed by "eyeballing" the plot, or a "least squares" line can be calculated mathematically.

A scattergram as described is shown in Figure 1. Each cross on the chart indicates the job points and the salary presently paid to one incumbent. The completed scattergram therefore represents the plotting of the total exempt and managerial group of employees. The best fit or least squares line is the current pay line.

When the current pay line is developed, the next step is to determine whether it is an adequate pay line upon which to build the pay structure. This determination is based on salary surveys and the organization's salary pay policy. Salary survey data can be used to relate the pay in the organization to pay in other companies. The comparison should be made using key jobs at different pay levels in the organization. For a complete picture two comparisons should be made. First, average salaries actually paid to incumbents in each of the key jobs should be compared with the average salaries paid by the other companies to their employees in each of the key jobs. Second, there should be a comparison made between the organization's pay line and the pay lines of the other companies. On the basis of information derived from these comparisons and the salary pay policy of your company, a pay structure line can be established at the level your organization wants to pay. An example will be helpful: The salary pay policy of the organization is to be 5 percent above the average of the companies surveyed. The salary survey shows that the organization's current pay line is 3 percent below the survey average at 200 job points and 5 percent below the survey at 500 points. Thus to establish the salary pay line where the organization wants it, a new pay line must be drawn or calculated which is 8 percent above the current pay line at 200 points and 10 percent above the current pay line at 500 points. This new line becomes the pay structure line.

From the pay structure line salary ranges can then be developed for either a pay line structure or for a salary grade structure. The pay structure line developed represents the midpoint of the salary ranges. The question now becomes, "How much spread is desirable from the minimum to the maximum of the salary range?" In other words, we know now what we want to pay on the average,

FIGURE 1   Scattergram Showing Current Pay Line

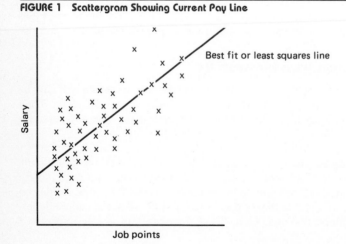

and we need to decide what is the minimum and the maximum salary for each job level. We will mention several ways this can be determined. There is no one right answer. It depends upon the circumstances and the thinking in the organization. Whatever the decision, it should be reviewed periodically for a few years to see that it is producing appropriate results.

It is generally accepted practice for the spread from minimum to maximum of a salary range to be greater for an exempt and managerial pay structure than it is for the wage or nonexempt pay structures. The premise for this is that the wage and nonexempt jobs are more standardized and, therefore, job performance varies in a narrower range.

One way of determining the range minimum and maximum is to set them in relation to the organization's present pay practice. The scattergram and current pay line developed earlier can be used to draw salary minimum and maximum lines. These would be drawn through the lower salaries at the various job point levels to produce the salary range minimums. The same process would be followed for the higher salaries at the various job levels to produce the salary range maximums. These ranges should be drawn or calculated in a manner that the current pay line is the midpoint of the salary range at any given job point level. An illustration of these ranges is shown in Figure 2. Since the minimums and maximums have been constructed on the basis of the current pay line, they then need to be increased by the percentages needed to bring them in line with the new pay structure line as described earlier.

Another way is to set the ranges based on information from the salary survey that was conducted. The survey data will show what other company minimums and maximums are for jobs you have compared. Also, a possibility is to decide you want a certain percentage spread from the minimum to the maximum of each range. Many companies today use a 50 percent spread from the minimum to the maximum of a salary range. For a 50 percent range spread at any given job point level, the range can be calculated by taking the salary at the pay structure line and applying a plus and a minus 20 percent. If the salary on the pay

---

FIGURE 2   Establishing Salary Ranges

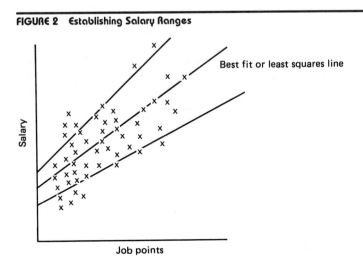

Best fit or least squares line

Salary

Job points

structure line at a certain job point level is $50,000, 20 percent of $50,000 would produce $10,000. The $50,000 plus $10,000 would give a salary range maximum of $60,000. Then $50,000 minus $10,000 would give a salary range minimum of $40,000. The net result is a salary range of $40,000 to $60,000 which has a 50 percent spread from minimum to maximum. To say it another way, the maximum is 50 percent higher than the minimum. Some companies use a larger constant spread. Others use a spread for beginning-level exempt jobs that continually increases throughout the various levels of jobs up to the top executive.

The foregoing discussion should provide good general direction for developing salary ranges. The final decision on the salary ranges to be used must necessarily be made in relation to the circumstances that exist within each organization.

Utilizing the Computer in Developing the Pay Structure   Using today's computer technology, the compensation specialist can accomplish quickly the task that can take days if done manually. With salaries and job evaluation points in the computer data base, a computer systems designer can develop a program which will compute the current pay line by the least squares method. The computer can print out the formula for the least squares line that is your current pay line. With a cathode ray tube (CRT) the scattergram and the current pay line can be displayed on the CRT screen. Further, with a printer connected, the scattergram and current pay line can be printed out, providing a hard copy with which to work. Further steps in developing the new pay structure line can be programmed or carried out manually. Once the new pay structure is developed, it can be programmed so that it also displays along with the scattergram. This is useful for analyzing current pay in relation to the new pay structure for either the total or part of the exempt and managerial payroll. It can be useful to examine the salaries of special groups, functions, departments, or certain geographic areas when this has been included as part of the program design. When the computer and printer have color capability, the salary structure can be programmed to display and print out in a color different from the current pay line or other data on the scattergram. The computer offers many useful opportunities in designing and maintaining pay programs.

Pay for Performance   Earlier in this chapter we noted that exempt and managerial employees have greater opportunity than do hourly and nonexempt salaried employees to be creative and show initiative in their jobs. Because of this, salary ranges need to be wide enough to properly reflect differences in job performance.

When structures are relatively narrow, it is likely that most people will reach the maximum over a period of time. The difference, then, is that the excellent performer will reach the maximum earlier than the average performer. The average performer will reach the maximum earlier than the below-average performer.

We have already observed that exempt and managerial salary ranges have more spread from minimum to maximum, and this is to provide more room to reflect individual performance in pay. There is still a problem that exists. The top performers in the lower exempt and managerial jobs are regularly promoted to larger jobs. Thus over a period of time many of these lower-level jobs will be filled by older employees whose performance has been only acceptable or somewhat better. This can be true throughout the structure, but it is more of a problem at the lower levels. There can still be the situation where, over a period of time, employees with different performance levels can reach the maximum of the salary range.

There needs to be some method of relating job performance to pay within the salary range. Job performance appraisal is of paramount importance. It is covered in Part D of this handbook. It is mentioned here to emphasize its importance in properly paying people within the salary ranges. In general, any performance appraisal system should be able to identify top performers, average performers, and below-average performers. The following example is one approach to relating performance to the pay structure: It could be established that top performers would be able to go to the maximum of the applicable salary range. The performance-level pay maximum for the average performers could be set at a point 85 percent through the salary range. Then for below-average performers, the midpoint of the salary range could be considered their performance-level maximum.

A system could be devised where available salary increases would be influenced by both performance and position in the salary range. This is a good technique in any organization, and it is especially helpful when instituting performance salary range maximums in a mature organization which has long-service employees high in their salary ranges. It has the effect of correcting for performance over a period of time rather than in a dramatic and more harmful manner to the organization.

The above approach to developing performance maximums was simply an illustration. The designer of the exempt and managerial pay structure must find an approach that will work in the situation that exists in the organization and that will be acceptable to top management. The important thing is to have an approach so employees are being rewarded in accordance with their contributions.

MAINTAINING THE STRUCTURE

Earlier in this chapter we pointed out that we might end up with one exempt and management structure for the entire organization. The alternatives were that we might have two or more structures for different countries, businesses, and geographic areas. We also indicated that the structures needed to be competitive and that surveys played a key role here. Once we have developed the structure, we must decide how to keep it up to date. How often it should be changed and by how much will now be discussed. Again, there is no one answer which fits all circumstances. We will cover factors that should be considered and give some possible answers. We will also take a look at supply and demand in relation to the pay structure.

When to Adjust the Pay Structure   The national economic climate probably plays the greatest role in this determination. With the rate of inflation we have had in the recent past, it has been necessary to adjust pay structures annually. In some countries in the world it has been necessary to adjust the structures even more frequently.

Generally, the change in the pay structure should take place at the beginning of the salary budget year. The change should be part of the compensation and salary budget planning that takes place in the months just prior to the start of a new salary budget year.

The Amount to Adjust the Pay Structure   There are a number of factors that must be considered in determining the amount of adjustment to an exempt and managerial pay structure. Some of these factors are external and some are internal. We will first look at the external market conditions which affect the amount the pay structure needs to be changed.

While it may not be controlling, one of the important external considerations is the rate of inflation. The change in starting salary necessary for adding new professional people to the organization is a second important consideration. Unless this is provided for, compression or inequities can result when new professional employees report to work and have higher salaries than employees with equal qualifications and longer length of service. An elaboration on compression follows later. Whether the salary test levels for exemption from overtime pay have changed is another consideration. The fourth and perhaps most important external check is how the structure compares with the structures of competing companies. Some companies design their pay structures based on their actual salaries. Others may not have as close a relationship between pay structure and actual salaries. This is mentioned to emphasize the necessity of obtaining both salary and salary range data when conducting salary surveys. Knowing the relationship between the two in each company surveyed is important to the decision as to the amount to increase the pay structure.

Before discussing the internal factors to be considered in deciding how much the exempt and management pay structure is to be changed, some discussion of compression is appropriate. The term "compression," as used in the compensation area, means that a lower pay structure, or at least the top part of a lower pay structure, has gone up faster than a higher pay structure. This alters what was previously considered to be the proper relationship between the pay ranges of adjacent jobs. Another meaning is that within the same pay structure pay has advanced at a faster rate to individuals in jobs lower in the structure than to individuals in jobs higher in the structure. There are two schools of thought on proper relationships between pay rates and pay structures. This refers to looking at the relationships on a percentage basis versus looking at them on an absolute dollar difference basis. It is well to discuss this subject and resolve it within the organization. Otherwise, it becomes a point of contention each time pay structure movement is considered.

There are several internal factors to consider in adjusting the pay structure. One of these factors is the amount that hourly or nonexempt wage or salary structures have recently changed. If they have not changed recently, then the amount they will change during the next salary budget year must be considered. The proper relationship needs to be maintained between the wage and nonexempt salary structures and the exempt and managerial pay structure. Thus the compression referred to above can be eliminated, or at least minimized. Another internal factor to consider is the organization's ability to pay. If business is good, then the organization's salary pay policy can be followed. In other words, the pay structure can be set based on how the organization wants to relate to structures of competing companies. However, if business is not that good, it may be decided to set the pay structure lower than it would otherwise be set. When this is done, usually this difference is made up later when business improves. Thus the organization's salary pay policy is maintained over the long term.

The final internal consideration we will discuss is closely related to the preceding one. It is the funding of the pay structure. Nothing is accomplished merely by setting the pay structure where we decide it should be. A fund or salary budget must be authorized for salary increases. This budget must be directly related to the change in the pay structure. Then when the salary increases are granted, the actual pay line moves to the level of the pay structure line (salary range midpoint line). Generally, it requires a salary-increase fund or salary budget of 1 to 2 percent more than the percentage increase in the pay structure line for the actual pay line to move to the pay structure line. The reason for this is that the organization's exempt and managerial group is not static. Employees, on the one hand, are receiving merit, promotion, and perhaps other types of salary increases. At the same time, some employees are retiring or there are terminations for a variety of reasons. Also, new hires are being added to the exempt group. The terminations of older employees at higher-than-average salaries and the employment of younger people at lower than the total group's average salary moderate the effect of the salary increases on the actual pay line. The degree of moderation will depend on the circumstances in the particular organization. A judgment in the 1 to 2 percent range can be made initially. This judgment can be measured at the end of the year. The next year's salary budget can then be set in relation to the first year's experience. Two or three years will provide enough experience to be able to calculate very closely the salary budget requirements to move the actual pay line to the desired pay structure level each year. We now turn to another aspect of maintaining the exempt and management pay structure.

Supply and Demand and the Pay Structure It can be expected, generally, in the exempt and managerial job market that supply and demand will be in balance between qualified candidates and job openings. There will be times, however, when this is not the case. When a scarcity of candidates in a certain discipline or specific professional area occurs and the need for these people is great, their salaries rise out of proportion to the general salary level. Likewise, salaries do not move up as fast as the general salary level when there is an oversupply of candidates in a particular job field. These situations where supply and demand are not in balance must be handled in a manner that will not be detrimental to the pay structure or pay system.

Where there is an oversupply in the market, an organization has the choice of continuing to pay new hires in that field at the rate at which the job evaluates or of paying them at the lower market rate. If the answer is to pay new hires in this field at the market rate, a depressing effect on the pay structure can be built into the compensation program. This may be a small enough group that the impact on the total pay structure is not significant. Where the group is significant enough to have an impact in time, and even where there will be no impact, one way to handle the situation is to pull the group out of the general salary structure. A special salary structure can then be designed for it.

The same approach can be taken for a group or groups where salaries have increased faster than the general pay structure. Special salary pay structures can be designed for these jobs also. See Chapter 49.

This approach to these out-of-balance supply and demand situations avoids any possible distortion to the general pay structure. Also, it keeps these situations in a highly visible position. Thus they will receive the proper attention and action to bring the salaries back into line when supply and demand are again in balance. There is the problem that increasing the number of pay structures complicates the compensation program. However, when the compensation program is computerized, these situations can be handled with relative ease.

We should strive to maintain the award of job points on the basis of content, in order to preserve the integrity of the job evaluation program. In those cases where market conditions demand high pay, then pay must be increased appropriately and a separate structure established. Job points should not be changed to allow higher pay.

IMPORTANT ASPECTS RELATED TO THE STRUCTURE

Three other items that are important to the subject of the exempt and management pay structure need to be mentioned. These are total compensation, special pay practices, and communications. We will discuss these items briefly.

Total Compensation and the Pay Structure   Preceding material in this chapter has dealt with base-rate or base-pay structures. It may be desirable, depending on the elements of the total pay program, to construct a total compensation pay structure. If the organization involved has little or no payment other than base salary, then the consideration is rather academic. However, if certain members of the exempt or management group receive significant monetary awards beyond base salary, the consideration becomes highly important.

Whether or not it is felt desirable to construct a total compensation pay structure, it is suggested that the organization's salary surveys cover total compensation if possible. Including total compensation in a survey or in a pay structure can be difficult. If each competitive organization involved paid people with only base rate and a cash bonus, the comparisons would obviously be practical and helpful. However, this is not likely to be the situation. Present tax laws allow the establishment of many different compensation programs. Some of these receive special tax treatment. In comparing total compensation the problem is one of comparing the value of a cash bonus with deferred stock, or with stock options, or with dividend units, or with some other form of special compensation. Even if a total compensation pay structure is not constructed, the compensation specialist will want to have knowledge of how the organization relates to competition in these areas of compensation.

Special Pay Practices   As we have just seen, the establishment of a pay structure does not require that all people within this structure be rewarded the same way. There may be many good reasons for trying to individualize the compensation treatment of many people insofar as this is possible and practical. We mentioned this may be particularly true for tax reasons. The higher the employees are in the structure, then the more difficult it is for them to realize appropriate aftertax income. For this reason, we may want to institute special pay practices which apply only above a certain level in the salary structure. In general, the percentage of incentive compensation to total compensation increases as job size increases.

It may be desirable for employees to participate in the decision as to how they are paid. Some employees might prefer all their income in current salary. Others might be interested in deferred compensation. When this is done, it becomes essential to ensure internal equity by calculating the dollar value of each specific practice or benefit.

Instituting special pay practices can create problems. The special treatment of certain people can cause hard feelings and hurt morale in the organization. It is necessary to be sure that the special pay programs will actually accomplish the desired results. Therefore, these programs should be thoroughly investigated and thought through before implementation. When improperly used, they can demotivate an organization. When properly used, they can both motivate and reward employees individually.

Communication   There is another important aspect related to the pay structure. The preceding material has been concerned with the mechanics and details of setting up and maintaining appropriate exempt and managerial pay structures. This is certainly a prerequisite for a successful salary program. However, a well-conceived and administered salary structure does not, by itself, guarantee a successful program. Perhaps the largest single factor in the success or failure of the administration of any salary structure is the communication necessary to get the job done. Presumably, a salary structure is ideal insofar as it maintains internal equity and the desired competitive relationship externally. At the same time, it can fail because no one really understands it or has confidence in it. Good communications are more important and more difficult to accomplish than anything else discussed in this chapter. See Chapter 60.

IMPORTANCE OF THE EXEMPT AND MANAGEMENT PAY STRUCTURE

In conclusion we offer a few final thoughts on the importance of the exempt and management pay structure. A poorly conceived or administered structure can do considerable harm to an organization. The future of any organization depends on its professional, managerial, and top executive staff. If the pay structure is poorly designed or managed, and if because of this the top performers leave the organization, the result can be very detrimental. If, on the other hand, the structure is well conceived and well managed, the result will be an exempt and managerial group that is more highly motivated than is true of these people in other organizations. This can give an organization an advantage of incalculable value.

chapter 20

Solving Technical Problems in Establishing the Pay Structure

Martin G. Wolf

SENIOR PRINCIPAL, THE HAY GROUP, PHILADELPHIA,
PENNSYLVANIA

This chapter assumes that the reader operates in a fairly sophisticated compensation environment where there is sufficient job diversity so that the organization is faced with a variety of different labor market pressures, perhaps somewhat contradictory at times. Within this setting, it is further assumed that there is a formal program of compensation administration, that there is a reasonably formal system of ranking jobs in terms of their relative contribution to the organization, and that accurate data exist on the pay practices of other organizations with which the organization must compete for the required talent. Should any of these facilitating administrative aids not be available, the reader is referred to the appropriate chapters of this handbook.

The comments and suggestions offered in this chapter assume an organization where management is free to use its best judgment in establishing pay rates for its employees. Thus the comments and suggestions offered do not apply to employees represented by a union, where wage rates are negotiated and defined by a labor contract. Further, the focus is on salaried, as opposed to hourly paid, employees, although some of the general principles involved would be the same with hourly employees.

Unfortunately, the problems of pay practice have grown with the inflation of recent years. Further, the market for employees, like many other markets, has become increasingly segmented. Thus pay structures have become more varied as employers have developed increasingly sophisticated methods to cope with the greater complexity of the labor market. The purpose of this chapter is to offer some practical advice on some of the rather technical issues which inevitably arise in the development and implementation of an effective pay system.

ISSUES IN ESTABLISHING THE PAY STRUCTURE

Once the job evaluations and the market rate information are at hand, and after the basic salary policy questions have been resolved, there still remains the step of establishing a system whereby specific dollars of pay are attached to specific jobs that are occupied by specific people. While many of the issues to be dealt with are essentially philosophical in nature, the philosophy that is applied has to be quite pragmatic. In finding answers that work in practice, it is quite important, however, to ensure that they have a logical conceptual base. An articulated compensation philosophy which guides one's practice provides a basis for treating recurring issues readily and consistently.

Grades versus Individual Job Ranges   The nonquantitative approaches to job evaluation, such as whole-job ranking or a grade description system, lead to clusters of jobs. With these types of job evaluation approaches, it is almost impossible not to group jobs into grades.

If a quantitative system, such as a point-factor or factor comparison approach, has been employed, the end result is a virtual continuum of jobs ranked by points. With these types of approaches, the pay structure can either develop individual ranges for each unique point level or jobs similar in points can be grouped together into grades. There are advantages and disadvantages to each approach.

The grouping of jobs into grades inherently abandons some of the precision of the quantitative job measurement method. That is, the job evaluation process identifies fine differences between and among jobs, resulting in differences in the points assigned to these jobs. Since all jobs in a grade are, by definition, treated alike for salary administration purposes, some of the ability of the measurement system to differentiate jobs is of necessity eliminated by the process of aggregating jobs into grades.

The reduction in the fine discriminations between and among jobs can be of administrative value, however. Particularly with nonexempt jobs, and to a lesser degree with the lower-level exempt ones, it is often desirable to be able to shift personnel back and forth between similar positions in differing parts of the organization. Because of slight differences between these positions as they exist, the job measurement system may assign slightly different point values to the jobs. The process of aggregating similar point values into a common grade can thus simplify the administrative process by allowing the free movement of personnel back and forth between the positions without any complications engendered by small shifts in the individuals' salary ranges as they move from one job to an essentially equivalent one.

A graded structure system also has an advantage where jobs are openly posted. Since most postings will attract a number of internal applicants, the salary range of posted positions quickly becomes common knowledge, even if the range itself is not part of the posting. Where jobs differ very slightly in content, and thus vary slightly in salary range, awareness of this difference on the part of an incumbent of a similar position to the posted one has the potential to lead to some dissatisfaction. In a relatively "closed" system, where job ranges are not normally common knowledge, the posting process can also lead to more openness about salaries than is desired.

The graded structure lends itself nicely to posting. The grade of the opening can be posted on the board, enabling applicants quickly to identify for themselves whether or not it represents an opportunity to advance. Similarly, the use of a graded structure can be of value in communicating an easy-to-understand policy on promotional increases so that employees can identify for themselves the rewards they are likely to reap if they assume the posted position.

As was suggested above, there are also some disadvantages to a graded structure. Unless one uses a very large number of grades, in which case the graded structure begins to approximate a unique salary range for each unique point level, the use of grades inevitably results in jobs of identifiably different job content being treated the same for salary administration purposes. For example, graded structures based on the Hay Guide Chart–Profile System of job evaluation generally use grade widths of 10 to 14 percent in job content points. Where two jobs are at the upper and lower extremes of a single grade, they can thus receive identical treatment despite relatively substantial differences in job content. Further, since a grade range is commonly based on the appropriate midpoint for the point level at the middle of the grade, all jobs within that grade but below the middle value will be paid somewhat more than they otherwise would be, while all jobs above that value would be paid somewhat less than they otherwise would be. While on the average this evens itself out, it is little consolation to the employees who are being paid noticeably less than their position otherwise would receive.

Of greater concern than the lack of pay distinction between two positions at opposite extremes of the grade is the relatively substantial distinction between two positions almost identical in job content that happen to lie on either side of the grade boundary. In the Hay Guide Chart–Profile System, for example, there are a variety of such occurrences, such as jobs evaluated at 393 and 396 points, 404 and 406 points, 464 and 466 points, etc. If one uses a logical approach based on a constant percentage grade width, it is almost impossible to create a graded structure encompassing jobs varying widely in job content without splitting (with a grade break) one or more of these natural job groupings. Inevitably, shifting the grade structure in terms of either its starting point or its percentage width to solve the problem with one such grouping will create a problem with another. It is extremely difficult to explain successfully to employees, or to an outside party in an EEO proceeding, why two jobs so close together in measured job content should receive quite disparate salary treatment because they happen to be placed arbitrarily in two different grades.

The choice of whether or not to employ a graded structure is a complex and difficult one. It is necessary to evaluate carefully the pluses and minuses of the graded versus the ungraded approach in light of the specific needs and pressures of the unique organizational situation. Items such as organizational values and history must be carefully studied. For example, some organizations have a long history of a graded structure. Where a new evaluation system is being employed, it might well be advantageous to translate that system into the familiar grades to ensure employee—and management—acceptance of the new process. Under some circumstances, however, just the opposite might be true, and it might be advantageous to break from the traditional graded structure and use individual ranges.

This is most likely to be true where the job grades are relatively public knowledge and where the reevaluation process results in significant shifts in the relative valuation of different jobs. Here the use of individual ranges can serve to mask the shifts in relative values by making the new relationships less conspicuous. For example, two jobs may historically have been in different labor grades. The new evaluation process may result in one being assigned a point value of 393 points and the one which historically had been in the higher grade being assigned a value of 404 points. Normally, two jobs so close together would be assigned to the same salary range if a graded structure were employed (though see the cautions above), thus making obvious a shift in the relative evaluation of these two jobs. The assignment of pay based on the unique points of these two jobs, on the other hand, preserves the tradition of the one being "higher" than the other, even though the resultant difference is much less than that required to be truly significant.

Job Rates versus Salary Ranges   Having determined whether to use a graded structure or an ungraded one, the organization must then decide the width of each salary level. Traditionally, certain hourly jobs have had a single rate. For example, it is not uncommon for all journeyman members of a craft to be paid exactly the same rate, either from their first day on the job or after a short probationary period at slightly below the journeyman rate. It has been equally common practice for salaried positions to have a relatively broad pay range. For lower-level positions, this has typically been about 35 percent from minimum to maximum, while higher-level jobs more commonly have a 50 percent spread from minimum to maximum.

In recent years, the traditional practices have broken down somewhat. In the hope of achieving greater productivity through greater employee identification with the organization, and not incidentally as a union avoidance mechanism, a number of organizations have put employees on salary in what traditionally were hourly paid jobs. In many instances, this has been accompanied by the initiation of a salary range, as opposed to a single wage rate or several step rates based on tenure. These salary ranges generally are part of a "merit" program.

While few companies have abandoned the policy of having a wage range for salaried employees, many have abandoned this concept in practice. As will be discussed later in this chapter, the rapid escalation of salary ranges from one year to another has caused many organizations to pay virtually all their employees well below the policy midpoint. Similar escalation has been at work in regard to the entry salaries for college graduates—which is among the problems addressed in Chapter 49. These forces have had the effect in practice of restricting severely the portion of the salary range actually used, resulting in something quite akin to a job rate despite an expressed policy to the contrary.

Given these issues, pragmatism suggests that the prudent salary administrator should think carefully about the size of the salary ranges used. Survey data should be examined carefully to determine how much variation in pay truly is needed to meet competitive practice. The analysis also should consider the effectiveness of performance measurement in the organization. If supervisors lack either the ability or the willingness to differentiate among employees in a given job category on the basis of performance, it makes little sense to provide them with a broad salary range. Similarly, if the average salary increase year after year is little or nothing more than the amount of the increase in the salary ranges, it will be impossible to move employees through a broad salary range. Under such circumstances, the availability of broad ranges is more often a negative from a morale standpoint than it is a positive factor. (In this regard, please see "The Problem of the Moving Target" in the next section of this chapter.)

Internal Equity versus External Competitiveness   As with the flag and apple pie, every salary program is foursquare behind both internal equity and external competitiveness. In today's world, however, these two desirable objectives are often incompatible.

Market forces ebb and flow in our economy. In response to these forces, the relative wages of certain occupations rise and fall vis-à-vis one another. In the late 1950s, the demand for geologists was so low that one of the author's friends who graduated in this discipline went to work for Sears, Roebuck. Twenty years later, the competition for geologists was so keen that the newly minted geologist could pick from an array of offers. Similarly, in the 1960s, many firms that would have preferred to hire a chemist hired a chemical engineer instead because they commanded a lower starting salary. By the early 1980s, the competition for chemical engineers was so intense that the new chemical engineering graduate was commanding a 30 to 50 percent premium over the newly graduated chemist.

While many other examples could be added, these should suffice to demonstrate the fickleness of the market. The company that responds appropriately to these external market forces does so at the expense of internal equity. For example, has the relative contribution of the chemist and the chemical engineer to any given company changed in keeping with the change in market pricing?

The salary administration process must cope as best it can as the irresistible force of the marketplace meets the immovable object of internal equity. While the solution is neither simple nor completely satisfactory, there is one basic principle which can significantly enhance the likelihood of success. That principle is to make explicit and fully identifiable the compromises with internal equity that are made in response to market pressures.

Adherence to this principle means the creation of special salary ranges for those positions which are repriced as a result of market pressures. Traditionally, most organizations have responded to market pressures by reclassifying their positions within the existing salary structure. Where grades are used, jobs have been upgraded. Where jobs are paid directly from the evaluation points, jobs have been reevaluated upward as a result of market pressures. In essence, organizations have used a job evaluation answer to deal with a job pricing problem.

The rub is that such solutions tend to linger long after the problem is gone. Further, these solutions tend to endanger the integrity of the job evaluation process. The upward evaluation of the market pressure position tends to result also in the upward evaluation of other jobs which are somewhat similar in nature but which are not subject to the same market pressures. The preferred solution is the assignment of the market pressure jobs to special salary ranges which are clearly designated as market responsive.

Returning to our example of the chemical engineer, let us look at a hypothetical organization which utilizes a graded system. In this organization, the job evaluation process places the entry-level chemical engineer at grade 10. However, the market price for chemical engineers is such that this organization would need to assign entry-level chemical engineers to grade 12 to be competitive. Rather than employing this reclassification, the organization would be better served were it to classify its entry-level chemical engineering position as grade 10M (for "Market"). By this means, the company can identify clearly, and quantify fully, the premium that it is paying as a result of perceived market pressures.

Unique Situations   Chapter 49 focuses on special compensation problems which may arise, requiring treatment outside the overall pattern adopted by the organization.

DEALING WITH INFLATION

In writing something which appears in a book, one is caught between the Scylla of wanting to be topical and the Charybdis of rapid change which may make the total discussion obsolete by the time it appears in print. Thus this discussion on coping with inflation is offered with some trepidation. While it is the author's fervent hope that this discussion be only of academic interest by the time this handbook is published, persistent inflation has been a pernicious enough problem in salary administration that it demands treatment here.

The Ravages of Time   In a period of inflation, it is axiomatic that all economic data are dated. Just as the topicality of this section is at risk due to the lead time in producing a book, in inflationary times, the lead time in producing a salary survey renders it obsolete even before it is published.

This fact renders it imperative that all salary surveys clearly specify the date of data collection. The salary administrator must then utilize this date in econometrically updating the salary survey data. To do this, it is necessary to identify the most probable escalation rate to apply for the period between the collection of the salary data and the time at which it is to be employed. This escalation factor can come from various econometric models, economic forecasts, special surveys, or simply the collective wisdom of those in whom the salary administrator trusts.

Whatever the source(s), this escalation factor can be used to move the salary survey data forward in time to the point at which comparisons are to be made. This is done by using the annualized escalation rate as the "percent interest" in any of the standard formulas for compound interest. (Those salary administrators who have not yet invested in a calculator which has a hard-wired program for compound interest should proceed immediately to their nearest discount calculator store.) The interval in years (or decimal fractions thereof) between data collection and the time at which the comparison is made is entered into the compound interest program as the "period." If 1.0 is entered as the "present value" in the compound interest program, calculation of the "future value" will yield the adjustment factor. This adjustment factor is multiplied by the actual survey data to move them econometrically to the time at which the desired comparison is to be made. Conceptually, this amounts to the calculation of x months' adjustment at a y percent annualized rate.

While the calculation of the update factor is quite straightforward (and relatively simple with a financial calculator), the choice of the time to which to update the data is less clear-cut. In updating salary survey data for salary policy purposes, there are three basic strategies one can adopt regarding the time to which the data will be updated. Figure 1 illustrates these three time-related strategies. The vertical axis represents the salary index, starting at 100. The horizontal axis is time, starting at T1 and continuing for three annual cycles. Alternative A assumes that the data are updated to the first day of the salary policy year, alternative B assumes that the data are updated to the middle of the salary policy year, and alternative C assumes updating to the last day of the policy year.

Alternative A constitutes an overstatement of the organization's true competitive level under any circumstance. That is, under this approach, the organization achieves its targeted competitive level only on the first day of the salary policy year. For the rest of the year, the organization falls progressively further behind its stated level of competitiveness.

Alternative B is applied appropriately in those organizations where most persons receive their salary increases at the same time, generally the beginning of the salary policy year. Under such circumstances, alternative B results in the

FIGURE 1   Three Alternative Time-Related Pricing Strategies: A, Chasing the Market; B, Matching the Market; and C, Leading the Market

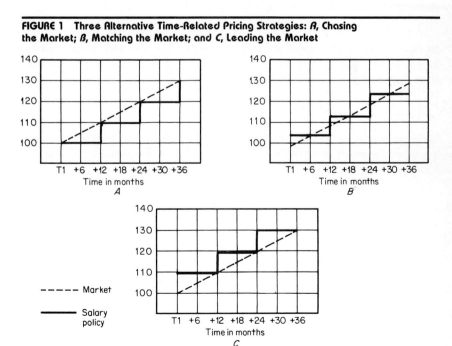

organization straddling its targeted competitive level, being somewhat above it for the first half of the year and somewhat below it for the last half of the year. Thus, on the average, the organization achieves its targeted level of competitiveness. However, if increases are granted throughout the year, alternative B somewhat overstates the true competitive position.

Alternative C is most appropriate where the organization grants salary increases on some sort of individual anniversary date, spread more or less evenly across the year. Under such circumstances, the organization will gradually "fill up" its salary policy throughout the year. As the organization's actual pay practice rises (through the granting of these increases) toward its stated salary policy, this rising practice will parallel the rising practice of other organizations and will thus track the desired competitive level.

The Problem of the moving Target   As virtually every salary administrator knows only too painfully, the rapid escalation of salary ranges from one year to another has resulted in many organizations paying virtually all their employees well below the salary policy midpoint. As outlined previously, a partial solution to this problem is the narrowing of the salary ranges, reducing the distance each employee has to traverse to reach salary policy midpoint. A fuller solution of this problem requires breaking the salary increase into its component parts. This enables the problem to be addressed analytically.

A salary range increase consists of two component parts: the range adjustment factor (RAF) and the merit increase factor (MIF). The RAF is the movement of the salary range, while the MIF is the movement through the salary range. A salary increase consists of the sum of these two components, plus their interaction or compounding. The formula is:

$$\text{Salary increase} = \text{RAF} + \text{MIF} + (\text{RAF})(\text{MIF})$$

In this equation, the salary increase, the RAF, and the MIF should all be expressed in decimal form (i.e., a 10 percent increase would be expressed as 0.10). Solving the equation algebraically to identify the MIF yields:

$$\text{MIF} = \frac{\text{salary increase} - \text{RAF}}{1 + \text{RAF}}$$

To illustrate, let us assume that the RAF is 10 percent and that a 12 percent increase is granted to an individual. Substituting in the equation to find the MIF, the result becomes:

$$\text{MIF} = \frac{0.12 - 0.10}{1 + 0.10}$$
$$= \frac{0.02}{1.10}$$
$$= 0.0182$$

That is, in the situation described above, the MIF granted the individual is 1.82 percent.

The implications of this type of analysis are eye-opening. For example, assume that this particular increase was granted to an individual at the bottom of his or her salary range. Further assume that the salary range is the typical exempt one of from 80 to 120 percent of salary policy midpoint. At this rate (RAF of 10 percent, salary increase of 12 percent, MIF of 1.82 percent), how long will it take the individual to move from the minimum of that range to the midpoint? Again, the financial calculator is useful. Returning once again to the compound interest program, enter the MIF of 1.82 percent as the "% interest," enter the present "compa-ratio" (or position in salary range) of 80 as the "present value," and enter the midpoint (or 100 percent compa-ratio) of 100 as the "future value." The calculation will reveal that it will take the individual moving at this rate 12.37 years to progress from the range minimum to the range midpoint.

Data from the Hay Industrial Compensation Comparison illustrate the problem:

Year	Average outstanding award	Average par award	Average midpoint change
1971	13.0%	7.0%	4.5%
1981	12.7%	8.8%	10.5%

In 1971, the typical "outstanding" performer received a 13.0 percent increase, almost 3 times the RAF, while the typical "par" performer got 156 percent more than the RAF. By 1981, the typical outstanding performer got 121 percent of the RAF, while the typical par performer lost ground—receiving only 84 percent of the RAF.

To solve the problem of inflation one must think in MIF terms. From this perspective, the salary administrator can work backward (from the allowable salary increase and the RAF) to determine the number of years it will take individuals to move through their salary range; can work forward (from the desired number of years to move individuals through their salary range and the RAF) to determine what the total increase must be; or can work sideways (from the desired number of years to move individuals through their range and the allowable increase) to determine how much RAF the organization can afford. (Reducing the RAF, of course, also reduces the organization's competitive level.)

COLA and Compression In recent years, many organizations in the United States, particularly those with unionized work forces, have had cost-of-living adjustments (COLAs) for their employees. In some cases, COLAs have been limited to hourly employees; in other cases, they have been extended to nonexempt salaried employees; in some cases, lower-level exempt employees have also been included; and, in a few instances, all employees have been included in COLAs. Except in the latter case, COLAs have resulted in salary compression. The differences in the extent of the group that received COLAs have resulted in the compression occurring at different levels in the organization, but the granting of COLAs to some employees and not to others inevitably has caused compression at the interface between the group that received COLAs and the employees who did not receive them.

The COLA-caused compression can be eliminated in either of two ways. One is to eliminate the cause of the compression by eliminating inflation, thus eliminating COLA payments. Unfortunately, this solution is beyond the control of salary administrators. The second method is to eliminate the symptoms of COLAs. This is done by making COLA payments (in a constant percentage, not an absolute dollar amount) to all employees. Unfortunately, such a solution is beyond the economic resources of most organizations.

Without one of these methods to eliminate the compression, the only response left to the salary administrator is to manage it. This can be done by tapering the COLA-related payments either to blend the reduction/disappearance of COLA payments in at those organizational levels where between-level pay differences are great enough to mask the effect of the COLA-caused compression or to move the compression to an organizational level where the dissatisfaction resulting from the compression is less likely to engender turnover. Such "solutions" are neither easy nor pleasant. They are, however, realistic responses to an unpleasant inevitability.

Further Discussion   See Chapter 65 for a further discussion of salary administration in an inflation-prone economy.

Appraising
Performance

chapter 21

History and Theory of Performance Appraisal

Jarold G. Abbott

PROFESSOR OF MANAGEMENT, COLLEGE OF BUSINESS
AND PUBLIC ADMINISTRATION, FLORIDA ATLANTIC
UNIVERSITY, BOCA RATON, FLORIDA

Fred E. Schuster

PROFESSOR OF MANAGEMENT, COLLEGE OF BUSINESS
AND PUBLIC ADMINISTRATION, FLORIDA ATLANTIC
UNIVERSITY, BOCA RATON, FLORIDA

Historically, few management problems have attracted any more attention than the effort to find valid, reliable, and practical ways to evaluate performance. This search has been marked by major shifts in the purposes and uses of the appraisal process and by significant refinements in the techniques. It is the purpose of this chapter to briefly summarize these developments in order to provide a perspective for evaluating the current status of performance appraisal.

HISTORICAL PERSPECTIVE

Robert Owens of Scotland developed the first recorded industrial system of appraisal around 1800. Later in the nineteenth century, a number of systems were developed for public administrators in the United States. For the private sector, the origins of appraisal have been traced to Frederick Taylor and his work measurement program.

Industrial growth in the 1920s led to increased formalization of the appraisal process. Some of the earliest formal appraisal plans employed either open-ended essay appraisals or some form of adjective checklist. Because these approaches lacked both objectivity and precision, the attention paid to psychometrics in the early 1920s led to the development of graphic rating scales. These scales employed a list of personal traits, but in addition the rater was required to judge the amount of each trait possessed by the ratee by marking a point on a graphic scale (or continuum) provided.

The human relations approaches of the thirties and forties led to greater emphasis on rating personality and behavioral characteristics of employees. Following World War II, the demand for qualified management and technical personnel resulted in a renewed interest in methods for assessing employee performance. Greater attention to more job-related characteristics accompanied the introduction of management by objectives in the fifties. And in the 1960s, the appraisal process was increasingly used to identify training and development needs.

By the seventies, performance appraisal had been formalized by most organizations, and significant changes in the legal environment had resulted in litigation regarding merit pay and promotion decisions. With this litigation came renewed concern about the subjective nature of the appraisal process and the need to make the appraisal process more valid and reliable. This intensified the effort to move away from trait-oriented appraisal toward job-related measurements, and toward techniques which recognized the "multidimensional" nature of performance. An example of this would be the development of behaviorally anchored rating scales (BARS). The experience with BARS was carefully studied to determine its effectiveness in reducing measurement errors and in providing a basis for identifying training and development needs.

Over the years, the continuing search for more accurate and practical appraisal methods has led to a variety of techniques, including such methods as the critical-incident technique, employee comparison (straight ranking, paired comparison, and forced distribution), and forced choice. Although not widely used, they are of interest and are discussed briefly in the next section.

ALTERNATIVE BUT LESS WIDELY USED APPRAISAL METHODS

Critical Incident Technique   In its simplest form, the supervisor is asked to record observations of an employee's behavior that are particularly good or perhaps need modification or improvement. Behavior which needs improvement should be amenable to change and should be related to mutually agreed upon objectives. These incidents become part of a "behavioral record" and provide the basis for appraisal. Despite its claims for more objectivity and reliability, the method is time-consuming and prohibitively expensive for many appraisal situations.

Ranking   For the "straight-ranking technique," the supervisor is asked to pick the best performer, second best, and so on until all employees have been appraised. The result is a list in order of high to low performance. A refinement of the straight-ranking technique is called the "alternative-ranking" method.

When using this approach, the supervisor first selects the highest- and lowest-ranked employees. These two are removed from further consideration, and the procedure is repeated until each employee has been ranked. Ranking techniques are desirable in that they reduce the tendency of many supervisors to give many of their employees the same rating. (The tendency to give very high ratings is called "leniency error," and the practice of giving most employees an average rating is called "central tendency error.") A major problem of the ranking technique is that differences in rank may either exaggerate or underestimate differences in actual performance. This creates problems for providing differential rewards for differential performance.

Paired Comparison   The supervisor compares each subordinate with every other subordinate to be ranked one at a time. The subordinate's final ranking is determined by the number of times he or she is compared favorably with another employee. Like the critical-incident technique, the paired-comparison method involves the very practical problem of getting the supervisor to take the time necessary to implement it properly.

Forced Distribution   The method is designed to force a normal distribution of appraisals around the average or mean performance of all members of the work group. The supervisor must assign each employee to one of several categories (such as low 10 percent, next 20 percent, middle 40 percent, next 20 percent, and high 10 percent). This method is deficient in that the distribution of performance within the work group may not correspond to that of the rating system.

Forced Choice   The supervisor is provided a series of statements about job behavior and is asked, Which statement is most descriptive of the subordinate for a particular job factor and which is least descriptive? The statements are designed to appear equally favorable or unfavorable in terms of a rating. Thus the supervisor is more likely to select the statement which is most descriptive rather than one which will result in a high or low rating. The method is advantageous in that it keeps indications of "favorability" off the rating form, yet it fails to distinguish differences in performance between individuals.

Unfortunately, the evolution of alternative approaches to performance appraisal has not been systematically studied, and a solid basis for developing a theory of performance appraisal has not been established. In 1978, DeCotiis and Petit observed the following cycle:

> A particular appraisal technique is first widely praised, then used and rejected, and subsequently replaced by a new more highly praised technique. As a consequence, the literature is a catalogue of performance appraisal formats, each with its assumed advantages, adherents, and critics. In the absence of assessed adequacy for the purposes of appraisal, it is difficult rationally to sort out, compare, and choose among available alternatives or to determine if development of a new format is warranted.[1]

---

[1]T. DeCotiis and A. Petit, "The Performance Appraisal Process: A Model and Some Testable Propositions," *The Academy of Management Review*, vol. 3, no. 3, 1978, p. 639.

All of this indicates the growing importance of performance appraisal and an awareness of the need to systematically review the purposes and methods of the process.

GROWING IMPORTANCE OF PERFORMANCE APPRAISAL

Changes in the work environment over the last 20 years have resulted in increased recognition of the importance of performance appraisal. Whisler and Harper have pointed out the following changes as significant:

1. Shifts in the occupational structure toward higher skills
2. Development of automation
3. Increasing size of organizations
4. Growth of unionization among the hourly work force
5. Increase in staff activities
6. Greater specialization in roles of organization members, combined with increasing technical education
7. Changes in the philosophy of management from scientific management to human relations, and then to quantitative decision techniques and overall corporate planning[2]

More recently, actions of the Equal Employment Opportunity Commission and subsequent court decisions have underscored the importance of accurate and objective records of employee performance in order to defend against charges of discrimination. All of this has led to increased recognition of the importance of performance appraisal and a corresponding awareness of the shortcomings of existing appraisal systems.

This awareness has resulted in an increase in empirical studies of the appraisal process and a concern for strengthening its theoretical foundations.

THE THEORY OF PERFORMANCE APPRAISAL

For many years, researchers and other students of performance appraisal have attempted to determine what methods are being used, why they are used, and to suggest what methods ought to be used. They have sought to answer such questions as:

What should be appraised and by whom?
When and how often should performance be appraised?
What are the sources of error in the appraisal process?
How can these errors be handled?

What Should Be Rated?   The vast majority of the earlier appraisal approaches have employed some form of trait rating. Basically the rating of personal characteristics, such as attitude, loyalty, and initiative, requires the superior to evaluate subordinates in some numerical or descriptive fashion. Two types of forms generally used for trait appraisal are shown in Figures 1 and 2.

---

[2]Thomas L. Whisler and Shirley F. Harper (eds.), *Performance Appraisal: Research and Practice*, Holt, Rinehart and Winston, Inc., New York, 1962.

FIGURE 1   Trait Appraisal Form

Rate the employee in the following traits, using this scale: 3 — Excellent
                                                      2 — Acceptable
                                                      1 — Needs Development
                                                      0 — Not Observed

Appearance	____	Ability to Learn	____
Self-confidence	____	Accuracy	____
Ability to Express Self	____	Meets Deadlines	____
Alertness	____	Health	____
Ambition	____	Enthusiasm	____
Initiative	____	Attitude & Acceptance of Responsibility	____
Energy	____	Use of Time	____
Knowledge of Department	____	Organizes Work to Get a Job Done	____
Contacts with: Superiors	____	Independence	____
Peers	____	Adaptable	____
Customers	____	Maturity	____

OVERALL EVALUATION

All factors considered, my overall evaluation of this employee is (circle one):

        1 – Outstanding

        2 – A Good Person Who Should Do Well

        3 – A Sound Person

        4 – An Adequate But Limited Person

        5 – Only Just Satisfactory

If reviewed, employee's reaction or comments

Reviewed with Employee by: _____   Date: _____

The wide use of trait appraisals disregarded numerous studies which had determined the job-related rating scales were superior. (The content issue is well summarized in the debate which took place between Kavanagh and Brumback over the relative merits of trait-oriented and job-oriented rating scales.)[3] In 1955, Ronald Taft had surveyed the extensive literature of research into human judgment and concluded that few individuals are qualified to judge the traits and aptitudes of others.[4] Although the alleged superiority of job-related

---

[3]G. B. Brumback and M. A. Howell, "Rating the Clinical Effectiveness of Employed Physicians," *Journal of Applied Psychology*, 1972, vol. 56, pp. 241–244; M. J. Kavanagh, "The Content Issue in Performance Appraisal," *Personnel Psychology*, 1971, vol. 24, pp. 653–668; G. B. Brumback, "A Reply to Kavanagh's 'The Content Issue in Performance Appraisal: A Review,'" *Personnel Psychology*, 1972, vol. 25, pp. 567–572. M. J. Kavanagh, "Rejoinder to Brumback: 'The Content Issue in Performance Appraisal,'" *Personnel Psychology*, 1973, vol. 26, pp. 163–166.

[4]R. Taft, "Ability to Judge People," *Psychological Bulletin*, vol. 52, no. 1, 1955, pp. 1–23.

FIGURE 2 Employee Performance Review Worksheet

EMPLOYEE PERFORMANCE REVIEW WORKSHEET

Employee Name	Department	Rated By	Date

INSTRUCTIONS:

1. Check the block beside each factor which contains the closest description of the employee WITH REGARD TO THAT FACTOR ONLY.
2. Enter rating points (0, 1, 2, 3) for each factor in the far right column.
3. Add the points in each section and divide the results by the figure shown. Round fractions as follows: 0.5 to 1.4 = 1; 1.5 - 2.4 = 2; 2.5 - 3.0 = 3. Should you not rate a job on a particular factor, divide by the number of factors rated rather than the figure shown.
4. Enter the "Rating" on the rating card.

QUALITY

FACTORS	POOR – 0	FAIR – 1	GOOD – 2	EXCELLENT – 3	RATING POINTS
APPEARANCE OF WORK	☐ Work is generally sloppy and incomplete. Employee has little or no regard for appearance. Work must be redone often.	☐ Some work is sloppy and incomplete. Employee tries to do acceptable work but rework is required often enough to cause repeated reminders.	☐ Work is generally neat and complete. Employee has pride in his work. Rework seldom required.	☐ Work is exceptionally neat, well organized and complete. Employee has exceptional pride in his work. Rework rarely required.	
ACCURACY OF WORK	☐ Continuously makes errors. Makes no effort to check own work. Work must be checked 100% by others.	☐ Frequently makes errors. Checks own work fairly often. Work must be checked 50% of the time by others.	☐ Occasionally makes errors. Almost always checks own work for accuracy. Only spot checking required by others.	☐ Rarely makes errors. Always checks own work. Little or no checking required by others.	
SUPERVISION REQUIRED	☐ Constant direction required with little effect.	☐ High degree of direction required to maintain a minimum level of quality.	☐ Needs occasional direction to maintain a high level of quality.	☐ Rarely requires direction to maintain outstanding level of quality.	
				TOTAL POINTS	
				DIVIDED BY	3
				RATING	

Recommendations for improvement

☐ Has improved
☐ Little or no change
☐ Has regressed

QUANTITY

FACTORS	POOR – 0	FAIR – 1	GOOD – 2	EXCELLENT – 3	RATING POINTS
VOLUME	☐ Volume of work is below acceptable level.	☐ Volume of work meets minimum acceptable level.	☐ Volume of work meets that of average worker.	☐ Volume is exceptional; exceeding average requirements.	
UTILIZATION OF TIME	☐ Frequently wastes time between assignments.	☐ Occasionally wastes working time.	☐ Wastes very little of available working time.	☐ Utilizes working time to the fullest.	
ORGANIZATION OF WORK	☐ Work not organized; rarely meets deadlines.	☐ Work is partially organized; frequently misses deadlines.	☐ Work is well organized; occasionally misses deadlines.	☐ Work is exceptionally well organized; rarely misses deadlines.	
WORK PACE	☐ Works at slow pace; frequently stalls. Indicates laziness.	☐ Works at easy pace.	☐ Works steadily.	☐ Works at an energetic pace.	
SUPERVISION REQUIRED	☐ Constant direction required to obtain quantity produced.	☐ Frequent direction required to obtain quantity produced.	☐ Occasional direction required to obtain quantity produced.	☐ Rarely requires direction to obtain quantity produced.	

Recommendations for improvement

☐ Has improved
☐ Little or no change
☐ Has regressed

TOTAL POINTS	
DIVIDED BY	5
RATING	

ALERTNESS

FACTORS	POOR – 0	FAIR – 1	GOOD – 2	EXCELLENT – 3	RATING POINTS
JOB KNOWLEDGE	☐ Grasp of job and scope very limited; requires considerable assistance and frequent instruction.	☐ Fair working knowledge of job; requires average assistance and instruction.	☐ Well informed on most phases of job; requires occasional assistance and instruction.	☐ Exceptionally well informed on all essentials of job; requires little or no instruction or assistance.	
ADAPTABILITY	☐ Can be used on routine tasks only; instructions must be repeated continually.	☐ Fairly adaptable to new tasks or changing conditions if properly prepared and instructed.	☐ Readily adaptable to new tasks or changing conditions with occasional assistance and supervision.	☐ Exceptionally adaptable to new tasks or changing conditions. Requires little or no help to adjust to new conditions.	
RESOURCE-FULNESS	☐ Unable to act independently in finding answers and solutions to problems; requires constant direction.	☐ Able to act independently on occasion in finding answers and solutions to problems; requires more than average direction.	☐ Able to act independently majority of the time in finding answers and solutions to problems; requires average direction.	☐ Acts independently in practically all cases in finding answers and solutions to problems; requires very little direction.	
JUDGMENT	☐ Decisions are usually unsound and not practical; no dependence can be placed on conclusions due to poor judgment.	☐ Decisions are usually sound and practical; exercises fair judgment in considering all factors and consequences before arriving at conclusions.	☐ Decisions are sound and practical in most cases; exercises good judgment in considering all factors and consequences before arriving at conclusions.	☐ Decisions are very sound and practical and well thought out. Judgment is always reliable.	
	Recommendations for improvement			TOTAL POINTS	
☐ Has improved				DIVIDED BY	4
☐ Little or no change				RATING	
☐ Has regressed					

CITIZENSHIP

FACTORS	POOR – 0	FAIR – 1	GOOD – 2	EXCELLENT – 3	RATING POINTS
WORK ATTITUDE	Complete lack of interest in his job and company. ☐	Minor interest in job and company. ☐	Some interest in job and company. ☐	Very interested in job and company. ☐	
PEOPLE RELATIONSHIPS	Does not get along well with others; not cooperative. ☐	Works fairly well with others; fairly cooperative. ☐	Works very well with others; fully cooperative. ☐	Works exceptionally well with others; goes out of way to cooperate. ☐	
CRITICISMS & SUGGESTIONS	Not responsive to criticisms or suggestions from supervision. ☐	Responds occasionally to criticisms or suggestions from supervision. ☐	Generally responds to criticism or suggestions from supervision. ☐	Always and enthusiastically responds to criticisms or suggestions from supervision. ☐	
PUNCTUALITY (Including Early Quits)	Continuously tardy (13 times or over during last 6 months) ☐	Frequently tardy (7 to 12 times during last 6 months) ☐	Occasionally tardy (3 to 6 times during last 6 months) ☐	Rarely tardy (2 times or less during last 6 months) ☐	
ATTENDANCE	Habitual absenteeism (7 occasions or over during last 6 months) ☐	Frequently absent (5 or 6 occasions during last 6 months) ☐	Occasional absenteeism (2 to 4 occasions during last 6 months) ☐	Rarely absent (1 occasion during last 6 months) ☐	
	Recommendations for improvement			TOTAL POINTS	
☐ Has improved				DIVIDED BY	5
☐ Little or no change				RATING	
☐ Has regressed					

ADDITIONAL COMMENTS

scales is still an issue for study, pressures in the legal environment are moving appraisal methods away from the subjectivity of rating personal characteristics.

Who Should Appraise?   Until recently, all appraisal practices have been based on the implicit assumption that the superior is the person in the best position to judge the performance and behavior of subordinates. Appraisals have thus emphasized the hierarchical relationship of superior and subordinate and have placed the superior in the position of passing judgment on the subordinate.

In the 1950s, social science research revealed that this reliance on passing judgment from above may reduce the effectiveness of the appraisal process in achieving its motivation and development goals. For example, the work of Likert and others at the Social Science Research Center has shown that hierarchical control may lead to lower motivation and may restrict rather than encourage individual development; on the other hand, these researchers assert that participative, supportive management tends to foster higher motivation and encourage development and personal growth.[5]

"Management by Objectives"   Efforts to increase employee involvement in the appraisal process were encouraged by the writings of Drucker and McGregor and the General Electric studies of Meyer, Kay, and French.

In *The Practice of Management*, Peter Drucker proposed a new approach to performance appraisal which he called "management by objectives and self-control." His recommendation was based on his observation that many effective managers required their subordinates to write a "manager's letter" twice a year.

> In this letter to his superior, each manager first defines the objective of his superior's job and of his own job as he sees them. He then sets down the performance standards which he believes are being applied to him. Next, he lists the things he must do himself to attain these goals—and the things within his own unit he considers the major obstacles that hamper him. Finally, he outlines what he proposes to do during the next year to reach his goals. If his superior accepts this statement, the "manager's letter" becomes the charter under which the manager operates.[6]

McGregor reinforced the application of management by objectives as an appraisal technique with his classic article, "An Uneasy Look at Performance Appraisal."[7] McGregor was concerned with the fact that most appraisal systems involved rating of traits and personal qualities and placed the manager in the untenable position of "playing God." This produced two main difficulties:

1. Managers were uncomfortable in this position and resisted making appraisals.

2. It had a damaging effect on the motivation and development of the subordinate.

---

[5]R. Likert, *New Patterns of Management*, McGraw-Hill Book Company, New York, 1961.

[6]P. R. Drucker, *The Practice of Management*, Harper & Row, New York, 1954.

[7]D. McGregor, "An Uneasy Look at Performance Appraisal," *Harvard Business Review*, vol. 35, no. 3, 1957, pp. 89–94.

McGregor felt that Peter Drucker's concept of management by objectives offered an unusually promising framework within which to seek a solution to this problem, and he proposed a new approach to performance appraisal based upon assumptions consistent with Drucker's philosophy. He described his proposal as follows:

> This approach calls on the subordinate to establish short-term performance goals for himself. The superior enters the process actively only after the subordinate has (a) done a good deal of thinking about his job, (b) made a careful assessment of his own strengths and weaknesses, and (c) formulated some specific plan to accomplish his goals. The superior's role is to help the man relate his self-appraisal, his "targets," and his plan for the ensuing period to the realities of the organization. . . . At the conclusion of the six-month period, the subordinate makes his own appraisal of what he has accomplished relative to the targets he had set earlier. He substantiates it with factual data wherever possible. The "interview" is an examination by superior and subordinate together of the subordinate's self-appraisal, and it culminates in a resetting of targets for the next six months. Of course, the superior has veto power in each step of this process. . . . However, in practice, he rarely needs to exercise it.[8]

Another landmark article in the literature of performance appraisal is Kindall and Gatza's "Positive Program for Performance Appraisal."[9] In a sense, this article began where McGregor's left off. Building on the philosophy stated by McGregor, they proposed a detailed plan for a five-step performance appraisal program based on McGregor's assumptions:

> 1. The individual discusses his job description with his superior, and they agree on the content of his job and relative importance of his major duties— the things he is paid to do and is accountable for.
> 2. The individual establishes performance targets for each of his responsibilities for the forthcoming period.
> 3. He meets with his superior to discuss his target program.
> 4. Checkpoints are established for the evaluation of his progress; ways of measuring progress are selected.
> 5. The superior and subordinate meet at the end of the period to discuss the results of the subordinate's efforts to meet the targets he had previously established.[10]

A typical set of forms used for the management by objectives approach to appraisal is shown in Figure 3. The forms used by different companies for this appraisal approach vary considerably, and some companies prefer to use only a blank sheet of paper. It will also be noted that these forms emphasize an explicit relationship between the appraisal of performance against objectives and the determination of incentive bonus. This direct tie between compensation and accomplishment of objectives is not uncommon; however, some make this tie less explicit and prefer to use appraisal data only as an input to a separate compensation decision process.

---

[8]Ibid., p. 91.

[9]A. F. Kindall and J. Gatza, "Positive Program for Performance Appraisal," *Harvard Business Review*, vol. 41, no. 6, 1963, pp. 153–162.

[10]Ibid.

FIGURE 3   Management by Objectives Form

TARGETS FOR 1982

Submitted by: _____   Title: _____

Dept/Div: _____   Supervisor: _____

TARGET (Ranked Importance____ & Weight %____)	PERFORMANCE CRITERIA

Review Dates	PROGRESS & RESULTS
FINAL (January)	

Work Planning and Review   One of the first reports in the literature of a company's effort to apply the management by objectives approach to performance appraisal was contained in a series of articles by Meyer, Kay, and French.[11] These articles report on the results of experimental research at General Electric regarding a positive approach to performance appraisal, such as that outlined by McGregor or Kindall and Gatza. The approach at GE, called "work planning and review," was a synthesis of McGregor's philosophy and the traditional need for administrative evaluations. In a sense, the research program at GE tested and proved many of the aspects of McGregor's philosophy which had been stated as hypotheses. It also validated the appraisal approach advocated by Kindall and Gatza. The program included controlled research to compare

---

[11]H. H. Meyer, E. Kay, and J. R. P. French, "Split Roles in Performance Appraisal," *Harvard Business Review*, vol. 43, no. 1, 1965, p. 123–129.

BONUS CONSIDERATIONS

Briefly outline each target below. List most important first; the least, last.	Please describe results obtained on each target and, in view of all circumstances, give your opinion of their adequacy.
	Comments by: _____ (Name)

the results of conventional appraisal with those of a work planning and review approach. The latter approach proved to be clearly superior for motivating and developing subordinates.

Behaviorally Anchored Rating Scales Behaviorally anchored rating scales (BARS) are designed to identify the critical areas of performance for a job and to describe the more effective and less effective job behaviors for getting results. Performance is evaluated by asking the rater to record specific, observable job behaviors of an employee and then compare these observations with a "behaviorally anchored rating scale." (Figure 4 provides an example of such a scale which has been designed to evaluate a department manager's ability to meet day-to-day deadlines.) As a result, the supervisor is in a position to com-

Summary appraisal	Bonus Percents by Grade and Performance							

Summary appraisal	Salary grade							
	10	11	12	13	14	15	16	17
Unusually high level of accomplishment on all targets. ☐ →	20–22.5%	33–37.5%	46–52.5%	65-75%	65–75%	78–90%	91–105%	104–120%
More than reasonable. Results against all targets were slightly better than normal expectations. ☐ →	17–19%	28–32%	39–45%	55–64%	55–64%	66–77%	77–90%	88–103%
Reasonable, normal achievement for managerial personnel. Did well on all the more important targets. ☐ →	14–16%	23–27%	32–38%	45–54%	45–54%	54–65%	63–76%	72–87%
Adequate performance against targets. However, achievement on the most important target could have been better. ☐ →	11–13%	18–22%	25–31%	35–44%	35–44%	42–53%	49–62%	56–71%
Results against several important targets could have been better. ☐ →	7.5–10%	12.5–17%	17.5–24%	25–34%	25–34%	30–41%	35–48%	40–55%
Failed to achieve minimum acceptable level of performance on all important targets. ☐ →	0	0	0	0	0	0	0	0

Bonus percent recommended: _____

pare the employee's actual behavior with behavior that has been previously determined to be more or less effective. Proponents of BARS claim many advantages for this approach. They argue that such a system differentiates between behavior, performance, and results and, consequently, is able to provide a basis for setting developmental goals for the employee. Because it is job-specific and identifies observable and measurable behavior, it is a more reliable and valid method for performance appraisal. For a description and evaluation of the methods used for developing a behaviorally anchored rating scale, the authors recommend a paper by John P. Campbell and others.[12]

---

[12]J. P. Campbell, M. D. Dunnette, R. D. Arvey, and L. V. Hellervik, "The Development and Evaluation of Behaviorally Based Rating Scales," *Journal of Applied Psychology,* 1973, vol. 57, no. 1, pp. 15–22.

FIGURE 4   Behaviorally Anchored Rating Scale for Meeting Day-to-Day Deadlines

NAME _____

In the job of department manager, how well does this person do in meeting deadlines? Consider only day-to-day or typical job behavior.

Write typical on the scale opposite the action that seems to fit most closely when doing a usual or typical job in meeting deadlines.

Could be expected never to be late in meeting deadlines no matter how unusual the circumstances.

Could be expected to meet deadlines comfortably by delegating an unusually high number of assignments to two highly rated associates.

Could be expected always to get his or her associates' work schedules made out on time.

Could be expected to meet seasonal deadlines within reasonable length of time.

Could be expected to offer to do the assignments at home after failing to get them out on the deadline day.

Could be expected to fail to schedule additional help to complete assignments on time.

Could be expected to be late all the time on weekly assignments for his or her department.

Could be expected to disregard due dates for assignments in his or her department.

Could be expected to leave assignments in a desk drawer for several weeks even when they had been given by a superior and called to his or her attention after due dates.

Empirical studies of BARS have provided a fertile ground for study by both theorists and practitioners. The BARS experience has helped to clarify three major controversies of the appraisal process. One was the previously discussed issue of rating content (trait versus job-related). A second dealt with the multidimensional nature of performance. The administrative uses of appraisal had encouraged rating systems to produce an overall ("global") measure of performance, which tended to mask differences in performance in the key result areas ("performance dimensions") which are critical to job results. The third dealt with the issue of the most effective way to anchor the rating scales (numerical or behavioral). By anchoring the scales behaviorally, the BARS approach was expected to produce more valid and reliable results by reducing measurement errors (leniency, halo effect, and central tendency).

In their review of the BARS literature, Schwab, Heneman, and DeCotiis found that "findings from research have not been very encouraging." Evidence regarding the effect of behavioral anchors on measurement errors, they reported, was inclusive. They hypothesized that the "major advantage of BARS may stem from the dimensions generated rather than from any particular superiority provided by behavioral versus numerical anchors."[13]

CURRENT PRACTICE IN PERFORMANCE APPRAISAL

The previous sections provide a historical perspective on the evolution of appraisal techniques and suggest theoretical guidelines for the development and implementation of performance appraisal systems. The purpose of this section is to describe current practice in performance appraisal. What appraisal techniques are being used at the present time by major American companies? Which employees have their performance appraised? What are the primary uses of appraisals? And, most important, what effect do the answers to the latter two questions have on the type of appraisal techniques used in a particular company?

Formalized Appraisal Programs   A study by Locher and Teel indicated that 89 percent of their respondents have formal performance appraisal programs.[14] This is consistent with a Bureau of National Affairs (BNA) study where 84 percent have "regular procedures for evaluating office employees."[15] However, only 54 percent of the companies in the BNA study have formal programs for evaluating production workers. The BNA study further reports, "For 81 percent of the office groups and 76 percent of the production employees, a standard rating form is used in making performance evaluation."

Types of Plans   Table 1 shows the types of appraisal plans used by companies surveyed by Schuster in 1968.[16] Somewhat surprisingly, 106 companies, or 34.9 percent, indicated they used only a management by objectives (MBO) plan, and

---

[13]D. P. Schwab, H. G. Heneman, III, and T. A. DeCotiis, "Behaviorally Anchored Rating Scales: A Review of the Literature," *Personnel Psychology*, vol. 28, 1975, pp. 549–562.

[14]A. H. Locher and K. S. Teel, "Performance Appraisal—A Survey of Current Practices," *Personnel Journal*, May 1977. (Findings based on survey of 696 organizations belonging to the Personnel and Industrial Relations Association of Los Angeles, of which 31 percent responded.)

[15]Bureau of National Affairs, *Employee Performance: Evaluation & Control*, PPF Survey no. 108, February 1975. (Report is based on responses from 150 employers who are members of BNA's Personnel Policies Forum.)

[16]F. E. Schuster, "An Evaluation of Management by Objectives Approach to Performance Appraisal," unpublished doctoral dissertation, Graduate School of Business Administration, Harvard University, December 1968.

TABLE 1   Appraisal Plans Used in 304 Leading Industrial Corporations*

Type of plan used	Responses	
	Number	Percent
1. Numerical or descriptive rating of only one general item, "How well does the ratee perform the job?"	16	5.3
2. Numerical or graphic trait ratings	27	8.9
3. Trait checklist	61	20.1
4. Forced-choice system of rating	11	3.6
5. Management by objectives	106	34.9
6. Other	8	2.6
7. Combination of (5) and another plan	75	24.7
Total	304	100.0

*Of the 316 respondents, 12 did not specify type of plan used.

75 companies, or 24.7 percent, indicated they used an MBO type of plan (for a part of the work force or a part of the organization) in combination with another type of appraisal plan. Thus 181 companies, or 59.6 percent, said that MBO served as the basis of performance appraisal for at least part of their work force. A total of 29 percent of the companies used some sort of trait rating, and this was the only alternative besides MBO chosen by a significant number of companies. Each of the remaining alternatives was chosen by less than 6 percent of the companies. It thus seems clear that in the late sixties MBO was by far the most common basis for performance appraisal in the largest industrial companies.

More recent studies provide conflicting evidence regarding the employment of MBO as an appraisal tool. The Downs and Moscinski study found MBO in use by 71.4 percent of the companies they studied, with more than half of the companies using a combination of MBO and essays.[17] The Locher and Teel study found that only 12.7 percent of their respondents used MBO as their "primary" appraisal technique, and concluded, "Perhaps the most surprising finding of the survey was the limited use of MBO as an appraisal technique."[18] Even the Downs and Moscinski study, which supported the Schuster study, found discrepancies in responses to their questionnaire:

> There is some discrepancy between the number of companies identifying MBO as their appraisal method and the number of companies emphasizing the setting of objectives. Forty-five (out of 67) companies say they use MBO, but only 32 companies report that setting performance objectives is a purpose of their appraisal system.[19]

---

[17]C. W. Downs and Paula Moscinski, "A Survey of Appraisal Processes and Training in Large Corporations," paper delivered to Annual Meeting of Academy of Management, Detroit, 1980, p. 3. (The study was based on a sample of companies obtained by cross-referencing the Fortune 500 companies with lists of members in the American Society for Training Directors. Questionnaires were mailed to 200 of the top 250 of the Fortune 500, and 67 questionnaires were returned.)

[18]Locher and Teel, op. cit., p. 247.

[19]Downs and Moscinski, op. cit.

Perhaps the inconsistent findings of the various studies can be explained by the grouping of production and office workers with differing levels of management. For example, the BNA study of office workers and production employees did not even report the use of MBO. By contrast, the Conference Board study in 1977, which looked only at systems for appraising managers, found "Objective Setting or MBO" being used by 40 percent of the companies for lower management, 53 percent for middle management, and 63 percent for top management.[20]

More than likely, MBO is still the most widely used technique for appraising managerial personnel, and Odiorne is probably correct in stating that MBO is the "dominant form" of management in the United States.[21] Nonetheless, there is strong evidence that MBO, as currently practiced, is failing to fulfill the high expectations which are often held for it. Kondrasuk reached the following conclusion after reviewing 185 studies of MBO:

> . . . we have found some evidence, but not conclusive proof, for the effectiveness of MBO. It appears we are headed toward a contingency approach to MBO. We still need to determine what aspects of MBO are most effective in which situations.[22]

For nonmanagerial workers, it is clear from all the studies that the rating scale in combination with some form of narrative comment is the dominant technique currently in use. Teel in 1980 noted a trend toward multiple appraisal techniques and an increasing employment of the narrative comment.[23] Other methods such as critical incidents, employee comparison, and forced choice are apparently used infrequently.

Purposes and Uses of Appraisals   For lower- and middle-management personnel, the Conference Board study ranked the following uses of appraisals in their order of importance: (1) management development, (2) performance measurement, (3) performance improvement, and (4) compensation administration.[24] This was also true for top management except for a reversing of the top two purposes. For top executives, performance measurement was ranked number one.

For office and production personnel, the BNA study indicated that performance appraisal is primarily used for "determining wage increases," "promotion decisions," and "determining training needs."[25] "Determining wage increases" was number one for office workers, whereas "promotion decisions" ranked first for production employees. Locher and Teel also concluded that

---

[20]R. I. Lazer and W. S. Wikstrom, *Appraising Managerial Performance: Current Practices and Future Directions*, The Conference Board, Inc., New York, 1977, p. 22.

[21]G. S. Odiorne, *M.B.O. II*, Fearon Publishers, Inc., Palo Alto, Calif., 1979.

[22]J. N. Kondrasuk, "Studies in MBO Effectiveness," *Academy of Management Review*, vol. 6, no. 3, 1981, pp. 419–430.

[23]K. S. Teel, "Performance Appraisal: Current Trends, Persistent Progress," *Personnel Journal*, April 1980, p. 297.

[24]Lazer & Wikstrom, op. cit., p. 11.

[25]BNA, op. cit., p. 9.

TABLE 2 Primary Use of Various Types of Appraisal Plans (Percent)

Type of plan	Not answered	Merit increases or bonuses	Counseling	Planning training or development	Promotion	Retention and discharge	Motivation	Improve company planning	Other	Total
					Primary Use of Appraisals					
Overall performance	25.0	50.0	0.0	12.5	0.0	0.0	6.3	6.3	0.0	100.0
Traits:										
Numerical	14.8	25.9	29.6	11.1	3.7	0.0	14.8	0.0	0.0	100.0
Descriptive	21.3	21.3	13.1	14.8	4.9	0.0	16.4	4.9	3.3	100.0
Forced-choice	45.5	9.1	0.0	9.1	9.1	18.2	9.1	0.0	0.0	100.0
MBO only	18.9	14.2	1.9	20.8	0.9	0.0	31.1	9.4	2.8	100.0
Other	25.0	25.0	0.0	12.5	0.0	0.0	25.0	12.5	0.0	100.0
MBO plus another	29.3	22.7	4.0	13.3	1.3	0.0	20.0	5.3	4.0	100.0
Total	39.0	17.4	5.5	12.2	2.0	0.5	16.6	5.0	2.0	100.0

appraisals are most widely used for compensation decisions and individual performance improvement programs, and "are being used today for essentially the same purposes that they have served for many years in the past."[26]

It is important to note that there appears to be a clear difference in viewpoint regarding the primary goal of performance appraisal between those companies using management by objectives alone and those companies using MBO in combination with other approaches. This can be seen in Table 2 where the modal response (31.1 percent) of companies having an MBO approach to appraisal was that the principal purpose of the plan is the motivation of employees. Another 20.8 percent of these companies said the principal purpose of the appraisal program was the planning of training and development of employees.

Significantly, MBO is the only appraisal approach for which the modal primary use is motivation. Only 20 percent of the companies having a combination of MBO and some other appraisal approach said that motivation was the primary goal of their appraisal programs; and the modal response (22.7 percent) of this group was that the program was used primarily to determine merit increases or bonuses.

What Is Evaluated?   Surprisingly, in spite of the growing recognition of the subjectivity and bias built into systems which rate personal characteristics, most rating scales are "trait-oriented" rather than "job-oriented." Even the Conference Board study of management appraisal systems reported widespread use of such personality characteristics as attitude, drive, stability, and integrity. Lazer and Wikstrom made the following comment on a list of terms which commonly appeared on rating forms which they reviewed:

> Many of these terms seem to refer to personality traits rather than to specific behaviors. It is possible, however, that these terms have more specific meanings in the firms that use them. At least, when asked directly to rank the importance of the performance areas they appraise, the firms in this study put "performance results–goal achievement" at the head of the list and "personal characteristics" at the end.[27]

From this and other studies, nonetheless, it appears that in many instances the stated preference for job-related factors is more "lip service" than reality. Both the Downs and Moscinski and the BNA studies found that quality and quantity of work are the items most widely evaluated.[28]

Who Is Involved in the Appraisal Process?   Locher and Teel observed that appraisals are primarily made by the superior of the employee being appraised, and without any direct employee input.[29] In a later study, Teel noted a trend toward a review by the manager immediately above the one who makes the appraisal.[30]

---

[26]Locher and Teel, op. cit., p. 246.

[27]Lazer and Wikstrom, op. cit., p. 20.

[28]Downs and Moscinski, op. cit., pp. 5–6; BNA, op. cit., p. 4.

[29]Locher and Teel, op. cit., p. 254.

[30]Teel, op. cit., p. 301.

Teel also concluded that the employee's role in the appraisal process is still a passive one.

> Most organizations follow a "tell and sell" approach, in which the manager completes the appraisal, shows it to the employee, explains the reasons for the ratings and/or narrative comments, discusses what might be done to improve performance, and asks for employee reaction. In short, the manager prepares the appraisal and tries to justify it to the employee.[31]

The BNA study described the following formal procedures for providing employee feedback regarding the appraisal:

> In nearly all the companies with evaluation procedures the evaluation is discussed with the employee; this is true for 97 percent of office groups and 24 percent of production; in many instances the employee must sign the evaluation form indicating it has been discussed with him. The evaluation or review form becomes part of the employee's permanent personnel record in 92 percent of both office and production groups.[32]

Many writers are reporting the increased use of both peer and subordinate appraisals. In fact, the Conference Board study provides a case study of the RCA "Talent Inventory" which provides for multiple assessment. The employee is rated by five to seven individuals within the employee's work network. Of these, two or three must be superiors, two or three must be peers, and one or two must be subordinates to the person being rated. Although many writers, including Craig Eric Schneier,[33] are recommending the use of multiple assessors, there is no evidence of their widespread use in current practice.

Rater Training   Less than half the companies responding to the Conference Board study report the existence of formal training programs for raters.[34] Similar findings were revealed by the Downs and Moscinski and Locher and Teel studies. Where training is provided, it primarily consists of short sessions involving two to four hours of instruction. Such programs are likely to include an explanation of the forms to be used, a discussion of measurement errors (e.g., halo effect, leniency error, and central tendency), and some help in conducting the appraisal interview.

Since current performance appraisal research clearly indicates the vital nature of rater motivation and skill, there should be increased interest in the development of effective programs for training the rater in the future.

The Dynamic Nature of Appraisal Systems   Both the Downs and Moscinski and the Conference Board studies conclude that two-thirds of the managers surveyed are reasonably satisfied with the appraisal systems currently in use. Yet all the studies seemed to describe systems in the process of changing. Teel reported a trend toward frequent yet evolutionary change.

---

[31]Ibid.

[32]BNA, op. cit., p. 6.

[33]C. E. Schneier, "Multiple Rater Groups and Performance Appraisal," *Public Personnel Management*, January–February 1977.

[34]Lazer and Wikstrom, op. cit., p. 39.

Of the 18 organizations surveyed, 6 have systems that have been in use less than a year, 7 have systems that have been in use for 1 to 5 years, and 5 have ones in use for over 5 years.[35]

Although there is no evidence of any significant effort on the part of companies to evaluate the effectiveness of appraisal systems formally, the tendency for companies to change their systems frequently does indicate an awareness of problems in the appraisal process and a desire to solve these problems.

PROBLEMS OF THE APPRAISAL PROCESS

Teel summarized the problems of the appraisal process as follows:

> One is how to arrive at a single overall performance evaluation, often needed for compensation decisions, based on a series of individual ratings and/or narrative statements. A second is how to get managers to follow a strictly merit philosophy, rather than giving approximately the same percentage increases to everyone. A third is how to get greater employee involvement in the appraisal process so that it will become more of a joint problem-solving discussion and less of a "tell and sell" session. The final problem is how to reconcile the developmental and administrative requirements of an appraisal system, since an approach that satisfies one often is unsuitable for the other.[36]

In addition to the problems of inflated ratings and rater bias, Downs found great concern for the lack of preparation on the part of raters, the pressures of time which made it difficult for raters to do the job properly, and the tendency for raters to view the appraisal process as an obligation rather than an opportunity.

CONCLUSIONS AND RECOMMENDATIONS

Our conclusions are that most companies do have formal programs for performance appraisal, and the larger ones in particular are working to make them more effective. MBO is still widely used for appraising managerial and professional personnel, and will probably continue to be the dominant form of management in the United States. Currently, the rating scale in combination with narrative statements is the technique most often used for evaluating both office and production workers. There is growing awareness of the subjective nature of the trait appraisals, and in response to pressures from the legal environment, there will be increased experimentation with "job-oriented" rating scales.

In order to make the appraisal system more effective, the authors make the following recommendations:

Management Climate   The effort to find the right form or the right system must be matched with an effort to create the right climate for appraisal. Rater motivation is critical to the evaluation process. To be effective, the type of appraisal plan adopted must be seen by all concerned as being consistent with the basic assumptions and style of management prevalent in the organization. Manage-

---

[35]Teel, op. cit., p. 301.

[36]Ibid., p. 316.

ment by objectives as an approach to appraisal, for example, works best in a climate which emphasizes participation and a high degree of mutual trust and confidence within a framework of basic commitment to management by shared objectives and self-control.

Training   Training programs must be developed which help the raters understand the importance of the appraisal and clarify both the purposes and methods of the system. In addition, the raters must be helped to develop the skills required, not only in the interview (e.g., asking questions, listening, responding to employee ideas, and handling defensive behaviors) but in developing a performance management system (e.g., setting goals, establishing performance standards, and documenting performance).

Evaluation   Formal evaluation procedures should be implemented which determine the effectiveness of the appraisal system. Is it integrated with the basic strategy of the organization? Is it consistent with equal employment opportunity guidelines? Does it apply sound principles of human resource management?

Investment   Be willing to commit the resources required to improve the system. It takes a considerable investment of time and money to do the job of communicating, motivating, and training which is required. Be prepared to undertake what often seems an overwhelming task of developing a job-oriented rating system.

Conclusion   The achievement and measurement of individual goals is an integral part of corporate strategy, which makes the appraisal process an inherent and inevitable aspect of management. The concern for productivity in the seventies will be intensified in the eighties, and the development of effective appraisal systems will be an important part of efforts to make organizations more productive.

BIBLIOGRAPHY

Books

Bureau of National Affairs: *Employee Performance: Evaluation & Control*, Personnel Policies Forum, Survey no. 108, February 1975.

Drucker, P. R.: *The Practice of Management*, Harper & Row, New York, 1954.

Lazer, R. I., and W. S. Wikstrom: *Appraising Managerial Performance: Current Practices and Future Directions*, The Conference Board, Inc., New York, 1977.

Likert, R.: *New Patterns of Management*, McGraw-Hill Book Company, New York, 1961.

Odiorne, G. S.: *M.B.O. II*, Fearon Publishers, Inc., Palo Alto, Calif., 1979.

Schuster, F. E.: "An Evaluation of Management by Objectives Approach to Performance Appraisal," unpublished doctoral dissertation, Graduate School of Business Administration, Harvard University, December 1968.

Whisler, Thomas L., and Shirley F. Harper (eds.): *Performance Appraisal: Research and Practice*, Holt, Rinehart and Winston, Inc., New York, 1962.

Articles

Brumback, G. B.: "A Reply to Kavanagh's 'The Content Issue in Performance Appraisal: A Review,'" *Personnel Psychology*, vol. 25, 1972.

Brumback, G. B., and M. A. Howell: "Rating the Clinical Effectiveness of Employed Physicians," *Journal of Applied Psychology*, vol. 56, 1972.

Campbell, J. P., M. D. Dunnette, R. D. Arvey, and L. V. Hellervik: "The Development and Evaluation of Behaviorally Based Rating Scales," *Journal of Applied Psychology*, vol. 57, no. 1, 1973.

DeCotiis, T., and A. Petit: "The Performance Appraisal Process: A Model and Some Testable Propositions," *The Academy of Management Review*, vol. 3, no. 3, 1978.

Downs, C. W., and Paula Moscinski: "A Survey of Appraisal Processes and Training in Large Corporations," paper delivered to Annual Meeting of Academy of Management, Detroit, 1980.

Kavanagh, M. J.: "The Content Issue in Performance Appraisal," *Personnel Psychology*, vol. 24, 1971.

Kavanagh, M. J.: "Rejoinder to Brumback: 'The Content Issue in Performance Appraisal,'" *Personnel Psychology*, vol. 26, 1973.

Kindall, A. F., and J. Gatza: "Positive Program for Performance Appraisal," *Harvard Business Review*, vol. 41, no. 6, 1963.

Kondrasuk, J. N.: "Studies in MBO Effectiveness," *Academy of Management Review*, vol. 6, no. 3, 1981.

Locher, A. H., and K. S. Teel: "Performance Appraisal—A Survey of Current Practices," *Personnel Journal*, May 1977.

McGregor, D.: "An Uneasy Look at Performance Appraisal," *Harvard Business Review*, vol. 35, no. 3, 1957.

Meyer, H. H., E. Kay, and J. R. P. French: "Split Roles in Performance Appraisal," *Harvard Business Review*, vol. 43, no. 1, 1965.

Schneier, C. E.: "Multiple Rater Groups and Performance Appraisal," *Public Personnel Management*, January–February 1977.

Schwab, D. P., H. G. Heneman, III, and T. A. DeCotiis: "Behaviorally Anchored Rating Scales: A Review of the Literature," *Personnel Psychology*, vol. 28, 1975.

Taft, R.: "The Ability to Judge People," *Psychological Bulletin*, vol. 52, no. 1, 1955.

Teel, K. S.: "Performance Appraisal: Current Trends, Persistent Progress," *Personnel Journal*, April 1980.

chapter 22

Appraising Hourly Performance

Bernard Ingster

CONSULTANT IN HUMAN RESOURCES MANAGEMENT,
PHILADELPHIA, PENNSYLVANIA

Major industrial organizations such as IBM and Gillette have had extensive satisfactory experience in paying salaries to *all* their employees, yet the practice of paying *hourly wages* and identifying employees as *hourly workers* is still dominant in the economy of the United States.[1]

The distinctions between salaried and hourly employment status usually influence the design of a broad range of corporate personnel policies and programs, including the use of formal methods for appraising individual performance to determine cash rewards. The slowly emerging U.S. management and union interest in experimenting with nontraditional forms of the organization of hourly work—particularly the expansion of worker participation in decisions at the work place—will test the continuing relevance of such appraisal methods. At the same time, there is likely to be renewed interest in devising reward systems that focus upon the performance of organizational units.

APPRAISING INDIVIDUAL PERFORMANCE

Typically, a newly hired hourly worker who participates in a formal appraisal program will be reviewed before the end of a 30- to 90-day probationary period

---

[1]Edward E. Lawler, III, "Reward Systems," in J. Richard Hackman and J. Lloyd Suttle (eds.), *Improving Life at Work: Behavioral Science Approaches To Organizational Change*, Goodyear Publishing Co., Inc., Santa Monica, Calif., 1977, pp. 186–188.

and annually thereafter. The immediate supervisor may record opinions about personal worker *traits* such as cooperation or enthusiasm and/or about the quality and quantity of personal production. The techniques used to establish such observations are diverse.[2]

Frequently, graphic ratings, showing performance standing along a relative scale from poor to excellent, are used. For example, the volume of work produced by a rough-grinder machine operator would be described on a continuous scale ranging from "fast setup time, uninterrupted operation" down to "long setup time between operations and frequent, lengthy delays for tool changes." The rating supervisor would mark the appropriate location along the line.

Other less frequently used but well-known techniques include the following:

1. *Ranking* all employees in a particular unit in a hierarchy from best to worst.

2. *Forced-choice comparisons* among either a set of individuals or sets of performance criteria. This is a difficult technique to use because it requires extensive research to determine what is good and poor performance for each operation. The research leads to a checklist which the supervisor marks and which is then analyzed against predetermined standards.

3. Descriptions of *critical incidents*—both of good and bad performance—during a specified period of work.

4. *Work-sample tests*, which are brief, formal examinations of a worker's skill in doing a set of tasks—actually, a test of what he or she *can* do, not of what he or she *does* day to day.

5. *Narrative descriptions* of overall performance.

6. *Objective measures of productivity*, such as units produced per hour.

7. *Scaled expectations*, for which scales of desired worker behavior are established. The scaled behaviors serve as "anchors" for the raters. These are complex techniques requiring extensive work in the construction of the scales.[3]

Such evaluation techniques tend to be used among larger groups of people in large organizations. In the case of a very small organization, judgments about the quality of worker performance are usually made very informally.

In appraising hourly worker performance, the use of peer rating or self-rating is not common.

USES OF PERFORMANCE APPRAISAL

Management's desire to appraise hourly performance comes primarily from a concern about maintaining and improving a certain level of productivity. This emphasis is illustrated by the common mandate given to first-level supervisors to control the departmental payroll tightly—a cost directly reflecting the work of people. It is widely held that supervisors can gain better cost control and

---

[2]Richard S. Barrett, *Performance Rating*, Science Research Associates, Chicago, 1966, pp. 58–59.

[3]Patricia C. Smith, "Behaviors, Results, and Organizational Effectiveness: The Problem of Criteria," in Marvin D. Dunnette (ed.), *Handbook of Industrial and Organizational Psychology*, Rand McNally College Publishing Co., Chicago, 1976, p. 761.

their subordinates will perform more closely to established standards if workers (1) understand clearly the objectives of the work they are doing; (2) regard the levels of desired output to be reasonable; and (3) are given accurate feedback about how they are doing.

A report from the famous Chicago Hawthorne Works of Western Electric Company[4] suggests additional reasons for using *hourly employee merit rating*— a term synonymous with *performance appraisal*. Western Electric believes that employees prefer knowing what the company thinks of them, and this need is fulfilled by the appraisal process. Further, supervisors are communicating with employees, giving them such information as where the company is going and what opportunity exists for them. In these discussions, employees learn of personal growth and development needs for present and future jobs, and supervisors discover employees' work aspirations.

At Hawthorne, supervisors may also get previously undisclosed information about the employee during the appraisal interview. This permits counseling, if appropriate, and allows for the strengthening of supervisor-subordinate interpersonal relationships. (At Hawthorne, employees were ranked in terms of whole-job performance—for example, a person is twelfth in a department of 25 press operators.)

Other uses for performance rating include wage and salary administration, promotion within a unit, transfer to another unit, layoff, discharge, and demotion.

KEY FACTORS FOR A SUCCESSFUL APPRAISAL PROGRAM

In companies where hourly performance appraisal is held to be an important contributor to overall corporate success, the appraisal programs generally share the characteristics discussed below.

Successful programs are acceptable to the people involved in them, and the acceptance seems to flow from the direct involvement of the participants in developing the system.[5] This includes top management, supervisors, the employees who are rated, and, performing a special role to be explained later, the personnel specialist.

The level of trust between the supervisor and subordinate is a significant variable in the successful use of performance appraisal, most particularly when the performance criteria lean toward subjective interpretation.[6]

Successful programs have explicit statements of the rating purposes and objectives. Further, these objectives are clearly related to the performance measurement criteria used in the program. In some cases, employees are rated for purposes of financial reward. If so, the criteria should be appropriate for such

---

[4]"The Nature and Interpretation of Employee Merit Ratings," from a publication of the Training Department, Personnel Service Branch, Hawthorne Works, Western Electric Company, Chicago, in Thomas L. Whisler and Shirley F. Harper (eds.), *Performance Appraisal, Research and Practice*, Holt, Rinehart and Winston, New York, 1962, pp. 21–27.

[5]Barrett, op. cit., pp. 134–140.

[6]Lawler, op. cit., pp. 197–199.

findings. If the rating is aimed at personal development (or acquisition of new skills), the rated employee must be confident that other kinds of conclusions will not be drawn from the appraisal. In general, participants must feel the criteria are related to desired outcomes. If, for example, a worker understands the need for a precision matching of a part he or she is making with one made at another work station, the criterion of quality of work can more readily be accepted as important in the performance review. Only what is truly important should be evaluated.

Successful programs ensure that employees have a complete and current understanding of how the company feels about their efforts. While hourly workers may be appraised at intervals of six months or one year—the latter being the most common—many managers believe that a really good supervisor lets employees know day to day how they are doing.[7] In companies with this kind of open interpersonal climate, formal appraisal discussions may be reserved for the exceptional cases—for the employee whose performance has been outstanding or for the employee whose work has been less satisfactory than that observed during a previous review.

In companies with unions representing hourly workers, a successful appraisal program requires careful conceptualization of the union role. Unions should be in a position to challenge the evaluation *decision,* but they *should not* be placed in a position of passing on the performance of their own members. It is management's responsibility to determine what the level of performance is. It is the union's role to challenge the standards against which worker performance is measured, as well as to challenge the objectivity of the supervisor making the rating. In this sense, the union is the advocate for "due process."

Beyond these roles, however, the union should be viewed as a principal communications link with hourly workers. Management must not only ensure a continuous flow of information to the union about the appraisal plan but also ensure significant involvement of the union in each stage of the plan's development and use.

Unions may not want, officially, to be a party to the design of the rating procedure, but by including unions on their (the unions') terms, management can gain important insight into what would or would not be acceptable to a particular group of employees. If unions are not involved in these ways, management's efforts to implement a merit review program will be so riddled with obstruction and grievance claiming that the anticipated values of performance appraisal will never be realized.

The personnel department is frequently the fountainhead for the development and maintenance of the successful program. It is the repository for the applicable, key research on work-related motivational questions. Personnel specialists usually convince top management of the practical usefulness of appraisal programs, and they organize the total effort required to launch the activity. The personnel department administers the program, including the development of appropriate forms and instructions. They pay particular attention to reducing the burden of extensive written detail. But most important, for the achievement of a truly successful effort, the personnel specialist ensures

---

[7]Paul Pigors and Charles A. Myers, *Personnel Administration—A Point of View and a Method,* 5th ed., McGraw-Hill Book Company, New York, 1965, p. 393.

that *raters are trained* to a level of full competence in working with all aspects of the program.

The rater must be well informed about the people and functions being evaluated. He or she must know, understand, and agree to the appropriateness of the standards against which the rating is being made. The rater must conduct the review in a businesslike manner, exercising care that the worker perceives the experience as being a *mutual* examination of *commonly held* performance goals. Such interviews are held in private to protect the employee from any embarrassment in case the discussions must deal with poor performance. The interview must be unhurried, to demonstrate that the matters being discussed are, in fact, important.

In the United States, the personnel specialist must be fully informed about the potential linkage between a performance appraisal process and the requirements of the Uniform Guidelines on Employee Selection Procedures adopted by a variety of federal enforcement agencies in 1978. While these guidelines were, primarily, the result of a federal interest in preventing unlawful discrimination in *preemployment* testing and selection, they *might* reach to an organization's *performance appraisal* program, if that program produces the principal records upon which judgments are made about transfers, promotions, or training for new assignments. The law concerning this matter is still developing as of the date of preparation of this chapter.

DETERRENTS TO PROGRAM SUCCESS

Raters who are unable to perform competently, of course, pose a serious threat to the success of an hourly performance appraisal program. And there are other factors that are equally jeopardizing. These can be divided among *internal* factors—that is, weaknesses inherent in the design or conceptual basis of the program—and *external* factors—those arising from challenges to the basic premise of merit rating. Let us take up the latter first.

External Factors: The Union   While an appropriate role for unions in developing rating programs has been described, it should be emphasized that unions almost universally do not support or encourage the establishment of such programs. Unions are particularly opposed to the use of performance appraisal for making administrative decisions about promotions, layoffs, or wage increases.[8] Long and serious work stoppages have occurred when companies have tried to use performance records to decide who keeps working when the company has a layoff to trim costs. Unions contend that seniority—the only objective measure easily identifiable—is the most equitable criterion for a layoff. Unions also contend that more experienced (i.e., high-seniority) workers will give the company the needed high production at quality levels because they are so familiar with the job to be done. Unions say long service means better work. (Not unlike the basis for choosing powerful committee memberships and chairpersons in the U.S. Congress, one might add.)

---

[8]Joseph Tiffin and Ernest J. McCormick, "Industrial Merit Rating," in Thomas L. Whisler and Shirley F. Harper (eds.), *Performance Appraisal, Research and Practice,* Holt, Rinehart and Winston, New York, 1962, pp. 4–7.

Unions usually charge management with the responsibility for detecting worker incompetence close to the time of hire, not after several years under an employee merit rating program. They urge management to focus on "reasonable and uniform standards of work load," not on the "subjective opinions" of supervisors as they appear in performance reviews. Unions may accept recognition of variability in worker performance under an individual incentive plan—if the union is integrally related to the development of work standards. But they resist the application of performance appraisal criteria for the multiple purposes suggested earlier in the chapter.

Internal Factors: Developing Equitable Performance Criteria   Weaknesses in the design of appraisal programs often grow out of the difficulty of establishing measurement criteria to be used. For example, if the objective of a program is to maintain and improve a given level of productivity, the questions must be asked: Is the employee who is being rated actually *able* to improve performance? If the worker is held to an established quantity of output, does he or she fully control the equipment being operated—its maintenance, the supplies, and the raw materials introduced into the process? Or does the worker suffer from "opportunity bias"[9] in his or her performance rating?

Opportunity bias is illustrated by two production punch press operators, side by side, working with similar dies but using machines which have significantly different operating characteristics. One machine may be easily affected by temperature shifts that make it difficult to hold specified tolerances. Management might need to rotate employees so that machine differences are equalized, not an uncommon annoyance in plants with standard-hour individual incentive plans. Or to cite another common situation: Two workers operating similar paper mills might have significant differences in output depending upon the characteristics of the pulp mixture each has been given by upper levels of management. One mill operator might need to work very much harder and with much greater skill than the other just to stay close to production standards. It is because of the great difficulty of choosing sound and appropriate criteria for individual hourly worker performance rating that many plans do not adequately tie together the measure used and the goal desired.

Internal Factors: Consistency in Ratings   Another major challenge to merit rating program administration is maintaining consistency and controlling variability of the ratings. The rating of "excellent" performance by the day-shift supervisor of a particular department may not be at all comparable with the "excellent" rating awarded by the night-shift supervisor in the same department.

Or consistency can be overdone. For example, a supervisor concerned about his or her *own* appraisal may be reluctant to show low ratings for the workers supervised. After all, the supervisor is supposed to train and develop employees' competence, and *their* failure, expressed on a review form, too clearly reflects on the boss. And, too, there are supervisors who are so concerned about "keeping peace" with their subordinates that they systematically avoid discussions of deficiencies.

---

[9]Barrett, op. cit., p. 55.

The importance of rater training has already been stressed, but it should be pointed out here that even effectively trained raters may not be able to measure various facets of performance consistently and reliably. Over a period of time, both the rater and the person being rated—and the job being done—undergo changes which might reduce the reliability of a measurement.[10] This points up again the importance of the *relevance* of measurement criteria.

Internal Factors: Periodic Revision   One additional problem with appraisal plans is the need for periodically revising the program just to overcome the boredom of supervisors and employees using the same rating scales and talking about the same things year after year. Since many hourly workers stay in the same jobs for many years, there is a tendency for job performance to stabilize at an individual-worker level. No significant gain in performance will be observed after about two or three years of using a particular score or technique of rating.[11] The plateau can be raised, however, by reexamining and, most likely, revising the program—particularly by including the workers being rated in the planning stage.

ORGANIZATIONALLY FOCUSED TESTS OF PERFORMANCE

The vast majority of hourly merit rating programs are "after-the-fact" appraisals. Very few programs force hourly employees to look ahead to yet uncharted achievement. If the latter is to be attempted, then the specific objectives of work must be clearly stated and worker agreement on both the definition of what is "satisfactory" accomplishment and how that accomplishment is to be measured must be secured. Such a framework for performance evaluation could lead to self-appraisal, a powerful motivational insight for personal growth and development. None of the appraisal techniques described earlier in this chapter have this quality in their designs.

Most of the traditional hourly merit rating programs stress individual effort in relation to a highly fragmented aspect of work—they are concerned with standardized, piece-part production efforts which give workers little control over the end results of their work.

Increasing numbers of U.S. companies—both union and nonunion—are considering a radical departure from the traditional organization of basic jobs. Most particularly, this usually involves the reorganization of *individual job functions* into larger, more complex jobs which offer workers a greater opportunity to understand the whole production unit of which they are a part.

On the transistor production lines of Texas Instruments, for example, the production flow was divided into segments, each of which encompasses a group of closely related, individual job functions. The segments became cooperative units of work, within which the individual operators were equally concerned with all steps of the process. They no longer thought only about doing their individual parts correctly. Each worker thought in terms of the *team* that was

---

[10]Ibid., pp. 18–20.

[11]Ibid., p. 124.

responsible for the productivity and quality of the whole unit. With such larger units of work the combined job content was great enough to allow decision-making power and individual responsibility to be exercised meaningfully. The feeling of being part of an interdependent group of important workers can be enhanced through such reorganizations. The emphasis in performance evaluation becomes the success of the *group* in achieving the production standards for multiple operations.

Further, these concepts lend themselves to the application of cash reward systems that support the achievement of both individual *and* group objectives.

One approach, known as the *Scanlon Plan,* has been in use for enough time to assess the organizational impact of group-focused production efforts. A Scanlon Plan is not a single plan but a philosophy of employee participation with various forms of attendant work practices. In such plans, management and employees jointly consider goals, problems, and activity programs. There is usually a committee system including departmental production committees and overall screening or steering committees. All effort is geared toward first, determining the current capabilities of a unit; second, agreeing on new levels of output needed for growth; third, agreeing on methods to achieve the higher productivity; and fourth, agreeing on an equitable distribution of the financial gains realized by the effort. The power of this strategy has been convincingly described in an article by Fred G. Lesieur, former president of the local union that cooperated in the first complete Scanlon Plan installation.[12] In each company reported on:

1. Workers took a broader view of the company's problems.
2. Management achieved a higher quality of production.
3. Indirect service groups—tool rooms, maintenance, etc.—strongly supported direct labor operations.
4. Automation was achieved without conflict over possible loss of jobs.
5. Company profits exceeded the growth patterns of competing enterprises.

Most companies would hope that their merit rating program could deliver similar results.

The previously discussed Texas Instruments program in many ways encompasses the philosophy of Joe Scanlon. It comes to grips very basically with the boredom and low motivation of workers doing highly repetitive tasks on machines and with the processes that control *them.*[13]

In these highly routine production-line situations, management is well advised to use traditional performance appraisal techniques on the machines rather than on the workers—the potential for productivity gains will be higher. (In a sense, the coming age of robots meets this recommendation.) If the jobs of

---

[12]Fred G. Lesieur and Elbridge S. Puckett, "The Scanlon Plan Has Proved Itself," *Harvard Business Review,* September–October, 1969, pp. 109–118.

[13]Two interesting case studies in non-American companies are described in John R. P. French, "Effects of Participation and Goal Setting in Performance," in Alvin F. Zander (ed.), *Performance Appraisals, Effect on Employees and Their Performance,* The Foundation for Research on Human Behavior, Ann Arbor, Mich., 1963, pp. 19–41.

hourly workers can be expanded, if the opportunity to assume significant responsibility and develop accountability can be designed into their jobs—then soundly constructed and administered performance appraisal programs can help achieve the impressive improvements in hourly productivity now so eagerly sought in the economy of the United States.

chapter 23

Appraising Performance of Clerical Personnel

R. C. Albright

DIRECTOR, HUMAN RESOURCES, STUDENT LOAN
MARKETING ASSOCIATION, WASHINGTON, D.C.

A good performance appraisal system for clerical workers is effective to the extent that it shows each employee what results are expected—and follows through by telling the employee how well the results have been achieved. It helps improve performance on the job and assists in long-range development. Secondary benefits to the organization include the identification of training needs and potential talent.

CRITERIA FOR SUCCESS

A clerical performance appraisal program can be successful only if it is implemented by those closest to the performance situation, the line supervisors. Since they will be responsible for carrying out the program, they should be involved in its initial development.

Line supervisors should participate in designing the appraisal form to be used in the program and in defining the terms to be used in evaluating performance. What do *average, excellent,* and *below standard* mean? Since words of this type do not necessarily have the same meaning for everyone, clarity of use and a common understanding of terms, especially those that are unique to the industry, assume significance. *Honesty,* for example, may have one meaning in evaluating a clerk-typist and quite another meaning when applied to a bank teller.

A supervisor's commitment to the program depends on an understanding of its value to himself or herself and to subordinates. Proper training will help develop this commitment as well as teach the supervisor how to do his or her part successfully. A supervisor who is inadequately trained is likely to fall into appraisal traps, thus seriously undermining the entire program.

A common problem often related to inadequate training is the tendency of a supervisor to be too generous in appraising, creating what is often called the *halo effect*. For example, the supervisor may give a favorite employee a higher rating than is truly justified or be blind to certain weaknesses which the supervisor shares. There is the danger that the poorly trained supervisor will place too much emphasis on an employee's past record and not enough on current achievements, or will tend to give higher appraisals to the employee who does not complain or have too many bright ideas than to the one who pesters but also gets the job done.

A second problem common to appraisal programs carried out by poorly trained supervisors is the *horns effect*. The supervisor whose standards are set too high may tend to give appraisal ratings that are unjustifiably low. The employee who does not do the job as well as the supervisor once did may be rated lower than those who do work that is unfamiliar to the same supervisor; and the maverick or nonconformist may get a lower rating. There is also a tendency on the part of the uninformed supervisor to give lower appraisal ratings to employees on a weak team and higher appraisal ratings to those on a winning team, regardless of individual performance. Allied to this is the danger of over-emphasizing *one incident* in evaluating an individual's performance: a recent mistake by an employee may cause the supervisor to forget months of good work.

What has to be remembered here is that one incident is only a small part of what the employee has been doing. One of the major purposes in formalizing an appraisal system is to compel the supervisor to consider the *entire job performance* of the employee rather than just one aspect of it.

Performance Standards   Generally speaking, there are three standards against which individual performance in clerical positions can be appraised:

1. In relation to other people in the same category of jobs
2. In terms of the work standards set for the job
3. In terms of absolute job-skill standards, such as the number of words typed per minute, number of units assembled per hour, or number of errors committed in a specific period of time

These work standards can be developed according to tangible factors—for example, what kind of record the individual has in productivity; or they can be developed according to judgmental factors—for example, how well does the individual plan, organize, direct, and control?

Clerical personnel are most often appraised in terms of job standards based on tangible factors, since judgmental factors are not apt to be as important a part of their jobs. Appraisals using job standards are also more versatile than comparisons with others on the same job or absolute standards, as shown in Table 1.

Changes in modern technology require periodic review of established job

TABLE 1   Uses of Different Types of Performance Appraisal

Possible uses	Job standards	Comparisons with other people in similar work	Absolute standards
Salary and wage administration	Yes	No	No
Promotion within unit	Yes	Yes	No
Transfer to another unit	Yes	Yes	Yes
Layoff	Yes	Yes	No
Discharge for cause	Yes	No	No
Administrative control	Yes	Yes	Yes
Performance counseling	Yes	Yes	Yes
Research	Yes	Yes	Yes

Comment

Job standards:	Generally the best— require clear understanding of what can be expected.	Absolute standards:	Limited because absolute standards are available for only a few jobs.
Other people in similar work:	Easy to use, especially if there are enough people on one job to rank them.		

standards. Incorrect standards can seriously damage the effectiveness of any appraisal program.

THE APPRAISAL PROCESS

Appraisal Participants   Experience and tradition have long suggested the line supervisor as the appraiser. Some feel, however, that at times it is appropriate for others to become involved, including:

1. *Supervisor's Supervisor.* By involving two persons, it is hoped that a more objective analysis of the subordinate's work can be obtained. Unfortunately, persons in higher positions do not always know the actual work performance of an employee who is several steps down the ladder in the hierarchy.

2. *Peers.* At the clerical level, appraisal by an employee's peers might be very difficult to implement. However, those advocating this type of appraisal claim it adds a new dimension that can facilitate objectivity if the peer group has sufficient interaction and stability over a long period of time.

3. *Subordinates.* Having his or her subordinates appraise an individual is again an attempt to obtain objective appraisal. The major drawback is that subordinates usually see only a part of what their supervisors do.

4. *Self.* More recent efforts to improve appraisals have included the request that employees rate themselves. At best, this provides another perspective on the individual's work.

In spite of the arguments put forth in favor of involving the individual, his or her peers, subordinates, and others, it is still generally agreed that the major responsibility for the appraisal should rest with the person most familiar with the individual's work—the immediate line supervisor. Others who may be less directly involved—either by providing a general framework for the appraisal or by using information generated in the appraisal—are discussed below.

The work force planning and development specialist.   Appraisal systems can, among other things, provide information for work force planning and development which is directly useful in determining future training and development needs of both the individual and the entire organization. The work force planning aspect of performance appraisal can be especially important at the clerical level, since this area usually involves a large number of employees. At current-day training costs, such planning is critical to the ultimate profitability of an organization. A well-trained staff that is motivated to develop itself further is an invaluable competitive asset.

The wage and salary administrator.   Today's salaries and benefits represent as much as half of the annual operating cost of an organization. Effectively rewarding an employee requires the ability to identify the degree of performance with appropriate salary increases. This is particularly true at the clerical level, in which salary increases are often looked upon as the only real measure of performance.

The wage and salary administrator provides the framework that can guide the line supervisor in making salary recommendations. This framework will inform the supervisor how subordinates' salaries stand in relation to salaries for comparable jobs in other companies. The supervisor is also informed of the grades of the subordinates' jobs and the ranges of their salaries within the organization. In addition, the wage and salary administrator can alert the line supervisor and the organization to possible violations of the law, such as the Equal Pay Act.

The personnel specialist.   Today's personnel specialist expends a great deal of time and energy in gathering information and developing data on personnel activities to guide management in making personnel-related decisions. Appraisals are necessary, as well as beneficial, to this function. They can provide an inventory of persons qualified for greater responsibilities and promotions, and of persons whose performance has been below par or unacceptable, which may lead to termination and the need for a replacement. Thus appraisal information can help in career planning and in the proper placement of talents and abilities as they are demonstrated by individual employees.

Alternative Systems   Stripped to essentials, the various approaches to the clerical staff can be characterized in terms of the appraisal forms used. Some of these approaches are discussed below, with examples shown from the banking field.

1. *The graphic scale*, as shown in Figure 1, is widely used because it is simply constructed and easy for the line supervisor to handle. The graphic scale has serious limitations, however, in the assumption that all factors have equal weight and that this is true in all jobs. Obviously, the importance of the different factors will vary with the results expected from the person on the job. Even though the section for subjective comments allows the supervisor to consider unique requirements of each job, the fact that these factors are given equal weight prevents graphic ratings, by themselves, from being useful in consistently obtaining accurate appraisals for large numbers of employees.

FIGURE 1   Graphic Rating Scale

Clerical Performance Rating

Entry date _____ Date of birth _____ Name _____

Division/Dept. _____ Present position _____

Instructions: Read carefully each of the factor descriptions and the explanations of each of the ratings. Judge the employee on the basis of the work now being done. Consider each factor separately; do not let your rating of one factor influence your rating of another factor. Rate each factor by circling the appropriate number.

In certain instances you might want to explain your rating. While you are not required to write an explanation, you are expected to be able to discuss any rating if called upon to do so.

* * * * * * * * * * * * * * * * *

Explanation of ratings:

1 – Superior: Outstanding, on a par with the very best.

2 – Above average: Very satisfactory, well above minimum standards.

3 – Average: Satisfactory.

4 – Below average: Marginally satisfactory at best. Needs improvement in this factor.

5 – Low: A serious handicap to job performance.

ABILITY TO LEARN: Consider how quickly employee learns (ability to retain instruction and information).

1   2   3   4   5   Comments: _____

INITIATIVE: Consider ingenuity (self-reliance and resourcefulness; ability to know what needs to be done).

1   2   3   4   5   Comments: _____

JOB ATTITUDE: Consider the interest and enthusiasm shown (attitude toward the bank and supervision).

1   2   3   4   5   Comments: _____

KNOWLEDGE OF JOB: Consider the knowledge of job and related work.

1   2   3   4   5   Comments: _____

INDUSTRY: Consider responsibility to duties (ability to apply time and energy).

1   2   3   4   5   Comments: _____

QUALITY OF WORK: Consider accuracy of work regardless of volume (ability to perform work efficiently).

1   2   3   4   5   Comments: _____

QUANTITY OF PRODUCTION: Consider the volume of work produced (ability to produce results).

1   2   3   4   5   Comments: _____

COOPERATION: Consider ability and willingness to work in harmony with and for others.

1   2   3   4   5   Comments: _____

PERSONALITY: Consider ability to get along with fellow workers (personal conduct, courtesy, tact, friendliness).

1   2   3   4   5   Comments: _____

APPEARANCE: Consider neatness, personal dress, and personal habits.

1   2   3   4   5   Comments: _____

Summary and Conclusion

A. Considering overall job performance, this employee is evaluated:

1	2	3	4	5
Outstanding	Above average	Average	Below average	Unsatisfactory

Write a brief paragraph giving an overall summary of the employee's job performance. _____
_____
_____
_____
_____
_____

B. Does this employee have further potential beyond the next step? _____ If yes, for what position? _____
_____

C. Is there any other work regardless of department or division for which you feel this employee would be qualified? _____
_____
_____

D. What are the employee's most serious limitations? _____
_____
_____

E. What can or should we do to help the employee improve where weaknesses are indicated and to prepare him for
advancement? _____
_____
_____

F. What can or should the employee do to improve or prepare for advancement? _____
_____
_____

G. Has the employee taken any academic subjects this past year? _____ Please specify _____
Accounting (name of course) _____ Stenography (name of course) _____
Finance (name of course) _____ Other (name of course) _____
Law (name of course) _____

H. Are there any limiting factors such as health, habits, or character that influence this rating? _____ If yes, explain: _____
_____

I. Number of days absent since January 1st _____ Tardy _____
Rated by _____   _____   Approved by _____   _____
         Initials   Date   Initials   Date

J. Summary of review with employee, including employee's reaction. Use quotations to summarize his reactions when
possible.
_____
_____
_____
_____
_____

Discussed with employee by _____   _____
                            Initials   Date

2. The *nonpoint scale*, shown in Figure 2, is a variation of the graphic scale form. It defines more fully the factors used in the rating form, and it allows for written comments by the rater.

3. The *checklist*, shown in Figure 3, is easy to complete and also provides a place for written comments.

4. The *narrative form*, shown in Figure 4, allows the supervisor to gear the appraisal to the specific job under consideration, but it does not require the use

FIGURE 2 Nonpoint Rating Scale

Performance and Merit Evaluation

Date _____19 _____

Name_____Office _____ Dept. _____

Position (designate concisely, such as teller, stenographer, etc.) _____

Is this employee's job properly described in the job description? Yes ☐   No ☐

Suggestions for Completion of Report

Read carefully the phrases describing qualities. Then on the basis of the person's actual performance on the job, place a check (✓) mark above the degree which most nearly describes the person's performance on that factor.

A check mark to the right indicates person: does not quite measure up to specification.

A check mark in the center indicates specification adequately covers employee.

A check mark to the left indicates superiority to specification.

Base your judgments upon the entire period covered and not upon isolated incidents alone. Be objective.

Rate on each factor separately. Do not allow judgment on one factor to influence judgment on other factors.

Amount of work

Consider number of assignments completed and volume of output in relation to nature and conditions of the work performed. Disregard quality of work.

Explanation

Extraordinary volume of work completed.	Consistently turns out a good volume of work.	Amount of work completed is satisfactory but not unusual.	Output barely acceptable.	Amount of work entirely inadequate.

Quality of work

Consider thoroughness, accuracy, and orderliness of completed job. Disregard amount of work handled.

Explanation

Unusually high-grade work is consistently performed. Quality is exceptional in all respects.	Quality is of high grade, but not exceptional.	Work is reasonably complete, accurate, and presentable.	Quality occasionally is unsatisfactory.	Work usually lacking in thoroughness, accuracy, or neatness.

Dependability

Consider the manner in which worker applies self to work, does jobs on time, and the amount of supervision required to get desired results.

Explanation

Justifies utmost confidence. A minimum of supervision required.	Applies himself well but occasionally needs direction and supervision.	Fairly reliable and conscientious. Normal supervision required.	Cannot always be relied upon to get desired results without considerable supervision.	Entirely undependable. Needs constant supervision.

Judgment

Consider the wisdom of decisions in the absence of detailed instructions and judgment in unusual situations, where discretion is allowed.

Explanation

Thinks quickly and logically in all situations. Judgment can always be depended upon.	Judgment usually of a high degree.	Judgment adequate in normal situations only.	Makes frequent errors in judgment. Works best with detailed instructions.	Judgment entirely undependable

---

Ability to learn

Consider mental ability in mastering new routine, grasping explanations, and ability to retain this knowledge.

Explanation

Brilliant and keen mind coupled with eagerness to learn.	Quick to grasp new ideas and methods.	Learns satisfactorily.	Learns by excessive repetition. Needs guidance.	Slow in learning even simple procedures. Needs constant guidance.

Attitude

Consider attitude toward job and bank.

Explanation

Enthusiastic about type of work; booster of bank.	Happy on job; favorable attitude toward bank.	Seems to be satisfied with job and bank.	Shows little interest in either job or bank.	Disgruntled on job; critical of bank.

Cooperation

Consider extent to which employee works harmoniously and effectively with fellow employees, supervisors, and others with whom in contact.

Explanation

Exceptionally successful in working with and assisting others.	Quick to volunteer to work with and assist others.	Generally works well with and assists others.	Cooperation must be solicited. Seldom volunteers to work with or assist others.	Fails to cooperate. Unwilling to work with or assist others.

Capacity and ambition for future growth

Review all the factors previously considered and judge employee's capacity and ambition for future advancement both in present department or branch and in the organization.

Explanation

Outstanding candidate for future development. Given opportunity, could be expected to go far in the organization.	Capable of developing beyond present level of work.	Has probably reached most suitable job or level of work.	Barely capable of handling present level of work.	Entirely out of place in present job. Should be moved to simpler work or dismissed.

Personal statement — to be filled out by employee in ink in own handwriting.

	Business development record
	Mos. ending

Full name _____

Address _____ Phone _____

Marital status _____ Name of spouse _____

Green slips
Cust. _____

Prosp. _____

Children:
Name _____ Age _____

Name _____ Age _____

Name _____ Age _____

Name _____ Age _____

Interviews
_____

Sales
No. _____

Amt. $ _____

Person to be notified in case of emergency:

Name _____

Address _____ Phone _____

List your outside activities such as:

Educational courses
Home study _____
Civic activities

Attendance record

Abs. _____

Tardy _____

Personal characteristics	Superior	Above average	Average	Below average	Unsatisfactory		Executive characteristics	Superior	Above average	Average	Below average	Unsatisfactory
Grooming							Initiative					
Manner of speech							Ability to organize work					
Tactfulness							Ability to develop others					
Self-confidence							Ability to delegate work					

Comments

What outstanding qualities will aid advancement? _____

What qualities or physical handicaps, if not corrected, will hinder future development? _____

Give any other pertinent facts which should be known concerning this employee _____

This performance rating was discussed with employee _____ By _____

Rated by _____ Reviewed by _____
(Department head)   (Officer in charge)

This space for use of personnel division only _____

of the same criteria by all supervisors, and therefore appraisal methods and factors may vary too widely. The form in Figure 4 also includes a simple variation of the forced-choice method.

5. *The forced-choice form*, shown in Figure 5, allows a narrative discussion of job accountabilities and objectives as well as a forced-choice appraisal of performance and work traits. One unique feature of this particular form is that it makes provision for updating accountabilities by extracting them from the person's job description and including them in the appraisal form each time it is sent to the line supervisor.

FIGURE 3   Checklist

Final Personnel Appraisal

Name _____   Date _____

Division _____   Job title _____

1. Transferred _____ To _____
   Date   Division

2. Left employ of bank _____ Reason _____
   Date

3. Do you recommend reemployment?_____ If not, why? _____

A. What was his performance?   Unsatisfactory _____ Satisfactory _____ Superior _____
   Comment:

B. To what extent did this person give indication of future development?
   None _____ Little _____ Moderate _____ Substantial _____
   Comment:

C. Have you any indication that this person might become unsuited for bank work? _____
   Comment:

The following checklist of traits is provided to help you confirm your conclusions above. It is assumed that the person was *satisfactory* in these traits unless you indicate by check mark any of them in which he *was unsatisfactory* or *superior*.

Unsatisfactory	Trait	Superior
	First impression	
	Ability to learn	
	Speed	
	Accuracy	
	Dependability	
	Ability to get on with others	
	Initiative	
	Cooperation	

_____   _____
       Supervisor   Division manager

                                   _____
                                       Operating officer

Difficulties can be encountered in the use of these forms. The narrative format, for example, can leave too much freedom for the rater who writes well and too little opportunity for expression by the nonverbal supervisor. A classic cartoon showed an employee talking to his supervisor: "The word 'lousy' is a bit general. Specifically, sir, what do you think of my work?" Examples that are even worse are the following excerpts from Army Officer Fitness Reports:

FIGURE 4   Narrative Rating Form

<u>Employee appraisal</u>

Name _____   Position _____   Anniversary _____
Date of employment _____   Years in present position _____   Transfer _____
Office _____   Previous position _____   Promotion _____
Reports to _____   Merit _____
Other _____

Attendance   ☐ Satisfactory   ☐ Marginal   ☐ Unsatisfactory

Performance, results, and methods — Give production figures (be specific).

1. What has this person accomplished in measurable results since last appraisal?
   (Consider quantity and quality of work.)

2. How does this person go about getting his/her work done?

3. How well does this person work with people?

4. List outstanding personal qualifications or characteristics that help or hinder
   this person.

5. Recommended action to improve performance in present position.

The performance and personal qualification sections of this appraisal have been
discussed with the employee by:

Name _____   Position _____   Date _____

Approved _____

"Deep down, he's shallow."
"Exceptionally well qualified, since he has committed no major blunders."
"Never makes the same mistake twice but seems to have made them all once."

Many specialists in the field feel that forced choice (Figure 5) is the most
effective method of obtaining objective appraisals from the line supervisor. The
forced-choice form is difficult and time-consuming to construct, and supervisors tend to resist its use because they do not like to be forced to make a choice
in their appraisal of any employee. Thus many forced-choice forms provide
space for written comments where the supervisor can qualify the forced
choices on the form. Despite these difficulties, many feel that of all the tech-

6. Current status (check one):

☐	Immediately promotable	This person is doing outstanding work in present position and can fill immediately a specific position in a higher salary range with only casual training.
☐	Promotable	Same as above except systematic and extended training would be necessary, or promotion would not be in best interest of bank.
☐	Satisfactory	This person is supplying what can be reasonably expected, but could not be considered beyond the present assignment in the near foreseeable future.
☐	Questionable	This person's performance in present position is not completely satisfactory, but may be able to improve.
☐	Unsatisfactory	Performance not acceptable in present position, and has not been able to improve under guidance. Management action (transfer, demotion, separation) is indicated.

7. Do you recommend a salary increase? _____ If so, in what amount $ _____

Proposed effective date _____

CONTROL
_____
Personnel department

_____
Committee

Supervisor _____

Officer in charge _____

_____
Payroll section

Date _____

_____
Department notification

_____
Employee notification

_____
Personnel file

Note: Return this report promptly to the personnel department.

niques available, a well-constructed forced-choice performance appraisal form can greatly assist the clerical supervisor to make reasonably objective appraisals of subordinates.

Appraisal Frequency How often clerical performance should be appraised depends on the objectives and needs as well as the administrative capabilities of your own organization. The *annual* performance appraisal is probably the

---

FIGURE 5 Forced-Choice Form

Performance Review

Employee _____ Date _____

Position _____ Department _____

_____   _____

_____   _____

Purpose   When completed, this performance appraisal form will serve as a guide for
          the review of a staff member's job performance and salary.

- -

The immediate supervisor should review the current job description and make
the primary rating with the senior officer's approval. The performance and
salary review forms should be filled out in ink and forwarded in a sealed en-
velope to the Personnel Department by the return date indicated on the salary
review form. These forms will be processed for appropriate review and approval
and returned to the department head.

A full and frank discussion with an employee concerning salary and performance is strongly urged since it is felt that, if conducted sincerely and
wisely, it will contribute toward a better relationship between the staff member and the immediate supervisor, senior officer, and the bank. The form
should then be returned to the Personnel Department for filing in the staff
employee's personnel folder.

1. Utilizing the key outlined on the following page, rate the level of
   performance of each accountability and work trait on the basis of
   work done during the past year. Try not to let your appraisal of
   one accountability or work trait influence your rating of another
   accountability or work trait. Do not try to consult or recall prior
   ratings. You will be more objective if you forget them. One individual rarely merits identical ratings in every accountability or
   work trait. Be selective! Make independent decisions on each
   rating.

2. Consider Current Overall Performance without undue emphasis on
   recent or infrequent occurrences.

3. Under Other Comments you may explain, if you wish, individual
   ratings and / or make recommendations for a promotion, transfer,
   or further training needs.

4. Any recent major Change in Accountabilities should be recorded
   on the last page for future review.

5. The rater(s) should sign this form at the bottom of the last page.

easiest to administer, but many feel this occurs too infrequently and is not apt
to motivate employees sufficiently.

Semiannual appraisals are more difficult to administer since they involve
additional paperwork; moreover, supervisors must be motivated to rate their
employees more frequently. Many people feel, nonetheless, that semiannual
appraisals are desirable, arguing that more frequent dialogue between supervisor and subordinate is vital to the proper motivation of the subordinate.

Quarterly appraisals can truly be an administrative burden. On the other
hand, if the forms used are simple and supervisors have been properly trained
and motivated, the appraisals can serve as an excellent communication vehicle
regardless of the size of your organization.

KEY:

1 — Outstanding, exceptionally high level (top 5%)
2 — Superior, exceeds the expected level (next 10%)
3 — At expected level (middle 70%)

4 — Below expected level (next 10%)
5 — At marginal level (bottom 5%)

1. ACCOUNTABILITIES (as listed in approved job description)   Performance

Other factors that should be considered in determining the interval between appraisals include:

1. *Length of Service.* Many firms feel it is logical to appraise more frequently in the first few years and then to taper off in the latter part of an employee's career. To some, however, such a policy is entirely unacceptable on psychological and administrative grounds. They feel it would be extremely difficult to motivate employees to perform well if they are appraised only once every few years.

JOB OBJECTIVES   Performance

II. WORK TRAITS (Please continue to use key to describe
                 performance.)   Performance

Attitude —	Willingness to adjust to changes: Degree of interest and enthusiasm —	
Communication —	Ability to convey ideas and plans Written — . . . . Oral —	
Cooperation —	Ability to work with and through others including: Supervisor — . . . . Peers — . . . . Subordinates — . . . . Government officials, educators, bankers, etc. —	
Delegation —	Ability to effectively assign work to others —	
Development —	Ability to develop attitudes, knowledge, and skills in: Self — . . . . Subordinates —.	
Organization —	Ability to effectively organize time and effort on Work assignments —	
Forward planning —	Ability to plan ahead in order to meet changing needs of banking industry —	
Judgment —	Ability to arrive consistently at a sound decision(s) —	
Volume of work —	Ability to produce expected results in a given time —	

III. CURRENT OVERALL PERFORMANCE

Having rated each accountability and work trait, please indicate what the employee's overall
performance is in present position.

1. ☐ Performs at an outstanding level (5% could be here)
2. ☐ Performs at a superior level (10% could be here)
3. ☐ Performs at expected level (70% should be here)
4. ☐ Performs at below expected level (10% could be here)
5. ☐ Performs at marginal level (5% could be here)

2. *Nature of Position.* How easily a clerical position can be evaluated depends on the complexity of the job and the skills required. Jobs that can be appraised with ease should be appraised more frequently.

3. *Size of Organization.* Size considerations can certainly help determine the frequency of appraisals. Obviously, paperwork can become a major problem.

IV. OTHER COMMENTS (i.e., long-range potential, readiness for immediate or future advancement, career
development recommendations)

```
4  ☐  Potential should not be evaluated at this time
3  ☐  Not promotable to a higher level of responsibility
2  ☐  Promotable but needs further development
1  ☐  Ready for immediate advancement
```

REMARKS:

V. CHANGE IN ACCOUNTABILITIES (Please list any recent major changes in the employee's accountabilities
that you feel should be reviewed in the future by the Evaluation Committee.)

IMMEDIATE SUPERVISOR   SENIOR OFFICER

Date _____

(Wernher Von Braun, the famous scientist, pointed out that the United States
faced only two major problems in conquering space—gravity and paperwork.)

4. *Number of Employees by Category.* It is easier to carry out a performance
appraisal when the same job is held by a number of people. Therefore, the
more people there are in the same job, the more frequently their performance
can be appraised.

THE APPRAISAL INTERVIEW

The crux of any appraisal system is the discussion held between the supervisor and the subordinate regarding the subordinate's performance. It is in this interview that the supervisor, as the person best qualified to appraise the employee, can provide direct feedback about the appraisal.

A real danger here is that a well-designed appraisal form can totally lose its effectiveness if the supervisor does not know how to use it properly and then discuss it meaningfully with the subordinate. Evidence today suggests, unfortunately, that too many supervisors conduct such interviews poorly—so poorly, in fact, that many managers feel that the appraisal interview should be either discontinued entirely or carried on only by professional counselors. Without the appraisal interview, however, there really would not be any appraisal program. Furthermore, subordinates have clearly indicated a desire to discuss their performance with their own supervisor in order to:

1. Find out where they stand.
2. Get recognition for good performance.
3. Learn how they can improve on the present job.
4. Find out how they fit into the "big picture."
5. Learn where they are not performing satisfactorily.

An appraisal program is in effect a medium of communication between supervisor and subordinate, and the appraisal interview is potentially the most effective way of implementing such a program. This is particularly true of personnel at the clerical level. Often the appraisal interview is their only opportunity to learn how they are doing. If this is true, then why do supervisors resist conducting appraisal interviews? Here are some thoughts expressed by supervisors themselves:

1. "No time—the work comes first."
2. "Dislike criticizing people."
3. "It's unnecessary and unimportant."
4. "Not interested in doing it."
5. "Fear of having an argument with the employee."
6. "Afraid of inability to conduct the interview."
7. "Don't like the feeling of embarrassment."
8. "Dislike being judge and jury."
9. "No one ever helped me—it's a cold, cruel world."
10. "Afraid that any compliments offered will result in a request for a salary increase."

These comments would seem to indicate that this resistance can be attributed to a lack of understanding of the purpose of an appraisal interview and a lack of training in effectively conducting one.

Perhaps the first thing to do is to identify what an appraisal interview should *not* be. This may help in understanding why the interviews often fail. They are *not*:

1. An attempt to turn the supervisor into an amateur psychoanalyst or social worker
2. An attempt to manipulate an employee

3. An effort to remake or remold adult personalities
4. A substitute for day-to-day coaching and counseling
5. An effort to discipline or threaten
6. A cure-all for all supervisory problems

After all, a person who is 30 years old has spent more than 250,000 hours developing behavior patterns. A 10-minute, a 30-minute, or one-hour appraisal interview is not going to change his or her work habits substantially.

As we indicated before, standards of job performance are developed to help measure the results expected on the job. The appraisal of an employee's performance is the next step in measuring the quality of performance. Once the program's objectives have been determined, they must be communicated to the supervisor so that he or she will be able to conduct an appraisal interview which meets those objectives. The supervisor then needs to be trained in the techniques of conducting an appraisal interview, including the preparation necessary for the interview, the environment in which the interview should be conducted, and the manner of conveying the appraisal to the subordinate.

In preparing for the appraisal interview, the supervisor should review the appraisal form's objectives and become familiar with the employee's background. In addition, the supervisor should consider the subjects that will be covered in the interview—specific incidents that will be discussed and broad questions that will be asked to encourage conversation.

The interview should be conducted in privacy with no interruptions. The supervisor should strive to create an informal atmosphere and convey a willingness to listen to the subordinate. In any event, the supervisor should avoid being dogmatic or, if the subordinate disagrees with what is said, becoming defensive.

Before turning to the actual performance appraisal itself, the supervisor should explain the purpose of the appraisal to the subordinate. Then the supervisor can evaluate the employee's performance on the job, stressing strong points and pointing out possibilities for improvements in weak areas. In no case should the appraisal become an evaluation of the employee's personality. At the end of the interview, the supervisor should summarize all the comments and indicate to the employee that the supervisor is always available for future discussions.

The character of the feedback during an appraisal interview is critical to the employee's acceptance of the supervisor's appraisal. The supervisor should not only discuss the employee's entire performance in an appraisal interview but also show the employee the completed appraisal form. Often a supervisor conducts a fairly good interview and the employee thinks he or she is performing the job satisfactorily; then the supervisor writes something entirely different on the appraisal form. This is why many employees place no faith in an appraisal program.

Honesty and frankness on the supervisor's part are vital to the success of an appraisal interview. A supervisor who is well trained and motivated by management will recognize the importance of candor. Although authority for developing an appraisal program lies with management, the responsibility for carrying it out lies with supervisors, and they cannot discharge the responsibility successfully if they are unwilling or unable to discuss job performance honestly with their subordinates.

CONCLUSIONS

There are no pat formulas for performance appraisal interviews or forms. They have only one consistent pattern—change! Yesterday's methods are not being used today, and more research and validation are critically needed. There is still far too much pseudo-professional expertise being practiced by ill-equipped supervisors. However, major steps have been taken toward implementing an effective appraisal program if we see to it that supervisors and subordinates know what the appraisal program's goals are, see that an appraisal program which achieves its goals will also be of benefit to them, and work in an environment that encourages open dialogue between the supervisor and the subordinate.

chapter 24

Appraising Executive Performance

Harry L. Judd

VICE PRESIDENT, PERSONNEL, UNITED STATES GYPSUM
COMPANY, CHICAGO, ILLINOIS

Appraising employee performance is probably as old as business itself. Anyone in business will tell you that some employees perform better than others. If some employees perform better than others and the difference is noticeable, then why have a formal performance appraisal program?

A systematic approach to executive performance appraisal can provide many benefits. It can help upgrade performance, identify those persons worthy of promotion, and improve total company results by motivating executives to achieve topflight performance. Moreover, a systematic approach facilitates objectivity in the appraisal process.

Over the years, our firm—United States Gypsum Company—has used many performance appraisal systems. We believe that our current program is vastly superior to any other system we have used, but we also recognize the possibility that a few years hence we will find even better ways of appraising and motivating executives.

This chapter will describe the performance appraisal system we use throughout our company—at all levels and in all functions for all exempt salaried employees. This approach, which we believe has been successful in its application to our company, may be termed a "results management" program. Thus it is a good deal more than just a method or system for appraising executive performance. The primary value of the program lies in its effectiveness as a management technique for achieving results.

The primary purpose of results management—an integral part of the total management process—is to contribute to the attainment of overall corporate goals through achievement of individual accountabilities and objectives.

Results management goes beyond many planning and appraisal systems, which focus only on selected portions of the individual's total performance. Traditional performance evaluation programs place their major emphasis on "how" an individual has performed. Typically, little attention is paid to planning performance or integrating individual performance with corporate and unit goals. These appraisal programs often become little more than measures of an individual's personality, in which personal characteristics—not performance—become the primary basis of the final appraisal.

By contrast, results management is a two-way process in which employee and manager meet several times a year to plan, review, monitor, and appraise all aspects of the employee's total performance against a set of jointly agreed upon accountabilities and objectives derived from—and coordinated with—unit and corporate plans and goals.

While the main purpose of results management is improved corporate performance, the program also serves as a:

- *Guiding tool* to assist individuals in establishing key priorities based on corporate and unit business plans
- *Communication tool* to foster and develop dialogue between manager and subordinate and between the various operating levels of management
- *Assessment tool* to permit measurement and evaluation of total performance results based on previously agreed upon criteria of performance
- *Management development tool* to help individuals plan and prepare for greater responsibilities and to assist managers in assessing employees' potential for more challenging future assignments
- *Management reward tool* to facilitate administration of corporate reward systems with the goal of relating pay to performance, and to provide employees some opportunity to control their achievement, recognition, and rewards

PERFORMANCE PLANNING

"Performance planning" is the first key step in the results management process and should be conducted at or before the beginning of the performance period if it is to lead to the development of accountabilities, objectives, and measures which truly direct performance.

Objectives, which are short-term goals, are typically derived from accountabilities, the ongoing results of the job. For example, a marketing manager might have an accountability to "staff, motivate, and develop a professional sales force." One of his or her specific objectives to fulfill that accountability in a given year might be to "recruit, hire, and place five new sales representatives by October of this year."

While accountabilities and objectives are distinct in their development and measurement, they are closely dependent on each other for their fulfillments. Thus it is recommended that the planning process begin with the development of the position's principal accountabilities.

ESTABLISHING PRINCIPAL ACCOUNTABILITIES

Statements of principal accountabilities are not simply a list of activities or duties, but rather they articulate what the employee is supposed to accomplish in the job. Accountability statements begin with an action verb ("staff," "ensure," "manage," etc.) and are general but succinct analyses of the desired

---

FIGURE 1   Sample Accountabilities Worksheet

NAME: ___Fred Smith___   YEAR: ___198X___   POSITION: ___Plant Manager___

A= PRINCIPAL ACCOUNTABILITIES   DEPT./DIV./SUBSID.: Eastern Division   UNIT: ___Gotham___

1. Manager and incumbent should review position analysis, making sure it accurately reflects current job accountabilities.
2. Accountabilities are to be summarized below.

PRINCIPAL ACCOUNTABILITIES	COMMENTS ON FULFILLMENT	UNSATISFACTORY	SATISFIES MOST REQUIREMENTS	MEETS REQUIREMENTS	EXCEEDS MOST REQUIREMENTS	SUPERIOR	OUTSTANDING
1. Establish and maintain safe working conditions and practices for and by all employees.	Established and aggressively pursued a comprehensive safety training and communications program. No lost workday or recordable injuries. Handled OSHA inspection effectively--only one minor citation.						X
2. Ship products which meet quality specifications and market requirements, and furnish service to customers as required to maintain market establishment.	Missed plant quality goal. However, performance substantially improved over prior year. Tighter quality controls have been implemented, but require further improvement.		X				
3. Produce at lowest cost consistent with customer service and quality requirements; achieve or exceed cost goals and cost standards.	Met cost and profit goals. However, more aggressiveness needed to capitalize on cost reduction opportunities.			X			
4. Preserve, maintain and use the plant property and facilities to produce at capacity on a dependable basis; assure neat and orderly conditions within buildings and on grounds at all times.	Preventive maintenance program is functioning beyond initial expectations. General housekeeping substantially improved.				X		
5. Furnish opportunity for individual growth and development of plant personnel, and contribute to Division and Company needs for trained operating and technical managers.	Planned job rotation and training program for new college graduates needs greater attention. More rapid development of Department Superintendents is required.			X			
6. Select, develop, retain and motivate an effective staff and work force, organized for optimum use of its capabilities, and insure adequate continuity of technical and managerial skills.	No college graduates hired during recruiting season due to rejection of low salary offers. Hourly turnover continues in excess of 30%.	X					
7.							
8.							

ACCOUNTABILITY FULFILLMENT

     X

UNSATISFACTORY   SATISFIES MOST REQUIREMENTS   MEETS REQUIREMENTS   EXCEEDS MOST REQUIREMENTS   SUPERIOR   OUTSTANDING

result. They often include the accountability's purpose ("to assure efficient and effective operations"), as well as any constraints ("in line with overall corporate sales and profit goals"). They also give broad direction on how the accountability might be fulfilled ("by scheduling and achieving production goals").

Accountabilities serve as criteria for determining the degree to which the employee has accomplished what is expected of him or her. Therefore, both the employee and the manager must have a clear understanding of what the accountabilities mean. Accountabilities can then also serve as a valuable communication link between the manager and the employee.

To maintain the focus on accountabilities, generally no less than five nor more than ten accountabilities should be determined. These should include not only operationally oriented accountabilities (profitability, reduced costs, market share, etc.) but also managerial accountabilities of a less tangible kind (improved organizational efficiency, development of subordinates, improvement of morale, etc.). (See Figure 1, Sample Accountabilities Worksheet.) Accountabilities should be worded so that their fulfillment will not conflict with the performance of other employees and should be controllable by the individual: Does he or she have the authority, resources, money, staff, time, and materials to do the job?

SETTING PERFORMANCE OBJECTIVES

In results management, an individual's objectives flow from the position's accountabilities and the unit's business plans for the year. After the employee's accountabilities are established, the manager and employee set the latter's objectives. An objective is a statement of specific results to be achieved—or a specific, verifiable accomplishment to be attained—within specified resource constraints.

There are several criteria in setting useful objectives.

First, a sound objective will clearly be related to the job, and the individual should see himself or herself as fully capable of achieving the desired end result by putting forth the needed effort.

Second, objectives should be descriptions of behavior that are specific enough to enable an employee or manager to readily verify accomplishment. In other words, a valid objective should be measurable.

Third, a good objective should state in detail what is to be accomplished, by when it is to be accomplished, and, if applicable, how it is to be accomplished.

Fourth, one or more objectives will likely be "assigned" to an employee by his or her manager for attainment of certain goals or results beyond the normal scope of the employee's accountabilities.

Finally, a well-conceived objective should specifically identify where the employee's priority effort should be directed. It will not necessarily cover the whole job, but it may indicate where emphasis should be placed.

Objectives can be short term or long term. Most objectives—particularly for line positions—are short term, with a time period of one year or less. Long-term objectives should concentrate on accomplishing a specific portion of the objective during the "performance year," even though the final result may not be realized until some future time.

Company goals should be translated into functional, divisional, or departmental objectives for specific groups, divisions, and corporate departments such as business systems, engineering, purchasing, etc., so that each executive knows the full extent of unit performance which is expected over the next 12-month period. Working with their employees, key managers, in turn, translate their unit objectives into more specific, and perhaps more detailed, objectives to be reviewed with subordinates—and so on down the management ladder until all exempt salaried employees have established annual objectives in line with the accountabilities of their positions.

Working from these plans and from the principal accountabilities already agreed upon for his or her position, the individual then develops a set of short- and long-term objectives for the coming year.

Most people tend to set too many objectives. It is advisable to set fewer objectives and to focus attention and effort on critical goals. Therefore, on the average, each position should have from six to ten short-term objectives and one or two long-term objectives.

In developing final objectives, the employee should keep in mind the following:

- Objectives should be specific, realistic, and (as we will see) measurable.
- Each objective should be commensurate with an established priority (i.e., "weightable") and compatible with all other objectives.
- The individual should be able reasonably to achieve his or her objectives.
- Objectives should not be set that require input or support from other units unless the other unit's commitment is relatively certain.

Besides being based on unit plans and position accountabilities, objectives may also be derived from:

- Areas where deficiencies now exist and improvement is required
- Areas where the manager and/or employee have ideas for change or development
- Areas where the manager and/or employee see unique opportunities for the unit and company

Once all the objectives for a job have been established, it will be clear that some objectives are more important than others and that not all of them have "equal weight" in terms of impact.

The results management program provides a numerical weighting system to rate the relative significance of each objective. The employee should list his or her objectives in descending order of importance. Then, with the manager's agreement, the individual assigns to each objective a numerical value which indicates its priority or impact—the "weight" of the objective. (See Figure 2, Sample Objectives Worksheet.)

Not only is the assigned weight an indication of the importance of an objective, it also serves to focus attention and emphasis on priorities—which, in turn, allow the employee to plan activities and the investment of time and resources. The sum of the weights of the objectives must equal 100.

If a weight of less than 5 points is assigned to an objective, it should be reexamined to determine if it should be dropped.

The simplest, most useful approach to discovering which objectives are critical is to ask: For which objectives would below-average performance hurt the

FIGURE 2   Sample Objectives Worksheet

NAME: _____Fred Smith_____ YEAR: ___198X___ POSITION: Plant   Manager

O = PERSONAL OBJECTIVES   DEPT./DIV./SUBSID.: _Eastern Division_ UNIT: ___Gotham___

1. Objectives are to be developed and mutually agreed upon by the incumbent and his or her manager, and then approved by the next level of management.

2. Approved objectives are to be summarized below. Attach separate pages, as necessary, listing the complete objectives with other pertinent information and documentation

PERSONAL OBJECTIVES (INCLUDE STANDARDS OF PERFORMANCE OR REQUIRED MEASUREMENTS WHICH APPLY INDICATE PLANNED COMPLETION DATE)	A OBJEC-TIVE WEIGHT (TO TOTAL 100)	REVIEW OF RESULTS ACHIEVED (USE QUANTITATIVE MEASUREMENTS WHEN AVAILABLE)	B OBJEC-TIVE RATING (0 TO 100%)	C ACHIEVE-MENT VALUE (COL A · COL B)
1. Achieve timely startup of plant expansion within allotted project cost. STANDARDS OF PERFORMANCE: Minimum Acceptable (0%) Target (100%) $1,000,000 $950,000 by 8-1-8X by 6-1-8X	30	Startup was achieved on 6-1-8X. Cost overrun was $17,000 over target cost of $950,000.	90%	27
2. Introduce cost saving programs in 198X to reduce burden expense. STANDARDS OF PERFORMANCE: Min. Acc. (0%) Target (100%) 3% reduction in 6% reduction in burden costs over burden costs prior year	20	Significant progress has been made in reducing excessive burden expense historically experienced at this plant. Total annual reduction was 6.2%.	100%	20
3. Improve quality controls to reduce complaints and improve market acceptance of product. STANDARDS OF PERFORMANCE: Min. Acc. (0%) Target (100%) 100% quality rating 150% quality rating	15	Implemented statistical quality control methods during 4th quarter and is making progress in bringing product quality into full compliance with bulletin specifications. Year-end rating 125%.	50%	7.5
4. Improve recovery from 95% to 96.5%. STANDARDS OF PERFORMANCE: Min. Acc. (0%) Target (100%) 95% recovery 96.5% recovery	15	Achieved excellent results in recovery through aggres-sive training and direction of operating personnel. Year-end recovery was 96.5%.	100%	15
5. Ensure completion of principal objectives of subordinates. STANDARDS OF PERFORMANCE: Min. Acc. (0%) Target (100%) 85% completion 100% completion	10	Completed 98% of subordinate plans. However, some key plans in quality area were not implemented.	70%	7
6. Work with Corp. Engineering Dept. to complete feasibility study for converting old calciner to rock dryer and make recommendations by 11/1/8X. STANDARDS OF PERFORMANCE: Min. Acc. (0%) Target (100%) Study Completed Approval by 11/1	10	Project never started.	0%	0

most? Answering that question isolates those objectives which are truly critical for job performance.

ESTABLISHING MEASURES AND STANDARDS OF PERFORMANCE

After the principal objectives have been developed and weights assigned, specific measures and standards of performance should be established. For most

NAME: ___Fred Smith_____ YEAR: _____198X_____ POSITION: ___Plant Manager_____

O = PERSONAL OBJECTIVES - CONTINUED   DEPT./DIV./SUBSID.: __Eastern Division__UNIT: ___Gotham_____

7				
8.				
9.				
10.				

TOTAL OBJECTIVE WEIGHTING	100	TOTAL OBJECTIVE ACHIEVEMENT VALUE (0 TO 100)	76.5

Special Projects and Personal Accomplishments

(Significant contributions which are separately identifiable and measurable - (1) Specific achievements not covered by approved objectives, and, (2) Attainment of results which substantially exceed intent and scope of original objectives).

After installation of equipment for plant expansion by contract engineering personnel, several serious process problems were encountered. Through exceptional personal effort, incumbent directed a "de-bugging" program that resulted in timely restoration of production at near capacity level. (20 points)

Raw material supplies were disrupted during second and third quarter due to operating problems experienced by suppliers. Incumbent successfully located alternative sources which alleviated shortage to the benefit of 3 division plants (15 points)

TOTAL SPECIAL ACHIEVEMENT (0 TO 50)	35
TOTAL SCORE FOR OBJECTIVES COMBINED OBJECTIVES AND SPECIAL ACHIEVEMENT	111.5

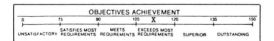

OBJECTIVES ACHIEVEMENT

0	75	90	105	X	120	135	150
UNSATISFACTORY	SATISFIES MOST REQUIREMENTS	MEETS REQUIREMENTS	EXCEEDS MOST REQUIREMENTS		SUPERIOR	OUTSTANDING	

objectives, performance is not an all-or-nothing matter, but one of degree. Thus measures and standards must be set to gauge how well each objective is achieved.

Measures and standards of performance are usually derived from unit objectives or from performance areas where there are problems to overcome or opportunities upon which to capitalize.

By jointly establishing sound measures and standards of performance, the manager and employee:

- Focus the employee's efforts on what is required to reach desired job performance against objectives
- Provide the employee with a reference to plan and review performance during the year so as to direct attention to problem areas
- Reach agreement ahead of time on how performance will be evaluated
- Facilitate performance evaluation by defining the desired standard of performance

Performance standards are intended to focus action on the achievement of the objective. They should be set at a level high enough to require the individual to "stretch" to reach them, but not so high that he or she will become discouraged. When standards are established at too difficult—or, for that matter, too easy—a level, they fail to motivate and focus effort properly.

The results management program has two standards of performance: "minimum acceptable," the lowest level of acceptable achievement against the objective in question, and "target," the goal the individual is striving to achieve. Measures of performance may be either numerical (quantitative) or descriptive (qualitative). Whenever possible, the measures should be numerical (dollar sales volume, number of units manufactured, percent increase or decrease compared to previous year) because these are observable and concrete.

But some objectives cannot be given a quantitative value and must be measured qualitatively. For example, a manager might be rated on how well he or she maintains morale. While there are some indicators of morale (turnover, absenteeism, etc.), there is no direct measure. Thus a description must be used.

MIDYEAR PROGRESS REVIEW

Approximately midway through the "performance year," the employee and manager should discuss the employee's progress toward achieving his or her objectives and informally review the individual's progress toward fulfilling his or her accountabilities.

The manager may want to conduct such progress reviews more often if problems appear to exist or if the employee would benefit from special coaching.

Periodic reviews allow for revision of objectives or standards of performance in those cases where business plans change or where there is a major shift in emphasis to react to some intervening variable. Such reviews also help the employee to redirect efforts and obtain assistance from the supervisor to meet specific performance challenges.

PERFORMANCE EVALUATION

At the end of the performance year, the manager will privately review the employee's performance against each accountability and objective in preparation for meeting with the employee in a performance evaluation session. The supervisor will rate performance against each accountability and objective separately and develop separate ratings for total accountabilities and total objectives to come up with an overall performance rating. The six performance levels used in the rating system, and their meanings, are as follows:

Outstanding	Clearly unique performance; far above other employees holding positions with like duties and responsibilities
Superior	Clearly and substantially above required performance
Exceeds most requirements	Very good performance, meets all, and exceeds many, position requirements
Meets requirements	Good performance which meets all, or practically all, position requirements
Satisfies most requirements	Generally acceptable performance, but some skills, performance factors, or position accountabilities require attention
Unsatisfactory	Marginally meets minimum standards

A properly accomplished evaluation can:

- Improve the employee's performance and morale
- Provide greater development of his or her potential
- Provide the basis for a fair and consistent reward system
- Provide management with greater knowledge of individual potential that can be utilized for promotion decisions

In evaluating the employee and assigning a rating, the manager must be careful to avoid the following errors which can arise from the subjective nature of the evaluation process:

- *Personal bias.* Because of personal likes or dislikes, the evaluator tends to evaluate a person too high or low. Some studies indicate that personal bias emanates from the "good" or "bad" credentials of a person. In other words, the evaluator is biased by preperformance expectations.
- *Halo effect.* This error is usually associated with positive bias and makes the evaluator tend to evaluate everything high because of a few strong points exhibited by the employee.
- *Central tendency.* The evaluator very seldom rates characteristics of anyone at the extremes of the scale.
- *Logical error.* The evaluator simply does not understand the accountability or is not able to translate the accountability into performance criteria.

EVALUATING GENERAL FULFILLMENT OF ACCOUNTABILITIES

First the manager assigns a rating for each accountability, then establishes a rating for total accountability performance. Most individuals will receive different ratings on individual accountabilities, and as a result, the supervisor must develop an overall rating which honestly and fairly summarizes the employee's total performance against accountabilities. For example, an employee who was rated "meets requirement" on most accountabilities but has shown "superior" or "outstanding" performance in a key accountability area may receive a final rating of "exceeds most requirements."

EVALUATING SPECIFIC ACHIEVEMENT OF OBJECTIVES

In judging the achievement of objectives, the manager evaluates the employee's performance against each of the objectives set at the beginning of the year. Because this evaluation uses the weights and standards previously agreed upon to measure performance, the objective achievement evaluation process tends to be less subjective than accountability fulfillment evaluation. However, procedures involved—as well as the benefits derived—are basically the same.

As with accountabilities, the performance of the employee against each objective is evaluated separately and is assigned a rating. (See Figure 2.) In this case, the rating takes the form of a percent score on a scale from 0 to 100 percent—0 percent is given for performance that is at or below the "minimum acceptable" standard, while a full 100 percent is awarded for meeting or exceeding the "target." Achievement levels less than target, but better than the minimum acceptable, receive a score between 0 and 100 percent based on the supervisor's best judgment.

An "achievement value" for each objective is then computed by multiplying the rating (percent) by the weight of the objective. Thus if an individual met or surpassed the target for an objective with a weight of 40, the achievement value for that objective would be calculated as follows:

$$
\begin{array}{rl}
100\% & \text{Rating} \\
\times \underline{40} & \text{Weight} \\
40 & \text{Achievement value}
\end{array}
$$

When the manager has completed the evaluation of the employee's performance against each objective, he or she should record the achievement value for each objective and then add them to obtain a total objective achievement value. Comments supporting the evaluation should be entered in a "Review of Results Achieved."

To guarantee the evaluation's validity, some recognition must be given to special achievements on the part of the employee which either fall outside the scope of the listed objectives or exceed their intent and scope (for example, substantially surpassing the approved target). Such achievements must be both clearly identifiable and distinctly measurable.

These special projects and/or personal accomplishments can be summarized and awarded points on a scale of 0 to 50 at the discretion of the supervisor. If the employee performed competently against all his or her approved objectives but, in the evaluator's best judgment, did nothing in excess or outside of the stated standards, no points at all may be given for special achievements. However, in most cases some special achievement points are awarded.

The total score for objectives then becomes the sum of total objective achievement value and the points awarded for special achievement. This total score can then be converted into a rating.

DETERMINING OVERALL PERFORMANCE

The supervisor now evaluates the results of the accountability fulfillment and objective achievement evaluations to arrive at a final overall performance evaluation for the subordinate.

FIGURE 3   **Results Management**

RESULTS MANAGEMENT
EVALUATION REPORT

NAME: _____ | YEAR 19 ___ ___ |

POSITION: _____

DEPT./DIV./SUBSID.: _____ UNIT: _____

Results Management is a <u>two-way process</u> in which each exempt salaried employee and manager meet several times a year to plan, review and appraise all aspects of the employee's total job performance.

Results Management is a combination of Accountability fulfillment and Objectives achievement. (A + O = R) The relative weighting or importance of each should be discussed with the incumbent at the beginning of the year and at year end when appraising performance.

<u>Performance Appraisal:</u> Considering Accountability Fulfillment (rating from Page 2) and Objectives Achievement (rating from Page 4) and the relative weight of each, assign an overall performance rating below:

	UNSATISFACTORY	SATISFIES MOST REQUIREMENTS	MEETS REQUIREMENTS	EXCEEDS MOST REQUIREMENTS	SUPERIOR	OUTSTANDING
Accountability Fulfillment						
Objectives Achievement						
RESULTS (OVERALL PERFORMANCE)						

COMMENTS ON OVERALL PERFORMANCE:

WHEN INCUMBENT'S JOB PERFORMANCE IS QUESTIONABLE/UNSATISFACTORY IN ONE OR MORE AREAS, SPECIFY REQUIRED IMPROVEMENT WITH TARGET DATE FOR ACTION:

ACKNOWLEDGEMENTS:

	Performance Planning		Year End		Interim Reviews	
	Signature	Date	Signature	Date	Dates	Dates
INCUMBENT						
MANAGER						
NEXT LEVEL MANAGER						

First, the relative weight previously determined for total accountability performance versus objectives should be considered. Using this weighting, the manager should consider both ratings awarded and determine the final rating for the performance period. (See Figure 3.)

For example, if a plant manager receives a "meets requirements" rating on accountability fulfillment and "exceeds most requirements" on objective achievement, a final rating of "exceeds most requirements" reflects the emphasis on objective achievement in a line position.

PERFORMANCE EVALUATION SESSION

After the manager has completed the evaluation, he or she should meet with the employee and discuss the results. The established accountabilities, objectives, and standards should be compared to actual achievement. The manager should communicate each rating and the reasoning behind it. It is important that the employee completely understand the reasoning, as well as the rating, so that he or she will know what can be done to sustain or improve performance in the coming year.

FIGURE 4   Annual Report of Exempt Employee Performance Ratings

ANNUAL REPORT OF EXEMPT EMPLOYEE
PERFORMANCE RATINGS

REPORTING UNIT: _____   DATE _____

NAME	POSITION	PERFORMANCE RATING					
		UN-SATIS-FAC-TORY	SATIS-FIES MOST REQUIRE.	MEETS REQUIRE.	EXCEEDS MOST REQUIRE.	SUPERIOR	OUT-STANDING

FORMULA FOR DETERMINING % OF AVERAGE RATING:

LINE "A" SUM OF EACH COLUMN ⟶

ENTER TOTAL OF LINE "B"   ENTER TOTAL OF LINE "A" TIMES 5

MULTIPLY BY THIS AND PLACE RESULT ⟶

| ×0 | ×2 | ×4 | ×6 | ×8 | ×10 |

HERE _ _ _ _ ⟶
LINE "B"

_____ ÷ _____ × 100 = _____ %

This feedback session is extremely important in the results management process and should be approached positively by both parties. The main emphasis should be on how the employee can improve, rather than on mistakes and failures.

COMPARATIVE EVALUATION RATINGS

For purposes of the results management program, let's assume that most employees fall just above or below the average on the rating scale. It is expected that most exempt salaried employees will fall into the "meets requirements" and "exceeds most requirements" groups. At either extreme, the normal distribution includes only a small percentage of the population; likewise, for the ratings of "outstanding" and "unsatisfactory," it is expected that only a small number of exempt salaried employees will fall into the two extremes—probably somewhat less than 5 percent will achieve the "outstanding" rating.

One method of obtaining a satisfactory distribution of ratings is to force them into the desired curve: a manager is told that a certain number of employees must be rated "outstanding," a certain number "superior," and so on. The problem with this approach is that, unless the rater is evaluating an exceptionally large group, the forced distribution will likely contribute to, rather than correct, error and distortion. Nevertheless, chances are that 30 percent of the employees will be in the "exceeds most requirements" or "meets requirements" categories, while only 4 percent of the employees will be in either the "outstanding" or "unsatisfactory" range.

COMBINED EVALUATION RATINGS

Following completion of the ratings for all exempt employees, an annual report of performance ratings is to be prepared by each plant, district, or department manager and submitted to the manager's superior for approval and forwarding to the corporate personnel department no later than February 1 of each year.

Managers should assign a value to each rating level which can be used to compute an average rating for the unit. It is recommended that the average employee rating be compared with the overall performance of the unit or department. (See Figure 4.)

CONCLUSION

Results management is one of the best tools available to assist exempt employees in the performance of their jobs. It is based on the belief that the company will operate more profitably and efficiently if employees know in advance the results that are expected of them, the yardsticks that determine whether they have achieved those results, and the specific plans to produce the results.

Rewarding Performance

chapter 25

Adjusting Wages and Salaries

William H. Hrabak

DIRECTOR, COMPENSATION AND BENEFITS, BANKERS
LIFE AND CASUALTY COMPANY, CHICAGO, ILLINOIS

Even in today's business environment of formalized and sophisticated compensation systems, many managers and supervisors—when faced with responsibility for reviewing, recommending, and approving employee pay increases—still make decisions with less than full consideration of the pertinent facts involved. Typically, pay decisions made by uninitiated managers will be based on oversimplified, subjective, or arbitrary factors which will result in overly generous or tightfisted pay practice administration. Allowed to continue, such practices will result in an inequitable and generally unsatisfactory pay structure which will adversely impact employee work attitudes and motivational levels.

Needless to say, salary levels and general salary information such as merit budgets are becoming more available to employees than has been usual in the past. Salary administration practices, therefore, need to be fair and equitable and well communicated to be a positive factor in the management of people. Individual salary-increase decisions need not be based on complex analyses. However, there are certain critical factors which are important and need to be given consideration by managers to produce consistently satisfactory salary adjustment results.

BASE-PAY REVIEWS AND INCREASES

Pay-increase judgments should be made with consideration of each individual's specific job level, the length of service, the date and amount of the last increase, and the pay levels of others on the same or similar jobs within the company. Consideration should also be given to pay levels of similar jobs within the industry, geographical area, and among other companies, which normally are used for comparisons, and—above all—the objective appraised performance level and potential of each individual concerned.

How to determine amount of pay increase. From a purely mechanical aspect, the amount of a pay increase should be influenced by the date and amount of the last increase. Also to be considered is the position of the current salary within the salary range, if ranges are used, or the relationship of the present salary to outside salaries for comparable jobs.

With regard to administrative procedures, it is more practical to make salary increases effective at the beginning of a pay period rather than to be encumbered with increases given in the middle of the pay period, which will result in payroll administration complications.

Merit, general, or promotional increases should always be expressed as a percent of salary and adjusted to a weekly, monthly, or annual multiple. For example:

1. A nonexempt accounting clerk earning $10,400 per annum or $200 per week should have a pay increase presented as 9 percent—$18 per week.

2. An exempt supervisor earning $24,000 per annum should have a pay increase presented as 11 percent—$264 per month.

3. A manager earning $40,000 per annum should have a pay increase presented as 12 percent—$4800 annually.

The amount of the increase should take into account individual performance (this important matter will be addressed more specifically later) plus the employee's salary history, position in the range, and *job level.* Assuming performance to be equal, a pay increase for an employee classified to a high-level job with a salary in the lower part of the salary range should normally be higher in percentage but given after a longer interval than for an employee on a lower-level job. As employees in higher-level jobs exceed their range midpoints or a calculated median for the job, the increase percentage should normally be lower, unless economic conditions or other conditions take precedence.

Salary increases should always be made with consideration for the net amount that the employee's paycheck will be increased. In no event should small pay increases be granted where the net increase in paycheck amount or "take-home" money will be extremely small or nonexistent. As a general rule of thumb, merit pay increases should be no smaller than 6 or 7 percent for an individual who merits to remain on the payroll, especially in highly inflationary economic conditions. If a manager wishes to recommend a small increase, serious consideration should be given instead to lengthening the time interval between increases rather than to reduce the percentage of increase.

Frequency and regularity of review. The frequency of review of an individual employee's pay level should be tied directly to the level of the job involved. Nonexempt jobs, such as clerks, secretaries, and technicians, should be reviewed at least every six to nine months. Exempt jobs, such as first-line supervisors, department heads, salespeople, engineers, exempt technicians, managers, and executives, should be reviewed no less than once each year.

However, a personnel appraisal review should not automatically generate a pay increase. It is rather a process of investigating each employee's pay situation to determine whether individual salary pay levels are proper within the context of formal company pay policies, if they exist, or within accepted company pay practices. Also to be considered is the comparison of internal and external pay for similar jobs.

Review of nonexempt salaries.   Reviews of employees in nonexempt salaried jobs should be made in different time frames from reviews of higher-level exempt jobs.

In addition, the nonexempt salary review should be done with consideration of hourly pay changes experienced in the unit or company (whether or not the hourly jobs fall under union organization), specific economic conditions (whether the economy is in an inflationary or deflationary period), availability of people to fill nonexempt jobs (which will influence the marketplace), and prevailing salary rates in the particular company or locality. All these factors have a bearing on pay review considerations at all job levels but have a more profound influence upon nonexempt jobs, in which the incumbents are less mobile and relate more to pay levels in the specific geographical area.

Employees in nonexempt jobs are hired locally and normally are not subject to job transfer. Therefore, their pay levels should be tied to prevailing salary levels for the specific locality and/or unit in which they work. Movement of pay levels for nonexempt jobs will generally be influenced by the above-listed factors.

Oftentimes it is more difficult to make merit-increase judgments for employees in nonexempt jobs because only minor differences in the quality of performance may exist between individuals, assuming the employees are performing well enough to remain on the job. Therefore, salary-increase practices for jobs at nonexempt levels should be more standardized than for jobs at exempt levels.

From a practical standpoint, it is generally agreed that of the two main variables associated with pay increases—the amount of the increase and the frequency of the increase—the latter is the more important consideration for nonexempt jobs. This is especially true for the lower or beginning level of nonexempt jobs. A higher degree of equity and employee goodwill will generally result if increases for nonexempt employees are given more frequently, such as at eight- or nine-month intervals, but for smaller percentage amounts.

In some cases, depending upon the sophistication of a company's salary administration program, the more practical approach from an administrative and internal-equity concern would be to grant nonexempt pay increases according to a formalized progressional increase system. A typical salary progression system would be tied to a series of separate salary schedules developed to meet each location's competitive conditions, with salary increases administered automatically through a series of steps within the salary ranges for different job levels. For example, suppose a particular salary range is:

Minimum	Midpoint	Maximum
$700	$840	$980

In this case, the progressional steps could be established in $35 increments between the $700 minimum rate and the $840 midpoint rate. The progressional step increase range would appear as follows:

		$35 Steps		
Minimum	1st	2d	3d	4th (midpoint)
$700	$735	$770	$805	$840

As an alternative, progressional steps may be established as a constant percentage. This serves the same purpose but becomes more complicated to administer.

The time intervals for administering salary increases can then be set at any point to conform with general company policy or philosophy. The intervals can be established at six, seven, eight, nine, or ten months as determined to be competitive and reasonable.

It is important in such a system that the minimum of the progressional range be established as the minimum going rate, below which no employee would be paid. However, depending on individual qualifications and rates being paid longer-service employees, a new employee could be started at a step higher than the minimum rate.

The progression in the above example extends only to the midpoint rate, since a midpoint normally represents the company's judgment on its average rate for the job in relation to the local labor market. Thus no automatic progression system should be carried to the maximum; the range between the midpoint and the maximum should be reserved for merit increases based upon individual ability and continued good performance.

A progressional increase system will avoid or help correct many equity problems and personnel relations difficulties which may creep into nonexempt compensation programs. Some major advantages of such a system are that it:

1. Guarantees that each individual's pay is reviewed automatically at periodic intervals. There is no chance that the supervisor may forget or overlook review dates.

2. Ensures that each individual's salary is automatically increased on the scheduled effective dates unless the individual's supervisor countermands the increase by positive action properly substantiated.

3. Guarantees that new employees receive a fair and equitable minimum starting rate without regard to supervisory whims or attitudes not based on good personnel management or compensation judgments.

4. Assures nonexempt employees of continuous and objective review of their salaries, provided that good job performance continues.

5. Enables employee recruiters and supervisors to clearly define the pay latitudes of specific jobs and the maximum pay potentials available.

6. Permits reduction of administrative detail and realization of cost savings, since this system is less time-consuming and eliminates unnecessary paperwork.

Of course, any automatic program has disadvantages, and a nonexempt salary progression system is no exception; however, most can be avoided with effective administration. The major pitfalls are:

1. Employees who do not deserve increases could receive them automatically under such a system. (This, however, would happen only through inaction on the part of concerned supervisors.)

2. All employees, regardless of performance, would receive the same amount of increase within the same time interval. (This is true only up to the midpoint of the salary range. This system can also be designed to permit a supervisor to delay an increase until the next review period or to advance an exceptional performer two steps, rather than one step, within the progression range.)

3. This system eliminates individual consideration and the personal contact between employee and supervisor on pay-increase matters. (This may be true. However, a thorough examination of most companies will show that the personal pay relationships in a nonexempt area are not as "personal" or as well handled as many supervisors may believe. From a personnel relations standpoint, the improvement in internal equity derived from a progressional increase system will far outweigh any loss of so-called individual pay treatment.)

In essence, the most important aspects in good administration of nonexempt pay increases are uniformity, consistency, frequency, and fairness. These are necessary in order to avoid inequities and assure competitiveness for all employees regardless of company operation or business area.

Review of exempt salaries below management levels. Exempt employees' salaries should be reviewed in a uniform manner. However, since exempt jobs are not grouped in as narrow a hierarchy as nonexempt jobs, different factors must be considered in making salary-increase judgments for different levels of exempt jobs. The lower exempt job hierarchy includes first-line supervisors, beginning salespeople, and junior accountants, while the next higher level includes senior salespeople, senior engineers, plant superintendents, territory sales supervisors, and accounting and office supervisors.

The traditional concept that the high degree of mobility of exempt personnel makes them part of a national market and that, accordingly, they should be assigned to a single exempt schedule, regardless of the number of diverse locations of company operations, is no longer considered realistic by many companies. Individuals in lower-level exempt jobs tend to be hired locally and often remain in the same area during their entire employment careers. Therefore, these employees tend to compare their status and pay levels with pay levels in their particular area rather than with the national market, of which they may not even be aware. For example, an exempt junior accountant hired in the New York metropolitan area will tend to remain in the New York metropolitan area and should be paid commensurately with pay levels in that area rather than according to a national average pay schedule for junior accountants. Likewise, a junior accountant in Phoenix, Arizona, should be paid according to the prevailing salary levels in that area. Only in the upper exempt position level, where jobs and people are truly mobile and are part of a national market, should salaries be compared with a national schedule. Companies which design their lower exempt schedule to be competitive nationwide will find the schedule to be higher than need be at some locations and lower at other locations.

Frequency and amount of pay increase for exempt employees should also vary with job level. Even though all exempt employees should be reviewed or appraised at least once a year, salary schedules should have a greater influence on pay increases for those in the lower exempt levels. Here again, for employees on lower exempt jobs, pay-increase factors similar to those mentioned above for nonexempt jobs (union contract pay levels, company and general economic conditions, and, of course, specific comparisons with internal and external pay for similar jobs for each company location) must be considered. For example, in reviewing a first-line shift foreman, consideration must be given to the effect of pay increases granted in the hourly ranks, whether affected by union contract or by unilateral company action. In addition, first-line foremen's pay ought to be maintained at a level sufficiently above the group of highest-paid hourly employees supervised to maintain an equitable differential between the different job hierarchies and to avoid pay compression problems. Nothing will defeat pay-equity principles quicker than for a first-line foreman to receive total direct income that is not sufficiently above the highest-paid hourly employees supervised. What is a proper differential between supervisor-subordinate pay levels will vary by company and/or industry but normally should be in a range of not less than 10 to 15 percent.

Pay increases for exempt employees should be based on appraisal judgments, and each increase should be substantial enough to have a definite motivational impact. For well-paid exempt employees approaching the maximum of their range, it may be more realistic to lengthen the interval between increases to 15 or 18 months but retain a reasonably high rate of increase. The concept of general salary increases should normally not be part of the salary compensation program for exempt employees. Automatic or general salary increases of 4 or 5 percent will not substantially increase the net paycheck or take-home pay of an exempt employee and will probably have a negative motivational effect on the better performers. It is therefore best to review exempt salaries regularly but within the policy that pay increases will not be automatic, especially in the higher exempt positions, and that individual salary increases should be substantial enough to have a significant increase in take-home pay.

Review of management and executive salaries. The administration of management and executive salaries in a systematic and professional manner has come to be accepted as part of the total responsibility of the salary compensation manager in the more progressive companies. In the not too distant past in many companies, the administration of executive salaries had been considered to be within the private domain of the company's chief financial officer or chief executive officer. In many cases, companies have maintained separate executive payrolls to protect the "confidentiality" and "uniqueness" of top-level jobs. As a result of this isolation of top executive salary and pay practices in past years, many otherwise successful companies have found that their pay practices in this most important area had become chaotic and inequitable. As a result, more and more companies are coming to realize that good, objective salary administration serves as a valuable management tool in the administration of executive salaries just as it does for salaries at lower levels. The advent of the compensation committee on company board of directors has also influenced the adoption of professional administration for executive compensation programs.

Salary administration for management and executive jobs, however, must reflect the fact that each position at this level is personalized, individual, and unique to itself and oftentimes unique to the job incumbent. Therefore, in order to maintain equitable and competitive pay levels in the executive job hierarchy, more sophisticated and individualized administrative and position comparison techniques need to be employed.

Executive Job Surveys   The survey, which has been employed in the wage and salary field for many years, has come into its own and gained acceptance by executives as a meaningful tool for management compensation. Various consulting firms and industry groups have developed systematic methods of surveying executive positions in order to provide companies with objective and meaningful data from which salary ranges and pay practices may be developed for their top management employees.

It is most important in determining executive salary ranges and pay practices for a company treasurer, vice president of manufacturing, vice president of sales, personnel director, research director, president, and also chairperson of the board to compare these positions with their counterparts in other companies on the basis of industrial classification, size of company in terms of revenues, and organization structure.

With regard to executive compensation surveying, it is important in comparing executive positions to understand whether the company's organization is completely decentralized, completely centralized, or divisionalized or operates in a manner which has been described as "controlled decentralization" (i.e., relatively autonomous divisions but with an overall corporate group responsible for developing, implementing, and administering overall policy).

When comparing executive positions, it is most important that company size enter into the picture. If a company's revenues are $300 million, its pay practices for top executives should be compared with those of other companies of the same size rather than with those of companies which have sales of $50 million or $5 billion.

In addition, it is important to recognize industrial classifications, because in executive compensation some companies have traditional (whether right or wrong) pay practices unique to their particular industry. For example, some industries have traditionally relied heavily on bonuses or incentive payments rather than on base salary. Other industries such as utilities rely heavily on base salary with very little bonus compensation. Other industries attempt to achieve a balance between base salary and bonus; and still others deliberately pay low salaries but extremely high bonuses in an effort to motivate executives to generate high levels of business and profit growth.

Also, in surveying executive compensation practices, it is important to look beyond job titles, which can be confusing and misleading. For example, the job of a treasurer in one company who reports to a vice president of finance will not be the same position as that of a treasurer in another company who reports to the president or chief executive officer. A marketing manager in one company who has no field sales responsibility will not be the same as a marketing manager in another company who has accountability for the line sales function.

In addition, it is becoming more important to understand the total compensation package of executives, since this has a bearing upon the base-salary or direct-pay package. Here again, some companies or industries establish high benefit and perquisite programs which may detract from salary levels, while others direct their executive compensation packages to heavy cash payments.

Another important factor to consider when surveying the executive field is the relative availability of executive talent as well as the mobility of this group. Compensation judgments should not be based on general tip-of-the-iceberg comparisons, but should delve as deeply into all compensation elements and company-size factors as are necessary to arrive at sound appraisals in the executive compensation field.

Actual Executive Salary Pay Practice Guidelines   It is extremely important that a company's executive pay practices be formalized and documented in the same manner as pay practices for other employee groups. This is essential to provide top management and the board of directors with uniform and meaningful guidelines and policies on which to base salary-increase judgments for individual executives.

A formalized executive compensation program is important for purposes of attracting executive talent from outside the company. It is also an extremely important safeguard in the event that federal wage and salary controls should ever again, God forbid, be imposed on our economy. When such controls were established in the past, companies which did not have a systematic, formalized executive compensation program found it difficult, embarrassing, and complicated to administer pay increases for their executives. Conversely, if a formal, documented program is in existence and working, wage control administrators normally have accepted it as a realistic and controlled means of administering executive salaries.

Executive salaries should be related to a salary range, as are other salary jobs, but with three differences:

1. Salary ranges (from minimum to maximum) should be at least as wide as those in effect for other employee groups—at least 50 percent and in some cases possibly as high as 66⅔ percent.

2. The term "merit increase" should not be used for executive salary increases. Merit is a term applicable to jobs at lower salary levels. At the executive level, *performance* is the name of the game and needs to be recognized and compensated. However, salary reviews should be made at least once a year for executive employees as they are for other exempt salaried employees.

3. The size of the increase is extremely important at this level. A small increase would have either no motivational effect or possibly a negative effect, since the take-home dollars would be insignificant after income tax and other payroll deductions.

A frequent problem in executive compensation is the case of younger, fast-rising executives who demonstrate rapid growth within the job. In such a case, is it wise to pay according to established company policies, even though the amount and frequency of the increases may appear abnormally high. At the very minimum, the executive's salary should be increased to the salary range minimum within a prescribed period of time, as determined practical through good salary administration. There is no logical business reason to underpay a top executive who truly is charged with the responsibility of the position and is performing the job in an acceptable manner. Below-minimum salaries not only invite dissatisfaction but will tempt the executive to look for greener pastures and make him or her ripe bait for professional recruiters or "headhunters." This is especially true at a time when proven executive talent is in great demand. In this same regard, it behooves any company to establish good pay practices for its executive employees, because true executive talent, regardless of the specific function or discipline involved, is readily transferable across company and industry boundaries.

A simplified example for use in the administration of a management performance increase program is shown in Table 1.

Relationship between Salary Reviews and Performance Reviews A definite relationship should exist and be workable between pay increases and employee performance appraisals. Nothing is more exasperating to a salary administrator or executive management than to see termination papers processed on an employee for reasons of incompetence when the same employee two or three months earlier had been granted a salary merit increase. This situation, which should not occur in a progressive business organization, happens more often than management would like to believe, primarily because in most companies there is not direct relationship between individual employee performance appraisal and salary increases.

Employee appraisal programs, whether formalized or not, have been practiced by companies for many years, but in many cases, employee appraisals have not been used in direct relationship to pay practice decisions. Personnel executives are finding, however, that pay practices and personnel appraisal systems must work in concert so that each program can be more effectively administered. Many new personnel appraisal programs have been developed and adopted by companies which merge individual performance with individual pay level. A salary performance increase program based upon formal, individual appraisal judgments should be governed by an established normal distribution range of evaluations. The ideal distribution for appraisals would be a bell-shaped curve which would provide a range of 5-15-60-15-5 percent for a five-level appraisal system for a representative group of employees. For a newly organized company with a large group of new employees, a true bell-

TABLE 1   Salary Performance Increase Guidelines and Distribution

	If Current Salary Is			
	Below range minimum	Range minimum to midpoint	Over range midpoint to maximum	Performance appraisal distribution
1. Salary reviewed at least every:	9 months	12 months	12–15 months	
2. Recommended salary increase range based upon performance appraisal:				
Outstanding	Up to 15%	12–14%	10–12%	10%
Superior	Up to 12%	10–12%	8–10%	20%
Satisfactory	Up to 10%	8–10%	6–8%	50%
Acceptable	Up to 8%	6–8%	6%	15%
Unacceptable	0%	0%	0%	5%

shaped curve may be feasible. However, for a more mature organization, the distribution of appraisals should more practically be established with a skewing to the high side as represented in Table 1.

It is important that a system linking performance appraisal with salary pay practices begin at the top of the organization, where performance is a truly measurable element, and be extended to all other job levels. Just as many companies have position evaluation plans to evaluate different job families at different organizational position levels, it is important that performance appraisal systems be designed for different position levels. Performance appraisal systems for executive and higher management and higher-level exempt positions should be quantifiable, business goal–oriented, and related to specific measurable factors contained in each individual position description and evaluation. For example, a sales manager can be measured on meeting sales goals, within price, quality, and service considerations. In the same sense, a manufacturing manager can be measured on meeting production goals within cost, production efficiency and quality levels, and overall profit considerations. A marketing representative can be measured on performance against sales volume goals in relation to price levels and market conditions, consistent with good supervisory support and guidance. Employees classified in lower-level exempt or nonexempt jobs should be evaluated by a different appraisal system, designed to consider specific, individual job duty and skill levels.

The ultimate goal is a direct correlation between individual performance and salary pay levels in which top performers would consistently receive higher salaries than poor performers. Unless this is achieved, personnel appraisal will not have the muscle it needs to be effective, and salary administration will be less equitable and inconsistent in its application.

Administering pay of unionized employees.   Administration of a pay-increase system takes on a different character for hourly or salaried employees covered by union contract. Union wage contracts are generally oriented toward the concept of one basic wage for each job. The base wage can be identified as the job rate, the qualified job rate, the journeyman job rate as applied to skilled trade jobs, or in other terms unique to the union and/or company and industry involved. In most cases, management has little discretion during the life of a contract to adjust employee rates, since union contracts provide for negotiated fixed pay increases to the job's qualified or maximum rate level. However, two mechanisms are available which can be employed to distinguish between varying job base rates in a union-organized operation.

The first is job evaluation, which has been described in Part B. Job evaluation offers a systematic tool to be used in partnership with labor relations negotiators, by which clear distinctions can be drawn between different levels of job duties. Hourly job evaluation can establish rational pay-rate differentials between different job and skill levels, but the qualified-rate concept will normally still prevail as the maximum job rate.

The second alternative is to establish a narrow hourly wage range. This approach is not foreign to hourly wage contracts and is desirable in that it will aid to maintain management control. The wage range would include a beginner hourly rate and wage increases in steps to a qualified or maximum job rate. An example of such a range is shown in Table 2.

TABLE 2   Sample Hourly Wage Range

Beginner rate	Steps			Qualified job rate
	1st	2d	3d	
$6.00	$6.16	$6.32	$6.48	$6.66

The spread of the range from beginning to qualified rate should be narrow—accordingly, the range depicted in Table 2 has an 11 percent spread. The step increments can be designed to comply with particular union-and-company-negotiated agreements and other pertinent company labor or market factors. However, it is normally a good practice to establish the steps with time increments no longer than six months. It is also prudent to have only one or two steps in the lower unskilled classifications and to gradually increase the number of steps to four or five in the highly skilled classifications.

The beginning rate should be used as a probationary hiring rate. In this case, no employee would be advanced beyond the beginning rate until a decision is made that the employee meets minimum qualifications to become a permanent employee, at which time the employee's job rate would begin increasing through the range according to established contractual procedures.

Another advantage of the concept of hourly rate range is that a new hourly employee need not be hired at the beginning rate or the qualified rate. Instead, the initial wage can be established commensurate with the employee's skills and abilities as determined by relevant testing and supervisory appraisal. For example, an employee without previous knowledge or job-related ability would begin employment at the beginning rate. Following this, the hourly rate would be advanced through the progressional pay steps as individual abilities develop until reaching the fully qualified rate. Another employee who is judged, when assigned to a job, to have satisfactory job skills to warrant the qualified rate could be paid the qualified rate immediately after the probationary period is satisfied. Employees' pay rates should be increased within the pay range as soon as they have progressed to higher performance levels as determined through job standard criteria established by the personnel department and as appraised by the employee's supervisor.

Pay increases within the range are not necessarily limited to one step at a time. If an employee is appraised by supervision as progressing faster to the proficient job level, the rate may be increased two steps at a time or at shorter time intervals. This will produce accelerated movement to the qualified job rate and should be used only in exceptional situations.

Employees who may have problems in learning the job should be moved less rapidly within the step progression. If the supervisor feels that an employee does not merit a step increase within the maximum period, consideration should be given to retraining, transfer to a lower-level job, or other appropriate action. Of course, when a union contract is involved, delays in rate progression due to unsatisfactory performance should be carefully documented by foremen and supervisors, consistent with contract language and specific union-employer relations.

In summary, a pay-increase program can be developed whether employees are organized or unorganized, but the system is more restrictive and limited in scope when a union is involved. In addition, it is advantageous for hourly wage adminstration programs and procedures to be as simple as possible so that day-to-day administration can be handled at the lowest-possible operational level.

BUDGETING IN ADMINISTERING PAY INCREASES

Budgeting of merit pay increases on a calendar- or fiscal-year basis is a vital tool of salary administration. To be most effective, the pay-increase budget and the methods by which it is developed and administered need to be consistent with the company's total financial control system, accounting procedures and practices, and personnel policies. Essentially, however, there are two basic forms of budgetary systems.

First is the formal control budget which is established after internal company and external job marketplace conditions are analyzed and company economic conditions appraised. The result is a total annual merit budget, represented as a percent of the new business year's beginning payroll. The merit budget allows a sum, usually expressed as a percent, that managers may grant as pay increases to their employees during the business year. An example of a formal budget calculation is shown in Table 3. The compensation costs represented in Table 3 should be the result of extensive analysis, to assure management that the 10.0 percent increase considers all relevant factors—employee turnover, increase or decrease in departmental size and level of employee performance, and mix of job levels.

A formal annual merit budget percentage should be considered by management as more than a cost factor.

A merit budget established after extensive research should be considered a viable management tool to position the company's base-salary levels in a real-istic and competitive posture.

The formal budget system may be most practical in organizations where salary administration is decentralized. This system has the advantage of establishing definite cost projections which normally will not exceed budgetary amounts, and in this regard it is strongly favored by financial management. However, it has the disadvantage of being inflexible. If later in the year the company needs to add or reduce personnel levels or to grant pay increases not anticipated when the budgets were developed, additional monies may be difficult to generate, especially if the merit budget is part of the company's total financial and corporate planning program. A second aspect of the formal bud-

TABLE 3   Annual Salary Budget Calculation

Total department annual salaries as of December 31 of previous year	$140,400
Addition of new employee to payroll, January 1	14,400
New total salary as of January 1	$154,800
New year's salary-increase budget:	
Percent and amount (10%)	15,480
New year's total annual salary cost	$170,280

get system, which can become a disadvantage, is that it delegates to unit managers broad authority for granting salary increases without review by higher management. This may result in inequitable pay situations. Of course these disadvantages can be controlled or avoided by the establishment of well-designed financial and salary administration policies.

A second budgeting method utilizes accounting budgetary principles to forecast salary-increase costs for a one-year business cycle. These estimated costs are built into accounting projections as a normal experience factor for cost control and overall cost and profit forecast purposes and may or may not be established as rigid cost projection factors.

The accounting budgetary system has the distinct advantage of being flexible in its administration while retaining an element of cost control which requires managers to plan salary increases on an individual basis rather than on an overall cost projection basis. An example of an accounting budgetary analysis for salary-increase purposes is shown in Table 4.

A shortcoming of the accounting budgetary system is that it cannot function equitably within reasonable cost boundaries unless other formal salary-increase policies and procedures are also practiced. These formal procedures should include time and percentage limits for granting salary increases, guidelines covering the use of the salary schedule, and a tie-in of personnel appraisal with merit-increase administration.

In order for accurate cost projections to be developed under any budgetary system, the makeup of the employee organization must be thoroughly investigated by specific unit, department, division, and the total company.

A most important variable to be considered for any merit budget system is employee turnover rates for separate company units. Employee turnover, if not analyzed correctly, can have a disruptive effect upon a formal budget system. For example, a unit which has a high degree of employee turnover would normally need a smaller salary-increase budget than a more stable unit which experiences low turnover. This conclusion is based upon the assumption that no general across-the-board increase would be granted. Of course, if general increases are planned, the cost effect upon the total budget can be easily projected. However, if the salary-increase system is based entirely upon merit or performance, studies have shown that employees on the payroll longer than one year will, on the average, receive increases at least 3 percent higher than those given to employees on the payroll less than one year.

COMPENSATION ADMINISTRATION IN DECENTRALIZED AND CENTRALIZED ORGANIZATIONS

The administration of pay-increase systems takes on different forms depending on how the company is organized. Generally speaking, a decentralized compensation program provides much wider administrative latitude for operating managers but costs more to administer than a centralized program. From a practical standpoint, most companies do not have a completely decentralized or completely centralized program, but a combination of the two, consistent with the company's operational needs and cost control programs.

A company's size, in terms of revenues or diversity of product line, is not

TABLE 4 Programmed Salary Increases and Accounting Budget, "Department A"

Name	Job grade	1981		1982											1982 total annual salary
		Dec.	Jan.	Feb.	Mar.	Apr.	May	June	July	Aug.	Sept.	Oct.	Nov.	Dec.	
R. Jones	4	$ 800									+$70 870				$ 9,880
J. Doe	5	1,100	+$100 1,200											+$100 1,300	14,500
J. Black	6	1,200				+$90 1,290									15,210
T. Williams	10	1,800		+$160 1,960											23,360
B. White	10	1,900											+$190 2,090		23,180
E. David	14	2,100					+$200 2,300								26,800
(New employee)	14	.....	1,735												21,050
C. Adams	20	2,800				+$300 3,100									36,300
Monthly totals		$11,700	$13,535	$13,695	$13,695	$14,805	$14,285	$14,285	$14,285	$14,285	$14,355	$14,355	$14,545	$14,875	$170,280

necessarily a good indicator of whether or not a pay-increase system should be centralized or decentralized. The primary consideration will normally be the company's organizational philosophy and needs, marketplace considerations, and diversity of businesses. These conditions do not remain static but are influenced in turn by industry position, employee needs, legal considerations and, most important, the basic "personality" of the company.

Also, many companies which have been organized or grown to become conglomerates have no choice but to administer their pay system in a decentralized mode. Other companies will remain with centralized programs regardless of their size. Some companies may decentralize from an operational standpoint but find it wise to remain centralized for their compensation and, more specifically, their pay-*increase* programs.

It is therefore generally accepted that no single system or program is best for all companies. In the sections that follow, we will describe the primary characteristics of decentralized and centralized compensation programs, how they are administered, and their advantages and disadvantages.

Administration in a decentralized organization. In a decentralized organization, wage and salary administration practices and programs, by necessity, are established to conform with the separate and individual nature of the units. If a decentralized unit is a separate and complete profit center and includes all operations of a staff and line nature within its structure, the administration of its employee direct-pay compensation program can also be decentralized. A decentralized pay practice operation need not be devoid of all corporate controls, but it does need to operate independently on a day-to-day basis. Normally the top corporate compensation function in a decentralized organization should guide the operating groups with research and development of new programs and techniques, and general policy development and guidelines. The corporate group should also assume responsibility for compensation auditing to assure top management that independent units operate within general company policy.

Unit management in a truly decentralized organization should have broad authority, within corporate policy guidelines, to establish direct-pay policies, including all necessary pay schedules, merit and promotional increase policies, and also to develop and administer job evaluation systems oriented to the decentralized unit's specific operational needs.

Normally, a decentralized company will not be concerned with job and pay equity or relationships between its major operating groups except at the very top management level. Normally, operating or line employees are rarely transferred between independent units or business groups of a decentralized company. The profit centers are established along separate and probably unrelated product lines, and even though they all are part of a total corporation in the eyes of the public, stockholders, and government agencies, the separate groups often are viewed by their employees as separate companies. In this regard, an employee hired for a particular level job in one unit of a decentralized company can move within that same group, be transferred to other plant locations within the same group, and rise to a management role in the same group, but seldom have contact of an internal business nature with members of other units of the same company.

Most decentralized corporations do not operate in such a completely decentralized manner. Nonetheless, the point is well taken that in a decentralized organization it is more important that pay administration practices conform to the patterns of each particular unit and its relationship to the industry and geographical area in which it operates than to standard and uniform patterns and practices which may be established for the total company.

It is extremely important in a decentralized organization that employee compensation costs be controlled through the use of a formalized budget system as described in the previous section. By necessity, corporate involvement in direct-pay programs focuses on broad financial aspects rather than on the individual worth or interunit equity of the program. Program needs and equity needs must be left to the judgment of each unit's management, which is closer to the market place and therefore better able to appraise compensation needs. In a decentralized organization corporate compensation management should deal primarily with total financial considerations—for example, increasing the corporatewide salary budget by 10 percent and requiring each decentralized manager to live within the budget limitations. However, an overall merit budget does not necessarily indicate that all units will be affected to the same degree. The merit budget for individual, decentralized units may vary depending on size of operation, makeup of the employee group, profitability of each group, future sales and profit growth of each group, and industry and union considerations. Of course, not to be dismissed is the negotiating ability of each group's management to influence budgets as reviewed and approved by corporate management.

Administration in a centralized organization. Administering a centralized employee compensation program involves the same functions as for a decentralized organization. In addition, the centralized group is involved in planning and developing new programs and systems and overseeing and controlling day-to-day administration. A centralized compensation program, administered uniformly through the corporation, is less complex and less costly to administer than a diversified, decentralized program. A centralized direct-compensation function can operate in a company that is engaged in the manufacture and sale of a multitude of products as well as with a one-product division type of organization.

The essential characteristic of a centralized compensation program is its uniformity and consistency of administration, promoting internal pay equity throughout the company. These elements are necessary to assure equitable administration of direct-compensation policies, which is essential in a company that transfers exempt employees across organizational lines.

In this type of organization the maintenance of internal pay or equity relationships takes precedence over external considerations. This does not, however, imply that a centralized compensation function does not relate its pay practices to those of other companies. External pay comparisons are important to a centralized organization in order for compensation management to be familiar with all external elements which may influence internal pay relationships. A centralized organization operating in more than one industry must establish a very sensitive balance between internal equity requirements and external competitive relationships.

A centralized compensation program is normally a highly structured operation which operates with formal and uniform compensation policies pertaining to job evaluation plans, pay-increase systems, incentive programs, and related employee benefits programs. Job evaluation or job ranking in a centralized organization will normally involve the use of one basic system or variations of the basic system, depending upon the job families or job hierarchies involved. This does not mean that only one job evaluation plan should be used to measure all jobs from top management to nonexempt clerks. It normally does indicate that the same job evaluation system is used with variations built into separate plans to evaluate different levels of job families. This technique also promotes the general theme of job evaluation consistency and pay equity in the determination of job values throughout the organization.

Salary schedules in a centralized organization need not be uniform or identical throughout the organization. Some variation is always needed for nonexempt jobs in different operational areas of the country. In addition, exempt salary ranges should vary according to the needs of job families, different geographical areas or industries in which the company operates.

A centralized direct-compensation system does not restrict operating managers in their responsibilities for compensating their employees. Policies should be developed to permit managers sufficient latitude to make direct-pay and other compensation judgments based on individual performance, economic conditions, and unit performance.

An important element of a centralized program is an approval system designed to assure that general company policies are applied consistently and pay increases are granted judiciously. All pay recommendations normally channel through a series of unit, divisional, and corporate management approvals and reviews prior to final authorization.

An important advantage of a centralized compensation program is that it provides a constant, up-to-date flow of information at corporate headquarters so that all pertinent employee information can be maintained in a central data bank. Individual employee data can be used for many purposes in the total human resources operation beyond the basic direct-compensation needs. In addition, centralized pay records facilitate close control of company pay-increase trends and policy compliance and can be utilized for frequent reporting of cost data to management.

Hourly compensation administration in decentralized and centralized organizations. Hourly compensation administration, if covered by union contract, normally is not affected by whether the company is centralized or decentralized. A highly centralized company may be required to have a completely decentralized hourly pay program because of the number and type of union contracts in effect or because of specific provisions contained in union contracts. In the same sense, a highly decentralized corporation with separate and distinct profit center organizations may have one major contract which applies to all units. Similarly, an hourly job evaluation system can be used differently in a centralized or decentralized organization depending upon the type and number of union contracts involved. Hourly pay administration under a formal union contract must of course conform to contract provisions and also follow administrative provisions, as covered earlier, without regard to company organization. However, if no union contracts exist, hourly pay practices normally can be administered in accordance with either decentralized or centralized program policies and guidelines as described above.

Payroll function. All pay-increase programs, regardless of their makeup or of company organization, ultimately lead to the preparation of the individual employee paycheck.

In a centralized compensation program it is essential that the payroll function be closely allied with the compensation department. A centralized program cannot produce the needed internal control and reporting mechanisms without easy access to records of a centralized payroll group.

In the case of the decentralized compensation operation, each unit should have its own separate payroll function over which its management maintains direct supervision.

PAY TREATMENT WITH JOB CHANGES

Within a company's total compensation system, the individual direct-pay increase is usually the only and most important aspect of an employee's total compensation which supervisors and managers can directly influence. Very little discretion can be exercised by operating managers over employee benefit programs, i.e., pensions, group insurance, vacations and holidays, premium pay, or in any other specific company programs which by necessity are established and controlled by inflexible formulas and are subject to contractual or governmental regulations. This is not intended as a criticism; it's simply a fact that managers do not have complete control over an individual's compensation package except to the extent that an individual's salary level influences his or her benefit level.

Pension programs usually cover all employees and are normally based on salary level and years of service. Therefore, salary increases not only affect career income but also determine retirement income levels. The benefits under a company's pension program do not and cannot measure whether an individual contributed more or less to the company's operations, but can only reflect the judgments implicit in salary treatment.

In the same sense, if a company observes 10 annual holidays, all employees, regardless of individual performance, receive 10 annual holidays. These benefit programs, therefore, do not distinguish between good and poor performers; and they should not, since benefit programs are established to meet employee security needs as well as competitive needs influenced by market conditions and socioeconomic factors.

Since direct-pay decisions not only affect individual pay levels but also influence most benefit programs, it behooves each supervisor and manager to use the pay-increase program, as covered by company policy or practice, to reflect meaningful distinctions between individual performance. Usually the supervisor's salary decisions involve merit or performance increases, as described earlier in this chapter. However, in cases of promotion, transfer, or demotion, managers have wider latitude to reward or penalize employees through pay adjustments based on individual performance.

Promotional pay increases.   The single best motivational tool that any supervisor or manager possesses is the promotion of an employee to a higher-level position. A promotion should increase the employee's income at least in 99 percent of the cases, recognizing the employee's increased worth to the company in the eyes of management, associates, family, and friends. A promotion not only enhances the employee's material well-being but also is ego-satisfying. In some cases it may be difficult to determine which of the two provides the greater motivational impact.

A promotional pay increase should be large enough to avoid being considered a hollow achievement in the eyes of the employee. The promotional increase should, in all cases, be substantially higher than increases given for reasons of merit or job performance. As a general rule, a promotional increase should be at least 50 percent higher than the merit-increase percentage budget in effect. If the merit-increase budget is 10 percent, a promotional increase should be a minimum of 15 percent. An alternative is to increase the employee's salary to the same position in the new salary range as it was in the previous salary range.

Promotional increases should not be combined with merit or general salary increases. It is sometimes a temptation for managers to schedule job promotions to become effective on a merit review or merit-increase due date and then grant the merit increase as if it were a promotional increase. However, this practice should be discouraged. This pseudo cost saving only detracts from the motivational impact of a job promotion and will classify the promotion as a sham in the mind of the employee. If a promotion must fall on a merit review date, one of two methods can be employed: (1) the merit increase can be given separately in one month with the promotional increase to follow in the next month or (2) the total increase can be built up to include both the promotional and merit increase. The latter method is more practical and should be followed in order to avoid misunderstandings and administrative complications.

An exception to the above may be justified if an employee is granted a public relations type of promotion in which there is a change in title but no change or possibly a decrease in job responsibilities. In this case the nature of the promotion should be clearly understood, and the employee made aware that the press releases do not warrant an increase in salary.

In summary, a bona fide promotion should always be accompanied by a healthy increase in salary level so that it is readily identified as a recognition of the employee's increase in job responsibility.

Transfer of an employee at the same job level, a lateral transfer, should not necessarily be accompanied by a salary increase if the move is made primarily to broaden the employee's exposure and experience within the organization. However, a lateral transfer in which the employee is required to change residences should be reviewed very carefully by management to be certain that the move is necessary. If no salary increase accompanies a lateral transfer, and if the company has no other programs for compensating an employee required to change residences, serious personnel and compensation problems will result. If at all possible, any employee job transfer should be organized and managed to involve a promotion so that the employee can be granted an appropriate pay increase. Any job transfer which involves a residence change results in both short- and long-term added expenses for employee and family. This is true *regardless* of whether the new area has a measurable or perceived higher or lower cost of living. Therefore, it is doubly important that managers carefully review the necessity of any lateral transfers which require a change of residence.

Employee demotion, accompanied by corresponding salary reduction, is one of the more difficult problems faced by a manager or salary administrator. In fact, it may be more difficult than an employee discharge. A discharge usually involves circumstances such as cause, dishonesty, insubordination, incompetence, which are generally clear-cut and justifiable. Many personnel experts contend that it is better from a total employee morale and management standpoint to discharge an employee than to reduce the individual's salary. An employee who is discharged can often find employment opportunities that are as good as or better than the former position, whereas the employee who has a salary reduction will more often than not continue to be a problem.

Demotions frequently are not clearly substantiated and can take on many forms. The most common reason for a demotion, of course, is that the employee is not able to accept the assigned responsibilities or perform the job. Other reasons for demotions include changes in organization which eliminate jobs; change or elimination of job responsibilities which reduces the position's value; and personality conflicts between the employee and subordinates, superiors, or peers, which adversely affect performance. Whether or not an employee's pay should be reduced at the time of demotion should be a highly individualized judgment on the part of management in the light of all the circumstances.

As a general rule, salary should be decreased if the demotion is clearly the result of the employee's inability to accept responsibilities or to handle them in an effective manner. The size of the reduction should vary depending upon the circumstances, but in no case should it be greater than the promotional increase, if that was the employee's last pay increase. The salary decrease should be large enough so that the new salary will not be higher than the maximum of the job salary range to which the employee is reassigned. If the demotion is for reasons of personality conflict, a decrease should not be made if it is possible to place the employee in a comparable position in a different department or operation of the company. If the demotion is the result of reorganization or elimination of important job responsibilities, salary should not be reduced unless a lower salary would position the employee to be considered for another responsible job assignment.

Due to the relationship between pay and benefits, a salary decrease as a result of the demotion should be analyzed thoroughly to determine its effect upon the employee's benefit coverage.

Other types of "demotions" are the transfer of a *competent* employee to a lower-level job in order to offer broader experience and the temporary transfer of a *competent* employee to a lower job to correct a bad operation within a stated period of time. In these cases, it may be advisable to grant salary increases. A demotional increase may also be considered when it is in the best interests of the corporation, and all personnel involved, that the employee be moved to a nonsensitive, lower-valued job which may carry a prestigious title.

In summary, a manager does not have a great deal of latitude with regard to varying the benefit portion of an employee's total compensation package. Therefore, the manager with the advice and guidance of compensation personnel should utilize to the fullest the motivational tools available when making direct-compensation decisions—including merit or performance increases, transfer increases, and especially promotional increases.

chapter 26

Planning and Budgeting for Merit Increases: An Integrated Approach

Allan T. Hauser

MANAGER, CORPORATE COMPENSATION PLANNING,
MERRILL LYNCH & CO., INC., NEW YORK, NEW YORK

THE BASICS: DESCRIPTIONS, EVALUATIONS, GRADES, AND RANGES

Position descriptions are the genesis of a salary administration program. They are usually prepared by employees who actually perform the jobs and then are evaluated and graded. Next, key benchmarks are priced with range midpoints reflecting the marketplace, and range control points are calculated from the midpoints.

The elements of any well-designed salary administration program should be fully integrated. Each element should be linked to the next as the program evolves step by step from its embryonic stages to a functioning, coordinated network of descriptions, evaluations, grades, priced jobs, and salary ranges. In their infancy, most salary administration programs appear to be homogeneous, but as they develop they recognize the culture of a particular organization, and the form, substance, and administration of the program change accordingly. This chapter will focus on two elements of a salary administration program which have evolved at Merrill Lynch, namely, the *planning* and *budgeting* of merit increases.

The objectives of this chapter are twofold: (1) to emphasize the importance of effective merit-increase planning and budgeting and (2) to describe the design and implementation of a fully integrated approach to the planning and budgeting process.

PAY FOR PERFORMANCE: CORNERSTONE OF SALARY PLANNING

Integral to effective salary planning is the concept of "pay for performance," which states that managers should grant salary increases based upon their observations of the demonstrated achievement of each employee.

Merit Increases versus Automatic Increases   By definition, merit increases are salary adjustments awarded to employees who, through demonstrated past performance over a given period of time, have earned the recognition of higher base salaries.

Merit increases must not be perceived either by managers or their employees as automatic salary adjustments (entitlements) granted on the basis of seniority or the anniversary of the employment date or the last increase date. However, if a conscious effort is not made to emphasize the importance of pay for performance, increases other than merit inevitably creep into the salary administration effort. Both managers and employees are often under the mistaken impression that an increase is an automatic event after a certain period of time has elapsed. As a result, so-called merit increases may deteriorate to perceived entitlements on the part of employees.

The concept of pay for performance is certainly not a complicated one for managers or employees to understand, but a mere understanding of the concept does not guarantee successful implementation. It must be committed to by senior management and communicated throughout the organization by word as well as action. An effective process for planning and budgeting salaries can help to reinforce pay for performance.

In many progressive firms, the concept of the automatic increase has been abolished from salary planning, and the pay for performance philosophy has become deep-rooted in managerial thinking. In this way, outstanding performers are given the highest-percentage increases; fully competent performers are given competitive increases; and marginal performers are given the lowest-percentage increases, if any. Those employees not meeting requirements are appraised as such, and managers are advised to exclude them altogether when planning salary increases. Important, significant differences must also be built into the guidelines governing increases so that employees can recognize and appreciate the impact of performance appraisal on the size and frequency of their merit increases.

Merit-Increase Grids   To eliminate automatic increases and to ensure that a pay for performance concept is maintained as the springboard on which all merit increases are planned and granted, the "merit-increase grid" has become recognized as a tool to assist managers in their thinking. It is used as a guideline in making decisions about the size and frequency of merit increases.

While a multitude of combinations of numbers for size and frequency of increases may be appropriate in different companies, the basic design of the grid is almost always standard. In most cases, the percentage of the merit increase is directly linked to the employee's performance rating, and the frequency of increases is tied to the positioning of the employee's current salary within the grade range. In this fashion, higher-percentage increases are granted to those employees who have demonstrated their capability, and more frequent increases are granted to those whose current salaries are low within the salary range.

This serves to bring employees earning significantly below the midpoint up to the market rate at a faster pace by granting more frequent increases. At the same time, it serves to motivate improved employee performance by granting higher-percentage increases to employees at each successive level of performance appraisal. Variations may, and do, exist in merit-increase grid designs, but the message is always the same: the better performers should be receiving the better increases.

Performance Standards Essential to the design of a merit-increase grid emphasizing pay for performance is development of a set of standards (both for exempt and nonexempt employees) which managers can use as the basis for assessing individual performance. Definitions of performance levels must be developed which clearly distinguish between the ratings, so that managers can objectively identify the appropriate classification for each of their employees.

This appraisal system must be in place throughout the firm in order for the merit-increase grid to be properly used by managers. Even more important, however, the appraisal system must be recognized as a worthwhile managerial tool, and the definitions associated with each performance level (as well as their distinctions) must be clearly understood both by the managers who use them and the employees who are appraised by them.

The concept of pay for performance, implemented by managerial adherence to a merit-increase grid, is the prelude to an integrated approach to planning and budgeting merit increases. The basic elements of any job evaluation and salary administration program are linked with the controls of planning and budgeting via salary grade ranges, and pay is administered within these ranges through the use of merit increase guidelines. Figure 1 illustrates these critical linkups, necessary to the successful maintenance of an ongoing compensation program.

WHY SALARY PLANNING?

Salary planning should be practiced at least annually by all managers who have people accountability. It should be extended to the lowest-supervisory level and should be completed for *each* employee. A good system allows those who assess the performance of individual employees on a daily basis to do the actual salary planning.

For the most part, salary planning programs which are administered on a group basis (e.g., allocation of a 10 percent merit increase "pot" for a group of employees) versus the individual employee basis, and which are participative only through a senior- or middle-management level, tend to be the least effec-

FIGURE 1   Phases of an Integrated Salary Administration Program

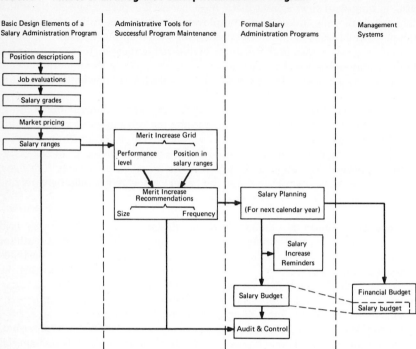

tive in accurately forecasting the salary increase needs of the firm for the upcoming year. Programs which allow first-line supervisors to become actively involved in planning will be much more responsive to the needs of the organization.

Objectives of Salary Planning   A good salary planning program should achieve the following objectives:

- Serve as the basis for the following year's salary and financial budgets
- Serve as an accurate forecast of actual and annualized expenses for merit increases, promotional increases, and total base-salary payroll for each employee in each department for the upcoming calendar or fiscal year and provide comparative data on this information from one year to the next
- Provide managers with planned staffing information from one year to another, detailing planned additions to staff as well as the average cost for new hires during the upcoming plan year

Timing of Salary Planning   The salary planning process should begin with the annual budgeting cycle. To start out, reports should be distributed to all managers, with projected new salary ranges for the upcoming year. This enables managers to plan increases in accordance with proposed ranges, in place at the time the increases are to be granted.

Since the actual salary planning figures for base salaries should be used as input to the compensation expense line on the manager's financial budget, the timing of salary planning should be coordinated with the financial budget so that these figures may be automatically input to the financial budgeting system. A computer linkup between the salary planning program and the financial budgeting program may accomplish the transition of the appropriate numbers from one system to another with administrative ease and efficiency.

Total Base-Salary Expenses versus Merit Increases   In salary planning as well as salary budgeting, the emphasis should be on total base-salary expenses. Although information is tracked and reported for merit and promotional increases, the primary focus should be on the total and not only on one segment of that expense.

In some companies, salary planning and salary budgeting reports tend to concentrate on the monitoring and control of only the merit-increase portion of base-salary expenses. However, this is a limiting practice, especially in those environments where high turnover results in additions to staff being paid more in salary dollars than the employees they replace. It also causes a problem in those rapidly growing companies where promotional increases and new hire rates may be much more significant than merit-increase amounts.

By monitoring only merit increases, these very significant shifts in total base-salary expenses could be "going through the ceiling" as a result of the types of activities cited above. For this reason, readers designing salary planning programs in their own firms are advised to concentrate on the major portion of compensation expenses (total base salaries) while being alert to the major components of this expense; namely, merit and promotional increases as well as additions to staff.

SALARY PLANNING MODEL

The purpose of this section is to provide the reader with a description of those elements that are integral to the good design of a salary planning program.

Segments of the Salary Planning Report   Merrill Lynch's salary planning report is divided into three segments:

- Current-employee data
- Current-year planning (through year-end)
- Future-year planning (i.e., salary planning for the upcoming calendar or fiscal year)

The *current-employee data segment* provides the following information on each active employee within the firm (on a unit-by-unit basis):

- Employee name
- Employee number
- Employee status (e.g., full-time or part-time)
- Job grade
- Current base salary
- Date of last increase

- Percentage of last increase
- Type increase (e.g., merit or promotional)
- Compa-ratio

As shown in Figure 2 (an illustration of the Merrill Lynch salary planning format), the above information is generated by the computer and is printed on the left-hand side of the salary planning report. Managers simply use this information as a reference source in planning future increases for their employees.

The *current-year planning segment* includes two columns which are used by managers to post proposed revisions to the salaries of those employees for whom increases are planned prior to the *current* year-end. These two columns include:

- Date of the current year's proposed increase
- New current-year annual base salary (after the planned increase)

Merrill Lynch, in refining its salary planning program, purposely designed these two columns for the current-year planning, as it reduces the number of errors that managers normally make when their attention is not focused on increases to be granted to employees prior to the upcoming year. Through experience, Merrill Lynch has learned that managers tend to overlook increases they plan to grant through the current year-end, and this results in automatic errors in the next year's salary planning for those employees.

The third segment of the report, *future-year planning*, provides managers with space to record the data for planned salary actions during the upcoming year. Using the merit-increase grid as a guideline, managers simply post the following information for each employee to the salary planning report:

- Planned percent increase
- Number of months to the next increase (from date of last increase)
- Projected performance rating
- Type of increase (e.g., merit, promotional)

A manager's proposals as to planned salary increases are, of course, subject to review and approval by those to whom the manager reports.

This information is input to the system, and a turnaround document (Figure 3) is provided to each manager, which takes the raw data cited above; performs the necessary calculations; and provides the following information for each employee:

- Projected increase date (calculated from number of months to next increase, as input by manager)
- Projected annual base salary (calculated from planned percent increase, as input by manager)
- Projected annualized increase dollars (projected annual base salary minus current annual base salary)
- Projected actualized increase dollars (actual salary-increase dollars to be expended in the upcoming calendar year)
- Projected compa-ratio (projected salary as a percentage of the next year's estimated midpoint)
- Second increase indicator (all planned second increases for employees are flagged in this column)

FIGURE 2 Salary Planning Report (Input Form)

THIS FORM MUST BE RECEIVED IN COMP ADMIN NO LATER THAN 7/13/81. FORMS RECEIVED AFTER THIS DATE WILL NOT BE INCLUDED IN FIRST SALARY PLANNING REPORT.

RUN DATE 06/15/81

SALARY PLANNING FORM

HRS FILE DATE 06/22/81

00565   EXEMPT

←— — — TO BE COMPLETED BY MANAGER — — —→

EMPLOYEE NAME	EMPL INIT	EMPL NUMBR 6-10	EMP STAT 11-12	JOB GRD 20-21	CURRENT BASE SAL 22-28	DATE OF LAST INC 29-34	% LAST INC.	TYPE INC 35-36	% MID	DATE OF 1981 PROPOSED INC 37-42	NEW 1981 BASE SAL 43-49	PLANNED % INC 50-52	NO. MOS TO NEXT INC 53-54	EST PERF RATING 55-56	TYPE INC 57-8	ORG CODE 59-63	ACT CDE 64	SECOND INC IND 80
						← — CURRENT DATA — →				← — 1981 PLANNING — →				← — 1982 PLANNING — →				
ARDEN	CC	23232	FT	25	18,500	01/12/81	12.1	NM	89	8-10-81	2',000	9.0	07	ER	NM	00565	–	–
MOORE	HF	11111	FT	27	22,000	03/23/81	15.7	NM	85	9-7-81	24,000	9.0	06	ER	NM	00565	–	–
COLLINS	BP	23233	FT	30	33,000	10/06/80	13.7	NM	86	6-29-81	38,000	14.0	06	FE	NM	00565	–	–

Planned Addition   FT   25   18,000   9/01/81   9.0   06   MR   NM   00565   A

**** KEY INSTRUCTIONS ****

TO DELETE   EMP — PUT "D" IN THE ACTION CODE COL 64
TO TRANSFER   EMP — PUT "T" IN THE ACTION CODE COL 64 AND WRITE THE NEW ORG CODE ABOVE THE OLD ORG CODE (COLS. 59-63) AND DRAW LINE THRU OLD ORG
TO ADD PLAN/ADD   — PUT "A" IN THE ACTION CODE (COL 64). FILL IN THE GRADE (COLS 20-21). HIRING SALARY UP TO GRADE MIDPOINT (COLS 22-28)
                     HIRING DATE (COLS 29-34), ORG CODE (COLS 59-63) AND COLS 50 THRU 58.
TO ADD 2ND INCR   — PUT "2" IN THE 2ND INC IND (COL 80) AND FILL IN UNDER THE FIRST INCREASE COLS 50 THRU 63
NOTE: ALL 1ST INCREASE DATA SHOULD BE ENTERED IN SPACE ABOVE DOTTED LINES, ALL 2ND INCREASE DATA SHOULD BE ENTERED IN SPACE BELOW DOTTED LINES.
   PLANNED % INC — COLUMNS 50-52 CAN BE A WHOLE NO. OR HALF NO. EXAMPLE — 08.0 OR 08.5

FIGURE 3 Salary Planning Report (Output Form)

00565   EXEMPT

EMPLOYEE NAME	INIT	1981 DATA								1982 SAL PLAN							RESULTS OF 1982 SALARY PLANNING				
		EMP NMBER 6-10	EMP STAT 11-2	JOB GRD 20-1	12/31/81 BASE SAL 22-28	DATE OF LAST INC 29-34	% LAST INC	TYPE INC 35-6	% MID	% INC PLAN	MONS. TO NEXT-INC	PERF RTNG 55-6	TYPE INC 57-8	ORG CODE 59-63	ACTION CODE 64	PROJECT INC DATE 65-70	12/31/82 BASE SAL 71----78	INCR ANNUAL	INCR ACTUAL	% MID	SEC INC 80
PLANNED ADDITION	CC	P0216	FT	25	18,000	09/01/81			81	9.0	6.0	MR	NM	00565	A	03/08/82	19,620	1,620	1,327	95	
ARDEN	CC	23232	FT	26	21,000	08/10/81	13.5	PR	81	9.0	7.0	ER	NM	00565		03/08/82	22,890	1,890	1,548	111	
MOORE	HF	11111	FT	27	24,000	09/07/81	9.0	NM	92	9.0	6.0	ER	NM	00565		03/08/82	26,160	2,160	1,769	101	
COLLINS	BP	23233	FT	30	38,000	06/29/81	15.1	NM		14.0	6.0	FE	NM	00565		01/11/82	43,320	5,320	5,174	113	

···· KEY INSTRUCTIONS ····

TO DELETE   EMP — PUT "D" IN THE ACTION CODE COL. 64.
TO TRANSFER   EMP — PUT "T" IN THE ACTION CODE COL. 64. WRITE THE NEW ORG CODE ABOVE THE OLD ORG CODE (COLS. 59-63), AND DRAW LINE THRU OLD ORG CDE
TO ADD PLAN/ADD — PUT "A" IN THE ACTION CODE (COL. 64). FILL IN THE EMPL STAT (COLS. 11-12), GRADE (COLS 20-21), HIRING SAL UP TO GRADE MIDPT 22-28
                 HIRING DATE (COLS 29-34), ORG CODE (COLS 59-63). COLS 55 THRU 58 AND COLS 65 THRU 78.

TO ADD 2ND INCR — PUT "2" IN THE 2ND INC IND (COL. 80) AND FILL IN UNDER THE 1ST INC THE ORG CODE COLS (59-63), AND COLS (55-58), AND COLS (65-78)
TO CHANGE 1ST INC — CROSS OUT PRINTED DATA IN COLS 55 - 78. IF NECESSARY, AND ENTER CORRECTED DATA ABOVE THE PRINTED DATA.
TO CHANGE 2ND INC — CROSS OUT PRINTED DATA IN COLS 55 - 78. IF NECESSARY, AND ENTER CORRECTED DATA BELOW THE PRINTED DATA.
TO REMOVE 1ST INC — CROSS OUT PROJ INC DATE (COLS 65-70), BASE SALARY (COLS 65-70), PLACE "6" ZEROS ABOVE COLS 65-70 AND "7" ZEROS ABOVE COLS 71-78.
TO REMOVE 2ND INC — SAME INSTRUCTIONS AS FOR REMOVING 1ST INC. EXCEPT PLACE ZEROS BELOW THE LINE AND CIRCLE THE "2" IN COL. 80.
NOTE: DATA INPUT CAN BE CHANGED ONLY IN NUMBERED COLUMNS. DO NOT CHANGE "1982 SAL PLAN" SECTION.

Distribution of Salary Planning Reports   Since the computer-generated reports are run on a department, section, and unit organizational basis at Merrill Lynch (so that the lowest-level supervisor can participate in the planning process), the pertinent compensation information for each employee is printed within the reporting area to which the individual is assigned.

For example, all employees in the compensation department of the firm are printed on one or two pages which can be distributed to the compensation manager to complete salary planning for employees who report directly to the compensation manager. These reports are channeled to lower-supervisory levels through middle managers (usually at the department level) who are accountable for the functions performed on each of the sublevels and who are responsible for reviewing and approving the salary planning before it is finalized.

On the point of distribution, it is important for the designer of the program to install a systems provision whereby managers appear on the salary planning reports of their superiors. Merrill Lynch, for example, uses the concept of the "reporting organization code" to ensure that a manager's information is not included on the same form as the employees reporting to that manager.

In other words, information on the compensation manager would appear on the salary planning report of the director of compensation and benefits who would be responsible for planning the compensation manager's salary increases. This, obviously, is a commonsense issue; however, it is easily overlooked in the design phase of a program, resulting in headaches at the time of implementation when all management employees appear on their own salary planning reports!

Salary Planning Systems Design Provisions   To ensure accurate salary planning and to minimize managers' administrative problems after the implementation of a program of this nature, it is advisable to engineer the following provisions into the design of the system.

First, the salary planning program should be developed so that managers have the capability of adding current employees who, for one reason or another, do not appear on the report. These situations occur much more frequently than one would, at first, imagine.

For example, an employee is *transferred* into a department by the time a manager receives the salary planning report, yet the paperwork on the transfer was not processed at the time the salary planning report was generated. The manager receiving the transferred employee should have a mechanism in the system which makes it convenient to add the employee to the list so that salary planning may be done for the employee for the future plan year.

As another example, suppose an employee is hired *after* the salary planning report is generated but is on the payroll at the time the manager completes the forms. Again, the manager must have the capability to add the newly hired employee to the salary planning list and to plan for that employee for the coming year. Considerable frustration on the part of the salary administrator, resulting from endless questions and complaints of user managers, can be spared if the designer of the salary planning program ensures that the system has a mechanism whereby managers can simply add current employees who do not appear on their reports.

Second, designers of salary planning programs should be reminded that employees, for one reason or another, are continuously moving in and out of jobs. As a result, the system should be developed so that managers can easily delete from their listings the names of employees who appear but whose transfer or termination has taken place since the report was generated.

Also, a preferred feature is to incorporate a provision whereby managers have the capability of deleting employees who they know will not be on their payroll in the upcoming year (for example, as a result of planned retirement, planned termination, transfer, etc.). For these employees, salary planning is not required and their current base salaries should not be included in the total salary figure which will comprise the unit's salary budget for the upcoming year.

Third, managers must have the capability of adding "planned additions" to their salary planning forms, based on their current-approved open requisitions and their projected staffing requirements for the coming plan year. In many planning systems this critical element is overlooked, resulting in a loss of credibility by line users. If summary totals of base salaries and planned increases are to be of any use to the manager, it is essential that the salary planning system be designed so that it will accommodate data on planned additions (defined as employees who are not yet on the payroll, but for whom the manager will be recruiting during the coming plan year).

Usually, managers must estimate hiring salaries for these employees, and the system can impose certain administrative restraints in this regard with respect to limits on projected hiring rates (e.g., up to the midpoint of the approved job grade). Likewise, the manager must estimate planned increase data, if deemed appropriate, or the system can be programmed to automatically plug in a certain percentage after a prescribed number of months have passed since the date of hire.

Fourth, the designer of the system should be wary of special classifications of employees for whom increases should be planned—but whose employment situation is such that they are treated as somewhat separate and unique when it comes to salary administration issues. For example, at Merrill Lynch, this is the case with part-time employees whose salaries appear on all personnel records as hourly rates.

This type of situation causes administrative salary planning problems in that the hourly rates must be converted, hypothetically, to annual figures based on a full workweek to enable the manager to relate to the salary structure, which is not printed using an hourly pay basis. In these cases, the hourly rate must also be multiplied by an annual formula (based on the actual number of hours worked each week) in order to be added to the total salaries of other employees so that the total annual base-salary calculation for the area is accurate.

Fifth, if a merit-increase grid incorporates the recommended concept of variable timing (e.g., more frequent increases to those employees lower in the range), then the designer of the salary planning program must provide managers with the capability of planning two or more increases per year for certain employees.

Normally, such a provision can be programmed into the system with relative ease; however, the designer of the system must, first, recognize that these two-increase situations can occur so that the programmer is made aware of this possibility. Second, a decision must be made with regard to the display features of the first and second increases. The Merrill Lynch system prints both increases, taking care that the increase amounts are prorated properly so that the total figures do not include "double counting" in terms of the annualized and actual amounts.

Unique situations of this nature should be examined closely, as neglect of these, at first, seemingly irrelevant issues can wreak havoc with the system once managers actually become involved with the complexities of the salary planning process for individual employees.

Salary Planning Summary Reports   While planning for merit and promotional increases should be done on an individual basis, good summary reports are critical to the success of the program. These summary reports enable management to understand the impact of individual planning done by managers, by providing them with "bottom line figures" for units, sections, departments, divisions, groups, and total company.

Items included on a typical salary planning summary report are usually broken down by exempt and nonexempt employee classifications but are also summarized for the total employee population. (Refer to Figure 4 for an illustration of the Merrill Lynch salary planning summary report formats.) Salary planning figures which should be included on these summary sheets for management's review include the following:

1. *Current plan year's total base salaries (as of year-end).* This figure establishes the salary budget base for the upcoming year.

2. *Projected plan year's total base salaries (as of year-end).* This figure establishes the projected annual base-salary level at the conclusion of the plan year.

3. *Plan year's annualized dollar increases.* This figure is the direct result of salary planning and is calculated by deducting (1) from (2).

4. *Plan year's annualized percent increases.* This figure is calculated by dividing (3) by (1) and provides a good gauge for managers in examining the overall rate of growth in salaries planned for their areas.

5. *Plan year's actual dollar increases.* This figure is the actual dollar amount to be expended during the plan year for salary increases.

6. *Plan year's actual percentage increases.* This figure is calculated by dividing (5) by (1) and gives managers a reading on the actual percentage rate at which salary increases are planned for the upcoming year.

7. *Current year versus planned year compa-ratio.* These figures will give managers an idea as to where actual salaries are in relation to grade midpoints, both prior to and after salary planning.

In addition to the above information, summary sheets may also provide data on performance appraisal practices of managers; for example, number of employees appraised at each performance level. Summary sheets may, also, present number of employees at the end of the current year, planned additions to staff during the plan year, and projected number of employees at the end of the plan year.

FIGURE 4 Salary Planning Summary Forms

RUN DATE 12/21/81 | SALARY PLANNING SUMMARIES | HRS FILE DATE 12/21/81 PAGE 002146

TOTAL DEPARTMENT

TOTALS — EXEMPT SUMMARY

12-31-81 BASE SALARY	12-31-82 BASE SALARY	1982 $INCR ANNUAL	% 1982 INCR ANNUAL	1982 $INCR ACTUAL	% 1982 INCR ACTUAL	ACTUAL SALARY AS % OF MIDPT (COMPA-RATIO)
101,000	111,990	10,990	10.9	9,818	9.7	106.4

TOTALS — NON-EXEMPT SUMMARY

12-31-81 BASE SALARY	12-31-82 BASE SALARY	1982 $INCR ANNUAL	% 1982 INCR ANNUAL	1982 $INCR ACTUAL	% 1982 INCR ACTUAL	ACTUAL SALARY AS % OF MIDPT (COMPA-RATIO)
0	0	0	0.0	0	0.0	0.0

TOTALS — EXEMPT/NON-EXEMPT SUMMARY

12-31-81 BASE SALARY	12-31-82 BASE SALARY	1982 $INCR ANNUAL	% 1982 INCR ANNUAL	1982 $INCR ACTUAL	% 1982 INCR ACTUAL	ACTUAL SALARY AS % OF MIDPT (COMPA-RATIO)
101,000	111,990	10,990	10.9	9,818	9.7	106.4

PERFORMANCE RATING HEADCOUNT SUMMARY

	FE	ER	MR	MM	DN
EXEMPT	1	2	1		
NON-EXEMPT					

HEADCOUNT AND SALARY INCREASE SUMMARY

	EXEMPT	NON-EXEMPT	TOTAL
EMPLOYEES AS OF 12-31-81	4	0	4
# OF SAL INCREASES IN 1982	4	0	4
# OF SAL INCREASES AFTER 1982	0	0	0
NO INCREASES GRANTED	0	0	0
EMPLOYEES AS OF 12/31/82	4	0	4

DIVISION/REGION DIRECTOR APPROVAL _____

SIGNATURE

THE MARKETING OF SALARY PLANNING TO LINE MANAGERS

Salary planning will only be an effective managerial tool within an organization if the line managers who must use it recognize and understand the benefits to be derived from their participation in the program. As such, a good salary planning program must be marketed to line managers in a fashion which will motivate them to want the system to be successful. The user must recognize that an identified managerial need will be satisfied if the required time and effort is expended on the program and participation is taken seriously. Some helpful techniques that have been used at Merrill Lynch in this regard are as follows:

First.   The salary planning program is linked to the financial budgeting program and to the salary budget, and managers are continually reminded that participation in salary planning will make it easier for them to complete the financial budgeting exercise.

For example, base-salary expense can be planned on an individual-employee basis by the manager; the computer will perform all the necessary calculations, and a total actual compensation expense figure for the next calendar year will be provided to the manager for his or her entire area. This compensation expense figure is automatically input to the manager's financial budget, which is used to measure managerial performance in the upcoming year by comparing actual to budget results.

Most of the work is done by the computer, and the manager can see that participation in the program will assist tremendously at the time of financial budget preparation.

At Merrill Lynch, the salary planning program has a meaningful and worthwhile outcome. Managers do not engage in the program simply to fulfill another in their seemingly endless quota of administrative requirements. From the inception of the program each year, managers are reminded of the end result of their efforts. And, of course, experienced managers recognize the time-saving features of the program from past use. Planning programs which exist for their own sake are not nearly as successful as those that are fully integrated and function as a part of the firm's overall management reporting system.

Second.   At Merrill Lynch, salary planning results in an adjunct monthly salary-increase reminder system. This reminder system focuses on the individual salary planning done for each employee and generates, on a monthly basis, follow-up reports which remind managers of the increases they had planned for their employees for each upcoming month.

These reports, as illustrated in Figure 5, include all the information necessary to complete the paperwork to process the increase, provided that the manager still deems it appropriate at the time it is to be granted.

The reminder system is a well-received byproduct of the salary planning program. It serves to keep the planning process alive during the year.

Third.   Most managers are line-oriented; they are interested in the operations of their units and, oftentimes, view systems such as salary planning as potential time wasters which deter them from their more direct accountabilities. At Merrill Lynch, the administrative aspects of the salary planning program have been streamlined in the following ways:

- A comprehensive "instruction kit" is prepared to accompany the salary planning reports, giving guidance to managers on the mechanical aspects of the

FIGURE 5 Salary Increase Reminder Report

COMPANY:
EVP GROUP:
DIVISION/REGION:
DEPARTMENT/OFFICE:
ORGANIZATION:

SALARY PLANNING INCREASE REMINDERS

SALARY INCREASES PLANNED FOR MONTH OF: **MARCH**

	(1)		(2)	(3)	(4)	(5)	(6) CURRENT SALARY DATA				(7) SALARY PLANNING DATA *						(8) PPR PROCESSING DATA				(SEE NOTE A)
							(A)	(B)	(C)	(D)	(A)	(B)	(C)	(D)	(E)	(F)	(A)	(B)	(C)	(D)	(E)
FOOT NOTE	EMPLOYEE NAME	INIT	EMPL NUMBER	JOB GRADE	POSITION TITLE	JOB CODE	CURRENT BASE SALARY	DATE OF LAST INCREASE	RANGE QUINT	TYPE INCR	PERF RTNG	# MONTHS FROM LAST INCREASE	% OF INCR	ANNUALIZD INCREASE	PLANNED DATE OF INCREASE	PLANNED ANNUAL BASE SALARY	PLANNED INCR AMT FOR PAY PERIOD	PAY PERIOD	PLA- NNED TYPE INCR	PLANNED INCREASE AMOUNT OF CHANGE	PPR TO BE PROCESSED NLT:
	ARDEN	CC	23232	26	ACCT.	60921	21,000	8/10/81	3	PR	ER	7.0	9.0	1,890	3/8/82	22,890	880.39	BW	NM	72.69	2/22/82
***	CUSMAN	DW	41509	25	JR. ACCT.	60921	18,000	9/01/81	2	NH	MR	6.0	9.0	1,620	3/8/82	19,620	754.62	BW	NM	62.31	2/22/82
	MOORE	HF	11111	27	SR. ACCT.	60922	24,000	9/07/81	2	NM	ER	6.0	9.0	2,160	3/8/82	26,160	1,006.15	BW	NM	83.07	2/22/82

FOOTNOTES:

* SECTION 7 INCLUDES SALARY PLANNING DATA ONLY. PLEASE REVIEW THIS INFORMATION CAREFULLY PRIOR TO GRANTING ANY INCREASES AND REMEMBER THAT ACTUAL MERIT INCREASES DEPEND UPON INDIVIDUAL PERFORMANCE AT THE TIME OF THE COMPENSATION REVIEW. AS SUCH, THESE INCREASES NEED NOT BE GRANTED. EVEN THOUGH PLANNED. IF CURRENT PERFORMANCE DOES NOT WARRANT AN INCREASE.

** FOR THIS EMPLOYEE, AN UNPLANNED INCREASE WAS GRANTED. AS A RESULT OF THIS UNPLANNED INCREASE, THE SALARY PLANNING DATA POSTED ABOVE MAY BE INAPPROPRIATE.

*** THIS EMPLOYEE WAS HIRED THIS YEAR. A MERIT REVIEW MAY BE IN ORDER AT THIS TIME. DEPENDING ON YOUR ASSESSMENT OF PERFORMANCE SINCE HIRE DATE.

**** THIS EMPLOYEE WAS TRANSFERRED TO YOUR AREA SINCE THE TIME OF SALARY PLANNING. THE INCREASE WAS PLANNED FOR THIS EMPLOYEE BY THE PREVIOUS MANAGER. (SEE FOOTNOTE *).

NOTE A: THE CURRENT PERFORMANCE RATING FOR THE EMPLOYEE SHOULD ALSO BE ENTERED ON THE PPR BEFORE IT IS PROCESSED. THIS MAY NOT BE THE SAME PERFORMANCE RATING PRINTED IN COLUMN 7-A.

KEY PAY TYPE: MO = MONTHLY, BW = BI-WEEKLY, HR = HOURLY. TYPE INCREASE: NM = NORMAL MERIT, PR = PROMOTIONAL, OT = OTHER RANGE OF QUINTILE: BM = BELOW MINIMUM, OM = OVER MAXIMUM, IG = INVALID GRADE.

program. The kit is indexed so that the user may turn quickly to the page which describes the topic on which a question is raised. This prevents the manager from having to leaf through a dozen-or-so pages to find the information needed. A copy of this index is included as Figure 6.

▪ In addition to this kit, abbreviated instructions on commonplace salary planning actions are footnoted on the bottom of each salary planning page (refer to Figure 3). Therefore, managers who are even vaguely familiar with the program can complete their salary planning forms without ever having to refer to the instruction kit.

▪ Each year, the first salary planning document is distributed along with a brief questionnaire which surveys managers' perceptions of the program with regard to its overall usefulness, as well as suggestions for its improvement. This questionnaire is helpful to salary administrators in terms of providing good, practical feedback on the value of the program from the line users. It also emphasizes to managers that the program exists to meet their needs; and changes in program are made as follow-up to many of the design suggestions received through this questionnaire approach.

FIGURE 6 Salary Planning Instruction Index

▪ INDEX ▪

General Information about the Report	*Page*
▪ The Three Sections of the Report	1–3
▪ Contents of Each Section	1–3
▪ Column Information Which May Be Changed	4
▪ Salary Planning Summaries Sheet	5–6
▪ Salary Planning Summaries for the Financial Budgeting Process	7–8
▪ 1982 Salary Planning Schedule	9
▪ Calendar of 1982 Payroll Dates	10
Reference Index for Specific Salary Actions	
▪ How to Add Newly Hired Employees not Appearing on Report	11
▪ How to Delete Terminated Employees	11
▪ How to Transfer Employees	12
▪ How to *Revise or Delete* Planned 1981 Salary Increases	12
▪ How to *Revise or Delete* Planned FIRST 1982 Salary Increases	13
▪ How to *Revise or Delete* Planned SECOND 1982 Salary Increases	14
▪ How to Add Planned Additions and Plan Their Salary Increases	14–15
▪ How to Delete Planned Additions	15
▪ How to *Revise or Plan* Increases for Part-Time and Limited-Hour Employees	15–16
▪ How to Add Planned Additions for Part-Time and Limited-Hour Employees	16
▪ How to Plan 1982 Salary Increases If Not Done on the First Salary Planning Report	16–18
Instructions on How to Return Completed Forms to Compensation & Benefits	18–19

■ All arithmetic calculations are automatically done by the computer. Managers need only post four pieces of information for each employee: namely, the percentage increase; the number of months to the next increase (from the last increase); the performance rating; and the type of increase. The system, then, performs all calculations—both for individual employees and for total summary figures for the unit. The user need not perform one clerical function throughout the entire process.

Fourth. The importance of quality in salary planning by managers is always emphasized throughout this process. Oftentimes, under systems which are administratively complex, users may believe there is a correlation between the number of turnaround documents and the overall quality of the salary planning. In practice, this is simply not the case; in fact, the converse is often true.

At Merrill Lynch, managers are typically given only two opportunities to revise their initial salary planning inputs for their employees for the upcoming year. The turnaround systems operate as follows:

■ The initial input document is normally distributed during the month of August for planning for the next calendar year. This document contains current employee data (refer to left-hand side of Figure 2). The manager uses this information along with the merit-increase guidelines to plan increases for employees for the coming year.

■ The first turnaround document is distributed near the end of September. The manager, on this document, has an opportunity to review the initial results (by individual employee and, also, by summary totals) and to make revisions, as appropriate (refer to right-hand side of Figure 3).

■ The second turnaround document is distributed near the end of October, and the manager has a final opportunity to review planning both by individual employee and in total for his or her area. Final revisions are then input and the last revision of the salary planning report is distributed in November, at the same time the managers are involved in the preparation of their financial budgets. If managers are in agreement with their salary planning totals at that time, these figures are then automatically input to the compensation expense line of the financial budget.

Depending on the size of the organization, of course, the number and timing of these turnaround documents can either be increased or decreased and/or moved up or back, although it is advisable to schedule at least one turnaround document so that initial salary planning errors can be revised by the managers.

Fifth. Proper communication to managers on the importance of such a program is always critical to its success. This also encompasses the need to *train* managers in an understanding of the value of the process itself. At Merrill Lynch, two communications vehicles have been used for this purpose.

The first medium is "instructional technology"—or the employment of the computer to enable managers to learn about the benefits inherent to them via participation in the salary planning program as well as to teach them, as their own time permits, the mechanical procedures of the process. Merrill Lynch has utilized Control Data's PLATO program in the design of a computer-based educational program which is administered to managers interested in learning more about the intricacies of the salary planning process. Additionally, this one-hour course is a requirement for all newly hired or newly promoted managers who have not previously been involved with this program.

The second medium is the personal presentation. On a periodic basis, representatives from the compensation department visit areas of the firm in order to deliver to managers an overview of the salary administration program. A key part of this presentation deals with the salary planning process. During these presentations, compensation specialists have an opportunity both to describe the benefits of the program in detail and to receive direct feedback from managers on the merits and deficiencies of the system. This one-on-one communication is invaluable to the salary adminstrator in fine tuning the program so that it remains in step with the ever-changing needs of the managers who must use it.

WHY SALARY BUDGETING?

As a result of the integrated planning and budgeting systems at Merrill Lynch, the salary budgeting program is simply an extension of the salary planning process. In other words, through salary planning, a manager plans the salaries of each of the employees for the upcoming calendar year. Then, once approved, these plans become the next year's salary budget against which actual salary expenditures are measured.

By definition, any budget is a forecast of the expense that will be incurred for the upcoming year. A salary budget, very simply, tracks the actual salary expenditures versus the planned expenditures and reports on the variance of these two figures. This variance is a common measurement of managerial performance.

Objectives of Salary Budgeting   The salary budgeting system at Merrill Lynch is designed to accomplish the following objectives:

■ Provide managers and their superiors with direct feedback on their performance on salary administration issues by summarizing overall actual versus budget base-salary expenditure data.

■ Provide managers with a control device whereby they are informed of variances which may exist between actual and budget salary expenses so that, if necessary, they can modify or seek an exception to their planned salary actions for the remainder of the year. In this way, managers are continuously aware of their performance on salary administration issues, and emergency or crisis situations are less likely to occur.

■ Provide managers and their superiors with direct feedback on actual versus budget *merit* and *promotional* increase expenditures so that attention can also be focused on the specific components of total base-salary expenses which may result in budget variances.

■ Enable managers to foresee the financial impact of actual year-to-date salary expenditures by projecting year-end estimates of compensation expenses.

This information makes it easier for managers to keep their actual expenditures in line with their original budgets. It also prevents them from having to postpone increases that are due in the latter part of the year because over-budgeted amounts may have been granted in the early part of the year.

Timing of Salary Budgeting   The salary budget evolves from salary planning, and at the beginning of the calendar year, the budget becomes the measuring stick against which actual expenditures are compared. Monthly, thereafter, salary budget reports are distributed to managers which describe activity for three different time periods:

- Year to date
- Year to date (actual) plus remainder of year (projected)
- Annualized result

Distribution of the salary budget reports on a monthly basis enables managers to receive continuous feedback on their actual salary practices so that variances are identified as they emerge, as opposed to appearing as "surprises" to management at a time when it is too late to remedy the situation.

Additionally, salary budget summary reports are distributed on a quarterly basis to senior management so that they are kept abreast of salary administration activities at the divisional or regional level. After reviewing these summary reports, senior management has the option of requesting additional information from their managers, if questions arise within specific areas of the firm.

SALARY BUDGET MODEL

The purpose of this section is to provide the reader with a description of some of the key features which should be incorporated into the design of a salary budget program.

Segments of the Salary Budget Program   Merrill Lynch's salary budget program consists of three interrelated reports:

- Salary budget summary
- Employee detail report
- Staffing report (by grade)

Salary budget summary.   This report (Figure 7) is the core of the Merrill Lynch salary budget program. In addition to the total information shown, separate data are furnished for the exempt and nonexempt groups, respectively.

The salary budget summary itemizes data for three expense areas:

- Total base-salary expenses
- Merit-increase expenses
- Promotional-increase expenses

While the focus of the salary budget program is on the total base-salary expense figure for each unit of the firm, both merit and promotional increases are also monitored as they represent the two types of salary actions that most often contribute to changes in the total base-salary level.

FIGURE 7 Salary Budget Report

SALARY BUDGET REPORT

(FROM 01/01/83 THRU _____)

TOTAL EMPLOYEES SUMMARY

COMPANY: _____
BUSINESS UNIT: _____
SVP GROUP: _____
DIVISION/REGION: _____
MGR GROUP: _____
DEPARTMENT/OFFICE: _____
ORGANIZATION: _____

AT-A-GLANCE KEY DATA - TOTAL EMPLOYEES	SECTION
— BASE SALARY % CHANGE OVER 12-31-82:	(I)
— HEADCOUNT % CHANGE OVER 12-31-82:	(I)
— % OF ANNUAL BASE SALARY BUDGET SPENT:	(II)
— % OF ACTUAL INCREASE BUDGET SPENT:	(III)
— % OF ANNUAL INCREASE BUDGET SPENT:	(III)

--- BASE SALARY/HEADCOUNT SECTION --- | --- SALARY INCREASE SECTION ---

I BASE SALARY/HEADCOUNT: COMPARISON OF 1982 & 1983 LEVELS

ANNUAL LEVEL	TOTAL BASE SALARIES	TOTAL HEADCOUNT
12-31-82 LEVEL		
CURRENT LEVEL		
— DIFFERENCE		
— % CHANGE		

II BASE SALARY/HEADCOUNT: 1983 BUDGET VS. ACTUAL

TIME FRAMES	BUDGET	ACTUAL	VARIANCE	% OF BUD EXPENDED
YEAR-TO-DATE				
— BASE SALARIES				
— HEADCOUNT				
THRU YEAR-END				
— BASE SALARIES				
— HEADCOUNT				
ANNUAL				
— BASE SALARIES				

III KEY TOTAL SALARY INCREASE DATA: 1983 BUDGET VS. ACTUAL

TIME FRAMES	INCREASE BUDGET $	%	#	ACTUAL INCREASES GRANTED $	%	#	INCREASE VARIANCE $	#	% OF INCREASE BUDGET GRANTED INCREASE #
THRU YEAR-END									
ANNUAL									

IV MERIT AND PROMOTIONAL INCREASE DATA: 1983 BUDGET VS. ACTUAL

TIME FRAMES	INCREASE BUDGET $	#	ACTUAL INCREASES GRANTED $	#	INCREASE VARIANCE $	#	% OF INCREASE BUDGET GRANTED INCREASE #
YEAR-TO-DATE INCREASES							
— MERIT							
— PROMOTIONAL							
— OTHER							
— TOTAL							
THRU YEAR-END INCREASES							
— MERIT							
— PROMOTIONAL							
— OTHER							
— TOTAL							
ANNUAL INCREASES							
— MERIT							
— PROMOTIONAL							
— OTHER							
— TOTAL							

This report provides managers with a snapshot of their budget and actual pay practices. It is subdivided into four sections:

Section I—Base salary/head count: Year-to-year comparison
Section II—Base salary/head count: Budget vs. actual
Section III—Key total salary increase data: Budget vs. actual
Section IV—Merit and promotional increase data: Budget vs. actual

The format of this report is simple and straightforward. At a glance, it gives the manager a "reading" on all pertinent salary budget indicators. By scanning the "Variance" and "% of Budget" columns in each section, the manager knows immediately if actual pay conforms with the planned actions. Additionally, if unfavorable variances appear on this report, the manager is also given the information to determine precisely those areas in which actual practices are deviating from the plan—for example, merit increases and/or promotional increases for either the exempt and/or nonexempt employee populations.

The manager, in reviewing this report, is given a concise, yet complete, overview of the status of actual versus budget pay practices. Depending on the variance data, the manager can decide whether or not an investigation of more specific salary practices may be necessary. If this is the case, the manager simply refers to the second report in the package, *the employee detail report.*

The employee detail report. As conveyed by its title, this report is a breakdown of the individual salary actions that are taken by a manager within the unit. Therefore, if a glance at the summary report concerns the manager, the employee detail report will provide all the backup information (employee by employee) which will reveal the specific reasons for the variances.

The detail report is also a handy reference tool regarding all personnel transactions within a particular area. In addition to providing actual versus budget compensation information on an employee basis, the report also summarizes personnel actions which have been taken (e.g., new hires; transfers, both in and out; and terminations). This report, on a monthly basis, chronicles all the salary and personnel actions that have actually taken place year to date within a unit as well as those which are planned to occur prior to year-end. As such, it is an invaluable reference document to be used by the line manager as a supplement to the summary report.

Staffing Report. This report provides managers with information pertaining to the staffing head counts within each unit. In the easy-to-read format, it details head count in job grade sequence (exempt and nonexempt) and provides counts for full- and part-time employees as well as counts on employees in miscellaneous payroll classifications. Three head-count periods are included on the report:

- Actual head count as of the end of the previous year
- Budget head count for the plan year
- Current head count for the plan year

In reviewing this monthly report, the manager is presented with an overview of actual versus planned staffing levels for the unit. Additionally, head-count variances are included and managers and their superiors can either take corrective action when significant variances begin to emerge or prepare an analysis as justification for the variance in planned staffing levels.

THE AUDIT AND CONTROL OF MERIT INCREASES

Merrill Lynch, in addition to its salary planning and salary budgeting programs, has designed and implemented an "exceptions-based" salary administration audit and control program. This program is comprised of monthly and quarterly reports to management detailing the specifics of those salary actions processed within each unit which are exceptions to the firm's salary administration guidelines.

Pertaining to merit increases, one special report (Figure 8) has been developed which compares the actual merit increases granted to each employee against the guidelines of the merit-increase grid. Where exceptions exist insofar as amount or timing of the actual increases versus the guideline, the particulars of the salary transaction are printed on this monthly exceptions report which is distributed to management.

While all increase transactions bearing the proper authorization are processed when submitted by managers (in accordance with the philosophy that a manager best understands the requirements of the unit and its people), all such salary transaction *exceptions* are flagged for future management review. As time passes, management is able to perceive trends in the pay practices of some managers, especially those who frequently grant increases which are not in adherence with the firm's guidelines. In these cases, management must exercise its good judgment in determining whether specific business conditions were the cause of noncompliance to the guidelines.

As noted in Figure 8, the merit-increase grid exceptions report provides the name of each employee for whom a merit-increase exception transaction was processed as well as the pertinent details of the merit increase. In column 10 of the report, the specific merit grid guidelines (in terms of percentage of increase and number of months from last increase) applicable to the individual employee's performance rating and salary positioning in range appear. In column 11, the actual percentage increase granted is printed along with the frequency in months. A quick glance down column 11 at the asterisked items alerts the managers as to the specific merit-increase exceptions processed during the previous month within the area.

Similar audit and control reports are also generated for other salary administration exception transactions, some of which include the following:

- Employees paid below range minimum
- Employees paid above range maximum
- Newly hired employees paid above range midpoint
- Employees with promotional increase exceptions
- Employees receiving retroactive increases
- Employees receiving increases in unevaluated jobs

The purpose of this system is not to impose police control over the salary administration practices of the managers within the firm. To the contrary, it is to provide managers with flexibility with regard to pay matters so that they may take the salary actions deemed appropriate in responding to the specific needs of their units. By the same token, management should be reminded on a regular basis that exceptions to the firm's accepted salary administration policies have been processed so that they can assess each individual situation and make their own determinations as to whether or not the exceptions are warranted.

FIGURE 8 Merit Increase Exceptions Report

COMPANY
EVP GROUP
DIVISION/REGION
DEPARTMENT/OFFICE
ORGANIZATION

JECAP MERIT INCREASE GRID EXCEPTIONS REPORT
REPORT NUMBER III
PPRS PROCESSED DURING MONTH OF NOVEMBER, 1981

(1)	(2)	(3)	(4)	(5)	(6)	(7)	(8)	(9)	(10) MERIT GRID GUIDELINES		(11) EXCEPTION TO MERIT GRID *	
EMPLOYEE NAME	EMP #	POSITION TITLE	SAL PRIOR TO LAST INCREASE	DATE OF LST SAL CHG	CUR JOB GRD	CURRENT SALARY	PERF RTNG	** PRV QNT	% OF INC	# OF MTHS FROM LST INCREASE	% OF INC GRANTED	NUM MTHS FROM LST INCREASE
SMITH AP	21428	JR. ACCT.	21,000	08/10/81	25	26,250	FE	4	13-15	11-13	25.0*	3*

** PRV QNT = PREVIOUS QUINTILE — PRIOR TO MERIT INCREASE GRANTED

SUMMARY

As emphasized throughout this chapter and as illustrated in Figure 1, the formal salary adminstration programs at Merrill Lynch are fully integrated with one another. In addition, the systems also interface with the firm's overall management reporting program. A summary description of the various phases of this integrated approach is as follows:

PHASE I: The "basics" of the salary administration program, as described at the beginning of this chapter, are integrated with the salary planning program via the salary grade ranges, and pay is administered within these ranges through the use of merit increase guidelines.

PHASE II: Salary planning is the basis upon which salary budgets are determined. Managers are given an opportunity to plan salary increases for employees during the last half of the year, and the results of their efforts, once approved, are translated into the salary budgets for their areas in the upcoming year.

PHASE III: Salary planning is used as direct input to the financial budget. The compensation expense entry in the financial budget is a reflection of the "bottom line" of each manager's salary planning efforts.

PHASE IV: The salary budget report, then, provides backup detail for the compensation information included in the financial budget. In other words, the financial budget states total year-to-date actual and budget base-salary expenditures (among other expense items), while the salary budget provides a separate, detailed listing which itemizes individual salary actions by employee. The financial budget reports the bottom line actual and budget compensation amounts for the entire unit, and the salary budget system details specific information for each employee. In this fashion, the salary administration program is a critical link within the firm's overall management reporting system.

PHASE V: As the last "link" in a fully integrated approach, even after actual merit increases are granted to individual employees, the audit and control system compares the amount and frequency of each increase against the merit-increase guidelines and reports all exceptions to management on a monthly basis. This system provides managers with the "freedom to act" when deciding upon those pay matters which are critical to the success of their own units' operations while informing management of the salary exceptions processed within their areas of responsibility.

Incentives

chapter 27

Relating Incentives to the Total Compensation Package

Roy Delizia

SENIOR PRINCIPAL, THE HAY GROUP,
PHILADELPHIA, PENNSYLVANIA

The total compensation package is composed of fixed and variable components. Salaries and wages, benefit programs, and perquisites all fit into the fixed category; incentives in whatever form compose the variable portion. In putting together a total compensation package, an organization should decide what is an appropriate balance between the fixed and variable components. Factored into this decision are several key elements: economics (How big a fixed component can I afford?); competition (What do the companies with whom I compete for talent provide?); stage of development (Are we a young, growing organization with little need to emphasize security?); and culture (What mix do we feel fits our value system best?). The fact that organizations have different economics, different competitors, are in different stages of development, and have different value systems results in the development of total compensation packages of enormous variety and complexity. the variable component is often the most complex.

Incentive defined. For purposes of this chapter, "incentives" are variable rewards related to the achievement of specific results. In order to have a true incentive program, the desired results must be known beforehand and the relationship between desired results and related awards must be clear. Otherwise, the program is likely to provide nothing more than after-the-fact rewards for achievements that happen to have occurred.

PREREQUISITES FOR EFFECTIVE INCENTIVES

While there may be situations where an incentive program is not appropriate as part of the compensation package, it is becoming increasingly difficult from a competitive standpoint for a company not to have an incentive program. This is an unfortunate situation in that many of the prerequisites for an effective incentive program are either missing or not present to the necessary degree. This can result in an organization seeing little or no return on its investment (time, effort, and money) in its incentive program. Among the critical prerequisites are:

1. Adequate, competitive floors in base salaries or wages and security areas (benefits).
2. Significant individual or group impact on key results areas.
3. Measurable results and appropriate yardsticks. Qualitative results are the more difficult to measure and require special approaches in an atmosphere of mutual trust.
4. Appropriate time spans. For top management, an appropriate time span may be three to five years; for hourly workers, a week or month may be the best.
5. Top-management commitment to all aspects of the program. This is vital to its success. It includes the commitment to setting the right goals, measuring and assessing performance, and determining the appropriate payouts.
6. A climate in which striving toward individual and group excellence is encouraged and recognized. Adverse peer (or superior) pressure can defeat the finest incentive program.
7. A management information system which can clearly track the measures selected for use in the program.

While it may be meaningful to use market share to recognize sales performances, if market share is not tracked or if no one places great reliance on the accuracy of the numbers, it is better not to use this measure. Many times, operations would like to use return on assets employed to measure division performance but are smart enough to back off when there is major disagreement as to "just whose assets are these?"

While the absence of these prerequisites may dictate that an organization should not consider incentives (without changing), having them is not a license to use incentives extensively. Because the cost is measured not only in dollars but in management time, top management must be selective in the use of incentives.

Before adopting an incentive program, a cost-benefit analysis is appropriate. We have mentioned costs, including dollars paid out and management time. The potential benefits will be discussed in the following sections.

IMPROVED COMMUNICATIONS

The goal-setting aspect of incentives provides management with a vehicle to communicate, in both quantitative and qualitative terms, just what results are desired. Individuals are often not clear as to what is considered critically important at this point in their jobs. Managements (and managers) have a way of saying one thing and meaning another ("Quality is of number one importance," "The customer is always right," "Service is our business," "How many did you ship today?"). A lot of lip service is given to a lot of things, and it is not always easy to discover what the name of the game really is.

Poorly designed compensation programs can be unrelated to or actually in conflict with the critical needs of the business. An incentive program which rewards people for increasing levels of shipments at a time when management is trying to increase cash flow through better management of its working capital is contraproductive. If an incentive program is being managed properly, then management will change the emphasis of incentive goals from shipments and sales to inventory turns and pretax margins. Changing the incentive goals provides instant communication to managers that their efforts need to be focused in different, yet specific areas. When critical areas and goals are made clear, management can become more productive. This can lead to the entire organization working more productively.

Incentives provide management with a vehicle for specifying not only desired results but what it is willing to pay for these results. The related "reward" aspect can be critical. Identifying a specific result area, say, lower production costs, creates awareness; putting dollars behind the achievement of the goals and actually paying those dollars provides credibility. An effective incentive program gives management one of the most important communication tools it has at its disposal. This is true at all levels of the organization, starting with the board in its deliberations with the chief executive.

No other part of the compensation package can facilitate communications in quite the same way. Furthermore, if incentive payments are made frequently (weekly, monthly, quarterly, or semiannually), the program carries with it the built-in requirement for regular communications. Every time an incentive payment is made, effective communication has occurred. Having to compute the amount of an employee's incentive award forces review and communication on a regular basis.

Effective incentive plans require periodic measurement and reporting. They also build in a demand for remedial improvement and utilization of all abilities to achieve it. Thus they are the essence of effective communication, if handled properly, to a degree not possible in most other components of the compensation package.

MORE EFFECTIVE PLANNING SYSTEMS

Incentive goals should not be developed in a vacuum. Having specific goals for an incentive program is nice, but your goals should also be the "right" goals. The acid test of "rightness" is how well incentive goals can be linked to the strategy of the company. If the company is emphasizing profitability, incentive goals should stress productivity, working capital management, and expense control. The linkage of incentive goals to strategy requires that the company have an effective planning process. The planning process must be able not only to piece together a viable overall strategy but also to analyze that strategy and assign the specific contributions needed from each unit to make it successful. However, this does not mean that a company must forgo incentives in the absence of such a process. The introduction of incentives may itself cause the company to improve its planning. As the planning process improves, so will the incentive program.

INCREASED MOTIVATION

Variable economic opportunity based on individual or group accomplishment can play a profound role in personal motivation. Money, or money equivalent, is itself significant. As a symbol of achievement, it has deep, added motivational penetration. People respond constructively to legitimate and exciting challenge. Confronted with a target (which they accept as valid, preferably because they participated in establishing it), they shoot at it.

Knowing what is expected of you, and what you expect of yourself, is a critical part of motivation. Incentives provide that information and provide visible, tangible rewards in recognition of achievement.

Furthermore, incentives tend to speak to the psyche of more and more of the younger members of today's work force. There is increasing interest in individual fulfillment, self-realization, and maximizing one's potential. There is an impatience with junior roles for juniors, a demand for responsibility with a real chance to have impact, limited only by competence and capacity.

Incentives provide that opportunity far better than any other form of compensation. Moving up in a salary range requires ability, no doubt, but it also requires survival and the passage of time. On the other hand, an incentive plan says simply, "This is what accomplishing these results is worth: if you do it, you'll get it; if you do more, you'll get more; and if you do less, you'll get less— but you have the same crack at it as everyone else in this job, regardless of age, or length of service, or time in the job."

Unquestionably, incentive compensation can be a significant motivator in and of itself. More important, it can be used in a supportive way in relation to other motivators in the behavioral, environmental arenas. People may be willing to work longer or harder or more carefully because there is a crisis (a hurricane destroyed the telephone lines) or because they know their work is critical to a project's success (the quality of equipment in a medical diagnostic system), but it also is supportive and comforting to know you are getting paid commensurately with your response to the challenge.

More immediate mileage in terms of improved results is often obtainable through incentive compensation than through other components of the total package. The basic security programs—pension, group insurance, and so forth—are necessary and desirable in the long run, but they are difficult to utilize for improved results in the short run and to identify with such outcome.

The base-salary program and opportunities for promotion have an important motivating impact when they are appropriately related to individual performance. A salary increase is, however, a permanent thing: once granted, it is rescinded only rarely. Most managers prefer to discharge a person rather than cut salary or rescind a promotion, and the higher one climbs the company ladder, the truer that is.

Because of their permanent impact, salary increases and job promotions tend to be based on fairly long-range judgments of performance, both in retrospect and in prospect. One's track record is examined over a period exceeding the most recent year, and one's probable future level of sustained performance is also considered. There is motivational pull in this, but it is long range by nature rather than immediate. Incentives recognize current achievement and the pay-off is prompt, unconditioned by other considerations. But it is not permanent. To get the same incentive award again next year, or next month, or tomorrow, one must produce comparable results.

MORE "BANG" FOR YOUR COMPENSATION "BUCKS"

If managed properly, giving a heavy weight to incentives in the mix of base to benefits to bonus in the total compensation package can be prudent and conservative financial management. Essentially, total compensation costs will vary according to specified end results.

An increase in the incentive rate may be more cost-effective than an increase in base pay if it raises productivity while utilizing the same space, equipment, overhead, and time. An equivalent outlay for added time off with pay (holidays, vacations, or shorter workweeks) is likely to be less cost-effective because of the lost production while maintaining the same overhead.

Application of the concept of real cost is even more dramatic in its implications at the salaried or sales level—and the higher in the organization you go, the more significant it is. The compensation of the chief executive officer and his or her immediate staff is not usually a variable cost—it is overhead—except when incentives are paid strictly according to greater results for the corporation or institution: if greater results are not realized, the incentive award is not paid. This is not true of base salary, and is true of benefits only when they are expressed as multiples of total compensation rather than of base salaries.

An interesting aspect of the typical American industrial experience is that greater thought has gone into the development of hourly incentives than incentives at the salaried level. This is true not only as to costs and directly measurable results but also as to the psychological and motivational aspects. Yet almost every aspect of the design, implementation, and administration of an effective hourly program has its counterpart at the salaried levels.

In developing effective incentive programs, a company needs to be aware of specific performance-reward relationships. What level of performance merits no incentive award at all? What will the incentive payout be if planned performance is achieved throughout the organization? What is the maximum award that can be paid out? How has maximum performance been established?

Management needs to be satisfied that for each performance level the potential payouts make economic sense both for employees and for stockholders. This kind of cost-benefit analysis needs to be done throughout the life of the incentive program.

MANAGEMENT CONTINUITY

An incentive system at its best can be thought of as a performance agreement between employer and employee. The employer stipulates the performance desired and the rewards related to this performance; the employee agrees that the goals specified are appropriate and achievable.

An individual's performance vis-à-vis agreement goals can provide management with a picture (even if incomplete) of how well the individual is performing against the basic requirements of the job. An individual who continually exceeds performance-agreement goals will not only earn sizable incentive awards but also demonstrate ability for the current job and for future promotion. While failure to perform well against the goals in a single year may not prove an individual's inability, consistent underperformance should be a red flag.

The performance agreement requires that dialogue occur between boss and subordinate on the front end to assure that the goals are appropriate (in terms of business conditions, the potential for improvement, and the individual's ability to exercise some degree of control over key factors). Performance then needs to be reviewed regularly during the incentive period to assure the validity of the goals and to discuss measures that can be taken to increase the individual's odds of success. At the end of the incentive period it is imperative that an individual's boss discuss each goal area to explain how awards were determined. It is at this point that key developmental needs can be discussed.

The important point about an incentive program is that it can force this important dialogue to take place through a structured approach to goal setting and performance review. And, in forcing this dialogue, it can provide substance to a management development program. Identifying today's and tomorrow's key managerial talent may be the best benefit of a well-designed and executed incentive program.

CUSTOMIZING THE INCENTIVE PROGRAM

A good incentive program is not mechanical. It should be tailored to the needs of the organization. The term "organization" in its broadest sense includes structure, management processes, people, value systems, and its overall strategy. Given the dimensions of organization, the statement that "no two organizations are alike" has immediate credibility. What this means in terms of incentives is that what works for one organization works because it is uniquely suited to that organization—and generally not suitable for any other organization.

The particular combination of elements (both real and perceived) which spur people on to produce desired results must be understood and captured in an incentive program. Is teamwork a key to success or is independent action stressed? Do we need to be concerned about rewarding individual contributors? Just how important is the stability of our management team to our long-term success? Is this the time to emphasize asset management instead of growth? Should incentives be completely mechanical (and quantitative), or is there room for management discretion in determining awards? These are only a few of the questions management must answer in order to know itself and thus be in a position to develop incentive programs attuned to the needs of the organization.

Diversity exists not only among organizations but also within a given organization. Today's organizations are more diverse than even ten years ago; and this trend is likely to increase. More geographical expansion, more intensive international competition, technological innovation, and acquisitions will combine to produce even more diverse organizations in the future.

Organizational diversity can be the bane of those people charged with designing incentive programs. This is because a basic aim in designing incentive programs is to "keep it simple." Armed with this dictum, the designer sets out to develop one program that will fit the needs of most of the units in the organization—the growth units, the mature units, units organized around profit centers, units using a matrix structure, etc. It is probable that one design scheme will not fit all units equally well.

This does not mean that developing meaningful incentive programs for various units within a single organization is impossible. A single format can get people to use the same design principles while having flexibility as to the specific goals, measures, performance standards, and reward mechanisms appropriate for individual units. The program must be managed if it is to be effective.

Thus in their most effective and sophisticated applications, incentives can be attuned to organizational needs no matter how diverse and, with this proper tuning, can encourage units to produce desired results.

SUMMARY

In summary, the total compensation package has two essential components: (1) the fixed portion consisting of wages and salaries as well as essential security programs and (2) the variable portion consisting of incentives in whatever form. The fixed component must be pitched at an adequate level to be competitive in the marketplace and also to provide a satisfactory standard of basic living. Once this condition is fulfilled, incentives, in the true sense of the word, can be incorporated into the total compensation package.

When designed and managed effectively, incentive programs can be a valuable management tool. Incentives can be instrumental in implementing a new strategy, in identifying current and potential managerial talent, in motivating people to produce desired results, in forcing management to decide what results are desired, in communicating goals, and in monitoring and feeding back information both on group and individual performance. Despite complexities in organizations, it is still possible to develop incentive programs that are appropriate for units with different requirements.

Incentives are not, of course, a panacea. They are not a substitute for but a critical part of effective management. Moreover, there may be circumstances in which incentives are inappropriate and result only in a waste of time, effort, and money. But when the circumstances are ripe and the climate supportive, incentives can provide a vehicle to draw from each employee his or her best and to reward it and, in concert, to accomplish the best for the total enterprise.

chapter 28

Designing Incentives for Hourly Workers

Ervin Seltzer

SENIOR CONSULTANT, THE HAY GROUP,
PHILADELPHIA, PENNSYLVANIA

WHAT IS AN INCENTIVE?

There is no shortage of theories why people work. For almost every theory one can find examples of how that particular incentive stimulated workers to be more productive, and for the same theory, examples of failures. Evidently, factors such as administrative policies and the social environment within the work force are critical components of any motivating system in addition to the incentive scheme itself.

An incentive plan is a program that provides extra pay as a reward for extra results. The premise is that both management and the worker will profit equitably from the arrangement: the extra cost of the incentive pay to the worker is offset, and more, by lower unit costs.

A prerequisite for any incentive plan, in fact for any equitable working arrangement for hourly employees with or without incentives, is the classification of all the jobs in a way which reflects the relative value of each job to the organization. A good evaluation system will consider the various levels of skill, effort, responsibility, and working conditions associated with the jobs and set base rates according to some rational, credible, objective plan.

In most organizations where there are significant numbers of hourly employees performing repetitive tasks and where payroll costs are an important cost factor, sooner or later—when the managers consider ways to increase productivity—the use of incentives will come up. This chapter looks at some of the more common programs for wage incentives for hourly personnel with comments on some of their counterproductive as well as productive aspects. Incentives may be paid to each worker, individually, with a direct linkage between the worker's personal performance and the pay. There are also group incentives where the output of a group produces some shared reward for the group members.

For convenience it is assumed that the incentives discussed here apply to hourly personnel in a manufacturing organization.

The care and feeding of such plans are discussed, with suggestions how successful ones operate. At the same time, mention is made of some of the hidden reefs which may be encountered and which may only be noticed after the plan is installed and the shakedown cruise is over.

The very notion of hourly worker incentives implies that for each task there is established some legitimate and predetermined output goal, with an arrangement to pay extra for exceeding that goal. In fact, the underlying theory of paying wages for work implies the concept of the worker providing a certain level of performance in return for equitable wages.

When a profit-making organization makes a quotation or sets a selling price for an article or service, there has to be a plan of just about what part of the cost will be based upon the hourly labor. For successful use, over a period of time, the performance goal must be measured or "engineered." For a successful plan it is essential that the worker have the same vision of a fair level of output as the employer.

The presence of a union is no inherent obstacle to the successful functioning of an incentive plan. But if there are adversary stresses or hostile attitudes between management and the union, weak administration may provide unwelcome occasions for conflict.

There are many managers who believe that setting good work standards is in the long run the best and only requirement for improving worker productivity. Management's job is to get the worker to meet the standard, and it relies on improving methods, machines, technology, and good administration to bring about improvements in productivity. This is known as the measured-day work system. Without incentives there is more freedom to make changes as needed. Another advantage claimed for working without incentives, under the measured-day work system, is that even in the best of installations it is rare that more than 60 or 70 percent of the hourly workers are covered by incentives. The balance of the workers are on operations which do not meet the criteria for setting measurements. They perform maintenance work, material handling, tool and die making, inspection, and similar operations which are difficult or impractical or impossible to measure.

VARIETIES OF INCENTIVE PLANS

In considering the design of an incentive plan, there are a number of alternatives: (1) There is the *individual plan.* In this, individual performance goals are set up for each operation with some additional pay for performance above a threshold amount. (2) *Incentives for groups.* Here instead of individual performance rates the performance goal is set for the output of a group working together. (3) *Profit sharing.* The well-known Lincoln Electric Plan takes this form. This is an interesting concept which appeals to entrepreneurial instincts but is not a strong motivator when there is a prolonged period without profits. For large groups, the plan tends to suffer because each individual's effort may not be clearly tied to profitable results. (4) *Gain sharing*, such as payoff to workers on the basis of value added by the entire operation. Sometimes the Scanlon Plan and the well-known Rucker Plan are in this category. These plans are believed to be weakened to the extent that influences such as selling prices, credit losses, and similar factors not under the control of the worker may seriously affect the reward. (5) *Productivity sharing*. This is a form of group incentive generally linking payoff to improvements in performance against standard costs, especially these components of the standard costs which are directly related to worker performance. It has the great advantage that results are linked to the workers' efforts regardless of problems such as competition, commodity prices, etc., which are beyond the control of the worker.

All of the sharing plans—profit sharing, gain sharing, productivity sharing—usually have the merit that, in addition to the offer of monetary reward, they are normally constructed in such a way as to involve the workers at the very grass roots level in producing ideas and helping make decisions regarding the work. Thus they tap not only the desire for more money but, perhaps of equal significance, the desire for participation and importance as members of the organization. This feature of involvement has been used with great success by the Scanlon Plan and Rucker Plan and by the Japanese with their "quality circles." Such indirect incentive plans are proven examples of the principle of using all the human resources at hand to motivate the worker and reduce costs.

In brief, the process is simple. Each natural production group (such as a department of ten or more persons) is encouraged at frequent intervals (weekly, if not daily) to review the work schedule and to help decide the most effective way to meet the goal. The workers' first-hand knowledge of the actual production processes is an important resource in optimizing the production plan. Causes of delays, poor quality, scrap, etc., are reviewed, and if internal to the department, corrections are considered; if outside the department, recommendations are made. In the latter case, management is expected to respond promptly or give reasons to justify inaction. Results, good and bad, are shared with the participants. Sometimes, for large groups, rotating representatives are selected who report back to their co-workers. For some groups, there is a conscious effort to have the group perform without the front-line supervisor. In others, the front-line supervisor is encouraged (and trained) to take a leadership role. The latter practice is favored by the author.

ESTABLISHING PRODUCTION STANDARDS

Any incentive plan which is designed for long-term use requires consistent, engineered work standards.

Industry has in the past turned to the stopwatch, which permits timing the operation and obtaining an accurate record of its various elements. A major difficulty which has been encountered with much stopwatch work is in adjusting every observation to a judgment of the pace of the worker. That is to say, if the worker is working faster than standard pace, the time has to be adjusted upward, and if the worker is working slower than the standard pace, the time has to be adjusted downward. This standardization of work pace is difficult to maintain uniformly from task to task and from observer to observer.

The use of predetermined time standards is an excellent tool for getting around this difficulty. "Methods time measurement" (MTM) and "work factor" are two systems of predetermined time standards which have been used with success for the various hand and body motions. With synthetic times all motions have been previously measured and standardized, and rather than taking a stopwatch study of the operation, it is only necessary to get a record of what motions are involved.

If there is any thought that the original times in the predetermined time standard are not appropriate, it is easy enough to put a uniform coefficient of correction on all the standards.

Managers have frequently found that the process of setting a standard in itself is highly likely to stimulate substantial improvements in productivity, largely by requiring a questioning look at the methods and by reducing obvious factors which cause delay in the repetitive operation.

Once the standard is set, it is important that the method used be recorded accurately and that the operator be instructed to conform to that method. It is not legitimate for the operator to perform by a different method from that authorized in the standard. Operator-originated method changes should be encouraged and welcomed, but must be reflected in the work standard. Private, unrecorded changes introduce all kinds of ills which later may plague the system.

The details of measuring work and establishing standards are outlined in many textbooks on work measurement and are summarized in handbooks, such as McGraw-Hill's *Industrial Engineering Handbook*, 3d ed., 1971, edited by H. B. Maynard.

There is something so simple, so "just" in the basic incentive idea, "extra pay for extra work," that it is difficult for most managers and for most workers to find a flaw in it.

The first step is to provide a goal which will be felt to be fair and equitable by management and the worker.

There are four preconditions: (1) The work must be repetitive. (2) The task must be measurable, and it must be feasible to describe exactly how the task should be performed. (3) The worker must follow the standard method. (4) There has to be some suitable method of counting the output.

The work standard itself can be set by stopwatch or by the use of synthetic time standards. It is not recommended that incentive standards be based on estimates, no matter how informed the estimator.

With good management and a clear understanding of the need for consistency and honesty in setting rates and a fidelity to the principle that when changes occur the rates will change to reflect those changes, it is possible for incentives to produce a substantial increase in output.

Often industrial engineers look for a performance that will average about 25 percent above that of an average day worker who is using good and well-engineered performance rates. Most work measurement practitioners consider it unlikely that a worker can consistently perform at a very much higher level. Outputs of 160 percent of standard and higher suggest that the standard may not be set correctly.

An output improvement of 15 to 25 percent is indeed very desirable. This improvement, however, does not come without its price. It requires a work measurement and methods organization capable of setting standards; it requires consistent management attitudes; and it requires the endorsement of the front-line supervisors in enforcing the standards and in "selling" the rates to the workers and in proving to the workers that the standards are indeed equitable.

If rates are not kept up to date or if the methods are not standardized, there are many problems which can arise to plague an incentive plan. Here are a few of them:

1. Waits and delays caused by the company stimulate discontent and grievances because the worker then cannot work against the standard. Workers accustomed to working under an individual- or group-incentive plan do not like to be deprived of their "incentive opportunity."

2. Workers may adopt ceilings on output because the rate has been set loose in the first place and they fear that the company may simply tighten the rate. To forestall this, it is common practice for the company to guarantee it will not change the rate unless the method or the materials or the equipment change.

3. Workers may claim that the standards don't fit the task, requiring the lifting of the incentive standard and costly reviews. This implies the need for an experienced industrial engineering staff whose work is understood and supported by management.

4. Demands to perpetuate the worker's former earnings opportunities could occur when the tasks change.

5. Workers may request payment of "average earnings" whenever nonstandard conditions arise or when the company asks a worker to do special tasks.

6. There might be work performance by other than the official methods (cutting corners). From the point of view of the worker, the extra earnings which come from an unrecorded change in the method are simply a well-earned reward for ingenuity. Management, however, can only regard such a practice as a violation of the terms of the incentive plan and as an inequitable treatment, compared to the other workers.

7. Runaway rates can occur. Sometimes incentive rates are set in error, and they provide extra pay without extra effort. Minor changes in method, too subtle to be recorded, or in materials or equipment, aggregated, often contribute to runaway rates. Great maturity on the part of both the worker and management is required to bring the situation within the normal, equitable range.

8. Banking of work credits for a rainy day can occur. Manipulation by the worker of reports on work performed (or materials used) tends to defeat the purposes of the incentive plan. In addition, the company loses control of work in process.

9. Managers have experienced that workers tend to sharply reduce their work pace when the standard rate is lifted or if the rate cannot be achieved.

10. For any incentive to work, it is recommended that the role of the front-line supervisor be carefully examined. It should not be thought that the existence of an incentive plan automatically will inspire the worker and the group to perform at top level. Management and leadership are essential.

The managers should only consider incentives where the worker has a decisive influence on the output. This generally means labor-intensive operations such as sewing machine work or hand assembly. Where the work is mostly controlled by a machine cycle or by a conveyor, there is comparatively little the worker, no matter how well motivated, can do to increase the output. When a plant has some jobs which are machine-controlled and others which are operator-controlled, the manager should be very thoughtful about introducing incentives for the latter, unless there is some provision for also rewarding and motivating the other production workers and, in addition, the 30 percent or so of the work force who are support people such as adjustors, maintenance workers, inspectors, and so on.

Perceptions of inequitable treatment within an organization, favoring one group over another, are often disruptive and demoralizing. Such conditions may act as more pervasive dissatisfiers than, for example, a pay scale which is below the community levels for comparable work.

It is sometimes feasible to pay a bonus to certain service or support jobs, such as machine adjusters, material handlers, etc., which is based on the average incentive earnings of the people serviced. In a great many cases, it is questionable how well such an arrangement really links reward with output. Even when the work of the service person is satisfactorily tied to the output of the workers serviced, there is the formidable problem of adjusting fairly the earnings as conditions change. Examples of changes which must be foreseen and agreed upon in advance are decreases or increases in the speed or number of machines, changes in product, materials, etc.

There are many possibilities in the formula to produce extra pay for extra work. Experience has shown that once a threshold is passed which represents a day work pace or a minimum incentive pace, the most acceptable arrangement to the worker is to pay off "one for one." For each percent output is increased, the pay is increased by a similar percent over base. Experience also suggests that it is unwise to impose a ceiling, or upper limit, on output and earnings. There are other formulas which can be considered. Many of them offer an incentive to get the worker above the 80 percent rate of output. Others pay off on curves, with diminishing rewards above some level such as 130 percent of base.

ALLOWANCES

When an operation is measured by predetermined time standards or by the stopwatch, in addition to the observed time corrected for pace, it is necessary to add in various allowances to cover factors such as:

Fatigue
Interruptions to the work
Personal requirements
Breakdowns of equipment
Delays of supplies
Idle time caused by line balance
Wash-up time

It is common in industry for such allowances to total 7 to 12 percent of the 480 minutes in an 8-hour workday. All information involved in setting a work standard should be open for inspection by both workers and supervisors. All have a right to see all the data and to satisfy themselves whether any corrections are needed.

ADMINISTRATION OF AN INCENTIVE PLAN

Once an organization has coverage on incentives, a steady operating state will determine the number of permanent personnel required in the rate setting and industrial engineering department. In general, using predetermined time standards or stopwatch studies of short-cycle operations (under about two minutes in duration), it is reasonable to expect that a rate-setter can establish standards for different operations at a rate of two or three per day.

For long cycles, five or ten minutes of work or longer, it may take one to five days for the rate-setter to gather all the information necessary for a rate. The number of operations and the level of changes in methods, machines, and materials will determine the number of people involved in the rate-setting activity.

Every rate should be reviewed or audited periodically and systematically at least every year or 18 months to verify whether it is still applicable and whether the method can be improved. The number of changes in equipment and materials are difficult to believe unless experienced. It is important for the health of the operation to conduct such an audit.

Ultimately, the success of work standards, whether for individual or group use, depends on the acceptance by those concerned of the fairness of the standard. Otherwise, there may arise a tremendous motivation to find ways to get around the system and to defeat it either fairly or unfairly by aboveboard or by underboard methods.

The best pay period for calculating incentive performance has been found usually to be the shift. If the pay period is stretched out to a week, a poor performance at the early part of the week may tend to demotivate the worker for the later part of the week.

In summary, incentives can be a powerful force for improving productivity for the right kind of labor-intensive operations, in combination with strong and experienced management skills. If labor relations are unsettled, an incentive plan is frequently a focus of discontent over real and fancied inequities. It is also well to decide in advance the strategy for equitable treatment of those workers not given incentive-earning opportunities.

chapter 29

Designing Effective Sales Incentives

John S. Rogers

PARTNER, THE HAY GROUP,
PITTSBURGH, PENNSYLVANIA

Robert J. Davenport, Jr.

PRINCIPAL, THE HAY GROUP, CHICAGO, ILLINOIS

The only certainty about business in the final decades of the twentieth century is that uncertainty is increasing. Inflation, interest rates, shortages, surpluses, technological advancement, obsolescence, and demographic shifts have all contributed to the sense of bewilderment felt by many sales executives as they try to formulate winning strategies.

Compounding the external problems are two internal problems. First, as U.S. industry matures, marketing is being pressed to produce more with less, and that usually means more pressure put on the sales department not only to justify its sales expense but often to cut it.

Second, just as the pressure on sales force productivity is increasing, a corresponding shortage of good, professional sales representatives is developing. Sales representatives are less willing to take risks; conservatism is the name of the game. The result is that traditional ways of rewarding and motivating a sales force do not seem to be producing the effect that they once did. Previously effective incentive plans, such as straight commission, have gotten so far out of control that they are damaging the integrity of the profit and loss statement, as well as creating an elitist group of salespeople who no longer aspire to growth and refuse to accept directions. On the other hand, many salary-plus-incentive plans have underpayed sales representatives and lost the ability to attract and retain the caliber of person necessary to compete effectively.

This chapter describes how to design a sales incentive plan that works—i.e., increases sales force effectiveness. The bulk of the chapter deals with cash incentives, because they are the more appropriate tool for long-term motivation and sales direction. Formulation of noncash incentives—which can be effective short-term motivators—will be described at the end of this chapter.

DESIGN OF AN EFFECTIVE SALES INCENTIVE PLAN

Well-designed cash sales incentives should accomplish two major objectives:

Earnings opportunity.   This provides a sufficient and competitive total cash-earnings opportunity to attract or retain the quality of sales representative necessary to compete in the marketplace.

Marketing support.   This reinforces goal-setting activity by paying for specific goal accomplishment. It encourages performance that is directly linked with—and supports—marketing strategies.

Steps in Incentive Design

The parameters to consider when designing a motivational, strategic sales incentive program are 25 percent compensation and 75 percent marketing and sales management. To be both effective and strategic, sales incentives should be designed using a formal process such as the one outlined in Figure 1.

Step 1. Understand Sales Force Climate   The unfortunate fact is that many sales executives do not really know their sales forces. There is no "typical" sales organization. Every company has a particular climate as a result of both internal and external conditions. And to design motivational incentives, it is essential that management knows which key factors affect (both positively and negatively) the effectiveness and productivity of a particular sales organization.

Sales force attitudes are shifting. Today's salesperson has an entirely different view of himself or herself than was prevalent a decade or two ago. Most salespeople view themselves as more professional, are highly involved with all

FIGURE 1   Steps in a Cash Sales Incentive Plan Design

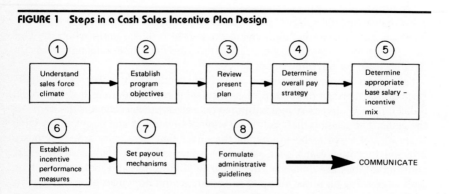

TABLE 1   Typical Sales Force Climate Issues

1. Clarity and realism of marketing strategy, goals, action plans
2. Sales management direction, training, and communication
3. Pressure, sense of urgency, and freedom to act in individual sales position
4. Importance and amount of promotional opportunity, career orientation
5. Degree and quality of support from nonsales organizational units
6. Current and ideal time management of selling and nonselling activities
7. Sense of sales force vitality, morale concerns, leadership, and competitive strength
8. Adequacy and competitiveness of both total cash and incentive opportunity
9. Risk orientation

phases of the marketing plan (more than a "peddler"), and have much more concern about career progression. As such, they respond less to traditional, volume-oriented incentives and more to multiobjective incentives which focus on the total sales task.

Some of the areas that would affect sales force acceptance and commitment to a performance-related incentive program are listed in Table 1. Unless you know your salespeople's perceptions of their unique strengths, weaknesses, developmental needs, and special motivational issues, incentives will be based only on *presumptions* of what excites, motivates, or "turns off" your salespeople.

Step 2. Establish Program Objectives   Companies have different market opportunities, competitive strengths, missions, organizations, and marketing plans. As a result, they have different sales incentive objectives.

Prior to the development of an incentive program, objectives must be clearly identified—and agreed upon—by marketing and sales management. The more specific the objectives are, the more effective the incentive program will be. Some typical objectives of a sales incentive plan are:

Attract and/or retain sales talent.   Depending on the nature of a company's selling activity and the type of individual sales profile, good sales incentives can be designed to not only help attract high-quality sales candidates but also to retain top performers. This can be an especially important goal when a firm finds itself in the position of losing good salespeople to the competition, or where the recruiting of qualified personnel has proved difficult.

Before a plan that meets attraction and/or retention goals can be designed, a profile of the appropriate sales incumbent should be constructed. This profile would include such factors as:

- Risk/independence orientation
- Technical skills
- Educational background
- Experience (industry or other)
- Compensation expectations
- Career expectations

Well-designed incentives closely match the needs of the sales representative's profile.

Achieve marketing priorities.   Obviously, marketing goals and strategies have to be clear (and internally and externally achievable) before a strategic incentive plan can be designed.

The current economic climate, with its swings and disruptions, often makes changes necessary in an organization's objectives. But while most companies' marketing plans change emphasis from year to year, more often than not sales incentive plans fail to follow suit. Thus there is an erosion of effectiveness until the problem reaches crisis proportions.

For example, one manufacturing company in a rapidly maturing market has changed its emphasis from volume growth to profit improvement—without changing its incentives. Not surprisingly, the incentive plan has failed to achieve its objectives, because its sales representatives have not changed their direction, working as they are under an old plan which is no longer appropriate and is not consistent with objectives.

Marketing priorities must also be realistic. This may sound simplistic, but most companies plan for substantial real growth, which is often not realistic. The business world is full of disappointed optimists.

In summary, marketing priorities must be clearly defined—and clearly measurable—prior to incentive development.

Motivate and sustain high energy level.   A sales incentive plan should do just that—provide an incentive for performance. When properly designed, with frequent payouts linked to objectively measured goals, incentives can help maintain a performance climate.

Support needed changes.   When a company is changing products or entire lines of business, or perhaps totally redirecting its market emphasis, a revised sales incentive program can be designed to help in the changeover. For example, a major group insurance carrier had traditionally expected its field sales force to spend most of its time attending to the service needs of existing major customers. As competitive activity increased and market share began to slip, an aggressive new business-oriented marketing strategy was formulated. A new incentive plan was then designed which emphasized and rewarded acquisition of new customers.

Reinforce managerial direction.   Sales management exists to provide sales direction, assistance, coaching, and counseling. An incentive, while never a *substitute* for sales management, should provide *reinforcement* of managerial direction. For example, assume that sales management wants a sales representative to focus his or her time on key products in key accounts which require disproportionately more selling time and effort. If, however, incentives pay off equally on all products to all customers, you can be sure that sales personnel will focus their efforts on activities which pay the rent or the mortgage the easiest. Nothing frustrates sales managers more than an incentive program which sabotages their own managerial direction.

In summary, objective setting is a key step in incentive plan design. Once objectives are clearly defined and agreed upon by top management, the task of developing an effective, performance-oriented plan will become easier.

Step 3. Review Present Plan   The obvious reason for developing new incentives is the fact that present incentives (or lack of them) are not producing cost-effective results.

TABLE 2   Most Frequent Problems with Commission Plans

1. Overpayment—often tens of thousands of dollars
2. Unwillingness to accept promotion
3. Overfocus on maintaining current accounts
4. Underattention to new products
5. Lack of company loyalty
6. Resistance to management direction

In straight commission-oriented incentive plans, inflation is driving up sales incomes far in excess of what productivity or real performance would warrant. Because of these and other problems with straight commission plans, a large number of companies have switched to salary incentive plans. Their experience has been disappointing. Incomes under these plans have generally failed to keep pace with earnings in nonsales jobs, because of poor goal setting. And when we examine incomes on a person-by-person basis, we find that windfall earnings in high-opportunity territories are frequently making an even poorer earnings picture for the majority of participants.

Tables 2 and 3 outline some of the problems companies are having with both types of plans. A helpful framework for determining what is wrong (as well as what isn't) with existing sales incentives is to examine strategic and tactical appropriateness (Figure 2).

Following such a review, you should have a good idea where remedial action is needed and whether the existing incentives should be totally scrapped, or perhaps only modified.

Step 4. Determine Overall Pay Strategy   To determine the size of the incentive opportunity, an overall pay strategy must be developed. Despite some contrary opinions, sales compensation is not profit sharing. It is a *planned cost expenditure*. As such, an overall sales force pay strategy should be formulated that accomplishes four goals.

- *Externally competitive* (industry, sales positions)
- *Internally equitable* (other organizational units)
- *Attract and retain*
  Keeps top performers
  Discourages poor performers
  Eases recruiting
- *Fits importance of salesperson*
  Based on individual job accountabilities and overall impact on sales

TABLE 3   Most Frequent Problems with Salary Incentive Plans

1. Underpayment
2. Poor goal setting, and quota gamesmanship
3. Extreme payment variations by territory
4. Turnover—loss of top sales representatives
5. Loss of drive and ambition
6. Inability to recruit quality people

FIGURE 2   Strategic and Tactical Appropriateness Checksheet

	Excellent	Good	Fair	Poor
Strategic Check		Results		
● Achieves marketing goals	☐	☐	☐	☐
● Fits marketing life cycle	☐	☐	☐	☐
● Externally competitive	☐	☐	☐	☐
● Internally equitable	☐	☐	☐	☐
Tactical check				
● Reflects individual effort	☐	☐	☐	☐
● Meets career income needs	☐	☐	☐	☐
● Simple and action-oriented	☐	☐	☐	☐
● Seen as fair	☐	☐	☐	☐
● Balances sales rep risk and reward	☐	☐	☐	☐
● Provides for territory variances	☐	☐	☐	☐
● Provides for territory management	☐	☐	☐	☐

The degree of overall total cash competitiveness must be determined prior to formulating the amount of cash opportunity which will be made available through an incentive program.

Competitiveness is an important concept in setting total cash strategy. For example, the pay practice of certain industries is higher than others. High-technology firms tend to pay among the highest average sales compensation in U.S. industry. Pay practice also reflects the relative importance of the salesperson. In the capital goods industry, for example, the retention of a stable, experienced sales force is essential. In other industries, such as consumer packaged goods, where promotion and other marketing factors dominate, pay strategy does not have to be as high.

Of course, the market position and sales strategy of the individual company are also important. Weaker competitors often must pay more than market leaders in order to attract high-caliber salespeople to do a tougher selling job. Also, some industries, such as the retail sporting goods business, can compete with relatively lower compensation practices because part of the reward of employment is working with products the salespeople enjoy in their leisure time.

The first step in determining pay competitiveness is to conduct a pay survey to determine the existing level of competitiveness. Although this can be done internally, third parties (industry groups, trade associations, management consultants) generally do a better job. When comparing pay levels by position, it is important to note that job titles may not provide the proper match. To be meaningful, pay comparisons should be made among jobs of equivalent content and accountability, regardless of title.

Step 5. Determine Appropriate Base-Salary–Incentive Mix   The percentage of total cash compensation paid out in incentive is called leverage. Leverage is usually expressed as the ratio of base salary to incentive reward, as a percent of total earnings, for competent performance. For example, a 60/40 plan is one in which the total cash compensation for competent performance is paid out as 60 percent base salary and 40 percent incentive. Sales compensation leverage ranges from the extreme of 100 percent incentive (a straight commission plan with no salary) to a plan that is all base salary. The amount of leverage should be consistent with the stages of a company's marketing life cycle. For example, a firm that is young and aggressive, and needs to grow quickly and reach new customers, will typically hire hard-driving salespeople. They will normally be given high levels of incentive opportunity, with relatively low base salaries. In contrast, an established company, whose main concern is to retain existing customers and protect its share of the market, will tend to pay higher salaries and hold down the proportion of incentive pay. The cyclicality of an industry can also be an important factor that determines the appropriate mix of base salary and incentive compensation. Incentive opportunity for sales incumbents in an industry characterized by relatively unpredictable, severe business cycles should generally be much lower than in industries which enjoy a more predictable economic environment. In cyclical industries, where total company results are difficult to forecast, standards of *individual* performance become almost impossible to establish. Nevertheless, many companies in such industries today still use incentives as a management tool. Standards of individual performance are allowed to change quarterly, based upon changes in key indices that track the business cycle. The result is a program that measures and rewards results relative to a moving target but is still reflective of individual performance.

The amount of incentive opportunity should also reflect the degree to which the salesperson is in a position to influence the sale. Figure 3 shows that relationship and also indicates the relative incentive opportunity usually provided by several industries. Generally speaking, the higher the incentive leverage, the higher the motivational effect. However, if a job has little impact on end results, a highly leveraged plan can actually be demotivational.

FIGURE 3   Individual Impact on Sale Helps Determine Incentive Leverage

Step 6. Establish Incentive Performance Measures   Historically, incentive measures for sales representatives, such as straight commission on sales volume, were fairly simple and did not reflect diverse marketing and sales force requirements. Some guidelines are useful to help design appropriate incentive measures.

As explained in "Step 2. Establish Program Objectives," the incentive measures should reflect overall marketing and sales goals. For example, instead of paying an incentive on sales volume, a company may consider paying incentives for achievement of other objectives:

- New product sales
- Profit margins
- Product mix (selling a certain amount or percentage of products in a territory)
- New customer development
- Customer penetration
- Customer retention
- Territory market share
- Target product sales
- Specific project objectives, e.g., closing sales to preestablished accounts, achievement of new product penetration goals, improvement of local-territory gross margins

In the formulation of performance measures, point systems can be useful in avoiding commission or payout problems caused by price inflation, varying profit margins, or changing product objectives. In a typical point system, a specific commission rate or dollar amount is paid for point accumulation. Points can be related to sales, by sales price, profit contribution, marketing emphasis, end customer, etc. Some group insurance firms, for example, use points to differentiate between the various risk profiles of their customer base. They can also be used to pay off accomplishment of special objectives, with higher point values being attached to more strategic objectives. Their major drawback is that points are one step removed from the primary sales measure—dollar volume.

One or several performance measures can be used, although more than three becomes cumbersome to administer and loses motivational impact. Territory performance measures should be designed and weighted by the importance of various marketing objectives. For example, a company that has a low relative market share and depends on key buying accounts to generate profits could attach the following weights to incentive components:

Territory Sales	20%
Territory Growth	50%
Territory Priorities	30%
	100%

Incentives are, however, only one part of a compensation program. When the overall accountabilities of a job are considered, some are necessarily measured and rewarded by base salary. In most sales jobs, incentives do not take the place of sound salary administration.

In summary, sales incentives may come in many forms. Those which are successful are:

- Measurable
- Directive
- Weighted by importance
- As few as necessary

Step 7. Establish Payout Mechanisms   Several structural options are available for payout incentives. Designing the components by which incentives are earned and weighted is only half the job. Equally meaningful are the specific payout rules. Depending on the nature and number of components, one or more of the following structures could be used.

Payout tables.   This type of mechanism establishes a predetermined payout for achievement at preset performance levels. It is typically linked to individual-territory characteristics and requirements or to certain specific sales representative activities. One form of payout table, a management by objectives (MBO) mechanism, usually ties in with activities that are one-time occurrences. Under this system five to seven objectives are identified, and specific dollar payouts are attached to the successful completion of one, several, and all of them. The key concept here is that the objectives be quantifiable and the accomplishment of the objectives be readily apparent—with limited subjective determination required.

Commission plans.   Three types of commission plans are commonly used and are sometimes combined.

1. *Commission from first dollar or unit (Figure 4).* This mechanism requires no goal setting, and is more of a "profit sharing" device than an activity-directed plan. It is appropriate where it is very difficult to establish sales forecasts or territory quotas. The proportion of base salary depends on the amount of leverage in the plan. Under this structure, sales representatives' incomes will rise and fall as a result of *both* individual performance and the economy. The commission percentage is usually small, so that the reward for incrementally improved performance is a very slight increase in total cash. The mechanism provides a very good method for limiting sales compensation expense to a fixed percentage, but may not be very motivational.

2. *Commissions above a minimum goal (Figure 5).* This mechanism incorporates a goal-setting process that enables management to assign accountability for achieving a portion of overall results to each sales territory. The individual

---

FIGURE 4   Commission on First Dollar or Unit

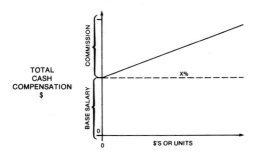

FIGURE 5 Commission above a Minimum

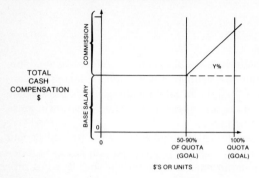

participant, however, is protected to a greater or lesser extent from earning zero incentive due to unrealistic setting of the threshold or from unanticipated swings in the economy. The commission rate generally gets higher as the threshold moves closer to the expected average sales level. The company has limited protection from upside payouts if overly pessimistic thresholds are established in a rising economy.

3. *Commission for extra performance (Figure 6).* With this type of structure, a commission is paid for performance which exceeds a quota based on the expected, competent level of performance. Under this type of system, the program tends to reward only half the sales force (assuming a normal performance distribution) and is viewed more as a "bonus" than as a planned and integrated part of total cash compensation. Quotas generally get harder and harder to achieve each year, and the expectation of earning a bonus becomes less motivational to the majority of the sales force. If quotas established under this system are below the expected level of performance, then the plan becomes similar to option (2). The drawbacks, however, are that the sales representative doesn't have a true yardstick of sales excellence and the quotas are not tied to the overall planning process.

A combination of options (2) and (3), with a basic commission rate above the minimum goal, and an accelerated commission rate above the average quota,

FIGURE 6 Commission above a Quota (Goal)

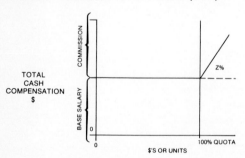

can be very effective in motivating—and rewarding—the achievement of outstanding results.

Bonus plans.   Under this type of mechanism, a bonus, or lump-sum amount, is paid out for exceeding a goal or a level of performance. Typically, bonuses are paid once during the year. Although they do serve as performance reminders, their motivational impact is lessened because of the infrequency of payout and their remoteness from the actual event that triggered the bonus.

Bonuses paid for performance beyond the direct control of the participant (such as a payout for companywide volume) have no direct motivational effect. In most instances such bonuses become part of expected income and are considered to be deferred salary.

Step 8. Formulate Administrative Guidelines Despite the best incentive design, unusual occurrences and special cases must be anticipated and provided for under any sales incentive plan. To prevent possible morale and management problems, administrative guidelines should be provided to cover such issues as:

- Transfers
- Territory splits
- Goal setting
- Windfalls or disasters
- House accounts
- Distributor accounts
- Price changes
- Timing of payouts

Communication

A frequently ignored element of incentive plans is the need for effective communications. The plan itself should be simple enough for the sales force to understand; if the plan cannot be presented on one page, it is probably too complicated.

It is not enough merely to announce revised incentives to the sales force; the incentives must be *sold* to the salespeople. An explanation of the plan's background (market conditions, company direction, sales role in marketing strategy, resulting payout) makes commitment to the plan much easier and can avert future incentive problems. Finally, all sales incentive plans should be thoroughly audited every two years to assure maximum sales effort and effectiveness. Companies cannot afford to wait for a crisis to develop to decide it is time for a change.

DESIGN OF A NONCASH INCENTIVE PLAN

Although cash is a prime motivator to salespeople, there are instances where one-time, or periodic, noncash incentives can be productive motivators.

They can take the form of trips, merchandise, prize points for merchandise, upgrading of the company car—even dinner with the boss. They are most effectively—and appropriately—used to generate excitement and activity about a particular sales event, as opposed to the overall sales management objectives rewarded by a cash incentive plan. Such events can include:

1. New product introductions
2. Special efforts for slow-moving products or services
3. Signing up distributors
4. Product demonstrations
5. Prospecting for new customers
6. Recharging a sales force (short time span)

Similar to the design of a cash incentive plan, a noncash incentive plan must be a planned event that takes into consideration the following issues:

1. Eligibility and rules
2. Goals (realistic *and* measurable)
3. Percentage of sales force likely to qualify—usually 10 to 60 percent (which, of course, affects the cost of the incentive)
4. Timing (enough time to communicate program and achieve results— reward should be as close as possible to goal achievement)
5. Communications (critical—program should be thoroughly promoted to establish and maintain excitement level throughout the plan)

CONCLUSION

There is no doubt that sales incentives can contribute measurably—both to sales force effectiveness and to a company's bottom line.

As shown, there are several approaches and countless modifications available in plan design. The key ingredient to success is *management*, both of the program and the sales force. The key to incentive success is to establish the critical fit between goals, sales force culture, and incentive measures that adds up to increased sales force productivity.

chapter 30

Designing Incentives for Banking

Victor P. Iannuzzi

VICE PRESIDENT, CITIBANK, N.A.,
NEW YORK, NEW YORK

BANKING IN THE 1980s—AND BEYOND

Banking is usually thought of as a straightforward business—the process of taking in money with one hand and lending it out with the other. Hopefully, the spread is sufficient to make a profit. It used to be that banking had a monopoly on both of these functions—deposits and loans. Because they possessed a unique power to create money, banks have become the most severely regulated privately owned institutions in the United States. The straitjacket has not changed much in 50 years, but unfortunately, just about everything else has, and banks no longer have a monopoly on either loans or deposits.

Banks take demand deposits and pay customers' checks drawn against them—so do credit unions, savings banks, savings and loans (S&Ls), the American Telephone and Telegraph Company, stockbroker cash management accounts, and money market mutual funds.

Banks take time deposits and savings deposits and pay interest on them—so do brokers, money market funds, and all the S&Ls owned by companies like Sears, Roebuck; National Steel; Beatrice Foods; and the Baldwin Piano Company.

Banks lend money secured by collateral—so do brokerage firms, leasing companies, factoring companies, captive finance companies, and aircraft-engine manufacturers.

Banks lend money to businesses without collateral—so do other businesses.

Indeed, business firms now lend to other firms more than $100 billion in the commercial paper market.

Banks make personal loans and offer credit cards—so does everybody else, from finance companies to department store chains. In fact, bank-issued credit cards account for only about 15 percent of the credit cards outstanding in the country. Banks deal in government paper. So do corporate treasurers, brokers, mutual funds, and the person in the street. The list is endless, because it covers every so-called banking service. It is doubtful whether anyone could come up with anything a bank can do that somebody else is not also doing—*and doing nationwide.*

Competition is fierce and for a good reason—the marketplace for financial services is enormous. In fact, commercial banks entered the 1980s competing with 28,000 other specialized depository institutions. Today, most of the Fortune 500 companies are combining commerce and banking in significant ways on many different fronts. Add to this the fact that there are 165 or more foreign banks in the United States today, growing much more rapidly than their domestic counterparts. Not long ago, 8 out of 10 of the largest banks in the world were American banks. Now there are only two. Telecommunications and data processing have made banking the easiest game in the world to play and almost any business can do it.

Restrictive federal banking regulations date back to 1864. Today there are state-chartered banks where regulations vary from state to state, federal charter restrictions, Federal Reserve requirements, the Comptroller of the Currency, and numerous other regulatory agencies.

Regulations impose deposit interest-rate ceilings which are far below market prices. As a result of a law passed in early 1980, ceilings are scheduled to end in 1986 on interest rates payable by banking and thrift institutions on deposits of approximately $1.6 trillion. Meanwhile depositors are leaving the banking system in droves, headed for money market funds. One might reasonably ask, How is it banks have survived if things are so bad? The answer is that many have not. Sixty years ago there were 30,000 banks; today there are about 15,000. And those that remain are steadily losing their share of the business.

If the banking industry is to be successful in the 1980s and beyond, it must be free to respond to the dynamic changes in technology, in telecommunications, and all other factors in the great revolution in financial services. The business of banking is fast becoming a high-technology industry, and it is one that can no longer be constrained by laws and regulations designed for a different time. Nor can it be constrained by outmoded compensation systems designed for a past era.

FORMS OF INCENTIVE COMPENSATION

There could not have been very many occasions in the history of commercial banking when the need for a performance-oriented management was as critical to the success of the business as it is today. Incentive compensation can play an important role in motivating bank executives, by providing a linkage between performance and reward. It may be useful at the outset to clarify just what the term "incentive compensation" means when used in the context of executive remuneration. (See Chapter 46 for a comprehensive discussion of executive compensation programs.)

The purpose of incentive compensation is to motivate individuals to perform in a manner leading to the accomplishment of specific business goals contributing to the overall success of the corporation. It provides an award based on measured performance against predetermined goals. Incentive compensation typically involves a commitment to reward the accomplishment of specific goals communicated before the fact and provides a predictable reward commensurate with the achievement of known, specific, and well-defined objectives. Individual control of performance against defined objectives is an important consideration in an incentive plan.

By contrast, a "bonus" is generally viewed as an extra payment. It is usually paid *after the fact,* as a reward for extra effort or as recognition for an extraordinary contribution of a nonrecurring nature. The individual doesn't customarily receive an advance commitment as to the potential reward for specific results. As you might suspect, few variable compensation arrangements are either purely incentive plans or purely bonus plans in the sense described above. Let's take a look at some common forms of incentive compensation used in commercial banking today.

SHORT-TERM INCENTIVE COMPENSATION: TYPES AND PREVALENCE

The typical short-term plan of incentive compensation generally provides an *annual* reward for the accomplishment of specific, predetermined objectives. In some organizations these plans frequently contain elements of a bonus plan; for example, participants receive no advance commitment regarding their potential award. The terms "annual incentive plan" and "annual bonus plan" are frequently used interchangeably in business today, even though the type of

FIGURE 1   Growth in Annual Award Plans, 1970–1978, by Industry

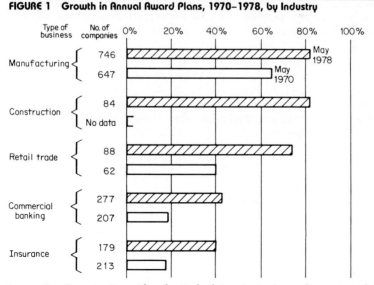

Source: *Top Executive Bonus Plans,* by Harland Fox, Senior Research Associate, The Conference Board, Inc.

TABLE 1   Annual Incentive Compensation Plans in the Top 200 Banks Ranked by Assets

Ranking	% with plan
1–50	90
51–100	91
101–150	69
151–200	52

SOURCE: "Executive Compensation in the Top 200 Banks," Meidinger, Inc.

plan referred to may be distinctly of one variety or the other. The growth of these plans over the last decade, in the banking industry compared to other industries, is shown in Figure 1.

As can be seen, the growth has been significant for banking overall, although there has been considerable difference in the prevalence of such plans among the top 200 banks. As shown in Table 1, 90 percent of the top 50 banks had an annual award plan in 1980, whereas only 52 percent of the banks ranked 151–200 had such a plan at the time.

The timing of awards and method of payment under short-term award plans generally fall into four categories.

Current Cash Awards   These are awards paid in cash immediately following the end of the year for which the award was earned. Payment may be in a lump sum or may be in installments beginning immediately and continuing for a fixed number of years during active employment.

Current Stock Awards   Current stock awards are paid in company stock immediately following the end of the year for which the award was earned. Payment may be in a lump sum or may be in installments beginning immediately and continuing for a fixed number of years during active employment.

Deferred Cash Awards   Awards paid in cash commencing at a future date specified by the company or the executive are known as deferred cash awards. Customarily, deferral is until retirement, and the amount deferred is credited with interest (possibly at the Treasury Bill rate, prime rate, internal rate of return, or other basis) in a manner specified in the plan. Eventual payment may be in a lump sum or in installments.

Deferred Stock Awards   These are paid in company stock at a future date specified by the company or the executive. Customarily, deferral is until retirement, and the amount deferred appreciates (or depreciates) with the value of the stock plus dividends payable over the deferral period. Eventual payment may be in a lump sum or in installments.

The prevalence of these various methods of payment, and their timing, is shown in Table 2, which compares the practices of the top 50 banks to the top 100 industrials. As may be seen, the banks, like the industrials, permit flexibility in the award timing and payment method. By far the most prevalent form of

TABLE 2   Annual Award Plans   (Timing and Method of Payment)

	% of Plans	
	Top 50 banks	Top 100 industrials
Timing of awards		
Current awards only	54	37
Deferred awards only	....	1
Both current and deferred	46	62
Method of payment		
Current cash awards	100	99
Current stock awards	20	44
Deferred cash awards	46	52
Deferred stock awards	15	45

SOURCE: "Incentive Compensation in the Top 50 Commercial Banks," Towers, Perrin, Forster & Crosby, *Survey Report—*December 1981.

payment is a current cash award, with virtually all the surveyed banks and industrials providing this popular payment option.

LONG-TERM INCENTIVE COMPENSATION

Long-term incentive compensation plans provide key executives with financial reward for making decisions that have a positive effect on the longer-range profitability of an organization. Results are always measured over a period of longer than one year and may be either financial or nonfinancial or a combination of these. Most frequently, organizations have *both* short-term and long-term incentive compensation plans. The reason for this is to motivate executives to make decisions that balance the need for short-term profits with the goal of continued long-term success. There is a seemingly endless variety of long-term incentive plans in use today. Generally speaking, the value of an award under such a plan is not determinable until after some future event. This may be because the award value is tied to the stock market (as in a stock option plan) or because the value is tied to some measure of company performance (e.g., earnings per share) for the period during which the award will be earned. Let's look more closely at some common types of long-term incentive compensation plans offered to bank executives.

Stock Option Plans   These give executives the opportunity to purchase company stock over a future period (usually ten years) at a predetermined price. Sounds fairly simple, doesn't it? Well, there are at least six variations on this theme that differ substantially enough to warrant separate mention:

Market value stock options.   This is the traditional nonqualified option where the price of the option is fixed at the publicly traded fair market value of a company's stock. The prices at exercise of the option and subsequent sale of the stock are also determined at the fair market value at the time of exercise and sale, respectively.

Formula value stock options.   The price of the option and subsequent price of the underlying stock are determined by some formula related to the financial performance of the company; for example, the formula might be book value per share. Disposal of the special class of stock used for this purpose is restricted. The stock must be redeemed through the company, using the same formula method.

Variable price options.   The price of the option varies depending on company performance, appreciation in the market value of the stock, or some other means.

Performance stock options.   Such options are granted to executives conditional on the attainment of specific, predetermined performance objectives.

Tax offset stock options.   These options contain a feature which pays the executive a sum of money equivalent to the personal income tax due at exercise, attributable to the appreciation in the option between its grant and exercise.

Incentive stock options.   An option receiving favorable income tax treatment under the Economic Recovery Tax Act of 1981. Such options must meet a number of stringent requirements in order to be tax-favored.

Stock Appreciation Rights (SARs)   This type of long-term plan gives the executive the right, usually in connection with a stock option, to an amount of money equivalent to the appreciation in the value of the underlying stock between grant of the option and the point at which the option would have been otherwise exercised, in lieu of exercising the option. When tied directly to a stock option grant, SARs are referred to as tandem SARs. These are the most common type of SAR today. An SAR that is not tied to a stock option grant is known as "free-standing SAR." These SARs are generally functional through a phantom stock arrangement which duplicates the conventional SAR except that actual company stock is not used.

Performance Unit Plans   These plans grant executives a number of units assigned an arbitrary value, and earned over a fixed period of time, contingent upon the achievement of predetermined performance objectives. The number of units earned may vary depending on the extent to which objectives have been achieved. Payment may be made in cash or an equivalent number of shares of company stock.

Performance Share Plans   Executives are granted a number of shares of company stock which are earned over a fixed period of time, contingent upon the achievement of predetermined performance objectives. The number of shares earned may vary depending on the extent to which objectives have been achieved. Payment may be made in shares of stock or their cash equivalent.

Restricted Stock Plans   Executives are awarded outright grants of company stock at no cost which can be sold only when certain restrictions lapse. The customary restriction is a fixed number of years of continued employment.

Phantom Stock Plans   These plans grant the executive the equivalent of company shares although actual stock is not used. The award to the executive, after a fixed period of time, is equivalent to the appreciation in the company's stock since the phantom grant and may include dividend equivalents. (The approach is similar in many respects to a free-standing stock appreciation right.)

Dividend Unit Plans   In this, the executive is awarded an amount equivalent to the dividend paid on a specified number of shares of the company's stock. Payment is in cash or an equivalent number of shares of company stock. Dividend units are frequently found in conjunction with other long-term incentive plans as opposed to a stand-alone plan.

The use of long-term incentive compensation plans in banks continues to increase. About 75 percent of the top 50 commercial banks have one or more such plans. Table 3 provides a breakdown of the prevalence of these plans in banking and diversified financial institutions.

As the table shows, stock options are the predominant form of long-term incentive plan used by the surveyed banks and financial organizations. Stock appreciation rights, typically granted in conjunction with stock options, are in use in about 42 percent of the surveyed organizations. Table 4 provides a name-by-name listing of the long-term incentive compensation practices of the 50 largest commercial banks. Table 5 summarizes pertinent scope data (eligibility, award size) for the various types of long-term incentive plans discussed here. It is worth noting that among the surveyed financial organizations, eligibility and participation in stock option plans is generally less restrictive than in performance share and performance unit plans. This differentiation pattern is typical among nonfinancial organizations as well.

DEVELOPING AN INCENTIVE COMPENSATION PROGRAM

With compensation expense representing one of the largest expenses on bank income statements, few people would quarrel with the importance of effective compensation systems in banks today. Because the human resource impact is essential to the success of any business, incentive programs directed toward motivation and reward must create a positive, performance-oriented climate. At the same time, the incentive system needs to be a natural extension of the business. It must be consistent with the bank's business strategy, recognizing

TABLE 3   Prevalence Breakdown by Plan Type   (Commercial Banking and Diversified Financial)

Type of plan	Number of plans	% of financial participants with plans
Nonqualified stock options	29	67.4
Stock appreciation rights	18	41.9
Performance units	7	16.3
Performance shares	4	9.3
Restricted stock	11	25.6
Phantom stock	2	4.7
Other (special)	5	11.6

SOURCE: "Survey of Long-Term Executive Incentive Plans, Highlights 1981," Hewitt Associates.

TABLE 4 Incentive Plan Practices of the 50 Largest Commercial Banks

Bank	Short-term incentive plans	Stock option plans	Stock appreciation rights	Performance-related plans	Stock grants*	Phantom stock plans
Citicorp	X	X	X			
BankAmerica Corporation	X	X	X	X	*	
The Chase Manhattan Corp.	X	X	X			
Manufacturers Hanover Corp.	X				*	
J.P. Morgan & Co., Inc.	X	X	X			
Continental Illinois Corp.	X	X	X			
Chemical New York Corp.	X			X		
Bankers Trust New York Corp.	X	X	†	X		
First Interstate Bancorp	X	X	X	X		
First Chicago Corporation	X			X	*	
Security Pacific Corp.	X	X	X			
Wells Fargo & Company	X	X	X	†	*†	X
Crocker National Corp.	X	X	X		*	
Irving Bank Corporation	X					
Marine Midland Banks, Inc.	X	X				
Mellon National Corporation	X		†	†		
First National Boston Corp.	X					
Northwest Bancorporation	X	X	X	†		
First Int'l Bancshares, Inc.	X	X	X	X		
First Bank System, Inc.	X					
Republic of Texas Corp.	X	X		X	*	
Texas Commerce Bancshares, Inc.	X	X	X			
First City Bancorporation of Texas, Inc.	X			X		
NBD Bancorp, Inc.	X					
The Bank of New York Co., Inc.	X			X		

Company						
Seafirst Corporation	X					
NCNB Corporation	X				*†	
Harris Bankcorp, Inc.	X	X		†	*	
Republic New York Corp.	X					X
Pittsburgh National Corp.	X					
Philadelphia National Corp.	X					
Southeast Banking Corp.	X	X	X			
Northern Trust Corporation	X	X	X			
Michigan National Corporation‡	X					
Valley National Corporation	X					
DetroitBank Corporation	X		X			
The Wachovia Corporation	X	X				
AmeriTrust Corporation	X	X				
First Pennsylvania Corp.	X	X				
National City Corporation	X	X	X			
Mercantile Texas Corp.	*	X				
Rainier Bancorporation	X	X				
BancOhio Corporation	X					
U.S. Bancorp	X	X		X		
Manufacturers National Corp.	X					
Mercantile Bancorporation Inc.		X				
First Wisconsin Corporation						X
Barnett Banks of Florida, Inc.	†					
The Girard Company	X	X	X			
Citizens and Southern Georgia Corporation	X	X	X	X		

*Grants of restricted stock.
†New feature adopted.
‡No plan publicly reported.
SOURCE: 1981 company proxy statements.

TABLE 5   Long-Term Incentive Compensation Characteristics for Commercial Banks and Financial Organizations

	Nonqualified stock options	SARs	Performance shares	Performance units	Restricted stock
Eligible employees					
(Average % of exempt)	12.4	N/A	0.5	1.1	11.4
Plan participants					
(Average % of exempt)	4.9	2.7	N/A	N/A	N/A
(Average % of eligible)	65.4	N/A	100.0	77.2	36.9
Lowest recipient					
(Average salary midpoint)	$44,829	$54,190	$85,000	$64,400	$44,613
Annualized award size					
(Average % of salary)					
1. Lowest	29.2	N/A	28.0	37.0	17.1
2. Highest	87.1	N/A	59.0	82.0	41.3

SOURCE: Adapted from "Survey of Long-Term Executive Incentive Plans, Highlights 1981," Hewitt Associates.

and accommodating new directions, and it must be compatible with the management style of the organization. For these reasons, it is crucial to establish incentive compensation objectives and programs in support of business objectives.

UNDERSTANDING THE CONSTITUENCIES

In organizing to meet the task of designing an effective incentive compensation program, it may be helpful to begin by considering the primary factors influencing design considerations, specifically the:

- Marketplace for talent
- Business
- Individual
- Stockholder

An amplification of these basic considerations will be useful in shaping a sound basic incentive compensation philosophy, and ought to provide a reasonable foundation for formulating specific objectives.

Marketplace Implications   In any reward system *the level of total compensation opportunity should be consistent with an established marketplace objective.*

This is not always as straightforward as it seems. Oftentimes the bank and the individual have differing definitions of the marketplace. Individuals will quite naturally have a tendency to associate the "marketplace" with only the most elite banking organizations in a particular market since they may view their peers as only the best talent in their field.

The bank, on the other hand, needs to have a broader perspective. Failure to do so could greatly distort the real competitive situation and the resulting compensation comparisons. Specifically, the marketplace should generally meet at least these criteria:

1. It should be a source from which talent is drawn into the bank (and to which the bank may lose talent).

2. It should include a reasonably broad cross section of banks and other companies, thereby constituting a fair representation of compensation practices in the community.

3. Individual firms comprising the marketplace should be as comparable as possible to the business entity in organizational terms—or we should be alert to the implications of the lack of comparability.

There isn't any right marketplace or compensation objective for every bank or necessarily for a single bank at its various stages of growth. These decisions must be made given the specific circumstances. What is important is that the proper considerations be focused on, and the principle of relating the level of reward to the marketplace not be taken entirely for granted.

Business Implications   In developing an incentive compensation program, it is necessary that the level of total compensation can be *supported by the business* and that the reward system *fits the overall structure of the bank.*

If incentive compensation programs are to reinforce the business strategy of the bank, they will need to do a lot more than add to staff expense. Properly constructed, a total compensation program actually should help make money for the bank by motivating performance above the norm and by assuring that a significant portion of an officer's total compensation potential varies with the results of the business. Relating the level of reward to the business is accomplished by assuring a proper balance of fixed versus variable compensation and assuring that the variable components appropriately reflect the bank's ability to fund them. This doesn't preclude recognition of individual performance, but puts such recognition in the context of overall business performance. It is extremely important for the financial control system of the bank to be congruent with the reward system to ensure that results are measured and reported as accurately as possible.

The far more difficult issue is the program's "fit" to the rest of the organization. It is imperative for the structural aspects of a company to fit the organization level at which performance is measured for reward purposes. It could be chaotic to attempt to reward for business unit results where there is a great deal of interdependency requiring substantial joint effort among various business units.

As a general rule, differentiated compensation in a bank makes most sense in a structural and management environment where:

■ A significant degree of product and/or market diversification exists, and the corporate role materializes as an allocator of resources among the businesses.

■ Top management wants to concentrate on developing new markets through entrepreneurship.

■ Business entities operate independently, and their financial results can be readily isolated and measured—generally in these situations there is not a great deal of interdependence requiring substantial joint effort among business units across the bank.

■ The need for mobility of talent among businesses can be balanced against the benefits of establishing separate reward systems among various business entities.

In the final analysis, there is no formula to replace the management judgment needed to arrive at decisions on differentiated compensation.

Individual Implications   In order to continue to attract the best talent to the bank, to motivate behavior consistent with new business objectives, and to retain a positive climate, *it will be important for incentive compensation programs to cause individuals to see a relationship between the level of their reward and their performance.*

There is abundant research evidence substantiating the belief that if pay is related to performance, it can contribute to organizational effectiveness. There are several things a reward system can do to effectively relate pay to performance, depending upon such things as the *climate, technology,* and *structure* of an organization.

The *people management climate* of a bank can be an important influence on the type of reward system that is right for a company. The potential for using pay to motivate performance is probably greater in a bank characterized by a collaborative style of management. There are any number of ways to promote the basic notion of collaboration, including more open communication of the compensation program, participative performance appraisal, or peer goal setting in an incentive plan. These approaches contribute to assuring that compensation is related to job performance behaviors that the individual perceives he or she is expected to exhibit. A compensation scheme can be made more effective by relating rewards to what the bank and individual jointly recognize as solid, comprehensive measures of performance. In this way meaningful differences can exist between the rewards for the best and worst performers, provided the organization is willing to accept perceptions of inequity on the part of some as a consequence of explicitly recognizing different levels of performance. Although it makes sense to talk about these general notions, actual practices must fit the conditions that exist in a specific situation. Expansion of the pay-for-performance concept should evolve naturally in an organization.

Technology can be an important influence on the appropriateness of the incentive program. For example, quite obviously it would make little sense to use a piece-rate incentive plan in a professional service organization, while it might make considerable sense in a mass production environment.

Finally, *organizational structure* should significantly affect a bank's reward philosophy. The degree of centralization or decentralization is relevant to formulating a compensation strategy because it generally affects the kinds of performance data available. In a highly centralized bank it is often difficult to measure the performance of a subpart because of the lack of an accurate, responsibility-based accounting system. This point is particularly important in a large bank where business unit or divisional performance as a criterion for variable compensation is practical only if the bank is decentralized to a substantial degree. In addition, decentralized banks can more easily tolerate different compensation practices in different parts of the organization. Indeed, an organization structure consisting of many decentralized business units would seem to encourage differentiated compensation programs tailored to fit the specific unit.

Stockholder Implications   It is essential *the compensation system adequately reflect the stockholders' interests.*

The stockholders who have entrusted a bank with their capital expect and are entitled to a reasonable return on their investment. Concern for stockholder interests is interwoven throughout a bank, from basic credit policy to developing business objectives.

The expense of an incentive compensation program should be a vital management concern. A responsible bank would not make any investment without being sure it was getting the best return possible. That is precisely what an effective incentive compensation program can do—assure the maximum return to the stockholder for the monies spent. By making the necessary investment in an effective incentive program, banks will be able to attract the caliber of individual needed to continue the industry's growth. That growth is part of their fiduciary responsibility to the stockholders.

Summary of Section   The key points in this section represent a set of design principles of incentive compensation that could be useful in formulating a specific program. Restating them here:

- The level of total compensation must be consistent with the established objective of the business as against the marketplace.
- The level of compensation must be supported by the business, and the reward system must fit the overall structure of the organization.
- Individuals should see a relationship between the level of their compensation and their performance.
- Stockholder interests must remain of paramount importance in considering new incentive compensation programs.

The usefulness of these compensation principles will be their broad application in the design of compensation programs which, in effect, impose norms of expected behavior on individuals. These programs can do this by conveying notions about what the banking business is all about, identifying who the competition is, and spelling out what kinds of performance are valued and under what circumstances. If properly designed, the structure of the compensation program will measure and reward the kinds of performance the bank values most.

DETERMINING SPECIFIC OBJECTIVES

In thinking through the elements of program objectives, the following general criteria may prove useful:

Performance Criteria   Plans may reward for corporate, business unit (divisional), or individual performance, or some combination of these. Rewarding for corporate performance generally provides the maximum visible shareholder protection and tends to reinforce a unified effort to achieve institutional goals. Business unit or individual performance criteria provide the flexibility to recognize outstanding achievement in a year of poor overall corporate results.

Performance Measurement   How performance is measured depends on what is being measured, of course. But within each of the three performance criteria, there are alternative measures. For example, if the criterion is corporate performance, the measurement could be earnings per share growth, return on assets, earnings improvement versus competition, etc. Business unit and individual performance can be more difficult to measure in a manner that assures equity for all participants.

Achievement Threshold   Once the performance criteria are established and the way performance will be measured is decided, the next issue is whether to establish a minimum level of performance before an award can be generated. Achievement thresholds are probably most useful where corporate performance is being measured. They are least discernible where individual achievement is the performance criterion.

Degree of Compensation Risk or Reward   Where placing a portion of a participant's compensation at risk is a desired objective, the type of plan selected is critical. In short-term incentive plans, making participants aware of a reward upon achievement of specific goals has as its corollary making them aware of a (compensation) risk if goals are not achieved. Almost by definition, after-the-fact bonus plans have no real degree of risk since there is no commitment to a defined reward.

Participant Control over Goal Achievement   This objective is highly interdependent with performance criteria. Where individual achievement is the performance criterion, the participant generally has maximum direct control over goal achievement. Corporate performance criteria generally provide the least amount of perceived individual control over goal achievement. The decisions on the number of people to be made eligible for participation in a plan and the number actually receiving an award are usually functions of the performance criteria and degree of participant control.

The objectives worksheet in Figure 2 may serve as a useful tool in reformulating existing objectives or for the commercial bank thinking about installing its first short- or long-term incentive compensation program.

FIGURE 2   Incentive Compensation Objectives Worksheet

Type of Plan:	Bonus Plan	Incentive Plan	
		Short Term	Long Term
Overall Objectives:	To serve as a means of providing extra payments as an after-the-fact reward for performance	To measure performance against specific, predetermined goals and to reward individuals commensurate with goals achievement	To provide a reward based upon the achievement of some contingent event (such as an increase in stock price) occurring over a period of time generally ranging from 3 to 10 years

Type of Plan:	Bonus Plan	Incentive Plan	
		Short Term	Long Term
Specific Objectives: ■ PERFORMANCE CRITERIA *What do we want to measure?* —*Banking group measure?* —*Corporate performance?* —*Banking group performance?* —*Individual performance?* —*Other?*			
■ PERFORMANCE MEASUREMENT *How will we measure performance?* —*Corporate: EPS growth, earnings vs. community, other?* —*Group: profits, nonfinancial goals, other?* —*Individual: judgmental, other?* —*Other: stock price?*			
■ ACHIEVEMENT THRESHOLD *When should the plan pay?* —*Corporate: min. growth, positive earnings, other?* —*Group: min. profit growth, budgeted profits, other?* —*Individual: min. rating, discretionary, other?* —*Other?*			
■ DEGREE OF RISK/REWARD *Do we want compensation at risk for failure to achieve goals?* *How much reward?*			
■ PARTICIPANT CONTROL OVER GOAL ACHIEVEMENT *How important is direct individual control over goal achievement?* *How many should be eligible/receive?* *Should there be flexibility to reward outstanding individual achievement in a year of poor overall results?*			

chapter 31

Performance Management:
Chasing the Right
Bottom Line

Robert H. Rock

PARTNER, THE HAY GROUP,
PHILADELPHIA, PENNSYLVANIA

Pay for Performance   For the past two decades, calls for "pay for performance" have echoed through the halls of management. Speeches in support of pay-for-performance philosophies and practices have been delivered by board directors, top management, stockholders, and special-interest groups. The proponents of pay-for-performance incentive plans offer a variety of rationales: attraction, motivation, and retention of people; control over variable compensation costs; recognition of contributions and achievements; and reinforcement of strategic goals and objectives.

Some managers and consultants hypothesize that incentive plans should be a process for implementing strategy; that incentive pay should be awarded for the accomplishment of preestablished standards of performance; and that the size of incentive payouts should be related to the degree of performance. In fact, there has been only a modest correlation between pay and performance.[1] At present, most incentive plans focus on pay, not performance. Moreover, those plans that do focus on performance frequently do so in such an offhand fashion as to provide merely a thinly veiled justification for the payment of

---

[1]Edward T. Redling, "Myth vs. Reality: The Relationship between Top Executive Pay and Corporate Performance," *Compensation Review,* fourth quarter, 1981.

bonus awards. Some cynics suggest that these so-called pay-for-performance plans devised by compensation consultants are merely elaborate schemes to sanitize the distribution of large sums of money to those senior executives who hired the consultants.

Performance Agreements   Despite these claims, many managers and many consultants are attempting to develop incentive plans which truly forge a link between pay and performance. As Figure 1 indicates, companies are gradually moving toward more structured performance management programs which reward managers for the accomplishment of preestablished measures of performance, particularly corporate and operating unit performance. Some of these programs devise "agreements" with individual managers, specifying performance objectives, measures, and standards and relating the accomplishment of these standards to varying incentive awards.

For example, the performance agreement for a chief executive officer (CEO) may include the information shown in Table 1. The CEO has the opportunity to earn a $40,000 bonus for A+ performance defined as a 20 percent return-on-stockholders equity (ROE) and a 60 percent market share. He or she would earn proportionately less for achievement of a lower ROE and a smaller market share.

Performance agreements can be devised for almost any position in an organization. These agreements define the link between pay and performance but require substantial support systems and significant management involvement to assure their implementation. Currently, few companies have adopted such programs, though some are experimenting with the concept, particularly at the top-management levels. To adopt the practice successfully, a company must improve both its "performance demand" and its "performance commitment." The former consists of the objectivity and specificity of results; the latter, of the commitment and trust between managers. As Figure 2 illustrates, the successful implementation of the performance agreement process depends on both the performance demand and the performance commitment, thereby moving the

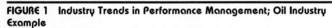

FIGURE 1   Industry Trends in Performance Management; Oil Industry Example

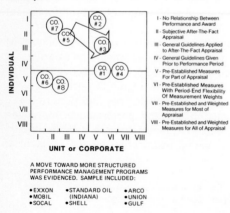

I - No Relationship Between Performance and Award
II - Subjective After-The-Fact Appraisal
III - General Guidelines Applied to After-The-Fact Appraisal
IV - General Guidelines Given Prior to Performance Period
V - Pre-Established Measures For Part of Appraisal
VI - Pre-Established Measures With Period-End Flexibility Of Measurement Weights
VII - Pre-Established and Weighted Measures for Most of Appraisal
VIII - Pre-Established and Weighted Measures for All of Appraisal

INDIVIDUAL

UNIT or CORPORATE

A MOVE TOWARD MORE STRUCTURED PERFORMANCE MANAGEMENT PROGRAMS WAS EVIDENCED. SAMPLE INCLUDED:

- EXXON
- MOBIL
- SOCAL
- STANDARD OIL (INDIANA)
- SHELL
- ARCO
- UNION
- GULF

TABLE 1   Performance Agreement for a Chief Executive Officer

Objective	Relative importance	Measure	Standard			Incentive Awards		
			C+	B+	A+	C+	B+	A+
Increase earnings	75%	ROE	10%	15%	20%	$0	$15	$30
Improve competitive position	25%	Market share	40%	50%	60%	$0	$ 5	$10
	100%					$0	$20	$40

organization from a position of "conflict," resulting from low clarity of direction and low trust among managers, toward a position of "challenge," reflecting acknowledgment and commitment to "stretch" targets. Few companies can claim that they have achieved the latter position.

One of the major reasons for companies not achieving the position of challenge is their inability or unwillingness to discriminate among performances and performers. In order to relate pay to performance, it is necessary to determine what constitutes performance, which in turn requires an understanding of the objectives, measures, and standards of the company and its underlying operating units. If realistic and meaningful objectives, measures, and standards can be determined, the resulting performance agreement could influence a manager's activities, priorities, and time frames and could be used to gauge successes and failures.

Performance Measures   Many companies have invested large sums of money and large periods of management time in the development of planning processes and support systems. These processes and systems are intended to generate strategies for the overall company and for each of the underlying operating units. For an incentive compensation program to reinforce these strategies, it is necessary to translate the goals and objectives of a strategy into measures of performance which can denote good, bad, and indifferent progress toward the achievement of these goals and objectives. Moreover, this translation must be meaningful, realistic, and valid; that is, the measure or measures must chase the *right* bottom line.

FIGURE 2   Performance Agreement Process

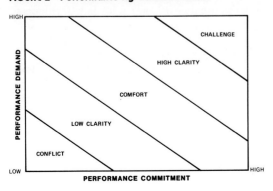

To assure the proper focus on the right bottom line, the selection of appropriate performance measures should meet the following criteria, listed in order of importance.

Usefulness	Can the measure appraise the most important results?
Sustainability	Can the measure accurately forecast the trend of results into the future?
Measurability	Can the measure be calculated from readily available data? Would different judges make the same calculation?
Controllability	Can management truly impact the results gauged by the measure?
Communicability	Can the measure be explained easily and clearly to internal and external audiences?
Universality	Can the measure be cascaded downward from the corporate level to the operating units?
Timeliness	Can the measure be applied annually even if it also can be used on a longer term?
Comparability	Can the measure be related to past performances and to competitive performances?
Constancy	Can the measure resist being unduly manipulated?
Volatility	Can results vary widely from one measurement period to the next, so as to adequately reflect changes in performance?

Currently, many companies use only measures derived from the profit and loss (P&L) statement as standards for the determination of incentive awards. Thus many incentive plans use earnings per share (EPS) or growth in earnings per share as the bonus bogey. Other companies have introduced measures derived from both the profit and loss statement and the balance sheet. These companies' incentive plans use return on equity or growth in return on equity as indicators of performance. Sometimes these measures are gauged relative to the performance of a competitive reference group of companies.[2]

A few companies are beginning to experiment with cash flow measures. These companies recognize the inherent shortcomings of earnings and related accrual accounting ratios, such as return on equity. These shortcomings are most visibly demonstrated when comparing cumulative net income with cumulative cash flow. As illustrated in Table 2, companies can report substantial earnings during periods when in essence they are incrementally liquidating their businesses. Moreover, companies can report significant growth in earnings per share (in the order of magnitude of 10 to 15 percent per year) when in fact they are destroying the value being realized by their stockholders.[3] When inflation is taken into account, a large number of companies have evidenced this destruction of shareholder value despite having reported seemingly buoyant earnings over the past decade.

With the increasing realization that P&L statement and balance sheet figures are inadequate gauges of performance, managers are exploring the possibilities of cash flow indicators. In times of high interest charges, high replacement costs, and high inflation, the distinction between earnings and cash flow is mag-

---

[2]Lawrence C. Bickford, "Long-Term Incentives for Management," *Compensation Review*, third quarter, 1981.

[3]Alfred Rappaport, "Selecting Strategies That Create Shareholder Value," *Harvard Business Review*, May–June 1981.

TABLE 2   Net Income versus Net Cash Flow

| Company | Cumulative, 1977–1981* | |
	Net income	Net cash flow
Alcoa	1779	(36)
American Can	509	(28)
Bethlehem Steel	385	(852)
Du Pont	4377	(1944)
Goodyear	1069	(329)
Sears Roebuck	3828	(2953)
Union Carbide	2874	(806)
U.S. Steel	1669	(1267)

*Cumulative net income and net cash flow from operations, in millions of dollars.

nified. Earnings may show how well a company is doing at making money; cash flow can demonstrate how real that money is. Ultimately, the purpose of a company is to generate cash for its investors, and consequently, a measure that reflects the generation of cash flow may better reflect performance. As indicated in Table 3, when tested against the aforementioned criteria, cash flow has advantages over EPS and ROE in terms of usefulness, sustainability, and universality and disadvantages in terms of measurability and communicability. To help lessen these disadvantages, Hay proposes the use of a cash flow performance management model that plans for, measures, appraises, and rewards performance at multiple levels in an organization, thereby supporting corporate, unit, and individual short- and long-term business objectives.

Cash Flow Performance Management Model   Figure 3 presents a schematic of Hay's cash flow pay-for-performance process. The process combines a "bottom-up" determination of cash uses and sources, evidenced in a company's long-term strategic plans, with a "top-down" valuation of cash generation required by the capital markets. The bottom-up determination starts with an evaluation of each strategic business unit's planned competitive positioning and the capital requirements needed to support these plans. These require-

TABLE 3   Responsiveness of Performance Measures

| Criterion | Measure | | |
	EPS	ROE	Cash flow
Usefulness	−	0	+
Sustainability	−	0	+
Measurability	+	+	−
Controllability	+	+	+
Communicability	+	+	−
Universality	−	−	+
Timeliness	+	+	0
Comparability	+	+	0
Constancy	−	−	0
Volatility	+	+	+

"+" = Good Fit; "0" = Adequate Fit; "−" = Poor Fit

FIGURE 3   Cash Flow Pay-for-Performance Process

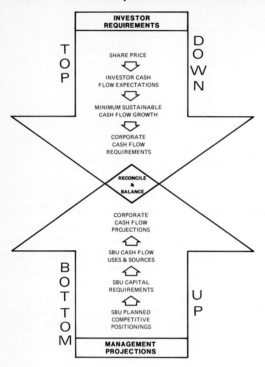

ments, in turn, reflect the potential cash uses and sources of each strategic business unit (SBU), and the aggregate of all the company's SBUs reflects the cash flow projection for the company over its planning horizon. The top-down approach starts with the company's stock market valuation and derives an expected growth in cash flow needed to support the stock market's expectations reflected in the company's share price. This growth in cash flow can be translated into a net cash flow requirement for the overall company. If the aggregate of the SBUs' cash flow projections derived from the bottom-up approach equals the expectation for cash flow evidenced in the top-down one, then cash flow targets can be set for the overall company and its individual SBUs. If the bottom-up target differs from the top-down one, then the overall corporate strategy must be redefined to meet market expectations, or else the company must communicate to the stock market its inability to meet these expectations (or conversely, its ability to exceed them).

Achieving a Balance   The bottom-up approach, developed by professors Alfred Rappaport and Carl Noble of Northwestern University, maintains that the present value of an SBU's strategy equals (1) the discounted value of all future cash flows attributable to the strategy during the plan period, plus (2) the discounted, strategy-positioned terminal value. By adjusting for the present value of the SBU's debt and equity, we obtain the so-called shareholder value contribution of the SBU's strategy. The aggregate of individual SBUs' shareholder value contributions equals the expected shareholder value contribution of the overall company. Some investors, particularly brokerage firms, try to estimate corporate cash flows as a basis for buying and selling corporate securities.

The top-down approach, developed by Marakon Associates and Strategic Planning Associates, maintains that a company's share price reflects investors' expectations for growth in "free cash flows" and uses the "constant dividend growth discount model" to derive the minimum sustainable growth required to support the share price.[4] Free cash flow is defined as cash from operations (after reinvestment necessary to maintain the company's existing productive base) that is available for either investment in growth opportunities or for distribution to investors. Therefore, a company's share price can be translated into a mini-mum-required growth rate which, in turn, can be translated into a corporate cash flow target.

Hay's cash flow pay-for-performance process combines the top-down and bottom-up approaches. The cash flows expected by investors must be recon-ciled and balanced with the cash flows projected by management. The process for reconciling the two approaches involves adjustments to the company's financial policies (e.g., dividend policy), its profitability demands (e.g., required return on net assets), and/or its investment community communications (e.g., announcements regarding future performance). Once a balance between mar-ket expectations and management plans has been determined, the growth rate or the absolute cash flows can be used to establish a meaningful, realistic, and valid corporate performance target. Moreover, since cash flow is applicable throughout all levels of a company, the corporate cash flow target can be devel-oped into divisional and unit cash flow targets. These targets can be used in performance agreements to reinforce management's drive to achieve the *right* bottom line.

---

[4]Eugene F. Fama and Merton H. Miller, *The Theory of Finance*, Dryden Press, Hinsdale, Ill., 1972.

Surveys and Their Uses

chapter 32

Conducting Surveys

T. Michael Fain

MANAGER, WAGE AND SALARY ADMINISTRATION, DUKE
POWER COMPANY, CHARLOTTE, NORTH CAROLINA

Conducting surveys of the marketplace is one of the most important and can be one of the more perplexing functions done by the compensation staff. Compensation policy should be designed to support corporate goals. Policy statements, supporting this concept, usually include language summarizing the ideas of internal equity and external competitiveness. Monitoring external competitiveness requires a knowledge of the marketplace which can only be obtained through surveys. Analysis of the marketplace is an imprecise art form requiring the practitioner to decide which marketplace and jobs to study, how to conduct a study, and how to interpret the results.

DECIDING WHETHER TO CONDUCT A NEW SURVEY OR USE EXISTING DATA

Previous studies of the survey process have concluded that some companies expend considerable effort in participating in and conducting surveys, in some cases using as many as a hundred surveys a year; and much of the information collected in the process is of relatively little value.[1] Determining how much survey work is enough is highly subjective. A company which relies on too few surveys may find itself sadly out of focus with its market. A company which uses too many surveys may generate enough conflicting information to produce

---

[1]David W. Belcher, *Compensation Administration*, Prentice-Hall, Inc., Englewood Cliffs, N.J., 1974, pp. 459–476.

the same results. Because a little bit of information is good does not necessarily mean that a lot is better.

No formula exists to tell the compensation professional how many surveys are enough. Experience and circumstances usually dictate the answer. One factor which contributes to survey overload is the idea of reciprocity. Asking another company to participate in your survey creates an obligation to participate in surveys conducted by that company. Good survey work is a delicate balancing act between quality and quantity.

Numerous sources of survey information are available from both public and private sources which can reduce the need for company-sponsored surveys. Chapters 36 to 42 review a number of specific public surveys and private surveys which are now available.

Who in the Organization Should Conduct Surveys? This is a question most often faced in larger, more diversified companies. Such organizations frequently have several personnel functions with responsibility for various aspects of compensation administration. Duplicate surveys conducted by the same company should be avoided if at all possible. Asking other companies to participate in duplicative surveys annoys those companies, makes you look foolish, and destroys the credibility of the personnel function when management is presented with different answers to the same question.

Some specific factors should be considered in determining who in the company should conduct a survey. It is of utmost importance that the highest-level staff reporting to the executive who will make policy decisions be responsible for conducting surveys. In some cases, this will be a corporate staff, in others a regional, divisional, or other staff. Other factors to consider include use of the staff capable of producing the best results, the sensitivity of specific issues involved, and the possible use of information gathered by other units within the company.

DEVELOPING SURVEY SCOPE AND PURPOSE

Once the decision has been made that a survey is needed and that readily available public or private resources cannot fill the need identified, some time should be spent fully developing the purpose and scope of the survey. Few events are more frustrating than hurriedly conducting a survey, only to learn that basic questions remain unanswered and that additional survey work will be required. Before development of a survey, knowledge of the underlying issues can be critical.

Surveys usually fall into one of several categories.

Benchmark surveys typically play a fairly direct role in the formulation of an important facet of overall compensation policy. Benchmark surveys usually tend to take a fairly broad shotgun type of approach in covering a wide range of jobs and/or issues; are normally done on an annual basis; are almost invariably conducted by mail; and are frequently conducted through industry or trade groups or by a third party. Since benchmark surveys tend to become routine and institutionalized, periodic reviews should be conducted of survey content to ensure continuing utility.

Special-purpose surveys typically address nonroutine questions regarding compensation for specific occupational areas or issues of general administration and play a less direct role in the establishment of broad compensation policy. These riflelike surveys are more likely to be conducted by telephone or mail in a shorter time frame than benchmark surveys.

A troublesome offshoot of special-purpose surveys is the *vested interest* survey. These surveys tend to be originated when a specific executive or employee group requests a survey be made of particular jobs at a specific company or companies. These requests usually reflect either the notion that the information gathered will support an effort to gerrymander segments of the salary structure or certain individual salaries. Occasionally, such requests may reflect the desire to gather information to assist in recruiting a specific person or to stave off losing a specific employee, an idea of dubious ethical substance. Vested-interest surveys should either be converted into special-purpose surveys or, if possible, resisted.

Once specific issues or questions to be resolved have been identified and a general determination has been made as to how survey results will be used, further development can begin.

DETERMINING THE SURVEY SAMPLE

In some rare instances, surveys which include all or virtually all members of the relevant population can be administered. This will produce the highest possible degree of reliability in the resultant information. However, most surveys cover only a portion of relevant companies and/or jobs. Thus the reliability of most survey data is directly influenced by the size and composition of the sample chosen as representative. Generally speaking, the larger and more representative a sample, the greater the probable reliability; that is, the more likely your survey will truly be representative of the entire population.

Statisticians try to construct surveys using an unbiased random sample approach in order to generate data which are most representative of the universe. Most private compensation surveys are intentionally biased, inasmuch as the desired results are intended to represent only a small part of the universe, i.e., the competition, which is usually defined as the organizations most similar in composition, goals, etc. An overreliance on narrowly defined surveys can lead to compensation policies in an industry or regional group that could seriously impair the viability of an organization. Keep an eye on the real world.

An analysis of employee groups within your organization can assist in determining construction of the survey sample. Consideration should be given in each instance to the source of the employees for the groups and to where departing employees tend to go. Typical "different" employee groups may include executives, which usually includes most employees with a substantial portion of "at risk" compensation; professional and managerial employees; craft employees, usually subdivided into represented and nonrepresented camps; and office employees. From time to time, subgroups may have to be created to cover employee groups with special skills or for which the demand is unique or whose members may appear in several groups, such as data processing specialists.

A careful review of the requirements of different employee groups will give guidance in determining whether a survey should be conducted on a geographic, industry, organizational size, or some other basis. A survey pertaining to executives might be constructed to reflect data for companies of similar technology, size, and industry, on a national scale. A survey pertaining to employees whose skills have a high degree of transferability, such as one covering CPAs, may be conducted without regard to the industry in which the company operates. And a survey covering employees with highly specialized skills, such as semiconductor design, might be confined to a single industry.

Management needs and concerns must be given careful consideration when constructing a survey. If, for some reason, the key issues to be resolved by a survey have not clearly been identified by all levels concerned, then every effort should be made to identify accurately questions to be resolved before proceeding further. Compensation surveys should be designed to assist the line organization in the prevention and resolution of problems affecting operations.

Decisions with respect to the composition of the survey sample should be made after giving careful consideration to the above factors. Comprehensive policy recommendations may on occasion require the integration of several smaller surveys covering specific areas. Comprehensive survey work can present specific problems for some larger companies and/or conglomerates that operate in several markets and industries.

METHODS OF DATA COLLECTION

Several factors will often dictate the method used to collect survey data. These include the urgency or amount of time available to do the survey, the cost associated with a specific approach, and the degree of reliability of the information which can be obtained from the different approaches. Other factors influencing the methods of data collection will include the number of companies participating in a survey, the number of jobs being surveyed, and, finally, the amount of detailed information to be collected. Certainly, the method of data collection should have a direct relationship to the purpose of the survey and the sample being surveyed. Several types of surveys are described below.

Telephone surveys usually offer the fastest and least expensive method of collecting information. This approach is best suited for short surveys collecting simple data about familiar jobs or subjects. The reliability of telephone surveys may be somewhat suspect, inasmuch as there is significant room for poor communication to affect the results. Telephone surveys are more reliable when the surveyor is personally acquainted with the individuals responding for the various companies. If the wrong person answers the telephone and answers survey questions, the results can be disastrous. One significant advantage of conducting telephone surveys when the respondents are known personally is that it affords the opportunity to develop information with respect to why certain actions have been taken or what actions are being actively considered, responses which normally might not be reduced to writing. Before telephone surveys are conducted, a form should be developed, just as with a mail survey, to ensure that the same questions are asked of each survey participant and that responses can be accurately compared.

Mail surveys are more suitable when a fairly large number of jobs are to be surveyed and responses are to include data which will require some research and preparation. Carefully prepared, brief job descriptions must be included to enhance the reliability of the data collected. This approach is also better suited to collecting data from a larger sample of participants. On the down side, mail surveys are usually more expensive and far more time-consuming than telephone surveys. Mail responses should be carefully reviewed, and questionable responses should be verified with the respondent by telephone.

A survey incorporating the best features of telephone and mail surveys is the *on-site visit*. This is an excellent method to use when conducting surveys demanding a high degree of reliability and whose content is extensive. This approach is particularly useful when excellent job matches are required. The on-site visit should also enable the surveyor to develop a high degree of understanding of the organization being surveyed. This is particularly useful when the reasons why organizations do certain things are being examined, as opposed to simply gathering straight statistical information. An important consideration in the conduct of on-site visit surveys is the selection and training of the personnel who participate in the survey. Consideration should be given to selecting individuals who will present a good impression of your company and who will be able to articulate the particulars of the survey. The on-site visit is a good way to initiate a benchmark survey which will be used for a long period of time and which in subsequent years will be conducted as a mail survey. Clearly, this approach is far more expensive than either telephone or mail surveys.

Industry and trade associations offer a forum for conducting surveys of a broad interest among companies with similar needs. This avenue is an excellent way to gather benchmark information while ensuring a high degree of reliability and participation.

Third-party surveys, while usually being the most expensive survey method, are sometimes the only way to ensure a high degree of participation when the information being collected is particularly sensitive. This approach may incorporate any or all of the features of telephone, mail, and on-site visit surveys. The third-party survey is particularly useful when a unique knowledge, background, commitment of time, or an extremely high degree of analytical ability, which is not available in the company conducting the survey, is needed. A benefit survey which is to include an actuarial valuation of various programs is an example.

DEVELOPING THE SURVEY INSTRUMENT

When a survey form is designed, the format is very largely influenced by decisions made with respect to the purpose, sample, and method of collection to be used. The survey instrument should be as short and simple as possible, while not omitting any important questions or explanatory information. A good technique for evaluating a survey instrument is to have a nonprofessional review your document prior to its use. The survey form should be easy to complete and, when developed, should give consideration to the method of survey analysis which will be used to ensure that all the data needed for various calculations will be gathered. If the survey is to be encoded for use on a computer, the format should be designed to facilitate keypunch or data entry. As a general rule, the longer the survey, and the more data collected, the poorer the response will be.

If the analysis of the survey data is to include the mode (the most frequent rate), then you must gather the individual rates of each company's employees.

The survey instrument needs to include questions addressing all pertinent issues. For example, if a survey of compensation rates for new graduates is being conducted, a question asking the rate paid for each degree, without addressing whether or not companies surveyed make use of add-ons for class standing or work experience, or how many graduates the company seeks, may lead your company to establish rates which are not realistic. One small, seemingly insignificant piece of information which is often omitted from surveys is the effective date of the current policy. Not knowing whether the policy rates gathered have just been approved or are 12 months old can significantly impair the validity of the data.

Selecting Positions to Be Surveyed   The number of jobs to be included in the survey should be tied to the method of data collection used. Jobs selected for the survey should be those positions for which a high degree of comparability exists in companies being surveyed and should be jobs which will be fairly prevalent among many of the participating companies. Many surveys include job descriptions for the sample which do not provide enough information. Since too brief a job description will lead to poor survey matches and too long a job description will perhaps eliminate some valid comparisons as a result of minor job differences, special attention must be given to the preparation of these descriptions. For this purpose it is useful to select benchmark jobs from a broad spectrum of different levels, to provide reference points which can be expected to be reasonably constant through time.

Factors other than base pay can also have a meaningful effect on the significance of the information gathered. Such things as production bonuses, hazardous duty pay, license pay, bonus payments, and unusual policies for the payment of shift premium and overtime pay can have a significant impact on the overall compensation levels in any organization. Failure to consider these factors may invalidate survey results.

Administrative procedures employed by various companies can also have a major impact on the interpretation of survey data. Certain factors, such as the frequency of pay period, can have a noticeable impact on the results. For example, a company that pays biweekly will have 26 pay periods in a year, which will result in an annual compensation 8⅓ percent greater than a company having bimonthly pay periods, or 24 pay periods in a year, and paying the same rate of pay per period.

Miscellaneous Considerations   Once the survey has been developed, a carefully constructed cover letter should be written to accompany the survey. Specific items often omitted which will improve the quality and the reliability of survey results would include a paragraph explaining the purpose of the survey, to help the participant better understand survey questions. The survey instrument should also include a definition of any unique terms used. Some items which may seem clear to the surveyor may have a very different meaning to the participating company. The survey instrument should also identify a contact person who can answer participants' questions with respect to any item of the survey. One other small but often overlooked detail of importance is to include the date when the information is to be returned.

ANALYSIS OF DATA

Extreme care should be taken in the analysis of data gathered by any survey. Complex and detailed calculations are easily made with the assistance of calculators and computers readily available to everyone today. Any statistical calculation can be carried to several decimal places with ease, giving the aura of precise, scientific results. One must remember that results should not be carried to more decimal places than the crudest element of the data being manipulated. For example, three companies report cost-of-living adjustments of 8, 9, and 11 percent. A quick calculation would yield an average adjustment of 9.333 percent. If the above-reported figures were rounded off from actual increases of 7.6, 8.6, and 10.6 percent, perhaps as a result of poor questionnaire design, the true average would only be 8.9 percent. Errors of even this magnitude, applied to a multimillion dollar payroll, can result in expensive bottom line results (approximately $250,000 for a $60,000,000 payroll).

Generally, the more complex and abstract the analysis, the harder it is to detect errors and the greater the likelihood that poor decisions will be made as a result of its use. Most surveys are not of sufficient quality to justify their use as anything more than indicators of general salary levels and trends. For this reason, simple statistical measures will suffice for the analysis of most surveys. Four common methods of calculating averages are discussed here.

The single most often used measure is the *arithmetic mean,* or simple average. This is calculated by taking the sum of the rates reported and dividing the result by their number. Thus the average pay of four workers paid $10.00, $11.00, $12.00, and $13.00 per hour would be $11.50 per hour ($10.00 + $11.00 + $12.00 + $13.00 = $46.00 ÷ 4 = $11.50).

Since most compensation surveys ask participants to report the average pay of all incumbents in a job, the *weighted arithmetic mean,* or weighted average, can be useful in analyzing survey results. The weighted average is calculated by multiplying the rate for each entry by the number of incumbents, then adding the products of the calculations, and dividing by the total number of incumbents. Table 1 illustrates this calculation.

In Table 1, the weighted arithmetic mean is $12,286 ($860,000 ÷ 70 = $12,286). This compares to an arithmetic mean of the average reported for each company of $13,000 ($52,000 ÷ 4 = $13,000). The resulting market rate reported can be quite different depending on the method used to calculate the result. In this hypothetical example, the arithmetic mean of the average is 5.8 percent higher than the weighted arithmetic mean.

TABLE 1   Calculating Weighted Average

Company	Number of incumbents (A)	Average pay (B)	Product of A × B
A	25	$10,000	$250,000
B	20	12,000	240,000
C	15	14,000	210,000
D	10	16,000	160,000
Totals 4	70	$52,000	$860,000

The *median* is the middle value of a set of numbers, in this case salaries, arranged in sequence. For example, if 5 workers earn $10,000, $12,000, $16,000 $19,000, and $20,000, the median value is $16,000. If there is an even number of values, then the median is calculated by averaging the two middle values. Thus the median salary of 6 workers earning $10,000, $11,000, $16,000, $18,000, $20,000, and $21,000 is $17,000. In this example, the arithmetic mean is $16,000.

The *mode* is the most frequently occurring value. For example, if 5 workers earn $12,000, $13,000, $13,000, $14,000, and $18,000, then the mode is $13,000. In this example, the arithmetic mean is $14,000.

The preceding examples illustrate the necessity of deciding the statistical method to be used in analyzing a survey before the survey instrument (form) can be designed. If the weighted arithmetic mean is to be calculated, the number of incumbents for each position must be collected in the survey. More sophisticated methods of statistical analysis are discussed in Chapter 58.

The statistical analysis applied to survey data should be appropriate to the use being made of the results and to the comprehensiveness of the data collected. If the survey is to answer a simple question, then only a simple analysis is required. If, on the other hand, a detailed analysis of a complex question is required, then a detailed survey which can support complex statistical analysis is needed.

CONFIDENTIALITY

Protecting the *confidentiality* of data is an important issue in the conduct of most compensation surveys. Compensation professionals usually assume as a "given" that information exchanged between companies will be maintained in a confidential manner. Therefore, if survey information is to be made public, that fact must be communicated when the information is collected.

Whenever survey information is reported back to the participants, information relating to specific companies should be coded, unless all the participants have agreed to the contrary. When codes are assigned to participating companies, the codes (such as Company A, B, C, etc., or 1, 2, 3, etc.) should be assigned in a random sequence. Never arrange company names in alphabetical order and assign codes in sequence.

Care must also be exercised when *encoding survey information.* If information unique to a given company (such as its number of employees) is given the same company code as its pay data, then it can easily be identified, and confidentiality is breached. Benefit surveys can be particularly tricky in this respect. If, for example, a survey of local companies, including one tire manufacturer, reports that Company "X" offers discounts on the purchase of tires, then Company "X" will likely decide not to participate in the next survey. If sensitive survey information cannot be encoded so as to protect confidentiality, then either the information should be omitted from the survey report or permission to publish it should be obtained from all participants prior to publication.

Confidentiality is also an issue from an *internal standpoint.* Normally, summaries of survey data used internally should also be encoded. Once such summaries leave the care of the compensation staff, little can be done to ensure that the information is not used improperly.

A *policy defining the company's position on the protection of confidential information* and specifying disciplinary action for intentionally disclosing it should be adopted. Such a policy accomplishes two objectives. First, the policy will communicate the importance to the company of protecting confidential information so that no room exists for misunderstanding. Second, in the unfortunate event that an employee is disciplined for disclosing confidential information, the company will have a better defense if the employee seeks redress.[2]

Surveys of executive compensation may pose special problems with respect to confidentiality. Executive surveys usually cover positions which are principally single-incumbent positions, and may well include details of "secret" incentive plans. Since many corporate directors, both inside and outside, hold directorships in several different companies, a breach of confidentiality in an executive survey must be thoughtfully guarded against.

SUMMARY

This chapter has attempted to outline the logical steps to be followed whenever a compensation survey is contemplated. The issues considered herein should be addressed at the appropriate time to ensure a quality product. Poor survey work can have significant adverse consequences with respect to the overall effectiveness of a company's human resource management. Compensation surveys are an art form. They result from the pooled judgment of a number of different people with varying backgrounds, experience levels, knowledge, and interests, relative to job content, abstract policies and procedures, and constantly changing information. Good compensation policy recommendations are the result of combining good survey results from different sources with a thorough knowledge of one's business, an appropriate awareness of the economy, and a touch of common sense.

---

[2]*Texas Instruments, Inc.,* v. *NLRB*, 80-1120 (1st Cir. 1981). In this case, the First Circuit Court of Appeals upheld a discharge of employees for distributing confidential survey information to other employees, in violation of company policy.

chapter 33

Using Information Derived from Surveys

W. T. Haigh

MANAGER, CORPORATE COMPENSATION, GENERAL
FOODS CORPORATION, WHITE PLAINS, NEW YORK

Today's compensation professional is inundated with survey requests and market information. It is not unusual for a major corporation to be asked to participate in more than 100 surveys each year. With this high level of survey activity, there is an increasing need for the compensation function to carefully balance its time between "production output" of surveys and the thoughtful management of market data to serve as an input to compensation planning.

With the abundance of available survey information and the extensive network of company contacts, line management and compensation planners need to determine to what extent market data should influence the company's compensation policy and pay levels. Increasingly, companies will move away from total reliance on market data and become more interested in the business reasons for paying the way they do. Even with this shift in direction, competitive market data will continue to provide an important frame of reference and an essential starting point for compensation planning.

COMPENSATION POLICY AND PRICING

There are a number of strategic compensation policy decisions that should be addressed first to provide a consistent, rational direction to a company's compensation planning and pricing practices. To determine an appropriate use of survey information, the following areas should be considered.

Defining the Labor Market A company should begin by defining the dimensions of its labor market. The principal considerations used to select comparison companies should cover the following factors.

Size. Companies of comparable size, not only in current financial dimensions but also in growth rate characteristics, should be selected.

Industry. The senior management and board compensation committee of most companies are interested in an industry benchmark, as a frame of reference, to provide assurance that practices are within reasonable limits. Finding companies with similar product or business portfolios has become increasingly difficult with the widespread diversification in many companies. *Value-Line* profiles and company annual reports are useful in determining comparability.

Functional sourcing. Consideration should be given to personnel sourcing practices by function. For instance, companies may look to the banking, investment, and diversified financial industries in staffing controller and treasurer positions. Top marketing talent may be sourced from consumer-oriented companies, while personnel professionals may have a more broadly defined market. Other functions, such as technical research and operations, may have more unique requirements found only in the company's industry group.

Personnel competitors. Attention should also be given to companies that compete directly for the same personnel across a broader functional range. Companies that engage in active college recruiting, for instance, may be head-to-head competitors, regardless of industry, in that particular market.

Location. A company should first define the geographic scope of its labor market. For larger companies, this market is typically national, reflecting the scope of business and recognizing the need to staff at many locations under the same salary program. For smaller companies, this market may more appropriately be confined to the company's immediate city or region of the country.

Management profile. Another less tangible but equally important factor is the reputation and image the company projects as being well-managed and a leader from a personnel relations standpoint. This would include companies which have consistently demonstrated over time their fairness and interest in employees and which provide attractive, well-crafted compensation and benefit programs.

Other considerations. Selecting companies which are represented on the board of directors will provide an insight into outside-director perspectives that may influence their actions in administering senior-management compensation. Also, from a convenience standpoint, using companies that belong to the same professional organizations may facilitate survey exchange.

Compensation Mix Determining the appropriate relative positioning versus the defined labor market should be done within the context of total compensation. The strategic mix of salary, annual incentive compensation, long-term incentive and capital accumulation plans, perquisites, and benefits should reinforce the management direction of the company and provide an integrated, well-balanced total compensation program. (Refer also to Chapters 40, 44, and 54 which expand on this idea and report on survey data incorporating benefit values as part of total compensation.) Figure 1 cites examples of total compensation profiles based on the growth characteristics of the company.

FIGURE 1   Company Growth Phases and Mix of Compensation

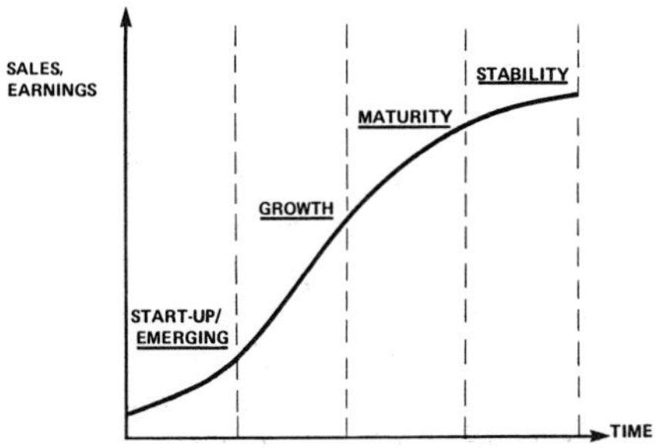

COMPENSATION				
– SALARY	LOW	AVERAGE	AVERAGE	AVERAGE
– INCENTIVE	HIGH	HIGH	HIGH	AVERAGE
– BENEFITS	LOW	AVERAGE	AVERAGE	AVERAGE

Each element should have a unique purpose and performance focus. The competitive positioning of salary must be determined based on the company's needs and within the framework of total pay pricing.

Positioning versus Market   With the rapidly expanding size of *most* major survey samples (for example, the Hay Industrial Survey has grown from 221 companies in 1971 to 490 in 1982), companies must exercise greater discretion in setting pricing targets and must guard against being overly precise and fixed in the way they translate these market data into internal compensation program actions. Placing more reliance on a select company sample that reflects the defined labor market characteristics is often a more prudent method of pricing. As a practical matter and from a compensation committee optics standpoint, pricing within a 50th–75th percentile range, depending on relative performance and quality of fit with the select sample, is a reasonable positioning to seek.

PRINCIPAL USES OF SURVEY DATA

The principal uses of survey data are listed below and are discussed in the following material.

1. Job evaluation
2. Salary range structure
3. Salary-increase budget
4. Starting salary rates (particularly college recruiting)

Job Evaluation   The market-pricing method of job evaluation uses survey data as the primary basis for determining a position's relative value in the company. Positions are assigned to salary grades based on the market value derived from survey analysis, as illustrated in Table 1.

In 1975, a survey of 275 companies conducted by the American Compensa-

TABLE 1   Assignment to Salary Grades, Using Market-Pricing Evaluation Approach

Position	Market value, $	Salary Grade	
		Grade	Midpoint, $
Brand group manager	62,000	8	61,000
		7	55,000
Brand manager	49,000	6	50,000
		5	45,000
Brand associate	39,000	4	40,000
		3	36,000
Brand assistant	32,000	2	32,000
		1	29,000

tion Association reported that 23 percent of the companies used a formalized market-pricing job evaluation system for their executive groups. The principal shortcomings of this approach are (1) the over-reliance on external equity that may not accurately reflect the position's internal importance and (2) the lack of precision in job measurement techniques used to determine job comparability in survey exchange.

Survey data are frequently used by other companies to validate evaluation decisions made under point-factor and ranking systems. Excessive turnover in a function may be a result of valuing the positions below their marketplace value and can be tested through survey comparisons.

In all cases where survey data are used as a basis for evaluating jobs—either under a formalized system or on a spot-check basis—it is critical that an effective method for determining job comparability be utilized. Such a method must provide a means for identifying differences in job responsibilities and relative impact of positions of similar function. Company organization and operating style will influence the importance and pay level of positions with the same title. These differences are most pronounced at the senior- and middle-management levels and exist to a lesser extent at entry-level exempt and nonexempt job categories.

Salary Range Structure   Most companies use survey data to adjust their salary range structures. This review is typically conducted each year, particularly with wage and salary movement in the 7 to 10 percent range over much of the last decade. In other countries with much higher rates of wage inflation—especially those in South America (for example, Argentina and Brazil, which are currently experiencing wage and cost-of-living inflation in excess of 100 percent per annum)—there is a need to adjust ranges on a more frequent basis, sometimes quarterly or even monthly.

A well-defined pricing policy for salaries will provide consistent direction to the periodic review and adjustment of salary ranges. In addition to the principles discussed earlier, the following are some technical considerations that will affect a company's actual salary range positioning.

Updating survey data for time.   Typically, at least four months elapse from the date a survey is conducted to the date a company adjusts its salary ranges. This time period (usually longer) is required to process survey inputs, publish results, analyze and develop salary program recommendations, gain management approval (and in some companies, compensation committee approval), and finally, communicate and implement.

Companies need to address whether the data should be updated for time. With the current 9 to 10 percent annual wage and salary movement, there is typically at least a 4 percent slippage if no updating is applied. If a company plans to update the survey data, it needs to decide the date to which it will update, whether (1) date of adjustment, (2) salary program midyear, or (3) salary program year-end, and the amount by which to update, whether (1) rate of past or current wage inflation or (2) projected rate of inflation.

Actual salary versus midpoint policy target. Depending upon the time of year, there is as much as a 5 percent difference reported in most surveys between actual salary and policy midpoint averages. Actual salaries are lower early in the year, reflecting a low compa-ratio position, and increase to a higher position by year-end. (See Chapter 20.)

Bonus versus nonbonus companies. While the difference has narrowed in recent years, companies that do not provide incentive compensation still pay higher base salaries than companies that do. Attention should be given to selecting a market sample that does not have a disproportionate number of non-bonus companies—unless, of course, the company is also nonbonus or happens to be in an industry such as finance or utility where the prevalence of bonus schemes is well below market practice.

Salary-Increase Budget   There are several ways to measure salary movement from year to year. Each approach serves a purpose in salary planning but is distinctly different. Attention should be given to these differences to minimize confusion and misunderstanding in survey exchange.

For total group (double snapshot). This measures the increase in the average annual salary paid to all employees. It is affected by turnover, promotions, and changes in population mix, as well as by individuals who do not receive an increase. This index most accurately reflects a company's salary-increase budget and what it plans to spend on total wage and salary payroll changes.

For position. This measures the increase in average annual salary paid by position. This movement is impacted by turnover and includes cases in which no increase was granted. This statistic is most frequently used as the basis for adjusting salary ranges.

For type of salary increase. This measures the amount of total-group payroll increase generated by each salary-increase program, e.g., merit, promotion, and general or cost of living. It provides a useful aid to companies in their allocation of salary-increase budgets.

Table 2 provides a summary of market movement trends under each of the above measurement categories.

Starting-Salary Rates   The same basic principles that apply to salary policy pricing also apply to the determination of starting-salary rates. It is equally important to ensure that the labor market is carefully defined—sourcing schools, educational degree specifications, target rank in graduating class, relevant work experience, etc. All these factors will influence the market rate and competitive climate in which a company will be engaging.

TABLE 2   Typical Annual Rate of Salary Change, 1970–1980

Salary change	Annual % increase
Average increase for:	
1. Total group	7–9
2. Position	6–7
Type of increase:	
1. Merit	
Total group	7–9
For those receiving an increase	9–10
2. Promotion	
Total group	1–2
For those receiving an increase	15–16

For this purpose, market data made available through university placement offices and statistics of the College Placement Council are often too generic to meet most companies' needs. As a result, industry-related surveys have evolved which provide more relevant information as a basis for setting starting rates.

CONCLUSION

The climate for survey exchange and the state of the art of how companies use survey data have progressed measurably over the past decade. Companies will increasingly focus on ways of ensuring a fair return on the compensation dollar as opposed to just keeping pace with the marketplace. This should lead to further advancement in salary policy design and provide for a more effective use of market survey information in compensation planning.

chapter 34

Achieving External Competitiveness through Survey Use

George E. Mellgard

PRINCIPAL, THE HAY GROUP, PITTSBURGH, PENNSYLVANIA

In any economic system that permits employees to choose their employers, every organization must compete for employees either directly or indirectly with all other organizations. In order to compete, a company must first identify its rivals and then determine their nature and caliber. External competitiveness and internal equity are therefore the principal aims of management pay policy. Equity has been discussed at length in earlier chapters; our concern here is with the need to be competitive and the means by which a company can define just what is competitive for it. The compensation survey is the tool most frequently used by management to find out who is paying how much for what jobs. Labor unions, like management, are interested in comparative pay practices, since they may provide the justification for "more" in wages and fringe benefits.

COMPETITIVE FACTORS: MONEY VIS-À-VIS OTHER REWARDS

In the vast majority of cases, a survey of competitive factors is the first step in establishing or changing wage, salary, or benefit levels. Competitive compensation factors typically include (1) cash—current or deferred, base or incentive pay—and (2) fringe benefits for personal and family security. Cash compensation and fringe benefits are competitive factors that can be measured in well-defined terms. Other factors which influence a company's ability to attract, retain, and motivate people—factors such as organization climate, management style, and opportunity for advancement—are not so easily measured or compared.

The relative influence of money as against intangible competitive factors varies according to job level. The higher the job, the broader its accountabilities and the more diverse the means of obtaining job satisfaction and a sense of accomplishment. In competing for managers, therefore, companies must keep in mind that money is only one of the factors that makes a job more or less attractive to them. Managers are also motivated by sheer job challenge, a belief in the value of the work they are doing, the drives for status and leadership responsibilities, and a competitive environment encouraging and facilitating achievement of specified end results.

Competition in the marketplace for higher-level people is based on compensation practice as well as on the intangibles mentioned above. At the lower levels, however, jobs are more narrowly defined, restricting the incumbent's autonomy and opportunity to respond to challenges and to exercise leadership. Since the intangible factors have less impact on the job, money becomes proportionately more important in the competition for production and clerical people.

In addition, the marketplaces for managerial, clerical, and production people are substantially different in character and scope. Executive pay must be competitive nationwide. Clerical rates, on the other hand, vary from one locality to another and, hence, must be geared to the local going rate. The competitive market for production people varies according to whether a union is involved. In major unionized industries like steel and autos, the competitive market is industry-oriented and nationwide; smaller, nonunionized companies tend to compete for labor in a local market, the going rate of which would be influenced by the presence or absence of larger unionized companies.

Because the jobs are different in character and the marketplaces vary in scope, different approaches must be taken in determining competitiveness. At the lower levels, comparisons generally focus on job rates; at management levels, comparisons look to salary structures and trend lines. The objective of these comparisons is always to relate compensation to specified duties at the lower levels and to more broadly specified accountabilities at the higher levels.

At all levels, then, money—because it is measurable—is the universal yardstick. Financial compensation, in the form of wages or salary and supplemental benefits and services purchased for employees, is the most tangible bond between employer and employee. Money is the factor most commonly described and compared by the parties to the ultimate bargain, since the nonfinancial competitive factors of present environment and future opportunity are difficult to appraise.

Moreover, there are many ways to recognize and reward superior performance, but there is no substitute for money (or other tangible rewards that can be easily measured in terms of money). The impact and value of these financial motivators can be enhanced or destroyed, depending on how well they are administered. Thoughtful design, consistency of practice, dependability, and ethics play important roles in successful administration.

C. H. Greenewalt casts more light on the role of money vis-à-vis the intangibles:

> We should recognize the importance of financial rewards in balancing other types of incentive, and so ensuring able candidates for every field of endeavor. Personal prestige, for example, is more likely to accompany success in the sciences, in universities, or in the professions than in business. Were we not able to offset this by increased financial reward, I suspect that business would have much greater difficulty filling its ranks with able people.
>
> If financial incentive is absent or greatly reduced, the number of candidates for top management positions will decrease since many men will have gone into vocations where the rewards seem more desirable. And the motives that remain seem less likely to produce the best in management for our business enterprises. Certainly the desire for power, or the desire for prestige, or admiration, are not characteristics that would be expected to lead to the kind of competence we need in business management.[1]

Base salary is the largest element in compensation. Furthermore, it is the pivot point for all compensation. All other forms—incentive compensation, profit sharing, deferred compensation, and fringe benefits such as insurance and pension plans—are to some extent related to base salaries. As one result, if the base structure is inequitable or noncompetitive, these secondary and dependent forms of compensation compound the anomaly.

Our chief concern here is motivational dollars—sensitive dollars above basic survival dollars which are tangible recognition of personal growth in a job and contribution to the organization. It is true that people are motivated by things other than money. But the obvious danger is that the employee who feels insufficiently rewarded in the material sense is apt to look elsewhere for more money.

STANDARDS OF COMPENSATION ADEQUACY

In making compensation choices, it is sometimes useful to conceive of general wage levels in geographic areas or industries or unions or companies, but it should not be supposed that such general wage structures actually exist, any more than a competitive price or a natural rate of interest really exists. Wage structures are intellectual constructs useful in thinking about wages and in arriving at decisions about them, but the spectrum of possible concepts and decisions is broad. Different industries, companies, and organizations seek different talents, and the levels of their compensation structures should reflect these variances. Some talents, moreover, are rarer than others. In making pricing decisions, a manager has one foot in general economic theory and the other in the highly practical considerations of labor-management relations and external supply and demand factors. The range of choices is considerable.

Although every wage rate is related to every other from a strictly statistical standpoint, some relationships are more significant than others. Suppose a window washer in Pittsburgh earns $4 per hour and a cotton picker in California, although paid by the hundredweight of cotton picked, averages $4 per hour.

---

[1]C. H. Greenewalt, "What Kind of Incentives?" a speech before the Illinois State Chamber of Commerce, 1951.

There is a statistical equality, but one which is fortuitous and meaningless. Suppose, however, that printing press operators employed by Pittsburgh and Chicago newspapers each receive $13 per hour. Here again is a statistical equality, but one which is important and meaningful. Similar examples may be drawn to illustrate many different types of relationships that influence the dimensions of wage structures—intraindustry, interindustry, rural-urban, between geographic areas, between occupations, between plants of a multiplant company, between large plants and small ones, between profitable companies and those less so—with every relationship having its own set of causes. Thus a company may test the adequacy of its compensation practice in a wide variety of comparisons, but the question is, With what organizations are such comparisons appropriate?

David W. Belcher[2] notes a number of standards employed by companies to determine whether their compensation is adequate to attract, retain, and motivate the people they need:

1. What other employers in the community and/or industry are paying
2. Union demands
3. Ease of recruitment
4. Labor turnover
5. Employee satisfaction levels
6. Product market competition
7. Profit prospects
8. Company prestige

Each of the standards or tests of compensation adequacy requires comparative knowledge of a labor market.

Pay comparisons can take a number of different forms. First, comparisons can be made in terms of relative wage and salary movements or in terms of absolute pay. Also, pay for similar jobs in different plants, industries, areas, or unions can be compared. Entire pay structures can be compared with each other, or comparisons can be made of a few key jobs in each structure. Also, comparisons may be made in terms of a gross concept of compensation costs that includes both cash and fringes, or cash and fringes may be compared separately. Although wages and fringes generally are bargained at the same time and are substituted for each other under some negotiating circumstances, basically they are subject to separate external comparisons.

Because employees understand and accept external comparison as an assurance of equity, external pay comparisons are to be valued. But a number of factors make it difficult to develop valid comparisons: problems of evaluating job content, established internal wage relationships, differences in stability of employment, corporate policies, prejudices, working conditions, variations in fringe benefits, and the financial conditions of the organizations involved. And even if these factors can be accounted for, variances from absolute external equity are inevitable as the applications of the data are modified through labor-management negotiations, bargaining between an applicant and the recruiter, or unilateral decisions of management. Other factors which influence how an

---

[2]David W. Belcher, *Wage and Salary Administration*, 2d ed., Prentice-Hall, Inc., Englewood Cliffs, N.J., 1962.

organization uses competitive pay data include the economic prospects for the economy as a whole, for the industry, and especially for the particular employer; the cost of living; technological innovation; the relative productivity of the employer and the competition; the standard of living of the workers involved; technical factors relating to specific jobs in the organization; the degree of unionization, internally and externally; historical relationships; standing differentials among firms, jobs, or areas; relative bargaining power of negotiators; ability to pay; and the present evaluations of the future of each of these factors in a dynamic system.

CONGLOMERATES' USE OF SURVEY DATA

Conglomerates face unique problems in the application of competitive pay data. Not only must they consider the multitude of factors mentioned above, but they must also develop compensation structures at the executive level that must at least permit, if not facilitate, transfer between divisions which may operate in entirely different industries. In the conglomerates, managerial compensation tends to follow industry patterns. Thus there may be a different design for each component. At the same time, however, there is a corporate-wide need to motivate the executives and managers of the decentralized, autonomous units.

In lower organizational levels, conglomerates' compensation decisions generally are influenced by long-established pay patterns which may result in vast differences between divisions—differences reflecting plant locations, union-management relationships, management philosophies, differing industries, labor markets, and economic capacity. In any case, acceptance of the comparative wages criterion by a multiplant company should not imply establishment of uniform pay rates throughout all company plants. With decentralized operations and/or diversifed products and/or markets within the same corporate structure, troublesome inconsistencies in pay structures might arise if compensation policies were not formulated which, while uniform in principle, would allow for variation and flexibility in administration.

BALANCING INTERNAL EQUITY AND EXTERNAL COMPETITIVENESS

Internal equity is best established by use of an evaluation or classification system to determine the relative value of all jobs by comparing the functional content of each job with that of other jobs in the organization. The end result is a hierarchy of jobs ranging from those requiring very little skill and responsibility to that of the semiprofessional tool and die maker or similar highly skilled trades; or, in the case of clerical, professional, and executive positions, ranging from that of mail clerk to that of chief executive officer. The objective of job evaluation is internal alignment.

A company usually conducts wage and salary surveys to compare its compensation practices with those of other organizations. The objective of surveys is to develop a competitive pay structure.

Used together, job evaluation and surveys equip a company with the information needed to develop a sound and consistent pay structure. Thus the employee is assured of being compensated on an equitable basis compared with colleagues and others in the area and industry, and the company is assured that its compensation cost is on a par with that of its competitors.

While both job evaluation and wage surveys attempt to achieve consistency in the wage structure, they use different criteria to evaluate consistency—i.e., internal versus external comparison. When internal and external comparisons yield conflicting results, the two must somehow be balanced to achieve a rate that reflects the job's value within the company as well as the going rate in the marketplace.

Some early pioneers in the field of job evaluation suggested that the prevailing community rate be incorporated into the job evaluation plan itself as a characteristic job factor. One may question, however, whether this does not defeat the basic purpose of job evaluation, i.e., *internal* consistency. Another extreme view is to focus primarily on market factors and use internal job evaluation only as a convenience for interpolation of survey results into the wage structure.

Experience seems to indicate that establishment of compromise rates in cases of conflict is probably the solution even in the face of a preference for evaluated rates. Internal consistency is more important than strict external competitiveness. The purpose of job evaluation is to provide a balanced pay structure within a particular plant or enterprise based on work which is typical of that plant or enterprise. Competitive practice is a general guide as to the adequacy of the whole pay structure—not necessarily of the pay for each individual job. It is essential that pay structures be flexible enough to bend when the need arises.

chapter 35

Acquiring Competitive Information from Surveys:
Maturity Curve Surveys

Charles R. Draughon, Jr.

SENIOR STAFF ADVISOR, COMPENSATION, EXXON
COMPANY, U.S.A., HOUSTON, TEXAS

Maturity curve surveys have traditionally been used for comparing salaries of engineers, scientists, and other professional groups. The methodology relates pay to years of experience, so that the marketplace survey will reflect ongoing pay levels for professionals with 5, 10, 15, or more years of experience. Using the data or curves produced from these surveys, organizations or individual professionals are able to compare their own pay levels with those of the general market. The curves are used to identify pay differences that may exist between companies, industries, or geographical regions. They will show differentials for masters and doctors degrees compared with bachelors degrees. The curves can also be used by organizations to establish policy pay-level objectives and to set up salary-increase programs to achieve those objectives. They may be used by individual professionals to seek out the location and type of occupation that will best meet their expectations with respect to pay. Chapter 53 also includes a discussion of the application of maturity curves.

One problem in the maturity curve process is the measurement of experience. The method most frequently used is to count the years after the first professional degree was obtained. It is assumed that the professional has been gaining in experience since the first degree. Age has also been used to measure experience, but a certain amount of judgment must be imposed. Engineers generally obtain their first degrees at age 22, but some other professionals, such as attorneys, typically obtain professional degrees at later ages. Adjustments must be made for such differences to obtain good correlations.

WHAT ARE MATURITY CURVES?

In the maturity survey, salary information must be sorted out to common experience levels. Salaries can be listed for each year of experience or listed in experience brackets spreading from three to five years. The median, quartile, and decile points are calculated for each experience bracket. Using these raw data points, smooth curves are calculated by a least-squares method and can be plotted graphically to show the spread of salary pay at each year of experience.

Figure 1 shows a chart from the 1981 survey conducted by the Engineering

FIGURE 1   Weighted National Average—All Engineers

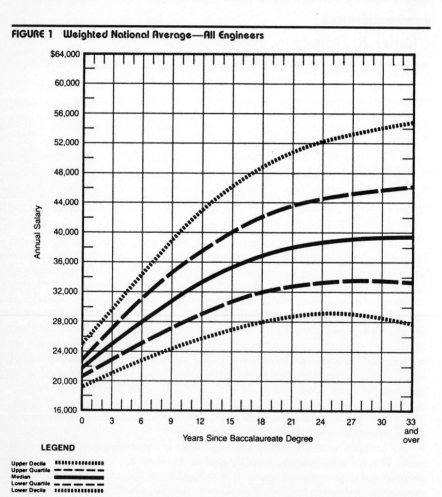

Reprinted with permission from "Professional Income of Engineers," Engineering Manpower Commission of the American Association of Engineering Societies, Inc. 1981.

Manpower Commission of the American Association of Engineering Societies, Inc. This chart is typical of maturity curve survey reports. In this case, the data represent nationwide pay for engineers for all degree levels. Five curves are shown on the graph to identify the median, two quartile, and two decile levels in the total array of data. These levels, or "cuts," in the data are defined as follows:

1. *Upper Decile, Sometimes Called the 90th Percentile:* The point in the array of data above which 10 percent of the salaries are located and below which 90 percent of the salaries are located
2. *Upper Quartile, or 75th Percentile:* The point in the array of data above which 25 percent of the salaries are located and below which 75 percent of the salaries are located
3. *Median, or 50th Percentile:* The point in the array of data above which 50 percent of the salaries are located and below which 50 percent of the salaries are located
4. *Lower Quartile, or 25th Percentile:* The point in the array of data above which 75 percent of the salaries are located and below which 25 percent of the salaries are located
5. *Lower Decile, or 10th Percentile:* The point in the array of data above which 90 percent of the salaries are located and below which 10 percent of the salaries are located

Sometimes an average, or mean, salary is determined for each year of experience and a sixth curve may be plotted with the other five described. However, the mean curve usually lies very close to the median, so there is little to be gained by using both of these. Also, high curves and low curves may be developed representing the highest and lowest salaries paid for different levels of experience. These could result in irregular data, since they are produced from isolated data points that may not be representative. Salaries falling between the 90th and the 10th percentiles represent the spread of pay for 80 percent of the people; this is regarded as the statistically reliable band for the range of pay of those included in the survey.

USES FOR MATURITY CURVES

Slicing the pay bands into the various deciles and quartiles serves a useful purpose. This allows the establishment of definitive pay targets within a rather broad spread of pay for any given experience level. Figure 1 shows that an engineer with eight years of experience would be paid $24,000 at the lower decile and $38,000 at the upper decile. This represents a spread of $14,000, or nearly 60 percent. However, when the quartiles and medians are determined, salary positioning becomes more meaningful. An engineer with a salary of $40,000 or more could have some satisfaction in the knowledge that this was in the top 10 percent of all engineers nationwide. A pay level of $34,000 would be in the upper 25 percent but below the top 10 percent. A salary of $30,000 would represent something close to the national median for engineers with eight years of experience. Some organizations will develop the median pay curve for their internal group of professionals and plot this on the same graph as the marketplace curves. This gives a picture of where their pay levels are positioned at all experience levels.

Employers can use maturity curves to establish pay objectives for professionals of different performance ratings and abilities. These employers will set up a "policy orientation" which says, for example, that they want to pay their highest performers at rates equivalent to the top 10 percent in the survey and their average performers at rates equivalent to the median, or survey average. Salary ranges and salary-increase programs can then be designed to accomplish these objectives. There is no need to limit these target objectives to one of the five percentile curves shown in the example in Figure 1. Other intermediate percentile curves can be developed, such as 70th, 60th, or 30th, if these would serve better than the five displayed.

When maturity surveys are conducted periodically over a span of time, they can be useful in establishing the trends or change patterns in pay levels for certain professional groups. Figure 2, a chart from the survey of the American Association of Engineering Societies, shows trends in the median salaries of engineers from 1953 to 1978. The solid lines are the median salary curves for the various survey years. These data show, for example, that the "median engineer" with 10 years of experience was paid about $6000 in 1953 and this was up to about $25,000 in 1978, which is more than four times the 1953 pay level. The recent trend data are probably more useful. The chart shows that over 35 percent of the salary growth took place in the last four years of the 25-year period.

FIGURE 2   Trends in Median Salaries of Engineers, 1953–1978

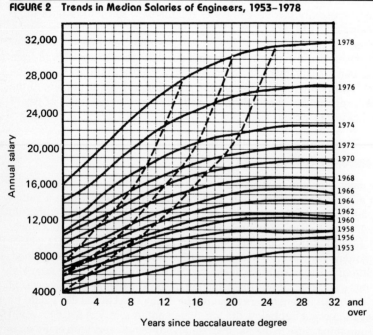

Reprinted with permission from "Professional Income of Engineers," Engineering Manpower Commission of the American Association of Engineering Societies, Inc., 1978.

TABLE 1   Analysis of Living-Cost Effect on Engineering Salaries by Decade

| Year start as an engineer | Percent Increase | | | | | |
| | Start Date to 1960 | | 1960 to 1970 | | 1970 to 1980 | |
	Current $	Constant $	Current $	Constant $	Current $	Constant $
1953	118.5	97.0	94.4	48.2	106.4	(3.0)
1958	26.5	23.8	97.8	50.9	137.0	11.3
1964	...	...	80.1	43.9	147.5	16.3
1970	...	...	...	...	172.9	28.2

From the survey report "Professional Income of Engineers," Engineering Manpower Commission of the American Association of Engineering Societies, Inc., 1981.

The dashed lines in Figure 2 indicate the pay progress of three example cases of "median engineers" who reach 1978 with different levels of experience. The rates of increase reflect the growth of pay for typical individuals as they gain experience through the years. The median engineer who started in 1953 at an annual salary of about $4000 reached a pay level of $31,500 in 1978. This reflects an average increase rate of 8.6 percent per year over the 25 years. The engineer who started in 1958 was increased at about the same rate over the 20-year period. The one who started in 1964 received an average annual increase of over 10 percent. However, due to price inflation and devaluation of the dollar, these increases are not representative of increases in real purchasing power.

Table 1 shows the effect of living cost on engineering salaries by comparing the increases in current dollars with the increases in dollars adjusted for constant purchasing power. The median engineer starting in 1953 received increases of 94.4 percent in the decade from 1960 to 1970, and this produced a gain in purchasing power of 48.2 percent. In the 10 years from 1970 to 1980 pay increased by 106.4 percent in actual dollars, but this was not sufficient to offset the higher rate of inflation during this period. A loss of 3 percent in constant dollars was realized. The figures demonstrate that in years of high inflation, much of the salary-increase money goes toward offsetting the devalued dollars. The amount left to represent real gain is greatly reduced.

SELECTION OF DATA GROUPS

Maturity curve surveys that cover very broad areas, such as engineers with all types of degrees employed in varied occupations and industries across the nation, have value for showing national and historic trends. However, they are too broad to be useful in establishing pay targets for specific groups or even for making pay comparisons by an organization. Some breakouts from the total data pool are required to serve these purposes. Three general categories are usually considered desirable. First, separation by degree levels, such as developing separate curves for bachelors, masters, and doctors degrees, may be useful. Second, separation by categories of employer is customary so that the pay levels in industrial companies can be compared with those in government and educational institutions, for example. Some users will separate large employers from medium and small employers. It is also possible to separate industries

TABLE 2 Data Groups Used in American Association of Engineering Societies' Survey

1. B.S. degree engineers	8. Nonmanufacturing
2. M.S. degree engineers	a. Construction
3. Ph.D. degree engineers	b. Consulting service
4. Large industrial employers	c. Mining
5. Medium industrial employers	d. Research
6. Small industrial employers	e. Communications
7. Manufacturing industry	f. Utilities
a. Aerospace	g. Pipelines
b. Chemicals	9. Government
c. Electrical equipment	10. Educational institutions
d. Electronic equipment	11. Geographic regions
e. Instruments	a. New England
f. Machinery	b. Middle Atlantic
g. Metals, basic	c. East north central
h. Metal products	d. West north central
i. Petroleum	e. South Atlantic
j. Auto and railroad	f. South central
k. Shipbuilding	g. Mountain states
l. Paper and wood	h. Pacific Coast

such as chemical, electrical, petroleum, food, and others. The third refinement involves separation by geographical regions to account for any pay differences that may exist across geographical boundaries in the United States. Many of the data groups included in the American Association of Engineering Societies' survey report are shown in Table 2.

Any organization or person making use of maturity curve survey data needs to give careful consideration to all the options and variables in the makeup of the survey. If the user is designing and conducting the survey, the format can usually be set up to suit the end purpose of the user. However, when use is being made of a survey conducted by others, one must sort through the data bank to select the data groups most appropriate for accomplishing the purpose of the particular user.

SELECTION OF PROFESSIONAL GROUPS

While the maturity curve procedures have been used to compare the pay levels of engineers and scientists for many years, similar methods are now being applied to other professional groups, including attorneys, auditors, economists, financial analysts, industrial relations specialists, public relations advisers, sales representatives, systems analysts, and others. In some cases, professional societies have instigated and conducted surveys in like manner to the American Association of Engineering Societies with their report "Professional Income of Engineers," which is updated periodically. In other cases, employers have designed and conducted maturity surveys as a method of checking the pay levels of their employees against the pay of competitor companies or the general marketplace users of the particular profession.

The maturity curve techniques are most adaptable and meaningful when the professionals are employed in similar organizations that have something in common. Job duties and responsibilities can then be defined in a few short sentences which are easily understood by all engaged in that line of business. Differences in pay result not so much from differences in job content but from variations in experience and personal contribution. Senior professionals can work with less supervision and direction. Their judgments and decisions are more readily acceptable, so they are more influential and accountable than the junior members of the same profession. The high-level performer will be more inventive or creative and will find answers more readily for the tough problems. Thus the ideal candidates for use of maturity curves are those professional job families in which job value can be measured in terms of personal experience and performance.

PROFESSIONAL ADVANCEMENT GUIDES

Many organizations utilize "professional ladders," which include a hiring grade with advancement salary grades extending above it. After the new professionals gain experience, they can achieve the journeyman grade, which designates fully competent individuals who can perform all the normal duties of the profession. Higher grades may be provided for those with unusual expertise and skills who make contributions of greater value than the journeyman types. The justification for these higher levels will depend upon the need and utilization in the particular business operation. Many of the organizations that need personnel with highly specialized professional skills will set up programs to train and develop such personnel within the organization.

Promotions on the professional ladder to higher salary grades will demonstrate to employees that they are progressing and will also serve to guide their salary treatment. Maturity curve surveys are useful in establishing guidelines for professional advancement to the various grades. Pay objectives or targets can be established for different levels of performance by using various percentile curves from a maturity curve survey. An example is shown in Table 3.

With specific pay objectives established for experience levels and performance ratings, the salary grade and range required to achieve pay at the objective levels can be determined. An example of guidelines developed in this manner is shown in Table 4.

In this table, the professionals are hired and placed in salary grade 1. Grades 2 and 3 may be achieved by all acceptable levels of performance, but different levels of experience would be required. A, B, and C performers may reach grade 4, while only A and B performers would reach grade 5 which is considered to exist for the recognition of high skills and expertise. The figures in the

TABLE 3 Salary Targets by Performance Rating

	Performance	
Rating	Description	Salary target
A	Outstanding	90th percentile curve
B	Above normal	70th percentile curve
C	Normal	50th percentile curve
D	Below normal	30th percentile curve

TABLE 4   Experience Required for Professionals to Advance

For advancement	Performance rating	Highest Advancement Expected		
		Salary grade 5	Salary grade 4	Salary grade 3
		Years to advance from grade 1		
To grade 2	A	1	2	3
	B	2	3	4
	C	...	4	5
	D	...	...	6
To grade 3	A	2	4	6
	B	4	6	8
	C	...	8	10
	D	...	...	12
To grade 4	A	4	6	
	B	7	9	
	C	...	12	
To grade 5	A	7		
	B	12		

table express the total years of experience required for advancement to the grade indicated. Individuals with C performance ratings who would eventually reach grade 4 could promote from grade 1 to grade 2 after 4 years, to grade 3 after a total of 8 years, and to grade 4 after a total of 12 years. The B performer going to grade 5 would promote through grades 2, 3, and 4 and could reach grade 5 in 12 years.

The actual table would be designed to fit the salary grades and structure of the organization making use of the method. The maturity curve survey data should be representative of marketplace pay for the particular professional group and should be chronologically in phase with the salary structure. Maturity surveys, like all other surveys, give a "snapshot" of the marketplace pay at the time the survey was conducted. One month later, the survey is slightly out of date, and 12 months later it is grossly out of date. Since it is not practical to have up-to-date surveys available at all times, estimates and adjustments are often necessary to bring the survey data and the salaries being compared into the same time frame.

SUMMARY

Maturity curve surveys differ from other surveys in that pay is related to experience or age rather than specifically to job content. Their application is limited to certain professional groups in which a degree of similarity in job content exists among those participating in the survey. The methodology of maturity surveys has been explained, and some uses of the survey data have been described. The intent is to provide enough information for salary administrators and other readers to gain some insight into the uses and limitations of maturity surveys.

chapter 36

Acquiring Competitive Information from Surveys:
Abbott-Langer Directory of Pay Survey Reports

John Yurkutat

PROGRAM MANAGER, THE HAY GROUP, PHILADELPHIA,
PENNSYLVANIA

The establishment of sound compensation policies and the implementation of these policies through comprehensive and integrated salary administration programs depend on an accurate assessment of an organization's position within the salary marketplace. This assessment of marketplace positioning is most frequently accomplished through use of salary surveys, which vary greatly in terms of content, format, and applicability to specific situations. The astute human resources professional considers the precision, comprehensiveness, timeliness, cost, and applicability of available survey data and selects the most appropriate sources for comparison. Where does the diligent researcher turn to discover what is available?

An annotated bibliography entitled "Available Pay Survey Reports," put out periodically by Abbott, Langer and Associates, is the most comprehensive reference work currently available that covers the spectrum of salary surveys. It is published in three volumes:

Part One: U.S. survey reports not produced by the federal government
Part Two: U.S. federal government survey reports
Part Three: Non-U.S. survey reports

Within these volumes, annotations have been indexed according to source of data, geographic area covered, type of employer, and job title or function. All surveys reported in the bibliography provide information on wages, salaries, or other direct or indirect forms of compensation.

Part One of the directory, which lists salary surveys produced by consulting firms, local employer associations, professional organizations, chambers of commerce, and other nongovernmental sources, is perhaps the most useful to the compensation professional. This volume includes annotations on approximately 650 survey reports produced by over 225 different organizations. By using indices at the back of the volume, the salary planner or compensation analyst looking for information on salaries for accounting clerks in Chicago will discover almost 100 surveys that contain data on accounting clerks, almost 50 surveys with salary data on the Chicago metropolitan area, and 9 surveys with specific data on salaries for accounting clerks in Chicago.

In addition to identifying potential sources of marketplace data, the directory also provides some information to aid in the process of evaluating the suitability of the data as a source for comparison. The bibliographic annotations typically include information on the number and types of positions covered by the survey, the number of participants in the most recent report, the date of publication, and the cuts of data used for analysis.

While this information may aid in the evaluation of the applicability of the survey, certain things should be noted here. The information provided in the annotation is dependent on the information received from the survey providers, which in some cases results in very sketchy information and in other cases results in no information on certain survey data sources. The annotations also typically do not contain information on whether the survey is based on a simple title match, a match to a summary job description, an evaluated job content approach, or some other methodology.

This directory is a useful references source that the human resources professional should be aware of, both for the identification of available sources of salary survey information and for the preliminary evaluation of the appropriateness of the survey as a basis for compensation comparison.

chapter 37

Acquiring Competitive Information from Surveys:
Administrative Management Society

Phyllis K. Bonfield
ADMINISTRATIVE MANAGEMENT SOCIETY,
WILLOW GROVE, PENNSYLVANIA

Doris M. Graff
MANAGER OF SURVEYS, ADMINISTRATIVE MANAGEMENT
SOCIETY, WILLOW GROVE, PENNSYLVANIA

In searching for clerical, administrative, and management personnel, most business organizations need to have access to timely and relevant salary and fringe benefit information. For clerical and/or administrative employees, companies typically compete at local and regional levels, while they often compete nationally for their management people. In addition, there is also competition for employees within various business and industrial groups. With economic conditions in constant flux, it is important for companies to review salary and fringe benefit packages regularly. Regardless of a company's size, well-maintained wage and salary programs do much to ensure the company retains a competitive edge in the marketplace.

Meeting the need for accurate, timely salary and fringe benefit information within the North American business community, the Administrative Management Society (AMS), a professional management association, undertakes two annual salary and benefits surveys, plus a biennial office turnover survey. The

TABLE 1   AMS Office Salaries Survey

	Job Category								
	Word processing trainee	Word processing operator	Lead word processing operator	Computer operator	Data entry operator	Programmer	Programmer analyst	Accounting clerk B	Accounting clerk A
	A	B	C	D	E	F	G	H	I
Average	192	217	246	259	209	355	405	100	242
First quartile	177	215	245	235	195	337	362	195	225
Median	185	215	245	255	195	362	425	195	235
Third quartile	205	215	245	275	225	387	425	205	255
No. companies	21	55	29	87	103	49	49	110	116
No. employees	56	942	826	382	931	390	496	1332	1033

SOURCE: Reprinted from the *1981–82 AMS Office Salaries Directory* with permission of the Administrative Management Society.

surveys are conducted through AMS's network of 145 chapters located in cities throughout the United States and Canada. Chapters solicit member and non-member company participation. Local reports are distributed as supplements to the international surveys which are issued through AMS's headquarters office in Willow Grove, Pennsylvania.

AMS OFFICE SALARIES DIRECTORY

Presenting results from the annual salary survey of office employees, the 1981–1982 directory reports on 20 positions (16 clerical, including 3 word processing, and 4 data processing) covering 498,760 employees with 5970 companies in 122 cities. Participating companies furnish data only on those jobs that substantially match the description supplied with the survey's questionnaire. (See Table 1 for the job titles covered by the 1981–1982 survey.) While not intended to cover the full spectrum of office employees, the survey provides weekly salary data for 20 carefully selected benchmark positions considered to be representative of jobs found in all types and sizes of business and industry throughout the United States and Canada.

The Directory   For each job, the directory presents four salary rates—the average weekly salary, the first and third quartiles, and the median salary. Also given are the number of companies reporting and the number of employees whose salaries are reported. The Minneapolis–St.Paul area is a typical example, as shown in Table 1.

The directory's statistics are presented in a number of ways: (1) nationally for the United States and Canada; (2) regionally for five large U.S. areas; (3) individually for all participating cities; and (4) by type of business, classified as manufacturing and processing; banking, insurance, and financial; retail-whole-

Secretary-level B	Secretary-level A	Executive secretary administrative asst.	Legal secretary	File clerk	Clerk B	Clerk A	Switchboard operator/receptionist	Clerk typist	Customer service representative	Photocopy machine operator
J	K	L	M	N	O	P	Q	R	S	T
215	247	290	269	178	188	217	198	187	244	183
205	235	275	245	167	172	195	195	185	195	162
205	245	285	255	185	185	215	195	185	235	177
225	265	312	295	185	205	235	195	185	285	195
94	116	114	23	65	92	96	136	69	53	26
1157	2521	906	339	741	1378	1042	984	1591	346	52

sale sales and distribution; government agencies; and education, employment, medical, and utilities.

Corollary Information   In addition to the salary data, the latest trends in company policies and practices are presented with figures on hours of work, paid holidays and vacations, unionization, and policies regarding payment of insurance benefits and pension plans.

Table 1—Range of Weekly Salaries for AMS Jobs, Minneapolis–St. Paul   In interpreting Table 1, consider job classification K, "secretaries-level A." In the Minneapolis–St. Paul area, 116 companies participated in the survey and reported data for 2521 level A secretaries. The "effective salary range" for this position is a weekly salary of between $235, at the 25th percentile, and $265, at the 75th percentile. The median (50th percentile) is $245, and the average (arithmetic mean) is $247. (Reference in Tables 1 and 2 to a given quartile means the top of that quartile.) The middle 50 percent of the secretaries surveyed earned within this effective range, which is considered the best guide to the "going" salary rate. The highest and lowest salaries are not shown, as these are considered extremes and not representative of the position in this particular area of the country. The median, $245, is the actual weekly salary of the middle employee in the distribution; the average, $247, is the arithmetic mean of the 2521 salaries reported for this position.

AMS GUIDE TO MANAGEMENT COMPENSATION

Since 1970 AMS has published the results of its annual salary and fringe benefit survey of management personnel. This survey provides the North Ameri-

TABLE 2   AMS Management Compensation Survey

	Job Category								
	Accounting manager	Auditing manager	Cost accounting manager	Payroll supervisor	Credit and collection mgr.	Personnel director	Employment manager	Customer service manager	Word processing manager
	A	B	C	D	E	F	G	H	I
Average	28.3	27.9	28.2	18.8	23.9	31.9	24.7	26.2	17.9
First quartile	24.5	22.5	23.5	14.5	19.5	25.5	19.5	21.5	15.5
Median	28.5	26.5	27.5	17.5	22.5	32.5	24.5	26.5	17.5
Third quartile	31.5	34.5	32.5	22.5	28.5	39.0	28.5	32.5	19.5
No. companies	121	33	44	56	78	100	48	49	14
No. employees	146	38	50	58	87	113	52	58	14

SOURCE: Reprinted from the *1982 AMS Guide to Management Compensation* with permission of the Administrative Management Society.

can business community with comprehensive information on middle-level management positions.

The guide reports on the annual base compensation for 20 representative benchmark positions found in all types and sizes of business and industry. Fourteen positions are of a general administrative nature, while six are plant- or factory-related jobs.

Findings in the 1982 survey represent 63,093 management employees with 3686 companies in 115 United States and Canadian cities. Salary information is furnished by participating companies on those positions that closely match the job descriptions supplied by AMS with the survey questionnaire. (See Table 2 for the job titles covered by the the 1982 survey.)

The Report   The report contains four rates for the annual base salaries of each position. Also given are the number of companies reporting and the number of employees whose salaries are reported. The Minneapolis–St. Paul area is, once again, a typical example, as shown in Table 2.

Data in the guide are presented with national totals for the United States and Canada, as well as breakdowns for five large geographic regions in the United States and by the individual city or area for the companies participating in the survey. By type of business, figures are reported using the following categories: manufacturing and processing; banking, insurance, and financial; retail-wholesale sales and distribution; utilities; and education, employment, government, and medical.

Corollary Information   Figures are given on up-to-date company policies and personnel practices for payment of insurance benefits, hours of work, sick leave, paid holidays, and vacations. Also, policies on pension plans and the basis for granting salary increases are presented.

Word processing supervisor	Manager, elec. data processing	Branch manager	Sales manager	Manager-admin. services	Warehouse manager	Plant manager	Foreman	General foreman	Purchasing manager	Buyer
J	K	L	M	N	O	P	Q	R	S	T
16.9	32.0	28.5	33.4	24.5	23.9	36.4	23.6	27.8	28.5	21.2
13.5	26.5	22.5	26.5	18.5	20.5	31.5	20.5	22.5	24.5	17.5
15.5	31.5	27.5	34.5	24.5	23.5	35.5	23.5	28.5	28.5	20.5
17.5	39.0	34.5	41.0	29.5	27.5	43.0	25.5	31.5	32.5	24.5
30	84	29	75	67	55	54	69	49	84	77
32	94	110	176	81	69	90	659	174	104	214

AMS OFFICE TURNOVER SURVEY

Since 1971 AMS has conducted the biennial office turnover survey through its North American chapter network. The survey provides a reliable guide on changes in the work force and assists companies in determining whether their turnover rate is too high, too low, or at a desirable level. The 1980 survey reported on 96,087 terminations among 561,878 employees with 2574 companies in 94 cities.

The survey presents turnover rates for the United States and Canada by geographic area, individual reporting cities, type of business, and size of office and for exempt and nonexempt employees. Statistics on reasons for employee terminations are presented with breakdowns by exempt and nonexempt status. Length of service at the time of termination is also given, broken down into categories of under one year, one to five years, and over five years of service. Turnover rates for Minneapolis-St. Paul, located in AMS's west central U.S. region, are shown in Table 3 as an example of this survey's findings.

Table 3—Annual Turnover Rate by Region and City, Minneapolis–St. Paul   The formula for figuring the overall turnover rate was calculated as follows:

$$\frac{\text{Total number of terminations}}{\text{Average annual employment}} \times 100 = \text{turnover rate}$$

For 1980 the national average turnover rate was 17 percent, a decrease of 2 percent from the 1978 figure of 19 percent. As Table 3 shows, the west central U.S. region ran slightly ahead of the national averages for 1978 and 1980. Minneapolis–St. Paul has a turnover rate 5 percent greater than the national figures for each of the two surveys.

TABLE 3   AMS Office Turnover Survey

	1980 turnover rate	1978 turnover rate	Number of firms	Total employment	Total terminations
West central U.S. (total)	18%	21%	510	84,348	15,558
Minneapolis–St. Paul, Minn.	22%	24%	108	19,027	4,127

SOURCE: Reprinted from the *1980 AMS Office Turnover Survey* with permission of the Administrative Management Society.

USE OF SURVEY INFORMATION

The data and other relevant information contained in the AMS surveys can assist companies in a number of ways:

- Comparing the company's overall salary structure and/or specific jobs with current community, regional, and national salaries in comparative types of business
- Checking the validity of a company's own evaluation of job rankings and salary ranges
- Appraising of going rates as the basis for establishing a company's salary ranges in new or revised job evaluation plans
- Comparing current company practices and policies with those of other companies

APPLICATION OF SURVEY INFORMATION

A considerable amount of judgment is required in interpreting and evaluating survey information. Thus it should be used with a degree of caution. For instance, recognize that small samples cannot be depended upon to produce meaningful mathematical measures.

REPORTING OF SURVEY INFORMATION

The published results of the Administrative Management Society's surveys are available through the AMS Headquarters, Willow Grove, PA 19090. Detailed descriptions of the jobs surveyed are also available. Inquires should specify the survey or subject matter on which information is desired.

chapter 38

Acquiring Competitive Information from Surveys:
Executive Compensation Service

J. A. Engel

DIRECTOR, EXECUTIVE COMPENSATION SERVICE, INC.,
NEW YORK, NEW YORK

WYCO's EXECUTIVE COMPENSATION SERVICE

The Executive Compensation Service (ECS) has been furnishing information on compensation and related subjects for well over 30 years. From a modest beginning in 1950, when 250 companies participated, the service has grown to the extent that approximately 10,000 companies in the United States and nearly 5000 foreign firms now actively participate in ECS activities. The service provides industry with over 60,000 reports on compensation subjects each year. It is a subsidiary of the Wyatt Company, (WYCO).

OBJECTIVES OF ECS

This service has recognized from the start that each company's management compensation problems are distinctly its own—that industry, size of company, competition, age and experience of individuals, and availability of qualified personnel are the primary influences on management compensation practices. The necessity for equitable position relationships within companies is of paramount importance; however, companies have found that it is impractical to isolate themselves from what others are doing.

The purpose of ECS is to provide an orderly basis for measuring a company's compensation practices against those of other companies of comparable size within their own industry as well as in industry in general. The service is intended as a guide in establishing levels of pay and in improving other methods of compensation.

WHAT IT IS

ECS provides up-to-date facts on a continuing basis on how much and by what methods management personnel are paid. The service covers positions from chief executive officer down through office personnel, including executive, staff, administrative, professional, sales, supervisory, technical, and office personnel. The following is a list of all the reports.

North American Compensation Reports

1. Top Management Report
2. Statistical Supplement to Top Management Report
3. Middle Management Report
4. Statistical Supplement to Middle Management Report
5. Hi-Comp Report for Middle Management Personnel
6. Professional and Scientific Report
7. Sales Personnel Report
8. Technician Report
9. Supervisory Management Report
10. Office Personnel Report
11. Hospital and Health Care Report
12. Reports on Current and Deferred Incentive Compensation
13. Reports on Stock Purchase Plans
14. Reports on Salary Administration and Control
15. Reports on Benefits and Employment Contracts
16. Corporate Directorship Report
17. Insurance Industry Compensation Report
18. Canada Executive Remuneration Report
19. Canada Professional, Scientific & Technical Report
20. Canada Office Personnel Report

International Compensation Reports

1. International Compensation Report
2. United Kingdom Report
3. Federal Republic of Germany Report
4. Brazil Report
5. Mexico Report
6. Belgium Report
7. Netherlands Report
8. Switzerland Report

9. France Report
10. Portugal Report
11. Puerto Rico Report
12. European Benefits Report
13. European Sales and Marketing Personnel Report
14. Office and Administrative Personnel—Europe
15. Scandinavia Report
16. Spain Report
17. Italy Report
18. Labour Relations: Europe
19. Termination of Employment: Europe
20. European Top Management Remuneration Report

NORTH AMERICAN COMPENSATION REPORTS

Top Management Report

1. Shows average compensation of approximately 20,000 executives in 75 top positions in 2000 companies

2. Classifies companies in different industries, each industry in a separate section; summarizes each of the industry classifications in complete detail and presents overall summaries of major industrial groups

3. Indicates the trend of sales and profits as a percent change from the previous year; relates profits after taxes to sales; shows average return on investment and relates all these figures to the trends in compensation

4. Reports compensation trends related to sales and profits over the last five-year period in the industry sections and summarizes trends in all industries since 1952

5. Breaks down compensation into average salaries and average bonuses

6. Shows five or more of the sales groups listed below for most industries:

Annual Sales (in Millions)

Under $2	$50 to $100
$2 to $5	$100 to $200
$5 to $10	$200 to $500
$10 to $25	$500 to $1 billion
$25 to $50	Over $1 billion

7. Itemizes average annual sales, profits after taxes, average invested capital, and average number of employees for each industrial classification and each sales group

8. Presents position descriptions for typical top management positions found in the report, with a chart showing typical organization relationships

In addition, a comprehensive summary contains all-industry sales, profits, and compensation trends; sections relating compensation to responsibility; and the application of salary administration policies.

For small companies (under $25 million in sales), the Top Management Report provides compensation of executives in companies classified in durable and nondurable manufacturing categories and also provides an all-manufacturing summary. The compensation data are analyzed by company size based on sales volume in five groups at steps of $5 million, from under $5 million to $20 to $25 million. In addition, average salaries and bonuses for 19 top management positions are broken down by function.

For large companies (over $500 million in sales), the report classifies companies into five industry sector categories and analyzes their data by size based on sales volume. Also, the report shows the relationship of salary to responsibility.

For divisional positions, comparison is made between compensation paid these positions and that paid similar positions in independent corporations. Compensation is related to responsibility, and average salary and bonus are reported for 14 top management positions by sales volume groups.

Middle Management Report   This report gives salary ranges for 81 middle-management positions. Each job category reported contains a complete position description and is analyzed in detail. In addition, the report includes:

- Vital trend information
- Data on general salary increases
- Merit-increase budgets
- Incentive compensation
- Total payroll as a percentage of sales

Professional and Scientific Report   Based on more than 1000 survey responses, this report gives up-to-date data on every kind of engineer or scientist, as well as the latest information on professional, administrative, and operating personnel from accountants to patent attorneys. Highlights of the report include data on:

- Current hiring rates
- Salary trends
- Cost-of-living increases
- Merit increases
- Salary range adjustments
- Overtime practices
- College graduate recruitment activity
- National and regional compensation

Statistical Supplement to the Top Management Report   This report translates the data that appear in the Top Management Report into industrywide graphic presentations. It provides a method for determining compensation rates for any given position at any given sales volume. Through the utilization of regression analysis, sample variables—which may temporarily distort segments of information for narrow-sized groupings—are minimized.

Statistical Supplement to the Middle Management Report   This report provides graphic presentations for over 80 positions, relating salaries to sales, employment, and other scope measures identified with middle-management positions.

Sales Personnel Report   Effective sales incentive programs and the amount by which marketing salaries have changed in the past year are included. It contains salaries, incentives, and commissions paid by more than 600 companies employing more than 64,000 people in a wide range of sales and marketing positions including the supervisory level.

Supervisory Management Report   Ranging from transportation equipment manufacturers to banking institutions, this report shows a classification guide for every function of production first-line supvervisors, trades first-line supervisors, service first-line supervisors, general supervisors, and office supervisory personnel. It also includes data on cost-of-living allowances, working hours, and work shift differentials.

Technician Report   Compensation practices for specific technical, craft, and supportive positions are included in this report. Broken down into national and local practices, the data cover such positions as technicians and technologists, electronic data processing, drafters and designers, equipment service personnel, and craftspeople and skilled tradespeople.

Corporate Directorship Report   Gathered through a confidential survey of corporations throughout the United States, the information in this report gives compensation trends for both inside and outside directors. The report includes vital statistics on the size of corporate boards by industry and company, the powers of committees and frequency of meetings, benefits programs for outside directors, and compensation for committee work.

Hospital and Health Care Report   This guide contains statistics on over 216,000 people filling more than 100 positions in the industry. The data are broken down by institutional size, region, and ownership and include information on such benefits as tax-sheltered annuities, pensions, overtime, sick leave, vacations, merit and cost-of-living increases, and uniform allowance.

Report on Current and Deferred Incentive Compensation   This report is a guide to all the types of current and deferred incentive plans in use today. It includes data on such incentives as bonuses, profit sharing and productivity plans, management incentive plans, incentive plans with deferred payment features, employment contracts, group deferred compensation programs, and unit or share plans.

Report on Salary Administration and Control   This report covers salary policies and practices, salary determination, personnel policies, and control procedures and maintenance. It includes data on merit increases, rates paid to new employees, shift differentials, overtime compensation, methods of position evaluation, and budgetary control.

Report on Stock Purchase Plans   This review of stock option and purchase plans contains exhibits of all known types of plans and programs, plus a guide to the administration of stock option plans. It includes reporting requirements, option price, eligibility of participants, stock purchase plans in closed corporations, and employee stock purchase plans.

Report on Benefits and Employment Contracts   This report shows information on company practices regarding the use of management employment contracts, basic provisions of pension and profit sharing plans, and an outline of company practices in the field of insurance programs.

INTERNATIONAL COMPENSATION REPORTS

1. The U.S. expatriate compensation section sets out guidelines for special benefits to American executives working abroad, including salary premiums, hardship differentials, allowances for housing and education, and sample expatriate compensation policies currently in use.

2. The international division section gives the latest salary and bonus figures for executives holding key positions in 10 critical areas of international management, including industrial relations and export sales. All data are classified according to international sales. It also includes special regression analyses of eight top international positions.

3. The third-country nationals section contains information on the compensation of third-country nationals, including tax equalization and tax reimbursement policies, a breakdown of various benchmarks used to determine housing allowances, and a method for pinpointing equitable cost-of-living allowances for third-country nationals based on home city and assigned indices.

European Top Management Remuneration   This report covers top management compensation policies, trends, and practices throughout Europe. It presents current comparative salary data for 15 top management positions, including information on fringe benefits, social security legislation, and supplementary pension schemes. A detailed sample description is given for every position within a country.

Labour Relations, A Handbook of European Practices   This topical guide to industrial relations covers the main aspects of labor and social law and practices in the following six European countries: Belgium, France, Germany, Italy, the Netherlands, and the United Kingdom.

PRACTICAL APPLICATION OF SURVEY DATA

Generally speaking, the most usable and effective survey is one conducted by the company that intends to make decisions based on the results. In this situation, key factors, such as comparability of participants in terms of company size, industry, and competition, can be carefully controlled. Benchmark positions included in the survey can be selected to ensure a representative coverage of the total number of positions to be affected. What is perhaps most important is that the survey questionnaire can be designed to minimize the effect of differences between jobs with the same title.

EVALUCOMP: A SYSTEM OF JOB EVALUATION

An adjunct to the ECS survey reports is the EVALUCOMP system of job evaluation. It offers a comprehensive system for installing and administering an internally and externally equitable job evaluation program.

EVALUCOMP starts with external analysis and then adjusts the results for internal equity by combining an uncomplicated technique of market pricing and positioning with the salary data bank in the Executive Compensation Service. As an integral part of EVALUCOMP, nine of the ECS compensation reports are provided.

Also furnished are training for the participating employer, a standard position description manual, and other assistance in implementing and communicating the system. The manual describes over 400 salaried positions in 12 major functional areas. Each position is summed up in a position description form which may be adapted, modified, or installed verbatim.

chapter 39

Acquiring Competitive Information from Surveys:
Bureau of Labor Statistics

George L. Stelluto

ASSOCIATE COMMISSIONER, WAGES AND INDUSTRIAL
RELATIONS, BUREAU OF LABOR STATISTICS, U.S.
DEPARTMENT OF LABOR, WASHINGTON, D.C.

The 1972 edition of the *Handbook of Wage and Salary Administration* provides descriptions of occupational pay surveys conducted each year by the U.S. Department of Labor's Bureau of Labor Statistics (BLS). The surveys—designed for use in wage and salary administration—focus on wages and salaries by occupation, one of the most important pay determinants in the U.S. economy. Survey results yield information for the nation as well as for other pay-determining characteristics: region, local labor market, and industry.

Since 1972, BLS has developed new survey efforts that also provide useful wage and salary information. The surveys include information on the details of employee benefits and on trends in employee compensation (pay as well as employer costs for employee benefits).

Survey results are published in a variety of formats, including news releases, summary tabulations, and free reports available from the Bureau of Labor Statistics, Washington, D.C. 20212, or from any of its regional offices.[1] Final com-

---

[1]Addresses of the eight BLS regional offices are 1371 Peachtree Street, N.E., Atlanta, Georgia 30367; 1603 JFK Federal Building, Government Center, Boston, Massachusetts 02203; 9th Floor, Federal Office Building, 230 S. Dearborn Street, Chicago, Illinois 60604; Second Floor, 555 Griffin Square Building, Dallas, Texas 75202; 911 Walnut Street, Kansas City, Missouri 64106; 1515 Broadway, Suite 3400, New York, New York 10036; 3535 Market Street, P.O. Box 13309, Philadelphia, Pennsylvania 19101; 450 Golden Gate Avenue, Box 36017, San Francisco, California 94102.

prehensive bulletins are typically issued for sale and may be purchased from the Superintendent of Documents, U.S. Government Printing Office, Washington, D.C. 20402, or from BLS regional offices. Many surveys are also summarized in the BLS *Monthly Labor Review*.

The following sections describe BLS occupational pay surveys, employee benefit surveys, and the employment cost index—a quarterly time series on changes in employee compensation and wage and salary rates.

OCCUPATIONAL PAY SURVEYS

BLS surveys on straight-time pay by occupation fall into three major categories: (1) the National Survey of Professional, Administrative, Technical, and Clerical Pay; (2) area wage surveys that present data for occupations common to a wide variety of industries in local labor markets; and (3) industry wage surveys that yield data for occupations characteristic of the industries studied. Although differing in occupational, geographic, and industrial coverage, the three survey categories form an integrated program of occupational pay surveys. A common set of survey methods, concepts, and definitions applies to each type of survey.

The PATC Survey   The National Survey of Professional, Administrative, Technical, and Clerical Pay (the PATC survey) has been conducted annually since 1959. It provides a fund of broadly based information on white-collar occupations in private industry. The 102 work categories currently surveyed include the following: accountants, chief accountants, auditors (internal and public), attorneys, buyers, job analysts, personnel directors, chemists, and engineers; engineering technicians, drafters, computer operators, and photographers; and a range of clerical jobs from messengers and routine file clerks to high-level secretaries. Definitions for the survey occupations provide for classification of employees into work levels based on such pay-determining job elements as duties, responsibilities, experience, and educational requirements.

Although reflecting job elements in private industry, the definitions are designed to translate into specific pay grades (GS grades) in the General Schedule covering federal white-collar employees. Thus the PATC survey provides information for use in comparing salaries of federal government employees with pay for their private-industry counterparts, a requirement of the Federal Pay Comparability Act of 1970.[2]

The PATC survey provides estimates of average monthly and annual salaries in private industry by occupational work level. It also presents distributions of employees by salary interval, e.g., $1000 to $1100 a month, $1100 to $1200 a month. The survey design yields only national estimates for establishments within the survey scope,[3] with separate detail for establishments in metropolitan areas and for those with 2500 employees or more. The survey does not

---

[2]For a description of the federal pay comparability process, see "Federal Pay Comparability: Facts to Temper the Debate," *Monthly Labor Review*, June 1979, pp. 18–28. The process illustrates the use of survey data in salary administration for more than 3 million federal employees (including the military).

[3]The survey covers establishments in mining, construction, manufacturing, transportation, public utilities, wholesale and retail trade, finance, insurance, real estate, and selected services. Minimum establishment employment sizes are 50, 100, or 250, depending on the industry.

develop information on employee benefits. Details on employee benefit plans are provided, however, in a separate BLS survey (described below) which covers the same scope as the PATC survey.

The annual PATC survey uses March as an average reference month. Initial survey results are included in a BLS news release, usually the following July. The comprehensive bulletin is published for sale in October.

Area Wage Surveys   The BLS annual area wage survey program covers over 180 localities for which separate reports are published. Seventy localities are Standard Metropolitan Statistical Areas (SMSAs, as defined by the U.S. Office of Management and Budget) and were selected to represent a cross section of local labor markets found throughout the United States. Area selection is also designed to yield national and regional estimates for all SMSAs combined. The remaining localities are surveyed under contract for other federal agencies and are a mixture of SMSAs and other geographic entities. Occupational coverage of these surveys differs slightly from coverage of regular BLS area wage surveys.

Area wage surveys provide information on straight-time pay (hourly or weekly) for occupations common to a variety of industries. The occupations are chosen from four employment groups: (1) "Office Clerical," e.g., file clerks, typists, secretaries; (2) "Professional and Technical," e.g., industrial nurses, drafters, electronic technicians, EDP systems analysts and programmers; (3) "Maintenance, Toolroom, and Powerplant," e.g., electricians, stationary engineers, tool-and-die makers; and (4) "Material Movement and Custodial," e.g., truck drivers, forklift operators, janitors.

Pay data are presented as averages, along with distributions of employees by wage or salary interval, for the occupations surveyed in the locality. Data are provided for all industries covered by the surveys[4] and separately (whenever possible) for manufacturing, nonmanufacturing, and transportation and utilities.

Area wage surveys are conducted annually, but every third year they include the following additional data for plant and office workers: work schedules; shift operations and differentials; and information on the incidence of paid holidays, paid vacations, and health, insurance, and pension plans. Surveys conducted for other federal agencies do not include information on work schedules and late-shift differentials.

The surveys are conducted throughout the year with payroll reference months varying by area. Individual area reports are typically issued within 60 days of the payroll reference month. Appendix A lists the individual area wage surveys conducted in 1981 and identifies reports as being either for sale or free.

Industry Wage Surveys   About 45 manufacturing and 25 nonmanufacturing industries are covered by this BLS program. The industries were chosen to give as broad a coverage of the nation's industrial makeup as possible within

---

[4]The surveys cover the following industries: manufacturing; transportation, communications, and other public utilities; wholesale and retail trades; finance, insurance, and real estate; and selected services. Establishments with fewer than 50 employees are excluded from the surveys except in the 13 largest SMSAs where the minimum establishment size is 100 employees in manufacturing, transportation, utilities, and retail trade.

resource limits. Most industries are surveyed on a five-year cycle, but several comparatively low-paid industries are surveyed every three years.

Nearly all manufacturing, public utility, and mining industries are surveyed nationwide, with separate estimates for regions, states, and/or areas of industry concentration. Surveys in trade, finance, and services, on the other hand, are typically limited to selected Standard Metropolitan Statistical Areas.

The occupations for which straight-time pay data are developed vary by industry. They are selected to represent the range of skills and pay rates, methods of wage payment (e.g., time or incentive rates), and major activities performed by employees in the individual industries surveyed. Selection also takes into account the occupations prevalent in the industry (e.g., numerically important) and those that are important reference points in collective bargaining and wage administration.

Like area wage surveys, the industry surveys present pay data as averages, along with distributions by wage and salary interval, for the occupations surveyed in the industry. Industry wage surveys also develop data on the incidence of establishment practices and employee benefits, e.g., work schedules, shift operations and differentials, paid holidays and vacations, and health, insurance, and pension plans.

Approximately 12 to 14 industry wage surveys are conducted each year. Preliminary survey results (summary or locality releases) are usually issued within six to nine months after the survey reference month. The comprehensive bulletin is typically for sale about nine months later. Appendix B lists the industry wage survey bulletins issued from 1975 to 1981.

EMPLOYEE BENEFIT PLAN SURVEYS

The growth of employee benefits over the last four decades has drawn increasing attention from individuals interested in wage and salary administration. Moreover, benefit costs (currently between 25 and 30 percent of total combined remuneration) have outdated the term "fringe benefits," coined in the 1940s. Benefits and their cost are now major considerations in developing pay administration systems.

The federal government—like other employers—has devoted increasing concern to benefits in pay administration for its more than 2 million employees. The concerns led to experimental efforts (in the late 1970s) to incorporate employee benefits, together with wage and salaries, in the federal pay comparability process. An experimental approach, known as "total compensation comparability," was developed by the Office of Personnel Management (OPM) in 1978. (See also Chapter 54.)

The approach required a unique survey effort by BLS to gather information on the incidence and detailed characteristics of employee benefit plans in private industry. Detailed plan characteristics were used by OPM to calculate dollar costs of providing federal employees with a level of benefits comparable to that in private industry.[5]

---

[5]The dollar costs were calculated by OPM using mathematical and actuarial models that took account of the demographic characteristics of the federal work force. See OPM report, "Total Compensation Comparability: Background, Method, Preliminary Results," July 1981.

As part of the new approach to federal pay comparability, BLS established a broad-based annual survey in 1979 on employee benefit plans in private industry. The survey covers the same scope[6] as the BLS National Survey of Professional, Administrative, Technical, and Clerical Pay—the PATC survey. It also is limited to nationwide estimates.

The survey provides estimates on the incidence and details of a wide variety of employee benefits: paid leave (lunch and rest periods, holidays, vacations, personal leave), short- and long-term disability benefits, health insurance, life insurance, and retirement plans. Separate survey estimates are presented for three major employment groups, i.e., professional-administrative, clerical-technical, and production workers. The amount of detail is extensive.

Employee Benefits in Industry, 1980, Bureau of Labor Statistics Bulletin 2107, published in September 1981, may be purchased from the Superintendent of Documents, U.S. Government Printing Office, Washington, D.C. 20402, or from BLS regional offices.[7] Publication plans for results of future surveys include issuing a BLS news release in the summer and following this with a bulletin available for sale in the fall.

EMPLOYMENT COST INDEX

The BLS employment cost index (ECI) is a quarterly measure of change in employee compensation rates—wages, salaries, and employer costs for employee benefits. Its development began in the early 1970s, when concerns about labor cost escalation were in sharp focus. At that time, federal policymakers expressed a strong need for a measure of labor cost trends that would:

- Be timely and comprehensive, covering all types of workers and industries in the U.S. economy and all elements of employee compensation
- Be fixed in weight, unaffected by employment shifts among occupations and industries with different wage and compensation levels
- Have internally consistent subseries (e.g., by occupation, industry, union-nonunion status) to provide insights into overall wage and compensation trends

To satisfy this need, the ECI was planned in stages: (1) development of its conceptual and statistical framework, 1971–1974; (2) initial publication of a continuing quarterly series on wage and salary change for workers in the nation's private nonfarm economy, 1975; (3) expansion to a quarterly measure of changes in compensation (wages, salaries, and benefit costs), 1980; and (4) introduction of state and local government coverage, 1981. In October 1980, the U.S. Office of Management and Budget designated the ECI a "principal federal economic indicator."

In addition to its use in policymaking, the ECI yields information valuable to individuals involved in wage and salary administration. It is a tool for tracking compensation and wage movements at the establishment, company, or industry level with more general trends in the U.S. economy. ECI subseries provide for tracking along occupational, industry, regional, and union-nonunion lines.

The ECI series on wages and salaries is limited to wage and salary rates,

[6]See footnote 3.

[7]See footnote 1.

defined as straight-time average hourly earnings. Straight-time earnings are total earnings before payroll deductions, excluding premium pay for overtime, work on weekends and holidays, and shift differentials. Production bonuses, incentive earnings, commission payments, and cost-of-living adjustments are included in straight-time earnings, whereas nonproduction bonuses (such as Christmas or year-end bonuses) are excluded. Also excluded are such items as payments in kind, free room and board, and tips.

The ECI compensation series includes employer costs for employee benefits as well as wages and salaries. Benefits covered include:

Hours-related benefits: Premium pay for overtime and work on weekends and holidays, paid holidays, paid vacations, paid sick leave, and other paid leave

Supplemental pay: Shift differentials, nonproduction bonuses, severance pay, and supplemental unemployment plans

Insurance benefits: Life, health, and sickness and accident insurance

Retirement and savings benefits: Pension and other retirement plans and savings and thrift plans

Legally required benefits: Social security, railroad retirement and supplemental retirement, railroad unemployment insurance, federal and state unemployment insurance, workers' compensation, and other legally required benefits such as state temporary disability insurance

Other benefits: Merchandise discounts in department stores

ECI data are collected for the payroll periods including the 12th day of the survey months of March, June, September, and December. A BLS news release is issued within two months of the survey reference month, e.g., March data are published in May. The releases are available free from the U.S. Bureau of Labor Statistics, Washington, D.C. 20212, or from its regional offices.[8]

REFERENCES

"BLS Handbook of Methods," Bureau of Labor Statistics, 1976, *Bulletin 1910.*

"Directory of Occupational Wage Surveys, 1974–79," Bureau of Labor Statistics, September 1980, *Report 606.*

"Major Programs," Bureau of Labor Statistics, July 1980, *BLS Report 552.*

---

[8]See footnote 1.

APPENDIX A: BLS Area Wage Survey Program, 1981

Area	Type of survey†	Reference month
*Alaska (statewide)	I	July
*Albany, Ga.	I	July
Albany-Schenectady-Troy, N.Y.	I	Sept.
*Albuquerque, N. Mex.	I	Sept.
*Alexandria-Leesville, La.	I	Feb.
*Alpena-Standish-Tawas City, Mich.	I	July
Anaheim-Santa Ana-Garden Grove, Calif.	F	Oct.
*Ann Arbor, Mich.	I	Oct.
*Antelope Valley, Calif.	I	Dec.
*Asheville, N.C.	I	May
Atlanta, Ga.	F	May
*Atlantic City, N.J.	I	Aug.
*Augusta, Ga.-S.C.	I	Feb.
*Austin, Tex.	F	Dec.
*Bakersfield, Calif.	I	Dec.
Baltimore, Md.	F	Aug.
*Baton Rouge, La.	I	Feb.
*Battle Creek, Mich.	F	Mar.
*Beaumont-Port Arthur-Orange and Lake Charles, Tex.-La.	I	May
Billings, Mont.	I	July
*Biloxi-Gulfport and Pascagoula-Moss Point, Miss.	I	Sept.
*Binghamton, N.Y.	I	Nov.
*Birmingham, Ala.	I	Mar.
*Bloomington-Vincennes, Ind.	I	Nov.
Boston, Mass.	F	Aug.
*Bremerton-Shelton, Wash.	I	Jan.
*Brunswick, Ga.	I	June
Buffalo, N.Y.	F	Oct.
*Cedar Rapids, Iowa	I	Mar.
*Champaign-Urbana-Rantoul, Ill.	F	July
*Charleston-North Charleston-Walterboro, S.C.	I	Sept.
*Charlotte-Gastonia, N.C.	F	June
Chattanooga, Tenn.-Ga.	F	Sept.
*Cheyenne, Wyo.	I	June
Chicago, Ill.	I	May
Cincinnati, Ohio-Ky.-Ind.	I	July
*Clarksville-Hopkinsville, Tenn.-Ky.	I	Mar.
Cleveland, Ohio	I	Sept.
*Colorado Springs, Colo.	I	Jan.
*Columbia-Sumter, S.C.	F	Feb.
*Columbus, Ga.-Ala.	F	Apr.
*Columbus, Miss.	I	June
Columbus, Ohio	F	Oct.
*Connecticut (statewide)	I	Mar.
Corpus Christi, Tex.	I	July
Dallas-Fort Worth, Tex.	I	Dec.
Davenport-Rock Island-Moline, Iowa-Ill.	I	Feb.
Dayton, Ohio	I	Dec.
Daytona Beach, Fla.	I	Aug.
*Decatur, Ill.	I	Dec.

See footnotes at end of table.

APPENDIX A: BLS Area Wage Survey Program, 1981   (*Continued*)

Area	Type of survey†	Reference month
Denver-Boulder, Colo.	I	Dec.
*Des Moines, Iowa	F	May
Detroit, Mich.	I	Apr.
*Dothan, Ala.	F	Dec.
*Duluth-Superior, Minn.-Wis.	I	June
*El Paso-Alamogordo-Las Cruces, Tex.-N. Mex.	I	Mar.
*Eugene-Springfield-Medford, Oreg.	I	Aug.
*Fayetteville, N.C.	I	Feb.
*Fort Lauderdale-Hollywood and West Palm Beach-Boca Raton, Fla.	F	Apr.
*Fort Wayne, Ind.	I	June
*Frederick-Hagerstown-Chambersburg, Md.-Pa.	I	Dec.
Fresno, Calif.	I	June
*Gadsden and Anniston, Ala.	I	July
Gainesville, Fla.	I	Sept.
Gary-Hammond-East Chicago, Ind.	I	Nov.
*Goldsboro, N.C.	I	July
*Grand Island-Hastings, Nebr.	F	July
Green Bay, Wis.	F	July
Greensboro–Winston-Salem–High Point, N.C.	I	Aug.
Greenville-Spartanburg, S.C.	I	June
*Guam, Territory of	I	Dec.
*Harrisburg-Lebanon, Pa.	I	Oct.
Hartford, Conn.	I	Mar.
Houston, Tex.	I	May
Huntsville, Ala.	I	Feb.
Indianapolis, Ind.	F	Oct.
Jackson, Miss.	I	Jan.
Jacksonville, Fla.	I	Dec.
Kansas City, Mo.-Kans.	I	Sept.
*Knoxville, Tenn.	I	Oct.
*La Crosse-Sparta, Wis.	F	Oct.
*Laredo, Tex.	I	Feb.
*Las Vegas-Tonopah, Nev.	I	Oct.
*Lexington-Fayette, Ky.	F	Dec.
*Lima, Ohio	I	Aug.
*Little Rock-North Little Rock, Ark.	I	Nov.
*Logansport-Peru, Ind.	I	July
*Lorain-Elyria, Ohio	F	Mar.
Los Angeles-Long Beach, Calif.	F	Oct.
Louisville, Ky.-Ind.	I	Nov.
*Lower Eastern Shore, Md.-Va.-Del.	I	Aug.
*Macon, Ga.	F	Dec.
*Madison, Wis.	I	Sept.
*Maine (statewide)	F	Dec.
*Mansfield, Ohio	I	Nov.
Memphis, Tenn.-Ark.-Miss.	I	Nov.
*Meridian, Miss.	I	Aug.
Miami, Fla.	F	Oct.

See footnotes at end of table.

APPENDIX A: BLS Area Wage Survey Program, 1981   (Continued)

Area	Type of survey†	Reference month
*Middlesex, Monmouth, and Ocean Counties, N.J.	I	July
Milwaukee, Wis.	F	May
Minneapolis-St. Paul, Minn.-Wis.	F	Jan.
*Mobile-Pensacola-Panama City, Ala.-Fla.	F	Aug.
*Montana (statewide)	I	July
*Montgomery, Ala.	I	Apr.
*Nashville-Davidson, Tenn.	F	July
Nassau-Suffolk, N.Y.	F	June
Newark, N.J.	I	Jan.
*New Bern-Jacksonville, N.C.	I	Mar.
*New Hampshire (statewide)	I	July
New Orleans, La.	F	Oct.
New York, N.Y.-N.J.	F	May
Norfolk-Virginia Beach-Portsmouth, Va.-N.C.	I	May
*North Dakota (statewide)	I	Aug.
Northeast Pennsylvania	I	Aug.
*Northern New York	I	Sept.
*Northwest Texas	F	Sept.
Oklahoma City, Okla.	I	Aug.
Omaha, Nebr.-Iowa	I	Oct.
*Orlando, Fla.	I	Aug.
*Oxnard-Simi Valley-Ventura, Calif.	I	Feb.
Paterson-Clifton-Passaic, N.J.	I	June
*Peoria, Ill.	F	Feb.
Philadelphia, Pa.-N.J.	I	Nov.
*Phoenix, Ariz.	F	June
Pittsburgh, Pa.	I	Jan.
Portland, Maine	F	Dec.
Portland, Oreg.-Wash.	I	June
*Portsmouth-Chillicothe-Gallipolis, Ohio	F	Feb.
Poughkeepsie, N.Y.	I	June
*Poughkeepsie-Kingston-Newburgh, N.Y.	I	June
Providence-Warwick-Pawtucket, R.I.-Mass.	I	June
*Pueblo, Colo.	I	July
*Puerto Rico	I	Dec.
*Raleigh-Durham, N.C.	I	Mar.
*Reno, Nev.	I	Jan.
Richmond, Va.	I	June
*Riverside-San Bernardino-Ontario, Calif.	F	Dec.
St. Louis, Mo.-Ill.	I	Mar.
Sacramento, Calif.	I	Dec.
Saginaw, Mich.	I	Nov.
*Salina, Kans.	I	Sept.
*Salinas-Seaside-Monterey, Calif.	F	May
Salt Lake City-Ogden, Utah	F	Nov.
San Antonio, Tex.	I	May
San Diego, Calif.	I	Nov.
San Francisco-Oakland, Calif.	F	Mar.
San Jose, Calif.	F	Mar.

See footnotes at end of table.

APPENDIX A: BLS Area Wage Survey Program, 1981   (Continued)

Area	Type of survey†	Reference month
*Sandusky, Ohio	F	Feb.
*Santa Barbara-Santa Maria-Lompoc, Calif.	I	Feb.
*Savannah, Ga.	F	Mar.
Seattle-Everett, Wash.	I	Dec.
*Selma, Ala.	I	July
*Sherman-Denison, Tex.	F	Dec.
*Shreveport, La.	I	Apr.
South Bend, Ind.	I	Aug.
*South Dakota (statewide)	I	June
*Southeastern Mass.	I	Sept.
*Southern Idaho	I	June
*Southwest Virginia	I	Sept.
*Spokane, Wash.	F	Sept.
*Springfield, Ill.	I	Aug.
*Stockton, Calif.	I	Aug.
*Tacoma, Wash.	I	Apr.
*Tampa-St. Petersburg, Fla.	F	July
Toledo, Ohio-Mich.	F	June
*Topeka, Kans.	I	Aug.
Trenton, N.J.	F	Sept.
*Tucson-Douglas, Ariz.	F	July
*Tulsa, Okla.	I	June
*Upper Peninsula, Mich.	I	Aug.
*Vallejo-Fairfield-Napa, Calif.	I	Sept.
*Vermont (statewide)	I	Sept.
*Virgin Islands of the U.S.	I	Apr.
*Waco and Killeen-Temple, Tex.	I	July
Washington, D.C.-Md.-Va.	F	Mar.
*Waterloo-Cedar Falls, Iowa	I	June
*West Virginia (statewide)	I	July
*Western and Northern Mass.	I	Jan.
Wichita, Kans.	I	Apr.
*Wichita Falls-Lawton-Altus, Tex.-Okla.	I	Nov.
*Wilmington, Del.-N.J.-Md.	F	Apr.
Worcester, Mass.	I	Apr.
*Yakima-Richland-Kennewick-Pendleton, Wash.-Oreg.	I	Aug.
York, Pa.	F	Feb.

*Asterisks indicate Service Contract Act surveys that are similar to those conducted under the Bureau's regular program but are more limited in number of occupations studied and types of supplementary benefits for which data are provided. Summary reports are available free. For areas without an asterisk, as well as Poughkeepsie-Kingston-Newburgh, more detailed bulletins are for sale individually or by subscription.

†The letter "F" designates a full survey of occupational earnings and establishment practices and employee benefits. The letter "I" designates an interim survey, limited to occupational earnings data.

APPENDIX B: BLS Industry Wage Survey Program, 1975–1981

Industry	Date of last survey	Expected year of next survey
Manufacturing		
Food and kindred products:		
Meat products	May 1979	1984
Grain-mill products	Sept. 1977	1982
Candy and other confectionary products	Aug. 1975	Discontinued
Tobacco manufactures:		
Cigarettes	June 1981	1986
Textile-mill products:		
Cotton and synthetic fiber textiles	Aug. 1980	1985
Woolen and worsted textiles	Aug. 1980	1985
Hosiery (full-fashioned and seamless)	July 1981	1986
Dyeing and finishing textiles	Aug. 1980	1985
Apparel:		
Men's and boys' suits and coats	Apr. 1979	1983
Men's and boys' shirts (except workshirts) and nightwear	May 1981	1984
Men's separate trousers	May 1978	Discontinued
Women's and misses' dresses	Aug. 1977	1982
Lumber and wood products:		
Millwork	June 1979	1984
Furniture and fixtures:		
Wood household furniture	June 1979	1984
Paper and allied products:		
Pulp, paper, and paperboard mills	Summer 1977	1982
Corrugated and solid fiber boxes	May 1981	1986
Printing, publishing, and allied industries:		
Newspaper printing*	Sept. 1980	Discontinued
Book and job printing*	Sept. 1980	Discontinued
Lithography*	Sept. 1980	Discontinued
Chemicals and allied products:		
Industrial chemicals	May 1981	1986
Synthetic fibers	Aug. 1981	1986
Paints and varnishes	Nov. 1976	Discontinued
Petroleum refining and related industries:		
Petroleum refining	May 1981	1986
Rubber and miscellaneous plastics products:		
Miscellaneous plastics products	Nov. 1979	1984
Leather and leather products:		
Footwear	Apr. 1980	1985
Stone, clay, and glass products:		
Glass and glassware, pressed or blown	May 1980	1985
Structural clay products	Sept. 1980	1985
Primary metal industries:		
Blast furnaces, steel works, and rolling mills	Feb. 1978	1983
Iron and steel foundries	Sept. 1979	1984
Primary smelting	Feb. 1981	1986
Rolling, drawing, extruding nonferrous metals	Feb. 1981	1986
Nonferrous foundries	May 1975	Discontinued

See footnotes at end of table.

APPENDIX B: BLS Industry Wage Survey Program, 1975–1981   (*Continued*)

Industry	Date of last survey	Expected year of next survey
Manufacturing		
Fabricated metal products:		
Fabricated structural metal	Nov. 1979	1984
Machinery, except electrical	Jan. 1981	1984
Electrical machinery:		
Transmission and distribution equipment	June 1980	1985
Semiconductors	May 1977	Indefinite
Nonmanufacturing		
Mining:		
Metal mining	July–Sept. 1977	Indefinite
Bituminous coal	Jan. 1976	1982
Oil and gas extraction	Sept. 1977	1982
Contract construction:		
Building trades*	July 1980	Discontinued
Contract construction	Sept. 1976–May 1977	Indefinite
Transportation, communication, electric, gas, and sanitary services:		
Local transit*	July 1980	Discontinued
Trucking*	Sept. 1979	Discontinued
Scheduled airlines	Sept. 1980	1985
Communications	Late 1980	Annual
Electric and gas utilities	Feb. 1978	1983
Retail trade:		
Department stores	May 1981	1986
Grocery stores*	Sept. 1979	Discontinued
Finance, insurance, and real estate:		
Banks	Feb. 1980	1985
Savings and loan associations	Feb. 1980	1985
Life insurance	Feb. 1980	1985
Services:		
Hotels	May 1978	1983
Contract cleaning	July 1981	1986
Computer and data processing	March 1978	1982
Auto dealer repair shops	June 1978	1983
Appliance repair shops	Nov. 1981	1984
Nursing homes	May 1981	1984
Hospitals	Oct. 1981	1984

*Annual or biennial surveys of basic (minimum) wage rates and maximum schedules of hours at straight-time rates, as determined by collective bargaining between trade unions and employers. Due to budgetary constraints, these union wage surveys were discontinued in fiscal year 1981.

Acquiring Competitive Information from Surveys:

The Hay Compensation Information Center

Lois H. Barker

PARTNER, THE HAY GROUP, PHILADELPHIA, PENNSYLVANIA

The Compensation Information Center (CIC), within the Hay Group, conducts a number of annual surveys to provide a data base of compensation information on jobs at all levels in many different functions, industries, and locations. CIC also conducts special-purpose surveys sponsored by individual clients or groups. Analyses focus on the relationship between the individual participating organization's compensation and the general marketplace and on compensation trends within labor markets. Analytical methods may include tabular percentiles and distribution statistics, as well as linear and curvilinear or multiple regression representations of company policies. Existing capabilities allow for conversion of foreign currencies to a U.S.-dollar equivalent and calculation of aftertax income based on the various social taxes (similar to social security) in a number of western countries.

The central building block is the relationship that exists between compensation and measured job content. The Hay Guide Chart-Profile Method is widely used to identify units of job content. Those units, or points, describe the relative importance and difficulty of jobs within companies, based on consid-

FIGURE 1 **Raw Scattergram**

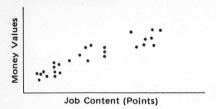

eration of common job elements. By using job content points, relationships can be established between jobs in different organizations, functions, occupations, and industries. This allows the linking of various survey data sets to provide a comparison base of well over 2 million jobholders in over 1500 organizations in the United States, as well as survey data collected by Hay offices in other developed economies worldwide.

HAY COMPENSATION COMPARISONS

The most widely known CIC surveys are the Hay Compensation Comparisons (HCC), available to organizations that control their compensation programs with measurements which can be converted to standard Hay job content points. Annual HCC publications summarize general cash compensation practices for management, professional, and exempt technical positions in all functions. Separate reports are provided for general industrial, utility, banking, insurance, Blue Cross and Blue Shield, and service organizations. The total data base is an accurate reflection of direct compensation in the national market. Participating organizations can also request special analyses that focus on particular industry, function, or location markets.

In response to an annual questionnaire, the participating organization provides detailed tabulations showing individual job titles and points, policy midpoints, actual base salaries, and total compensation payments. For each of these categories, money values are paired with the points of measured job content (Figure 1) and lines of central tendency are identified using techniques that combine direct statistical analysis and expert judgments (Figure 2). These lines represent the organization's compensation practice. The annual Hay survey

FIGURE 2 **Existing Compensation Practice**

FIGURE 3   Policy Structure (Administrative Guide)

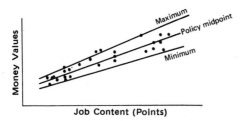

Job Content (Points)

consolidates all such practice lines and shows graphically how each organization relates to appropriate markets.

The survey focuses on three aspects of direct compensation:

1. *Policy Midpoint:* The salary structure or near-term goal against which base salaries are administered (Figure 3).

2. *Actual Base-Salary Practice:* The central tendency of base salaries plotted against job content points. It shows what actually is happening (Figure 2).

3. *Total Cash Compensation Practice:* The sum of base salaries plus supplemental cash payments, such as sales commissions, discretionary bonuses, and incentive awards, determined on the basis of individual, division, or company performance.

Data in HCC reports are analyzed in many different ways.

Charts   Values are taken from lines of central tendency for participating organizations at standard Hay reference levels in standard job measurement points. For broad purposes the reference levels can be interpreted as:

Hay Points	Generic Job Group
100	Entry professional
200	Journeyman professional, basic management
400	Seasoned professional, middle management
600	Advanced management
1000	Strategic professional, executive
1500	Senior executive—middle-sized organization
2000	Senior executive—large organization

Charts are developed by identifying averages and selected percentiles in distributions of compensation at standard reference levels and by interpolation between the standard intercepts. They provide a graphic representation of the distribution of organizations' compensation practices. The sample chart shown (Figure 4) illustrates the wide diversity of salary practices for similar measured job content when employers in all types of industries are considered together. A second sample analysis shows *average* salary practices for the different major types of industries (Figure 5).

History and Trends   Organizations that participate in the HCC have large enough employee populations to be important competitors in their particular

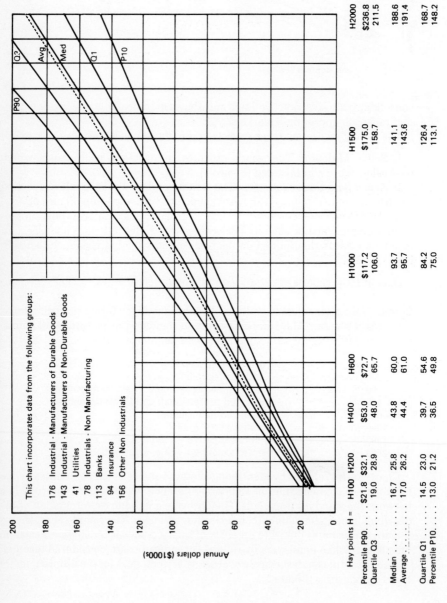

This chart incorporates data from the following groups:

176	Industrial - Manufacturers of Durable Goods
143	Industrial - Manufacturers of Non-Durable Goods
41	Utilities
78	Industrials - Non Manufacturing
113	Banks
94	Insurance
156	Other Non Industrials

Annual dollars ($1000s)

Hay points H =	H100	H200	H400	H600	H1000	H1500	H2000
Percentile P90	$21.8	$32.1	$53.0	$72.7	$117.2	$175.0	$236.8
Quartile Q3	19.0	28.9	48.0	65.7	106.0	158.7	211.5
Median	16.7	25.8	43.8	60.0	93.7	141.1	188.6
Average	17.0	26.2	44.4	61.0	95.7	143.6	191.4
Quartile Q1	14.5	23.0	39.7	54.6	84.2	126.4	168.7
Percentile P10	13.0	21.2	36.5	49.8	75.0	113.1	148.2

40/4

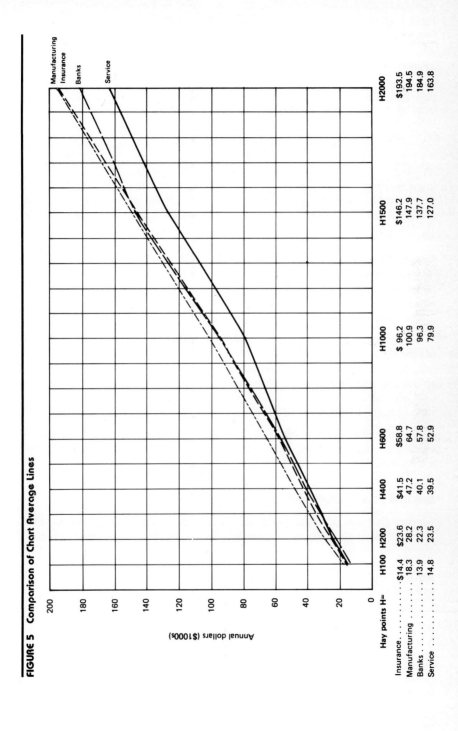

FIGURE 5 Comparison of Chart Average Lines

Annual dollars ($1000s)

Hay points H=	H100	H200	H400	H600	H1000	H1500	H2000
Insurance.	$14.4	$23.6	$41.5	$58.8	$ 96.2	$146.2	$193.5
Manufacturing	18.3	28.2	47.2	64.7	100.9	147.9	194.5
Banks.	13.9	22.3	40.1	57.8	96.3	137.7	184.9
Service	14.8	23.5	39.5	52.9	79.9	127.0	163.8

TABLE 1   Summary Percent Changes in Average Total Cash Compensation in Industrial Companies

Period	General professional and management, %	Executive, %
1981–1980	9.9	8.1
1980–1979	8.9	10.7
1979–1978	7.8	10.7
1978–1977	8.1	7.7
1977–1976	8.0	12.8

labor markets. They manage compensation in systematic and rational ways. Their continuing participation in the survey provides an accurate history of compensation changes on a basis that is not distorted by sample changes (Table 1).

Compensation Facts   Participating organizations also provide supplementary information about the patterns and considerations that govern their compensation programs. Analyses of prevalence and effect are provided as part of the annual HCC publication. (Table 2 is one example.)

The annual report provides each participating employer with:

1. A clear picture of its own internal compensation relationships and practices
2. A comparison of its compensation practice to all other participants or selected groups of participants (i.e., the competition)
3. Supporting tables and charts to give perspective in considering compensation program changes

The combined analysis of internal equity and external competitiveness provides the foundation for compensation programs that are satisfying and motivating.

EXECUTIVE COMPENSATION SURVEYS

Surveys that are published annually from the executive data base contain information on all forms of compensation (salaries, bonuses, short-term incen-

TABLE 2   1981 Average Bonus as Percent of Base Salary in Bonus-Paying Industrial Companies

Job content level	Bonus as % of base salary
Entry professional	4
Journeyman professional, basic management	6
Seasoned professional, middle management	13
Advanced management	21
Strategic professional, executive	33
Senior executive—middle-sized organization	40
Senior executive—large organization	46

tives, long-term incentives, benefits, and perquisites) for specific corporate line and staff executive positions. Separate reports are regularly provided for industrial, utility, banking, and insurance organizations. Information received from companies is more accurate, complete, and current than compensation information from proxy statements. However, proxy information can be used to supplement specific survey data to conduct custom-designed analyses.

The annual Hay Survey of Directors' Compensation reports fee and retainer practices for the corporate board and its various committees. Additional information analyzed includes benefits and perquisites available to board members, supplemental payments to the board and committee chairpersons, and board organizational characteristics.

NONCASH COMPENSATION COMPARISON

An annual noncash compensation comparison (NCC) summarizes all types of benefits, perquisites, and personnel practices. The major content is a detailed analysis of all principal programs and their chief design elements. Additionally, using actuarial models, CIC calculates the cash-equivalent value of such benefits and perquisites. *By adding this value to cash compensation, companies can compare total remuneration (the cash plus cash-equivalent value of all compensation and benefits).*

The cash-equivalent approach was developed by Hay to translate the complexities and variations among noncash compensation practices into a uniform, quantitative evaluation. It provides a basis for comparing and combining the provisions in different types of plans and for comparing total benefit programs and overall remuneration practices. The use of actuarially determined standard values eliminates the distorting effect of differences in purchasing effectiveness and employee demographics among various plans and coverage groups.

The noncash compensation values are based on the employer's share of cost alone. If benefits are financed entirely or in part by employee contributions, their value is reduced approximately by the proportion paid by the employee. Some credit is still given to fully contributory plans in recognition of their value to the employee when offered at group rates. Values for the employer-paid portion of social security benefits, workers' compensation, and unemployment compensation are also included in the report.

Linear analysis enables comparison of an individual organization's total remuneration, noncash compensation, and cash compensation with other participants at a broad range of job content and pay levels. Also, by comparing noncash and cash competitive positions, firms can determine to what extent they emphasize one over the other and how they affect position in terms of total remuneration. The noncash total remuneration analysis and benefit-level analysis can be used in conjunction with the employer-paid benefit-value analysis to provide a full perspective on the noncash element of compensation. A comparison of the benefit-value results from the 1980 and 1981 surveys is useful to illustrate some analytic capabilities (Table 3).

Overall analyses are also provided in the NCC showing the average employer-paid values by major benefit area for industrial, financial, and service organizations, as well as the average pension benefit levels, including

TABLE 3   Benefit Value as Percent of Salary Level

Salary level	Industrial Companies		Financial Companies		Service Organizations	
	1981	1980	1981	1980	1981	1980
100,000	32.0	31.0	34.8	33.3	30.7	30.3
70,000	33.4	32.4	35.8	34.6	32.6	31.9
50,000	35.9	34.2	38.5	36.2	34.7	33.8
30,000	40.6	37.7	42.7	39.3	39.4	37.3
20,000	43.7	41.0	44.4	42.0	42.3	40.5
10,000	54.5	50.0	54.2	49.0	52.3	49.0

social security. In addition, the average replacement income ratios of total survivor benefits based on basic, supplemental, executive life, survivor income, and social security survivor benefits are shown.

Comparisons can be made against a wide variety of subgroups such as the electronics industry, banking, or individually selected regional groups. Comparisons of employer-paid benefits and total benefit values can be done separately on any or all benefit areas. For example, a utility company may compare the values of its pension and health care plans with those of other utilities in the survey data base to confirm suspected strength or weakness in these areas. A benefit-value comparison for each benefit area is particularly effective in identifying the trade-off value of one area against the other.

OTHER SURVEYS AND SERVICES

The majority of CIC surveys do not require that participants use Hay job content measurement methods. Models of occupations and functions and of common organizational patterns of industries support job matching. The total CIC data base also identifies information for specific industries, occupations, occupational categories (including blue collar and clerical), and geographic regions.

Acquiring Competitive Information from Surveys: Project 777

James R. McMahon

CONSULTANT, MANAGEMENT COMPENSATION SERVICES,
SCOTTSDALE, ARIZONA

As the compensation function has gained greater prominence in the corporate setting and the need to pay competitively has become clearly recognized, accurate and timely survey data is now a requirement for most large companies.

Since 1968, Management Compensation Services (MCS) has provided national and international survey data and specialized compensation studies to those executives responsible for decisions in executive compensation and salary administration throughout American industry.

PROJECT 777

Our comparative studies range from those targeting a few carefully selected organizations to a broad cross section of Fortune 500 companies operating in the United States and overseas. The study MCS is perhaps best known for is Project 777, an annual survey of executive compensation among large manufacturers.

In the early 1960s, executives from seven leading American manufacturing firms met in Room 777 of a Cleveland airport hotel and began a cooperative venture aimed at exchanging confidential information regarding executive compensation. Stemming from that exchange, *Project 777* was launched in 1964. In 1981, this survey included 392 participants (52 percent of the Fortune 500) and ranks as the most comprehensive data source on executive compensation in manufacturing businesses.

ESSENTIAL ELEMENTS

MCS believes that certain elements are essential in conducting as successful and high-quality a study as Project 777. These include:

■ *Comparability.* Criteria must be established to assure that reasonable comparability exists among participants.

■ *Confidentiality.* The confidentiality of highly sensitive information must be assured by the organization conducting the survey.

■ *Responsiveness.* A post-survey conference should be held for the participants to assure that the survey is adaptable to changing needs.

■ *Data editing.* Great care must be taken in reviewing the data submitted to assure that survey concepts and requirements are adhered to and that companies are reporting on a comparable basis.

■ *Results.* The survey results must be presented in such a way that participants can interpret them easily while retaining precision.

■ *Data base.* The data base should be large enough to be representative of the marketplace and large enough to permit experimentation with new methods of analysis. To preserve the continuity of the data base, casual participation in which companies are in and out in alternate years should not be permitted.

The following pages discuss these elements in more depth and the MCS approach to meeting them.

MCS APPROACH

Requirements for Membership In order to join Project 777, three eligibility requirements must be met:

■ The organization must be a corporate entity not owned or controlled by a higher-level organization unless such organization is headquartered outside the United States or Canada.

■ The organization's sales volume must be at least $100 million.

■ A minimum of 30 percent of sales must be generated by a product the company manufactures.

Confidentiality Great care is taken to protect the confidentiality of private information. It is never revealed to other participants, government agencies, or consultants (including consultants from our parent company, Hewitt Associates). No one outside of the MCS production staff has access to the data.

Thus the study attracts both publicly held companies and large privately held organizations that are extremely sensitive about use of their data.

Steering Committee   To assure that Project 777 is highly responsive to its members' needs, the MCS staff works closely with members of the steering committee. The members represent a variety of size, geographic, and industrial interests and assist in the planning of survey modifications, organize the annual all-participant meeting, and review applications of potential members.

Data Collecting Process   Each participant receives a coded data collection form and instructions. The form is reproduced for as many organizational units as will be reported.

The upper portion of the form, shown in Figure 1, gathers information as to the unit's organization level, sales, employment, and industry. On the lower portion, space is provided for reporting specific compensation information on executives matched in any of the 34 functions.

Each item of incoming data is then edited manually, compared with the previous year's submission, and run through a series of computer checks. Where doubt exists regarding the actual compensation data or the job match, the respondent is contacted by telephone.

Presentation of Results   Two formats are used—tabular and graphic. Each displays the results according to organizational level, size, industry, and form of compensation.

FIGURE 1   Data Collection Form—Project 777

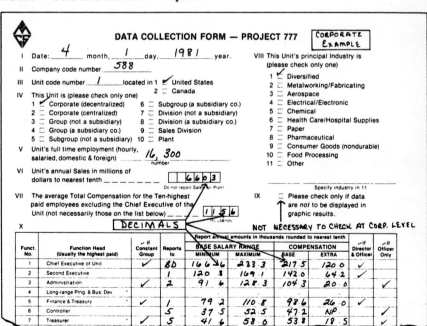

The tabular report (shown in Figure 2) presents average compensation data—for base salary, as of April 1, most recent short-term incentive payments, total compensation, and base-salary ranges—bracketed for various company sizes. If the use of averages is acceptable and there are adequate data within the bracket, the tabular report—a very concise, easily understood method of data presentation—can be used.

If more precision is required and there is a need to reflect data from all organizations, large and small, the graphic presentation should be used. The graphic report (shown in Figure 3) is based on the statistical technique known as regression analysis, or "least-squares." If a strong correlation exists between an independent variable (sales) and a dependent variable (pay), the value of the dependent variable can be predicted from the value of the independent variable. This enables a compensation value to be obtained for any included sales volume. Moreover, the compensation value will be based on all the data, not just the cases within a certain bracket. The tabular and graphic formats both have advantages and serve as supplements to one another.

Data Base   As mentioned earlier, 392 companies, including over half of the Fortune 500, reported data on over 37,000 executives in the United States and Canada in 1981. The surveyed executives are organized in 34 position levels at the corporate, group, subgroup, division, and plant levels. Data are broken down for the following industries: diversified, metalworking and fabricating, aerospace, electrical and electronic, chemical, health care and hospital supplies, paper, pharmaceutical, consumer goods, and food processing.

All-Participant Meeting   A unique feature of Project 777 is the annual all-participant meeting. Topics discussed include an analysis of the study results, prevailing compensation practices and trends, and ideas for improving the study. The meetings provide an excellent opportunity for representatives from participating companies to share experiences, ideas, and problems concerning executive compensation. Together with the steering committee meetings, the all-participant meetings assure that Project 777 remains reponsive to participants' needs.

OPTIONAL REPORTS

Statistical Supplement   As participants become more sophisticated in their data analysis, their needs for additional statistical information increase. The information contained in the statistical supplement includes measures of dispersion, coefficients of correlation, and formulas for calculating the regression value. Many participants find it more useful and much more precise to calculate the regression value on their own, rather than simply to read it from a graph.

The supplement also outlines the methodology of calculating percentiles around the regression curve and provides the information necessary for this calculation. Only a rudimentary understanding of statistics and an inexpensive desk-top calculator are required.

FIGURE 2 Tabular Report

U.S. Group Comb.	Sales in Millions				Chief Executive							Consolidated Industries	
								****Earnings in Thousands****					
							*******All****	****Bonus Eligible*******					
Sales					*Nonbonus* Eligible				***Bonus Paid***				
From—	To	No. Cos.	Avg. Sales	Avg. No. Emp.	No.	Avg. Base	No.	Avg. Base	No.	Avg. Total Comp.	% TC of Base	Avg. Total Comp. All	
16.0	31.9	10	23.3	570									
32.0	63.9	27	45.0	796									
64.0	127.9	58	93.2	1634									
128.0	255.9	82	193.8	3093									
256.0	511.9	91	367.8	5507									
512.0	999.9	80	707.3	9757									
1000.0	1999.9	48	1319.3	17260									
2000.0	3999.9	16	2569.1	28447									
4000.0	7999.9	6	5837.2	41974									
8000.0	and over	3	12600.5	104608									

FIGURE 3   **Graphic Report of Group Chief Executives**

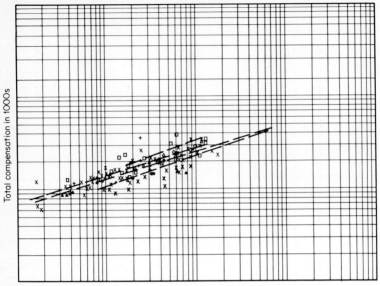

Sales volume — millions/billions

Multifactor Analysis and Multiple Regression Analysis These two optional reports are refinements to the regression analysis utilized in the base study.

Compensation specialists have long realized that many of the variables that are used to measure company size and performance could also be used to predict compensation. The most widely recognized of these variables are sales and number of employees. There are, however, numerous situations in which a company might like to focus on additional factors.

The *multifactor analysis* extends the regression analysis beyond sales and number of employees and takes into account a total of 14 size and performance measures. This report is a result of a series of simple, one-to-one regressions between compensation and each financial measure. The user has the flexibility of working with only those factors that are viewed as important in the company's environment.

In the *multiple regression report* a combination of size and performance measures are taken into account simultaneously. The resulting compensation prediction is the most accurate one possible, given today's state of the art. This report yields the highest correlation and therefore also yields a greater explained variance than simple regression.

During the more than 10 years of research involved in this report, we have experimented with a number of alternative variables and methodologies. We have settled on a method using the same six measures in each equation and holding them constant from year to year. This approach provides the stability and consistency necessary to enable users to apply this powerful statistical technique to their own situations. The measures include three size measures—sales, assets, and number of employees—and three performance measures—one-year return on sales, assets, and capital.

Because data on the factors utilized in these reports are readily available only at the corporate level, they do not extend to lower organizational levels.

Special Studies While Project 777 is able to meet the needs of many large manufacturing companies through its basic design, it cannot address all the compensation problems that arise in each and every participating company. However, because the data base is large and easily manipulated, many companies have found that specific compensation questions can be answered through tailor-made special studies. Provided the confidentiality of the individual data can be preserved, companies can custom-design their own survey.

These studies often take the form of a limited sample of companies, frequently 15 to 30, based on characteristics such as size, industry, geography, or performance criteria. (A minimum of ten companies is required to protect the confidentiality of the data.) Often these studies will be limited to one to two organization levels and perhaps five to ten positions; however, any information included in the data base can be tapped. For example, a study could involve only corporate finance and treasury executives who are also directors of their own firms. Another situation might call for information on division chief executives who report directly to the corporate chief operating officer. Still another example might involve an analysis of administration executives who have responsibility for both legal and industrial relations. There are endless possibilities, and these studies are often the most cost-efficient and readily accessible way of obtaining data.

OTHER MCS STUDIES

Middle Management This study, which began in 1974 and, as of 1981, has 189 participants, provides compensation data on management positions below the level covered in Project 777.

The basic study is very similar to Project 777 in terms of design and major concepts.

Retail, Engineering and Construction, Travel and Transportation Studies These three studies provide compensation data on top executives in these industries in a fashion very similar to the way Project 777 provides data on executives in manufacturing. As with the middle-management study, they are modeled after Project 777. Each study has its own criteria for membership, and its own steering committee and all-participant meeting. The measures of magnitude vary by industry, and the organization-level definitions, of course, are tailored to the needs of the specific industry.

A complete summary of 1981 MCS studies is shown in Figure 4.

FIGURE 4 Capabilities Summary

Name of study	Type of study	For	Participating companies	Membership fee	Application due	Data due	Results shipped
Project 777	Executive compensation survey	Manufacturers with sales over $100 million	392	$1050 Optional statistical supplement—$200	March 1	April 6	July 15
Multiple regression & multifactor analysis	Analysis of executive compensation using 14 financial measures in simple regression (MA) or 6 measures in multiple regression (MR)	Project 777 participants	—	MA—$300 MR—$400 BOTH—$600	—	—	September 1
Executive perquisite study	Biennial survey of executive perquisite practices and policies	Manufacturing, retailing, banking, insurance, utilities	125	$375	October 1	November 1	December 15
International study	Executive compensation in 45 countries; Nationals, TCN's & expatriates	Industrials with operations outside their home country	167	$250 1st country then $100 each with maximum of $800	April 15	May 22	August 1
International executive perquisite study	Biennial survey of executive perquisite practices & policies in 28 countries	Industrials with operations outside their home country	41	$500	August 15	October 15	December 15
Middle management study	Management positions below the level covered in Project 777	Industrials with sales over $25 million	189	$700 Optional statistical supplement—$150	May 15	July 1	September 15
Field sales study	Sales and sales management compensation	Industrials with own field sales force	114 (411 Sales units)	$400	July 1	August 1	October 15

Study	Description	Coverage	No.	Price			
Long-term incentive study	Biennial survey of long-term incentive plans	Industrials & retailers	50	$700	November 1	December 1	February 1
Retail study	Executive, merchandise management & buyer compensation	Retail industry	56	$850 Optional statistical supplement—$150	June 15	July 15	September 1
Engineering & construction study	Executive & project management compensation	Firms engaged in the engineering and/or construction of industrial properties	23	$850	June 15	July 15	September 15
National engr. const. salary survey	Engineering, drafting, scheduling, estimating & purchasing compensation	Firms engaged in the engineering of industrial properties	16	$1,350	—	July 1	August 15
Houston engr. constr. salary survey	Semi-annual survey of engineering, drafting, scheduling, estimating & purchasing compensation	HECSS members	16	$550	—	February 1 July 1	March 16 September 1
NCA survey	Non-manual salaried positions	National constructors association members	28	$400	July 15	August 15	October 15
AAMA study	Executive & middle management compensation	American apparel manufacturers association members	42	Established by AAMA	April 1	May 1	July 1
PICA I PICA II	Executive, management & professional positions from CEO to sales reps.	Paper industry compensation association members	15 12	$1,200 $1,250	—	May 1	June
Transportation/ travel industry study	Executive & middle management compensation	Firms in the transportation, travel & hospitality industries	22	$900	November 1	December 4	January 22

SOURCE: Management Compensation Services 1981.

Acquiring Competitive Information from Surveys:
An Empirical Approach

Kenneth E. Foster

DIRECTOR, COMPENSATION PLANNING, TOWERS, PERRIN,
FORSTER & CROSBY, NEW YORK, NEW YORK

Because internal job measures have no intrinsic dollar value, salary surveys are indispensable to an effective compensation program. Companies are compelled to look outside their own organizations to obtain salary information. With external data so important, surveys must be carefully planned and conducted to provide meaningful, comprehensive, and timely information at the lowest possible cost.

CHARACTERISTICS OF A GOOD SURVEY

An organization planning to conduct a survey must first make a number of key determinations: What is the survey's purpose? What information do we need to obtain? From whom will we obtain it? What jobs will we survey? How will we ensure job comparability? And, of course, the survey methodology must be decided upon.

In addition—and this is a must if survey results are to be used wisely—the organization should plan to measure the effectiveness of the methodology. Otherwise, it will not know how much of the reported pay variation can be attributed to the compensable factors used to match jobs or explain differences in pay. One way to gauge this relationship is to correlate actual pay rates with adjusted or competitive rates, based on the compensable factors employed.

The correlation coefficient indicates how actual and adjusted rates relate. By squaring the coefficient, the organization can tell how much of the variation in actual rates of pay is attributable to the factors used to match jobs or otherwise explain pay differences among survey participants.[1] Without such a process, it is virtually impossible to evaluate survey results.

IMPORTANCE OF JOB COMPARABILITY

Job comparability is the single most important aspect of a reliable survey; in fact, the survey's credibility is directly proportional to the level of comparability attained. But determining comparability is a difficult task, especially for positions that have the same job titles but are seldom alike in different organizations. Middle-management and executive positions are good examples.

Because the specific duties and responsibilities of management positions vary greatly, some type of job evaluation process must be used to equate such positions across companies. Most prevailing processes have several drawbacks. The evaluations they produce are inherently subjective, time-consuming, and costly, and because of the volatility of job configurations at management levels, they must be repeated each time the survey is conducted.

Fortunately, there is an alternative that establishes job comparability by using a combination of objective, quantitative compensable factors and computer-based analytical techniques. It also indicates how well the matching process works, so that participants always know the degree of comparability attained.

Naturally, other factors influence survey results. Perhaps the most obvious is the survey sample—the participating organizations. Their selection is important from three standpoints: size, industry, and pay policy. Management views survey results more favorably if the participants are of comparable size, in the same industry, and have similar pay policies.

These factors play an important role in obtaining accurate data. Surprisingly, many surveys seriously miscalculate this role. Some surveys, for example, concentrate on controlling for company size at the expense of attaining job comparability. Others stress comparability but neglect size or industry differences. Surveys seldom deal effectively with all these considerations at the same time.

To illustrate the need to do so, let us take a look at the impact of job comparability and of company size, industry, and pay policy on survey results. Our methodology will focus on salary range midpoints and total cash compensation (base salary plus annual bonus) as they relate to managerial and executive posi-

---

[1]If the correlation coefficient (r) equals 1.0, the square of r also equals 1.0, showing that the compensable factors account for all (or 100 percent) of the differences in pay, and actual rates are the same as adjusted rates. But if r equals .70, the square of r equals .49, indicating that only 49 percent of the differences in pay can be accounted for by survey factors. A survey that explains 90 percent of the reported differences in pay can be used with much more confidence than one that explains, say, 40 percent of the variance.

tions. We will call this methodology a "job evaluation plan," although it is not job evaluation as traditionally defined. It does not review the worth of jobs to the organization but takes for granted that reported salary range midpoints reflect the true internal worth of positions.

JVI CONCEPT

Our job evaluation plan is simply a quantitative technique to compare and match the relative ranking of positions, across organizations, on a standardized basis. How is this job evaluation plan constructed? For ease of illustration, we will ignore job incumbent characteristics in our example.

In step one, we convert the salary range midpoints reported by each survey participant to relative job value points. The conversions are done mathematically on an organization-by-organization basis, and the resulting points are called the job value index (JVI). By converting dollar values to points, we eliminate the effects of differences in pay among organizations and establish which positions have the same relative value within their respective organizations.

In other words, we are separating the job evaluation process from the job pricing process. This is important because, as already noted, how much a position is actually paid is influenced by factors other than job value—organization size, for instance. In determining relative job value, the influence of these other factors must be excluded.

Technically, the JVI reflects how many standard deviations (a statistical measure of dispersion around the mean) a given midpoint is from the arithmetic average, or mean, of the salary range midpoint distribution. Because salary range structures vary greatly, their means and standard deviations also vary. But from organization to organization, positions that vary uniformly from the mean of their salary range structures—say, one standard deviation above— have exactly the same relative value within their respective firms. This is true even if the actual salary range midpoint for the position is $60,000 in one company, $80,000 in another, and $100,000 in a third.

HOW THE PLAN IS DEVELOPED

After all relative job values have been calculated, we must determine which combination of quantitative compensable factor proxies (Table 1) best explains why, from one organization to another, the JVI of the same position—say, the vice president of marketing—varies. This is accomplished with the aid of a computer and a statistical process called "multiple regression analysis."

Multiple regression analysis allows us to correlate compensable factor proxies with actual JVI points. The results of a few such correlations are shown in Table 2.[2] Clearly, some of the proxies there are strongly related to JVI points.

---

[2]Although these correlations are derived from one particular set of companies, they are typical of those found among companies in general.

TABLE 1   Some Basic Compensable Factors and Their Quantitative Proxies

Compensable factors	Quantitative proxies
Job content	
Job importance and impact	Reporting level
	Board of directors membership
	Officer status
	Job code (primary duties and responsibilities)
	Unit level (corporate, group, division, plant)
	Bonus eligibility
Accountability	Number of exempt employees supervised
	Number of nonexempts supervised
	Total number of employees supervised
	Number of managerial levels reporting to the position
	International responsibility
	Unit size
Incumbent*	
Training and experience	Education
	Age
	Length of service
	Time in position
Performance	Bonus receiver

*The compensable factor proxies pertaining to the incumbent are not used in salary range midpoint evaluation models.

TABLE 2   Relationship Between Selected Compensable Factor Proxies and Salary Range Midpoint JVIs

Compensable factor	Correlation
Job code	.93
Number of managerial levels reporting	.75
Log of the number of exempts supervised	.72
Member of corporate board of directors	.69
Log of reporting level	.68
Unit	.30
International responsibility	.30
Log of unit sales	.29

Job code, for example, correlates .93 with JVI, and the number of managerial levels reporting to a supervisor correlates .75.[3]

Starting with the compensable factor that correlates most highly with actual JVI, the computer develops an equation or model that estimates actual JVI points based upon this single factor. The computer then builds a second equa-

---

[3]The reader should be aware that a number of these factors overlap (or correlate with) one another in varying degrees. Therefore, once one factor is held constant, the correlation of the remaining factors with JVI will change. Some of these second-order correlations increase; others decrease.

tion, retaining the first factor, but adding a second factor that, along with it, will most improve the accuracy of JVI estimates.[4] The computer continues to add factors to the JVI equation until the addition of another factor no longer improves the accuracy of the estimates.

Finally, the computer produces an intercompany job evaluation equation that looks something like this:[5]

> Estimated JVI points (for salary range midpoints) =
> .731 × job code of position
> + .108 × log of unit sales of position
> + 12.456 × log of the number of exempt employees supervised by position
> + 150.123 (if incumbent is corporate director)
> + 20.246 (if incumbent has international responsibility)
> + 3.257 × log of reporting level of position
> + 210.834 (constant)

That this process works exceedingly well is evident from Figure 1, which shows a scatterplot of estimated JVIs versus actual JVIs for 1400 cases. Data for these cases were supplied by 14 companies in the same industry. The scatterplot

---

[4]The regression coefficient for the first factor will be different in equation two.

[5]This is an illustrative equation only. The actual model typically contains 15 to 20 compensable factors, depending upon the sample size and other considerations.

FIGURE 1   Scatterplot of Estimated Evaluation Points versus Actual Evaluation Points—14 Companies in the Same Industry

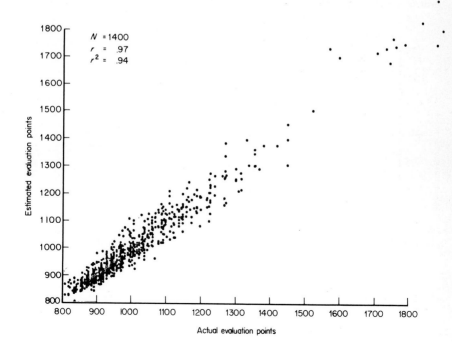

reveals a very close correspondence ($r = .97$) between predicted or estimated JVIs and actual JVIs, indicating that we can place a great deal of confidence in relative job values attained through this process.[6] Interrater reliabilities of trained evaluators using the same job evaluation plan seldom, if ever, achieve this degree of consistency.

The correspondence between actual and predicted JVIs will often be even closer within one company. Figure 2 illustrates this. There the correlation between actual and estimated JVIs is .99.

Because job evaluation points, whether actual or estimated, have no intrinsic dollar value, dollar amounts for the points must be obtained by comparing the pay of jobs of like relative value. There are several ways of doing this.

POINTS VERSUS DOLLARS

One way of determining the average dollar value of JVI points is to "regress" actual dollars against them. Regression analysis provides a trendline that relates points to dollars. We developed such a trendline between the salary range midpoints and JVI points of more than 24,000 managers and executives

---

[6]These findings also support the appropriateness of the methodology used to construct actual JVIs. If the actual JVIs were improperly developed, they could not be simulated with such accuracy.

FIGURE 2   Scatterplot of Estimated Evaluation Points versus Actual Evaluation Points—One Company

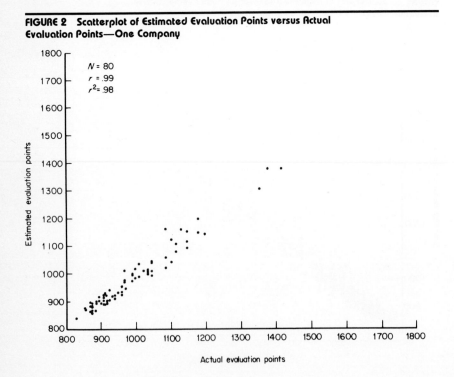

Actual evaluation points

in Towers, Perrin, Forster & Crosby's (TPF&C's) Compensation Data Bank (CDB). This group represents more than 350 organizations. Figure 3 shows the results of the analysis.

The figure indicates a strong relationship between points and dollars—despite the fact that diverse pay policies are represented. The correlation is .82, meaning that 67 percent (r squared) of the variance in salary range midpoints can be attributed to differences in relative job value.

So relative job value explains about two-thirds of the variance. What about the one-third that remains? To what can we attribute that?

POINTS VERSUS DOLLARS AND SIZE

Further analyzing the CDB organizations, we found a great disparity in company size. The smallest firm reported annual sales of less than $20 million; the largest, $60 billion. The overall mean was $3.4 billion; the overall median, $1.6 billion.

To study the effects of company size on pay, we broke out two groups from the total sample: companies with sales of less than $200 million (Small Group) and companies with sales of more than $6 billion (Large Group). We then repeated the analysis, relating JVI points to salary range midpoints in each group. Figure 4 shows the results.

FIGURE 3   Relationship of Salary Range Midpoints to Relative Job Value Points (JVI)—Total Survey

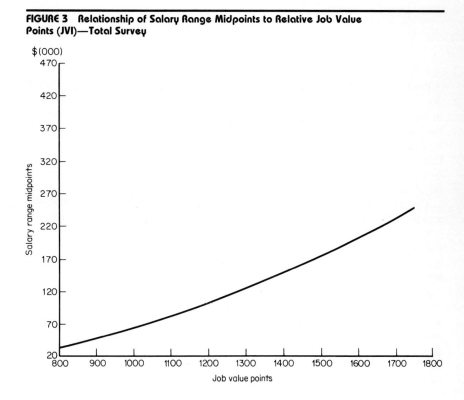

FIGURE 4   Relationship of Salary Range Midpoints to Relative Job Value Points (JVI)—Small versus Large Companies

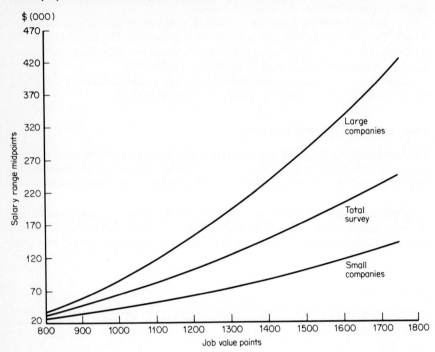

For the Small Group, the correlation between points and dollars increased to .93, meaning that relative job value accounted for 86 percent of the difference in midpoint dollars—a 28 percent improvement over the 67 percent figure for the total sample. For the Large Group, the relationship between midpoint dollars and JVI points was even stronger—r equaled .95. Thus among organizations in this group, JVI points accounted for 90 percent (.95 squared) of the differences in salary range midpoints—an improvement of 34 percent over the comparable figure for the total sample.

The relationship between size and pay—for clearly such a relationship exists—is a positive one. Large firms tend to pay more than small firms for jobs of equal relative value. If this tendency is not taken into account when conducting a salary survey, comparisons with smaller organizations will result in underestimates of market rates and comparisons with larger ones will have the opposite effect.

Differences in pay among small and large organizations are even more pronounced among highly paid positions. In the Small Group, for example, the average midpoint is $140,600 for a job with 1750 JVI points (typically the chief executive officer). This is 43 percent less than the total sample average of $245,600 for 1750 points. The average for an 800-point job (typically a general foreman level of position) in the Small Group is $26,600, which is only 17 percent under the overall survey average for such a job. On the other hand, in the

Large Group, a 1750-point job averages $423,200—72 percent above the overall survey average—and an 800-point job averages $35,900—12 percent more than the total survey average.

POINTS VERSUS DOLLARS AND INDUSTRY

To study the effects of industry on survey results,[7] we correlated the JVI points and salary range midpoints of 1080 managers and executives in 14 large food companies. The correlation coefficient equaled .98. Thus JVI points accounted for 97 percent of the midpoint differences.

Because these were all large food companies (median sales of $3 billion), the high correlation stems from the fact that relative job value, type of industry, and organization size have been, in part, simultaneously controlled. To some extent, the effects of business results have also been controlled because all 14 companies had similar business results during the preceding fiscal year.

POINTS VERSUS DOLLARS AND PAY POLICY

To illustrate the impact of pay policy on survey results, we analyzed the relationship between JVI points and salary range midpoints for 1190 managers and executives in 13 large organizations with similar pay policies. Each of the 13 sought to pay substantially more than general industry averages. They ranged in size from about $1 billion to more than $20 billion in annual sales, and were engaged in such businesses as communications and the manufacture of business equipment, of consumer products, of diversified products, and of pharmaceutical products. They were above-average performers in terms of return on sales and return on equity.

In spite of the wide dispersion in size and business, the correlation between JVI points and salary range midpoints was .96, meaning that the evaluation explained 92 percent of the variance in midpoint dollars. This is slightly better than the 90 percent explained among all firms in the Large Group.

When we analyzed the relationship between evaluation points and total cash compensation in these 13 high-paying companies, the correlation was a phenomenal .99. Thus we could attribute 98 percent of the differences in total cash compensation among the 1190 executives to differences in relative value points. By contrast, among the Large Group, only 89 percent of the differences in total cash compensation could be so attributed.

CONTROLLING FOR JOB COMPARABILITY AND ORGANIZATIONAL FACTORS

Thus far, we have illustrated the extreme importance of job comparability in conducting salary surveys. We have demonstrated how comparability can be attained by an objective, quantitative methodology. And we have shown that relative job value is only one determinant of actual pay. Such organizational

---

[7]As companies become more and more diversified, such comparisons will become increasingly difficult to make on a meaningful, corporatewide basis.

factors as size, industry, and pay policy also have a substantial impact on pay. Therefore, both job comparability and organizational factors must be taken into account by the survey process. How can this be done?

An obvious way of controlling for organizational factors is through the selection of survey participants. For example, to control for size, industry, or pay policy, you survey only those firms that meet your criteria for these factors. As long as enough firms that meet these standards are available, a meaningful survey is possible. But survey participants that meet all the desired selection criteria often cannot be found. Even if enough companies are found, adequate samples for certain key jobs may not be available. Consequently, the survey methodology must be able to control for organizational factors among disparate companies.

To ensure adequate samples for key jobs, some surveys incorporate pay data for a particular job title from organizations of different sizes. Then to control for size differences, pay data are regressed against annual sales or some other size measure. Unfortunately, this approach fails to take differences in job content into account. Because jobs with the same title frequently differ significantly from one organization to another, it is not unusual to find that organizational size accounts for no more than 50 percent of reported pay differences among similarly titled positions.

This single regression approach can control for industry or pay policy differences by segmenting the data base by industry category or pay policy and regressing pay against appropriate size measures. Still, it cannot simultaneously control for differences in job content or business results among the companies. Moreover, for single regressions to be meaningful, at least 25 cases are necessary. The participant population would therefore have to be very large to ensure adequate job samples for regression analysis after the population is divided into particular groups.

AN EMPIRICAL APPROACH

TPF&C has developed a methodology that surmounts these difficulties. Our approach takes job content and organizational factors into account simultaneously. In addition, it is more effective than conventional methodologies in controlling for industry and pay policy through participant selection. This is because it can produce accurate results from small job samples. Therefore, survey participants can be segmented by industry or pay policy and, in most cases, still provide reliable, high-quality data.

Under this TPF&C approach, relative job value (as determined by each survey participant), company size, and corporate business results are taken into account simultaneously using multiple regression analysis. This process generates an equation or pay model that typically looks something like this:

Log of pay (base salary, total compensation, or midpoint) =
.1125 × log of corporate sales
+   .0005 × return on stockholder equity
+   .0683 × evaluation points
+ 10.253 (constant)

When positions are simulated through this model, it produces highly accurate estimates of actual pay. For example, we developed a model that accounted for 98 percent of the differences among approximately 3600 salary midpoints reported by 42 organizations with annual sales of more than $6 billion. This is a significant improvement over the 90 percent variance that we were able to explain by job value alone among the Large Group of CDB participants. Errors in midpoint estimates derived from our composite model are about 50 percent less than errors in estimates based on the single-factor JVI model.

Such results are more than adequate if each survey participant is willing to accept the relative position evaluations of the other participants. Few are willing to do so. Most organizations want to be sure that survey results are based upon comparable jobs.

To ensure comparability, we reevaluate each position using the empirically derived job evaluation plan described earlier. If our evaluation produces a different index for a given position, we substitute this figure for the original evaluation index in the pay model. The resulting market estimate indicates what other organizations exactly *like* yours would pay for a position exactly *like* yours.

WHAT PARTICIPANTS GET

In addition to raw data summary tables, bonus practice data, and other information, TPF&C CDB participants receive an "Incumbent Comparison Table" for each position they submit, providing there are at least five cases in the relevant job code. Figure 5 shows the information that the Incumbent Comparison Table provides.

These tables permit CDB participants to see how their individual positions compare with general industry patterns. In the lower right-hand corner of Figure 5, for example, the actual and estimated JVI points for the XYZ Company position are shown for base salary, total compensation, and salary range midpoint. Toward the bottom of the "Mean" column, the average evaluation rankings (actual JVIs) for the 102 cases in this job code are shown. The consensus industry evaluations for this position are 1275, 1289, and 1289 JVI points, respectively, for base salary, total compensation, and salary range midpoint.

All three of the actual JVI points (1290, 1314, and 1303) for the XYZ Company position exceed the corresponding survey averages but not the corresponding estimated JVI points (1356, 1364 and 1396). In fact, the actual JVIs for this position are, respectively, 5, 4 and 7 percent below the estimated values.

The estimated JVIs were generated by the three job "evaluation" models (base salary, total compensation, and salary range midpoint) developed from the data submitted by all the companies in this sales group ($1 to $3 billion in annual sales). Using the information listed in the "Your Data" column for the XYZ position (Reporting level, Number of management levels reporting, etc.), this position was simulated through these evaluation models to produce the estimated job evaluation points.

XYZ's position came out with more than the average amount of evaluation points because it is a bigger job than the average reported position of multiprofit

FIGURE 5 Incumbent Comparison Table—XYZ Company

POSITION TITLE:	Multiprofit Center Head	JOB CODE 0101	NUMBER OF CASES: 102

SALARY, SCOPE, & INCUMBENT INFORMATION

	YOUR DATA	25th	Mean	Median	75th	YOUR GOING RATES	% DIF
Base salary	$144,000	$106,921	$132,606	$125,000	$151,250	$142,500	1
Bonus	$70,380	$38,250	$60,089	$54,750	$73,575		
Total comp	$214,380	$152,292	$192,695	$180,925	$225,160	$215,000	0
Midpoint (N = 87)	$147,920	$107,800	$137,014	$130,430	$153,200	$145,500	2
Reporting level	3	3	3	3	2		
No. of management levels reporting	8	5	6	6	7		
Unit level	2	2	2	2	2		
Unit size (in $ millions)	557	206	512	435	689		
No. of exempts supervised	3281	433	1873	1237	2405		
No. of nonexempts supervised	8309	1748	5982	4586	7814		
Total no. employees supervised	11590	2439	7855	6198	10605		
Age	57	48	53	53	57		
Years of company service	42	12	21	22	30		
Years in position	8	2	5	4	6		
Education	Some college	B.A.	M.A.	B.A.	M.A.		

	YOUR DATA	25th	Mean	Median	75th	ACTUAL JVI POINTS	ESTIMATED JVI POINTS	DIF
Base JVI	1290	1189	1275	1268	1373	1290	1356	−5
Comp JVI	1314	1206	1289	1293	1363	1314	1364	−4
Mid JVI	1303	1216	1289	1298	1362	1303	1396	−7

Board/officer status

YOUR DATA	MEMBER OF PARENT BOARD (%)	MEMBER OF SUBSIDIARY BOARD (%)	CORPORATE OFFICER (%)
PARENT BOARD	26	13	49

International responsibility

YOUR DATA	FULL (%)	PART (%)	NONE (%)
FULL-TIME	13	59	28

Bonus eligibility

YOUR DATA	ELIGIBLE (%)	RECEIVED (%)
BONUS ELIGIBLE	100	98

center head. The XYZ position, for example, has 8 levels of subordinate managers versus a survey average of 6; it manages a unit with sales of $557 million versus a survey average of $512 million; it supervises 3281 exempt employees versus a survey average of 1873, and it supervises a total of 11,590 employees versus a survey average of 7855.

Figure 5 also shows that both the XYZ position and its incumbent are paid more than the survey average—which is quite appropriate in view of the position's higher estimated evaluations. In the upper right-hand corner are the market rates for XYZ's position based on the evaluated points. XYZ's actual pay rates are all within 2 percent of these estimated market rates.

SUMMARY AND CONCLUSIONS

Job comparability is the sine qua non of an effective salary survey. We have shown how high levels of comparability can be attained by using an empirical methodology that is less time-consuming and more cost-effective than other job-matching approaches. And because pay is influenced by organizational factors that are completely unrelated to job size or content, these factors must also be taken into account when determining appropriate pay levels. The multiple regression approach that we have described enables an organization to do this successfully.

Noncash Compensation

chapter 43

Types of Noncash Compensation

Herbert F. Crehan

PARTNER, THE HAY GROUP, BOSTON, MASSACHUSETTS

NONCASH COMPENSATION

The term "noncash compensation" has really only achieved common usage within the human resource vocabulary during the last decade. Previously, the definition "fringe benefits" was commonly used to describe employee benefit plans, personnel policies, and the myriad of other special programs. As these types of programs continued to grow in breadth and depth, it became clear that this form of remuneration is anything but a "borderline activity." With noncash compensation values commonly ranging in worth between 30 and 50 percent of cash compensation, this area is certainly within the mainstream of total remuneration planning and strategy.

In its broadest sense, noncash compensation could be defined to represent all the elements of the total remuneration package which are not considered to be a form of cash compensation. This would seem to eliminate only base salary, annual incentives or bonuses, and other special forms of cash payments. However, in order to provide a focus for this chapter and to allow for important details, the balance of this discussion is generally limited to plans and programs that apply to a majority of the employee population. While executive capital accumulation plans are described briefly, this specialized area is afforded detailed treatment elsewhere in this handbook.

HISTORY

While formalized noncash programs in the United States first appeared early in the twentieth century, informal practices have existed since the very first employer-employee relationships. Examples of gratuitous payments to the survivors of a deceased employee, severance awards to superannuated employees, and special treatment of disabled employees are well documented for U.S. industry in the nineteenth century. However, these practices were rare in occurrence, totally unilateral on the part of the employer, and generally of a modest amount.

A number of pace-setting employers adopted formalized noncash programs in the early 1900s. These included American Express and Montgomery Ward among others. Several states, most notably Wisconsin and New York, also pioneered in providing employee assistance programs through state-sponsored programs.

The large growth in noncash programs during the latter part of the first half of this century was largely influenced by government action. Examples of governmental impact include:

1. The enactment of the Social Security Act in 1935 providing old-age benefits, widow's income, and death benefits
2. The World War II wage freeze which motivated employers to adopt employee benefit plans in lieu of wage increases
3. Escalating graduated federal income taxes which made it attractive to add tax-exempt plans and policies

The next significant factor in the growth of noncash compensation was the National Labor Relations Board (NLRB) ruling in the *Inland Steel* case in 1948. In this case, the NLRB ruled that employee welfare plans were negotiable items for purposes of collective bargaining. From that point to the present, organized labor has played a significant role in the evolution of noncash compensation programs.

Over the years, the most important element in the expansion of noncash compensation has probably been the initiation of new programs by progressive employers. Employers who maintain aggressive noncash programs generally cite the following reasons:

1. *The Competitive Edge.* Providing a competitive noncash package gives them an advantage in attracting and retaining key employees.
2. *Tax Efficiency.* A dollar expended on a tax-sheltered benefit provides the employee with the full value of the dollar while the same dollar expenditure in cash provides only a partial dollar after payment of income tax.
3. *Enhanced Employee Security and Morale.* When employees feel that their employer has provided a measure of protection from the economic insecurities of death, disability, health care expenses, and superannuation, their morale is increased and their anxiety is reduced.
4. *Management Efficiency.* When uniform plans and programs are in place and understood by employees, management does not have to expend time deciding policy on a case-by-case basis.

TABLE 1   Average Values of Employer-Paid Benefits

Annual base salary, $	473 industrial companies, %	162 financial companies, %
10,000	54.5	54.2
20,000	43.7	44.4
30,000	40.6	42.7
50,000	35.9	38.5
70,000	33.4	35.8
100,000	32.0	34.8

NONCASH COMPENSATION VALUES

In any general discussion of noncash compensation, at some point the issue of the value of the package expressed as a percentage of cash compensation is bound to arise. In most cases, the comparative figures used are developed by dividing the employer's noncash compensation costs by the employer's cash compensation expenses. Depending upon the conventions adopted, the plans included, and a number of other factors, the result of this calculation may produce a percentage ranging from the low teens to over 60 percent of cash compensation! The results vary so greatly for a number of reasons:

1. An employer's demographics, e.g., young average age and short service versus higher average age and long service, greatly influences plan costs.
2. Costs are also influenced by the employer's purchasing skill, and sheer volume may produce economies of scale.
3. Some comparisons will include the costs of statutory plans, while others may exclude them.
4. Some calculations exclude time-off with pay programs (e.g., holidays and vacations), while others include them, and still others adjust the numerator and denominator for these programs.
5. Some approaches include every conceivable form of noncash, while others are limited to the principal programs.

The problems cited above have created a trend toward benefit-modeling techniques that eliminate the biases of cost comparisons. Using this approach, "typical" cost factors (or average values) are developed and applied to the actual benefit levels of employee programs in order to produce comparable results. An example of this is the Hay/Huggins Benefit Value Technology which is applied annually to our data base. Table 1 illustrates the effects of the application of this methodology based on the 1981 Hay/Huggins Noncash Compensation Comparison.This approach is extremely useful in defining competitive position, identifying internal equity issues, and developing program revisions to respond to strategic objectives.

SOCIAL SECURITY: THE FOUNDATION

When social security was enacted by Congress in 1935, the system was intended to ensure a basic level of income for retired workers. Over the past four and a half decades the program has been expanded again and again by vote of Congress. The following is only a partial listing of the additions over the years:

1950   Expansion of coverage to include an additional 10 million workers
1954   Compulsory coverage of most self-employed persons
1961   Provision for early retirement as early as age 62
1965   Introduction of medicare
1973   Maximum taxable wage base first surpasses $10,000 (i.e., $10,800)
1978   General benefit increases tied to consumer price index
1984   Expansion of coverage to include federal government workers and all employees of nonprofit organizations

At the same time that the scope of the program has been extended, social security contribution requirements have increased dramatically. In 1937, the first year the social security tax was assessed, employers and employees were required to contribute 1 percent of annual compensation up to $3000, or a maximum of $30 each. By 1983, the contribution had risen to $2391.90 each, 6.7 percent of $35,700. As a result of the Social Security Amendments of 1983, the tax rate is scheduled to reach 7.65 percent by 1990; meanwhile, the maximum taxable wage base will continue to rise annually in proportion to increases in the average wage level.

Social security retirement benefits.   While social security costs and contributions have gone up significantly since the inception of the system, benefit levels have also grown. In 1940—the first year social security benefits were paid—the maximum annual primary benefit payable to a 65-year-old retired worker was $494.40; by 1983, the corresponding amount had increased to $8508.

Full retirement benefits are currently available to qualifying retired workers at age 65. The nature and scope of the program have expanded to the point where these benefits represent a substantial source of retirement income. The following illustrates the estimated level of primary social security benefits payable to a 65-year-old retired worker in 1982 expressed as a percentage of earnings:

$10,000	$15,000	$20,000	$25,000	$30,000
49%	43%	37%	31%	26%

While full retirement benefits are available at age 65, eligible workers may elect to receive reduced retirement benefits as early as age 62. In the case of such an election, the benefit is permanently reduced. The reduction is equal to ⅚ of 1 percent for each month that retirement precedes age 65, or 6⅔ percent for each full year. Conversely, employees who elect to defer retirement and postpone receipt of benefits receive an increase of 3 percent for each year they work beyond age 65, up to age 70.

Social security survivor benefits.   The 1939 amendments to the Social Security Act expanded the program to include income continuation to the survivors of deceased workers. In order to qualify, the deceased worker must have been either fully or currently insured under the social security requirements (depending upon the category of benefit). Survivor benefits are available to a spouse with unmarried dependent children under age 16, children under age 18 (19 for full-time high school students), a spouse age 60 or over, and dependent parents age 62 and over. Benefit levels are directly related to the primary insurance amount of the deceased worker; the maximum total benefit payable to all survivors is roughly equal to 175 percent of the primary insurance amount.

Social security disability benefits.   The 1956 amendments to the Social Security Act added disability benefits for workers age 50 or over; in 1960, the minimum age requirement was eliminated. Payments are related to the primary insurance amount earned by the disabled worker, and additional payments are available on behalf of the spouse and dependent children. The maximum family disability benefit may not exceed 150 percent of the primary insurance amount.

Social security health and medical services.   Through medicare, social security also provides important health and medical benefits for persons age 65 or over, certain disabled persons, and those afflicted with specific chronic illnesses. Medicare coverage includes two categories: Part A for hospitalization benefits and Part B for supplemental medical insurance. Special rules under the Tax Equity and Fiscal Responsibility Act of 1982 govern the payment of medicare benefits to workers age 65 through 69 who are also covered by employer-provided health plans. Ordinarily, the employer plan must be the primary provider and medicare the supplementary provider for such workers.

Response to economic and demographic trends.   Economic trends and demographics in the last decade have brought on a funding crisis for social security. These events have included inflation (with prices rising faster than wages), unemployment, and a growing ratio of retired workers to active workers. The Social Security Amendments of 1983 include both short- and long-term measures to keep the old-age, survivors, and disability insurance programs solvent. For example, the amendments provide that starting at the turn of the century the age for full retirement benefits will gradually rise, eventually reaching 67 for those born in 1960 or later. In 1990, the benefit increase for deferred retirement will begin to go up from its current level of 3 percent per year to 8 percent in 2008, giving an added incentive to postpone retirement. However, revisions will still be needed in the *medicare* program before the end of the current decade, to keep *it* solvent.

Further changes to social security are inevitable in the coming years, as the system responds to the shifting age mix of our population and the ongoing public policy debate on the appropriate level and extent of social insurance programs.

EMPLOYER-SPONSORED EMPLOYEE BENEFIT PLANS

As previously stated, the value of the employer-provided noncash compensation package typically falls in a range of 30 to 50 percent of cash compensation, including the employer contribution toward social security. The following discussion provides an overview of the private plans included in a noncash compensation program.

Health Care Programs   Health care benefits have expanded significantly over the past 50 years. The original health insurance plans provided limited hospital and surgical benefits. During the 1950s, they were enhanced to cover additional medical benefits through the vehicle of the major medical plan. During the past decade, the alternative health delivery system of the health maintenance organization grew substantially. In addition, dental care plans have moved rapidly toward status as a standard benefit, and esoteric programs such as vision care have achieved limited acceptance.

Hospital and surgical benefits. Hospital and surgical benefits are covered under the basic medical plan. The earliest hospital and surgical plans required payment of a deductible before benefits commenced, and then the plan reimbursed a portion (e.g., 80 percent) of the covered expense. Over time, typical practice shifted toward first dollar coverage and full payment of the covered expense based on a fixed dollar amount or a "usual and customary" standard. More recently, the distinctions between these two approaches have blurred as employers have selectively reintroduced deductibles and limited coinsurance. At this point, hospital and surgical plans are almost universally available to employees. Usually hospital room and board coverage ranges from 120 days to 365 days or more, and surgical fees are covered on a usual and customary basis. Cost sharing arrangements between the employer and employee vary widely, but the most common approach is to provide employee coverage on a noncontributory basis and to require employees to pay a portion of the additional premium for dependent coverage. While hospital and surgical benefits have been traditionally insured under group contracts, including Blue Cross and Blue Shield, more and more employers are instituting self-insurance and other combination funding vehicles.

Major medical benefits. This type of plan is typically superimposed on the basic plan, i.e., it picks up specific medical expenses over and above hospital and surgical charges. Usually, the participant must satisfy an annual deductible (e.g., $100) before benefits are available, and there is a maximum annual family deductible (e.g., $200). Once the deductible is satisfied, the major medical plan reimburses a portion of the covered expense (commonly 80 percent), although in recent years the trend is towards 100 percent coverage once major medical expenses reach a certain level, e.g., $5000. Major medical maximums are generally stated in terms of lifetime amounts, and coverage has grown to the extent that $250,000 limits (with possible reinstatement provisions) are the rule rather than the exception.

Health maintenance organizations (HMOs). The concept of HMOs is to place an emphasis on preventive care. While the traditional health care program reimburses participants when they are ill, HMOs attempt to reduce medical expenses by encouraging regular examinations and identifying medical problems early on. The pioneer in this area is generally recognized as the Kaiser Permanente Plan which introduced the HMO approach on the West Coast in the 1940s. In 1974, the U.S. government attempted to facilitate the expansion of HMOs by making federal funds available to "qualified" HMOs. In addition, this legislation required employers to make qualified HMOs available to employees as an alternative to the tradtional health care plan. As a result of this government action and a general change in societal attitudes toward health care delivery, the number of HMOs and the amount of employee participation have grown dramatically during the last decade.

Dental care plans. This coverage has probably enjoyed the most dramatic growth of any employee benefit plans in history. In 1976, one-third of the participants in the Hay/Huggins Noncash Compensation Comparison reported a dental plan; by 1981, this proportion had more than doubled to 69 percent. This tremendous growth is largely attributable to the following factors:

1. Early dental plans were plagued by overutilization and antiselection. As experience emerged, plan design techniques became more sophisticated and cost-efficient.

2. Labor unions placed the addition of dental benefits high on their list of demands.

3. Employers recognized dental plans as a tax-efficient means of providing additional remuneration dollars and enhancing their competitive standing.

The typical dental plan is characterized by deductibles and coinsurance with coverage levels structured for specific treatments. Annual benefits are generally restricted (e.g., $1000), and more sophisticated procedures such as orthodontics are limited or not covered. The vast majority of dental plans provide employee participation on a noncontributory basis while dependent cost sharing is evenly split between noncontributory and employee sharing in contributions. Most dental plans are insured but many include elements of self-insurance.

Other health care plans.   A minority of employers have adopted additional health care programs such as vision care and prescription drug plans. However, these types of plans are generally seen as outside the mainstream of classic health care hazards, and their future growth is likely to be modest.

Disability Income Programs   Plans to provide continuing income to disabled employees have evolved over time both to provide employees with enhanced security and to provide employers with a systematic means of dealing with this issue. Pay for absence attributable to occupational hazards is covered under workers' compensation laws and five states have mandated short-term disability benefits for workers. The occasional employee absence is generally treated by employer policy, while the formal programs described below apply to more lengthy spells of absence.

Accident and sickness (A&S) plans.   This type of program is most common for the nonexempt employee population. Benefits typically commence on the first day of absence for accident and on the eighth day of illness. A&S plans usually provide a continuing percentage of salary (e.g., 50 to 70 percent) up to a limited weekly maximum amount, e.g., $150 to $200. The maximum duration is generally 26 weeks, which coincides with eligibility for long-term disability benefits. Most A&S plans are noncontributory, and the typical plan is funded through an insurance contract.

Short-term disability (STD) plans.   This type of program is most often provided to the exempt population, and it generally applies to periods beyond the casual absence. Most STD plans provide benefits based on the length of service of the employee; payments are often at full or partial (e.g., 50 to 70 percent of salary) pay for a specific number of weeks based on service. Most employees with a meaningful length of service are fully protected during the waiting period for long-term disability benefits. Virtually all STD plans are noncontributory and they are self-insured.

Long-term disability (LTD) plans.   LTD plans became a standard element of the noncash package during the 1970s. Prior to that time absences of a longer duration were handled under the pension plan or by ad hoc employer decisions. LTD benefits are generally available after six months of a disability which prevents an employee from performing the duties of his or her own job for the first two years and the duties of any job for which the employee is "reasonably suited" thereafter. Benefits are expressed as a percentage of pay (e.g., 60 percent), and since social security disability benefits are substantial, nearly all LTD plans are integrated with (offset by) social security benefits. Monthly maximum LTD benefits vary widely; a representative range would be $2500 to $3000 per month. LTD plans are most often noncontributory, but a substantial minority of plans require employee contributions. A majority of plans are fully insured, but there is a trend toward consideration of self-insurance for at least a portion of the benefits.

Other disability provisions. Disability benefits are generally provided under a number of other employee benefit plans. For example, the pension plan may provide accrued benefits for long-term disabilities, but more often there will be a provision for continued service credits for periods of disability. Profit sharing and thrift plans usually have a disability provision, and group life insurance is most often continued in full for disabilities before age 60. Many employers also continue health care benefits during periods of long-term disability.

Death Benefit Programs Death benefits are provided under a number of employer-sponsored employee benefit plans. The primary objectives for these benefits are to provide funds for final expenses and to provide a source of continuing income for survivors. Secondary objectives include providing estate liquidity and estate creation itself. Most basic death benefit programs only partially address these secondary objectives.

Group life insurance. The principle vehicle for employee death benefits is the group life insurance program. In most cases the amounts of group life insurance are related to employee earnings, although nonexempt employees are often covered by flat dollar amounts, e.g., $5000 to $10,000. Earnings-related plans are expressed as a multiple of earnings (e.g., 2 times annual base salary) either by a schedule of salary brackets or as a direct product, often being rounded to an even multiple of $500 or $1000. One design consideration is the fact that death benefit needs vary considerably from one employee to another: factors include age, marital status, number and ages of dependents, etc. An additional consideration is that group life insurance amounts in excess of $50,000 result in imputed income for federal tax purposes under Section 79 of the Internal Revenue Code. One approach is to provide basic group life (e.g., 1 or 2 times earnings) on a noncontributory basis and optional supplemental group life (e.g., 1, 2, or more times earnings) on an employee-pay-all basis. Benefits are usually funded by the group term life arrangement of an insurance contract which is partially experience-rated and partially "pooled."

Accidental death and dismemberment (AD&D) insurance. Most employers sponsor AD&D insurance which pays the full face amount in the event of death due to accidental means and a portion of the face amount for dismemberment through accident. Usually AD&D coverage is a component of the group life program (basic and sometimes supplemental group life), and it is equal to the principal amount of group life insurance (although a lower maximum amount may apply). AD&D is funded under a group insurance contract and experience is invariably pooled.

Survivor income plans. This type of program provides continuing income over a period of time rather than a lump-sum payment. Typically, the surviving spouse receives a percentage (e.g., 20 to 25 percent) of the worker's earnings before death, and additional amounts (e.g., 10 percent of earnings before death) are payable on behalf of dependent children. Benefits continue for a limited term (e.g., remarriage, attainment of age 19 by children), and total benefits may not exceed a stated percentage and maximum monthly amount, e.g., 40 percent of earnings and $2000 per month. While often discussed, this type of program is provided only by a minority of employers. Funding is either under a group insurance contract or a 501(c)(9) trust, and cost sharing varies from noncontributory to fully contributory.

Business travel accident (BTA). A majority of employers provide BTA insurance for employees traveling on company business. Principal amounts are usually substantial (e.g., $100,000 or more), and coverage is either a flat amount or a multiple of earnings, e.g., 5 times base salary.

Other death benefit provisions. Death benefits are available through a number of other company programs. For example, some companies provide dependent life insurance plans covering the spouse and dependent children, while others make available employee-pay-all plans such as personal accident insurance. Other potential sources of death benefits include the pension plan, profit sharing or thrift plan, and in some cases the LTD plan. Social security survivor benefits represent a substantial source of income, but this program is seldom directly reflected in the employer-provided death benefit program.

Retirement Programs Employer-provided retirement benefits represent the most complex, the most highly regulated, and generally the most expensive element of the noncash package. Most larger employers provide a basic retirement plan which is generally a pension ("defined benefit") plan *and* a supplemental ("defined contribution") plan such as an employees' thrift plan or a qualified profit sharing plan. Complexities arise because these plans must conform with a host of governmental regulations and provide reports to a variety of regulatory agencies (IRS, Department of Labor, etc.) as well as to plan participants.

Pension plans. Pension plans are maintained by a majority of employers, to provide a defined level of benefit at retirement age. The defined level of benefit is generally expressed as a percentage of earnings near to retirement, e.g., 5 highest years of earnings during the 10 years preceding retirement. The percentage of earnings is generally related to the employees' years of service, e.g., 50 percent of final average earnings for 30 years of service or 1⅔ percent of final average earnings for each year of service. Private pension plans are generally "integrated" with social security retirement benefits, since the latter represent a substantial source of income and a significant employer expense. The two primary methods of integration are the direct offset (e.g., 50 percent of final average earnings *minus* 50 percent of primary social security) and the indirect method (e.g., 30 percent of final average earnings *plus* 20 percent of final average earnings in excess of the average social security wage base). The age for full normal retirement benefits is usually 65 although employees cannot be retired involuntarily due to age prior to 70 (with the exception of certain highly compensated executives).

Pension plans typically include a number of other features in addition to normal retirement benefits. For example, a majority of plans allow for retirement benefits prior to normal retirement. A common early retirement provision would define eligibility as age 55 with 10 or more years of credited service; the accrued benefit payable early would be "actuarially" reduced (or partially reduced by a company-subsidized factor) to reflect the fact that it starts sooner and is likely to be paid over a longer period. Another important provision is "vesting," or the nonforfeitable right to an accrued pension. The Employee Retirement Income Security Act (ERISA) introduced three alternative vesting requirements, one of which must be provided by a "qualified" pension plan. Most employers elected a vesting provision requiring 10 years of credited service; as a practical matter, the IRS sometimes requires a more liberal vesting schedule before it will issue an advance determination letter which encompasses the vesting provision. Finally, ERISA introduced important requirements regarding death benefits for surviving spouses of plan participants. First, participants who have been married for at least one year at retirement must have their benefit converted to the joint and 50 percent survivor annuity option form of payment (the participant may elect another form of payment but otherwise the joint and 50 percent survivor option is automatic). Further, employees who are otherwise eligible for early retirement must be given the opportunity to make an election (at their expense unless the employer chooses to pay the cost) which will cause the joint and 50 percent survivor option to operate as if they had elected it the day before death: this provides the spouse with continuing income in case the participant dies prior to retiring. Investment of the pension plan assets is an important issue, and banks, insurance companies, and other investment managers compete vigorously for these funds.

Qualified profit sharing plans.   Some employers use this type of plan as their primary vehicle for retirement income, but a majority of qualified profit sharing plans serve as a supplement to a pension plan. These plans are generally subject to the same requirements as qualified pension plans with the important exception of the minimum funding requirements. The absence of a minimum annual contribution accounts for a large part of profit sharing's appeal: if profits warrant, a contribution is made; if not, no funds are contributed. A majority of profit sharing plans include a profit-related formula which determines the annual contribution, but a sizable minority leave this totally to the discretion of the board of directors of the company. Typically, employees are eligible to participate after one year of service, and the annual contribution (if any) is credited in direct proportion to the compensation of the participants (e.g., $100,000 contribution, $1,000,000 in participant compensation: each participant's account is credited with an amount equal to 10 percent of compensation). Vesting must comply with one of the ERISA requirements, and as a general rule it tends to be more liberal than pension plan vesting. Member accounts are usually invested through the vehicle of a trust fund, and in many cases employees may allocate their accounts among alternative investment funds. Benefits are paid at termination (or subsequent retirement age), but accounts are often fairly accessible during employment, for hardship or other reasons. Profit sharing plans are almost never contributory, but a great number allow voluntary employee contributions.

Employee thrift plans.   Next to dental benefits, the fastest-growing employee benefit in recent years has been the thrift plan. Reasons cited include its responsiveness to differing employee needs, its straightforward nature, and its low (relatively) cost. A qualified thrift plan is also subject to extensive rules and regulations, e.g., eligibility, vesting, etc. In its most straightforward form employees with one year of service may elect to join by contributing an amount of salary between the minimum (typically 2 percent of salary) and the maximum (usually 6 percent of salary). In turn, the employer matches the employee contribution with some proportion of contribution, most often $0.50 for each employee $1. The employee and employer accounts are invested (like a profit sharing plan) and fund balances are payable at termination. In general, however, account balances are even more accessible than profit sharing funds while the employee is still actively employed. An increasingly popular version of the thrift plan is financed by elective *pretax* exclusions from employee pay rather than aftertax payroll deductions.

Employee stock ownership plans (ESOPs), Tax Reduction Act stock ownership plans (TRASOPs), and payroll-based TRASOPs (PAYSOPs). An ESOP in its simplest form is a profit sharing plan with participant accounts invested principally or entirely in the stock of the employer. A "leveraged" ESOP extends this concept to include a loan by a third party. The company guarantees the loan and makes tax deductible contributions to the trust which are used in part to amortize the loan. A variation on this approach is the TRASOP, which is funded through tax credits over and above the normal investment tax credit. TRASOPs have appealed mainly to capital-intensive organizations. However, tax credits for ESOPs are being changed from an investment basis to a payroll basis for 1983 through 1987 and are then scheduled to cease.

Unfunded retirement plans. ERISA established limitations on the maximum annual benefits payable under qualified pension plans and the maximum annual additions to qualified defined contribution plans. In addition, ERISA contained explicit conditions for the establishment of unfunded, supplemental retirement benefits for groups of "highly compensated executives." These two provisions have motivated a growing number of employers to adopt unfunded, supplemental retirement arrangements to cover senior executives. In many cases, these plans simply make up the difference between the ERISA maximum and the plan benefit otherwise payable, but other employers are extending these arrangements to attract executives in midcareer and to otherwise enrich the basic retirement program.

Other retirement programs. Employers utilize a number of other programs to supplement retirement income, including stock purchase plans and stock bonus plans. Programs such as retiree health care coverage and retiree group life insurance provide additional retirement benefits. Finally, the Economic Recovery Tax Act (ERTA), including provisions dealing with tax-deductible employee retirement contributions and employer tax credits for ESOPs, will undoubtedly influence future retirement planning.

Time-Off with Pay Programs   Changing employee demographics and societal pressures for more leisure time have caused many changes in time-off with pay programs. All indications are that this trend will continue throughout the 1980s.

Holidays. Perhaps more than any other noncash program, holidays are extremely sensitive to regional differentials. For example, a majority of companies in the south provide fewer than 10 holidays, while a majority of companies in the northeast provide more than 10 holidays. In addition, a growing number of employers provide one or more "floating" holidays (or "personal days"); most often employees may elect to use these additional holidays on the day of their choice.

Vacations. Over time, vacation schedules have become more and more liberal. In almost every case, the number of weeks of vacation is related to service with the company. For the exempt employee population, three weeks of vacation after five years of service now approximates typical practice. A number of employers have extended their vacation schedules to include a fifth or even a sixth week of vacation for truly long-service employees.

Other time-off with pay programs. Employee sabbaticals are an often discussed but seldom introduced program which may receive further attention in the future. The concept of flexible work schedules may simply reallocate rather than reduce the workweek, but it certainly responds to changing employee needs. Additional programs cover jury duty, military commitments, and bereavement leave with pay.

Executive Noncash Programs   A number of noncash programs are applicable to the executive classification. These plans respond to the facts that (1) the basic noncash package is focused on the general employee population and (2) high marginal income tax rates apply to this group. Examples of executive noncash compensation include financial counseling, physical examinations, and company-provided automobiles. A program which allows executives to defer compensation which would otherwise be payable currently may be considered as an element of noncash compensation. Executive stock options and other capital-oriented plans are covered elsewhere in this handbook.

Cafeteria Approach   The clear trend during the 1980s will be toward more flexible noncash compensation program offerings. The traditional program has been designed around the male breadwinner with a dependent wife and children. In 1982 this profile fit only 15 percent of the U.S. work force. As a result, many noncash programs fail to respond the needs of the participants, and employees are often covered by plans they neither want nor need.

The ultimate response to changing demographics and divergent needs is a cafeteria compensation (or flexible benefit) program. In its purest form, employees literally study a "menu" of different benefits and select the combination that matches their needs. The end result is a tailor-made program for each employee. To ensure some measure of protection, a core of benefits (statutory benefits and basic coverages) is usually provided.

While in theory the cafeteria arrangement offers the best of all possible worlds, there are of course some obstacles to overcome. One potential problem is the cost-increasing effect of antiselection, i.e., employees selecting only those benefits they are likely to use. Another issue is the mammoth task of simply keeping track of all the employee selections. Still another concern is the absolute requirement to communicate all the choices to all the employees effectively. Despite these difficulties, a number of progressive employers have successfully implemented cafeteria compensation programs.

A variation on the theme of cafeteria compensation is the noncash compensation program which offers a maximum number of choices within the framework of the traditional noncash program. Many employers offer multiple health plan options, several levels and kinds of death benefit plans, and various capital accumulation options. In addition to maximizing the various options available, these companies communicate extensively and intensively. By taking this approach, it is possible to achieve many of the advantages of a cafeteria plan with less complexity. In any event, the trend toward more flexible noncash programs is irrefutable and irreversible.

Other Noncash Compensation Programs   We could compile a very long list of noncash compensation programs *not* discussed in this chapter. It would include such important programs as tuition reimbursement, subsidized cafeterias, credit unions, day-care facilities, and company products. In all likelihood the eighties will produce an array of new programs. Noncash compensation design seems limited only by the imagination of its practitioners, the funds available to finance the plans, and the inhibiting effect of government regulations.

SUMMARY

Noncash compensation will continue to increase in value and expand in scope during the decade of the eighties. Skilled managers and human resource professionals will thoughtfully integrate noncash programs within total remuneration planning. Plans must be properly related to employee needs, cost efficiency achieved, tax efficiency maximized, and plans effectively communicated to employees. Noncash compensation has truly outgrown the fringe category.

chapter 44

Benefits as Part of Total Remuneration

Michael F. Carter

VICE PRESIDENT, HAY/HUGGINS, PHILADELPHIA,
PENNSYLVANIA

Kenneth P. Shapiro

PARTNER,THE HAY GROUP, AND GENERAL MANAGER,
HAY/HUGGINS

In the first half of this century, employee compensation consisted primarily of "cash"—wages, salary, and bonuses—modestly supplemented by "fringe" benefits. Since World War II, however, employee benefits have increased significantly, moving from the "fringe" to the "fabric" of employee compensation.

Today, the average U.S. employer spends an additional 30 percent of payroll on benefits such as pensions; health, disability, and life insurance; thrift, profit sharing, and stock plans; and mandated benefits (social security, workers' compensation, and unemployment compensation). Morever, paid time off (vacations, holidays, and sick leave)—representing 10 percent of payroll costs—brings the total benefit expenditure of the average employer to 40 percent of payroll.

Despite the size of this expenditure, management generally has not actively planned or managed benefits programs but, instead, has reacted to current trends and practices. Reasons for this reactive approach include:

- The gradual nature of the increase in benefits over the years
- Constant changes in legislation and regulations

- Inflation
- Social security changes
- Pressure from unions
- The low priority that benefits traditionally have held in relation to other compensation elements

However, due to the growing size of benefits in the total remuneration package; differing employee needs; benefit program complexity; and legal, tax, and competitiveness issues, it is now clear that benefit planning must be not only thoughtful but *proactive*.

THE PLANNING CYCLE

Benefit planning, like most planning, should not be a one-time exercise, but rather an ongoing process. The steps in that process are illustrated in Figure 1 and discussed in detail in the remainder of this chapter.

Because of the cost of benefits, and the importance of business strategy and management style in the total renumeration planning process, remuneration planning should be conducted by senior management as a group, rather than by benefit and compensation specialists alone. Such a committee approach should ensure that the organization's goals and strategies are supported by an effective remuneration program and that the program will be attractive to, and suitable for, the kinds of employees that are best for the organization. A "right" program will reinforce the objectives of the organization.

Determining Strategy   To be most effective, benefit planning should be conducted as a part of a total remuneration program—base salary, incentives, benefits, executive perquisites, and intangible rewards. The ultimate goal of a total remuneration program is to attract, retain, and motivate employees to fulfill the organization's goals and objectives. Attracting and retaining the *right kind of people* is aided by developing a total remuneration program with a mix of compensation elements that best fits the organization. Determining the "best mix" is a step-by-step process that starts with an analysis of the organization's business cycle and business type and includes primary consideration of management style (as demonstrated in Figure 2).

FIGURE 1   The Benefits Planning Cycle

FIGURE 2   The Process of Determining Total Remuneration Strategy

Business cycle and business type

Business strategy

Management style

Total remuneration strategy

Examples of how to best match the total remuneration mix with the organization's style and characteristics are shown in Figure 3. For instance, an industrial company with a competitive product in a growing market would be in a developing business cycle and therefore would probably have a strategy of investment and growth. An appropriate management style could be entrepreneurial, requiring dynamic risk-taking individuals. An appropriate total remuneration mix under these circumstances would be a lower level of benefits and a higher level of cash compensation—particularly incentive compensation. The

FIGURE 3   Orienting Compensation Mix to Organizational Style

| Type of Organization | Working Climate | Reward Management Components | | | |
| | | Cash | | Noncash | |
		Base Salary	Short-Term Incentives	Level	Characteristics
Developing industrial	Growth, creativity	Medium	High	Low	Short-term-oriented
Mature industrial	Balanced	Medium	Medium	Medium	Balanced
Conservative financial	Security	Low	Low	High	Long-term, security-oriented
Nonprofit	Societal impact, personal fulfillment	Low	None	Low–medium	Long-term, security-oriented
Sales	Growth, freedom to act	Low	High	Low	Short-term-oriented

SOURCE: *Hay/Huggins Bulletin,* December 1980.

benefits provided could be short-term-oriented, stressing medical and dental coverage and time off.

In contrast, a conservative financial organization would have very different business characteristics and, thus, would be best served by a different total remuneration mix. Business strategy here, which might be controlled growth coupled with protection of assets, would generate a conservative management style and require security-oriented individuals. The total remuneration package in this kind of organization might stress benefits rather than cash compensation. In particular, it would probably be appropriate to have a limit on cash incentives or to avoid them altogether. The benefits provided could be long-term and security-oriented, emphasizing retirement income and "protection" coverages such as life and disability insurance.

Finally, in determining the total remuneration strategy, management must consider developing different programs for different businesses and employee types within the total organization. For example, the total remuneration mix is often different for sales positions than for other jobs in the company.

Setting Objectives   Once strategies are set, specific objectives should be developed. A checklist of major benefit-objective issues is shown in Figure 4.

One primary objective concerns *competitive position*. The organization's desired competitive compensation position is a result of its total remuneration mix (as determined in the previous step).

Related to competitiveness is benefit *adequacy*. Decisions are made here regarding the desired level of disposable income replacement after retirement, disability, or death; appropriate levels of health insurance; and the level of employees' responsibility in protecting themselves through their own personal savings, individual insurance, premium cost sharing, and/or deductibles and coinsurance.

Flexible benefit programs can be considered in the objective-setting phase. Most companies already offer some modest degree of flexibility by allowing a choice of an insured medical plan or health maintenance organization, a supplemental life insurance or other plan, and other options.

There is a growing awareness that most firms are composed of a divergent employee population of various ages and different marital and dependents sta-

---

FIGURE 4   Checklist of Benefit Objective Issues

- Competitive position
- Adequacy
- Flexible benefits
- Funding
- Cost containment
- General plan design
  —Early or late retirement
  —Benefit comparability for different employee groups
  —Benefit taxation

tus. These employees, therefore, have very different benefit needs. To better address these needs, and thereby achieve greater employee satisfaction and awareness, additional forms of flexible benefits should be considered. One caveat: Although the advantages of flexible benefit programs can be great, setting up administrative and communications procedures can be expensive and very time-consuming.

When setting objectives, management may want to bring employees into the planning process by surveying their benefit preferences and perceptions. Such employee involvement can be very valuable in determining the range of employees' needs and desires. Employee opinions can be used to ensure the company makes changes that provide employees with the benefits they most want and need.

If employee input is desired in the planning process, the most reliable approach is to use a written questionnaire. Wording must ensure that the right questions are asked in the right way. In addition, management must be prepared to respond to issues that employees raise; otherwise, because expectations may have been raised and then not fulfilled, the project will be self-defeating.

Management also must develop objectives about *funding issues.* Certainly all employers want their programs to be effectively funded. There may, however, be a trade-off between lowest cost and administrative convenience. Where cost savings are absolutely critical, the organization should seek the lowest possible cost regardless of administrative difficulties. Where cost savings are not as critical, the organization may want to choose one carrier—or perhaps two—for all coverages, even though the overall cost of this approach may be slightly higher than using separate carriers and trustees for each.

The use of self-insurance should be reviewed during the funding analysis. If used, the appropriate balance of insurance and self-insurance can be determined at that time. A related matter concerns *cost containment.* Deductibles and coinsurance are commonly used to control benefit costs—particularly for health care. Requiring employees to pay part of the premium cost is another way to control benefit costs. An objective that aims to maximize such cost savings may, however, cause a conflict with the desire to provide a competitive plan. Other cost containment approaches include using an effective plan design to avoid overuse or abuse of the plan or encouraging employees to use a less expensive form of medical treatment—such as outpatient services, home care, preventive medicine, and generic drugs.

Finally, there are several *general plan design* objectives that should be addressed. Management must develop an appropriate approach to encouraging or discouraging early, normal, and late retirement. Provisions in pension and other plans can then reinforce the company's retirement orientation.

Another example of a plan design issue is whether to give different benefits to different employee groups. For instance: Should you differentiate between exempt and nonexempt groups; among those in different locations or different divisions; among those in different job groupings; or among those who are in a union and those who are not?

Also important is the degree of tax effectiveness desired. If the firm feels that a goal of total remuneration should be a high degree of tax effectiveness (primarily for higher-paid employees), then more benefits and nontaxable perquisites—rather than incremental cash compensation—could be emphasized.

Program Analysis   After specific objectives have been set, the organization's current benefit program should be reviewed to find out if the plans are consistent with those objectives.

A major step here is to analyze whether the firm's benefit program compares with the average practices of other employers (selected by region, industry, etc.) at a level which is consistent with the firm's objectives. A benefit program includes several major plans (pension, medical, etc.), which in turn consist of dozens of major provisions. Attempting to compare a benefit plan by comparing the individual provisions can be very difficult, while comparing overall benefit programs this way is virtually impossible. In order to make such an overall program comparison, a "bottom-line" approach is necessary.

This is accomplished by comparing an organization's program using an actuarial model that develops "average costs" of providing benefits. Using this approach, all of the provisions can be valued in common terms. For example, a company's pension plan that has a below-average benefit formula could maintain a favorable competitive position because of above-average vesting, cost-of-living adjustments, annuity forms, early retirement subsidies, and other plan provisions.

In addition to helping compare whole benefit programs, this approach also has the advantage of allowing a comparison of *total remuneration*. Because benefits and perquisites are stated in dollar-value terms, they can be added to cash compensation to derive a total cash and noncash compensation position (as illustrated in Figure 5). For example, a company may want to stress security and provide slightly below-average pay, offset by above-average benefits. The

FIGURE 5   Analyzing Total Remuneration

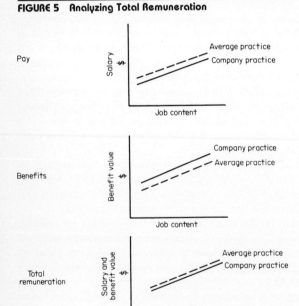

total remuneration-valuing approach would enable this organization to see if its benefits are high enough to offset a less competitive pay position.

The adequacy of benefits can be assessed by determining what percentages of disposable income immediately before retirement, disability, or death, respectively, the program should provide. These target "replacement ratios" can then be compared with the ratios which the firm's pension, death, and disability plans actually provide. For example, a pension plan that provided 35 percent of final pay, with social security providing 20 percent, would result in a combined replacement ratio of 55 percent. This can then be compared with the preretirement disposable income target for a specific age, service, and income level.

When considering a flexible benefit program, a company should conduct an employee benefit preference study to determine (1) whether there is a call for the program and, if so, (2) where the major variations in need and interest occur. Such a study could compare the *perceived value* with the *actual* cost of benefits to determine this firm's "return on benefit investment."

Funding effectiveness can be determined by analyzing the financial characteristics—rates, reserves, retention, and cash flow features—of the existing funding arrangement and then comparing them with the alternatives. Alternative approaches include changing carriers, consolidating coverages, splitting coverage among separate carriers, incorporating cash flow features, and revising to a different degree of self-insurance. Such an analysis is best done by an experienced third party.

The remaining areas of cost containment and plan design can be reviewed through a general benefit study. In such an analysis, the organization's program plan design can be reviewed for consistency with objectives in all areas. Any problem areas can then be reconciled. When the analysis has been completed, desired plan changes may be developed to produce a program which is consistent with the firm's objectives.

Implementation and Communication   Once plan changes are implemented, they should be communicated. However, communications should not be limited to the changes only; communication should be a continuous activity. It should reinforce the idea that benefits are part of a total remuneration package—benefits and pay. Such an approach would present pay and benefits separately—to emphasize their particular characteristics—as well as in total—to emphasize their interrelationship and cumulative effect. Good communication of benefits enhances employee understanding and appreciation; a failure to communicate deprives the employer of full value for the substantial cost of those benefits.

Employee Feedback   As the final step in benefit planning, employee feedback can be either a formal or an informal process. However, like communications, employee feedback must be ongoing—using informal channels, exit interviews, perhaps a question-and-answer column in the house publication, and formal questionnaires every few years.

Feedback is the link that closes the planning chain shown in Figure 1. The planning cycle, however, must be an ongoing process—one that considers the continual changes in the work force, competitive practice, government regulation, tax treatment, the general nature of the individual business, management style, and the content of employee feedback itself.

SUMMARY

Benefits have become an important, an expensive, and a complicated part of an organization's reward system for employees. Benefit planning should, thus, be an ongoing proactive process that is conducted in a total remuneration context. To be oriented to a company's management style and personnel needs, an organization's total remuneration program should be composed of the right mix of elements—including benefits.

chapter 45

Cost of Employee Benefits

Robert H. Selles

CONSULTING ACTUARY, THE HAY GROUP,
SAN FRANCISCO, CALIFORNIA

The purpose of this chapter is to consider the cost of employee compensation, other than cash and deferred cash compensation, from the following points of view:

- Historical perspectives on costs
- Recent trends in new coverages and legislative developments
- Efforts to contain costs

GROWTH OF EMPLOYEE BENEFITS

A retrospective glance at recent trends in benefit costs relative to total payroll reveals that they are no longer a small, insignificant appendage to the wage and salary structure (see Tables 1 to 3). As recently as 1929 the only legally required payments were workers' compensation and government employees' retirement. Vacations and paid holidays were usually limited to office workers, with the one-week vacation common and paid holidays considerably fewer than today. There were no old-age and survivors insurance and unemployment compensation programs. The U.S. Chamber of Commerce estimated that if allowance for time not worked, including vacations, holidays, and sick leave, was included in noncash compensation, then benefits as a percentage of total compensation nationwide would have increased from 3 percent in 1929 to 32.3 per-

TABLE 1   Growth of Employee Benefits, 1929 to 1980

Type of payment	1929	1959	1969	1979	1980
	(Percentage of Wages and Salaries)				
1. Legally required	0.8	4.2	6.6	9.4	9.4
Old-age, survivors, disability, and health insurance (FICA taxes)	0	1.7	3.5	4.8	4.8
Unemployment compensation	0	0.9	0.7	1.2	1.1
Workers' compensation	0.6	0.6	1.0	1.0	0.9
Government employee retirement	0.2	0.8	1.1	2.1	2.3
Other	0	0.2	0.3	0.3	0.3
2. Agreed-upon	0.4	4.2	5.1	8.1	8.3
Pensions	0.2	2.6	2.7	3.6	3.6
Insurance	0.1	1.3	2.1	4.1	4.2
Other	0.1	0.3	0.3	0.4	0.5
3. Rest periods	1.0	3.0	3.3	3.8	3.8
4. Time not worked	0.7	6.6	7.7	9.4	9.9
Vacation	0.3	3.5	3.9	4.8	5.0
Holidays	0.3	2.2	2.7	3.2	3.4
Sick leave	0.1	0.8	0.9	1.2	1.3
Other	0	0.1	0.2	0.2	0.2
5. Bonuses, profit sharing, etc.	0.1	1.0	1.3	1.1	0.9
Total benefit payments	3.0	19.0	24.0	31.8	32.3
	(Billions of Dollars)				
Wages and salaries	50.4	258.2	509.0	1,227.4	1,343.5
Total benefit payments	1.5	49.0	121.0	390.0	435.0

SOURCE: Estimated by Chamber of Commerce of the United States: "Employee Benefits, 1980."

cent in 1980 for all industries combined, including federal, state, and local governments (Table 1).

Note that the data in Table 2 represent a "same company" sample over a 22-year period, whereas the data in Table 3 represent a current sample of 983 employers. The data generally pertain to employees not exempt from the Fair Labor Standards Act and to nonsupervisory employees for certain industries.

COST EFFECTS OF PROGRAM DESIGN: GENERAL CONSIDERATIONS

There are wide differences of opinion regarding just what constitutes fringe benefits and how their cost should be computed. Some employers consider workers' compensation, suggestion awards and shift differentials, overtime premium pay, and similar items to be fringe benefits. Others do not regard total payroll as the correct base in computing fringe benefits but would use straight-time pay for time actually worked. In the 1980 Chamber of Commerce study, sampling 983 companies from all sectors of the economy, fringe benefits, including an allowance for time paid but not worked, amounted to 37.1 percent of cash payroll. However, if the computation base is changed to "straight-time pay for time worked," this percentage is increased to 45.2 percent; if overtime premium pay, shift differentials, holiday pay, production bonuses, and other miscellaneous payroll items are considered fringe benefits, the percentage becomes 50.8.

Also note that, as a result of rising wage rates, fringe benefits as cents per payroll hour and as annual dollars per employee increase far more rapidly than as a percentage of payroll.

Cost Variations by Region and Industry Groups   Table 4 indicates industry and geographic variations in the cost of fringe benefits as percentages of annual payroll. These percentages must be interpreted with caution. In addition to the general level of benefits provided, the age, sex, salary, and service characteristics of employees and the ratio of retired to active employees of a particular company will determine cost. Companies with identical benefit packages may experience substantially different costs as a result of variations in demographics of the groups of employees involved. Also, certain costs, such as those for employee pension plans, may, within limits, be varied from year to year, depending on the rate and level of funding.

To the extent that noncash compensation is designed to improve the efficiency of employees by relieving them, to some degree, of concern over what might happen to themselves and their families in the event of their illness, retirement, or death and to help in attracting and holding capable employees in a competitive labor market, it is necessary to be able to pinpoint the cost of specific benefits aimed at specific individuals or groups to facilitate sound decision making in this area. Benefits must be cost-effective, and costs are very much a function of plan design.

Use of Waiting Periods for Cost Control   To a limited degree the existence of an employee benefit plan that provides some form of compensation against the loss of income through illness, accident, retirement, or death will have a favorable effect on employee morale and on the organization's ability to attract and retain qualified personnel. The rate of employee turnover is usually a function of age and length of service and is usually highest among newly hired, younger employees. A considerable amount of administrative effort can be avoided by the introduction of a "waiting period" before the employee becomes eligible to participate in these plans. Such waiting periods may vary from a few months to a number of years, depending on the plan involved. For instance, it is not unusual to have a requirement of one year of service or the attainment of a certain minimum age, such as 25, for eligibility in a pension plan. On the other hand, group life and medical insurance plans usually have waiting periods of less than six months.

Funding Medium   Any employee benefit plan may be self-funded by the employer or insured by an insurance company. The choice will depend in part on tax considerations but also on the employer's ability to absorb possible fluctuations in annual cost, including substantial claims in any one year. An outside organization is usually better equipped to provide impartial claims administra-

TABLE 2 Comparison of Employee Benefits for 186 Companies, 1959 to 1980

	1959	1961	1963	1965	1967	1969	1971	1973	1975	1977	1979	1980
	All Industries (186 Companies)											
1. As percent of payroll, total	24.7	26.6	27.4	27.7	29.2	31.1	33.1	35.3	37.9	40.0	41.3	41.4
a. Legally required payments (employer's share only)	3.5	4.0	4.5	4.2	4.9	5.3	5.6	6.6	7.0	7.6	8.1	8.1
b. Pension, insurance, and other agreed-upon payments (employer's share only)	8.5	8.9	9.1	9.4	9.7	10.4	11.5	12.2	13.4	14.5	15.1	15.2
c. Paid rest periods, lunch periods, etc.	2.2	2.6	2.6	2.6	2.9	3.1	3.2	3.3	3.8	3.8	3.8	3.8
d. Payments for time not worked	8.4	8.9	9.1	9.3	9.5	10.1	10.6	10.8	11.3	11.6	11.8	11.9
e. Profit sharing payments, bonuses, etc.	2.1	2.2	2.1	2.2	2.2	2.2	2.2	2.4	2.4	2.5	2.5	2.4
2. As cents per payroll hour	62.0	70.8	79.2	85.9	100.6	118.4	141.4	174.0	219.7	260.4	330.6	355.2
3. As dollars per year per employee	1,268	1,461	1,637	1,782	2,084	2,467	2,927	3,640	4,553	5,368	6,871	7,633
	All Manufacturing (73 Companies)											
1. As percent of payroll, total	24.1	25.8	26.7	27.3	29.5	31.4	33.8	36.4	39.5	41.6	42.8	42.9
a. Legally required payments (employer's share only)	4.0	4.5	5.0	4.7	5.4	5.8	6.4	7.4	8.0	8.6	9.1	9.2
b. Pension, insurance, and other agreed-upon payments (employer's												

share only)	7.2	7.4	7.7	8.1	9.0	9.8	11.4	12.5	13.9	14.9	15.4	15.6
c. Paid rest periods, lunch periods, etc.	2.9	3.5	3.5	3.6	3.7	3.9	4.0	4.0	4.2	4.2	4.2	4.1
d. Payments for time not worked	7.3	7.8	8.0	8.4	8.9	9.4	9.9	10.2	10.8	11.2	11.5	11.7
e. Profit sharing payments, bonuses, etc.	2.7	2.6	2.5	2.5	2.5	2.5	2.1	2.3	2.6	2.7	2.6	2.3
2. As cents per payroll hour	60.2	69.0	76.6	83.7	97.0	117.2	142.9	173.6	222.2	265.3	341.2	362.8
3. As dollars per year per employee	1,254	1,435	1,610	1,783	2,072	2,493	3,016	3,711	4,685	5,506	7,210	7,567
All Nonmanufacturing (113 Companies)												
1. As percent of payroll, total	25.2	27.1	27.9	27.9	29.2	31.0	32.5	34.6	37.0	39.1	40.1	40.5
a. Legally required payments (employer's share only)	3.2	3.7	4.2	3.9	4.6	4.9	5.1	6.0	6.4	6.9	7.4	7.5
b. Pension, insurance, and other agreed-upon payments (employer's share only)	9.4	9.9	10.0	10.2	10.2	10.7	11.5	12.1	13.1	14.3	14.8	14.8
c. Paid rest periods, lunch periods, etc.	1.8	2.0	2.0	2.0	2.5	2.7	2.7	2.9	3.5	3.5	3.5	3.5
d. Payments for time not worked	9.2	9.6	9.8	9.8	9.9	10.6	10.9	11.2	11.7	11.9	12.0	12.1
e. Profit sharing payments, bonuses, etc.	1.6	1.9	1.9	2.0	2.0	2.1	2.3	2.4	2.3	2.5	2.4	2.6
2. As cents per payroll hour	63.3	71.9	80.8	87.3	102.1	119.2	140.5	174.4	218.0	257.2	323.8	350.2
3. As dollars per year per employee	1,299	1,479	1,654	1,781	2,093	2,450	2,870	3,596	4,468	5,279	6,653	7,677

SOURCE: Chamber of Commerce of the United States: "Employee Benefits, 1980."

TABLE 3 Employee Benefits, by Type of Benefit, 1980

Type of benefit	Total, all companies	Total, all manu-facturing	Total, all nonmanu-facturing
Total employee benefits as percent of payroll	37.1	38.2	35.9
1. Legally required payments (employer's share only)	8.9	9.9	7.6
a. Old-age, survivors, disability, and health insurance (FICA taxes)	5.8	5.9	5.7
b. Unemployment compensation	1.4	1.7	1.0
c. Workers' compensation (including estimated cost of self-insured)	1.6	2.2	0.9
d. Railroad retirement tax, railroad unemployment and cash sickness insurance, state sickness benefits insurance, etc.†	0.1	0.1	*
2. Pension, insurance, and other agreed-upon payments (employer's share only)	12.6	13.0	12.3
a. Pension plan premiums and payments not covered by insurance-type plan (net)	5.4	4.8	6.1
b. Life insurance premiums; death benefits; hospital, surgical, medical, and major medical insurance premiums, etc. (net)	5.8	6.8	4.7
c. Short-term disability	0.4	0.5	0.2
d. Salary continuation or long-term disability	0.3	0.2	0.3
e. Dental insurance premiums	0.3	0.4	0.3
f. Discounts on goods and services purchased from company by employees	0.1	0.1	0.2
g. Employee meals furnished by company	0.2	0.1	0.3
h. Miscellaneous payments (compensation payments in excess of legal requirements, separation or termination pay allowances, moving expenses, etc.)	0.1	0.1	0.2
3. Paid rest periods, lunch periods, wash-up time, travel time, clothes-change time, etc.	3.5	3.6	3.5
4. Payments for time not worked	9.9	9.5	10.3
a. Paid vacations and payments in lieu of vacation	4.9	5.0	4.8
b. Payments for holidays not worked	3.4	3.5	3.2
c. Paid sick leave	1.3	0.8	1.9
d. Payments for State or National Guard duty; jury, witness, and voting pay allowances; payments for time lost due to death in family or other personal reasons, etc.	0.3	0.2	0.4
5. Other items	2.2	2.2	2.2
a. Profit sharing payments	1.2	1.4	1.1
b. Contributions to employee thrift plans	0.3	0.2	0.4
c. Christmas or other special bonuses, service awards, suggestion awards, etc.	0.4	0.4	0.3
d. Employee education expenditures (tuition refunds, etc.)	0.2	0.1	0.3
e. Special wage payments ordered by courts, payments to union stewards, etc.	0.1	0.1	0.1
Total employee benefits as cents per payroll hour	295.8	306.3	283.7
Total employee benefits as dollars per year per employee	6,084	6,314	5,820

*Less than 0.05%

†Figure shown is considerably less than legal rate, because most reporting companies had only a small proportion of employees covered by tax.

SOURCE: Chamber of Commerce of the United States: "Employee Benefits, 1980."

TABLE 4   Employee Benefits as Percentage of Payroll, by Region and Industry Groups, 1980

Industry group	Total, all regions*	North-east*	East north central*	South-east*	West*
Total, all industries	37.1	39.0	38.7	34.7	35.1
Total, all manufacturing	38.2	40.7	40.1	34.3	34.7
Manufacture of:					
Food, beverages, and tobacco	36.4	44.9	38.0	35.3	33.9
Textile products and apparel	31.9	38.5	33.8	28.5	35.5
Pulp, paper, lumber, and furniture	35.0	35.7	32.8	29.2	42.8
Printing and publishing	35.7	39.3	39.1	32.6	33.4
Chemicals and allied products	43.3	45.8	45.1	44.6	32.1
Petroleum industry	48.0	†	†	49.6	45.6
Rubber, leather, and plastic products	36.7	37.3	37.4	35.8	†
Stone, clay, and glass products	37.8	41.4	37.7	34.3	37.0
Primary metal industries	45.1	48.9	48.1	37.6	†
Fabricated metal products (excluding machinery and transportation equipment)	39.4	41.3	40.3	34.1	32.7
Machinery (excluding electrical)	38.0	38.2	40.4	30.3	35.8
Electrical machinery, equipment, and supplies	36.9	40.1	38.2	29.0	33.9
Transportation equipment	38.8	34.0	43.8	42.2	33.8
Instruments and miscellaneous manufacturing industries	36.4	40.7	33.3	†	30.9
Total, all nonmanufacturing	35.9	36.8	36.5	35.0	35.5
Public utilities (electric, gas, water, telephone, etc.)	41.3	42.5	41.8	40.2	41.5
Department stores	31.3	†	39.5	†	†
Trade (wholesale and other retail)	31.3	27.5	39.1	29.8	26.3
Banks, finance companies, and trust companies	40.3	41.6	40.2	39.8	39.4
Insurance companies	37.6	41.4	35.5	36.2	35.8
Hospitals	29.6	30.4	31.0	26.6	29.2
Miscellaneous nonmanufacturing industries‡	32.7	34.6	30.4	32.0	33.3
Number of companies	983	273	273	208	229

*States in each region are as follows: *northeast:* Connecticut, Maine, Massachusetts, New Hampshire, New Jersey, New York, Pennsylvania, Rhode Island, and Vermont; *east north central:* Illinois, Indiana, Michigan, Ohio, and Wisconsin; *southeast:* Alabama, Arkansas, Delaware, District of Columbia, Florida, Georgia, Kentucky, Louisiana, Maryland, Mississippi, North Carolina, Oklahoma, South Carolina, Tennessee, Texas, Virginia, and West Virginia; and *west:* Alaska, Arizona, California, Colorado, Hawaii, Idaho, Iowa, Kansas, Minnesota, Missouri, Montana, Nebraska, Nevada, New Mexico, North Dakota, Oregon, South Dakota, Utah, Washington, and Wyoming.

†Fewer than three companies reporting.

‡Includes research, engineering, education, government agencies, construction, etc.

SOURCE: Chamber of Commerce of the United States: "Employee Benefits, 1980."

tion and necessary legal, investment, and administrative services and, most important, is in a better position to absorb large deviations from expected claims. Special considerations applicable to pension plans are discussed later.

COST EFFECT OF PROGRAM DESIGN: PENSION PLANS

Since pension plans constitute the most costly fringe benefit for most employers, careful plan design is of great importance in this area. In the case of union-negotiated plans the bargaining is frequently conducted on a "cents-per-hour" basis so that the cost comes first and the benefits are determined later. However, nonunion pension plans have an infinite variety of possible provisions, and it is important for an employer to have some knowledge of the effect of these provisions on costs.

Social Security Integration   One of the chief concerns of pension plan designers is to avoid duplicating social security benefits. Pensions may be integrated with social security benefits in a nondiscriminatory fashion so that the total retirement income, including social security benefits, bears a reasonable relationship to actual earnings prior to retirement for all classes of employees. What this relationship should be is a question requiring a decision not only on the level of benefits to be provided but also on how benefits should be allocated between long-service and short-service employees, between those retiring from active service and those retiring after having terminated service, and between newly hired employees and employees who were in service prior to the introduction of the plan.

As previously mentioned, an employer desiring to recognize the substantial benefits and costs of social security in designing a pension plan is confronted with complex and restrictive rules. Even though compliance with these rules becomes increasingly burdensome, the cost of social security to an employer (6.70 percent of the first $35,700 of each employee's earnings in 1983 and scheduled to increase to 7.65 percent by 1990) is great enough to virtually force a private plan to have lower benefits on the first $35,700, or less, of annual earnings than on earnings in excess of the limit.

Normal Retirement Age   The determination of the normal retirement age has a major bearing on the ultimate cost of a pension program, since a change of a single year in the normal retirement age may make a difference of as much as 10 percent in cost. The question will arise as to whether the retirement age is to be mandatory. Federal legislation (Age Discrimination in Employment Act, or ADEA) generally prohibits termination of employment solely on account of age before age 70. Some states extend this protection to virtually all ages. The effect on the company's operations of the loss of key personnel through retirement must be measured against the possible advantage of creating advancement opportunities for younger employees. The same type of question must be resolved with regard to the company's attitude on the subject of early retirement with or without a reduction in benefits.

Employee Contributions   Primarily because of tax considerations, most pension benefits in the United States are funded by employer contributions. Employee contributions come from aftertax dollars, whereas employers receive tax credit for their contributions.

Although employee contributions will automatically reduce an employer's burden in providing a given level of pension benefits, they usually have the complication of being fully refundable—with interest—on termination of service (including death) before retirement. Furthermore, they add significantly to the cost of administering a pension plan, since each employee's contributions must be accounted for individually.

The Economic Recovery Tax Act (ERTA) of 1981 created an opportunity for employees to make voluntary tax deductible contributions to an individual retirement account (IRA) or to a voluntary employee contribution account provided by the employer's pension plan.

Vesting The employer's sense of responsibility to employees terminating service prior to retirement also has a significant impact on cost. The Employee Retirement Income Security Act of 1974 sets minimum vesting standards, generally based on length of service.

A liberal vesting provision would have virtually no additional cost if employee turnover is light. On the other hand, minimum vesting may involve an indirect cost, namely, "labor immobility," the retention of less productive employees and difficulty in acquiring new talent.

Funding Medium The choice of the funding medium is significant from the viewpoint of benefit costs. Funds may be accumulated under a trusteed plan in which the administrator is responsible for managing the invested assets and benefits are paid directly from the fund. Any mortality risk is, therefore, borne by the fund and, indirectly, by the employer. On the other hand, funds may be deposited with an insurer under a variety of pension contracts, including individual policies. Under some of these arrangements the insurer merely plays the role of investment medium, with or without the insurer's guarantee to underwrite mortality and investment losses. Investment performance may be based on the overall performance of the insurer's invested assets or may be based on the performance of a separate account, consisting of pooled assets of similar plans. The latter arrangement often gives the employer the option to choose a blend of various types of securities, consisting primarily of bonds, mortgages, and stocks.

In recent years interest rates increased considerably, in response to a rising tide of inflation and the expectation of continued future inflation. Under these circumstances, employers questioned (1) the extent to which the relatively high yield on investments should be used to reduce employer costs of traditionally fixed postretirement benefits under a pension plan and (2) the extent to which investment performance should be reflected in upgrading pension benefits to offset the erosion of purchasing power of such benefits. A number of equity-linked products and cost-of-living–related annuities have been developed to add to the wide array of options available to the employer in deciding on the design which will meet the objectives of its pension plan.

Administration A pension plan should preferably be designed to minimize the amount of record keeping and to maintain sufficient investment flexibility to optimize the investment return consistent with safety of capital and cash flow requirements. At the same time, the plan should allow the employer some latitude in determining the rate at which funds are accumulated in the light of current business conditions and within the limits prescribed by income tax rules and regulations.

The degree of flexibility in these areas will depend on the funding medium selected by the employer as well as the actuarial cost method. The latter determines the rate at which funds are accumulated to build up the assets required to cover liabilities incurred on account of pension credits for past, current, and future service. Such investment and funding flexibility does not detract from the fact that a pension program is essentially a long-term commitment for which the ultimate cost is determined by plan design, investment return, mortality, administrative expenses, and the characteristics of the employee group, regardless of the amount allocated to the program in any particular fiscal year. The amount contributed in any one year under a qualified plan affects the employer's tax liability for that year, the required contributions for future years, and also the investment earnings on the accumulated fund.

COST EFFECTS OF PROGRAM DESIGN: DISABILITY INSURANCE

There are other benefits, such as short- or long-term disability plans, where the size of the benefit has an effect on claims frequency. As benefits increase in relation to income, both the frequency and the duration of claims will also generally increase. Reduction in the waiting period before benefits commence will have a similar result. It is interesting to note, for instance, that a long-term disability plan with a relatively long waiting period superimposed on a short-term disability plan which provides benefits during that period costs considerably more than a similar long-term disability plan which is not so superimposed.

The criteria for determining disability and the continuation of disability are largely subjective matters influenced by the attitudes of both the company and the employee. Nonetheless, these criteria play an important role in determining the cost of the program and the success of rehabilitating the disabled employee. For a corporation to maintain employee incentive to return to work, disability benefits paid to the employee must be somewhat less than take-home pay after various payroll deductions and must be reduced by disability benefits payable under other salary continuance programs, workers' compensation, social security benefits, and any other benefits to which the employer contributes. The importance of sound administration and claims control is brought out by the fact that there is a correlation between disability claims costs and swings in the economic cycle, which indicates the possibility that disability insurance tends to be transformed into unemployment insurance. To prevent a plan from also being converted into a retirement program, cease disability benefits as such at retirement age (or soon thereafter, as allowed by ADEA). At that time, the pension plan should provide the retirement benefits, which ideally would include credit for the period of disability and hence represent a "full" pension.

Recovery from disability may be encouraged by the inclusion of a rehabilitation provision under which partial benefits are paid when the employee returns to work on a part-time basis.

COST EFFECTS OF PROGRAM DESIGN: GROUP LIFE INSURANCE

One of the oldest forms of supplementary compensation is group life insurance. The traditional form is term insurance, without cash or loan values and without the requirement of evidence of insurability on individual risks. Where coverage is elective, it is necessary to obtain an average cross section of mortality risks. The individual is required to join the plan within a certain time of becoming eligible, provided he or she is then actively at work, and the amount of insurance is usually determined by a fixed schedule, generally salary-related. If the employee wishes to join after the eligibility date, evidence of good health is required. Furthermore, successful operation of a group life plan requires the participation of a minimum number of eligible employees, often set at 75 percent. Employee contributions, if any, must be small enough to attract even the younger employees, with the balance paid by the employer, to prevent a situation in which some employees would prefer to buy individual insurance at lower rates, thus increasing the average cost for the remaining employees. The latter situation would give rise to further dropouts, raising the average cost for remaining employees still further. An "assessment spiral" of this type would destroy the basis of a group life plan.

Inclusion of Pensioners   Costs are increased substantially by the inclusion of pensioners under a group life plan. Recognition should be given to the fact that the need for insurance is generally less after retirement, and benefit amounts should be graded down at or after retirement in order to lessen the impact on the premium rate, which is generally determined each year as a rate per $1000 of insurance in force.

There are a number of alternative methods of providing pensioners' insurance. Pensioners may be excluded from the term-insurance portion of the plan entirely, and the cost of future benefits provided by the employer at retirement through a single lump-sum premium. Another approach is to use employees' contributions during their working years to purchase permanent life insurance that will remain in force after retirement without further premiums. The employer could then buy term insurance equal to the amount by which the total insurance to be provided exceeds the paid-up insurance purchased by the employee.

Disability Benefits under Group Life Plans   One final comment on the effect of plan design on the cost of a group life insurance program concerns the inclusion of disability benefits. Before long-term disability plans gained wide acceptance, it was customary to provide for a monthly disability income under group life policies. This was achieved by providing that upon total and permanent disability the face value of the group life certificate, or a portion thereof, would become payable in fixed, periodic installments. Upon recovery, the unpaid balance would then be reinstated as term insurance. This benefit has proved to be costly and less flexible than those provided by current long-term disability plans with benefits related to earnings and integrated with other benefits. Modern policies usually provide for a one-year or, more commonly, a long-term waiver of premium without any changes in the scheduled amount of insurance, sometimes with reduced benefits after retirement.

COST EFFECTS OF PROGRAM DESIGN: MEDICAL INSURANCE

In recent years we have witnessed rapid increases in the cost of various medical services. This has been due in part to inflation in the cost of goods and services, but it is also a reflection of the introduction of more advanced medical techniques and more intense utilization of medical facilities.

The need for some type of prepaid medical services plan is now as great as ever before. During the last few decades, hospital- or doctor-sponsored and insured medical plans have been expanded widely. In addition, public demand is growing for coverage against all losses, including those of a minor nature which would normally not have a disastrous effect on the individual's budget. To control costs and prevent undue utilization of medical facilities, it has been found desirable to involve the employee in the cost of medical benefits. Such participation may take the form of deductible amounts and limited coinsurance. These features avoid the administrative cost of handling small claims, reduce the frequency of claims, and allow available resources to be channeled to areas of greater need, including coverage for costly procedures or long-term chronic conditions.

Open-ended liability under these plans may be avoided by imposing benefit-year or lifetime-maximum benefits, the latter often with a provision for gradual reinstatement. There are usually also provisions requiring notification and proof of claim within a certain reasonable time after a claim has been incurred. Overlapping coverage under more than one policy has been found to increase claims frequency and should be avoided by a "coordination of benefits" provision.

Various alternative devices have been used in an attempt to reduce costs. These include self-insurance, a combination of self-insurance with a stop-loss insurance arrangement, administrative services only (ASO) provided by an insurer, use of health maintenance organizations (mandatory dual-choice option provided by law), minimum funding with retroactive credits or charges to ease cash flow, use of second opinions before surgery is authorized, and peer review to discourage unnecessary treatment.

RELATIONSHIP BETWEEN WAGE ADJUSTMENTS AND FRINGE COSTS

Designing a supplementary compensation program acceptable to both employer and employees requires careful consideration of a large variety of alternative benefits. Limited resources must be directed into areas where they will be most effective in achieving specific objectives. Many benefits are salary-related. Any revision of salary scales, therefore, involves a change in the cost of noncash compensation beyond the immediate effect on cash payrolls. In the interest of proper financial planning and cost control, the employer must be aware of projected benefit costs and of the accrued and future liabilities arising from current plan revisions and extensions.

chapter 46

Executive Compensation

David J. McLaughlin

NATIONAL DIRECTOR AND GENERAL MANAGER,
STRATEGIC COMPENSATION SERVICES, THE HAY GROUP,
PHILADELPHIA, PENNSYLVANIA

Ever since there have been organizations, special compensation arrangements have been used to attract, retain, and motivate top management. Military organizations provided some of the early models. For example, Julius Caesar, who is credited with creating the professional army, pioneered one of the world's first formal pay systems—with his centurians and generals paid at successively higher levels of denari. Men at these ranks also received special bonuses and perquisites.

The modern organization has followed this tradition. As the corporation evolved in the United Kingdom and, particularly, in this country, organizations began to create incentive schemes for the emerging professional management cadre. The large industrial companies of the 1920s (Bethlehem Steel, Du Pont, General Motors, and General Electric) created special executive compensation programs for their top management class. These early programs were relatively simple. In addition to a base salary, there usually were an annual bonus and some special arrangements to acquire stock.

Executive compensation, as we know it today, got a big boost in 1934 when the Securities and Exchange Commission (SEC) required public corporations to publish pay data and other information each year. Before then, the details of executive pay had been rather secretive. The SEC disclosure requirements created the first data base for "executive" surveys, a phenomenon that has mushroomed to literally hundreds of surveys over the years.

During this same period, the number of ways in which executives have been compensated has also multiplied. Like most things in our late-twentieth-century society, the tendency has been toward greater complexity—in this case, in both the form and the timing of executive pay. Take, for example, that early tool of executive compensation, the stock option. Stock options evolved from an isolated and unusual technique, through a period when there was broad use of a specific type of plan (the restricted stock option, circa 1950 to 1964), to a multifaceted combination of plans (described under the umbrella heading "long-term incentive") in the 1970s. Today there are an almost infinite number of plan combinations.

The chief executive, the corporate board member, or, for that matter, the individual executive who wants to develop a basic perspective on this somewhat arcane field called "executive compensation" faces three broad questions:

- *What is included in executive compensation in today's corporation?* What are the elements of top management pay? How prevalent are the various plans, and what are they worth in the total package?
- *What are the characteristics of executive compensation programs?* What makes these programs different from broader employee compensation schemes, and what "forces of change" does one need to understand?
- *How should the corporation approach the design of the executive pay program?* What guiding principles exist; what planning framework can a company use to develop an effective program when forced to tread through an often bewildering array of plans and plan combinations?

This chapter will address these three issues.

Executive compensation, at a minimum, includes top executives—the chief executive officer (CEO), the chief operating officer (COO), and their immediate staff. Many companies consider their corporate officers as a group to be the core executive population. Others use a broader definition to include the key line executives in each of their divisions or subsidiaries. Most larger companies have at least two and sometimes three levels of executives who participate in progressively more executive compensation (in terms of number and type of plans, levels of reward, and dollar value of the total package).

PROGRAM ELEMENTS

In today's typical corporation, executive compensation programs can be based on 25 or more possible plans. Experts tend to group them into five broad categories:

1. Base salary
2. Bonuses (or annual incentives)
3. Long-term incentive plans
4. Executive benefits
5. Executive perquisites

Table 1 lists common executive compensation programs by category. Most industrial organizations have some type of incentive plan for executives, in addition to benefits and perquisites.

TABLE 1   Typical Executive Compensation Programs

Annual incentives	Long-term incentives	Executive benefits	Executive perquisites
Formula	Stock options	Key person	Assigned company
Goal-based	Restricted stock	insurance	car
Discretionary	grants	Split-dollar	Chauffeur
	Phantom stock	insurance	Club memberships
	options	Directors' and	Executive dining
	Stock appreciation	officers' liability	room
	rights	insurance	Financial counseling
	Performance units	Supplemental	
	Performance shares	retirement plans	
	Long-term cash	Executive physical	
	incentives	exams	
	Junior common stock	Special executive	
	Subsidiary stock	medical	
		reimbursement	
		Financial assistance	
		Deferred	
		compensation	

The Hay annual compensation surveys show that over 75 percent of all industrials have an annual incentive or bonus plan. Although financial institutions historically have relied on profit sharing to give management extra compensation in profitable years, annual incentive plans are also becoming prevalent. Our most recent surveys show that more than 50 percent of all financial institutions have an annual incentive or an annual incentive combined with a profit sharing plan.

Many corporations use long-term incentives to promote sustained performance and encourage more far-reaching executive decisions. Table 2 shows the prevalence of major types of long-term plans among 105 industrial companies with sales of $1 billion or more. The appendix at the end of this chapter briefly describes the variety of plans included in the ever-expanding array of executive compensation "tools."

PROGRAM CHARACTERISTICS

The decision maker confronted with the awesome list of program characteristics is further confused by the realization that the vehicles for executive pay

TABLE 2   Prevalence of Long-Term Incentives

Type of plan	Percentage in 1981
Stock options	78
Stock appreciation rights	60
Performance unit	21
Restricted stock	13
Performance share	10
Long-term cash	7
Phantom stock options	5
Other	1

seem to change continually. A recent example of this phenomenon is the emergence in 1981 of a new form of long-term incentive—the incentive stock option (ISO)—part of the Economic Recovery Tax Act (ERTA). What is behind this constant change and evolution of executive compensation programs? What is happening in executive compensation?

Legal Issues   Executive compensation is heavily influenced by legal considerations—often too much so—as companies strive to adopt plans that will qualify for special tax treatment. Since 1969 there have been six major changes in tax laws affecting the form and amount of taxation in executive pay schemes. When Congress introduced the concept of a maximum tax on earned income in 1976, even such straightforward executive pay as base salaries and cash bonuses were affected. (Subsequently, in ERTA, this same 50 percent maximum was extended to other "ordinary" income.) One consequence of the legal and tax options of executive pay is that the planning environment has been in flux. Tax developments (including IRS rulings) have led to experimentation, particularly with long-term incentives, and the rise and fall of particular vehicles for delivering these incentives.

Regulatory Issues   The actions of the SEC and the accounting profession—through the Financial Accounting Standards Board (FASB)—also influence the form of executive pay. Under its mandate to protect shareholders, the SEC is responsible for establishing disclosure rules, issuing regulations concerning the purchase and sale of stock by insiders, and so forth. FASB has become more involved in executive compensation by establishing reporting standards and promulgating rules that offset the impact of certain long-term incentive plans on the corporate balance sheet and income statement. Almost single-handedly, these bodies can reduce the popularity of a particular executive pay plan. For example, in 1970 FASB required that performance shares be valued using the company's share price at the time they were vested (usually three to five years after grant) rather than at the time of the initial award. This change meant that the future cost of the payouts was unknown; consequently, the growth of these plans slowed.

Board and Shareholder Involvement   Senior executive compensation plans require special approval in all publicly held companies. The board of directors (or sometimes a compensation committee of outside board members acting under its authority) must approve special plans and actual awards. Specifically, these groups always set the pay of the CEO and usually a broader group that might include all officers or all executives above a certain salary level. All plans involving company stock must be submitted to shareholders for approval; some companies choose to obtain stockholder approval of other special plans.

Public Record   Many aspects of executive pay are a matter of public record. Under current rules the compensation of the top five executives must be disclosed, as well as certain information on compensation plans. In recent years business journals, such as *Business Week*, *Forbes*, and scores of local publications, publish this information.

Outside Involvement and Review As a result of the above factors, executive pay has become highly technical, complex, and controversial. Program change typically involves outside management consultants, attorneys, and the company's public accounting firm, as well as inside staff experts. Redesign of an executive program can be arduous, extending over a minimum of three to four months. Because the various aspects of executive pay are interrelated, companies are increasingly looking at the total package, further complicating and extending the process. Most companies require this kind of fundamental overall review either every three to five years or more frequently if they are growing rapidly or there has been a major change in the planning environment (as there was recently on account of ERTA).

Counseling and Communications One characteristic of executive compensation programs is obvious but often overlooked: the accumulations and payouts under these plans account for the single largest source of executive net worth. For years, companies designed and administered executive plans in a way that left the individual responsible for his or her own financial affairs. With the maddening complexity of the programs themselves, this has become more difficult, requiring more expertise and time than the typical executive can provide. Thus we have seen a growth in company-paid executive financial counseling and an increase in communicating aspects of executive pay. Today there are booklets to explain stock plans, computer models to aid in the option exercise decisions, and a variety of other communications materials.

Planning Elements Another aspect of executive pay that goes largely unrecognized is the extent to which it involves trade-offs for both the corporation and the executive. As we move further from simple cash compensation, we need more detailed calculations to assess the impact of each plan on the company's expense structure, on reported profits, on the balance sheet, and on shareholder dilution—to say nothing of the principal objective, keeping and motivating the executives (where the considerations are less quantitative, but where experience with what works is required).

The financial implications for the individual vary according to differences in his or her cash flow, taxes, and risk preferences. The risk factor alone has been an important element of program design in the 1970s. Nonqualified stock options are just one example. The exercise of these options and the sale of stock obtained therefrom are limited for directors and officers by the insider-trading rules of the SEC. The insider-trading rules prohibit the "purchase and sale" or "sale and purchase" of stock within a six-month period. With the growing number of horror stories—about executives stuck with large blocks of stock newly purchased under options, as well as large blocks of unexercised options, when prices plummeted in the 1974–1975 recession—companies began to turn to other, longer-term plans. Stock appreciation rights (which give the recipient all or part of the gain directly in lieu of an option) are one example.

Performance Issues While all the above considerations have shaped the evolution of executive pay, we must note that most companies want compensation to be related to performance. In a simpler era—in the decades following World War II—the model was fairly straightforward. The annual bonus was related to company performance through a formula. During this period, particularly in the Eisenhower years, companies believed that stock price correlated reasonably well with earnings per share. Stock options were then viewed as performance-related. But a decade of sustained high inflation has eroded the relationship between executive pay and performance in most companies. At the same time, most organizations have become more sophisticated in their corporate planning—both for the overall enterprise and for each division (or what companies now like to call strategic business units, or SBUs). New plans, less heavily influenced by uncontrollable external events, have emerged. We have entered an era in which performance will again be a dominant consideration in the design and administration of pay.

Industry Differences   Wide differences exist between and among industries and business sectors. Pay for executives has never been as heavily influenced by location as is the case at lower employee levels (although it may become more so). However, executive pay has always been significantly affected by the business characteristics, profit economics, and performance of the business sectors in which companies compete. For example, industries such as drugs or petroleum have typically enjoyed higher margins, lower personnel costs, and greater growth; this has permitted them to pay more. Other business sectors and industries—such as steel, transportation, and insurance—have been more constrained. In some cases—utilities, for instance—regulation has further dampened executive pay. As a result of the major sectoral shifts taking place in the world economy, these differences appear to be widening. An interesting phenomenon is that multibillion-dollar companies are faced with widening sectoral differences within their own array of divisions and groups, forcing a rethinking of the advisability of internal parity at various executive levels.

Selectivity and Individualization   Finally, when reviewing the changes in executive compensation, one must conclude that it has become increasingly selective and has been tailored to each company's situation. For companies within the same industry group there is a wide dispersion in the level of executive pay. As they adopt different plans and plan combinations in their executive compensation programs—for both the short and the long term—the total and type of rewards one can realize from company to company will continue to widen.

PROGRAM DESIGN

Given these complex, interrelated factors affecting executive compensation, how should companies approach the design of executive pay? The simple answer, of course, is carefully and with a lot of reflection. This includes an analysis of what works and what does not work in the current program, along with an extended study of alternatives. Too many executive pay developments in the last decade have been externally driven and reactive in nature (largely because of tax law changes and other technical developments). Clearly, this approach has eroded the pay-performance linkage, subjecting companies and their boards to growing criticism. Worst of all, this approach has blunted what could be a valuable tool in reinforcing or changing the strategic direction and long-term results of the enterprise.

Compensation program design should focus on what we call the *strategic compensation* variables:

- Positioning of total compensation, for the company overall and for each major business unit
- Time frame of the incentive structure, involving the appropriate mix among current (annual), intermediate (two to three years), and long-range (three to ten years) plans
- Mix of pay between fixed and variable elements, by executive level and by business group
- Degree to which the reward structure and actual payouts will relate to corporate, business unit, team, and individual performance
- Selection of performance standards and goals, and tailoring rewards to these criteria
- Degree of flexibility and judgment that is appropriate in determining the actual payout
- Role of stocks or stock equivalents in the overall program

When formulating the correct response to these strategic compensation variables, five broad aspects of a corporation should also be considered:

1. *The ownership structure of the company itself.* Is the company privately or publicly held or a division or subsidiary of another enterprise? Also, to what extent is ownership concentrated? Answers to these questions particularly affect the mix of short- and longer-term rewards and the extent to which stock options or other stock-based plans can be used.

2. *The stage of growth of the company.* While every situation is unique, there are four stages of general evolution of most businesses; compensation requirements tend to change at each stage. (See Table 3.)

3. *The status of the business itself and its overall strategy.* Such factors as growth rate, company profitability, and the degree of diversification affect both what is required and what is feasible. In addition, the degree to which the company's basic strategy is fixed or is in transition is crucial. These considerations particularly affect the performance standards (both internal and relative) that are appropriate, the degree of incentive leverage required, and the flexibility that needs to be built into the program.

4. *The industry or industry sectors in which the company competes or intends to compete.* This affects the types of plans required. (For example, stock is used especially in high-technology companies; special participation and override arrangements are common in exploration and production companies.) It also affects how a company needs to manage cash compensation, since pay levels and the rate of increase vary a great deal by industry sector.

5. *The overall management style, culture, and human resource environment.* Table 4 lists some of the factors that can increase or decrease the relative importance of pay, influence the role and design of the overall pay program, and affect the feasibility of plans that theoretically might be superior but actually do not fit a given culture or management style.

Taking all these factors into account requires a formal process of study that must involve the chief executive and the company's compensation committee. So that the proper requirements can be documented, ample time should be

TABLE 3. Compensation Program Evolution

	Founding start-up phase	Building phase	Emergence phase	Pacesetter phase
Typical compensation requirements	Minimize cash flow Maintain flexibility	Meet competitive pressures Recognize middle managers Balance option gains with other incentives	Create edge (profit sharing) Become more competitive Provide significant incentives Reinforce changing performance measurement requirements	Meet inflationary pressures Meet diverse needs, tiers Control costs; direct rewards selectively Integrate compensation into total personnel system

Compensation Program Changes

	Founding start-up phase	Building phase	Emergence phase	Pacesetter phase
Level of pay	Low salaries	Competitive to premium pay	Competitive salaries and leveraged bonuses	Performance-based premium pay
Competitive positioning	Entrepreneurial	Industry and local	Industry	Industry, national, international
Plan emphasis	Stock grants and options	Salary judgmental bonus and option	Salary, formal bonus plan and long-term incentive	Multifactored
Short- vs. long-term mix	3–5 years	1–3 years	1–5 years	Balanced
Performance relationship	Company	Company, team, individual	Company, division, individual	Company, group, division, individual
Administration	Informal, individually managed	Formal and centralized	Formal and divisionalized	Systematic, decentralized

TABLE 4   Nonmonetary Factors Impacting Executives

Top-management leadership
Company growth rate and market share
Industry characteristics (i.e., cyclicality, degree of concentration)
Organization structure
Functional orientation and values (i.e., sales and marketing vs. technical)
Career and work ethic
Technical challenge
Management challenge
Systems
Rate of promotional opportunity
Location
Facilities
Communication environment
Flexibility
Quality emphasis
Degree of formality

allowed for an objective assessment of the current program and the overall process of business and organizational change. Changes should not be approved in a piecemeal manner but developed and implemented within the context of an overall strategy that uses executive compensation to reinforce the goals and direction of the company.

APPENDIX

Stock Options

Stock options involve the right to purchase a specific number of shares of a corporation's stock at a specified price and during a specified period of time.

Qualified stock option.   Under current law, qualified stock options are "dead" (any qualified option granted under prior plans had to be exercised no later than May 21, 1981, in order to receive favorable tax treatment). Nevertheless, since the qualified option has been so prevalent, an understanding of how it worked is useful. Qualified options were options that qualified for favorable tax treatment under Section 422 of the Internal Revenue Code. Some of the major requirements of this section were:

- Option term could not exceed five years.
- Option price had to be at least 100 percent of fair market value at the time of grant.
- Plan with specified requirements had to be approved by shareholders.
- Lower-priced option could not be exercised ahead of previously granted higher-priced option.

Nonqualified stock option.   A nonstatutory stock option that does not meet the above requirements of Section 422 of the Internal Revenue Code. Nonqualified options usually have a ten-year period and are sometimes priced at less than 100 percent of the fair market value at the time of grant.

Variable-priced nonqualified stock option.   A nonqualified stock option granted at 100 percent of the fair market value, but which provides that the option price will reduce depending upon market price appreciation, earnings-per-share growth, or other measures.

Discount stock option.   A nonqualified stock option granted at less than 100 percent of the fair market value at the time of grant.

Incentive stock option.   The Economic Recovery Tax Act of 1981 provides for a new tax-favored "incentive stock option (ISO)." If certain holding requirements are met, ISOs will have no direct tax consequences either when granted or when exercised, and the executive will be taxed at capital gains rates when the stock received on exercise of the option is later sold. However, the difference between the option price and the fair market value at time of exercise is an item of tax preference for purposes of determining the executive's alternative minimum tax liability. No business expense deduction will be allowed to the employer with respect to an ISO. The maximum value of ISOs that can be granted to an executive in a given year is $100,000, based on the fair market value of the stock at grant times the number of shares. They can be granted for up to ten years, allowing either full exercise or an installment-exercise provision (such as 20 percent a year).

Phantom Stock Plans

Phantom stock plans generally are awards made in artificial shares, units, or rights, rather than in cash, stock, or rights to purchase stock. These plans are classified in terms of appreciation, income, and asset plans, described below.

Appreciation Plans   A phantom stock plan in which the award is based on the formula appreciation of some share or unit (typically, appreciation in market or nonmarket value of company stock) is an appreciation plan. No underlying amount or value is provided, other than the payout formula. Typical phantom stock appreciation plans include phantom stock options, book value, and stock appreciation rights.

Phantom stock option.   A plan that grants to an executive a number of units, each of which provides a payment equal to any appreciation that occurs in the market value of a share of company stock between the date of grant and some future date, often accompanied by dividend-equivalent payments.

Book value plan.   A plan that grants to an executive a number of units, each of which provides a payment equal to any appreciation in unit value between the date of grant and some future date, using prices determined by book value or other nonmarket evaluation.

Stock appreciation right.   A right coupled with a nonqualified stock option to receive an amount equal to the appreciation in fair market value since the date of grant in lieu of, or in addition to, exercising the corresponding stock option. Stock appreciation rights are sometimes referred to as alternate stock rights or buy-back rights.

Income Plans   A phantom stock plan in which the award is based on the "income" from some unit, share, or right is called an income plan. No underlying amount or value is provided, other than the income formula. Such plans may be awarded independently, but are more commonly attached to other appreciation, asset, or incentive plans.

Dividend equivalent. A phantom stock income plan that grants to an executive a number of units, each of which provides a payment equal to any dividend paid on a share of the company's stock.

Asset Plans Asset plans are phantom stock plans in which the award starts with a basic grant of shares or units and there is an agreed value to be earned under stated conditions, not necessarily based on appreciation.

Performance shares. A phantom stock asset plan that contingently grants to an executive stock units which will provide actual shares of stock or their cash equivalent at the time of payment (i.e., unit value may appreciate or decline) if predetermined objectives are achieved. How many of the units become payable depends on the extent to which the objectives are achieved.

Performance units. A phantom stock asset plan that contingently grants to an executive units which will provide cash payments or their equivalent in stock valued at the time of grant (unit value remains constant) if predetermined objectives are achieved.

Book value asset plan. A performance share plan that values stock units according to nonmarket measurements such as book value of stock.

Real Stock

Real stock involves plans in which awards are made in the form of actual shares of company stock.

Restricted stock. A real stock plan in which actual shares of company stock are currently transferred to the employee but carry restrictions, such as prohibition against disposition or rights of first refusal, and may be subject to a substantial risk of forfeiture.

Junior stock. Similar to restricted stock in a special category or class of stock that usually has subordinate liquidation rights, lower dividend payout, and other provisions that limit its immediate value. Upon the achievement of pre-specified events, junior stock converts to regular stock (for example, the attainment of a cumulative earnings-per-share goal).

Cash Plans

Cash plans are longer-term incentive plans in which awards are stated in terms of dollars, percentages of pay, or similar terms (even though actual payments may be in the form of stock or part stock, part cash, etc.). Longer-term cash incentives are sometimes known as performance allotments or sustained achievement awards.

chapter 47

Evaluating an Executive Compensation Program

Donald R. Simpson

PARTNER, THE HAY GROUP, PHILADELPHIA,
PENNSYLVANIA

"Executive compensation" refers to the pay and related rewards which are designed specifically for either the officer group or the top executives of an enterprise. It includes salary, cash supplements, benefits, perquisites, short-term incentives, and long-term incentives. See Chapter 46 for an analysis of the principal components of an executive compensation program and how they are selected to meet the needs of a particular enterprise.

In addition to constructing an executive compensation program from appropriate elements, it is important to focus on the "total result" of all the rewards provided—to ensure that the program is integrated within itself and produces a close relationship with performance in terms of the company's strategic objectives. A thoughtful program for executive compensation should therefore be based on the answers to questions such as the following:

- What are the company's tactical and strategic plans in the marketplace?
- What kinds of people are needed to achieve these goals, both short term and long term?
- What kinds of compensation programs and levels are necessary to attract, retain, and motivate the caliber of people needed (and what should be done with those in the organization who do not meet the current needs, e.g., retrain, redeploy, terminate)?
- How can the conflicts in multiple short- and long-term factors be best balanced in program design?

Pragmatically, there should be an ongoing process of assessment and design, concurrent with administration, and an item-by-item analysis of the broadly based plans, examining each from the special perspective of the executive group. In that way, special plans can be soundly based, maximizing the likelihood that the desired results will indeed be encouraged and achieved, so that the substantial actual or potential costs of the plan will be profitable for the company.

Most industrial companies, and an increasing number of financial and service companies, provide some form of annual bonus opportunity for a relatively large or small group of executives. Similarly, most companies provide at least one form of longer-term incentive. Such a longer-term plan usually includes stock options, but increasingly, other long-term incentives are provided in addition.

It is desirable to reflect the needs and perceptions of executives in designing such benefits. (This can be complex when considering perquisites, because of the emotional connotations they carry.) Companies are finding preference surveys a useful tool in determining the relative value of a benefit or perquisite from the perspective of the executive group—so programs can be tailored to the executives' circumstances, giving due regard to economics and other factors.

The design of bonus plans has been evolving for years, toward clearer relationships between pay and performance, and introducing measures of performance other than stock price or a year's reported earnings. Establishment of realistic measures is not easy. Nevertheless, an increasing effort is being devoted to developing and testing various measures, including cash flow impacts, related to a company's plans.

FORMS OF LONGER-TERM PLANS

The area broadly categorized as "longer-term" plans includes almost innumerable combinations and permutations. Each special combination tends to have its own nomenclature, but most longer-term incentives can be grouped into major categories. For example, one categorization is:

- Asset plans (cash or stock award to be earned out)
- Appreciation plans (award whose value depends on some kind of appreciation, usually stock)
- Income plans (award whose value is primarily in a stream of income)

Another categorization is:

- Cash (value expressed or paid in cash)
- Stock (stock payments or stock options)
- Phantom stock (value expressed in some form of artificial stock)

But popular nomenclature blurs these distinctions and generally treats certain forms or combinations as separate categories. Table 1 shows the five-year trend (1977–1981) in the major popular forms of plans, using the Fortune 100 industrials. As can be seen, stock options are still the overwhelming choice of most companies, and with the reestablishment of tax-favored options (in the form of incentive stock options, or ISOs), options are likely to continue to be a "standard benefit."

TABLE 1   Longer-Term Incentive Plans for Executives   (Fortune's Top 100 Industrial Companies)

Alternative	Number of Companies Reporting*		
	1977	1979	1981
Stock options	86	87	87
Qualified	65	44	N/A
Nonqualified	81	84	87
Variable Price	2	1	1
Discount	5	3	3
Restricted Stock	8	10	16
Cash Plans	3	6	4
Phantom Stock	61	77	88
Appreciation	49	67	81
Phantom stock options	6	7	10
Stock appreciation rights	46	65	73
Book value	1	1	4
Asset	20	28	42
Performance shares	10	12	11
Performance units	9	16	31
Book value	1	1	0

*Note that the numbers are also percents of each year's 100-company group.

COMPARING TOTAL PROGRAMS—VALUING ALTERNATIVE FORMS

For some years, insufficient attention was paid to the relative value of the particular plan as part of the overall program. Comparisons were almost always item by item, more in the nature of a "bean count." Eventually, as it became common to compare salaries, and the total cash of salary plus bonus, methods were devised for comparing the value of so-called fringes—group insurance, pension, and other benefits plans. Thus it was a natural evolution that methods for comparing the value of longer-term incentives would be developed also, particularly since such comparisons permit a more realistic evaluation of a total program. Comparisons of a total program are much more complex than comparisons on a component-by-component basis, because of the different variables among the components.

■ Salary comparisons are relatively easy, using actual salaries. Often ignored, however, are the range midpoints, which indicate the announced or approved policies for salary opportunities. A comparison using only actual salaries can be misleading since these are affected by performance assessments, tenure, and short-term economics; but on the other hand, the "policy" may be honored more in the breach than in the observance.

■ Total cash introduces a complication when one attempts to examine any references beyond the actual salary paid and the actual bonus paid, since surveys of bonus opportunity typically relate only to bonuses as a percentage of salary rather than to the bonus equivalent of a range midpoint. For example, many bonus and incentive plans do not provide for a "par," an average or normal bonus to be expected, while other plans use par as the minimum bonus to be expected, and there are still other plans in which the expected bonus is totally unattainable during poor economic conditions. The main comparison problem is that bonus or incentive plans, by design, are intended to provide significantly varying amounts, depending upon performance criteria (which may be tough or easy, purely profit sharing or highly subjective). Thus, survey averages, or even overall company averages, can mask the true range of practice.

■ In benefit plans the use of actual costs can be substantially misleading as to the real worth of a program, due to demographic accidents of a cycle, funding policies, underwriting policies, or other local cost circumstances. Further, of course, many companies don't even have data available for a comparison of actual benefits costs. Accordingly, the most common "value" comparisons use only the equivalent of a range midpoint, i.e., a standard cost based on actuarial factors or other conventions.

■ Long-term plans can range in valuation from an actual cost that can be budgeted (such as for dividend unit plans), to a cost that needs to be estimated in accruals, to costs that will never be recorded (such as for stock options). Thus there are both real cost and accounting cost factors which need to be considered.

Nevertheless, with all the caveats and weaknesses of the assumptions which must be made, there are meaningful comparisons which are evolving as reasonably reliable representations of program values, using relatively consistent applications of data. Also, these comparisons now incorporate several years of data, so that year-to-year changes can be assessed. Finally, data are now available in large enough samples for statistical conventions to apply, and potential errors may be offset.

Specifically, one series of comparisons is developed from the following concepts and assumptions.

1. All data are related to specific pay. For example, data may be drawn from the Hay Executive Compensation Comparison which compares actual pay for incumbents of selected "generic" jobs (CEO, COO, head of finance, etc.). Thus thousands of individual pay situations can be compared in the aggregate measurements.

2. The actual salary rate is used, plus the previous year's bonus if any. (Eventually, it is hoped that sufficient reliable data on bonus *opportunity* can be developed, which will permit additional comparisons using a bonus equivalent of the salary ranges, including a design average or expected par, a minimum and a maximum.)

3. Comparisons for benefit plans and perquisites are confined to the theoretical standard costs rather than attempting to introduce all the problems of an actual cost (even where such can be ascertained in an aggregate number).

4. Longer-term plan values are portrayed in at least two forms: the actual awards realized and the present value of grants made—the "salary-equivalent value."

Realized gains. Realized gains fall naturally into this kind of comparison, added to actual salary rates and actual bonus paid in the most recent year. In essence, the philosophy is that there is a "bottom line" which must be considered—what has actually been gained in a year. In theory, these individual totals should fluctuate substantially from year to year and from cycle to cycle.

However, in terms of overall averages (lines of central tendency for survey purposes), there hasn't been as much fluctuation as one might expect.

Present value of current grants.   Determining a present value of stock options or other plans is a much more complex issue. In order to start the process of developing widely acceptable comparisons, a number of assumptions and conventions were made, including the following:

- Stock prices would be consistent with the past, i.e., the price earnings (PE) multiple would be exactly the average of the previous five years' PE multiple. (This won't be the exact PE multiple, of course, and in fact market conditions or market "fashions" may make the PE multiple substantially different, but at least there is a basis for consistent application that should be meaningful in an aggregate survey context.)
- Company earnings per share will continue on a straight-line basis consistent with the earnings of the past ten years. For most companies this means a straight line from ten years past to the present and extended for the next five to ten years. (For a comparison point which is during or just following a depressed cycle, the straight line will be inappropriate, of course, but, again, from a survey perspective a representative pattern should still be present.)
- Gains from performance shares, performance units, dividend units, and similar plans will be the 100 percent value (some plans provide for more than 100 percent in actual opportunity). Stock option and stock appreciation rights (SAR) profits were assumed on the basis of exercise at the end of the year in which a 50 percent price increase occurred.
- Interest and risk factors should be combined into an overall discount rate in a manner similar to rates of return for various risk levels of investments. Thus a high-risk plan would use a high discount rate similar to a venture capital rate, whereas dividend equivalents would use a low-risk rate, essentially the current value of money. (Inflationary periods place a great strain on these assumptions in terms of year-to-year comparisons, particularly because when discount rates exceed 25 percent and several years are involved, the resulting present value is so low that it lacks credibility.)

In theory, over a period of years the calculated present value should be essentially the same as the realized gains after adjusting for increases in general compensation levels due to inflation. In fact, while the years to date have produced numbers in the present value calculations which seem credible, the numbers have been substantially higher than those reported in the realized gains comparisons—on an order generally of 150 to 200 percent of realized gains.

Another factor not yet clearly resolved in determining present value is the impact of various patterns of making grants. Some companies make grants annually, others biennially, and others sporadically or sequentially. Thus while an annual grant should be valued in full each year, it also seems more appropriate that a grant intended to apply for two or more years should be somehow spread over those years—if one is sure that the policy will actually be applied, i.e., that a change in policy or practice will not occur.

Thus more studies are needed to produce more realistic and credible numbers. And it is likely that refinements will evolve to provide greater credibility to projections. This credibility is needed particularly for intercompany and industry comparisons, for establishing the comparative values of different longer-term plans, and also for comparing the overall value of a company program, including salary and bonus as well as benefits, perquisites, and longer-term incentive plans.

In the format described above, there are five years of comparisons available, even though the studies to date are still experimental. In these five years the trend seems to be to provide a perceived opportunity on the order of the annual bonus opportunity, i.e., balance the short-term and long-term opportunities equally. Actual payments, however, have tended to fluctuate from year to year, as shown in Table 2.

The percentages in Table 2 are derived from actual data reported for 21 "generic" jobs covered in the Hay Executive Compensation Comparison (e.g., CEO, COO, head of finance) and cover all the industrial companies each year whose revenues exceed $1 billion and for which complete data were available (105 companies in 1981).

Some of the variations may be due to impacts of the "voluntary" wage controls during these years, which probably affected degrees of awards. Also, of course, variations could be due to changes in mix. In fact, the calculations of overall program value—salary, bonus, and longer-term incentives combined—seem to indicate that the longer-term plans are being used to reverse the long-

TABLE 2   Average Short- and Long-Term Incentive Values as Percentage of Base Salary   (Billion Dollar [Revenues] Industrial Companies in Hay Executive Compensation Five-Year Comparison)

Approximate 1981 salary level		Short-term (annual) bonus	Realized gains of past long-term grants	Present value of year's long-term grants
	1981	19.5	2.7	8.2
	1980	21.0	1.5	7.5
$66,000	1979	22.3	2.3	8.1
	1978	13.8	10.2	25.5
	1977	19.1	9.1	15.8
	1981	31.1	11.7	19.1
	1980	35.0	8.2	18.6
$103,000	1979	34.0	3.8	29.7
	1978	29.0	10.9	28.8
	1977	32.0	16.7	37.7
	1981	41.0	19.3	28.2
	1980	47.0	13.7	27.9
$194,000	1979	44.0	5.0	47.8
	1978	42.0	11.5	32.4
	1977	43.0	23.0	55.9
	1981	46.4	23.5	33.2
	1980	53.0	16.6	32.7
$377,000	1979	49.0	5.6	57.6
	1978	48.0	11.7	32.2
	1977	49.0	26.3	65.4

term drift of compensation to an ever-flatter slope (i.e., progressively less pay for job content as job size increases), which has been apparent from comparing cash compensation alone.

Thus it seems clear that an important impact of longer-term plans is to supplement the cash compensation—salary plus bonus—in ways which will provide a greater consistency between pay and job content, so that while wage and salary increases at the lower levels may continue to exceed those at the higher levels, the apparent deficits are being made up—in aggressive compensation programs at least—by higher opportunities in both short-term (annual bonus) and longer-term plans.

Of course, since the eligibility for special plans is often confined to a relatively small core-management group, there are still inequities and anomalies in many programs. Thus the challenge of those involved with executive compensation will be to continue to rationalize all the multiple forms into a cohesive whole, consistent with the philosophies of society and both motivating and rewarding to those who share primary accountabilities for the success of an enterprise.

chapter 48

Executive Financial Planning

Paul Thompson, II

DIRECTOR, EXECUTIVE FINANCIAL PLANNING, THE HAY
GROUP, PHILADELPHIA, PENNSYLVANIA

THE OBJECTIVE

*Our plans miscarry because they have no
aim. When a man does not know what harbor
he is making for, no wind is the right wind.*
—SENECA

The objective of financial planning is to provide order and direction to the life-time task of personal asset management. When we travel, we determine our destination, the duration of the trip, the mode of transportation, and the accommodations that may be needed. We also decide upon the pace and style of the journey. In stark contrast to this ordered preparation is the executive financial odyssey which lacks both direction and purpose. Should not financial travels receive more thoughtful care and attention?

   Although an affirmative answer is inescapable, only a few executives utilize effective financial- and estate-planning techniques. There must be a reason for this contradiction. It is our belief that the problem is caused by the combination of too little time and too much ignorance. Most executives spend the majority of their waking hours on their jobs and in their career pursuits. This has made them successful as corporate managers. Little time—and usually poor-quality time—remains. Therefore, unless an individual has special motivation, time is not allocated to explore the lore and logic of personal financial planning. If an executive is unwilling or unable to open the doors that lead to knowledge and opportunity, how can one know what is beyond the doors or where those paths may lead? How can a person keep up to date or ask for help?

The solution to this problem is to include executive financial planning as an integral part of management education, training, and development programs—and not for the top tier alone, but throughout the organization. Many corporations require periodic physical checkups. Is it not equally important to encourage and support regular financial checkups?

Let us now examine the problems and the solutions in more detail.

THE PROBLEMS

"Now! Now!" cried the Queen, "Faster!
Faster!" And they went so fast that at last
they seemed to skim through the air, hardly
touching the ground with their feet ... "Now,
here, you see, it takes all the running you can
do, to keep in the same place. If you want to
get somewhere else, you must run at least
twice as fast as that!"—Alice Through the
Looking-Glass, LEWIS CARROLL

Few executives come from an environment of economic wealth. Many begin their careers with a residue of debt from the education process and soon incur substantial expense and debt to establish a home and raise a family.

As an executive continues up the ladder of success, increasing compensation generates discretionary income and provides the seed for capital accumulation. Some investments are made where the executive is comfortable by dint of experience or knowledge and some as a direct result of the sales activities of those in the investment or life insurance business.

The corporate environment includes a total compensation package which provides a sophisticated array of attractive benefits and opportunities. A comprehensive health insurance plan minimizes the need for personal coverage and reduces the individual's financial risk in the event of illness or injury. Disability benefits provide some measure of protection in the event of a disabling injury or illness. Significant life insurance coverage is available to the executive population—usually as a multiple of salary. As in the disability situation, peace of mind results and the need to investigate individual coverage is diminished. Added to these basic benefits is a variety of capital building opportunities. For lower management levels, these are usually limited to savings and thrift plans, stock purchase plans, and the like. As the individual progresses through the executive ranks, additional perquisites such as stock options, deferred compensation, and other special benefits may become available.

Although this panoply of benefits offers substantial protection and opportunity, it may, by its comprehensive nature, allow an executive to become complacent about personal financial affairs. The complexity of many financial offerings and the manner in which they are marketed may leave a person somewhat bewildered. Thus the unsophisticated investor may find comfort and security in "riskless" investments such as savings accounts, certificates of deposit, and other guaranteed investments. As a corollary, there may be an even greater fear in addressing the estate-planning process. All too often it is presumed that a simple estate plan—one which leaves everything to the surviving spouse and family—does the job. Here again, few executives have any useful knowledge of the estate-planning process. One result is that only 11 percent of the executive population—based on our statistics—have effective estate plans.

Financial advice is offered by individuals in a variety of professions. Many of these individuals present themselves as financial planners and some who do not are assumed to be. While many executives are seeking answers, too few are seeking the knowledge which will allow them to ask the proper questions. The financial planner should be a source of both—knowledge and answers.

Of great concern is the relationship in which an executive assumes that a professional adviser has knowledge which that adviser may not have. This is too often true in one's relationship with an attorney. Few attorneys are, in fact, qualified financial advisers, and only a small number of attorneys are competent estate planners. This is not an indictment of the legal profession but, rather, a recognition that lawyers specialize in specific areas of the law and that clients should not assume or presume that they are omniscient.

Compounding the problem and widening the knowledge gap have been the significant and often confusing tax reforms in recent years—especially from 1969 to the present. The United States has one of the most complex sets of tax laws in the civilized world. Indeed, for almost any given situation there are a multitude of exceptions, variations, and special ground rules. By and large, only persons who are professionally charged with the need to understand the laws take it upon themselves to do so. If it is difficult for the professional, consider the quandary of the executive! And then, to this mix of uncertainty, we add the dramatic impact and destructive results of inflation.

The 1980 Hay Compensation Comparison shows that taxes and inflation have canceled the real benefit of significant compensation increases. The following chart displays the compensation changes during the decade of the seventies for two management positions. After adjusting for taxes and inflation, each position suffered a reduction in real buying power and the middle manager was hardest hit.

Title	1970 compensation	1980 compensation	Buying power
Senior executive	$84,800	$179,500	96%
Middle manager	33,300	68,400	88%

THE SOLUTIONS

Over and over again the courts have said that there is nothing sinister in so arranging one's affairs as to keep taxes as low as possible. Everybody does so, rich and poor; and all do right, for nobody owes any public duty to pay more than the law demands: Taxes are enforced exactions not voluntary contributions. To demand more in the name of morals is mere cant.—JUDGE LEARNED HAND

Although Judge Learned Hand articulated a very basic right and privilege, tax planning does not resolve the stated problems; rather, it is a financial-planning tool which can be used when the underlying problems have been identified.

The first step in resolving the problems is education in the basic concepts of personal financial planning. Without this education, ignorance and uncertainty will continue and opportunities will be lost.

The second requirement is to provide individual guidance and direction to assist the executive in achieving those goals and objectives which have been identified. In response to these needs, the role of the professional financial planner has evolved.

Two separate and distinct individuals have a need for the services of the professional financial planner—the person of future rights and the person of current property. It is important to draw a distinction between these individuals because their needs are often quite different. Typically, the person of future rights is the corporate executive who has significant total compensation, enjoys an array of valuable benefits, and may, but usually does not, have a net worth commensurate with his or her income. This person may over a period of time accumulate wealth by virtue of participation in a variety of company benefit programs such as thrift plans, stock option plans, deferred compensation, and pension plans. Therefore, the professional financial planner must recognize the very significant impact of the corporate benefit structure.

The person of property, on the other hand, is the individual who has current wealth and enjoys the financial planning opportunities that wealth bestows. Whether this individual has earned income or not may be totally academic. The important thing is that he or she has the wherewithal to pursue financial opportunities. The problems and needs of the person of property may, therefore, be very different from the problems and needs of the person of rights.

Although financial planning has been practiced for hundreds of years, it was not until the late 1960s and early 1970s that it was added to the list of corporate perquisites. As a result of significant changes in the tax laws, many aspects of compensation and benefits changed dramatically. Thus the need for personal financial-planning assistance has been growing.

In the early years, personal financial-planning services were directed to the most senior executives in many of the larger U.S. corporations. Financial planning evolved as a one-on-one service through which the counselor assumed responsibility for:

- Educating the client
- Determining the client's objectives
- Analyzing the client's present circumstances
- Recommending changes, new ideas, and improvements
- Assisting in the implementation of accepted recommendations
- Monitoring results achieved and responding to new objectives

Typically, this process results in the preparation of a lengthy and comprehensive report which deals with all aspects of the client's affairs. In the process, it provides an educational overview of available opportunities and the tax climate under which the opportunities must be assessed.

One of the most important aspects of an effective financial-planning relationship is that the counselor must provide assistance in developing a plan which is compatible with the hopes, the aspirations, and the realities of the client. A plan which is good for one may not be good for another; and tax savings and tax planning alone should not provide the motivation for the decision-making process. In short, one must distinguish between the "hard facts"—the numbers—and the "soft facts" which embody the hopes, the aspirations, the dreams, and the prejudices that one brings to the planning process.

An emerging alternative to the one-on-one counseling process is the combination of a seminar or workshop followed by individual counseling. A distinct advantage of this alternative is the increased emphasis that can be placed on the process of understanding and awareness. A typical workshop runs two full days—enough time to permit a detailed examination of the lore and logic of financial planning and estate planning. In preparation for the workshop, a case study is created to reflect the probable circumstances of an average executive in the group that will be convened. Specific information is obtained from the company about the individuals involved, the benefit plans in which they participate, and the degree to which they participate in those plans. In addition, the case study will incorporate assets and liabilities which are appropriate to an individual in a given compensation range. The ideal workshop group size is 15 couples—and we emphasize *couples*—seated around an open U-shaped table so that there can be free exchange of ideas between the workshop leaders and the participants. The objective of the workshop is to share ideas, to provide new knowledge, and to allay the uncertainties that may be harbored about the goals and objectives of the financial-planning and estate-planning processes. As the program analyzes the affairs of a hypothetical individual—who may be similar to the individuals assembled—it does not intrude upon the personal affairs of any individual. Therefore, the discussion can be open and objective.

After completing the workshop, the executive and his or her spouse are prepared to take advantage of the individual follow-up counseling opportunities. Experience shows that this is an effective form of counseling because advice and guidance can be focused on those issues which are paramount in the executive's mind, many of which may have been suggested by the workshop process.

Financial planning as a corporate benefit has expanded considerably in recent years and will expand dramatically in the years ahead. An ever-increasing number of individuals are being paid salaries, bonuses, and benefits which make them candidates for personal financial planning. Thus companies may wish to provide a variety of opportunities to their management personnel. For some executives, it may be individual counseling or a workshop program, followed by extensive and ongoing personal counseling. For a second tier of executives, the corporation may elect to provide workshops plus some form of individual counseling, perhaps on a somewhat limited or defined basis. For a third level, it may be appropriate to develop a program of one-day workshops or seminars which are oriented to either financial-planning or estate-planning issues, depending upon the ages and needs of the participants.

With regard to the future, the emergence of customized benefit plans and diverse executive compensation strategies heightens the need for personal financial planning. Today's better-managed corporations coordinate the executive compensation package with the overall strategic plan for the organization and then provide executives with personal advice and counsel to ensure the success of the strategy.

Cafeteria benefit plans let individuals choose what is best for them. This concept, however, is often frustrated by the inability of participants to make appropriate choices and by the failure of the employer to provide the ongoing communications that are requisite in the operation of a multiple-choice plan. Personal financial planning addresses these problems in a unique way.

Corporations, by the extensive nature of their compensation and benefit plans, are creating a sheltered financial environment for their middle- and upper-management executives and are shouldering many of the responsibilities that a laissez faire society imposed upon the individual. Although executives benefit from this system, they are also deprived by it.

Personal financial planning is a never-ending task. In our complex world, change is the order of the day and today's plans become tomorrow's history. The responsibility of the financial planner is to provide order and direction and to know "which wind is the right wind."

part 1

Special Compensation Programs

chapter 49

Handling Unique Compensation Situations

C. S. Dadakis

MANAGER, COMPENSATION, HOWMET ALUMINUM
CORPORATION, GREENWICH, CONNECTICUT

Roger L. Bobertz

DIRECTOR, CORPORATE COMPENSATION DEPARTMENT,
UNION CARBIDE CORPORATION, DANBURY,
CONNECTICUT

No matter how carefully conceived or executed a compensation program is, situations will arise which cannot be accommodated within the normal patterns of the plan. The real test of the system and its administrators, then, is their ability to deal with these special situations without jeopardizing the operation and acceptance of the total program by the organization.

This is not to say that most variations in job market, employee performance, or grade structure cannot be handled within the context and procedures of the normal program. Problems in compensation are usually a matter of degree. Judgment must be used to decide when the variations are severe enough to tax the mechanics and logic of the existing procedure.

An effective program must be flexible enough to permit exceptions based on careful analysis and reason. But the integrity of the whole compensation plan will depend on how well the exceptions are integrated into the system. Caution should be exercised to avoid solutions which compromise any of the basic principles or challenge the fundamental equity of the program.

Most cases which require special consideration have one or more of the following underlying circumstances in common:

1. *Job market change*.   A sudden sharp change in the outside market for a specific function or a group of jobs.

2. *Special career development*.   A need to provide accelerated career paths for certain individuals beyond the salary limitations and normal promotional opportunities of the existing job.

3. *Salary compression*.   A reduction in actual pay spread between levels, caused by a disproportionate increase in such factors as starting salaries, hourly rates, or amount of overtime.

4. *Professional insulation*.   A sense of detachment from the company salary scales, affecting persons whose professional contribution is peripheral to the mainstream of the organization. Such persons usually identify more closely with the profession than with the company.

5. *Unique performance pattern*.   Individual performance which varies sufficiently from the typical to require special attention.

In any of the above cases, it is difficult to say precisely when the situation becomes unique and requires special handling. Problems arising from such circumstances have been encountered and solved by other companies. The few cases below will illustrate the sort of approaches that have been used.

JOB MARKET CHANGE

Example 1: The compensation treatment of computer specialists in a rapidly rising job market.   Here we are dealing with rapid change in the market price of a specific function or profession, resulting from an acute imbalance in the supply of and demand for trained personnel. (We are not, for the moment, considering the overall rise of the salary structure due to inflation or the increase in annual productivity which affects all groups in the salary population.)

Over the years, as companies sought to increase their computer capabilities, the demand for trained personnel in this field became extremely heavy. Job offers and salaries started an upward spiral which exceeded by a substantial degree the inflationary rise in the remainder of the salary structure.

At first, companies tried to maintain hiring rates and job ranges as originally evaluated, but this resulted in heavy attrition as employees sought better opportunities elsewhere. Companies then made it a practice to hire in the middle of the range and to pierce the top of the range for existing jobs in order to hold employees. In similar situations in the past, such temporary expedients seemed to afford relief until the supply and demand balance returned to normal. But in the case of computer personnel, the shortages continued year after year as computer operations were expanded. It became obvious to many companies that a more permanent solution was needed.

One way of meeting the problem was to remove the jobs from the regular classification tables and treat the group on an ad hoc basis. This did not work well, however, because it permitted employees with the strongest bargaining power to receive the greatest rewards. Also, managers were often at a loss to know whether their compensation practices were fair or in line with those of the rest of the industry. A more comprehensive solution was needed to achieve an acceptable and viable compensation plan for these employees.

One company solved the problem by removing the jobs from the salary evaluation procedure and setting up a separate ladder, distinct and apart from the regular program. This ladder was formed of typical nonsupervisory jobs somewhat as follows:

Junior programmer
Programmer
Programmer analyst
Senior programmer analyst
Consultant

The jobs were then compared with the outside market in a survey with careful regard for job content. On the basis of the survey information, realistic ranges, reflecting current market conditions in the area, were set for each level. This assured managers that the salaries they were offering were in line with the market. The ranges were reviewed every six months and adjusted to maintain market competitiveness.

However, the departmental problem was one not only of figuring valid ranges for each level but also of defining criteria by which incumbents could be slotted into the levels. Many of the employees were seeking promotional opportunities based on their increasing experience and rising qualifications.

To meet this problem, a work force table was developed for the department which set forth the number of employees required at each level for optimum operating effectiveness. This was done for present operations and estimated for each successive year for the next five years.

Using this work force table as a guide, managers were able to appraise more precisely the promotional opportunities existing currently in the department and expected over the next five years. They could discuss current careers and future openings with the employees and indicate opportunities which would be available to those who qualified.

In effect, the managers' approach to stabilizing employment and improving morale in the department was twofold:

1. Realistic ranges in line with the market, on which merit increases would be based with the firm knowledge that the salary represented competitive compensation for each job.

2. A reliable estimate of present and future promotional opportunities, based on the work force tables, which could reasonably be discussed with and provide incentives to the employees. Employees could then relate these opportunities to their own rising qualifications and decide more intelligently how to react to outside offers. Many such offers in the past were pseudo promotions intended only to gain their services immediately. Now they could respond with a better knowledge of what their future would be if they chose to remain with the company.

The managers had the advantage of feeling more secure in their staffing at each level for both present and future operations. If they were unable to make a promotional offer to an employee who voluntarily terminated in order to accept a higher-level position outside, they did not feel as vulnerable as they had in the past. Previously, such a loss was looked upon as a major catastrophe. Often, last-minute offers and promises were considered to entice employees to stay.

Under the new plan, with use of the work force tables, it was recognized that the loss of certain employees would not cripple the organization if the work force chart indicated that the department was sufficiently staffed at that level. In fact, certain terminations could serve as a "safety valve" to provide openings and advancement for others in the department.

The experience with computer personnel is not the only example of a sharp change in job market conditions. At one time or another, this phenomenon has occurred for certain types of engineers, mathematicians, lawyers, and those in other specialized professions. In no case, however, has the shortage lasted quite as long or its impact been as severe as in the case of computer specialists.

Generally, the solution to the problem has been more or less the same. The jobs have been segregated temporarily from the existing range structure. A separate evaluation and survey analysis has been undertaken to determine market value. Salary treatment has been in line with what was being paid in the market for comparable talents and contributions.

Usually a shortage in a particular trade or profession is neutralized within a few years by an influx of people into that field. As the supply and demand situation comes into balance, it is possible to place the jobs back into the normal structure, usually at the grade or point level at which they were originally pegged. Sometimes a slight change is needed either to correct an earlier error in evaluation or to allow for a permanent change in the market value of such jobs.

Example 2: The compensation of M.B.A.s.   For many companies, the hiring and salary treatment of selected M.B.A.s has become a major problem. These M.B.A.s are different from the business graduates in the past whom many companies assigned to well-defined jobs in accounting, credit, or related business departments.

Most companies engage relatively few M.B.A.s each year. Often a company is interested in finding the best-qualified candidate available. Competition for these relatively few candidates can drive rates sharply upward. If the company can be satisfied with a slightly lower level of qualification, the field becomes broader and the starting rates more reasonable. By having available a range of starting rates based on level of qualification, a company increases its chances for a successful recruiting effort.

When candidates accept employment, the company is faced with the problem of maintaining correct compensation to keep them on the payroll. Although it is possible to administer salaries on the basis of the company's regular exempt program, merit increases may be based on a special program for this particular group. In either case, it is important for the company to hold candidates until it can judge whether their contribution justifies their relatively higher starting rate and salary.

Attracting M.B.A.s may depend largely on the salary offer, but holding them requires more than salary. Of greater importance are the type of work they are doing, the environment in which they operate, and the challenge the job offers. If these variables are satisfactorily fulfilled, salary must be high enough to enable employees to resist the temptations of the outside market. Demand for such people is heavy, and they tend to be more mobile than the typical exempt employee.

Special treatment accorded M.B.A.s may appear to confer on them "crown prince" status. This should be avoided as much as possible by discreet handling of salary matters as well as by firm insistence on performance equivalent to salary. Otherwise, the charge of favoritism may be justified. On the other hand, unless special treatment is granted to high-quality employees, it will not be possible to compete for them in the market, either in recruiting or in retaining candidates after they have joined the company.

SPECIAL CAREER DEVELOPMENT

Example 1: Paying the up-from-the-ranks supervisor versus the college graduate engineer who starts as a supervisor.   There is a marked difference between the career paths of the up-from-the ranks supervisor and the trained engineer who starts as a supervisor. It is therefore unwise to evaluate both on the same basis or to reward them according to the same criteria simply because they occupy the same job.

The supervisor is generally at the top rung of his or her career. He or she may rise one more level (to general supervisor), but most supervisors in today's mass production factories accept their positions as career-terminal jobs. They are limited by their formal education and the technical demands of the higher-level positions. Engineers, on the other hand, are at the beginning of their careers. They have a vast reservoir of untapped knowledge and potential. The job of supervisor is assigned to them more as a learning exercise than as a job in which they can demonstrate their full capabilities. Nevertheless, they are usually expected to perform the job more capably than their counterparts from the ranks.

At least for the first few years, engineers in supervisory jobs should be treated in the same manner as their engineering peers in the rest of the organization. That is, they should be treated the way college graduates in engineering, research, sales, or administration are treated within the company. Frequently, the salary ranges for beginning engineers in production are very close to those of production supervisors. In a typical job evaluation scheme, the experience and skills acquired by supervisors during their careers often are equivalent to the academic learning of engineers directly out of college. Although the salary range may be similar, the merit-increase treatment of engineers will often differ from that of supervisors. Supervisors are usually paid for a satisfactory and stabilized performance of the engineer's job. Engineers, on the other hand, are paid for performing a supervisor's job, but they are also recognized as one of the cadre of professionals within the company from whom further growth and contribution are expected.

In the early years, engineers should be related to the college graduates in the company and receive any special merit treatments which are awarded to that group as a class. This means that their rate of pay should include normal merit increases as well as special adjustments influenced by new college hiring rates or unusual market considerations based on the supply and demand of candidates.

Sooner or later, however, a decision will have to be made as to whether the engineers will continue as supervisors indefinitely and cast their lot with the production hierarchy, or whether they will move to other areas of company operations to widen their background and experience. If the former decision is taken and they remain as supervisors, they will have to climb the ladder of jobs as they exist in the production part of the business. Their progress will depend on their own performance and the immediate openings which may occur in that part of the organization. If they remain as supervisors for any protracted period (usually three years or more), they must begin to conform to the pay levels and salary treatment of the other supervisors in the organization. Although at the start they may merit higher salary increases than their counterparts who came up from the ranks, after a few years such preferential treatment will have to be justified by their superior contribution on the job rather than by their technical background as members of a college-trained group.

Example 2: Paying the senior bookkeeper versus the entry-level accountant.   The salary structure of an accounting department is sometimes unsettled by the introduction of one or more entry-level, college-trained persons. Much day-to-day accounting work is routine in nature, and it is hard for many staff members of the department to conceive that the new, college-trained employee can make a different kind of contribution.

Yet unless the college-trained accountants are called on to innovate and to participate in decisions which have meaningful impact on the total accounting function, the company is not fully utilizing the talents their formal education brings to the job.

Except for the initial training period, therefore, the college-trained accountant occupies a different position from the senior bookkeeper, and this fact should be recognized. The job description should reflect the difference in job content, and even the title should differ from that of the bookkeeper. Although there will be instances when the two seem to be doing the same work, the depth of application and the scope of the two will be dissimilar. The jobs should be evaluated separately, and the merit treatment in each case should be related to the particular incumbent and job.

One word of caution: In setting up professional accounting jobs in the department, remember that college-trained employees expect to move up the ladder to more demanding and rewarding jobs. There have been many instances in which a company had staffed lower job echelons in accounting with college-trained, eager incumbents only to have these employees discover in a few years that they had no place to go. Feeling stymied, many of the best candidates quit, causing disruption and temporary demoralization of the whole department. The years spent in early training were lost to the company solely because it had sought out overqualified employees for the lower-level jobs.

It is best to limit the professionals in the department to the number that can reasonably expect upward movement and progress. The remaining jobs should be staffed as far as possible with people whose background and ability permit them to remain in career jobs over long periods of time.

SALARY COMPRESSION

Example 1: The squeeze on supervisors' salaries as a result of an increase in hourly rates, shift allowances, or overtime.   In most companies, supervisors are considered part of management and their salaries are tied to the managerial ladder (i.e., the exempt group in the structure). However, this often produces a dilemma because it is difficult to maintain a reasonable gap between the supervisors' compensation and the compensation of their highest paid subordinates.

At certain times, supervisors may earn scarcely more than their top operators, and sometimes, when unusually heavy overtime occurs, they may even earn less.

Companies have sought to solve this problem by continuing supervisors in the exempt ranks but tying their compensation to the hourly structure. This is usually done by relating supervisors' minimum or starting salaries to a percentage above the rate of the highest-paid hourly workers they supervise. This percentage may be anywhere from 10 to 35 percent, but the most prevalent in industry is 15 to 25 percent. The top of the supervisors' range, on the other hand, is usually related to the exempt salary structure, if possible. If this causes a compression problem within the structure, the top of the range can be set as a certain percentage of the minimum rate. Usually the supervisors' range spread is 35 percent, but this will vary and may be as high as 50 percent, depending on company policy.

When setting the starting salary or minimum of the range as a percentage of the hourly rate, companies usually include any shift or holiday allowances which may be a permanent part of the hourly rate. Some companies also figure in "average overtime" to make sure the "total package" of hourly compensation is representative. However, if overtime is extremely heavy or erratic, its inclusion in the average hourly rate may distort the basis of the calculation. In such cases, it is best to adopt a policy of supplemental income payments to the supervisor to counterbalance the effects of overtime. Supplemental pay to counterbalance overtime is also advisable if hourly rates are very high. If this is not done, and supervisors' ranges are set high enough to offset average hourly overtime, supervisors' salaries may reach levels which are seriously out of line with other comparable jobs.

Supplemental pay may be made at straight time or at time and one-half or a combination of both. The objective, of course, is to maintain a reasonable spread between the total compensation of the hourly worker and the immediate supervisor. Since the hourly worker is usually paid at time and a half for all hours over 40, one way of maintaining the spread is to pay time and a half on that portion of the supervisor's salary which is roughly equivalent to the hourly employee's base pay. For example, some plans provide time and a half on the first $1200 or $1500 of monthly salary and straight time on the balance. The plan often sets a limit on the amount of additional overtime compensation payable in any month regardless of how many hours have been worked. For example, the limit may be anywhere between $500 and $1500 a month. Also, there is usually a salary cutoff, above which a person is not eligible. For example, supervisors and general supervisors might participate, but plant managers or assistant plant managers and their equivalent levels would not be eligible.

It is wise to stipulate that supplementary payments will be made for scheduled overtime only. Unless overtime is carefully controlled, the need for overtime may be interpreted too loosely, resulting in high costs and inefficiencies. In any supplementary plan, the need for overtime should be strictly controlled and authorized only by persons who do not participate in the overtime payments.

Another way to deal with overtime compression is to introduce a form of additional income for first-level supervisors. A bonus plan for first-level supervisors need not be limited to considerations of overtime. Preferably, a bonus should be a reward for total performance which is measured rather precisely.

For example, performance goals can be set for specific items, such as production costs, level of quality, percentage of scrap, or timeliness in meeting production schedules. This bonus can be calculated by simple mathematical formulas which measure how well the department meets these goals. Although such a bonus plan is not related directly to overtime, it does increase the supervisors' total compensation and offers a means for providing a respectable spread between their overall reward and that of the people they supervise.

If a company already has a bonus plan for middle management, the supervisor can be made eligible to participate in the plan. Such middle-management bonus plans usually have the following characteristics:

1. They are selective in the people who are rewarded, so that a supervisor may or may not get a bonus in any one year, depending on management's view of his or her total performance.
2. They are variable in the amount of payment to each individual. Most plans pay approximately one-half month's to three months' salary (4 to 25 percent of annual pay) to first-level supervisors.
3. The payment usually is not considered part of the base income on which benefit plans are calculated. Thus a supervisor cannot build up a greater stake in the pension plan or in the savings plan of the company through his or her bonus payments.

Some companies have attempted to alleviate the overtime compression problem by granting extra time off to supervisors. Theoretically, this does not cost the company additional money. However, many busy supervisors can hardly find enough time for their normal vacations and holidays, let alone schedule days off for overtime previously worked. In most cases, these supervisors accumulate long backlogs of earned time off, which they are never able to exercise. As this builds up, companies find it necessary either to buy off the time by some type of cash equivalent or to gradually forget about it by quietly letting it drop into limbo. The problem usually cannot be solved by the latter approach. Although the supervisors' reaction may not be overt, manipulating their earned time off usually undermines their loyalty to the company. The long-term result is often deterioration in the organizational health of the department.

Example 2: Compression of salaries of recent college graduates due to rapid increase in starting rates for college-trained employees. Since most companies adjust the exempt salary structure over a broad spectrum of jobs, a serious compression problem arises when the starting rates of a particular group increase more rapidly than those of the rest of the structure.

Starting rates for college graduates have for many years increased at a faster pace than rates for the rest of the exempt population. As a result, graduates who have been out of school for two, three, or four years are often faced with the prospect of earning only nominal amounts more than the graduate just entering without any experience. For example, if starting rates rise 12 percent while the rest of the salary structure rises only 9 percent in a particular year and this is repeated for several years, the salary progression ladder for the first few years may well become uncomfortably flat. When this occurs, years of experience are rewarded very slightly if at all.

To compensate for this, many companies set up a series of special payments to college graduates during the first one to five years. Other companies provide a special merit program which accelerates salary increases to keep a proper motivating distance between classes. Eventually, of course, all salaries must be melded into the regular structure, but this is usually done after about five years on the payroll.

Three ways by which yearly salaries of college graduates can be adjusted to keep up with starting rates are detailed below:

1. New graduates are granted a first increase in six months to bring them up to the hiring rate expected to be paid the following June. They then receive a regular merit increase at the end of another six months. For the next two to four years, each class is kept a certain dollar figure ($50 to $100 a month) ahead of the previous year's class.

2. The first-year graduate is given an adjustment (in addition to merit increase) equal to the full amount of the rise in starting rates. Each successive class is given a decreasing percentage adjustment. For example, the size of the adjustments might be:

Years out of college	Adjustment as percentage of base salary
1	10
2	7
3	4

Generally, after the third year is reached, adjustments phase out and the incumbent takes his or her place in the regular exempt salary structure.

3. The merit program is made strong enough to maintain a proper distance between classes, taking into account individual performance. This requires that management be alert to changing starting rates and also courageous enough to give the size increases required to maintain equity. One way to help managers carry out such a policy is to provide a list of graduates with up to five years' service who have not kept reasonably ahead of the increase in starting salaries over the period of their employ. By using this list as a guide, managers can take the necessary action to bring young graduates into proper relationship with each other, assuming individual performance and contributions are satisfactory.

PROFESSIONAL INSULATION

Certain professional employees, such as lawyers and doctors, often relate more closely to the pay structure of the profession than to that of the company.

Example 1: Medical doctors.   Doctors, whose duty it is to look after the general health of the employees, conduct physical examinations, and handle emergency disabilities, are usually far removed in their interests from the line objectives of the enterprise. Although many companies have tried to incorporate evaluation of medical doctors into the overall company structure, such evaluations are often fictional and intended only to prove that all jobs can be evaluated under a plan rather than to determine the real worth of the medical job. It is far more realistic to try to relate the doctor's job to the going rates for similar jobs in that area. This cannot always be done by comparison with the highly specialized market of industrial medicine. Depending on location, the market value of an industrial physician may be influenced more by local doctors' incomes than by industry rates for doctors.

A survey of the area should include both private and industrial physicians, if possible, to provide sufficient data to determine a fair level of pay. At best, such a survey will indicate a general range for the job. The actual pay level will depend on the individual, his or her skills, reputation, and experience, as well as the negotiating position based on the current supply-and-demand situation. Most companies do not want to compromise on the quality of a physician and would rather pay a reasonable amount above what appears to be an average rate to obtain a competent physician than to adhere rigidly to a present range which would limit their choice and selection.

Example 2: Lawyers.   Members of the legal profession are often found in various managerial and administrative positions in industry. Such jobs are evaluated like other company jobs, since they relate directly to the operations of the business. Where lawyers are used strictly to provide legal counsel and guidance to others who make decisions or take actions, their role is more nearly that of a member of an outside law firm who may be hired on a retainer by the company.

The most effective approach to compensation for this latter group of lawyers will vary from company to company. When the law department is large and there is a regular hierarchy of levels from beginning lawyer to senior attorney, the jobs can be evaluated as staff jobs, similar to other staff jobs in personnel, credit, accounting, etc., and related to the total structure. In this way, companies create a law structure which is part of their overall staff structure. It is then priced as part of the overall company line, and the ranges for lawyers bear a relationship (i.e., are internally equitable) with the other professional, executive, and administrative jobs in the company.

When the number of lawyers is small and a hierarchy does not exist, companies have found it more effective to consider the jobs as specialists' jobs to be related to the outside profession rather than to the company structure. An area survey of rates for lawyers in law firms and in industry should provide sufficient background data to set up equitable ranges.

It should be remembered, however, that lawyers vary widely in professional ability and reputation. In many jobs, the incumbent does make the job. A lawyer's education, experience, and standing in the profession determine his or her level and capacity to serve the company. It would be hard to evaluate a lawyer's qualifications or the level at which he or she serves without closely observing the modus operandi. Therefore, the exact pay level must be left to the person making the selection and evaluating the performance. A survey can serve only as a general guide. In most companies, the lawyer's actual compensation is related to the manner in which the company utilizes his or her services. In certain companies, law departments are equivalent to and comparable with the finest outside law firms. In others, the lawyer is intended only as an adviser to act as intermediary between the company executive and one or more outside law firms which conduct most of the company's law operations.

Over the years, the demand for legal services has risen sharply. This has put upward pressure on lawyers' salaries in industry, which has been more than matched by rising incomes in private practice and private law firms.

It would be wise, therefore, to develop separate market data on lawyers' incomes to ensure that company ranges and actual compensation are in line with the market. It should not be necessary to design a new structure to keep up with the market, but it would be helpful to have information on what is happening in the market so that the manager or the person administering the lawyers' salaries can act accordingly. Many companies include lawyers' positions in their bonus plans. They are, therefore, able to supplement the salaries with reasonable bonuses which reflect performance and also help to keep current remuneration in line with total compensation of professional counterparts in the outside market.

UNUSUAL PERFORMANCE PATTERNS

Although most merit programs operate with little difficulty and are able to distinguish variations in performance and to award increases accordingly, some plans are deficient in properly recognizing sharp differences in performance.

Example 1: Extraordinary growth in performance. Companies pay lip service to the concept of rewarding the outstanding performer but often back away when it comes time to pay the salary demanded by such performance. Much of this reluctance is understandable, since companies closely examine present performance but also like to look at the employee on a career basis. However, certain managers, particularly those who have lived through the Depression, suffer from a weakness which might be called "dollar fear"; i.e., the total amount of dollars required to bring an outstanding performer into proper relationship, particularly a new incumbent, frightens the manager. Philosophically, the manager goes along with the idea that a substantial boost in salary is needed to match the level of performance. But emotionally, the "rend of parting" is too great for the manager to recommend the full amount of increase which is needed.

In order to help the manager meet this situation, some companies have set up percentage guides for various levels of performance. For example, a typical merit-increase guide might be:

9% for satisfactory performance
12% for commendable performance
18% for outstanding performance

By applying these percentages, the manager feels less "guilty" in awarding the amount of money which the situation demands.

Of course, percentage guides should always be used in conjunction with time-span considerations. A merit increase has two dimensions: money and time. If elapsed time since the last increase is disregarded, the percentage loses meaning. Therefore, it is best to specify elapsed time limits for each class of increase and to think in terms of a percentage per year of time since the last increase. In other words, if it has been one and a half years since the last increase and the incumbent is worthy of a 10 percent annualized increase, the real increase should be 15 percent. If he or she has been an outstanding performer and the last increase was 15 months ago, the new increase should be 22.5 percent ($1\frac{1}{4} \times 18$ percent) to cover the time span since the last increase.

Example 2: The rapidly promotable individual. Whenever possible, it is best to give an increase at or very close to the time of promotion. The old concept of "wait until they prove they can do job" has fallen into disfavor as a valid approach to rewarding promotable personnel. The reason is that much of the incentive generated by a promotion is wasted if the increase which should accompany that promotion is late. Furthermore, if the salary is below the minimum for the new job, there is a strain on the credibility of the salary program and the company may be vulnerable to an EEO charge. In general, when there is a good reason to delay an increase and maintain a person below the minimum of the range, three months should be the maximum waiting time. Otherwise, the employee not only is underpaid in relation to his or her colleagues but also may be earning less than the people he or she supervises. Such situations very quickly lead to disenchantment with the salary program. The entire motivating impact of a promotion may be dissipated, and the company will stand a good chance of losing a good employee in the not-too-distant future.

The situation becomes even more critical when the promotion is a substantial one. The employee may jump over the heads of two levels of subordinates—a "double jump promotion," as it is sometimes called. Here the gap between actual salary and the minimum of the range may be so great that a single increase to bring the employee up to the minimum may be unreasonable. In such cases, it may be better practice to give the increase in two awards—one at the time of promotion and the other approximately six months later. In other words, when responsibility increases substantially, it is wise to look at the employee's salary from the viewpoint of his or her total career. A single large increase at the time of promotion may make all subsequent increases of a more normal nature pall by comparison. Therefore, judgment should be used to provide a series of merit increases as a reward for excellent performance.

Example 3: Short bursts of extraordinary performance.   The performance of most employees will vary over the course of a few months. These variations are usually minor and hold to a standard pattern readily identifiable under one of the performance rating categories in use by the company. On occasion, however, some employees will, for short periods of time, perform at levels far beyond their normal pattern. This is usually in response to an extraordinary challenge of some sort—a special "crash" project, a need to fill in for a boss or an associate who is unavailable for several weeks, or a "once-in-a-lifetime" innovative idea.

Many companies feel that there should be some compensation response to these short bursts of extraordinary performance. Compensation programs typically take a longer view, however. Managers usually are encouraged to look at performance for an entire year in making salary decisions. A short burst may be overlooked or may create a "halo effect" on the balance of the employee's performance as seen by the manager. Either case could produce a less-than-optimal salary decision.

An effective response by many companies to these short-burst situations is a special bonus program. Such programs frequently provide for bonus payments to employees soon after the short burst occurs. Some companies, however, have good results with special bonus programs that pay all recipients at the same time once a year.

Bonus amounts will vary among companies. The amount of publicity given to the programs themselves and to the recipients also varies. One typical program provides a minimum bonus of $2500 and a maximum of 20 percent of annual base pay. The program is communicated only among managers, and no announcements are made concerning recipients. Since fewer than 5 percent of the employees participate, it is felt that nonrecipients would tend to be frustrated were knowledge of the program and the limited number of recipients more widespread.

The special bonus programs of most companies do not include the bonus payments in the pay on which benefit plans are based.

Since bonus recipients are typically few in number, a rigorous management approval process for bonus awards is normally included in the program design of most companies.

Example 4: A sudden downturn in performance and contribution.   There are occasions when a person who has been doing a good job over the years suddenly demonstrates a sharp downturn in performance. This may be the result of a variety of factors such as personal problems or illness. However, once all appropriate management steps to improve performance have been taken and it is certain that performance is not going to improve, the employee must either be reassigned to a job he or she can do (probably lower rated) or be terminated.

Most companies will permit a reassigned employee to continue at his or her existing salary, but the employee must remain at that salary as the structure moves upward until the salary is in line with the new range. However, other companies believe in giving the employee a pay cut to put the current salary in line with the new job. Then, on the basis of future performance, the employee is eligible for merit increases as ability on the new job is demonstrated. Such action eliminates the need for waiting for the structure to catch up, and it often has a salutary effect on the employee as he or she strives to do well on the new job. On the other hand, the shock of a pay cut often is severe, and unless the employee is psychologically prepared and willing to take such a cut, it could have a devastating effect on his or her morale. The manager will have to select the best approach. Results have been good with both procedures, but the choice depends basically on the individual employee and the environment in which he or she works.

Example 5: A static condition in which growth has plateaued or in which the employee has reached the top of the salary range and cannot be promoted.   In both of these situations, we have what might be called a "stabilized performance" condition. In one case, the employee's contribution remains satisfactory but there is very little, if any, growth in performance. In the other case, although growth may be present, the employee is already bumping the ceiling of the job. Normally, the top of the range in any properly designed salary program is good pay for that job and is the level at which high performers on the job should be rewarded. It would be unwise to pierce the top of this range except for extraordinary career situations. Occasionally, some companies will pierce the top by a certain amount, usually a maximum of 10 percent. However, in most cases, the incumbent must await an opportunity for promotion to a higher-level job. In the meantime, he or she continues to get increases equal to the movement of the structure, thus maintaining a position at the top of the range. Under these circumstances, it should be explained that the employee is already at the top of the range and that an opportunity for greater reward will occur if and when a higher-level job for which he or she qualifies becomes available.

The employee who has plateaued in performance, and whose salary is at an appropriate level within the salary range for the job, should receive increases no greater than the movement in the structure. This will keep the employee at the same relative level in the economy. Theoretically, "real" dollar pay will be maintained, since the structure tends to move in line with changes in the economy. However, in order to obtain a higher income in "real" money, it will be necessary for the employee to demonstrate a higher level of performance to justify a merit increase. This is hard to tell someone, but the message will soon get through. It is one of the built-in motivators of a good salary program.

The examples we have given of unique cases requiring special consideration in compensation all revolve around the single factor of flexibility in the salary program. A successful salary program is fundamentally a system of job and performance measurement. The program enables management to set up a meaningful hierarchy of jobs and to set dollar ranges and actual salaries for these jobs which are both internally equitable and externally competitive.

By various schemes, most programs are able to set up these relationships to cover a wide spectrum of jobs and to permit managers to administer salaries fairly. In most cases, the system is self-sustaining and self-correcting. Whether the jobs are clearly defined line jobs or less distinct jobs with intangible content, ranges can be reviewed and changes made to maintain an up-to-date and workable system.

Unfortunately, the job market never stands still. Career patterns of individuals vary widely. Therefore, situations arise which cannot be adequately fulfilled by normal application of the rules and procedures of the program. Most of these problems can be solved if the program is based on understanding and has a built-in flexibility to allow variations. Such variations, however, should meet the test of good common sense and should not strain the credibility of the program merely to take care of special interests or petty differences of opinion.

chapter 50

Employment Contracts

Lawrence W. Muth

DIRECTOR, CORPORATE ECONOMIC RESEARCH AND
STATISTICAL REPORTING, JOHNSON & JOHNSON, NEW
BRUNSWICK, NEW JERSEY

Employment contracts have been given an increasing amount of attention in the professional press and business literature in the past decade.

There are a variety of possible reasons for this. They include:

1. An increased awareness of the need to address a subject that had received little "press" in the past
2. The result of publicity concerning recent top-level management changes
3. The increase in merger activity and its potential impact on executive positions

These discussions and writings generally address the topic of using employment contracts, or they report the details of specific incidents. This leaves unanswered the questions of how frequently such contracts are used and which circumstances company managements feel warrant their use.

In an effort to respond to these questions, the author surveyed 155 companies in the latter half of 1981. The companies surveyed included 138 listed in the *Fortune* top 400 industrials and 17 listed in the *Fortune* nonindustrial categories of the top 50 life insurance companies, utilities, retail concerns, and transportation companies.

A similar survey on a smaller scale was conducted a decade ago. The current survey gives an opportunity to determine whether the intervening years and events have had a material effect on company policy. To facilitate this comparison, the underlying principles of the original survey were maintained.

In the current survey executive employment contracts were again separated from field sales employment contracts. Separating the two categories allows a distinction to be made between circumstances in which a specific person or group of persons is involved and those in which a company has sales representatives who, because of personal contacts and attachments, might have significant impact on a company's volume. In the latter instances, companies may use employment contracts as a protective device to avoid the possibility of significant loss of market when such sales representatives leave the company.

It was also determined that it would be desirable to distinguish between employment contracts and what are commonly called "security" or "patent" agreements. Trade and professional associations, including The Conference Board and the Executive Compensation Service of the American Management Association, have conducted surveys on the use of security and patent agreements. These kinds of agreements are generally restricted to protecting knowledge gained or inventions produced by employees while in the employ of a company. While such agreements may, on occasion, relate to employment contracts, they generally contain no commitment on the part of the company to retain the employees involved for a specified period of time, nor is there any commitment on the part of the employees to perform prescribed functions or assume responsibility for specified activities.

For the purpose of this survey, security and patent agreements are not considered to be employment contracts. This study is confined to those contracts containing special provisions which go beyond the items covered in normal employer-employee situations.

ITEMS COVERED BY EMPLOYMENT CONTRACTS

Specifically, an employment contract is considered to contain an agreement covering an individual's duties and the functional area for which he or she is responsible. It also spells out the compensation the individual is to receive, and it covers such items as salary, bonus, stock agreements, and perquisites.

Regulations and restrictions are sometimes incorporated into the contract to help define in more precise language the relationship between the company and the individual.

The period of time during which the contract is to be in effect is included in the agreement as well as the procedure to be followed in amending, terminating, or extending it.

FREQUENCY OF USE

Once again the spirit of cooperation so often found in personnel executives is clearly evidenced by the 108 individuals who responded to the request to have them participate in the survey.

The increase in the number of companies surveyed (155 vs. 100) broadens the coverage and adds a further degree of confidence to the value of the survey. It may also be the reason for the slight reduction in the rate of responses, from 75 percent in the earlier survey to 70 percent in the present survey, as shown in Table 1.

A comparison of the responses, however, shows a marked increase in the number of companies using employment contracts for executives. The number

TABLE 1   Survey Participants Rate

1971 Survey				1981 Survey			
Companies contacted		Companies participating		Companies contacted		Companies participating	
Number	%	Number	%	Number	%	Number	%
100	100	75	75	155	100	108	70

increased from 20 to 49 and the proportion of participants rose from 27 percent in the earlier survey to 45 percent in the current survey, as shown in Table 2. This seems to bear out the statement that employment contracts are of increasing importance in today's economy.

Despite the marked increase in the use of employment contracts for executives, the use of employment contracts for sales personnel continues to be very limited, as shown in Table 3.

An interesting sidelight can be drawn from the data by separating the results into industrial and nonindustrial concerns. This is shown in Table 4.

The ratio of participants to companies requested to participate is high for both the industrial and nonindustrial concerns. This high percentage of participation is an indication not only of the common interest in this subject but also of the fact that the need for information on employment contracts transcends commercial classification. The figures alone indicate the frequency of contract use; the reasons for using contracts, which follow, give substance to the raw data.

TABLE 2   Use of Employment Contracts for Executives

1971 Survey				1981 Survey			
Companies participating		Participants using employment contracts for executives		Companies participating		Participants using employment contracts for executives	
Number	%	Number	%	Number	%	Number	%
75	100	20	27	108	100	49	45

TABLE 3   Use of Employment Contracts for Sales Personnel

1971 Survey				1981 Survey			
Companies participating		Participants using employment contracts for sales personnel		Companies participating		Participants using employment contracts for sales personnel	
Number	%	Number	%	Number	%	Number	%
75	100	6	8	108	100	7	6

TABLE 4   Use of Employment Contracts in Industrial versus Nonindustrial Concerns

	Contacted		Participated		Participants using employment contracts for			
					Executives		Sales	
	Number	%	Number	%	Number	%	Number	%
Industrial	138	100	95	69	47	49	7	7
Nonindustrial	17	100	13	76	2	15	0	0

REASONS FOR USING EMPLOYMENT CONTRACTS

The survey questionnaire gave respondents the opportunity to expand on the answers to specific questions.

A substantial number of respondents who indicated that their companies used employment contracts said that these contracts applied to top executives in acquired companies. This may reflect a concern on the part of the acquiring company's management for the leadership of the acquired company to continue to be available for at least a specified period of time. It may also be a necessary part of the agreement negotiated by the two companies and may, in fact, be a reflection of concern for job security on the part of executives in the acquired company.

A second reason given by respondents for their companies' use of employment contracts was to facilitate the hiring of top executives from outside the company. Such contracts may be necessary to satisfy the desires of the executives being hired, particularly if the talents and experience of the prospective employees are in short supply and the perceived needs of the company require such action.

Employment contracts are also used when retiring executives take on a specific project for which their experience or talents are particularly appropriate. This procedure may enable a company to retain the expertise of executives who reach retirement age under the company pension plan. In addition, it may ease the transition from full employment to retirement in certain instances. This process may take on increasing importance in the next decade as the need for seasoned managerial talent continues to be a priority item.

The overwhelming majority of the "yes" responses indicated the use of employment contracts was restricted to the upper levels of management. The definition of the level varied among the respondents—in some instances, the level was determined by salary; in others, by position within the organization; and in a few instances, by geography, i.e., expatriate rather than domestic employees.

ADVANTAGES TO THE COMPANY

In discussing advantages gained by the company from the use of employment contracts, the respondents pointed out that these contracts were an instrument which permitted the company and the employee to agree in writing on the precise details of what the employee is expected to accomplish and the time frame within which that activity is to take place. By putting the agreement in writing, misunderstandings and misinterpretations can be eliminated or at least substantially reduced.

It was generally felt that avoiding such problems with individuals whose talents and knowledge can play an important role in the future of the company is worth the effort involved in preparing such contracts. An employment contract also emphasizes the need for both parties to pay careful attention to all aspects of the contract and to agree on the meaning of what is put in writing.

Another advantage to which several of the company executives referred can be broadly classified as "holding power," i.e., assurance that the special talents, knowledge, or ability of the individual covered by the contract will continue to be available to the company.

Company executives also feel that the use of an employment contract makes the employee more aware of the fact that something out of the ordinary is being made available. This is not meant to imply that the contract should be used as a status symbol but rather to point out that unusual items have been agreed upon and this agreement put into writing. This is borne out time and again in the responses of the companies using employment contracts. Phrases such as "used only for the highest-level executives," "used only in exceptional cases," and "used only to meet special situations" indicate that the individuals covered by such contracts are indeed being treated in a manner that differs from normal policy.

The respondents generally accepted the fact that certain job applicants may request an employment contract as part of an arrangement to change from one company to another. This desire for job security was—in the main—accepted as part of the hiring process in such cases.

On the other hand, one of the personnel executives took the contrary view, expressing the feeling that an individual who felt it necessary to ask for an employment contract was showing a lack of confidence in the organization. Such an attitude did not—in the opinion of that personnel executive—seem to be a sound basis upon which to build a good employer-employee relationship.

ADVANTAGES TO THE INDIVIDUAL

Personnel executives indicated that the formality of spelling out the agreement not only underlined the employee's commitment to the company but also defined the company's obligation concerning remuneration—and in a fashion sufficiently precise to eliminate questions during the life of the contract.

This reminder of the employee's personal commitment does not reflect an undesirable employer-employee relationship. Rather, it appears to be an indication of the value attached to having a mutually agreed-upon area of responsibility put into writing to avoid future misunderstandings.

In addition, some respondents stated that the primary advantage of such contracts was the increased sense of security resulting from putting the agreement into writing.

SUMMARY AND CONCLUSIONS

The scope of participation in the survey seems deserving of mention. Utilities, transportation companies, insurance companies, retail concerns, and manufacturing organizations all showed their interest in this subject by responding to the questionnaire. In fact, each of the categories of commerce included in the makeup of the survey is represented in the responses. What may perhaps be an even more significant indicator of the interest in this subject is the number of instances in which the participants included in their response a request for a copy of the survey results. This, in spite of the fact that the letter requesting their participation stated that "a copy of the completed results will be furnished to each participating company."

It is, therefore, quite apparent that employment contracts are of considerable interest to personnel executives. This interest may stem from any of the following reasons:

1. Personnel executives wish to stay informed on a phase of company action involving people.

2. Contracts may be a desirable part of a company philosophy concerning its relationship to key executives.

3. Contracts can be useful in the consummation of a merger or an acquisition.

4. Contracts are sometimes made public when executive changes take place at the top levels of some of our major corporations.

These expressions of interest do not reflect a high incidence of the use of such contracts, since the survey responses overwhelmingly carried notations such as "top executives only" or "only for executives above a certain high salary." It does, however, seem appropriate to conclude that they reflect a continuing desire on the part of personnel executives to remain alert to anything related to personnel activities that may be of value to their company. This thought was perhaps best expressed by two of the responding executives who commented that they were anxious to obtain the results of the survey to help them decide whether to recommend the use of such contracts in their companies.

It would be inappropriate to conclude this study without attempting to put the restricted use of employment contracts into proper perspective.

The fact that the companies using such contracts limit them to key executive positions should not be considered an indictment of employment contracts. This would be almost as grave an error as concluding that since company officials numerically represent only a small proportion of a company's total employees, it follows that company officials are not too significant in the scheme of things.

What seems to be a more reasonable conclusion is that employment contracts serve a useful purpose in certain specific circumstances. These circumstances will vary from company to company, but the use of such contracts indicates that some unusual or extraordinary action was deemed appropriate. Their use, therefore, seems to be another manifestation of management's ability to face up to unusual situations and, through the exercise of judgment required to direct the successful progress of an organization, find an acceptable solution.

Compensation for Retail Sales Personnel

Harriette A. Weiss

PARTNER, THE HAY GROUP, NEW YORK, NEW YORK

Alan Langer

FORMER CONSULTANT, THE HAY GROUP, BOSTON, MASSACHUSETTS

No compensation program can hope to be effective unless it takes into account the problems of the industry in which it is applied. In order to get a better perspective on the retail industry, let us step back for a moment and look at its problems.

Decline in Retail Profits   Back in 1969, *The New York Times* reported that the retail sector's return on capital invested *continued* to run below other industries—with a return, for example, which was 11.6 percent lower than that of manufacturing concerns.[1] More recently, from 1979 to 1981, net profits for four of the leading mass merchandisers (Sears, K-Mart, Woolworth, Montgomery Ward) declined more than 50 percent.[2]

The long trend of intensified competition is a principal cause of this squeeze

---

[1]"Retailers Are Facing Up to Sweeping Social Changes," *The New York Times*, Jan. 5, 1969, Section 3, 1:1.

[2]"The Retreat of the Mass Merchants," *The New York Times*, Feb. 21, 1982, Section 3, p. 1.

on profits. In the 1950s and 1960s, discount and self-service stores grew into prominence; in the 1970s, off-price *chains*, which sell brand-name merchandise at discount prices, entered the picture. Factory outlets and catalog showrooms are also offering expanded alternatives to in-store shopping. All of these are increasing the pressure on retail stores and adding to the uncertainty of adequate profits to absorb rising costs during the 1980s.

Nonstore Shopping   In a 1981 survey, the critical issues relating to "nonstore shopping" were found to include the need to cut down on driving and use of gasoline and the growing number of working women with reduced discretionary time. As consumers continue to spend their leisure in ways other than visiting stores, shopping by mail plays a more important role and perhaps will grow to 8 to 20 percent of in-store sales.[3] The increased variety of catalogs and of the goods they offer appeals to the rising number of two-income families and to affluent singles. Shopping by mail may be the fastest growing area of U.S. retailing, accounting for some 18 percent of all *general* merchandise sold. Mail order companies are enjoying a profit of 6 percent on sales as compared to the 3 to 5 percent profit of conventional retailers.[4]

In 1980, Federated Department Stores acquired an interest in Comp-U-Card of America to test an additional means of nonstore shopping. Comp-U-Card operates an electronic shop-at-home service providing home computer users, cable TV subscribers, and conventional telephone customers with access to product specifications, discount prices, and home delivery of more than 30,000 consumer products. Sears Roebuck and J. C. Penney are testing the QUBE system of Warner Amex Cable (a joint venture of Warner Communications and American Express), which is a two-way interactive cable system. According to some estimates, as much as one-third of general merchandise sales could be nonstore generated by the year 2000.

Productivity   Perhaps the biggest challenge is to increase the productivity of existing retail stores. Years ago the successful formula for profits seemed to be the addition of new stores. This is reflected in the increase of shopping centers in the United States over the last 20 years. In 1960 there were 3700; in 1970, 12,000; and in 1980, an estimated 20,000.[5] While the number of new centers rose more than fivefold in 20 years, the consumer population expanded at a much lower rate, resulting in an "overstored" condition in many areas. Also, because construction and land costs are steadily increasing, it has become more expensive to establish stores in new locations.

With the increased costs of construction, the slowdown of the population movement to the suburbs, higher overhead costs, and fewer sites on which to locate additional facilities, retailers are looking for methods of increasing productivity in their existing units. Store sizes are becoming more compact as retailers begin to emphasize return on investment.

---

[3]"Customers Dial N-O-N-S-T-O-R-E-S-H-O-P-P-I-N-G," *Chain Store Age Executive,* March 1981, p. 95.

[4]"Is the Store Becoming Obsolete?" *Time,* Nov. 27, 1978, p. 94.

[5]"The Challenge for Retailers," *The New York Times,* Dec. 16, 1980, Section D2:1.

need for Sales Training   Not unexpectedly, there is a new focus on the training of sales personnel in an effort to set one's own store apart from the competition, to improve employee morale, and to generate increased sales and profits.

In the past, sales training was not given a high priority by retailers, who dismissed it as a costly waste. They cited the fact that turnover among selling staff continued to average approximately 60 percent annually. Department store employees, who have a great deal of contact with the public, were often considered only for their operating roles and not for their marketing influence on customers.

In more recent years, by contrast, retail employers have begun to recognize that improved productivity is partly the result of better performance by sales employees. Training programs that focus on salespeople's friendliness, product knowledge, and enthusiasm about both the company and its merchandise can create an environment which encourages improved performance.

However, while top management may be aware of the role of training in getting the best out of employees, middle management is often unable to implement the necessary programs. Managers who are pressured to perform in a slow-growth, high-inflation economy tend to divert their attention from the need for increased productivity and to focus on external matters. If companies become even more impersonal and less communicative, the gap between the capacity of the employees and the utilization of their potential will widen.[6]

Traditional Low Pay   Over the last 10 years, retail employment has risen by 4 million workers. As many as 15.6 million persons are now employed in retail sales, and the value of what they sell represents about one-third of the gross national product.

However, despite the acknowledged importance of the retail employee's performance and its effect on the company's productivity, retail trade employment is well known for its relative instability, partially due to the industry's low earnings profile. Over a recent 10-year period, the number of retail employees who worked fewer than 35 hours weekly has risen from 29 to 35 percent. The reduction in the average workweek of full-time employees has been only partially offset by increases for part-time employees. The retail worker's average workweek has decreased from 37.2 to 35.1 hours. Electronic equipment, such as computerized inventory control systems, eliminates a certain amount of manual work, reducing the time required to complete sales transactions. Therefore, while store hours and output continue to expand, per-employee hours have not increased.

Moreover, salespeople are generally compensated less than they would be for equal work in other industries. As recently as the late 1970s, retail workers' median weekly earnings were only 59 percent of those for all wage and salary workers. Earnings of full-time retail workers were found to average about 73 percent of those for full-time workers in other industries. This reflects the occupational mix of relatively low-skilled, low-paying pursuits within retail sales— service, sales, unskilled labor, and clerical work.[7]

---

[6]"The Use of Human Resources and U.S. Productivity: The Gap Is Widening," *Women's Wear Daily*, Feb. 18, 1981, p. 30.

[7]Barbara Cottman Job, "Employment and Pay Trends in the Retail Trade Industry," *Monthly Labor Review*, March 1980, pp. 40–43.

Need for New Approaches   The outlook for retailing in the 1980s is not good. For the economy as a whole, the 1970s were characterized by a rise in employment and real income, easy credit, and consumer confidence in asset appreciation; but the early 1980s were plagued by decreases in disposable income, escalating interest rates, and inflationary pressures. Sluggish sales, coupled with the increased cost of doing business, compound retailers' problems. Retailers are therefore at a crossroads. They can continue traditional methods of recruiting, training, and paying salespeople, thus foregoing the chance to motivate their personnel and improve service; or they can recognize the characteristics of the new work force pool and gear compensation and training programs toward improved consumer service.

Current compensation practices vary widely, and some have been effective in meeting the needs of employees and motivating them. By and large, however, retailers' thinking on sales compensation has been confined to setting the hourly rate and deciding the items on which commissions should be paid. Generally speaking, retail salespeople are either paid straight salaries (usually for small-ticket items in department, self-service, and discount stores), salary plus some commission (on big-ticket items such as fur coats and white and brown goods), or straight commission (in a few large chain stores). A few retailers have gone beyond this formula in an effort to motivate their people. Sears Roebuck, for example, has for years provided its permanent employees with profit sharing. While Sears's profit sharing plan has been recognized as a farsighted, imaginative way to make employees profit-sensitive, it does not necessarily motivate individual performance. Also, it does not address nonmaterial needs, which—for the people among whom the retail industry must now do its recruiting—may be even more pressing than material needs and whose fulfillment may be prerequisite to even considering employment. These may include transportation to and from work and child care during working hours.

Given the retail trade's reputation for relatively unstable employment, compensation becomes one of the most important and sensitive issues facing the industry today. Changing expectations on the part of the work force, continuing inflation, the ongoing necessity to improve productivity by improving employee performance, and the need to ensure that payroll dollars are spent effectively—all impact on decisions regarding the pay of employees.

Pay System as Part of Strategic Planning: The Performance Contract   In general, retailers are known to have a very short-range outlook. In order to ensure a company's future share of business and its return on investment, management is in need of long-range strategic planning. Such planning must include the fundamentals of how to structure a pay system which will maximize organizational effectiveness by attracting and retaining a qualified work force, increasing job satisfaction, and rewarding individual performance. There is a trend among the more aggressive retailers to link compensation to performance in ways that focus employee attention on business objectives. Our experience shows that it is possible to reinforce a selling and servicing culture by providing significant opportunities that directly reward the achievement of specifically planned results.

Increasingly, retailers are anxious to reward profit generation rather than volume increase per se, as is understandable in a time of escalating costs and shrinking margins. Simple, easy-to-communicate, "snappy" sales incentive plans are taking the form of the performance contract, setting forth mutually agreed upon, job-related performance targets, the achievement of which will pay off in predictable amounts.

The idea is to define expected performance in concrete terms and to link it directly to pay, using a format that captures the employee's attention. Focusing on improved *sales* performance through pay-related arrangements follows the concept of variable rewards which underpins the majority of *management* incentive and bonus plans. Through a participative approach that involves salespeople and management, group and individual performance targets can be set, with earnings opportunities based upon achievement against the targets. This encourages a combination of team cooperation and individual effort and it provides management and the employee with a "score-keeping" system for evaluating and rewarding the success of the business and the salesperson.

Productivity per Square Foot ... Total Employment Opportunity   Let us close this chapter by citing the opinions of two prominent retail executives, both of whom are leaders in human resource management.

The vice chairperson of a chain of up-scale, nationally recognized specialty stores considers the compensation of sales personnel to be an integral part of the chain's people-related challenges. While different retail segments may vary in their approaches to pay and recruitment, *productivity per square foot* is today's measure of business performance and will more and more in the future determine the level and format of sales compensation. The obstacle to moving in that direction centers on the systems, both new automated and revised manual, that are prerequisite for the performance measurements necessary to underpin the reward structure.

The senior vice president of a leading mass-merchandising chain observes that the retail industry is in the early stages of a cultural change, which will impact not only on pay but also on sales job design, career pathing, and training. This executive sees the level of pay in this labor-intensive industry as the straightforward consequence of what is economically feasible—and sees a particularly great need to focus on the total employment opportunity. The intent is to shape the work experience to be more meaningful and human through redesigning jobs, clarifying expectations, and training beyond basic product and skill.

We believe that while the future of retailing as we know it today is largely dependent on economics, management can achieve a significant impact on that future by "merchandising" employee potential. The attention of customers and employees alike can be captured by inventiveness in merchandise and presentation and in employment opportunities that focus on business objectives while responding to human needs.

chapter 52

Designing an Integrated Sales Compensation Program

R. G. Jamison

CORPORATE DIRECTOR OF COMPENSATION, ROCKWELL
INTERNATIONAL CORPORATION, PITTSBURGH,
PENNSYLVANIA

The sales force is critical to the growth and success of most companies. Compensation must be carefully planned to reward the type of performance essential to the objectives of the organization. Pay plans that are well suited to a young company probably won't be adequate for a mature one. A policy that might work well for a consumer organization will not be appropriate for a company in the semiconductor business. As there are an infinite number of products and services to be sold, it is not surprising to expect that the sales job and, consequently, the design of sales compensation plans, will vary tremendously among them.

Sales managers and compensation specialists are required to rely on intuition rather than science in designing salespersons' compensation plans. To quote General E. W. Rawlings, former president of General Mills, Inc., "In this highly competitive world, it is clear that in motivating our sales force, we have no exact formula or exact science to guide us. Human judgment is still involved. You can't use computers to do this job; they may help, but they won't do it for us."

The sales manager's success represents the collective results of all the sales representatives under the manager's direction. Consequently, the motivation and efforts of the subordinates are critical to the effectiveness of the manager. Small wonder that the correct design of a pay plan for sales personnel receives the constant attention of the senior sales executives in most organizations.

In spite of the complexities that follow the design of sales plans, there is usually one important advantage: successful performances can be measured. The measures may be in direct procurement of sales, customer calls, servicing orders, convention activity, etc. In most cases, the measure of results can be supported in quantified terms. Consequently, the annual objectives of the salesperson are more precise than most other positions. This lends itself to compensation plans that reward the achievement of these goals. This is fortunate since salespersons in the field are located away from headquarters, frequently at considerable distances. Additionally, they are on their own much of the time and have a great deal of latitude in action and self-management.

It is important to keep in mind that the most critical step in the design of any sales plan is determining precisely what management wants the salesperson to achieve. This might mean heavier emphasis on high-margin products, new product introductions, expense control, total volume, or other objectives. The design of the compensation plan should complement these objectives and in a real sense communicate management's directions to the salesperson through a monetary reward system.

The cost of a sensible, effective incentive plan is not an expense. Such a plan is a good, sound investment for which a fair return is expected. It should stimulate sales, add profits, attract highly qualified personnel, and, of course, build for the future. Only poorly planned and badly executed programs are really costly. It is an accepted fact that the salespeople who are expensive to the company are usually those in the low-income group, while the least costly are the few top earners.

LEVELS OF COMPENSATION

Numerous surveys indicate rather significant differences in compensation levels of salespeople in various industries. One cannot help being impressed by the difference between the compensation levels of a pharmaceutical product salesperson and those of a person in jewelry sales. However, these industrial differences seem to be getting smaller. Surveys by industrial groups may tend to perpetuate the status quo in that unsound compensation practices can be supported by comparisons within each industrial group.

To determine a company's relative position with regard to compensation of its salespeople, one needs to conduct a survey or an analysis of reliable surveys on compensation. Such an evaluation must consider the total compensation of the salesperson, not just base salary alone. Market competitiveness is vital for sales positions because salespersons can be highly mobile. Many are motivated, perhaps more than people in other jobs, by the prospect of more money.

In designing a sales compensation plan, management needs to make some basic decisions regarding the amount of money a salesperson might earn. That is, what is the most that the company would be willing to pay for truly outstanding performance? There is the age-old question of whether a salesperson should ever be allowed to earn more than the boss. Many times, one hears a sales manager tell with great pride of the salesperson who earns a great deal more in total compensation than the president of the company. At first blush, this sounds very exciting, for there can be no question about the outstanding incentive opportunities available in this company. One cannot help but wonder, however, how many of these situations simply reflect a poorly designed incentive plan that permitted exorbitant and unreasonable amounts of compensation to occur.

"Sound travels faster than light" seems to be true within a sales organization, regardless of what happens in the world of physics. Unreasonably high earnings by certain salespersons because of inconsistencies or indiscriminate use of sales credits in the compensation plan are much discussed within sales organizations. Managers sometimes delude themselves into thinking that sales compensation can be kept confidential. It cannot.

In considering compensation levels for salespersons within a company, some rather elementary questions need answering:

1. Can the company afford to hire untrained and inexperienced salespeople, or does it have an immediate need for highly experienced professionals?

2. To what extent does the salesperson have a direct and final impact on sales?

3. Will the company be able to afford to bring its more successful salespersons into the sales management group without destroying appropriate internal relationships?

4. Does the company want to compensate its salespeople at its own industry level, or at the level of salespeople in all industries?

ELEMENTS OF COMPENSATION

Base Salary Only   Base salary provides the security and opportunity for a salesperson to establish a desirable level of living and social participation. It removes concern for the peaks and valleys and, therefore, permits personal budgeting for monthly mortgage and other fixed payments.

In 1946, over one-third (37 percent) of the 443 manufacturers in a National Industrial Conference Board (NICB) study used a salary-only plan for salespeople.[1] By 1981, only 23 percent of 159 companies surveyed by Hay Associates reported salary-only plans.[2] Nevertheless, a number of companies are still enthusiastic about such plans—and rightly so—for their particular situations.

Adequate compensation for performance of essential nonselling tasks required of salespeople may be overlooked in compensation plans that put undue emphasis on incentives. These tasks include missionary work, new accounts, service, complaints, meetings, travel, conventions, training other salespeople, record keeping, etc.

Compensation plans which provide for base salary only may provide realistic and fairer compensation relationships between salespeople on the basis of their performance and experience, etc., rather than on the serendipity of a particular sales territory. Another reason why some companies look favorably on the salary-only plan is that with it changes can be made within the sales territories without detriment to the compensation of other salespeople. The sales manager is more directly in control of these kinds of changes.

---

[1]National Industrial Conference Board Report, "Salesmen's Compensation Plans," *Studies in Personnel Policy*, no. 81, 1946, p. 13.

[2]"Sales Compensation Comparison—Industrial," Hay Associates, 1981, p. 38.

Therefore, management must at least consider some of the advantages of salary-only plans. Since straight-salary plans do not use supplemental compensation to motivate salespeople, the responsibility falls on sales management to provide this motivation. Some advantages worth considering are:

1. The salesperson has a steady, predetermined income and can establish a living level without the uncertainties of varying income.

2. Salespeople are more easily controlled and directed. For example, a salesperson may carry out assigned nonselling tasks without loss of income.

3. The sales force is more willing to engage in teamwork.

4. There is reduced likelihood of overstocking customers by using high-pressure selling methods.

5. The accent is on continuing service to an account.

6. Inequities because of differences in the time necessary to make a sale are reduced.

7. The differences in the level of education and the length of training required for various types of selling receive recognition.

Base salary is also important in salary-commission and salary-incentive plans. Clearly, a base-salary structure must be sound if it is to serve as the underpinning of an effective incentive plan. Moreover, a company's base-salary levels affect its ability to attract outstanding salespeople. Base salary should reflect the long-term values of both the salesperson and the job, and it should be high enough to free the salesperson from more serious money worries while he or she is building up the territory to productive levels. Ideally, it should also be part of an established range that will offer room for promotion and not impede desirable transfer of personnel between sales and other functions in the company.

Draw A drawing account provides money advances to a salesperson to be paid regularly like salary and later deducted from total commission earnings. If a salesperson fails to earn sufficient commission to cover the draw, he or she is theoretically expected to reimburse the employer for the overdraft before receiving additional commissions.

The drawing account is, therefore, used only where neither base salary alone nor salary in combination with incentive or commission is paid. A drawing account does provide greater stability in the salesperson's income, but at a risk. The drawing account was far more popular at the turn of the century than it is today.

Commission Plans Technically, a commission program pays a calculable amount for achieving quantifiable objectives. A commission is generally a specific percentage of the dollar volume generated by the salesperson's efforts. It always deals with specific measurable factors.

In 1946, companies with straight-commission plans represented 15 percent of the companies surveyed by the National Industrial Conference Board. By 1981, only 1 percent of the companies included in the Hay Compensation Comparison reported sales plans that paid commission only.

There seems to be a common frustration among sales managers because commission salespersons, as a group, feel they are free agents and consequently lack loyalty to the company or customer. It is interesting that manufacturers of furniture and apparel and companies oriented toward door-to-door sales have traditionally used the straight-commission plan.

The commission plan does not provide salespeople enough earnings when the orders dry up. Conversely, earnings may rise unduly in periods of prosperity or heavy demand. Sometimes a straight-commission plan has a built-in bias toward building volume on easy sales while ignoring the most profitable items. When a company wants to open up sales in new outlets, it is difficult, if not impossible, to induce the commission employee to do the necessary missionary work.

Some of the advantages found in a straight-commission plan are:

1. With its all-or-nothing approach, it tends to attract professional salespeople. High performance levels result in high earnings and a complete freedom of action.

2. Especially with new companies, the salesperson is asked to share the risk with the company and, conversely, to participate more favorably in the rewards of the company if it becomes successful.

3. Commissions allow the unit cost of sales to be predetermined. This is especially good for a small, struggling firm.

4. Straight-commission plans are probably most effective in taking care of incompetent salespersons; they eliminate themselves.

5. Commission plans have worked well in highly competitive industries where aggressive selling and strong incentive are needed.

Bonus Plans   Commission-bonus compensation usually considers the combination of subjective elements and quantifiable objectives. Normally, a certain percentage of the person's earnings is determined by precise sales accomplishments and may relate to a quota or be based on a percentage of sales. In addition, a portion of the incentive is based on factors such as new accounts, expense reduction, and other nonsales performance measures. Individual earnings, therefore, reflect the combination of specific sales results and other performance criteria.

A company may gauge a person's record—in part, at least—by customer services, numbers of calls made, organization of territory, and customer potential. The company can then base incentive payments on the results achieved in these areas as well as on sales volume.

Bonus plans are common in technical service and sales positions, where the salesperson may spend a large part of his or her time on nonselling activities. A bonus plan is almost always used in combination with a base-salary plan. Some of the advantages of bonus plans include:

1. Such plans seem to be a happy marriage between the straight-commission and base-salary–only plans, recognizing the importance of sales results as well as nonselling activities.

2. They provide an understandable target for salespeople to use in accomplishing the sales objectives of the company.

3. They establish a direct relation between individual performance and compensation.

4. While usually not affording the same earnings potential as straight-com-

mission plans, commission-bonus plans do allow better earnings when sales are poor—if the salesperson has done other important functions well.

5. Bonus plans promote teamwork among sales and service functions.

Combination Plans   A survey conducted in 1981 by Hay Associates showed that approximately three-quarters of the companies questioned provided compensation programs that combine salary and commission or salary and bonus. This compares with 38 percent of 443 similar companies surveyed by NICB in 1946. Obviously, companies are striving to tailor their compensation plans to fit their own particular objectives.

Combination plans recognize the importance of the fixed portion of an employee's earnings and the incentive value of a variable such as bonus or commission. As was discussed earlier, base salaries can be used to reflect the long-term values of the employee and to protect the salesperson while he or she is building the territory. The variable provides a reward for specific accomplishments over a predetermined period of time.

Judging from the trend toward combination plans, it does appear that managers must be concerned not only with the type of plan but also with the percentage they want to pay in more or less fixed amounts (salary) and the percentage they are willing to pay in variable amounts (incentives).

Based on the 1981 Hay Compensation Comparison, variable compensation represents approximately 20 percent of base salary in combination plans. However, there is a fairly wide range among various industries.

BALANCING FIXED AND VARIABLE PAY ELEMENTS

Pay plans are in a state of flux. Even though most companies are at least "satisfied" with their sales pay plans, only 16 percent rate their current sales compensation plan as "excellent."[3] During the period of 1975 to 1980, the majority of changes to plans were in the direction of a greater percentage of incentive. (See Table 1.)

Because there is no one compensation plan that is best for all firms, each company tries to find the one best suited to its own purposes. There is no single ratio of salary to variable pay that would or should apply. Therefore, after determining the total compensation level for a salesperson, a company must

---

[3]"Sales Compensation '80—An RIA Survey." Reprinted by permission of Research Institute of America. Copyright 1980 by the Research Institute of America.

TABLE 1   Direction of Change in Pay Plans   (All Companies)

	1980	1975
Toward more salary	30%	32%
Toward more incentive	55%	42%
No change in proportion	15%	26%

SOURCE: "Sales Compensation '80—An RIA Survey." Reprinted by permission of Research Institute of America. Copyright 1980 by the Research Institute of America.

decide the method of paying it. Some basic requirements must be met if a salesperson's compensation plan is to be effective. The plan should:

1. Provide a method of payment that motivates personnel to work toward the specific objectives determined by management
2. Have flexibility that operates equitably for both the salesperson and the company in all stages of the business cycle
3. Give realistic recognition to the relative impact the sales force has on the final sale and the extent to which the sales results are influenced by marketing and service support
4. Be relatively and appropriately consistent with practices used by other companies in the industry
5. Provide fair treatment of foreseeable future developments, such as introduction of new products, changes in territory or method of distribution, and split-territory sales
6. Be understandable and acceptable to the sales force
7. Provide an equitable level of compensation commensurate with both the size and the profitability of the company

The portion of total compensation that is commission, incentive, or bonus should reflect the degree to which the individual can directly influence the actual sale of the product. For example, certain technical sales personnel must have a heavy technical background and often spend much time in a service role. It would be foolish to place a large portion of such personnel's compensation in a variable form which could fluctuate widely with sales volume.

The weight of salary versus incentive or bonus should and does vary greatly among industries. Perishable or limited-shelf-life products do not lend themselves to the same degree of commission or incentive payment emphasis as do heavy equipment, insurance, hardware, and other nonperishable products. Food companies must consider turnover and freshness of product among factors influencing the balance between salary and incentive pay components.

Other factors also influence the balance between fixed and variable components in the total compensation package for sales plans—especially the type of selling to be done and the basic objectives of the company.

Isolating the company's particular needs and objectives is an important first step. It is critical because it requires a precise definition of the selling task at hand. Moreover, going through the exercise of defining the sales task tends to get all members of sales management thinking the same way about today's selling job. In the absence of the discipline of writing down a sales specification, company sales executives often think that each understands the other's views of the selling task when in fact there is a wide variation in the understanding of what is basic.

Objectives must then be communicated to the sales field. Trite as it sounds, it is nevertheless mandatory that a salesperson understand the job accountabilities precisely. This understanding may come through an effective manager, a position description, or a well-designed incentive plan. But there must be a clear understanding of the job expectations.

Behavioral scientists write much about the motivational aspects of incentive plans. In addition to providing motivation, a well-conceived incentive plan is one of the most effective communications devices we have. A good incentive plan, properly designed, will tell the salesperson in very precise terms how the company expects sales efforts to be spent and which results will be most favorably regarded by the company. A plan designed strictly on the basis of volume tells the salesperson that the company is most concerned about total dollar sales as opposed to the mix of the product sales or the development of new accounts. The name of the game in this particular company would be: Obtain sales volume.

A well-designed incentive plan provides a mutual understanding between sales management and sales personnel of key objectives and priorities. The compensation program should reward each individual for the degree of success in accomplishing these desired objectives. Conversely, failure of a salesperson to perform well should mean a penalty in the form of decreased compensation.

Low incomes resulting from lack of industry, lack of skill, or lack of planning may be regrettable, but the responsibility must be placed on the salesperson, or the sales management, and not on the compensation plan. Administrative decisions to protect below-average sales efforts are detrimental to the motivation of good salespeople and foolish from a business point of view.

As a general rule, therefore, the more directly a salesperson can actually influence the sales results, the greater should be the opportunity for variable compensation. There is no balance in the percentage of salary and variable that applies equally well in all companies. Even within a multidivisional company, the design and the percentage of base to variable will differ.

MANAGING SALARIES

Modern job evaluation techniques make it possible to evaluate a sales position in the same manner as other management jobs. These evaluations consider and weight a number of factors, such as the amount of knowledge that is required in the position, the human skills requirements, the extent of problem solving, the size of dollar impact, etc.

If the organization is properly structured, there will be a reasonable ladder of progression of positions. This offers the beginning salesperson an opportunity to move through the sales organization to reach the optimum management level. There should be a distinguishable difference between jobs. Often a temptation exists to differentiate jobs in a manner which simply reflects that one salesperson is more experienced than another. Unless there is a distinct difference in the requirements of the positions, experience is best recognized by movement within the salary range. Once the positions have been correctly evaluated, a dollar value for the jobs can be assigned. Most companies include sales positions in the same schedule as is used with other management jobs. A company is well advised to confirm the competitiveness of the assigned job values. In certain industries it may be necessary to use a structure that is different from the management structure in order to recognize competitive practices.

Typically, companies work with ranges having a 50 percent spread from minimum to maximum. This seems to give enough flexibility for movement of salaries while still protecting the proper salary relationship between jobs.

Let us consider this example: Sam Spade, a salesman for a cosmetics firm, currently earns $1500 a month. Last year he was his company's leading salesperson, eclipsing his quota by some 20 percent. Because of his sales results, he earned $6000 in commission payments. His total earnings were a respectable $24,000. His manager must now decide whether Sam should be given a merit increase, and how much. It could be argued that his performance has been outstanding and that he deserves a high adjustment. However, his manager is fearful that if Sam's salary is raised too high, the company will not be able to move Sam to a district supervisor's position. Such is the dilemma of many managers who must decide how much consideration should be given to the amount of incentive earned in arriving at a proper base salary.

In Sam's case, we need first to know what the policy guideline is for the job. His salary in relation to the guideline should be based on his overall performance. Now the manager can give consideration to many factors that may not be included in the incentive or commission plan, such as sales management potential, constructive ideas submitted, or other special criteria.

One company requires a ranking of salespeople in each of its districts (see Figure 1). On the basis of these appraisals, which cover both selling and nonselling factors, the sales manager makes decisions regarding the salesperson's base salary. A person may receive a relatively small incentive and yet receive

---

FIGURE 1 *Performance Review and Salary Budgeting Program*

District _____   Performance Review and Salary Budgeting Program

Date _____

Name	Accomplishment against objectives	Use of innovation and new ideas	Mgt. of terr.	Selling complete line	Customer relations	Keeping up-to-date on company, competitors, and customers	Overall perf.	Health status	Sales mgt potential

3 best professional salesmen

_____

_____

_____

3 who need most improvement

_____

_____

_____

Definitions

Accomplishment against objectives
- Achieving or exceeding quota
- New product deliveries
- Generating new business

Keeping up-to-date on company, competitors, and customers
- GMI organization and policies
- GMI products, services, and related technical information
- Competitors' policies, prices, tactics organization, and sales trends
- Each customer's operations, products, and market requirements

Management of territory
- Credit control
- Control of expenses and care of auto
- Developing sales plans
- Submitting required reports and keeping district manager informed of conditions in territory
- Effective use of time

Customer Relations
- Servicing customers by prompt handling of claims, technical assistance, expediting orders, etc.
- Cultivating those within a company who influence a buying decision

a large merit increase. Conversely, it is theoretically possible that there would be little or no merit adjustment, even though the actual sales results were good.

It is a mistake to omit making a change in the salesperson's base salary simply because the incentive was good and consequently it produced a relatively high total compensation for the year. As much as possible, incentive results should be kept separate from base-salary considerations.

Consideration for merit adjustments in sales positions should be on the same time schedule as in other exempt positions. If the salary structures are reviewed and updated each year, the assigned job values will reflect the current competitive salary level of the jobs. The size of the merit increase is then determined by the performance rating and the salary relationship to the midpoint of market value. This salary relationship is often referred to as the "compa-ratio." Generally, an employee who is fully satisfactory in the position would have a compa-ratio of 100 percent.

By definition, a promotion is a movement to a higher-level position. It therefore seems logical to give a promotional increase to recognize greater responsibilities. The size of a promotional increase will typically be in the range of 10 to 15 percent. The actual amount should be determined by a review of the job value for the new position, the length of time since the candidate's last adjustment, and the person's qualifications for the new job.

TRENDS IN SALES COMPENSATION

In the 1980 survey by the Research Institute of America cited above, 39 percent of the companies reported recent changes in incentive plans. This was a big jump from the 24 percent that reported pay plan changes in the 1975 and earlier surveys. This continual rate of change suggests that management is continuing to seek improvement in the sales compensation area.

Today's salesperson worries about the way he or she is paid. Although money is certainly a factor, the opportunity for a positive measurement of individual performance is an even bigger and more desirable element of incentive compensation. Everybody likes to keep score, even for fun. The salesperson's earnings provide a desirable yardstick.

The job of the salesperson is changing. The days of the Willy Lomans are gone. Salespeople in the future will become problem solvers rather than order takers. The salesperson will be much more of a manager and will have a much greater influence on the management of his or her time, territory, sales efforts, etc. As these changes occur, it is likely that plans will be designed to recognize a number of measures, in addition to volume alone, in determining appropriate compensation. As a greater amount of advertising support is given, there will be less of a need for commissions to generate sales. Sales management will have to look for better ways to motivate the salesperson than money. It is reasonable to expect that companies will continue to strive for the compensation plan that is most effective in motivating salespeople to expend their best efforts.

chapter 53

Compensation Programs for Scientists and Professionals in Business

Harold B. Guerci

DIRECTOR, SALARY ADMINISTRATION, BELL TELEPHONE
LABORATORIES, MURRAY HILL, NEW JERSEY

Salary administration problems are concerned with how employees' salaries compare with each other and with the market. These problems, like administrative problems generally, tend to be repetitive and so are best dealt with against a background of standard practices designed to provide the advantages of uniformity and efficiency in their resolution. The idea of expanding an administrative system to accommodate particular variant situations is seductive. Unfortunately, complex systems tend to multiply the variety and complexity of problems which are addressed to them. Moreover, the tendency in personnel administration, under pressure from creative managers and from labor contract bargaining, has been in the direction of liberalized policies and practices. For a compensation plan not to be an impediment to its own administration, therefore, its design should be characterized by simplicity and flexibility.

A great deal of inventiveness has gone into the salary administration plans which are in use, and they exhibit great variety. One then asks, "In what way are scientists and other professionals in business enterprises different from other employees, and what administrative systems serve them, and the enterprise, best?" The latter part of the question is clearly the more difficult.

Some key words from the Fair Labor Standards Act define professional work as: original and creative; depending on invention, imagination, or talent; predominantly intellectual and varied in character; and the output or results of which cannot be standardized in relation to a given period of time. A useful distinction concerning such workers is that their potential for significant contribution, and the value of the upper limit of their achievements, cannot be readily fixed as it can for other kinds of work. This suggests the need for broad, objective position descriptions, performance criteria, and salary practices for scientists and others acting as "individual contributors," and it makes the application of management by objective tenuous for them. On the other hand, few professionals perform in an ambiance of unconstrained creativity.

EXTERNAL COMPARISONS

A reference for salary levels paid by a company must ultimately be found outside itself, so the cultivation of salary surveys as a basic resource is essential. The survey needs only to provide a single line, its line of central tendency, which may be the mean or median, to be of value. Of greatest importance is to find a survey of companies that include the desired scientific or professional activities, whose caliber of personnel is as similar to one's own as possible, and to assure that the positions defined in the survey are specifically comparable. The establishment of comparability is not always done critically by surveyors. For scientific and professional categories, any survey of salaries should be preceded by a conference visit to each company by the surveying organization. Once comparability is thus established, it should periodically be critically reexamined.

Surveys of salaries frequently present their results as maturity curves since such curves provide a common ground among a variety of dissimilar practices in the participating companies. (See Chapter 35.) Companies that use different plans can usually apply the survey data readily if only in relation to preestablished peg points, and certainly to measure the extent of annual change occurring in the external market.

The survey may collect data from participants at the wrong time of year relative to the review cycle of the user and thus be out of phase as a timely measure of market movement. If this is so, the mean or median of the survey can be readily plotted for each of the last several surveys conducted, on the same sheet and using the same graphic coordinates. This set of curves will permit, by extrapolation, an estimate of the survey's position at a desired month in the future.

Salary surveys are often conducted among other employers in the same industry or profession. Prior to the use of such a survey its composition should be carefully appraised as to the nature of the participants, its suitability in terms of the sizes of the organizations participating, the representativeness of the samples submitted, the survey's degree level and discipline mix, the coverage (whether regional or national), and the amount of care exercised in specifying criteria for comparability.

Some technical societies also conduct surveys, not among companies, but of their individual members, and these represent a broad and diverse base. Of necessity, since participation by individuals is optional, the survey sample is demographically incomplete.

Third parties are increasingly engaged to perform the surveys. A sponsor pays for the collection and analysis of data and chooses which companies will be asked to participate. The sponsor, as well as the participants, receives only composite survey results. This arrangement relieves the sponsor of responsibility for protection of the companies' detailed data in the event of required disclosure in bargaining negotiations. It also avoids the situation in which possession of the data could be construed as providing an advantage that could be misused in the competitive pricing, among rivals, of a product. Still other surveys, conducted as an enterprise, are available to all who wish to buy the results.

The surveying of scientific and professional management positions will be difficult, since organizations differ in the number of rungs in their management hierarchy. The result is that the magnitude and content of responsibility at all but the lowest levels may differ considerably. The way in which one surveyor copes with this difficulty is by estimating the relative size of nominally similar positions and assigning fractional rung differences as salary weighting factors.

INTERNAL EQUITY

Job Evaluation The range of the kinds of individual work given to scientists and professionals is so broad, specific assignments may change with such frequency, and the matter of measuring personal skill levels is so difficult that the formal evaluation of such jobs may be impractical. Generic descriptions are therefore commonly used, both for systems using *grades* and for *maturity-based* plans.

Position descriptions of hierarchies of the work of nonsupervisory grades often hinge semantically on words conveying a progression from simple to complex. Thus they will say that the work of grade B is more complex than that of A, but less than that of C, without defining an objective reference for any grade. However, a statement often follows such as, "The work of this grade usually requires six to eight years of experience," which probably is, along with a high merit rating, the operative element in supporting the promotion of individuals to a higher grade. Such generic descriptions, although widely used and obviously serviceable, are of questionable validity in defining a sequence of skill levels.

Nonetheless, practical graded systems are in common use and may be designed beginning with a hierarchy of job description categories such as Junior, Intermediate, Senior, and, for the cherished few, Distinguished Scientist. The exact titles used are, of course, optional. In application, classification problems occur in individual, border-straddling cases. This is a natural consequence of having borders. Some relief is provided since graded salary structures have overlapping salary ranges, thereby permitting an employee to be paid within the range of the next-higher grade. Maturity curve plans which have only a single composite classification, i.e., a continuum, have fewer borders and so are less subject to this particular difficulty.

Pricing the System The first requirement in establishing salary levels is to conduct a careful study of the market, narrowly focusing on the professional specialty involved. Where several pertinent salary surveys are available, it will be discovered that the results reported in them are different. This may be due to several causes, among which are different participants including notably a difference introduced by large versus small companies, regional variations, survey data collected at a different time in the same year, or definitional inconsistencies. It is preferable, then, to select one survey as a primary reference, with one or perhaps two others for corroborative data. A common criterion is that the preferred survey be concerned with that specific sector of the market with which one competes for scientific or professional talent of the caliber desired.

The second requirement is to make a critical decision: At what level in the range of the survey does the company intend to, or can it afford to, pay its own professionals? A policy statement that their company "pays salaries which are competitive" is satisfying to employees. However, "competitive" may simply mean the ability to hire and retain employees, and for different companies this will correspond to pay levels which may be above, at, or below the market median.

After this decision has been made it is a matter of judgment how to fit the group of professionals harmoniously into the corporate grade structure. Alternatively, if a maturity-based system is used for this group, the question becomes, of course, "At what level in comparison with the survey should one's own line of central tendency be placed and kept?"

Individual Appraisal   Comparisons of the worth of the contributions of individual scientists and other professionals to the objectives of an enterprise may seem especially difficult because of the widely differing and often abstract work involved. However, because we are dealing with *relative* rather than absolute value, the systematic comparison of the contributions of a number of employees by several supervisors acquainted with their work will usually permit agreement. It would be counterproductive, of course, for the appraisal of creative work to be made except by managers who are themselves scientists or members of the same profession.

The appraisal review is best done before the salary review, and as a separate exercise, so that the quantitative mood and constraints of the latter do not impinge on the qualitative aspects of the former.

Many methods have been devised which seek to assure that the appraisal process has validity, reliability, and objectivity, and business and social science research literature includes many items which provide valuable background information on this subject (see Part D).

Before deciding which appraisal method is to be adopted, a decision should be made as to what the process will be used for. The most appropriate uses are:

- Establishment of merit hierarchies for salary administration purposes
- Motivation of employees
- General counseling
- Growth and development assistance

A starting point of universal utility is to provide a form on which the scientist or professional records principal activities and contributions to the goals of the organization since the previous review. Papers published in learned journals or given before meetings of professional societies, committee activity in the latter, and honors received and patents granted should also be recorded. The narrative should, of course, be directed largely toward results in the current assignment or toward stipulated objectives. Such an annual exercise provides a unique occasion on which the employee may present a personal assessment of worth and sets the stage for subsequent discussion and redirection, as necessary, of the employee's effort.

After the appraisal review has taken place, a second form should be completed which reflects management's final consensus on the scientists's or professional's performance and upon which the salary review will be based. A meeting should take place between the supervisor and employee and the written appraisal shown and discussed. The form should include the supervisor's statement of the current assignment, accomplishments during the year, and a brief statement of strengths and areas for improvement. Finally, plans for personal development and growth should be formulated with the participation of the employee to the extent possible. The form should be signed by both the supervisor and the employee.

A number of appraisal techniques are in current use. However, with regard to scientists and others a single method of comparison enjoys such widespread use that it deserves mention. This is the method of ranking, which is a procedure of systematically comparing the performance of peers and deciding on their *relative* value. Peers are here identified as individuals in the same professional grade, classification, or level and are limited to groups that have approximately the same experience. The decisions are arrived at through the combined judgments of those managers who know the work of the individuals. In practice a list of names is arranged in a ladder of descending *relative* merit as perceived by supervisors. A second ladder, of the same names, is arranged in order of descending current salary. Differences observed in the two orderings become the basis for a commitment to take corrective action in the salary review. Reasonableness in the process is maintained through overall budget limits, forestalling any imbalance in assigning upward as opposed to downward adjustments in the merit ladder.

THE PLAN FRAMEWORK

Use of Salary Grades Not infrequently, the practices through which the majority of employees are classified into graded levels are unsuitable for scientists and some other professionals. However, notwithstanding the difficulty of writing meaningful individual job descriptions for employees who deal creatively with abstract ideas, an objective can always be stated for work to be done, no matter how unstructured the work arrangement. For convenience and uniformity, therefore, many companies encompass their scientists and professionals in the corporate salary grade structure (see Part C), placing them in grades which accommodate the market cost of such employees. Where the grades of such nonsupervisory personnel have overtaken those of managers, a "dual-ladder" arrangement may be used to accommodate the need for the additional salary range. The dual ladder, where position grades are used, permits retention of outstanding individual contributors *as such*, rather than dissipating their talents in managerial positions to which they might otherwise be promoted solely because of an inflexible salary plan.

Employees classified to a particular grade level comprise a small universe which requires for its functioning a full set of administrative practices. The practices may be the same for other grades but must include criteria for entry and promotion, merit appraisal and salary review, and control lines of one kind or another. These controls delineate merit boundaries, regulate salary progress within the grade level, and may use a natural unit of time—Years In Level— as the time variable.

The grade plan may have only two curves, as well as a minimum and a maximum rate, for each grade (see Figure 1). However, where the grades are each associated with a stipulated control or reference salary rate a universal set of curves may be derived by relating the entire span of salaries to that rate (see Figure 2). Thus for all grades there is provided a single completely prescribed time-dependent (maturity) salary structure.

The growth portion of the curves is seen to flatten and become horizontal. The point at which this occurs may be selected for convenience but is more rationally the number of years required to achieve full grade-level maturity in the work performed.

The advantages of the use of grades for scientific or professional employees include:

- The psychosocial reward of a title and rank
- Compatibility with the corporate plan
- Organic controls which are uniform across multidivisional companies

Maturity-Based Salary Administration   Maturity curves that describe salaries statistically are quite common. These curves are derived from the salary data which are represented by related raw points to which a smooth line must be fitted. The fitting process can be simple or sophisticated, but in either case a choice must be made as to whether the central line is to be a mean or a median.

FIGURE 1   Prescribed Curves for a Grade

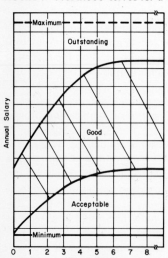

FIGURE 2   Universal Salary Chart

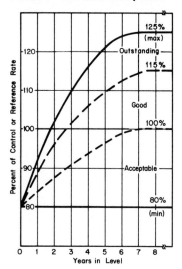

Because of the adverse effect of the appearance or disappearance of outlying salary points for whatever reason on the stability of a *mean* (for example, due to the changing population of successive years), the use of the *median* is often given preference. The median is said to be more robust, i.e., resistant to the vagaries of changes, especially in the salaries of small populations.

The salary maturity curve is so named because the independent variable (the horizontal axis) is stated in units related to the time spent in the profession. For this reason it is particularly well suited to the design of salary programs for scientists and professionals. These units may be years since B.S., Ph.D., or LL.B.; years in a particular level, grade, or function; or years of experience as an engineer, practicing attorney, or manager.

However, since different employers use different measures, the common denominator essential for the pooling of data in a survey may be age. The explicit use of age is not favored in the administration of salaries because of concern for the implication of contamination of the process with age discrimination. Nonetheless, it is inescapable that a variety of factors, such as hiring-rate escalation, loss by promotion from among the best paid, caps on the perceived value of a position, labor-cost limitations, and general cultural expectations, contributes to the shape of pay curves which consequently tend to be less steep as they progress from left to right, regardless of whether time is a factor at all in the rate review process.

Decile Curves   A family of nine lines which divide the salary distribution into 10 closely equal parts is shown in Figure 3. Each smooth decile line is the result of fitting to the raw decile data in the same way as the median line was. Note that the form of the resultant curves has been kept simple intentionally by the use of second- or third-degree curves, even though more undulatory, smoothed

FIGURE 3   Salary Decile Chart

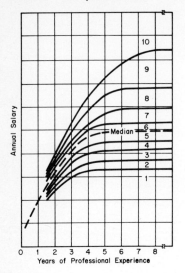

curves would have tracked the raw data with greater accuracy. Inherent in this simplicity is a compromise, the price of which is that in some sequence of years the smooth curve will fit less well than in others. Nonetheless, the mathematics of curve fitting will provide the best possible numerical division of the data, overall, into 10 parts. Smaller populations may justify fewer divisions, perhaps only a median, or perhaps a median and two quartiles. Larger ones suggest the further division of each decile into a number of parts. Certain lines may optionally be identified by the user as delineating merit categories. For example, occupants of the two upper deciles may be considered outstanding.

Deciles, or other derived fractional measures of a population, are maturity-curve forms both sound in conception and useful for defining the salary boundaries of equal parts of a homogeneous population, such as all nonsupervisory members of a professional classification. Their use may be judged to imply, however, that there are 10 clearly distinguishable levels of performance in the homogeneous group and that the population is, in fact, equally distributed in quality of performance within those levels. This is patently incorrect, since demographic changes will result in a new population mix that will have decile lines which are different from those of the original. This could readily result in changes in the relative position of the lines with respect to individuals in the original population without there having been a change in their performance. Thus although one may well adopt the use of deciles, it should be done with the understanding that they are artifacts.

It should also be remembered in the use of maturity curves that they, and the distribution of salaries which they represent, are only a "snapshot" of a point in time and not a history of salaries, nor do they permit the prediction of salaries.

The advantages of maturity curves, i.e., curves which are fractional divisions of the population, are:

- A line of central tendency of the data (the median) is intrinsic.
- The curves describe the literal distribution and level of salaries.
- The vertical spread of salaries can be accurately determined.
- Through management of the above elements, control can be effected.

Tiers   The compartmentalization of a population into equal segments by statistical methods, which occurs from the use of deciles, may be found inconsistent with perceptions of the way in which performance, i.e., value, is actually distributed in the population. For example, it is likely that over a central span in the range of performance there is a large part of the population who appear more alike than different. This suggests a variant maturity plan in which a functionally homogeneous population is divided not by the attribution of grade levels, or by equally populated segments, but by ranges of salary based on relative value. These ranges are called tiers, and they are characterized as having no limit to the number of individuals who may occupy each one. The central element is a true median, and each higher or lower tier boundary is a constant percentage of the median salary value, or of the tier next closer to the median, as shown in Figure 4. Thus there is formed a family of curves of constant percentage difference that derive their identity from the median. The percentage is a variable to be selected but may be in the order of 5 to 7 percent depending on the number of tiers desired.

In application the middle tier may be prescribed to have double the normal width in order for it to contain half or more of the population. Also, as an

FIGURE 4   Salary Tiers

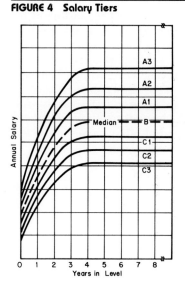

optional feature, the median may be made horizontal at the number of years corresponding to maturity in the work performed, as shown in Figure 4. The salary value at the horizontal is the single median of the entire population in the mature region, all considered as an undifferentiated group, i.e., independent of their Years In Level. The ascending curve is a fitted median in its own range of Years In Level. The tiers may be likened to grades, except that no job specifications are required and no formal and laborious apparatus is needed for the movement of individuals from a lower to a higher tier. Accordingly, there are no boundary problems. Most newly hired employees start in the middle double tier and move with time to a higher or lower tier, or do not move, depending on relative merit.

Under this plan, performance and salary differentiation is done in the same way as with other plans but emphasis is not placed on making distinctions where none are seen. This does not mean, however, that the existence of a considerable vertical spread in salaries is not important but, rather, that a distribution *within* the range of the spread has not been determined or limited artificially. Control is effected through the annual review budget and determination by management of the level of the median.

The advantages of the tier maturity plan are:

- Tiers are based on a statistically derived line of central tendency (median) of the actual population.
- The plan derives from the concept that individual salaries should be in proportion to relative contribution or value to the enterprise.
- The tier boundaries are not constraints.
- Compared to deciles, tiers are less disrupted by demographic change, since only the movement of the median is reflected in them.

THE ANNUAL SALARY REVIEW

The steps which precede the annual salary review are (1) completion of the analysis of salary survey information, (2) decision by corporate management fixing the company's market-related percentage of payroll to be provided in the review, (3) resolution of the relative merit standing of employees through a performance review, and (4) determination of the review's overall cost. The latter includes, in one way or another, the market and the merit components of the review, either reckoned individually for each employee or derived statistically from summary information. (See Chapter 20.) This will require analysis and application of the geometry of the particular kind of salary curves in use and the specification of controls relating raise percentage to merit category.

chapter 54

Compensation Programs for Public Employees

Richard I. Henderson

PROFESSOR, DEPARTMENT OF MANAGEMENT, GEORGIA
STATE UNIVERSITY, ATLANTA, GEORGIA

John T. Chandler

MANAGER OF COMPENSATION AND BENEFITS, COX
CABLE COMMUNICATIONS, ATLANTA, GEORGIA

Unusual challenges confront individuals responsible for designing and administering employee compensation programs in the public sector. The methods and techniques utilized are generally comparable to private-sector applications, and the similarity between public- and private-sector programs has grown stronger in recent years by such developments as widespread public-sector emphasis on point-factor job evaluation systems (in lieu of traditional position classification systems), performance-based pay increases (in lieu of traditional tenure or longevity-based increases), and treatment of fringe benefits as an integral part of the employee compensation package. Public-sector compensation administration occurs in a political environment, however, and this, along with an unusual allegiance to traditional practice, gives rise to compensation strategies, issues, and problems which are, for the most part, peculiar to the public sector.

Public-sector organizations are labor-intensive, with as much as 75 to 85 percent of the budget often going for payroll-related expenditures in local governments and school districts. During the last two decades, the public sector grew rapidly in size and complexity, particularly at the state and local levels, where employment more than doubled in this period. Along with this growth came dramatic increases in compensation expenditures, and these have been increasingly criticized as a major determinant of the escalating cost of providing public services. In addition to the major influence of rapid government expansion on public payrolls, this growth in compensation expenditures was also attributable to such factors as (1) significant increases in the number of higher-salaried professional and technical jobs in government and the requirement to compete with private industry for highly skilled individuals to perform these jobs; (2) emphasis on developing comparability in pay between the public and private sectors, particularly in the federal government General Schedule ranks, where "catch-up" increases were substantial during this period; (3) high inflation rates; and (4) rapid expansion in the size and influence of public-sector labor unions. Until recently, public employment levels and salaries continued to escalate, with only very limited setbacks occurring; experience continued to support the traditional viewpoint that the demand for public-sector labor was wage inelastic.

The late 1970s brought social, economic, and political conditions which influenced the ability of governments to continue to finance the level of services offered and, in particular, to continue the rate of payroll growth which had become common. Taxpayers began to vocally question the value of public services and the efficiency of government at all levels. A widespread tax limitation movement was organized by voters, and measures, such as tax and expenditure limitations, were used to effectively express displeasure with government. In addition to the impact of the tax limitation movement, many local government units began to experience serious erosion of their tax bases during a period of rapidly rising costs. New York City, for example, was very near insolvency by the mid-1970s when the state and federal government came to its rescue; this financial crisis was attributable in part to spending increases associated with the large concessions made to labor during the preceding years.

In most governments, legislators and top elected and appointed officials tend to exert considerable influence on employee compensation policy, either directly or indirectly. In addressing policy decisions regarding funding levels for employee salaries and benefits, these officials face substantial contrary demands from organized public employees and organized taxpayers. The compensation systems that have for many years satisfied public compensation managers, politicians, taxpayers, and public employees are being criticized, reviewed, and updated. The traditional idiosyncrasies of public pay plans are much less acceptable under today's scrutiny than they were in previous social, economic, and political climates.

COMPENSATION COMPONENTS

The compensation programs designed for public-sector employees are, for the most part, similar to those offered to private-sector workers. Government compensation information, including the salaries of many public employees and officials, is generally public information; therefore, there exist a more enlightened work force and more enlightened outside critics of public compensation than would be found in the private sector. As in the private sector, compensation plans for public-sector employees vary by kind of organization, geographic location, goods or services provided, collective-bargaining situations, and the specific activities performed by employees. Nationally, the federal government has been a trend setter with regard to pay for jobs assigned to lower and middle pay grades. Individuals working in the craft and trade areas in the federal government have also benefited by federal pay policies. For upper levels of management and professional employees, however, some major state and local governments and numerous single-purpose, public-sector agencies provide total compensation packages far superior to those offered by the federal government. In fact, some governments provide *all* their employees with compensation programs superior to those of the federal government. The total compensation package for public-sector employees, similar to that offered to most workers in the private sector, includes base pay; base-pay add-ons; pay for time not worked; disability income protection; loss-of-job income continuation; retirement income; spouse (family) income protection; medical, hospital, and surgical insurance; and assorted components that may be grouped under an area titled "perquisites."

Two major differences between a public-sector compensation plan and one designed for the private sector are the absence of components that relate to corporate equity and profits and, to a significant degree, the absence of pay-for-performance bonuses or other compensation-related rewards that tie directly to demonstrated, observed, and identified behaviors and the results of such behaviors. As a whole, this does not significantly influence employees who would normally be classified in a nonexempt or hourly category or even administrators, managers, and professionals in the lower and middle levels of the organization, because their counterparts in the private sector seldom benefit from stock acquisition or merit pay awards. If they do, these awards contribute minimally to their total compensation packages. A brief review of the major components of a total compensation program assists in determining similarities and differences between public- and private-sector compensation practices.

Base Pay   A number of critical factors influence base-pay determinations. To begin with, many local governments have copied the federal approach to job classification as a basic foundation for their merit systems and for minimizing political influence in the setting of rates of pay. Although the approach of local governments is frequently not as precise, orderly, and well developed as the federal Position Classification Plan, jobs are analyzed, described, and then assigned to a specific pay grade. Each pay grade is defined as to levels of activities that will be found in jobs assigned to the specific grade. Relative to required job activities, incumbent knowledge and skills are also identified and described, thus permitting an understandable and supportable approach for establishing job worth.

In the past decade, as described in Chapter 14, the federal government has moved toward the use of a point-factor job evaluation method for determining comparable worth among different kinds of General Schedule (GS) jobs. This movement has also been followed by state and local governments and independent public-sector agencies. A number of these organizations have adopted intact the federal Factor Evaluation System (FES) or have implemented a modified form that they find to be more suitable to their own environment. Other jurisdictions have adopted other point-factor methods that have had widespread use for many years by a wide variety of private-sector organizations. With the movement toward the use of point-factor job evaluation plans and the pressures emanating from the Equal Pay Act of 1963 and Title VII of the Civil Rights Act of 1964 as well as amendments to these acts, both public- and private-sector organizations have been spending more money in the analysis and description of their jobs.

Like their counterparts in the private sector, public-sector organizations use surveys to establish competitive or market rates of pay. Although state and local governments recognize the rates of pay and other compensation components offered by private-sector organizations with whom they compete in the labor market, most public-sector organizations focus primarily on the pay and total compensation practices of relevant state and local governments. On the other hand, the federal government has historically surveyed only large private-sector employers in its regular survey program for both General Schedule and wage-grade jobs. Only recently have the salaries of state and local government employees been added to the federal survey data base.

Pay Structure Design   Most state and local governments, like their federal counterpart, use a grade-and-step pay structure plan. While the federal government utilizes several different pay plans, it is not unusual for a state or local government to have one pay schedule for all merit system employees. The design characteristics of a pay structure normally include a progression between midpoints of pay grades that varies from 5 to 10 percent. A common range for a pay grade is 50 percent, or ± 20 percent around the midpoint, although many government units still maintain shorter ranges. Pay grades, typically, will have from five to ten steps, with equal amounts or equal percentage differences between steps.

As in the design of private-sector grade-and-step pay plans, the midpoint usually represents the competitive market rate of pay. Employees with no prior experience on a job are normally hired at the minimum wage rate. The lowest rate of pay offered to an incumbent at the most unskilled entry-level job normally approximates the minimum wage established by the Fair Labor Standards Act (FLSA). (Since state and local governments are exempt from the minimum wage requirements of the FLSA and since state minimum wage laws generally provide for a lower rate than the federally established minimum, this position is usually adopted out of social responsibility or as a necessity to compete for workers, or both.) Upon completion of a probationary period (normally 90 days, but for some jobs it may be as long as six to twelve months), the employee advances to the next step in the pay grade. Movement through the steps in the pay grade frequently coincides with an annual review of the employee's performance. The review date may be on the anniversary date of entry into the job, or it may be a common review date for all employees. In most public-sector organizations, if the employee has performed in a satisfactory manner, he or she receives a pay adjustment to the next step in the pay grade. With a typical 50 percent spread in the range and with an approximate 5 percent difference between steps, it takes an employee working in a satisfactory manner approximately eight years to reach the top of the pay grade.

In recent years, with high rates of inflation, some public-sector organizations, in attempting to keep their workers "whole" (maintain employee real income, i.e., purchasing power), have made annual adjustments to their pay structures.

In some of these cases, employees have received their in-step increase along with a structural adjustment. Other organizations have simply used the step increases for pay adjustments. Some organizations have given a flat dollar increase (i.e., $500, $1000, etc.) to all workers, while others have used a percentage increase. An across-the-board, common increase distorts an existing pay structure. When a general increase of a specific amount is granted to all employees, those in lower pay grades receive a relatively larger increase than do employees in the higher pay grades. This approach to pay adjustments has a very definite ring of equality ("everybody is paying more for bread, gasoline, etc.") and it is politically expedient because of the large number of employees at lower pay levels (relative to higher levels), but it destroys the equity concept in pay structure design and leads to the compression problem that will be discussed in the final section of this chapter.

A major pay structure problem with pay schedules relates to the fact that all jobs do not logically require the same probationary period nor do all jobs warrant the same range or number of pay steps for employee pay advancement.

While this section has focused upon the widespread practice of a single, uniform pay schedule, it is important to note that there are numerous cases of multiple-schedule compensation approaches, and there is apparently a trend in this direction. (Such a trend may well reflect the influence of unions that desire to negotiate only for the compensation interests of selected groups of employees.) The most common examples are found in schools and colleges (where there will usually be separate schedules for teachers, administrators, and nonacademic personnel) and in municipalities (where a separate police and fire schedule is relatively common). Salary schedules for teachers are generally characterized by longer ranges with more numerous, but smaller, step increments and a direct relationship between pay level and the level of education of the individual teacher. This structure recognizes the idea that additional education significantly improves a teacher's performance and also addresses the fact that virtually no promotional opportunities exist for teachers to permit vertical movement within a pay schedule. Some jurisdictions have established separate schedules for labor and trades, police and fire, executive and managerial, and white-collar jobs. In addition, some public organizations have established separate schedules for physicians and dentists because of extraordinary market conditions in this area; the Veterans Administration medical and surgical schedule is an example of such a plan at the federal level.

Base-Pay Add-Ons   A major difference between the pay plans of public-sector employees and those of private-sector workers relates to such add-ons to base pay as overtime, shift differentials, and premium pay for working on holidays and weekends. Because state and local governments are exempt from the overtime requirements of the FLSA, time-and-a-half payments for all hours worked in excess of 40 in a workweek are not common. Many public-sector organizations permit salaried employees to earn compensatory (comp) time in repayment for hours worked in excess of 40. Employees are usually permitted to accumulate comp time, which is normally provided on a one-to-one basis (one hour of comp time for each hour of overtime worked). Many comp time plans are operated on an informal basis with specific operating procedures established by the involved department.

Shift differentials and weekend and holiday premiums may also not take the same form or be as lavish as those offered in the private sector. Certain services must be provided on a continuous 24-hour basis. Public safety (police and fire) and public welfare (utilities and health) require employees to be on the job at all times. In some cases (fire), the job rates of pay and work schedules reflect the hours that must be worked by the incumbent. Within the past five years, nurses and other hospital workers have been recipients of improved treatment with regard to shift and weekend work. The improvement in this area of compensation has been gained by workers in both public and private hospitals.

Pay for Time Not Worked   Historically, public sector employees have received more paid time off than employees in the private sector, and surveys indicate this pattern still exists. It is common for public employees to average 11 or 12 paid holidays per year, while private-sector employees average 9 or 10. (Individual public-sector practices of interest are the federal government with 9 legal holidays and the Virgin Islands with 22.) A few public-sector organizations have also adopted the private industry practice of a floating holiday, and many conform with the federal Monday-holiday law which has been quite popular with employees. In recent years, increasing liberality in private-sector vacation and annual leave plans has resulted in comparable treatment for both public- and private-sector groups. Two to four weeks per year is common as is a graduating accrual schedule providing longer vacations for longer service. While most jurisdictions cover all employees with a uniform vacation and annual leave schedule, it is not uncommon to find a more generous schedule for police and fire personnel.

In addition to paying for holidays and vacations, governments provide several other types of paid time off, most of which are less common or less generous in private-sector organizations. Paid sick leave is discussed in the following section regarding disability income protection. Governments also provide military leave with pay for members of military reserve and National Guard components (typically 15 to 30 days per year); jury duty and court appearance leave with pay (typically unlimited); educational leave; and, frequently, either a holiday or several hours of paid time off on election days.

Disability Income Protection   Traditionally, disability income protection has been an area of major concern for employees in the public and private sectors. Now, however, a variety of short- and long-term disability plans provide workers in both sectors with improved protection. In addition, changes in workers' compensation and social security have provided improved disability protection. Income plans for long-term disability are common in the private-sector at a small cost to the employee; however, such plans are not common in the public sector. Governments continue to rely on pension plans to provide disability retirement for permanently disabled employees who have several years of service.

A plan found more often in public-sector organizations than in the private sector is sick leave, which is designed primarily for short-term protection. A typical public-sector sick leave plan grants an employee one day of sick leave for each month worked. In the past, it was fairly common for public organizations to allow employees to accumulate sick leave and to retire early on a day-for-day trade-off. Many governments did not place a limit on the number of sick leave days that could be accrued; however, the right to accumulate sick leave is now more restricted. Employees are entitled to "bank" a maximum of 60 to 120 days, and they lose everything beyond the maximum. (Because of the potential abuse of sick leave and the high related cost to the employer, a number of public-sector organizations have initiated plans to control its use.) In some cases, any unused sick leave is forfeited at the end of the year; in other cases, organizations pay employees at the end of the year or at termination, if earlier, for unused sick leave. Other jurisdictions offer the opportunity to convert accrued sick leave to annual leave or vacation time credits at a rate less than day for day (e.g., trade three days of sick leave for one day of annual leave).

Loss-of-Job Income Continuation Public-sector employees who lose their jobs as a result of forces over which they have no control frequently receive less protection than do their private-sector counterparts. State unemployment insurance programs covering the private sector provide protection for the first 26 weeks of unemployment. Some governments provide severance pay, but it seldom exceeds two weeks of income. A number of public pension systems have provided generous early retirement benefits for employees who lose their jobs after a limited period of service. This is discussed in the following section.

Retirement Income Most employees of state and local governments receive the pension protection provided by social security. In addition, their employers generally reinforce social security by some kind of pension plan. Public-sector pension plans usually require employee contributions, which frequently equal those made by the employer (typically 5 to 7 percent of salary); private-sector plans usually do not require employee contributions.

Social security coverage for employees of public-sector organizations requires an agreement between the state involved and the federal government. Until enactment of the Social Security Amendents of 1983, public-sector organizations also had the option to *terminate* such agreements—and a number had done this in recent years. Under the 1983 amendments, the option of terminating social security coverage was withdrawn.

The pension provisions for *federal* civilian employees depend on when their service started. Those hired up through December 31, 1983, are not covered by social security but are included in the Civil Service Retirement System only. Those hired after December 31, 1983, are covered by social security. It is therefore expected that the Civil Service Retirement System benefits and contributions for those now covered by social security will be amended to differ from the benefits and contributions of those not covered by social security.

Public employees are generally eligible to retire earlier than private-sector workers. Frequently, public-sector retirement plans permit retirement as early as age 55 without a reduction in benefits because of age, and some public plans permit employees to retire after 30 years of service at any age without penalty. As a consequence, public employees, unlike private-sector workers, often retire in their fifties. Whereas public employees who retire at age 55 with 30 years of service typically receive full pension benefits, their private-sector counterparts under the same early-retirement circumstances would typically receive, perhaps, 40 to 65 percent of a full pension. In addition, public pension plans frequently provide generous benefits to employees who lose their jobs through no fault of their own before they meet the normal age and service requirements for full retirement benefits. For example, federal civilian employees are eligible for involuntary retirement at age 50 with 20 years of service or at any age if they have 25 years of service. If the employee is age 55 or older, there is no pension benefit reduction; if less than age 55, the annuity is reduced by ⅙ of 1 percent for every full month the employee is under age 55. Other public pension plans are even more generous, and a great deal of concern has been raised about the threat this poses to plan solvency as layoffs in the public sector and attendant involuntary early retirements have become more numerous.

Similar to many other compensation components, retirement income treatment for public-sector employees in lower-level jobs is equal to, if not better than, that for private-sector employees performing similar kinds of work. However, in moving up the ladder to the ranks of top management, variation in treatment is noted. Since retirement income is almost always predicated on prior earnings, the higher base-pay earnings of private-sector managers and professionals result in significantly higher retirement income. The more highly paid private-sector retirees often benefit from supplementary retirement plans, annuities, and deferred compensation plans that can greatly increase income available upon retirement. These private-sector plans typically include large employer contributions, which are not offered by government employers. Police officers and firefighters are normally covered by a separate, more generous retirement program because of the potential for a shorter working life based on the physical requirements and hazardous duties associated with their work.

Spouse (Family) Income Continuation   In case of death of the public worker, his or her spouse or family is usually protected by life insurance, which has been provided at little or no cost to the employee. The face amount of the life insurance is usually one to two times the annual earnings of the employee. Employees are usually given the opportunity to obtain more life insurance at advantageous group rates. In these cases, employees pay the additional premium.

Additional spouse or family protection is provided through the retirement plan, social security, and workers' compensation programs. This kind of protection for dependents of nonexempt and lower-level administrators and management personnel is comparable to that offered in the private sector, but, typically, dependents of middle- and upper-level management personnel in the private sector receive better protection through increased amounts of insurance, annuities, and deferred income plans.

Medical, Hospital, and Surgical Insurance   Most public-sector employees are protected from the ever-increasing costs of health care through some kind of medical, hospital, and surgical insurance plans. These plans are designed to pay the costs or the majority of costs incurred for services received in overcoming some kind of problem resulting from sickness or accident. In recent years, many plans have been expanded to provide increased coverage in such areas as dental and ophthalmologic care and for emotional problems.

Public-sector employees typically contribute 25 to 50 percent of the cost of these plans. Private-sector employers often provided this coverage in the past at no cost to the employee, though employer contributions are being supplemented with employee contributions more frequently now. Other changes in this area are the increased opportunity for employees to select features they consider to be of value and the right of employees to choose among one or more providers of insurance in addition to a health maintenance organization (HMO).

Perquisites   Very few of the special set of highly prized compensation components grouped under the title of perquisites are usually made available to public-sector employees.

One perquisite available to some public-sector officials is the use of a government vehicle. Because of the nature of the work of these individuals (i.e., on call 24 hours a day, reporting or overseeing activities at various locations), the agency provides and maintains a vehicle. A chauffeur is usually provided for only a limited number of top officials (e.g., mayor, governor, etc.).

Other rewards offered by public-sector organizations that could be listed under perquisites are free or subsidized parking, subsidized dining facilities, tuition assistance for education improvement programs, and payment of expenses incurred to attend professional meetings.

The list of perquisites available to public-sector employees is extremely limited in comparison with those available to private-sector employees. Since perquisites are primarily granted to top officials, the limited range of available perquisites has the greatest influence in the total compensation package provided to senior public-sector officials.

TRENDS IN PUBLIC-SECTOR COMPENSATION

The various forces and procedures that influenced changes in compensation practices have had their impact on public-sector compensation, and it is quite likely these will continue to influence practices in the 1980s. Among the more important factors are:

1. Ability to pay—budget restrictions
2. Collective bargaining
3. Compensation compression
4. Pay for jobs in critical demand
5. Comparable worth and other legislative and judicial initiatives
6. Pay for performance (merit pay)
7. Social security and other retirement options
8. Total compensation analysis
9. Modern compensation practices

Ability to Pay—Budget Restrictions   In the latter part of the 1970s, taxpayer dissatisfaction with increasing taxes and widespread perceptions that government was too large and inefficient resulted in occasional legislation that legally restricted government spending. More often, candidates for public office who campaigned on a platform of reduced taxes and public spending were elected.

Such efforts have slowed the growth in or even reduced the size of public employment and have made it more difficult for public officials to increase the amount spent on employee compensation.

In the 1980s, however, public employees are affected by inflation the same as their counterparts in the private sector. These employees pressure their employers for pay adjustments commensurate with changes in the cost of living. Increasing costs in all aspects of government and restrictions on available public-sector income require public officials to closely review the compensation offered to their employees. These reviews are further complicated by union demands, comparable-worth issues, demands by taxpayers for improved services, and the necessity to emphasize employee productivity by recognizing different levels of performance through true merit pay programs.

Collective Bargaining   The 1960s and 1970s witnessed an explosion of unionization in government. Not only were public-sector officials required to negotiate with assorted crafts, trades, and laborers, but public safety workers (police and fire) and professionals (teachers and nurses) took lead roles in demanding improvements in their pay and benefits.

The success of these groups of employees led to further pressures by other employees to make demands on compensation policymakers and top elected and appointed officials. A major component negotiated by some public-sector unions that followed the success of the more powerful national unions was a cost-of-living adjustment (COLA) clause. With the advent of high inflation, the COLA became a highly desired addition by union members to their contracts. In turn, it caused many public-sector pay plans to become difficult to manage and balance, especially with reduced or restricted compensation or labor budgets.

Compensation Compression   Employees who are not protected by union contracts, or who have had the least influence in pay negotiation, or who have had legal or administrative barriers restricting the movement of their pay are the principal victims of the high inflation of the seventies and early eighties. This group of employees in the public sector usually includes those at all levels of management, but possibly those most affected are at middle and upper levels of management.

This problem is called pay compression, and it manifests itself in the continuing shrinkage of the designed, equitable difference in compensation between the individuals responsible for directing the work of others and the subordinates they manage.

Pay compression occurs through a variety of actions, pay policies, and even statutes. Union activities normally result in larger pay and total compensation adjustments for members than for employees and managers who are not members of a bargaining unit. Elected officials gravitate toward the idea of across-the-board pay adjustments. When these adjustments are equal in dollar amount and are not a percentage of current rates of pay, the compression problem is aggravated. Frequently, there are statutes that establish maximum limits to rates of pay. These statutes require that the rates of pay for senior elected officials, such as the mayor, governor, president of the council, or chairperson of the commission, equal or exceed those for high-level managers. Thus highly visible elected officials who fear repercussions from the electorate if they raise their own pay effectively limit the rates of pay for top career employees. Perhaps the most severe case of such compression in the public sector is found in the federal government. Since Congress is reluctant to vote itself a raise, government executives have their salaries frozen. According to the Office of Personnel Management (at the time of this writing), 34,000 federal managers and executives at seven different levels of responsibility were frozen at the same salary. Because of this, there is little incentive for these managers to accept positions of greater responsibility and authority. Moreover, these individuals were leaving government at an alarming rate.

The problem of pay compression can probably never be eliminated in government, but it is critical that it be reduced in order to attract and retain competent mangers, executives, and other highly paid personnel. It will be very difficult, but it is necessary to gain acceptance of the fact that there are federal executive and judicial branch jobs that warrant substantially higher salaries than those of members of Congress. A few municipal governments have recently made significant strides in this area by such actions as taking into account salaries of private industry executives rather than just those of other public-sector organizations; disregarding the mayor's salary as imposing any ceiling or barrier to the salaries of other top jobs; and utilizing a citizens advisory board on salary policy for top officials, which tends to add to voter acceptance of council actions such as establishing six-figure salaries for government officials. Such advisory commissions on the compensation of top government officials are not uncommon in state and local governments. However, after these commissions of personnel executives and other citizens submit their recommendations each year, the legislative body or executive branch officials who are responsible for setting salaries for top officials will typically determine that the voters would prefer to offer a much smaller increase than that recommended.

Pay for Jobs in Critical Demand   All too often, public-sector organizations find themselves operating expensive schools for training employees in jobs of high demand. This is especially true in jobs related to computer-based information systems (CBIS). CBIS-related employees, such as programmers, analysts, information system managers, and even computer operators and skilled word processing operators, are able to move from restricted pay ranges in their public-sector jobs to considerably higher rates of pay in the private sector.

The jobs for well-trained and experienced data processing personnel place a demand on public-sector compensation plans that is frequently impossible to meet. Even when jobs in this area are carefully analyzed and frequently reclassified into higher pay grades, the pay adjustments are inadequate to meet the demand for the workers skilled in these exotic jobs.

Comparable Worth and Other Legislative and Judicial Initiatives   The 1970s found public-sector organizations taking lead roles in the expansion of the civil rights movement in the workplace. State and local governments and other public-sector agencies were required to offer their employees and job applicants nondiscriminatory equal access to all employment rights.

The two major pieces of federal legislation—the Equal Pay Act of 1963 and its amendments and Title VII of the Civil Rights Act of 1964 and its amendments—placed all kinds of employment-related demands on public-sector employers. The workplace civil rights movement of the late sixties and early seventies primarily focused on recruitment, hiring, selection, training, and promotion opportunities. Although activity in these areas certainly influenced compensation practices, this influence could have minimal effect relative to the rise of the comparable-worth issue in the late seventies and early eighties. See Chapters 62, 63, and 64.

Comparable worth differs from equal pay for equal work in that equal pay for equal work requires workers to be performing essentially the same kind of work—secretary vs. secretary, claims agent vs. claims agent, nurse vs. nurse, and not secretary vs. plumber or nurse vs. heavy equipment operator—before a government agency or court can review the case as to the legality of pay treatment.

The major issue is no longer that of differences in pay for the *same* jobs because of sex, race, national origin, physical or psychological handicaps, or veteran status. The issue instead is differences in pay for different jobs, where the incumbents have traditionally been of one sex and, occasionally, of one race. The question especially relates to the worker's sex. If 70 to 80 percent of the incumbents are female, it is not uncommon for their jobs to be paid 60 percent of what jobs of comparable worth (e.g., equivalent job evaluation points) are paid if males comprise 70 to 80 percent of the incumbents. The standing and unresolved problem is the ability of organizations, courts, or government agencies to determine the comparable worth of jobs differently from the way they have been doing it.

The majority of judicial decisions regarding comparable worth in the late seventies and early eighties relate to public-sector employers. Although the federal government has changed its approach to enforcement of Title VII, the issue of comparable worth may well continue to be of major concern to public employers.

The issue of affirmative action in the area of employment has become less critical because of revised federal administration policy. Changes in federally assisted and reviewed programs at the state and local levels have also meant less demand by the federal government to follow specific federally oriented personnel practices. The result is reduced pressure to conform to certain merit system pay and compensation practices.

Pay for Performance (Merit Pay)   The pay-for-performance dilemma in the public service began to bubble forth in the last half of the seventies. This was in response to citizen pressure for reduced tax burdens and improved services and public employee pressure for increased pay and improved benefit packages. Public-sector pay practices traditionally relate more closely to seniority than to merit. Although the broad personnel system is called the "merit system," this term refers less to merit than to the distinction between an impartial approach and one controlled almost entirely through patronage. In a patronage, or "to the victors belong the spoils," approach, the elected official influences every phase of the employment system. The merit approach significantly reduces the politician's influence over the day-to-day operation of the personnel practices of public agencies, even though it is still essentially a seniority system.

From a pay perspective, however, the words of wisdom of "keep your nose clean and stay out of trouble" are sufficient advice, if followed, for public-sector workers to receive available pay adjustments. Frequently, there is little to no difference in the compensation received by the barely satisfactory or proficient worker and that received by the superior contributor. To improve the performance of public-sector employees and to increase levels of organizational productivity, considerable attention is now focusing on pay programs that relate pay changes to demonstrated behaviors and actual results achieved.

With profit-based or production statistics unavailable to public-sector organizations where so much of worker effort relates to providing services rather than producing an identifiable good or product, employee performance is not easy to identify, observe, and measure. The inability of public-sector managers to accurately and validly measure performance is a major barrier that must be overcome before pay-for-performance or merit pay plans can be initiated with a minimum of unjust, even illegal, action by those responsible for measuring and allocating rewards. In addition, public-sector employers must assure that compensation is competitive with the relevant labor market; without competitive salaries, a merit pay plan cannot operate satisfactorily.

Retirement Issues Other than base pay, none of the various compensation components offered by public-sector organizations has been a more fertile ground for dissension than the retirement programs.

Until enactment of the Social Security Amendments of 1983 state and local governments covered by social security had the option to withdraw. Considerable pressures were placed on compensation decision makers to remove their organizations from the social security program. This option has been eliminated by the 1983 amendments.

A problem that persists with continuing inflation is the improvement of the pensions of government employees, so that their purchasing power is not eroded completely by inflation. Increasing the amount of the retirees' income in recognition of the devastating impact of inflation could cause unacceptable changes in funding of existing pension programs or a drain on money available for the compensation of current employees. While a number of public pension plans provide periodic cost-of-living adjustments for retirees, very rarely do they provide regular adjustments geared to the consumer price index or the average wage index, which is the practice of the federal employee system and of social security.

Adequate funding, the extended life of retirees and their beneficiary spouses, increased pension payments for inflation, early retirement, and even the opportunity for employees who continue to work after 65 to increase the size of their retirement payments add to the funding problems related to the retirement programs of public-sector organizations.

Total Compensation Analysis Recognizing that compensation includes far more than base pay and base-pay add-ons became an important issue in the mid-1970s. The traditional fringe benefit program had been consuming 20 to 25 percent of the total dollars available for labor costs; by the late sixties, however, benefit costs started an upward climb, and by 1981 the benefits package was taking 35 to 40 percent of the total labor budget. (Public-sector benefits packages are generally somewhat higher than those in the private sector, with 40 to

45 percent of payroll being fairly common; also, it is common for police officers and firefighters to receive benefits superior to those of other employees.) With inflation squeezing the value of base pay, more concern had to be directed toward the allocation of every dollar for compensation purposes. This, in turn, caused policymakers and compensation managers to focus on the total compensation package.

The federal government initiated action to improve an understanding of total compensation practices in two major areas. In 1974, the U.S. Civil Service Commission (the predecessor of the Office of Personnel Management, OPM) began a study of white-collar compensation that focused on total compensation comparability (TCC). The goal of this project was to analyze and compare the pay and supplemental benefits of federal compensation with nonfederal compensation. The study had the following findings:

1. TCC is a feasible process for the federal government.
2. TCC is also desirable, since it would result in a closer degree of comparability than can be achieved through a system based on salaries alone.
3. The federal government should have a TCC system. The major components included within the TCC study were annual leave, sick leave, holidays, retirement, health insurance, life insurance, and premium pay. (It is interesting to note that federal benefits were found to average 4.7 percent more than private-sector benefits, primarily because of the larger employer retirement contribution.)

In 1975, the Bureau of Labor Statistics of the U.S. Department of Labor introduced the employment cost index (ECI). The purpose of the ECI was to provide a measure of change in total compensation (wages, salaries, and fringe benefits). The index has been modified since its introduction in December 1975 to improve its ability to identify national changes in total compensation practices. See also Chapter 39.

A nonfederal government leader in this area has been the state of California. In 1974, the Berryhill Compensation Act established the state policy that benefits and other nonsalary compensation components receive equal attention along with direct compensation in the ongoing consideration for adjustment of salaries for state employees. Agencies of the state government are responsible for comparing the salaries and benefits provided by both private and public employers in California. From their studies, the state personnel board makes integrated recommendations for total compensation decisions. On the basis of these studies, total compensation is negotiated with employee organizations in California. This is also the practice in Canada.

The total equivalent compensation (TEC) studies that began in 1975 reviewed not only salaries but such benefits as group life, accidental death and dismemberment, travel accident, hospital-medical, dental and ophthalmologic care, short- and long-term disability, and other health care insurance plans. (While there are several approaches to comparing benefits, California, as well as Canada and the federal government, elected to essentially follow the standard cost method.)

The federal TCC and ECI and the state of California TEC studies are an indication of the direction all compensation managers and systems must take to ensure that their employees receive the best possible program or set of compensation components to meet the specific needs of each and every employee.

Modern Compensation Practices   In light of the wide variety of pressures being exerted on compensation systems, it is logical to expect public-sector organizations to use the best of modern compensation practices, and there is clear evidence that such a movement has begun. The move to point-factor job evaluation permits improved evaluation of job worth and the need for more precise position and job definitions. The move away from general class specifications and toward very specific job descriptions not only will assist in the classification of jobs and their assignment to appropriate pay grades but will improve the design of selection criteria and the establishment of performance standards that adequately and accurately reflect job content requirements. The application of improved methods and adequate resources appears to present substantial opportunities for improvements in both equity and economy in public compensation programs. For example, studies by the federal Office of Personnel Management estimate that approximately 11.5 percent of federal white-collar jobs are overgraded and that 3.3 percent are undergraded. This misclassification and overgrading problem is estimated to cost taxpayers $500 million a year.

Pay structure design will transfer emphasis from lockstep pay-grade plans to those that reflect the needs of the organization. Pay grades with no step-and-pay adjustments related to position within the pay grade, and appraised performance, will reduce the dependence on seniority. The use of administrative techniques such as the compa-ratio (actual use of the pay grade) and range index (individual or group range penetration) will assist public-sector compensation administrators in improving their ability to monitor existing programs.

Although flexible or cafeteria benefit programs have had an extremely slow start in the private sector, the 1980s will witness more and more use of the concepts underlying these programs. Some public-sector organizations are already making limited use of flexible benefits. Employees are being granted certain amounts of money to purchase certain kinds of benefits (particularly options in life insurance; medical, hospital, and surgical insurance; and disability insurance). The need to relate the available benefits to the specific demands made by employees will become a more critical issue as total compensation dollars decrease and the demands of employees increase.

In the face of rising health care costs, containment procedures will become an increasing responsibility of public-sector compensation managers.

To ensure an improved understanding of how they are competing in the labor market, more and more public organizations will be improving their total compensation survey practices and unifying salary- and benefit-setting responsibilities in one central authority rather than continuing the common government practice of separate treatment in evaluation and decision making for pay and benefits. They not only will be attempting to ensure that they truly are comparing like jobs occupied by employees performing with similar levels of ability but will be analyzing total compensation packages.

Public-sector compensation practices must treat managers and professionals in a more equitable manner. The responsibilities, experience, talents, and contributions of these employees must be recognized in the compensation practices of the organization.

chapter 55

Compensation Programs for International Organizations

C. Ian Sym-Smith
GENERAL PARTNER, THE HAY GROUP, PHILADELPHIA,
PENNSYLVANIA

Mark S. White, Jr.
DIRECTOR OF INTERNATIONAL COMPENSATION, THE
HAY GROUP, PHILADELPHIA, PENNSYLVANIA

Direct business investment abroad by U.S. financial, industrial, and service businesses has grown throughout the 1970s and into the 1980s, but at a diminished pace from the growth that marked expansion abroad during the 1960s. In recent years, U.S. business organizations have undertaken activities in what is thought of as the nonfree world, including the People's Republic of China (a presumed-to-be-closed market 16 years ago).

Since the United States represents an excellent market, with reasonable degrees of financial and labor stability, and of course political stability, foreign investments in the United States have been outpacing American investments abroad. Investments in the United States by foreign industrial and financial organizations have taken mainly two forms: the purchase of shares in existing businesses and the outright purchase of manufacturing, commercial, and financial organizations. The overseas organizations making these investments are emulating the American multinationals in developing a network of businesses in countries outside their homelands.

Many of the more recently established international organizations come from countries, such as some of the Arab states, that are new to multinationalism.

They, as well as the long-established American and foreign multinationals, encounter similar problems in paying their staffs and workers in their overseas organizations. However, this chapter is written from the particular perspective of the U.S. organization operating abroad.

SPECIAL COMPENSATION PROGRAMS

The employees of multinational organizations used to be categorized into three subgroups: (1) U.S. expatriates—Americans working outside the United States; (2) third-country nationals—natives of country A working in country B for parent companies headquartered in the United States; and (3) local nationals—employees of U.S. business organizations working in their native countries. However, these distinctions have become blurred, particularly as regards American expatriates and third-country nationals.

Statistics are not available regarding the relative proportions of these groups in the overseas operations of U.S. multinationals. Considering only the equivalent of an "exempt" staff, it is reasonable to assume that expatriates and third-country nationals would rarely comprise 5 percent of the work force—while nationals would represent 95 percent or more—in any overseas subsidiary or affiliate. Although there are still multinationals that concentrate most of their attention on remuneration problems involving employees who are expatriates or third-country nationals, the number of such employees is declining. The sheer size of the local national group and, perhaps more significant, the fact that more local nationals occupy senior management positions have made it necessary for international managers to give local nationals increasing attention—commensurate with the importance of this group of people to the company.

COMPENSATION OF EXPATRIATES

An overseas assignment requiring special financial considerations for the employee and his or her family depends upon its duration. A commonly used guide defines the length of a foreign service assignment as a period of at least 18 months, usually continuing for a minimum of three years. Depending upon the policy of the organization, the overseas assignment may be continued for an additional three years, the individual may be transferred to another country, or less frequently, the individual may be rotated back to the United States and subject to subsequent reassignment abroad. Some companies have a group of employees who constitute a virtual international cadre and spend their careers with the employer working outside their home country; this concept has not grown as it had once been expected to.

A frequent development of the past decade was the situation in which the large U.S. multinational brought outstanding foreign national executives to the headquarters office and these executives then became senior officers and even chief executives of the worldwide organization. Somewhat similarly, the truly global-minded business organization may promote U.S. executives—who have had international business experience or successful overseas assignments—into worldwide management positions.

The criteria for defining a "foreign" assignment may include distance and cultural difference. For example, many companies do not consider an employee posted in Canada as being on a foreign assignment, but they may consider an American transferred to a Mexican company as being on a foreign assignment. Similarly, Puerto Rican assignments may qualify for extra compensation or expatriate compensation while Hawaiian assignments may not. Yet Alaska, because of the extremes of the winter season, may qualify for some financial consideration.

Some multinational companies may limit special expatriate compensation to intercontinental transfers: movements of employees within the European continent may not qualify. (However, special concessions may need to be made in order to continue a standard of living customary in the home country, including assurance of the same relative aftertax income and possibly a relatively even purchasing power.)

The core of a remuneration program for employees assigned abroad is, of course, the base salary. For the American expatriate, base salary logically, and almost without exception, relates to the relative size of the job in the organization (internal equity) and therefore to the amount according to the domestic salary structure for that size position. A number of premiums or allowances may be paid separately or in combination in addition to the base salary. Whether these premiums and allowances should be paid and are appropriate to individual situations may be determined by distinguishing three types of expatriates:

1. The career international employee. This individual has chosen to pursue a career abroad, typically with a company which has an international division or global organization.

2. The temporary international employee. This individual accepts an overseas assignment as a step in the career path; the immediate goal is training and experience to accelerate or enhance development of the career in the organization. In certain international companies, particularly those which compete internationally, foreign service is more and more a requirement for moving up into top management positions.

3. The short-term international employee. This individual is assigned abroad only for a specific project of limited duration (e.g., for a plant start-up). Both the individual and the company expect that the prior position held in the United States will be resumed when the project is completed.

The elements most commonly found in an expatriate compensation plan or policy include foreign service premium, hardship post premium, cost of living allowance, housing allowance, dependents' education allowance, home leave, and income tax allowance.

However, before considering such elements we must have an individual qualified to receive them. The selection process is the most important aspect of the program. The individual must have the technical qualifications demanded of the position in the foreign country; must possess personal qualities, interests, attitudes, and goals which enable an adaptation to its business and cultural environment; and in most cases must be able to communicate in another language. Equally important are the qualities necessary for the spouse and each member of the family. The selection process is further complicated by two-career families, which can obstruct or interfere with transfers even within the United States, much less a continent away. Many companies take special efforts in acquainting the employee and the family with the business, cultural, social, economic, and educational environment of the host country in which they will reside. This orientation may be in the form of special seminars and/or language instruction or even inspection trips to the location abroad.

Foreign Service Premium   With the emergence and expansion of expatriate compensation along more systematic lines following World War II, the overseas bonus, foreign service premium, or cash inducement to accept an overseas assignment became more and more a fixture in the total package. The premium represents a percentage of base salary, with or without an upper limit, or occasionally a lump sum paid prior to departure abroad in lieu of the percentage payable monthly. Originally, this bonus was the minimum required to persuade even the most adventuresome to accept assignments in foreign countries. More than any other special financial consideration given to the expatriate, this allowance has come under attack. Its justification takes the following forms: everyone pays it; or it is necessary to offset or ameliorate special expenses which are incurred in the host country and not otherwise compensated or fully compensated; or it is compensation for the cultural differences that must be borne by the family in the host country and recognition of the loss of relations, usual contacts, and way of life in the home country.

Critics ask why it should be necessary to pay someone a special premium to live in London, Paris, Geneva, Melbourne, or Mexico City. Further, they point out that extra pay as a basic right tends to be counterproductive, attracting employees for the wrong reasons and retaining the mediocre employees. The premium is costly, particularly when other allowances for extraordinary expenditures are required in the expatriate compensation plan. In a sense, the foreign service premium offends the national pride of the host country, implying that special financial inducement is necessary to enlist the services of an American in that country.

Nevertheless, this special payment probably will continue as long as the need to "keep up with the Joneses" philosophy persists among international managements.

The individual posted abroad for a single project may be considered to have a personal need which is different from that of the career international employee or the individual working overseas for purposes of personal career development. The foreign service premium in this case may be the reasonable and perhaps logical way to compensate for inconveniences, and it may be the necessary inducement to accept an assignment involving an extended absence from home and family.

Hardship Post Premium   There are certain locations around the world to which Americans may be assigned that are defined as hardship areas. The U.S. Department of State, for its foreign service officers and staff, has developed a set of criteria which has become accepted within and without the federal service. Some of these criteria are:

- Distance from a major metropolitan area
- Undesirable or unhealthy hygienic or hazardous environment

- Risk of civil strife or armed warfare
- Severe and persistent undesirable climatic conditions
- Inadequate facilities and supplies of items necessary for daily living

The degree of hardship is expressed by the Department of State as a percentage ranging from 5 to 25. This factor is applied to base salary in order to determine the amount of the premium, usually paid monthly.

Cost-of-Living Allowance   This allowance is the first of the few elements in the expatriate compensation package or policy which departs from the usual philosophy and practice of American management in remunerating employees. The cost-of-living allowance involves the personal affairs of the family. It begs solution of a very difficult question: How does one determine the personal financial needs of a family for day-to-day living? Even more, how does one determine the cost of day-to-day living for an American family in another economic environment? Additionally, American executives in foreign countries are frequently the "official" representatives of their multinational employers in the business and social community and, together with family members, are required to act as hosts in certain circumstances and situations (dictated to a degree by the size of the community). Such obligations go beyond the demands placed upon similar executives in the United States.

Despite the pervasive availability in the states of the various cuisines from around the world, which are at least sampled by most Americans, the employee and family who take up residence in the host country still prefer typical American fare: dry cereals, sliced bread, peanut butter, catsup, hamburger, iceberg lettuce, and other so-called typically American food items. Further, they ask for houses equipped with appliances and closets, as well as electrical outlets, central heating and air conditioning, prompt and reasonable repair service, and other goods and services commonly associated with the "typical" American way of life.

During the early evolution of the expatriate compensation plan, a cost-of-living allowance, as such, rarely was required. Very few areas were basically more expensive to live in than the United States (and most of them were clearly hardship areas as well). The foreign service premium usually sufficed. The extra expense peculiar to satisfying the needs of the American, and the costs associated with the status as a company representative, normally could be handled through an expense account liberalized for that purpose.

For quite a few years now, a great number of areas of the world cost as much as the United States, or more, for daily living requirements. Accordingly, elaborate procedures have been developed to determine the extra costs to which the American expatriate is exposed and to offset some of these additional expenses through the cost-of-living allowance. Two separate items in cost of living are recognized: the cost of goods and services on the one hand and the cost of housing on the other. During the recent past, the Department of State (see below) altered its study of cost-of-living comparisons by segregating housing costs from its survey.

There is still a problem in selecting the items to be considered as "common, usual, and necessary" for the American's way of life and in determining what portion of the family income may be reasonably expected to be devoted to these necessary purchases. Both of these factors are included in the formula for arriving at the cost-of-living allowance.

The most common reference source is the Department of State, which periodically (through its embassies, consulates, and other government agencies posted around the world) conducts surveys of the local price for a market basket of "American" goods. The market basket comprises the same items of goods and services throughout the world, to the degree practical and available at each location, as in Washington, D.C. With Washington as the base, the local-currency price of the market basket is converted to dollars at the rate of exchange prevailing at the time of the survey and related to the cost of the items in Washington. This comparison results in an index.

During the years 1972 to 1974, the Bureau of Labor Statistics, assisted by the Department of Commerce, conducted an extensive survey of the spending habits of American families throughout the United States. The sample consisted of families of various sizes and income levels. This study is the source of the spending norms in the United States for food, cars, gasoline, personal services (e.g., haircuts), etc. Through appropriate factoring or changes in cost of living, these amounts of spendable income may be updated as the reference for the cost-of-living formula.

It should be noted that the Department of State conducts two separate surveys of cost of living: one is for government employees who have access to supplies available through government-controlled sources and post exchanges; a separate survey is conducted among the local sources—shops, stores, vendors, and so on—that the civilian American residing in that area would be compelled to use. In addition to the Department of State Local Index, cost-of-living information is provided by several consulting firms in the United States who conduct surveys through their staff visits abroad, conduct client personnel surveys of costs of goods and services, or adapt or modify the Department of State indices.

There are some who argue that the American's spendable income must be determined on the basis of actual purchases made at the overseas post. Such an approach no doubt would produce a more precise basis for determining the amount of the allowance. However, how does one determine an appropriate amount of extra compensation for a family, when each one is so different from another? In setting up a plan, it should be recognized that these allowances do not offset dollar for dollar, or pound for pound, or franc for franc, the extra expenditures incurred, but they indicate the employer's genuine intent to ameliorate the extra costs incurred.

On a different tack, it is sometimes argued that after residing in a city or country for a prolonged period, international employees presumably adapt to local customs and their purchasing and consumption habits are closer to those of locals than to the customary American way of life. If this is so, the cost-of-living allowances should eventually be reduced to virtually nil. In fact, some multinationals do have a declining expatriate package after an employee has completed four years in one location.

Housing Allowance   The cost of real estate—buying, renting, or maintaining it—is enormous, particularly if a change in residence is required. This condition exists not only in the United States but in all developed and developing areas of the world. Ten years ago, at the time of the first edition of this handbook, a trend was perceived toward encouraging Americans being relocated abroad to retain their U.S. residences. This was to preserve their position in a real estate market of rapidly rising prices. Now, with higher mortgage costs, it has become the norm to encourage home retention. The encouragement may take the form of financial assistance in renting out the property during the period of overseas assignment and may go to the extreme of denying reimbursement of expenses incurred if the property is sold.

Financial assistance for the expenses incurred for housing in an overseas location, like the cost-of-living allowance, is virtually a universal consideration among American multinationals. It begins with the cost incurred in shipping personal possessions abroad. More and more often, if the employee decides to rent the U.S. property, it will be offered on a furnished basis. If it is not, then consideration is given to subsidizing the cost of storage in lieu of shipping because of the exorbitant charges—not only the transportation costs but, in many areas of the world, the import duties.

Such consideration requires the employer to become involved in the personal affairs of the employee: What kind of housing accommodation is appropriate for the employee and the family? What degree of subsidy will be provided by the company: for rent only, or including utilities? How many bedrooms are necessary for the size of the family? Because of the degree of judgment involved, general practice requires the country manager, or the regional manager, to approve the housing accommodation as appropriate for the family concerned.

As may be expected, the size of rooms and the comforts and conveniences of housing to be found in many areas of the world are somewhat less than what Americans are accustomed to. Outside the United States, American-style housing frequently exceeds the economic range of most executives. The housing situation is further complicated in many areas by severe shortages that contribute to rents which are enormously expensive by any standards.

Because of the temporary nature of most assignments and the complications entailed in the purchase and sale of residences in other countries, most housing accommodations are rented. Purchasing may be prohibited for foreigners, or severely restricted, and more complications arise from scarcity of mortgage money and its cost—considerably higher than in the United States during the early 1980s.

The amount of the allowance, of course, is a function of the size of the family and the number of rooms therefore required. The allowance may take the form of a specified amount; more usually, it is reimbursement of housing expense, or rent and utilities, exceeding a certain percentage of base salary, usually derived from statistics of housing expenses in the United States. Each method has its advantages and drawbacks, and both require proper and prudent administration to preserve equity. The local housing situation frequently dictates which method is more appropriate. Some companies substitute a maximum limit in place of a "rule of reasonableness."

Relocation Allowances   Relocation allowances granted to Americans moving abroad usually conform to the reimbursement allowance plan for domestic relocation, with certain modifications. A special payment may be made in lieu of shipping the employee's car; the company may reimburse the difference between the Blue Book value of the American car and the purchase price of a comparable car in the host country. The employee may not be allowed to ship items of major weight or cubic capacity—e.g., a boat, machine shop, or baby grand piano—and there may be a maximum shipping weight based upon family size.

The employee and family, after receiving passports, visas, and physical examinations at the expense of the company, may be housed temporarily, prior to departure and upon arrival at the overseas location, at company expense. The daily living expense in the host country usually is limited to the time required to ship household goods and/or obtain suitable accommodations. The mode of travel is more frequently economy or business class air fare.

Dependents' Education Allowance   Another virtually universal allowance reimburses the employee for the education of children at a school offering a curriculum which will enable the students to transfer back into the American educational system with ease. Usually the most available of such schools are the American schools, a number of which are sponsored by the Department of State and by multinational companies. Customarily, the company pays tuition and fees with the employee frequently paying the cost of books. However, some multinational companies resort to a complicated formula, taking into consideration only costs exceeding the taxes the employee would have paid for public education at home.

In the event that an American school is not conveniently located, nor a school offering a similar type of curriculum, the cost of educating the children at a private school nearby is partially or fully subsidized (tuition, room and board, and transportation from the host country to the location of the school, usually twice a year). This allowance covers attendance at elementary and secondary schools. The only consideration given to tertiary or university level students is one round trip per year to the parents' overseas home.

Income Tax Allowance   The income tax liability for Americans living and working abroad has gone through major changes since the midseventies. Up until then an American could exclude $20,000 or $25,000 of foreign earnings from U.S. taxable income, depending on the continuous period of residency abroad. This exclusion was eliminated in 1978, and regulations were introduced which severely limited the amounts of foreign tax credits an American could claim against U.S. income taxes. Accordingly, the cost of maintaining the expatriate abroad became huge for the American multinational corporation, which had to grant a tax allowance—reimbursing the expatriate for taxes paid in excess of the amount that would have been due if residency had been in the United States and taxes had been paid only on base salary and bonus.

The tax allowance is determined on a basis either of tax protection or of tax equalization. Under the tax protection concept, exployees are guaranteed that they will not pay more taxes as a result of their foreign assignment than they would have paid had they continued to work in the United States. In effect, they receive foreign service premiums and allowances tax-free; the company pays the taxes on these items. The taxes to which they would have been subject, had they been residents in the United States, are calculated only on base salary, and bonus if any. If foreign taxes on company-earned income exceed the hypothetical United States tax on this income, the employee is reimbursed by the company for the extra taxes. The reimbursement, of course, includes any added tax which *it* generates. Expatriates are responsible for filing their own tax returns.

Under the equalization concept, the company usually withholds monthly an amount approximately equivalent to the home country tax on the employee's base salary. When the time comes for the payment of taxes, either foreign or at home, the company will either pay the actual taxes directly or let the employee pay the bill and then collect reimbursement. This method involves the company more directly, but the employee does not stand to gain from any savings from lower local tax structures or from inclusion of specific premiums, since amounts equal to United States taxes are deducted from the United States–equivalent income. (Again, the tax payment or reimbursement by the multinational employer includes any added tax which *it* generates.) Companies which use the equalization approach feel that it is more equitable and also that it may encourage the employee to be more conscientious about paying local taxes (to the benefit of the company's image).

In recent years, only the Americans among industrialized countries have paid federal income taxes at home for earnings during periods of foreign employment residency. But starting in 1982 the American expatriate was again able to exclude a significant amount from U.S. taxable income. The maximum exclusion was $75,000 plus a portion of the housing allowance in 1982, and it rises in steps to $95,000 plus a portion of the housing allowance by 1986.

As a result of this change, expatriates assigned to certain countries again have the opportunity to enjoy what was formerly known as a "tax windfall." This can occur in areas of very low or no personal income tax (e.g., Hong Kong and the Middle East). The above exclusion protects much or all of the expatriate's income from U.S. taxation, and the income tax of the host country is lower than the U.S. tax which would apply if the expatriate had been a resident of the United States. Unless the multinational company uses the tax equalization principle described earlier in this section, there might be difficulty in persuading an expatriate to leave the low-tax country for employment in a high-tax country such as the United Kingdom or Canada. The tax equalization concept forestalls such a problem.

Other Allowances and Considerations   Many multinationals fully subsidize instruction in the language of the host country for the employee and, less frequently, for the spouse.

While abroad the expatriate may have access to a business and/or social club—a perquisite to which the position may not be entitled according to company policy in the United States. Similarly, the employee may have use of a company car at no cost, and in certain countries prudence would dictate that the employee have an assigned driver.

Because of financial commitments in the United States, as well as restrictions on movements of currencies in some countries, the company may arrange a split payroll, paying a portion of the salary and allowances in dollars deposited to an account in the United States. Another perquisite, usually reserved for senior corporate members in the U.S. but often available to the expatriate, is assistance in preparing income tax returns in the host country, as well as in the United States, along with attendant legal counseling. Counseling is also available regarding other personal legal matters in the host country. The rationale for providing these considerations is that they are required only because of the foreign service.

COMPENSATION OF THIRD-COUNTRY NATIONALS (TCNs)

Compensation practices for third-country nationals vary widely, largely because such employees come from so many different countries and backgrounds. Thus different pay practices and levels were required to attract them to their new jobs, and companies tended to treat their compensation on an ad hoc basis. However, their numbers grew rapidly, greatly encouraged by U.S. tax laws for Americans abroad. Policies had to be established for TCNs.

Basically, there are four approaches which can be taken. The third-country national can be paid: (1) on U.S. standards for salary and benefits, which, in effect, eliminates this classification of employee and joins the employee to the expatriate group, a practice followed by a number of companies; (2) on standards of the country of citizenship; (3) on standards of the country to which assigned; or (4) on an artificial standard created to facilitate transfers within a given geographic area, e.g., the Common Market. The choice among these alternatives should be based first on whether the person in question is hired by the corporation as part of its reservoir of international talent available for assignment anywhere or is hired by a subsidiary for its own needs. A second consideration is whether, regardless of citizenship, the person is hired within the country to which assigned or is hired at home for assignment elsewhere. A third consideration, which may or may not be controlling, depending on the first two considerations, is whether the person plans to retire at home or abroad.

The area of third-country national compensation is filled with contingencies, which is the primary reason why an underlying pattern is not readily apparent. For example, a superior executive is often simply placed on the expatriate roll and treated as an American regardless of actual nationality. On the other hand, if the salary structure in the country of employment is higher than in the home country, the executive may be treated as a local national with no premiums or allowances (except possibly a commitment to offset losses of local social security upon retirement). Often the decision as to status is made on the basis of original employment—if hired in the country of employment, the person is considered a local employee, but if recruited from the country of origin (or the United States), the person is considered an expatriate. (This policy also typically applies to U.S. citizens who may be residing abroad at their own choice.)

However, if the individual is recruited from a third country, and particularly if recruited for a job typically held by an expatriate, the question of expatriate allowances inevitably arises sooner or later. Because of this, many companies establish special sets of allowances using a separate salary structure for third-country nationals. The salary structure may be that of the local country or the home country, or a special structure may be developed for the situation. Usually a foreign service premium is paid only for real hardship stations (but still on the non-United States base) and allowances are more restrictive.

From the mid-1970s, when the value of the dollar began to deteriorate in relation to the currencies of European countries (the source of the greatest number of third-country nationals), it became rather difficult to persuade Europeans to accept a U.S.-oriented dollar salary. After all, the dollar equivalent at prevailing rates of exchange of their home country salary greatly exceeded the base salary of the American, at times by as much as 50 or 75 percent. However, beginning in the first quarter of 1981, the "snake" (predecessor of the European Monetary Unit) began to turn and those dollar-equivalent salaries in Europe plunged rapidly downward, closer to the level of American salaries for similar-sized jobs. Accordingly, managements that opted to change the base-salary orientation of the Europeans to their home country practices no doubt will be forced to rethink this policy in the event that the dollar-equivalent salaries in Europe fall below the base-salary rates for the same-sized jobs in the United States—which had been their historic relationship.

A different form of expatriation has evolved during the recent past whereby U.S. multinationals bring employees of overseas subsidiaries and affiliates for headquarters work assignments rather than training. Among these organizations, both industrial and financial, there are some that—contrary to historical practice—treat the transferred foreign national as an expatriate, qualifying for many of the expatriate compensation allowances ordinarily paid to the American expatriate abroad. Of the usual American expatriate allowances provided for these transferred nationals, there is the notable absence of any provision for a cost-of-living allowance.

Such transfers are usually for a predetermined period and tend to create a link between the foreign national employee and the parent organization before the individual becomes too deeply entrenched in the home country organization. This can help minimize the adversary relationship sometimes found between the overseas management group and the corporate staff in the parent organization in the United States.

COMPENSATION OF LOCAL NATIONALS

In the past, international managers concerned themselves only with remuneration plans for senior management groups of their overseas business units and left to those groups the responsibility for managing the remuneration of the balance of the work force. Thus long-established operations follow local compensation practices and patterns. Newer companies in a country tended to make judgments concerning compensation that were based upon expediency and experience and not necessarily attuned to local situations, sometimes creating disturbances in local practice. With the emergence of reliable surveys in most of the countries of the industrialized world, new companies have sources available in order to develop remuneration plans properly. The older-line companies now find the need to contribute to these data banks and use them as a resource for maintaining external competitiveness. These overseas remuneration plans more frequently have come, according to policy, under the direction, cooperation, or prior review of the international manager back in the United States.

Compensation practices among highly industrialized countries vary widely. If the total amounts paid do not differ significantly, the forms the payments take can be very different. Even considering only base salary, one will find in some countries a general use of a thirteenth month (and sometimes a fourteenth and a fifteenth), besides obligatory (or customary) Christmas payments and double vacation pay. One cannot, as in the United States, take the monthly salary, multiply it by 12, and call everything else either bonus or fringes.

Base salary is always the principal form of payment, but the social and taxation climate and practices of a country can and do influence significantly its relative importance. If taxes are high, other forms of compensation become more critical within the total package—hence the emphasis in The Netherlands or Britain on cars and pension programs (which generally include widow's benefits and, to counter the effects of inflation, are geared to terminal salary) as parts of total remuneration.

Another significant difference is the relatively high rate of change of salaries abroad. While U.S. salaries increased 100 percent during the 10-year period ending in 1981, European salaries rocketed 120 percent in Germany, 193 percent in France, and, almost incredibly for industrialized countries, 233 percent in England and 295 percent in Italy.

Salary structures and practices in different countries differ not only in amount and form but also in the slope of the structure (the relationship between increases in job size and increases in compensation). Thus one cannot use a single (multiplier) factor to convert from amounts in one country to those in another. Compared with the practices of most other countries, the slope in the United States is flat. While salary structures abroad tend to be steeper than in the United States, in some countries the structures are considerably steeper than in others (being largely dependent on social and taxation mores). The result can be that whereas wages in country A may be significantly higher than in country B, the reverse may be true for management salaries.

Thus compensation abroad is very different from what it is in the United States, and practices and customs vary widely from country to country. Because of this, it is difficult for the U.S. salary administrator to make valid judgments about local national compensation. However, the international compensation manager in corporate headquarters currently has become much better informed concerning the national practices of the countries in which there are business units. Because of this multicountry exposure, these managers have become a more helpful guide to the local national managers of human resources.

As experienced international executives in the United States and in other countries have grown in number, they have also grown in knowledge of business activities, including local remuneration practices, within and among the various countries. A natural outgrowth has been improvement in the system of cash compensation in foreign business units through revised design and better administration. The trend is satisfying the needs which a system of remuneration must serve abroad. These needs are comparable or similar to those in the United States: to assure that compensation is (1) consistent and equitable within a company, (2) competitive externally, (3) personally motivating, and (4) adequately controlled as to policy and cost. Companies in domestic organizations have, within limits, a choice between operating in a relatively centralized or relatively decentralized fashion, but in international operations the range of choice is considerably narrowed. The distances and differences involved naturally dictate a high degree of decentralization in all areas of management. In the area of compensation the aim should be to delegate to local management, subject to review, a high degree of latitude in designing and administering a program that accomplishes all the remuneration objectives of the company.

THE HEADQUARTERS-SUBSIDIARY RELATIONSHIP

If compensation actions are to be decentralized effectively, corporate and foreign subsidiary management must understand each other's needs and, on the basis of this understanding, develop a sound, workable relationship.

Corporate or international management of the multinationals must set compensation for the top executive of each overseas subsidiary and, in addition, must review—before the fact—the top executive's recommendations on compensation for each key lieutenant. This review should concern itself with how the compensation plans for the group of key executives fall within the framework of the organization's cash compensation practices, the labor market, and the total economic environment of each country.

The subsidiary's top executive needs the same standards for guidance in formulating compensation recommendations to corporate management. Standards for the top jobs, therefore, must ensure that the job relationships established are appropriate and the pay levels are competitive—i.e., sufficient to enable the company to attract, retain, and motivate the kinds of people it needs. Up to this point, corporate and subsidiary needs are the same.

Below the top people, at whatever level that cutoff is defined, the needs of corporate and subsidiary managements differ, not in principle, but in detail. Corporate management needs to know enough to be sure that what is being done is sound and effective, but not in the same detail it needs for matters on which it must make the actual decisions. Subsidiary management needs the same assurance of soundness and effectiveness but needs, as well, detailed standards to guide it in individual compensation decisions.

Thus, subsidiary management must develop and be able to use a sound method for establishing job relationships; corporate management needs only to know that the job is being done. Corporate management must be satisfied that the general level of compensation is both adequately competitive and not too costly, but it can delegate to the subsidiary the task of determining how these conditions are met. Subsidiary management, in fulfilling this delegated accountability, must do whatever is necessary to ensure that the unique characteristics of the national environment, and the subsidiary's competitive position therein, have been properly identified and measured in fixing the general level of the subsidiary's compensation and the form it is to take. Finally, corporate management must assure itself that the subsidiary has some effective means of relating opportunity and performance and reward. But, again, it does not have to prescribe the means; it confines its involvement to establishing criteria of effectiveness, which the subsidiary can meet as it sees fit.

Establishing the Pay Structure   Given this relationship between the parent organization and its overseas operations and the concomitant necessity for decentralization, it is necessary to provide corporate management with some assurance that the local compensation structure is appropriate.

The first step is to evaluate at least the top jobs in subsidiary companies on a common basis, and on the same basis used for domestic jobs. This helps establish compensation standards needed by both corporate and subsidiary managements. It is helpful for noncompensation purposes as well. Interchanges of personnel among subsidiaries are most likely to take place at the highest levels, and job evaluations are helpful in deciding whether a particular transfer represents good utilization of work force and management talent.

Evaluations of the top jobs are also essential to decentralization. Salary ranges developed on the basis of these job evaluations establish ceilings to which all lower jobs must be related in some sensible fashion. Once corporate and subsidiary managements agree on proper compensation for the top jobs in subsidiaries, they have gone a long way toward giving corporate management the assurance it requires about the adequacy and propriety of compensation for jobs below the top, and toward giving subsidiary management the reference point it needs to establish compensation for these lower jobs.

It is important for subsidiary management to be involved in these evaluations for several reasons. First, their knowledge of jobs in their companies and in the environment of the countries in which they operate is necessary to ensure the validity of evaluations. Second, local managers must participate, since one of the chief purposes of evaluating these jobs is to arrive at mutually understood and agreed-upon standards to help local managers make intelligent recommendations which corporate management can approve.

Finally, the job evaluation process yields a common language for discussing compensation, job content, and related issues; overseas managers must be involved in the process to understand and use the language.

Sound evaluations of the highest jobs, then, are the first prerequisite to a decentralized compensation program. The second is agreement on the general competitive level at which these jobs will be compensated. (References to top subsidiary jobs exclude the top executive, who should not help evaluate and price his or her own job.)

Corporate management should make the initial determination of where this level should be. But to gain acceptance and to confirm that it takes into account both competitive pay practices and other environments of the particular country, the competitive level should be reviewed with local management, not just imposed upon them.

BENEFIT PLANS

In many foreign countries (unlike the United States) the benefit program is provided primarily through government plans—i.e., a social security system—including health care for the employed and their dependents, pensions for total disability and old age retirement, lump sums as well as pensions for survivors, monthly cash family allowances according to the number of children, and lump sums at termination of employment determined in accordance with length of service. Thus the employer must be prepared to assess the need for supplementing these government-provided benefits and must be guided by the level of adequacy for all ranks of jobs within the organization and the cost impact on operating expenses and profitability. The statutory benefits are funded through a tax levied on the employer and the employee somewhat in the same manner as in the United States, but historically the tax rate and tax base have been significantly higher than in Americia.

Typically, the need for supplementation concerns the inadequate level of pension benefits from social security for positions that would be categorized as exempt and senior management in the United States. The private pension plan supplements disability as well as old-age retirement and survivor benefits. Pensions for widows have a long-standing history in industrialized countries other than the United States and Canada.

Another aspect of benefit plans that is not common in the United States but more prevalent in other countries is a pattern of benefits (i.e., relation to earnings). For example, a typical pension accrual rate among the British Commonwealth countries (excluding Canada) amounts to one-sixtieth of pensionable earnings for each year of service. In addition, the employee's contribution to the pension fund is deductible from taxable income.

The next most commonly found employer-provided benefit plan, especially in developing areas, is so-called group life insurance—so-called because the underwriting and the premium calculation are not always on a group basis. In some areas the premiums are higher than they would be by American standards.

Of the total remuneration program, the most complicated element is indirect compensation. It is affected by the social security system peculiar to each country, the labor law, the income tax both from the employer and the employee, and funding methods. Accordingly, close cooperation must exist between the international management group and the subsidiary managers in each country, who, guided by competent advice, design the necessary benefit plans to complement the total remuneration program of a company and meet its reward management objectives.

Because of the very high income tax rates in most areas of the world, greater emphasis is placed, particularly among the industrialized nations, on executive perquisites. There has been a better practice of conservation of aftertax income in these countries than in the United States. For example, the company car assigned to most levels of senior management has been an accepted mode of remuneration in many countries. In several countries over 90 percent of the participants surveyed provide company cars to executive groups with or without charges for personal use.

BONUSES

Over the years—and with relatively little resistance—American multinationals have succeeded in introducing and expanding into their foreign subsidiaries the same management techniques that had contributed to the success of American business in the United States. The initial reluctance on the part of nationals at executive levels to accept variable executive compensation appears to be eroding. A trend may be evolving to develop executive incentive compensation as an integral part of the total remuneration plan for this group. The number of "bonus-paying companies" increases gradually year to year, particularly in the European area. In comparison with domestic practice in the United States, the individuals eligible are fewer in number, the amounts and portion of total cash compensation are smaller, and the tax bite is greater. If the socialist-controlled governments prevail with their objectives of egalitarianism and redistribution of income, this seeming trend will vanish.

The chief executive officers of the giant multinational organizations in

Europe, as well as the American multinational managers, have seen the base salaries of their senior management rising constantly. By contrast with their American counterparts, European senior managers have tended to receive the same percentage salary increases as those granted to their employees in order to preserve purchasing power during inflation. The costs of this practice can be very high where senior officers are involved. Such costs might be controlled, however, if the salaries of senior management are held constant or increased only marginally; the "difference" is made up by bonuses, which can reflect the business success of the operation rather than the cost of living.

The Compensation Program in Action

chapter 56

Keeping the Compensation Program Up to Date

James H. Davis

GENERAL MANAGER, COMPENSATION, ALUMINUM
COMPANY OF AMERICA, PITTSBURGH, PENNSYLVANIA

An effective corporate compensation program depends upon a compensation philosophy or state of mind as well as upon good administrative procedures. There are three different states of mind that produce different physical and organizational structures. The first might be called "monument" thinking. The idea is to chisel the structure in stone. No thought is given to possible renovation, updating, or modernization.

The second state of mind might be characterized by the management of a successful ball club. The idea is to replace aging or less effective players with younger, more effective players. The same positions must still be played. The manager's task is to maintain a high level of performance in a relatively unchanged environment.

The third state of mind is response to and anticipation of changing conditions. This might be illustrated by a homeowner's response to or anticipation of legislation imposing pollution control. Many communities prohibit the burning of leaves and rubbish by homeowners. Other communities are likely to take such action in the future, as the density of population and motor vehicles increases. One of the responses to this new legislation is the use of polyethylene bags for leaves and refuse. Thus a new market enjoys new growth in response to a new set of conditions.

Compensation history has been dominated by monument thinking. This was a natural, but little recognized, outgrowth of poorly conceived compensation programs. The objective of most compensation programs was to establish or to administer relationships. It became increasingly clear that paying wages and salaries, particularly to large groups of people, without adequately devised and controlled programs, generally produced a variety of unsatisfactory situations. Random rates were common in the past; people doing the same work were paid different amounts, often for obscure and indefensible reasons. Favoritism was a charge frequently laid to salary and wage administration. High turnover of employees has often been due to poor understanding of adequate compensation practices or, indeed, to poor practices in spite of adequate understanding.

It was assumed that such problems could be relieved by adapting or revising the compensation program. The question of pay increases based on seniority versus pay increases for greater accountability has been long debated. Only recently has the weight of opinion swung in favor of accountability.

Compensation practice rests on a fundamental premise that the person who pays is the boss. Proprietors naturally and frequently resist sharing or explaining the compensation program because they recognize this fundamental principle. In corporations, managers and administrators often vie for authority for determining pay because they recognize that it provides a base for their own accountability. In this atmosphere, inequities are often caused by an owner's or manager's style of compensation practice.

Recent studies, surprisingly, suggest that there is an inverse correlation between full disclosure and productivity; organizations that don't reveal all the evaluation and salary range data seem to have more improvement in performance. Nevertheless, undue secrecy or inadequate communication makes it difficult to convince employees they are properly paid. Whatever its cause, this lack of understanding has been a dominant producer of employee unrest, as expressed at the bargaining table, in management discussions, or in the rate of employee resignation. Contributing to the lack of understanding was the great tendency of bosses to delegate only what they did not want to do themselves, usually the mechanical part of the compensation program. This has produced a generation of salary administrators dominated by monument thinking.

Monument thinking merely exchanges old problems for new ones and, indeed, ignores many identifiable problems. It produces a concern expressed by managers and employees alike that their jobs, careers, and compensation are boxed in by a job description, a salary scale, or a promotional table insensitive to their contributions.

Monument thinking does not easily adjust to economic changes, particularly rapid rises in the cost of living and inflation. It is insensitive to the change in people and jobs. It does not respond to organizational change, so common in industry today. It persists in tolerating and reinforcing the problems that the first mechanical salary administration program was supposed to relieve. Thus we conclude that something must be added to the monument approach.

Owners, executives, and compensation managers with ball-club mentalities strive to keep the compensation program as good today as it was yesterday. This calls for diligent effort to maintain and administer yesterday's programs to achieve credible answers to today's problems. Obviously, job descriptions, performance ratings, and job values must be current or this objective cannot be achieved. Yesterday's compensation program will not work today unless it has been revitalized by a subtle infusion of problem-solving modifications.

Included in such changes should be considerations of internal as well as external factors, such as company growth, diversification, organizational realignment, and governmental and legal regulations, in addition to the variable competitive relationships inherent in the marketplace.

Owners, executives, and compensation managers must be sensitive to changing needs—those which are permanent, not just fluctuations—in order to make programs do tomorrow what they did not have to do today. This suggests anticipating changes and successfully planning the implementation of such changes. Assuming that the existing compensation plan is a good one, change should not be made lightly or capriciously. Dramatic changes must be either carefully planned for presentation to managers and employees or avoided altogether, because if they are not adequately explained, the reaction could be opposite to the desired effect. If dramatic changes are instituted, employees may reason that the previous system must have been pretty bad. Thus proposed revisions must be pretested and explained carefully to ensure their being accepted and supported wholeheartedly by the management groups responsible for implementing them.

POLICY CONSIDERATIONS IN MAINTAINING THE PROGRAM

With state of mind identified and philosophy established for the compensation program, several factors are critical to maintaining it in an up-to-date condition.

Policy Approval　This fundamental requirement must exist before any meaningful compensation program can be maintained. History is full of the wreckage of compensation programs where the policy of the organization did not provide the guidance and support that could sustain the program under stress.

Competitive Position　A principal requisite of a compensation program is to define the market in which a company intends to compete. For example, if a company chooses to compete with the top 25 percent of national industrial manufacturing companies, it provides itself a broad base with which to compare its own practice. Or, if it intends to compete with the retail stores of a particular geographical marketing area, it is provided a definable measure of comparison.

Promotion policy is a key factor in determining competitive objectives. The company that promotes from within must develop a compensation program that provides orderly progression and supportable differentials between jobs. The company that routinely hires for assignments at all levels has a different kind of hiring and compensating objective.

The transfer of employees also requires constant attention to the differences between a locally competitive and a nationally competitive program. This becomes more important and complex when the company transfers people between countries.

Philosophy　The salary program is a management tool and, as such, must be designed to reflect overall corporate philosophy and the policies which embody that philosophy. Those responsible for corporate or institutional compensation programs should be responsible for devising or revising objectives which become part of approved policy. Objectives not in tune with approved policy are wasted effort. Policy not implemented by goal setting and the establishment of achievable objectives becomes so much verbiage.

PROCEDURAL MEANS OF MAINTAINING THE PROGRAM

To assure the necessary sensitivity to change described above, the manager of compensation must share in the accountability for job descriptions that will meet the needs of the organization. The manager must have accountability for reviewing the evaluation of all positions covered under the various evaluation plans of the company and for establishing the salary policy lines for nonbargaining employees.

Pay Relationships between Bargaining and Nonbargaining Employees   It is also important, for purposes of internal equity, that the compensation manager be involved in any bargaining to establish wage lines. In the typical industrial company with a unionized hourly work force, the bargained agreement provides the basis of compensation for the existing hierarchy of hourly jobs. These jobs represent a base-compensation group with which certain other similar, related, and associated personnel groups have logical and/or historical salary relationships. By virtue of these relationships, salary structures for such personnel groups should be updated in a manner which recognizes equity in relation to the bargaining unit. Comparison with hourly compensation is particularly important in establishing structures for *nonexempt salaried personnel* and *supervisory personnel:*

1. *Nonexempt Personnel:* This is usually a nonbargaining group performing secretarial, clerical, or routine technical work and having job value levels corresponding to the hourly work force. In businesses that do not have an hourly work force, the nonexempt salary structure is usually updated according to community wage practices as determined by local salary surveys.

2. *Supervisory Personnel:* This group normally includes the direct supervisors of hourly and nonexempt salaried personnel. Adequate salary differentials between supervisors and those supervised are required. Typical practice in industrial organizations is to maintain differentials ranging from 15 to 25 percent.

Employee Performance Results   Accurate and current evaluations of employee performance are essential to a well-ordered, up-to-date salary program. This input is most difficult to achieve because it requires perceptive and unbiased managerial effort to obtain complete and useful results. At the very least, each employee's performance should be appraised at the time salary action is being considered and as often as practical for each individual case.

Participation in Maintaining the Program   How up to date a compensation program is will depend a great deal on who is involved in maintaining it.

The *salary administrator* or *compensation manager* can be a primary force in carrying out policy, meeting objectives, and monitoring the use of the compensation tools described above. This can be done unilaterally to assure that the program is effective and up to date; if this approach is taken, the program's success will depend heavily on the salary administrator's own experience and acceptance by other managers.

The department head can have the entire responsibility for evaluating people and administering salaries within the department in much the same way as the proprietor did in smaller and less complex situations in the past. This plan has the advantage of providing the department head with some of the tools of the proprietor, but it has a conspicuous defect—which is magnified in a large organization—of creating or at least permitting wide variations between departments in the relationship of pay and contribution.

One device designed to give the compensation program the appearance and substance of top-level concern is the review of jobs, evaluations, and salaries by a *blue-ribbon committee* of key company executives. In a small organization this is a proper role for a group of executives who have direct knowledge of the people and positions concerned. In a large, multilocation organization the top executives often have little contact with the jobs or the incumbents. Here it is a time-consuming artifice which may provide the illusion of concern by top management but very often results in the domination of the committee's action by one or another of its members.

A series of committees, each made up of managers in a specific area of the business (for example, a committee of sales managers), may be charged with the responsibility for maintaining the compensation program in their respective areas. This approach tends to allay some of the problems caused by having a single manager perform these functions, but the relief provided is simply one of degree. Although all the departments in the same area of the business will be in step with each other, there is still the risk that whole areas will be out of step with the rest of the company.

A corporate committee which includes the compensation manager, the manager of the position in question, and others who provide a broad base of experience with the job appears to be the best compromise. Such a committee is usually composed of a small permanent corps plus varying members and tends to be more responsive to the levels of work being examined. The presence of the manager of the position in question assures that the job is properly considered in relation to others, and the presence of other managers on the committee also assures that problems within the department are being compared with problems in the other departments. In this arrangement the primary responsibility for results must remain with the compensation manager.

A probable dividend of this participative device is organizationwide communication and understanding of compensation policy and procedures. Also, key managers' firsthand knowledge is carried over to other employees, thus enhancing employees' understanding of the compensation program.

A NECESSARY CATALYST

To all the considerations mentioned in this chapter there should be added a needed catalyst: a generous application of openness, candor, and mutual respect. Those responsible for keeping a compensation program up to date need continuing endorsement of the program and honest feedback from managers who use it. Fairness and impartiality in the administration of a plan are musts even though they will produce unpopular decisions from time to time. For managers to accept these results, as well as more favorable ones, both managers and the compensation organization must recognize that a compensation program is not precise and neither is it controlled by a set of measures outside the tolerance of human judgment. Emphasis should be placed on reasoned usage of the systems involved and a seeking of facts as they exist. When this emphasis is achieved and all parties concerned are willing to review decisions and to amend previous results if new information is obtained or the situation has changed, a truly responsive compensation plan can come into being and be used as a vital force in the effective management of the enterprise.

chapter 57

The Role of the Compensation Manager

James E. McElwain

ASSISTANT VICE PRESIDENT OF COMPENSATION AND
BENEFITS, NCR CORPORATION, DAYTON, OHIO

Other chapters of this handbook have discussed the principles, approaches, techniques, and procedures pertinent to the compensation field. It is the role of the compensation manager to ensure that these are brought together to create a coherent whole—tailored to the organization and the personnel serviced.

The small firm provides a useful perspective from which to launch our discussion of the compensation manager's role. In the smaller company the compensation function as such may not exist or be required as a distinct, specialized activity. Normally, compensation will be one of the many "hats" that a personnel manager who is a generalist will wear. Likewise, in the smaller company the service, sophistication, and formal system required are typically less. The same principles of internal equity between jobs, external competitiveness for jobs, individualized pay for performance, and so forth, are applicable. However, because of its small size, it is likely that the company's individual jobs are known and understood by the line management in greater detail than is possible in a company with many divisions, many products, and large or far-flung operations. Less effort is required in job description. Similarly, job measurement (or job evaluation) to achieve internal equity can be approached more directly. The number and type of internal relationships are fewer and more readily identifiable. Line management is in a position to perform more of the compensation responsibilities, with less reliance on "system" and service from a specialist organization.

MANAGING THE COMPANY'S COMPENSATION DOLLAR

The conclusion which can be drawn from this review of the compensation function in the small firm is that compensation is basically and principally a line management responsibility. This conditions orientation of the compensation function under every set of circumstances. The corollary is that the compensation function exists to facilitate sound line management decisions concerning the relative value of jobs and, in turn, the value of individual performance and contribution in the job. The aim is to develop sufficient system, policy, and procedure to facilitate sound decisions—line management decisions. As with any staff or service function, the tendency which is ever present, and the risk which is to be guarded against, is that of providing more system or policy than is necessary—the tendency to get involved in technique, methodology, and system to the point where these take on a life of their own.

The role of the compensation manager is to participate with the line management in managing the company's compensation dollar. It is the centralization in a specialist organization of specific planning and control activities to meet the need for direction and coordination beyond that which is likely or possible if left entirely to each individual supervisor. On the other hand, each supervisor must be held accountable for accomplishing the work under his or her purview. This requires that the supervisor have authority to secure, measure, and compensate performance and contribution. To the degree that the supervisor's authority is diluted or diminished in this matter, his or her function as a supervisor is undermined and rendered less effective.

This leads to another important point about the compensation manager. Pay is the most basic and significant representation of the overall employment relationship of each individual. Additionally, the matter of pay implies "worth." Consequently, by nature this militates against system or centralization. It can be said that the company's compensation plan or compensation system is in reality determined and materialized at the point of the specific interaction of the individual manager and the individual employee in each of the tens, or hundreds, or thousands of individual interfaces which take place over time. It is at that point that the company's compensation posture is translated into an individually meaningful context, for better or worse.

It is easy for the compensation manager to veer from this perspective in discharging his or her responsibilities. It is easy to assume that the system of classification, evaluation, and pay has a significance, or in fact an existence, apart from its application. The fact remains that the employee generally understands, interprets, evaluates, and judges the company posture on the matter of compensation primarily in terms of its application to him or her individually. The compensation manager therefore must guard against the assumption that the compensation system is itself good or bad; that the plan itself will or will not accomplish something; that what the company needs is "system A" instead of "system B." This danger is equally likely if the line manager comes to depend on and expect the plan to do the job.

Thus compensation is relevant only to the individual, and the individual judges the system according to the compensation decisions which affect him or her. The compensation plan is little more and little better than its actual use, case by case. In view of this, the compensation manager's chief responsibility is to prepare each line manager to discharge compensation responsibilities most effectively. Techniques and systems do not by themselves provide the line manager with the tools to do the compensation job. Reliance on technique often leads to blind application of policy and substantial efforts to fit the individual to the system, rather than translating the policy meaningfully with respect to the individual for services performed.

What has been written to this point should not be interpreted as denigrating the importance and contribution of the compensation manager. The intent is merely to place the role and function in a proper perspective as a basic starting point. We begin from that point because the importance of the matter of compensation needs relatively little emphasis. Its importance is generally quite evident. The importance of pay in the operation of the total economy; the fact that the largest single component of national income is wages and salaries; the fact that in many businesses the largest single cost is wages and salaries; the fact that among the most important decisions a company makes are those which will or will not afford the firm the opportunity to attract, retain, and motivate the people required to accomplish its objectives; the fact that pay decisions are remarkably complex in their elements and so far-reaching in their effects—all these highlight the critical need for attention, expertise, and rational system, which are the substance of the compensation manager's role.

EVOLUTION OF THE COMPENSATION ROLE

The compensation function has emerged rather recently in business history, in response to the growing size and complexity of business organizations. Because of its relatively recent vintage, there is limited understanding generally of the functions of the compensation manager except by those closely associated with the activity. Due to these same circumstances, the compensation role exercised in different companies will vary significantly in content and impact. Also, the speed with which the problems have emerged and the degree of change that has occurred have created a situation where the tools, techniques, and solutions have hardly been able to keep pace. For these and other reasons, the nature and scope of the compensation function vary from company to company. The compensation manager may simply take care of clerical functions (organizing and maintaining pay records), have technical responsibilities (classification, grading, and surveying) or advise top management on strategic matters of policy dealing with human resources and labor economics.

Viewed from a historical perspective, the compensation role might be described as evolving through the above three phases. Any given organization might be, and might by design remain, at any of the three stages.

The first stage might be identified as records or information orientation. In this stage, one finds a centralization of pay data—data concerning salaries, increases awarded, employee pay groupings, and so forth. The primary thrust is statistical, and the impact is related to the availability and reporting of information. Such information is often used by others for analyses and decision making. Often, and quite naturally, this phase leads to a control orientation, since the data generated and reported are typically put to that use by the management serviced.

The second stage might be identified as survey orientation. By utilizing the data available within the organization as a base for comparison, attention begins to be directed to the outside labor market. However, to ensure that the jobs surveyed are comparable with jobs in the organization, it becomes increasingly necessary to develop groupings or classifications of like activities and jobs similar to those in other organizations. The thrust at this point is often to build an internal structure (or microstructure) within the firm which will reflect or conform to the assumed external labor market (or macrostructure). At this stage, the limited information and control orientation is exceeded and the service begins to take on an advisory orientation.

The third stage is one to which relatively few organizations have evolved, and only to varying degrees. We would identify it as the integrated professional compensation role. This is the stage in which the function becomes one of explicit policy development. It includes a balance between planning and control. It is this last stage which seems most reasonable to elaborate upon in our effort to define the role of the compensation manager.

AUTHORITY PLATEAUS

Before proceeding in that effort, it might be worthwhile to note the implications of the evolution described above. There is a pattern of evolution in staff roles which applies to a greater or lesser degree to all functions. The emergence of the compensation function is but one example. In terms of responsibility and impact, what emerges can be described as "plateaus of authority." There appears to be not only a chronological but also a natural progression from the "informational or recording plateau" to the "advisory plateau" and thence to the "policy plateau." There is, of course, a final plateau where the policy plateau is exceeded and actual operational decisions emerge. At that point, staff in effect functions as line. That final plateau may be necessary in certain types of enterprises because of an unusually critical need for control or because of the sophistication of technology. The exercise of such authority might be appropriate under extreme conditions, such as if the survival of the firm is at stake. It would normally seem, however, that in matters of human resources this last stage is not advisable and should be consciously avoided. In our view, this is particularly true of the compensation function.

THE INTEGRATED PROFESSIONAL ROLE

As visualized here in the integrated professional role, the compensation manager functions at the policy plateau, with considerable emphasis on planning and control. This role is integrated in the sense that it relies upon and welds together the theories, facts, discoveries, principles, and considerations of many allied disciplines. It integrates these in arriving at sound, meaningful, and effective policy recommendations across a broad spectrum of compensation matters. It implies anticipating, as opposed to simply reacting to, conditions. It implies assessment of future conditions and their impact on the firm. It implies a depth and a breadth of analysis and action which go beyond studying the labor market, collective bargaining, and applying standard techniques. The compensation role as it functions in this context is multifaceted and incorporates labor economics, organization theory, behavioral science, social science, and the total personnel function.

There is often some reluctance to claim the relationship between compensation and these disciplines—possibly because it has been suggested on occasion by members of those other professions that compensation practitioners engage in the superficial and shallow pursuit of each of these disciplines. There is some truth to this. On the other hand, the principles and findings of each of these fields have application to compensation issues; and, if such findings are to get beyond the laboratory or theory state, the compensation manager is the one likely to effect their application. In using theory to develop a practical working system in a real organizational environment, the compensation manager must deal with and relate such factors as cost of labor to price of services offered; the dynamics of organization design to relative job worth; the psychology of individual human needs to compensation rewards; and subtle institutional forces and changing demographic and social patterns, both internal and external to the organization, to appropriate monetary treatment. Finally, the compensation manager must consider the total mix of compensation in all its elements, since no aspect of the employment relationship is entirely divorced from the matter of compensation.

The Compensation Manager and Labor Economics   A substantial portion of compensation responsibilities is related to labor economics, an area emphasized in survey orientation. Although compensation is now recognized as encompassing a good deal more, it still deals with the basic economic issue of setting a price for a factor of production. From the employer's point of of view, compensation must be treated as a cost which is associated with units of production. From the employee's point of view, compensation is a price established for the offering of services. Thus we have the concept of a labor market with the dynamic tension of supply and demand.

The compensation manager must first identify the segments of the labor market in which the firm deals both directly and indirectly; the manager must then monitor as closely as possible labor price fluctuations as they occur. If pay levels are too low relative to that labor market, the firm is likely to fail in attracting and retaining human resources of the proper number and quality. If they are too high, the competitive position of the firm in terms of its product cost and selling price is likely to deteriorate. Primary responsibility for the economic instrumentation which enables the firm to identify and maintain this delicate balance rests with the compensation manager. It is a key and primary role.

This is not to imply, as is often assumed, that the labor market is in any sense simple or orderly. Quite the contrary. The problems of identifying and measuring the market are substantial, and few present approaches are adequate to the task. The typical tendency to identify market practice on the basis of job title or a sketchy job description is less than satisfactory at best. It makes basic assumptions concerning job comparability which are often subject to serious question. Thus, for example, a nationally published survey recently reporting on salaries of EDP occupations showed quite astonishingly that the pay reported for the job identified and described as "director of EDP" had a spread of 400 percent. An average was calculated including the extremes of the pay spread! This same survey showed the highest salary reported for the "junior keypunch operator" as higher than the lowest salary reported for the "director of EDP." Although this type of market data makes interesting reading, the compensation manager must develop and use substantially more refined measurement techniques to provide the basis for critical decisions on pay policy.

The labor market is imperfect in many respects. Not only is the employer's knowledge of the market incomplete, but the employee is likely to experience even greater difficulty in determining the basis for establishing a price for his or her services. There are traditional group relationships which tend to dilute the effect of supply and demand. Also, there is the effect of collective bargaining—which in some cases results in pay only remotely related to basic market factors. Beyond these, and possibly of more fundamental and pervasive significance, is the approach in which pay levels are related to living costs. This discounts the basic concept of a labor market and implies a concept of compensation based on need rather than on the type, level, or availability of work performed.

The compensation manager, then, must provide the firm with the tools necessary to maintain that precarious balance between a compensation level high enough to compete for needed human resources and one low enough to allow the company to be profitable.

The Compensation Manager and Organization Design   A sound compensation program must begin with and build from the work performed. The nature of a business organization is to take that work and to segment it into manageable elements which can be performed individually while being integrated toward a common objective. Although certain basic organization principles are commonly followed, the division of work and the design of jobs in an organization are to some degree uniquely a function of the particular product or service it supplies, the specific skills and resources available, and the particular management style. Further, since these factors are dynamic, the organization itself is constantly in the process of adapting and rearranging its design to accommodate and reflect shifting conditions. Periodically, the organization is formally realigned. However, more subtle and less evident shifts are continually in process as the organization acts and reacts through time.

Compensation, if it is to be meaningful, must relate to what people do, and what they do is intimately tied to the unique organization of work. Thus the compensation manager must have a thorough understanding of the work of the firm and the organization structure through which this occurs. A compensation program that is not grounded in the realities of organization relationships will be a "paper program."

The compensation manager must ensure that the classification and compensation system is uniquely fitted to and reflective of the organization of work. Of course, organization is inherently dynamic, and therefore it militates against the static description and classification of work; it is therefore essential to recognize that any such classification program is constantly dying. It can maintain its vitality, usefulness, and meaning only to the degree that the compensation role is sensitive to the organization process.

Just as the matter and manner of compensation may encourage or discourage effective individual performance, it may similarly enhance or impede effective organization in terms of the division of work and job design. The role of the compensation manager is to ensure that the factors of pay are selected and applied in such a manner as to facilitate effective organization patterns and to discourage ineffective patterns—e.g., under- or over-specialization, empire building, and the like.

The Compensation Manager and Behavioral Science   Many behavioral scientists feel that the chief responsibility of the compensation manager is to spread dissatisfaction as evenly as possible throughout the organization. There is possibly some element of truth in this viewpoint. A good deal is known about the place of compensation in the employment phenomenon and its effect on individual behavior. Enormously more has been hypothesized. Although there is not complete agreement as to the nature and degree of the effect of pay on individual employee behavior, the very concept of pay for services performed inherently links the two.

The role of the compensation manager is to assist the firm in achieving a compensation framework which positively reinforces effective performance and, equally important, discourages ineffective performance. As was stated earlier, however, the compensation program itself does not accomplish this. The proper and effective relationship of pay to performance is accomplished only by each line manager's application of the compensation framework on a case-by-case basis.

In dealing with the matter of compensation and individual behavior, it would appear that historically the compensation practitioner has been concerned primarily with one aspect of motivation. This aspect might be termed the "motivation to participate," i.e., to accept employment and join the firm. This is achieved through proper identification of the market and a competitive pay structure. Equal attention should be given to pay in terms of its effect on the motivation to perform and the motivation to develop.

Similarly, the compensation manager must create and foster recognition that compensation is enormously more than a matter of absolute dollars of purchasing power to the employees. It is in a sense a basic representation of the overall employment relationship. To state this another way, compensation, in addition to being a medium of exchange, is a symbol of how the firm views the employee's effort, performance, contribution, and potential. For this reason, very small differences or increments of pay take on a seemingly disproportionate significance. For this same reason, very large increments of pay can have little effect or significance if granted to all employees.

The tendency to deemphasize compensation as a factor in motivation and satisfaction and to emphasize other factors, such as achievement and recognition, must take into account the fact that compensation is a symbol of these—it is part of the language (the most tangible part) which confirms, reaffirms, or denies these for the individual. The compensation manager's job, therefore, is to create an awareness and sensitivity to the behavioral implication of compensation and to ensure a compensation system which effectively marshals these characteristics to further the work of the firm.

The Compensation Manager and Social Science   The compensation role has deep overtones in the matter of social patterns. In a mobile society and one which is economically advanced, social levels are strongly related to economic factors, notably employment income. The compensation manager must be sensitive to the social implications of compensation and at the same time attuned to the implications of changing social patterns relative to compensation. Specific factors which might serve to exemplify this area include: the changing nature and makeup of the work force; the aging population; the prevalence of the two-wage-earner family; the thrust to accommodate the part-time worker; the emergence of the female worker as the full partner; the generally higher educational level; the emergence of the "knowledge workers" and the decreasing demand for raw labor; the effect of economic advances and affluence on the work relationship and motivation; and increasing professionalism and its implications of group affiliation or scientific affiliation as a dimension additional to that of employer affiliation.

These changing social patterns will influence the role of compensation and the makeup of and approach to compensation much as did the emergence of collective bargaining in the past.

In addition to the changing social patterns external to the firm, the internal social system is of equal significance. The firm is a complex of social institutions and groups striving to maintain traditional relationships in some cases or to secure more favorable relationships in others. These phenomena are closely associated and interrelated with the matter of organizational dynamics mentioned previously. As products change, product mix shifts, technologies disappear or emerge, organizational format shifts, and new authority relationships develop, the nature of the work of individuals, occupations, and groups is affected and their relative responsibility, impact, and contribution are enhanced or diminished accordingly. A compensation program which is not attuned to such matters or is not adapted to accommodate them will not remain internally equitable or externally competitive very long.

The Compensation Manager and the Total Personnel Function   The compensation role is characteristically located within the personnel or industrial relations function of most large companies. Apparently this is because compensation (despite its significant financial aspects) deals primarily with the classification, evaluation, and pay treatment of the firm's human resources. Since no aspect of the employment relationship is entirely separate from compensation, the role of the compensation manager requires that he or she work closely with the various other personnel activities. The job description and job classification become a basic input and point of reference for the activities of the other personnel functions. Let us review the compensation manager's role as it relates to the other, more typical personnel functions.

The employment or placement activity and the compensation activity require extremely close interaction. On the one hand, the employment function will rely directly upon job descriptions and job specifications to aid in identifying qualified candidates. On the other hand, the employment function, since it is dealing daily in the labor market, can be a source of direct and immediate feedback to the compensation function concerning the competitiveness of the company's compensation posture. It will be recognized, however, that the difference in missions of these two activities means they often will be at odds. This is because the compensation function—through the establishment of wage or salary ranges—places limits on that segment of the labor market which is willing to avail itself of employment with the firm. Such constraints can be viewed by the employment function as obstacles to the accomplishment of its mission.

Compensation is also closely related to the organization planning activity—so much so that often these functions are found in combination. Sound, explicit, clearly delineated organization is essential to proper and equitable compensation. Difficulties in job description and job evaluation are often symptomatic of deficiencies or confusion in organization and job design. Similarly, the job description and job evaluation processes elucidate overlaps or gaps in organizational responsibility. The compensation manager can function effectively only when this association is close and continuous.

The compensation manager must also work closely with the labor relations or employee relations function. The labor relations activity is found primarily in companies that operate under a labor agreement with a union. Of the bargainable items (wages, hours, and working conditions), the so-called economic issues—i.e., primarily wages and benefits—are most often the subject of greatest contention and strife. A sound, well-conceived, explicitly defined, and properly administered compensation program is a prerequisite to labor harmony. Interestingly, although management and union groups often differ dramatically on other issues, both parties often concur on the need to establish a reasonably formal and explicit basis for satisfying the requirements of internal equity and fairness. Where this is done effectively, a sound and workable framework exists for resolving differences on the key issue of wages. The compensation manager's role in labor relations is therefore critical, and he or she will normally function as either the principal representative or a key participant in the resolution of economic issues.

THE ROLE OF THE COMPENSATION MANAGER FROM A TOP MANAGEMENT PERSPECTIVE

It hardly needs stating that pay is very high on the employee's list of things that are important. How high might be subject to debate, but there is no doubt that it is high—whether for senior vice presidents or junior clerks. As a result, compensation represents a powerful device for top management as an attention getter and a message giver. Pay systems provide an important tool for management to use when there is a need to shift direction, support business plans, convey standards of performance and behavior, reinforce what the organization must accomplish, and the like. The role of the compensation manager is to assist management in using this tool to convey its messages most effectively. The message which top management gives the compensation manager might therefore be that the effectiveness and success of the compensation function will be measured more by what it contributes toward fulfilling the firm's mission than by "good" compensation practice in any other context. This might suggest less attention to external markets and more to internal requirements and opportunities.

SUMMARY

This chapter has attempted to define the main characteristics of the compensation manager's role. Our description has projected the role as it might be performed in a highly professional context and typically in a large and complex organizational environment. This should allow for variations, of course, where size or other requirements dictate the need for expansion or contraction of the compensation function to meet particular circumstances.

In attempting to put it all together, the compensation manager's role might be summarized as follows: to perform a staff service that provides line management with a policy framework and a practical working system of total compensation which satisfies the economic, organizational, human, and social realities of the particular firm, its labor market, and its employees and which achieves necessary central control of labor costs, while reserving as fully as possible the operational decisions on individual compensation to line management.

chapter 58

Keeping Records for Administration and Research

Richard C. Fremon

PAST CHAIRMAN, ENGINEERING MANPOWER
COMMISSION, NEW YORK, NEW YORK

The principal importance of record keeping and data processing in salary administration lies in the information they provide for equity auditing and decision making. Such useful information includes statistical descriptions of structural and paid salaries within and outside the organization and stable historical and trend data, as well as statistical answers to questions of all sorts.

In record keeping and data processing the scope of objectives that can be set realistically and the range of techniques that can be used are determined by the capabilities of computers and their associated apparatus. A brief description of computers and their uses, with particular reference to salary administration, is therefore included in this chapter prior to a discussion of record keeping and statistical procedures.

COMPUTERS

The principal value of a computer is its ability to do large numbers of ordinary arithmetic and other simple number manipulations at great speed and low cost. Computers are most efficient when used in procedures that involve manifold repetition of the same or very similar elemental steps. Computers thus make possible certain valuable kinds of mass data processing which would be impossible to do by hand. The peripheral equipment usually associated with a computer can offer a large variety of ways of feeding in, storing, and presenting data and thus extend the time and cost advantage to these operations as well.

The computer art offers a dazzling array of hardware, system configurations, and input-output possibilities. To get the most service from a computer installation, one should rely on the advice of an expert who is familiar with the installation. To be able to use computers most effectively, a salary administrator should know at least their general uses and capabilities and their principal limitations.

Uses and Capabilities   Computers and associated equipment can be used to store information in a form which permits rapid and inexpensive access by and use within the computer. Information may be stored on magnetic tape, discs, or other magnetic devices, or even in files of punch cards. These means of storage differ from each other in respect to ease of access, cost, and the volume of information they will hold, and each has its own mechanical characteristics and hazards.

The choice of a particular means of storage for large masses of data should be made by an expert. Factors to be considered include (1) the amount of information or number of items, (2) how often the file will be updated, (3) how the information is to be used—i.e., what means of retrieval will be necessary—and (4) with what other collections of data the file is to be associated and in what ways.

For smaller amounts of information, particularly if the file is to be used infrequently, one should choose whatever means of storage are physically most convenient. Magnetic media are available in a variety of sizes and degrees of portability, and although punch cards are going out of style for large files, one should consider them, too, for applications that call for the stability, flexibility, and low cost that punch cards offer. An example would be a historical file from which elements are to be chosen and freely arranged for studies.

A large computer can be programmed to manipulate data in any way that is necessary in salary administration. All ordinary arithmetic operations can be performed with whole or decimal numbers, lists can be sorted, and computer decisions based on relationships among the data being processed can be made. Combinations of these elemental operations can be programmed to accomplish all kinds of standard mathematical calculations, as well as special procedures designed for particular problems.

Computer output is delivered in a number of different forms, depending on the peripheral equipment used. All installations have facilities for placing the output (i.e., any information that is in the computer at the time) on magnetic tape, punch cards, or paper. Some installations have the means to plot graphs and to record graphic or text output on microfilm and display it on a cathode-ray device. Remote input-output terminals are generally worthwhile for rapid access to one's data. All output methods offer a great choice of formats, which can be varied to suit specific needs or preferences. (Chapters 26 and 59 also offer illustrations of the use of computers to store, organize, and retrieve information relevant to decision making in the compensation field.)

Limitations   The most important limitation in computer applications is cost. A large computer installation is inherently expensive to operate per unit of time.

Each routine used requires the preparation of a program, the cost of which must be justified by the extent of the program's use. Extensive manual preparation of data is expensive, as is the transformation of large amounts of data from one form to another, i.e., between printed or written copy and a machine-readable medium.

Time scheduling also is often an important consideration. One should not forget that programming can be a slow process, particularly for large and complicated routines, and that the final preparation of a program for use (debugging) usually cannot be brought to an end at a precisely predictable time.

All data storage devices are subject to partial or complete loss of contents. One should always be sure to have backup data so that lost material can be replaced or reconstructed. This means having duplicate files or being prepared to reassemble part or all of a collection of data in an efficient way.

Programming Programming consists of all the procedures that go into the preparation of a program or sequence of operations for a computer to perform. The steps are:

1. Analyzing the problem and sketching a system or logical procedure to solve it
2. Designing the system or procedure and diagramming its structure
3. Writing the procedure or program in a programming language or code
4. Testing and debugging, i.e., correcting logic and coding errors

For particularly demanding applications (large amounts of data or large numbers of operations), the programming should be done by a professional. The salary administrator should be prepared to provide: (1) a complete statement of the problem, (2) a description of the input data, (3) a detailed specification of the nature and format of the output desired, (4) an estimate of the expected volume of use of the routine, and (5) a statement of possible closely related future problems. The salary administrator should also participate in the analysis of the problem and the selection of approaches to its solution.

Most programming is done in one or another specialized "higher" language. A program written in one of these languages is subsequently converted in the computer, by means of a special, internal routine called a *compiler*. This routine transforms the higher language into the detailed steps which the computer will follow in actual operation. Programming languages are designed for specific kinds of applications, some primarily for scientific or technical work and some for business use. For a given computer installation one can use only the languages for which a compiler is available. For most ordinary applications, it is not critical which computer language is used. The choice of language is important only when esoteric procedures are required or huge amounts of data must be processed.

During the life of a system or program, it is often necessary to change it to keep up with changes in the business environment and in the program output requirements. One should therefore arrange at the outset to ensure the continuing future availability of programming resources to take care of this maintenance work. This process is less expensive if one uses general instead of single-application programs to the greatest extent possible.

RECORDS

Records pertinent to salary administration include organized collections of detailed data about individuals and historical statistics on past salary actions, market surveys, and other economic information. Both individual and statistical records should contain all items that might reasonably be used. Flexible and efficient retrieval arrangements are important.

Individual Records   An essential part of the arrangements for keeping records of individuals is a central data base containing a large collection of information about each employee, stored in some machine-readable form, from which working requirements for information are supplied mechanically. Accordingly, the first question bearing on the nature of salary administration records is whether they are an integral part of the central data base or a separate deriv-ative of it. In the latter case the salary administrator need only provide storage for the items that he or she uses, whereas in the former there is a concern with storing all kinds of information as well as maintaining its timeliness and accu-racy. The following material assumes an interest in the whole process involved in keeping the data base.

In general, the data base should contain all information about each employee that might reasonably be found useful in managing the organization. Table 1 offers a list of possible choices. At any given time the data base should contain current information on each item for each person. It has been found useful to associate each principal item with its date of record so that the user can always judge whether it is really the latest information. Backup records are kept in the form of (1) contents from past key dates and (2) chronological lists of changes with suitable identifying data (also in machine-readable form). These backup records are, of course, also useful for studies of such personnel events as res-ignations, promotions, and transfers.

For economy of storage space, as much nonnumerical information as possible should be coded. It is not necessary that the codes be numerical. For some applications alphabetical codes are more efficient, and in any case mnemonic codes enhance accuracy. Coded information can be restored mechanically to

TABLE 1   Examples of Items in a Master Personnel Information File

Payroll account number	Regular or temporary
Name	Details of educational status
Sex	Completion of company training programs
Birth date	Present salary*
Citizenship status	Previous salary*
Company service date	Bonus status and history*
Social security number	Termination or leave category (if any)
Home address*	Job evaluation data*
Department number*	Performance rating*
Company location*	Security clearance status*
Occupational classification*	How employed
Organizational rank*	Work limitations
Standard hours per week	

*These items should be accompanied by their dates of record.

plain language in the process of retrieval or analysis. Encoding of material en route to the master file can also be done mechanically, although not quite as easily as in the reverse process.

For efficiency and accuracy, input information for a data base should come directly from the primary written source via a single keyboard manipulation into a machine-readable form. Personnel forms should accordingly be designed with the machine record format information preprinted.

Present practice is to have the main items in a personnel data base updated through on-line terminals by clerks who are trained in the routines involved. This procedure plus nightly file consolidations done automatically by standing programs ensures optimum timeliness for the ongoing business operations that need it. For the sake of efficiency, on the other hand, small or infrequent changes to items whose timeliness is less important should be accumulated and entered in batches. The maintenance cycle for these items, however, should not be made too long lest troublesome inconsistencies occur between the two types of data items.

Checking and auditing are of paramount importance in computer-kept records. Entirely new input (first recording of a new employee) should be confirmed with the source, preferably using data fed back from its ultimate location in the data base. A change in an existing record should be sent into the computer accompanied by several other associated items, particularly the expected present content of the item that is being changed, and, if these do not check, the change should be rejected automatically. Consistency checks are useful parts of the maintenance computer program and might include, for example, a routine that will reject information that an employee is 10 years old or has a salary of an impossible size. The maintenance program should also check the form of the input and should reject numbers where alphabetic characters belong, and vice versa.

Figure 1 is a schematic diagram of a working data-base maintenance routine. Although the diagram does not show it, there should be a security mechanism included in the maintenance program. This is an arrangement which keeps the data base itself in a changeable code and thus makes the information in the file available only to authorized persons who have the key. Security coding should not be confused with coding to save storage capacity, mentioned above.

Recorded information liable to change—for instance, educational status—should be audited periodically. This is done by sending each employee a printout of the changeable data that appear in the file for him or her and asking for verification.

Retrieval   One natural concomitant of the existence of a computer-oriented employee data base is the rapid expansion of management interest in using it to obtain selected listings and categorical studies in an expanding variety of specifications. This means that the retrieval routine must be flexible in all its operations and, at the same time, highly efficient, so that a large number of searches through a massive number of items can be carried out at reasonable cost.

The basic retrieval operations are (1) selecting a subpopulation specified by a number of parameters, (2) reading selected information about each member of the subpopulation, (3) sorting the data in a desired manner, (4) decoding, (5)

FIGURE 1   Master File Maintenance System

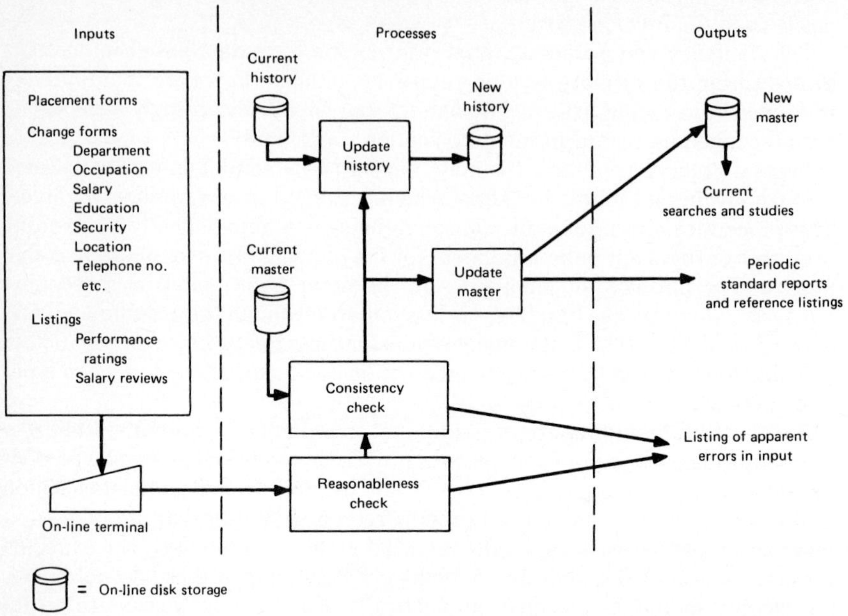

making calculations from the selected data, and (6) delivering output in one or more forms (printout, microfilm, or cathode-ray terminal) with some flexibility as to titles, headings, and format. The options available in the overall retrieval routine and the ways of calling for them can be organized so that the activity can be assigned to a clerk or clerks.

Historical Statistics   As a resource for studies of relationships between current situations and actions and corresponding ones of previous times, standardized collections of compressed statistics kept in machine-readable form are useful. The computer reduction and analysis of the details of a personnel action or a collection of market data can, with minuscule extra cost, be made to produce a condensed statistical representation which can be stored cheaply and used as input in the computer analysis of a later action or survey of the same kind to give data about changes over time. To set up such a statistical record, one should gather and record a relatively large number of categories of information so as to permit a flexible choice of groupings for later study and comparison. For example, for a salary survey that is repeated every year, one might choose to keep a record, on punch cards or tape, of the average salary and number of salaries reported for each combination of (1) occupational classification, (2) age, and (3) respondent organization.

STATISTICS

Formal statistical procedures are used in compensation administration to make generalized descriptions of detailed data, usually for the purpose of comparing groups of people in some way, and to assess the precision of such generalizations and comparisons.

Among the most troublesome problems commonly encountered in developing statistics for use in managing are the maintenance of credibility and the avoidance of credulity. In the former interest it is better to adopt for regular use a relatively small set of generally explainable statistical techniques and always be careful about the accuracy and relevance of the input data. For the latter, i.e., to combat the apparently natural human tendency to attribute undue accuracy to numbers as such, the analyst should cultivate the habit of estimating the statistical precision and the real significance of calculated results.

There are usually several good statistical approaches for any given situation. The selection of the one to use should depend on the feature of the data that seems most meaningful in terms of the management decisions to be made or most interesting to those who will be responsible for making the decisions.

In designing a statistical analysis, the first question is, Which variables should be treated explicitly, and, of these, which one or ones are assumed to be caused (i.e., dependent) and which are assumed to be causes (i.e., independent)? The choice of independent variables usually involves a trade-off between showing more detail and making the presentation simpler and easier to absorb. If, in a given case, an additional independent variable does not improve the overall precision of the analysis, it should be rejected. Variables measured on continuous numerical scales are the most convenient, but discrete categories can also be analyzed either as such or by giving each a numerical value.

It often seems desirable to average together or otherwise combine data which come from different sources or which represent different categories of people. In making such combinations, one must always decide what relative weighting to use for each source or category. Sometimes a natural weighting is clearly the right choice—for example, equal weight to each category or weights proportional to the populations of the respective sources. On the other hand, the question of weighting is often so difficult or controversial that the data of the different categories are best reported separately and not combined at all.

Using a particular mathematical expression or graphic form to report the essence of a collection of actual measurements of some set of variables implies that the principal relations among the variables are described at least reasonably well by the chosen expression or form. Thus if one speaks of the average salary of some classification of employees, it implies that a particular general level of salary is a principal characteristic of the classification. Likewise, using a curve of a given form to describe the relationship between experience and salary in some population suggests that that form of curve shows the main form of the relationship between those variables for such a population.

Measures of the dispersion of the actual data away from the generalized statistical statement (average, fitted curve, etc.) are related to the precision that may be attributed to that statement. In the practical case, the greater this dispersion, the poorer the precision. On the other hand, precision usually is improved by having larger amounts of data or larger samples of facts. One should, moreover, distinguish carefully between statistical precision and real significance. An observed difference between two averages, for example, might be highly significant statistically and utterly inconsequential in practical terms.

The following sections describe the more common ways of presenting statistical data, classified in terms of the number of variables that they involve.

Single Variable   Data on a single variable, such as the various individual salaries within a given occupational classification or the various market starting rates of the employers of a community for a particular level of skill, are most often reduced to some measure of central tendency. If the collection of items defined by the variable shows no central tendency, i.e., if no one value or range of values is more common than others, it ordinarily should not be expressed this way. Further, if there are two or more separate concentrations of data items among the values of the variable, one should suspect that the population represented by the data is really two or more different populations mixed together and seek ways of separating them.

The most commonly used measures of central tendency are:

1. *Mean:* the sum of the measurements divided by the number of them.
2. *Median:* the middle of a list of the measurements put in numerical order. If there is an odd number of measurements, the median is the middle one. If there is an even number of measurements, the median is midway between the middle two of them.
3. *Mode:* the quantity or range of quantities which is found in the data more often than any other.

For collections of data that exhibit a clear central tendency and in which the distribution of items is about the same on both sides of it, the mean, median, and mode are all about the same and the mean is usually the most accurate measure to use. Conversely, when the data items are distributed differently on the two sides of their central concentration, the three measures may be significantly different from each other, and one should use whichever one of them is consistent with the intended sense of the analysis.

The dispersion of measurements of a single variable is commonly expressed in terms of interquartile range or standard deviation.

The *interquartile range* is simply the difference between the value of the variable at the upper quartile and that at the lower quartile. The *upper quartile* is defined as that value of the variable which cuts off the highest one-quarter of the data items in an ordered list, and the *lower quartile*, the lowest one-quarter of them.

The *standard deviation* is the measure of dispersion that is most commonly associated with the mean, and it is estimated as follows:

$$\text{Standard deviation} = \sqrt{\frac{\Sigma(X - \overline{X})^2}{N - 1}}$$

where: Σ = summation over all items of data
X = each data item in turn
$\overline{X}$ = mean of data
N = number of data items

If one thinks of the data on hand as a sample of the data that would be obtained by measuring a very large population of the same kind, then the mean of the actual data may be viewed as an approximation of the mean that would apply to the larger universe. The precision of this approximation is estimated by the *standard deviation of the mean*, calculated as follows:

$$\text{Standard deviation of the mean} = \frac{\text{standard deviation}}{\sqrt{N}}$$

The connection between this quantity and the precision of the mean may be understood in the following way. Two-thirds of the time, on the average, the mean of the sample data will be within one *standard deviation of the mean* of the mean of the larger universe. Nineteen-twentieths of the time, on the average, the two means will be less than two *standard deviations of the mean* apart.

To estimate the precision of the difference between two means, one calculates the *standard deviation of the difference*, as follows:

Standard deviation of the difference
$$= \sqrt{(\text{std. dev. of mean \#1})^2 + (\text{std. dev. of mean \#2})^2}$$

The comparison of this quantity with the difference between the means indicates the *statistical* significance of the difference. If, for instance, the standard deviation of the difference is much larger than the difference itself, the variables in question might as well be assumed equal. If the standard deviation of the difference is equal to the difference itself, about one-sixth of the time the true difference between the variables is opposite in direction to the observed difference.

It must be noted that the estimates described in the preceding paragraphs are only approximations, which are better for larger samples. Textbook methods are available for assessing statistical significance more precisely, particularly for small samples.

Least-Squares Method Taking the mean of a set of measurements is the simplest example of a class of statistical techniques known as "least-squares methods." The name is taken from the fact that the estimates obtained have the minimum sum of the squares of differences from the actual data.

This least sum of squares of deviations corresponds to the idea of least error or best overall description of the data for a given form of representation.

Two Variables—Curve Fitting Simplified representations of two-variable (one dependent and one independent) data are obtained by fitting lines or smooth curves. The most common methods used are (1) visual smoothing, (2) group or moving averages, and (3) least-squares polynomials.

Smoothing by eye is the most flexible and least exact of these methods. It is particularly unreliable with respect to data that exhibit great dispersion.

Group averaging involves grouping the data in brackets or at intervals along the scale of the independent variable and then taking the mean of each variable in each group. The resulting group representations can be smoothed further by eye or by linear interpolation.

A moving average is constructed by calculating the mean of each variable at each of a progression of overlapping intervals of the independent variable. Usually these intervals are all of the same length along the independent scale, and each starts at a value that is one unit higher than the interval before it. An illustration of the calculation of a moving average is shown in Table 2. In this example the actual data are arranged in order of the independent variable (X), and the series of overlapping intervals is indicated by the numbered brackets. The values of the moving average for the first bracket are $X_a = 2$ (the mean of 1, 2, and 3) and $Y_a = 12.0$ (the mean of 11, 13, and 12). For simplicity, the example assumes equal weights for all the data. Unequal item weights, on the other hand, would have to be included in the calculation of both X_a and Y_a.

TABLE 2   Calculation of a Moving Average

Actual Data			Moving Average	
X (independent)	Y (dependent)	Intervals	X_a	Y_a
1	11			
2	13	(1)	2	12.0
3	12	(2)	3	13.0
4	14	(3)	4	13.0
5	13	(4)	5	13.7
6	14	(5)	6	14.0
7	15	(6)	7	15.7
8	18	(7)	8	16.7
9	17			

Group averages and moving averages are highly flexible with respect to preserving the apparent fine detail of the data but often are harder to interpret than a properly chosen simpler form, such as a polynomial curve.

The algebraic statement of a polynomial of kth degree is

$$y = a + bx + cx^2 + \cdots + zx^k$$

The best-fit coefficients, $a, b, c, \ldots z$, are calculated by solving the simultaneous equations:

$$
\begin{cases}
aN + b\Sigma X + c\Sigma X^2 + \cdots + z\Sigma X^k = \Sigma Y \\
a\Sigma X + b\Sigma X^2 + c\Sigma X^3 + \cdots + z\Sigma X^{k+1} = \Sigma XY \\
\quad \cdot \qquad \cdot \qquad \cdot \qquad \qquad \cdot \qquad \cdot \\
\quad \cdot \qquad \cdot \qquad \cdot \qquad \qquad \cdot \qquad \cdot \\
\quad \cdot \qquad \cdot \qquad \cdot \qquad \qquad \cdot \qquad \cdot \\
a\Sigma X^k + b\Sigma X^{k+1} + c\Sigma X^{k+2} + \cdots \quad z\Sigma X^{2k} = \Sigma X^k Y
\end{cases}
$$

where: X = independent variable
Y = dependent variable
N = number of data items
Σ = sum of values of expression to its right for all of data items

Standard computer programs are available for setting up and solving these equations for a variety of values of k.

The graphic representation of the equation for $k = 1$ is a straight line; for $k = 2$, a simple parabola; and for higher values of k, progressively more flexible and potentially more complex curves. The simpler polynomials tend to yield the truest fit around the midvalues of the independent variables, with wider variations from the actual data at the extremes. On the other hand, the higher polynomials, which generally improve the fit, sometimes introduce undesirable local peculiarities into the shape of the curve.

Figure 2 is an example of curve fitting by moving averages and by first-, second-, and third-degree polynomials.

More Than Two Variables   It is possible to fit algebraic expressions of two or more independent variables to observed data, reflecting the assumption that the dependent variable (salary, for instance) has two or more important causes (perhaps age, experience, and length of education). The expressions that work

FIGURE 2   Curve Fitting

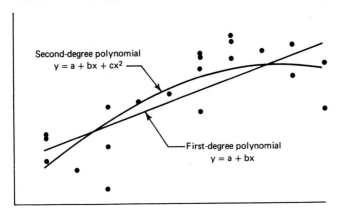

Second-degree polynomial
$y = a + bx + cx^2$

First-degree polynomial
$y = a + bx$

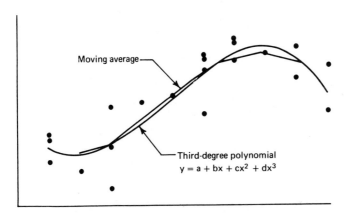

Moving average

Third-degree polynomial
$y = a + bx + cx^2 + dx^3$

well, however, are generally complex, hard to understand, and difficult to show graphically. On the other hand, when a very precise idea of the relative influences of several causes is needed, these more complex algebraic expressions give the best results. Their selection and calculation, however, should be left to a professional statistician.

For ordinary purposes, multiple-cause data can best be handled by grouping them into intervals or brackets of all but one of the independent variables and then studying the relationship between the dependent and the remaining independent variable, for each combination of the others, by the methods discussed above for the two-variable case.

Discrete Variables   Some information falls naturally into discrete categories. Examples are levels of education, occupational classifications, and organizational ranks. Discrete variables can be assigned numerical values by judgment and thus made analyzable by continuous-variable methods (the preceding section discussed making continuous variables discrete by bracketing), or they can be analyzed as discrete variables.

A discrete dependent variable is usually reported in terms of the number or percentage of cases in the various discrete categories of the independent variables.

If the data represent a sample from a larger universe, precision may be estimated from the appropriate standard deviation, as follows:

Standard deviation of the number in a category $= \sqrt{Np(1-p)}$

Standard deviation of the percent in a category $= 100 \times \sqrt{\dfrac{p(1-p)}{N}}$

where: N = size of total sample
$\quad\quad\;\; p$ = proportion of sample found in category

These formulas are reasonably good if the number in the category in question is at least 5 and the number in all the other categories together also is at least 5.

These standard deviations are related to the precision of the respective results (the number of individuals of the sample found in the category for the first and the proportion of the individuals of the sample found in the category for the second) in the same way that the *standard deviation of the mean* is related to the precision of the mean, as discussed earlier.

chapter 59

Supporting Business Strategy with Human Resource Inventory

James H. Davis

GENERAL MANAGER, COMPENSATION, ALUMINUM
COMPANY OF AMERICA, PITTSBURGH, PENNSYLVANIA

Larry L. Wyatt

MANAGER, HUMAN RESOURCE PLANNING, ALUMINUM
COMPANY OF AMERICA, PITTSBURGH, PENNSYLVANIA

John M. Rosenfeld

PARTNER, THE HAY GROUP, PITTSBURGH, PENNSYLVANIA

The supply, location, and qualification of personnel can provide the difference between growth and stagnation for industrial organizations—and, indeed, between survival and extinction. The rapid increase in labor costs and the loss of market share experienced by some organizations in the latter half of the 1970s have, in the 1980s, focused on productivity as the principal problem on the industrial scene. Growth in productivity is vital to cost reduction and has been lagging. Output per hour of work, measured on an annual basis, has risen by more than 3 percent only once during the eight years from 1974 to 1982, whereas in the 26 years before that, the feat was accomplished 16 times.[1]

---

[1] *U.S. News & World Report*, Mar. 8, 1982, p. 35.

Programs have been developed to improve productivity through people—programs which have required thoughtful business strategies and in many cases organizational changes. Planning the use of human resources to achieve organizational changes depends on an accessible inventory. It must be designed to provide timely needed information and to avoid dependence on irrelevant information. For example, most inventories identify the year of college degree, but candidate selection is rarely controlled by that fact.

CHARACTERISTICS OF A SUPPORTIVE INVENTORY SYSTEM

Data Bank The data bank consists of an inventory of jobs and an inventory of people.

Job data. The job data include title and evaluation. The evaluation is the key to defining job families (described in more detail in "Concepts," below). The data bank identifies the organization level and progression track to which the job belongs. It contains a job number so that a narrative description and other noncomputer information can be cross-referenced with the data base.

People data. The people data consist of personal information. Much of it is provided by the individual, who must update it annually. It includes salary and work history and appraisals of performance. Its accuracy and currency are assured by maintaining it at a level adequate to drive a computer-based payroll system. Also included (principally for high-potential people) are predictions of attainment in the present job and estimates of job families and/or jobs that are (in the opinion of supervisors, human resource specialists, and consulting analysts) attainable within five years.

Concepts

Job structure. A clear concept of job structure is essential to building an economical data bank, one which includes needed information in a concise form. There are a small number of key ingredients common to all jobs, and their mix defines the family of jobs. The ingredients, and their relationship, can be measured through a systematic analysis of job characteristics.

Organization levels. A manageable number of job levels descriptive of the organization should be clearly designated and defined.

Tracks of progression. Tracks of progression identify the paths in which job families (and specific jobs) fall, whether they are production, sales, technical, financial, or other types of jobs. (The organization should designate a manageable number of separate tracks, distinguishing between the principal types of activity which characterize its operations.) Each job family falls within one track or another; each individual is more likely to succeed in certain tracks than in others.

Job family. If there are several jobs which share significant characteristics, the group can be described as a "family." For example, a job family on the "technical management" track includes people who have solid knowledge in their particular disciplines, such as accounting or electrical engineering. The job family is placed at a given level within the organization and shares the characteristic of supervising the work of subordinate professionals and integrating their outputs with other disciplines. Jobs in the family have about the same value in the job evaluation system and approximately the same proportions of technical know-how and managerial accountability. If their number is large enough, they can be divided into separate disciplines within the job track; thus an accounting manager and the chief electrical engineer might belong to the same family, but they would fall into different discipline categories. Neither discipline is presumed to be the logical source of candidates in the other field, but each of these disciplines is part of the family comprising the technical management track.

Emphasis and Impact

The inventory's emphasis.   We have mentioned that the inventory of people should include appraisals of actual performance and of estimated potential for alternative assignments, tracks, or promotion. Realism and imagination at this step can enhance the inventory's usefulness in strategic planning by demonstrating a balance in emphasis. For example, some inventories have emphasized promotability to an extreme. Employees whose appraisal indicates they aren't likely to be promoted two levels may thus be prohibited from advancing one level. People who are satisfactory at their present level but are appraised as nonpromotable may be considered to block the promotion of others from a lower level, to the detriment of the organization.

However, a balanced inventory identifies all the people at each level, on each track, in each job family. Thus it emphasizes that most jobs are filled to accomplish an immediate economic purpose, not only to train the incumbent for promotion. You could reasonably expect a broader base of support, more universal interest in keeping data current, and less temptation to blame the inventory for the consequences of selection or training decisions if the inventory is generally perceived as a comprehensive, rather than selective, data base.

Organization structure's effect on staffing.   The inventory of jobs should focus on the effect of structure on staffing, not only to perform the work today but to replace individuals in the future. It should provide an early warning of the consequences of restaffing within the existing structure; it should also predict the consequences of an organizational redesign to avoid or alter restaffing needs.

Improving the reliability of appraisals.   Appraising individuals for promotability in their current tracks or in alternative tracks, and coding such appraisals for the data bank, can be challenging but can also determine the inventory's sensitivity in producing needed information for management decisions.

Appraisals are the responsibility of supervisors. Appraisals within particular disciplines are often the accountability of functional management. For example, the chief financial officer is frequently accountable for appraisals, assignment, and development of plant controllers even though the individual controller reports to a plant manager.

The inventory's influence on human resource planning.   Key elements in the usefulness of the data bank are currency and responsiveness. It usually takes longer to query the inventory than to make an intuitive decision. Therefore, unless the information is reliable and up to date, management will lose confidence in it and will rely on intuition, impulse, or other data for decisions to promote, transfer, demote, hire, or fire. The inventory data should be the most reliable input from the human resource department. If the department doesn't, or can't, influence staffing decisions, then it must live with the consequences.

The department will have to be satisfied with a reactive role rather than the participative role in human resource planning to which it should aspire.

Information Retrieval   Information from the data bank can be retrieved in various useful forms.

Inventory charts.   A chart along the following lines identifies people according to their readiness for promotion.

Ready for promotion now	Ready in 1–3 years	Ready in 3–5 years	Additional staff
Jones Lewis	Kuzma	Goodman	Evans Butler Carlini

It guides management and planners in preparing for changes. Take training, for example. For employees identified as ready for promotion now, training presumably won't improve their eligibility. It might be useful to provide skill training (e.g., report writing or speed reading) that could be interrupted if a promotion suddenly appears. Or, if the most logical promotion path is not likely to open up for a long time, the promotable person might take on an unrelated task (e.g., be loaned as an executive to the National Alliance of Business, the United Way, or government) as an alternative to overtraining, boredom, or discontent.

The most useful training for employees who need one, two, or three years on the job to become promotable is in the very definition of *on the job*. Such persons shouldn't be diverted from the pursuit of excellence in their own jobs. Reassignment could mean unrelated experience that doesn't improve the chances of promotion or an expensive transfer with the prospect of a second disrupting move when the promotion comes.

On the other hand, individuals expected to be ready in three to five years probably still have time to be shifted to other useful assignments that are performable and measurable and help prepare them for promotion.

The additional staff, who are identified as not being ready for promotion within the next five years, are not necessarily poor performers. They represent the remainder of the personnel currently deployed to staff the organizational level. The chart provides a preview of the organization's ability to perpetuate itself in its present form. Alternatively, it offers useful input for estimating the possible impact of organizational changes that may increase or decrease the number of people necessary to operate at various job levels.

Inventory grid.   An overview of the total organization or of a particular broad sector of the organization can be extracted from the data bank in the form of an inventory grid. This is a two-dimensional listing of job families, positions, or people in which the vertical axis identifes levels in the organization and the horizontal axis identifies the various job tracks under consideration. In each box representing a stated organization level within a stated job track, the names of individuals can be listed or job titles can be listed showing the number of persons holding each title (if more than one).

The grid gives a "snapshot" of the organization or the part of the organization that it covers and can be extremely useful in appraising current design and making plans either to maintain it or to revise it.

FIGURE 1   Integrating Personnel Activities by Job Evaluation System Linked to Human Resource Inventory

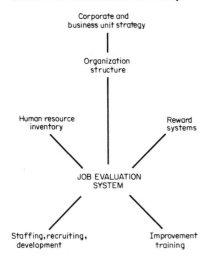

STRUCTURE, STAFF, AND STRATEGY

A well-defined job evaluation system, linked to the type of human resource inventory discussed here, should provide the hub used by human resource management to integrate the personnel activities that produce a structure needed to carry out corporate strategy. (This is illustrated in Figure 1 and explained in the following comments.)

Organization Structure   Organization structure is the personification of business strategy by which the objectives of the corporation and its units are converted into action. Analysis of the structure and its elements produces a list of human resource requirements. In this process, there must be interaction between the management of individual business activities and corporate management to harmonize their respective needs and to establish the total requirements of the corporation.

Human Resource Inventory   This defines the available population. Individuals can be described in terms of their current capabilities, future potential, and personal interests. By using the same analytical tools to define individuals as are used to define jobs, there is a common language which permits the requirements and the inventory to be matched. In the inventory's most useful form, there is extensive interaction between individuals and their supervisors that focuses on performance and career planning. Individuals can take an active role in identifying and improving their personal resources, thereby upgrading the value of the inventory and increasing their accountability for their own careers—and perhaps also bridging the issue of corporate goals versus individual aspirations.

Staffing, Recruiting, Development   This process matches requirements of the organization with the inventory. Current needs are identified; future needs are forecast; and acquisition and disposition are accomplished. Past work force planning was quantitative in nature. Current planning, facilitated by job evaluation, is qualitative as well. No staffing process is 100 percent successful, and the analytical job evaluation technique provides a way to highlight and explain the nature of any mismatch. It also identifies the need for organization or job redesign if staffing fails because the job can't be performed. Modern staffing should assure that individuals are developed for new responsibilities by having useful, measurable assignments.

Improvement Training Training—usually in specific skills ranging from machine operation and report writing to interpersonal relations and managing—complements the individual development that is achieved by job placement. It produces improvement in performance and an attendant increase in the value of the individual as part of the human resource inventory.

The analytical process defines the generalized skills required to grow within a track or to switch from one track to another. The difference between the individual's skills and the skills required by the job family can be measured, and a training program developed in response. This enables training to be much more specific and business-related than in the past.

Reward Systems The bond between reward systems and business strategy is well established in many organizations. Where it is not, the linkage through job evaluation contributes to the development and maintenance of responsive reward systems.

A systematic, consistent job evaluation method is the key to integrating the major elements of human resource activity to assure that the organization structure is perpetuated by qualified individuals and that corporate strategy is supported promptly and economically by an effective cadre.

THE ALCOA EXPERIENCE

Development of Alcoa's human resource inventory, and integration of its human resource activities, has been evolving over 20 years. Originally employed to link compensation and organization analysis, our job evaluation plan (Hay Guide Chart–Profile Method; see Chapter 15) provided an analytical tool that was later identified as the linkage that brought compensation, inventory, training, and staffing together to produce an organization to reflect corporate objectives. Since 1960, we have described jobs in terms of a limited number of characteristics: know-how, problem solving, and accountability. Through the profile technique we have identified a common thread in families of jobs and have measured the ingredients consistently over time and in worldwide company locations.

Subsequently, we developed the two-dimensional grid to display the hierarchy of jobs in the organization. The jobs clustered at each intersection on the grid can be described in consistent guide chart terms and the profiles are fairly uniform, regardless of the discipline. These intersections constitute the families of jobs mentioned earlier.

In Alcoa, the vertical axis consists of 10 major bands, spanning the organizational structure from corporate executive management to manual labor.

Within each major band, two levels of jobs are recognizable and identifiable. In general, they are differentiated by the scope and impact of their particular assignments relative to other jobs at that level, while representing similar degrees of skill.

We developed five major tracks in the horizontal axis, ranging from business management (where jobs are principally concerned with running a profit-accountable organization) to technical development (where jobs are principally concerned with pushing out the frontiers of knowledge). Individuals can usually operate successfully on more than one track. However, Edgar Schein's career anchor research suggested to us that there is usually one track that is the most comfortable for the individual.[2] Therefore, the likelihood of top performance and maximizing potential should be greatest on that track, and Schein believes the career anchor (the choice of the appropriate track) serves to stabilize and direct a career in predictable ways.

Many positions have characteristics that are described by more than one horizontal level or vertical track. A key to the development of an inventory system that is supportive of business strategy is the identification of major elements of the job which clearly place it at a single intersection. In job evaluation (guide chart-profile) terms, technical know-how, problem-solving environment, and freedom to act all increase progressively up the vertical axis of the grid. For example, these describable characteristics all increase for the sales representative jobs as incumbents deal with successively more important volume, price, and quality considerations. The relative importance of managerial know-how, human relations know-how, and accountability increases from the technical development track to the business management track. Jobs of similar total worth (expressed in evaluation points) emphasize different characteristics. The manager requires more skill in solving people problems because he or she accomplishes many objectives through others. The technical development jobs require more skill in solving product or process problems and therefore require more knowledge about such things as product, process, equipment, the economy, or finance. The problem-solving challenge increases from the business management track to the technical development track, as well as vertically with freedom to act. That is, at a given level, supervisory jobs meet many problems repeatedly, and previous solutions and experience permit the incumbent to solve the current question by "peeling off" know-how. The peer technical development job more often meets new problems that require new solutions. Similarly, the novelty of problems and range of solutions increase from the supervisory to the executive level. The profile, which describes the relationship among know-how, problem solving, and accountability, ranges from heavy emphasis on know-how and problem solving and light emphasis on accountability in the technical development track to the reverse in the business management track.

We built the inventory to permit an emphasis on families of jobs rather than individual jobs. The family concept is very important in any large, complex, multilocation, multidisciplinary organization. (Earlier attempts at inventory systems that identified individual employees for individual positions proved to

---

[2]Edgar H. Schein, "Increasing Organizational Effectiveness Through Better Human Resource Planning and Development," *Sloan Management Review*, vol. 19, no. 1, 1977.

be impossible to maintain at an acceptable level of credibility because of the continual change in the status of identified candidates. In some cases, the same individual was a candidate for many jobs, to the exclusion of other qualified candidates. At the opposite extreme, arbitrary rules limited the individual's candidacy too much, barring his or her availability for less conventional career shifts. These inventories often assumed a mobility and deployment that was unrealistic and almost always ignored the evolution in content or emphasis of the position to be filled.) The family idea includes jobs that have similar characteristics and a range, albeit a narrow range, of size, as expressed in evaluation points.

The job family significantly reduces the work and lends itself to computer storage and retrieval. The computer is a key element in manipulating data quickly to reflect changes in job design and in the availability of candidates. A significant objective is that of identifying the candidates in the inventory who are currently qualified for promotion. We have found the Hay Manpower Assessment, Planning and Development System (MAP-D) to be a meaningful and acceptable method of recognizing potential as well as performance and of expressing them in the same evaluation terms as those used to describe jobs.[3]

The Hay Manpower Assessment, Planning and Development System is an integrated, cohesive approach that identifies existing assets and deficiencies of management personnel through systematic comparison of individuals with the jobs they now hold, or might hold, using a standard language of description, measurement, and communication—the Guide Chart–Profile Method.

With the results of a MAP-D in hand, we are able to:

- Make full use of present management personnel
- Rationally plan for organizational and personnel needs
- Engage in systematic career planning and development for individuals

Although the process is time-consuming and involves the participation of several people, it usually produces a consensus and balances out the extreme favorable or unfavorable appraisal that is possible with a single evaluator.

Alcoa has developed generic titles and generic evaluations that provide an umbrella for a variety of more specific titles within each family. For example, in the technical development ladder there are a number of titles that are broadly grouped in the "senior fellow" family. At the same level in the organization, but on a different track, there is a group of business management jobs generically considered to be "senior business managers." These families have approximately the same worth expressed in total evaluation points, but the proportions of know-how, problem solving, and accountability are different.

The organization structure can also be described using generic titles, and the job evaluation system links structure with inventory. Although structure usually controls the shape of the inventory, it is possible to use the inventory to identify pockets of talent that are available to staff a venture not previously contemplated in corporate strategy. The challenge of utilizing available human resources to exploit opportunities for improved profit and productivity is an exciting alternative to changing the size of the organization, with its attendant human and economic costs.

---

[3]John M. Rosenfeld, "The Hay Manpower Assessment, Planning and Development System," Hay Associates, 1977.

chapter 60

Communicating the Total Compensation Program to Employees

Leonard Zimmerman

PARTNER, COMMUNICATIONS, THE HAY GROUP,
PHILADELPHIA, PENNSYLVANIA

An organization's ability to attract, retain, and motivate the people required to achieve its goals depends to a great extent on its ability to effectively communicate its reward system. Fully developed, the reward system includes nearly all the factors that contribute to the appeal of one organization over another: competitive salary and benefits, career opportunity, organizational style, image, and many other factors.

While pay and benefits constitute a major part of the reward system, the compensation communications plan must also ensure that employees at all levels understand and support company goals, objectives, policies, and practices.

If employees feel they have access to organizational information which puts their jobs in context, increased job satisfaction, pride, and support for business objectives will result. This, in turn, usually leads to improved perceptions of work-life quality. In turn, these improvements in employee satisfaction and perceived quality of working life can increase productivity.

The task of communicating with various segments of the employee population is no longer a matter of merely circulating information and letting employees draw their own conclusions. A complex labor relations environment, higher employee educational levels, and a more aggressive employee work force require a carefully planned and implemented employee communications program.

COMMUNICATIONS PROCESS

Communication can be defined as the process by which information is transferred within an organization through a system of mutually understood codes, words, or symbols. This concept is diagrammed as:

$$\text{Sender} \rightarrow \text{Message} \rightarrow \text{Channel} \rightarrow \text{Receiver} \rightarrow \text{Feedback} \rceil$$

In this model, there are several variables involved in the communications process: the sender, or the originator of the message; the message, or the information being communicated; the channel, or the method by which the message is encoded and transmitted; the receiver, or the one who hears, sees, and hopefully understands the message; and feedback, or the receiver's reaction to the message. Feedback reduces the number of misinterpretations between the sender and the receiver by allowing the sender to modify and send again a message based on the receiver's response.

When all the elements are present, the process is a continuous dialogue between the sender and the receiver which takes into account the values and attitudes of both the sender and the receiver as well as psychological and environmental influences which may affect the message transmittal. Whether the communication is between two individuals, involves specific groups, or is done on a mass basis, this model has relevance in understanding and managing it.

The communication flow within an organization may be categorized as follows.

Downward. Management sends a message to employees. For example, once senior management has decided upon the objectives of the compensation program, it must communicate these objectives to employees to gain understanding and acceptance.

Upward. Information travels from lower to higher levels in the chain. This enables employees to discuss their attitudes and concerns, misunderstandings, ideas, or suggestions with management. In the case of compensation communications, it is the feedback necessary to ensure that management's message is understood and accepted.

Lateral. Employees on the same level exchange information. Since this often occurs face to face among peers and has immediate feedback, it is a very effective method of communicating.

COMMUNICATIONS SYSTEM ELEMENTS

There are four elements which should be present and identifiable in any successful communications program:

Research: Formal and informal data gathering on a continuing basis using such techniques as audits, surveys, and interviews

Planning: Designing the overall program, drafting communications policy and objectives, and identifying those actions which meet specific needs and budgetary requirements

Implementation: Bringing the program to life once it has been approved

Feedback: Encouraging and planning for the responses of the target audiences

We will now examine these elements and how they relate to communicating the compensation program.

RESEARCH

The first element in program development is research. Included in this process are a review of general communications practices within the organization, an analysis of employee attitudes, an analysis of the objectives and strategies of the project, and an assessment of the impact of the proposed program.

Study the Compensation Program   A careful review of the compensation system should be made. The communications planner must gather the information needed to:

- Develop an objective analysis of the current situation
- Support statements that will be made about the status of the compensation program
- Deal with employee perceptions

Some of the questions that might be asked are the following.

Communications. How does the organization communicate with employees about salary, benefits, company policies, future growth, and direction? What are the formal and informal methods used?

Salary. Is the program fair? Is it consistently applied? What are the major components of the salary program? How do they work? What are the objectives of the program? What is the organization's competitive pay objective? How does it compare to actual salary practice? Have there been any recent changes? Why? Was there any problem in the past? Has it been corrected?

Benefits. What does the benefit program consist of? How does it compare to programs offered by other organizations locally, nationally, and by industry? Are all employees covered by the plans, or are certain benefits reserved for special groups? What is the cost of benefits? Have there been any recent changes? Why? What is the organization's benefits philosophy? If the benefits are low, is total compensation about average?

It is important to know where the organization stands. If the system is poorly designed, manipulated or inadequate, the communications plan cannot correct the problem. The organization's policies and practices are powerful instruments of nonverbal communication. Through its behavior, the organization constantly sends messages to employees about its reward system.

Determine Employee Attitudes and Perceptions   Whether a new compensation program is being installed or the existing one is being updated, it is important for the communications planner to take into account employee attitudes and perceptions. This helps the planner design a message that satisfies the information needs of employees and corrects false impressions.

The success or failure of any communications effort depends on the attitudes and perceptions of the receivers. It is therefore vital, before designing a communications plan, to know what employees think about their salary, benefits, the organization in general, and its communication with them. Often, what management believes is being communicated is not what the employees are hearing.

Some of the key areas that may be probed are the following.

Communications. How do employees view the overall organizational communications function? Do they think that management has a commitment to establishing open, two-way communications? Do they feel they receive sufficient information about the organization's goals and objectives?

Salary. Do employees understand the salary program? Do they view it as objective? Do they feel the program provides competitive pay?

Benefits. Do employees know which benefit plans they have? Do employees understand these benefits, and do they know how the plans interrelate?

Organization. Do employees feel that the organization has a commitment to them? Are there career opportunities for growth and advancement?

Having information of this nature is valuable when an organization is trying to determine whether its compensation program needs revamping or whether the communications about existing programs need enhancement. Obviously, if employees do not understand a program, it will not be fully appreciated.

Define Basic Goals of Communications Program   What are the potential effects of a compensation communications program? There are several. Such effects may serve as objectives that form the basis or rationale for a compensation communications program.

1. Ensure consistent understanding. It is often appropriate to communicate different aspects of the compensation program to different employee groups and for some groups to receive more detailed information than others. However, a well-planned overall communications strategy is necessary to ensure that the information provided to the various groups is consistent.

This is particularly important in larger organizations where most employees are removed from the policy-making process. And since it is generally true that as information travels downward it is subject to increased distortion, employees may lose an important part of the message. Therefore, the communications planner must ensure that the compensation message is delivered in a consistent manner to all employees and thus minimize misunderstandings which can reduce the motivational value of the compensation program.

2. Enhance individual motivation. In order for employees to develop a sense of loyalty, they must first know the organization's overall goals and objectives, feel they belong to the organization, and believe they are fairly rewarded for their efforts.

By communicating information about the compensation program in objective and concise terms, the company gives the employee some perspective on how his or her salary is determined and how performance is related to pay increases. This can lead to increased individual motivation, since each employee can assess his or her situation and feel confident of being fairly rewarded if realistic goals are successfully met.

3. Improve or reinforce organizational climate. It is vital for the communications planner to understand the organization's philosophy and style. This will assist in designing a compensation communications program that management will endorse and which is representative of the spirit of the organization.

Identify Audience Levels and Needs   Not every employee group needs the same amount of information on the compensation program. It varies according to level, responsibility, and involvement in the program. (However, as noted earlier, it must be consistent.)

When planning a communications program, it is necessary to separate the various employee levels and outline their information needs. The following breakdown is an example of how an organization might group its employees for this purpose.

Employee Group	Compensation Data Needs
Top management	Sufficient information to understand and support the objectives of the plan and to make broad policy decisions
Middle management	More detailed information to achieve a fuller understanding of the program in order to participate in its implementation as well as to make policy decisions
Compensation administrator	An in-depth knowledge of the workings of the program for administration and fine tuning
First-line supervisors	A full comprehension of the program to answer questions and to make program recommendations
Employees	Overview of the program, a detailed reference source, and opportunity for feedback to ensure that they understand it is fair and competitive

Review the Organization's Communications Style   It is important when designing a compensation communication program to view communications as a series of interrelated events and not as isolated messages. A compensation communications program cannot be totally successful if other employer-employee communications are poorly designed and sporadic in nature. Poor communications in other areas will adversely affect the reception of the compensation message.

Also, when designing a total compensation communications program, the planner should be aware of the many factors that can negatively influence the transmission of a message. The following items should be addressed:

- What are the expectations of the employee audience?
- How will this program fit in with existing communications programs?
- How can existing communications channels be used?
- What are the in-house capabilities?
- What type of production quality is the audience accustomed to?
- Should the production quality be changed?

PLANNING

Research and planning are correlated activities. The information gained through research helps the planner set objectives and priorities, assign responsibilities, design the program, and select the appropriate media.

Establish Communications Objectives   The first step in designing any type of communications program is to establish the overall objectives. What is management trying to accomplish by instituting the program? Are these objectives realistic?

Sample objectives include:

- Attract, retain, and motivate employees.
- Gain support and cooperation from all employees to ensure smooth program implementation.
- Provide managers and supervisors with the knowledge, understanding, and communications skills needed to support the program.
- Ensure that all employees receive a consistent message.
- Promote employee understanding of how the compensation program works.
- Ensure that the compensation communications program is consistent with other communications efforts.

Identify the Subject Areas to Be Communicated   A typical compensation program combines general organizational information with specific details of the compensation program. The communications planner must decide which topics are to be specifically addressed. For example, some general subjects include:

- Objectives and goals of the organization
- Role of the individual in the success of the organization
- Relationship between growth of the business and individual growth

Topics specific to compensation include:

- Compensation program objectives
- Job documentation
- Job evaluation
- Internal equity
- Salary ranges for individuals or grades
- External competitiveness
- Program policies and procedures
- Merit or promotion increase policy
- Performance appraisal program

In selecting which subjects to cover in communicating the compensation program, the communications planner will have to distinguish among the specific groups such as high-skilled workers, first-line supervisors, and middle managers in certain functions.

Select Media   Which medium is best suited to deliver the compensation message to employees? Since we live in a visual age, it is logical to consider the use of video, slides, and film for the primary delivery medium. Printed materials can be used to reinforce and provide details.

Audiences respond differently to various media. Some react positively to sophisticated multimedia presentations, whereas others prefer a more personalized approach. The following generalizations can be made about the various media.

Senses affected.   A successful communications program usually stimulates two senses. When designing a program, the communications planner should remember the following: printed materials affect only the eyes; slide-tape presentations affect the eyes and ears; and face-to-face communications can stimulate all the senses.

Feedback opportunity.   This is an important consideration, since it promotes a true exchange between the sender and the receiver. Face-to-face communications, such as supervisor-subordinate meetings, provide the maximum opportunity for feedback.

Receiver control. The receiver has more control with certain forms of communications than others. In a face-to-face exchange, the receiver can ask questions or direct the discussion to ensure that he or she receives the type and amount of information desired.

Printed material provides the receiver with the opportunity to reread and dissect the material. However, further clarification may be needed.

The receiver has very little control over most audiovisual presentations because they are usually designed to run without interruption. However, when presented in group meetings, the audiovisuals help to control time and to give information in a consistent manner to all audiences while allowing many of the advantages of face-to-face exchange.

Researchers agree that a combination of several channels (face to face, print, and audiovisual, for example) is the most effective method of communicating.

Written Communications   It is often impractical because of either time or geographic limitations to communicate the compensation message through an audiovisual or a live presentation. Under these circumstances, it is better to rely on written communications as the primary means of communication. Cassette tapes or records to the home could supplement the major written pieces and are discussed under "Oral presentations," below.

Written communications can provide as little or as much information as the organization wishes and can be reviewed, analyzed, and referred to by employees as often as they wish. In other words, a written piece can be an educational and a reference tool.

There are numerous types of written materials, including:

1. *Employee Handbook:* This piece provides the opportunity to present the compensation plan in detail. Employees can refer to the handbook if they have questions or if they require additional information.

2. *Booklets:* A booklet can range in size from a one-page foldout to several pages. The compensation brochure could discuss the details of the plan, how it works, and perhaps answer some of the more frequently asked questions.

3. *Highlights Folder:* This piece is intended to complement a visual presentation by doing exactly what its name implies—highlighting the key compensation issues discussed at the audiovisual presentation. It also serves as a summary and reference piece for employees.

4. *Individualized Total Compensation Statements:* These include the specific dollar amounts an employee can expect to receive from each benefit plan, as well as the employer's cost for providing such coverage. This medium emphasizes the portion of an employee's compensation that is often forgotten because it is not seen in the paycheck. Organizations maintaining written job descriptions can include the description and the employee's principal accountabilities on the statement, thus giving the employee the opportunity to review and confirm the job description annually.

5. *Company Newspaper or Newsletter:* Most organizations have an internal newspaper in which articles about the compensation plan can be placed. Although this medium is not appropriate for detailed information, it works well for introductory or highlight pieces.

6. *Company Magazine:* A more detailed article regarding the compensation system or one particular aspect of it can be placed in the company magazine.

7. *Payroll Stuffers:* A payroll stuffer is an excellent means of communicating compensation information, since it arrives when the employee receives his or her paycheck. It is a good announcement, highlight, or reinforcement piece.

8. *Bulletin Board Notices:* Bulletin boards provide a good communications opportunity if they are up to date and neat. They are excellent for making announcements but not for supplying an in-depth analysis of the compensation plan.

Audiovisual presentations.   Film, video, and slide-tape presentations are all very effective ways of communicating compensation; they permit the audience to both see and hear the message and thereby increase the likelihood that the message will be understood and retained. The information content of such presentations is usually high and can often be used as the primary communications piece.

There are drawbacks, however. Some organizations do not have the proper setting or equipment to make presentations. Also, because of the generic nature of the information, it can be distorted by the receiver. However, this can be corrected if the audiovisual is presented in a group meeting with a question and answer session.

Visual presentations.   This category includes posters, flip charts, and displays. These items provide quick and inexpensive ways of communicating one particular idea. They are not recommended for use when trying to communicate complex material unless developed in a series.

Oral presentations.   The oral (live) presentation is an effective communications format. It provides for immediate feedback, thereby increasing the accuracy and effectiveness of the communication.

The different types of oral communications which an organization can use are:

1. *Supervisor-Employee:* This is the best way to inform individual employees about the compensation program and how it affects them. Employees can ask questions about the complexities of the program and receive immediate responses. In this setting, an environment can be developed where trust, creativity, and personal initiative are fostered.

2. *Specialist-Employee:* There is usually at least one person who is a specialist in the salary administration or benefits program. This person can provide in-depth information that furthers understanding of the details.

3. *Small Group:* Although this type of communication is not as desirable as the above one-on-one approaches, it is an effective way of disseminating compensation information. The meeting can generally accommodate up to 20 people and can incorporate an audiovisual presentation and a discussion afterwards.

4. *Large Group:* This is a faster way of transmitting compensation information to a sizable number of employees. Since a wider group of people is addressed, the information has to be generic for the broadest application. This form is an efficient one, but not the most effective.

5. *Other Types:* Other voice channels used to transmit compensation information are telephone hotlines with prerecorded messages, a telephone number

to a specialist who is available to answer questions, and cassette tapes or records with an overview or message. When properly designed, cassette tapes or records can be entertaining and informative.

Whichever medium is selected, the decision will be influenced by the following factors:

- Audience profile
- Employee locations
- Current facilities
- Organization style
- Budget
- Future use(s) of the program
- Customary communications procedures

IMPLEMENTATION

When the program is implemented, all the pieces fit together. Each organization's program will differ from that of any other organization. However, it is valuable to look at a typical communications plan for a salary administration program.

Salary Administration Communications Model

Phase I—During Installation

1. *General announcement.* The president's letter at the beginning of the installation announces the study and its purposes. This letter is designed to allay fears of pay cuts or other adverse salary actions.

2. *Managers' memo or meetings.* Explain the importance of the project, ask for cooperation in recruiting and making available job analysts and evaluation committee members, and elicit support for the project.

3. *Notices to participants.* Managers notify employees who have been selected as job analysts and evaluation committee members, discuss the importance of the project, and the participant's valuable contribution.

4. *Quarterly updates.* Keep employees informed about the progress of the study by using company publications or memos.

Phase II—Completion of Project

1. *Supervisors' meeting.* Review audiovisual for employee presentation (see item 3, below). Answer questions. Hand out and briefly review Salary Administration Manual. If time permits, review case studies.

2. *General announcement of employee meetings.* Using publications, memos, posters, or brochures, announce that meetings will be held to explain the salary program.

3. *Employee meetings.* Using audiovisuals, provide an overview of the salary program. Follow with question-and-answer session. Then distribute highlights folder at the end of the meeting.

4. *Distribute detailed information.* Add sections to employee manual or produce a booklet covering the details of the salary program.

5. *Evaluate communications.* Review questions asked during employee meetings, conduct surveys and interviews, use other existing feedback mechanisms (e.g., exit interviews) to evaluate and adjust the communications program for future use.

Phase III—Ongoing Communications

1. *Orientation and training.* Use audiovisuals, highlights folder, and employee handbook for orientation on a quarterly basis. Continue to hold periodic meetings for new supervisors to review the Salary Administration Manual.

2. *Periodic meetings.* Continue to inform all employees about the salary program through memos, publications, posters, payroll stuffers, etc. Feature issues like performance appraisal during the salary review period. The first article could cover the employee meetings at the completion of the study and could highlight questions and answers from the meetings.

3. *Feedback mechanisms.* Encourage feedback on communications program and salary program through hot lines, supervisors, exit interviews, etc.

FEEDBACK

Feedback is the expression of employee ideas, attitudes, and concerns and should be planned and encouraged. It allows management to know whether messages are understood and accepted by employees and which topics may require further communication efforts. It creates a two-way flow.

Having sufficient feedback channels is particularly important because of the many natural barriers to communication, i.e., differences in knowledge levels, language codes, and experiences and their effect on message transmittal. There will always be a certain percentage of employees that will misunderstand a communication because of these innate barriers. This is compounded when the message concerns one's compensation, since it is a highly subjective and emotional topic.

Employees tend to judge a compensation plan by how it affects them and not by its merits. To compensate for these unavoidable distortions, the communications planner should create an environment in which employees feel comfortable either asking questions or expressing their opinions.

Supervisors play a major role in encouraging feedback from employees. Because of their daily and close contact, employees instinctively seek out their supervisors for advice or information. The supervisor's attitude greatly determines how open the communications will be. This becomes a key element in compensation communications. Usually, the supervisor knows the employee's needs, concerns, and abilities.

This helps the supervisor communicate the compensation plan in a way that is meaningful to the employee. The supervisor can transform abstract and technical concepts into understandable and pertinent information. Since this is such a critical link in the compensation communications chain, it follows that this is where most breakdowns occur. What are some of the causes?

- Quite often the supervisor has had too little training in the compensation plan and does not fully understand it. It is therefore impossible to inform his or her employees or to answer their questions.

- Some supervisors simply do not want to become involved, and they neglect their communications and managerial responsibilities.
- Some supervisors are not given the authority to execute compensation decisions, and they lose their credibility among employees.
- Many supervisors are unaware of their responsibility to inform, educate, and guide employees regarding job duties and performance and their effect on employees' salaries.

A supervisor must know the compensation plan. This will enable him or her to intelligently answer questions and earn the employees' respect.

A supervisor must also take action when an issue is raised, regardless of whether or not it is a pleasant task. This is one of the best ways to demonstrate a sincere commitment to the communications process and to the employees.

Also, a supervisor should develop a positive attitude. For example, how does he or she react when an employee has a question? Are the nonverbal communications clues, i.e., checking the time or tapping a pencil, indicative of an overall lack of interest? If employees sense that a supervisor is not really listening, they will soon stop talking.

A supervisor should look for any nonverbal feedback that employees send. This type of feedback is often more honest than any verbal or written comments. If supervisors are sensitive to it, they can ascertain whether employees understand and accept the compensation message.

The following behavioral patterns are examples of nonverbal feedback that indicate the compensation message was poorly understood or mistrusted:

- Tardiness
- Absenteeism
- Carelessness
- Increased accidents
- Reduced interest in job performance

If a supervisor spots an increase in any of these behaviors, he or she has a good indication that there has been a communications breakdown and should attempt to identify and solve the problem.

The supervisor is a critical factor, not only in communicating the compensation plan to employees but also in encouraging feedback. There are, however, other ways of gathering feedback information, including:

- Attitude surveys
- Employee interviews
- Evaluation forms
- Employee hot lines
- Question-and-answer columns in the company newsletter or magazine

SUMMARY

Although there is the need to regard certain aspects of compensation information as confidential, a good deal of it can and should be communicated to employees. All too often, an organization may create an atmosphere of distrust and discontent by labeling compensation information "top secret" and refusing to have honest and open discussions with employees. The result is not a lack of information but a flood of distorted and inaccurate compensation information, which causes much more erosion of employee morale than no information at all.

The communications planner should encourage management to develop a proactive approach to communications. Instead of waiting for something to happen or for a crisis to occur, organizations should adopt a corporate strategy based on well-planned and continuous communications.

When employees begin to understand and appreciate their compensation through effective communications, the organization will have achieved a major step in managing its most important resource—its employees.

Trends and
Issues

chapter 61

Changing Trends in the Total Compensation Program

Robert C. Ochsner

PARTNER AND REGIONAL DIRECTOR, STRATEGIC
COMPENSATION SERVICES, THE HAY GROUP,
PHILADELPHIA, PENNSYLVANIA

*Forecasts are dangerous, especially about the
future.*—SAMUEL GOLDWYN

More, more, always more.—SAMUEL GOMPERS

Compensation programs have matured and broadened substantially in every decade since World War II. This chapter, therefore, provides:

- Listings of recent and projected future trends
- A look at the factors which cause them
- A way of understanding and evaluating change when designing and maintaining a compensation program

Looking ahead through the 1980s, mindful of Mr. Goldwyn's warning, we believe that the eighties will differ from the seventies in some important respects. Mr. Gompers' demand, which has proved to be a forecast for nearly all seasons in compensation, will be met more selectively and through delivery of compensation in a variety of new forms.

WHAT WERE THE COMPENSATION TRENDS OF THE SEVENTIES?

Table 1 shows a listing of important trends we have observed. One thing stands out: most of the trends originated *outside the organization*. Three kinds of outside factors had considerable impact on compensation programs in the seventies.

Economic Forces Economic forces were at work on a scale unknown since World War II. Very significant for compensation were *inflation* and the *shift to a services economy*. The latter may or may not represent an indication of the ultimate role of the United States in the postindustrial world of the twenty-first century, but it has already spawned twin trends on the compensation front:

- Compensation expense in service businesses is a high percentage of total revenue—generally greater than pretax profit; the opposite is true in most asset-intensive businesses. This leads to a search for "pay-for-performance" compensation plans in industries where productivity is difficult to measure.
- The proportion of managerial, professional, and technical jobs (generally requiring college or other advanced education and classified as exempt) to other jobs in the work force is much higher, even a majority, in these industries. This requires much more effort in designing and managing compensation plans and has led, for example, to a proliferation of sales incentive plans and to a new, multidimensional approach to *internal equity* based on the construction of career ladders and accompanying compensation plans in critical profes-

TABLE 1   Compensation Trends of the Seventies

Origin	Trend
Internal	
Employee-generated	ADEA
	Aftertax protection
	Due process
	EEO
	Inflation protection
Company-generated	External competitiveness
	Internal equity
	Pay for performance, productivity, incentives
External	
Government-generated	Corporate law
	IRS: Benefits regulation
	Taxation of fringes and perks
	Unreasonable compensation
	SEC: Disclosure rules
	Other
Company-generated	Accounting rules
	Compensation committee involvement
	Mergers and divestitures
	Stockholder involvement

sional and technical job families. Inflation response has created *inflation-pro-tection* mechanisms and, coupled with the rapid escalation of effective tax rates, has led to *aftertax protection* of compensation in some cases.

Demographic Realities   As the post-World War II "baby boom" entered the work force, demographic realities had to be reckoned with. Great attention was focused on the number of births from about 1948 to 1955, and the people born during that period are often called the "me generation." These new workers seemed to expect more commitment and consideration from their employing organizations than they were prepared to give, causing great consternation among their elders who remembered war, depression, and employment conditions of another era. Part of this phenomenon may be traced to youth, part to changing social standards, and part to the much lower percentage of first children in this birth cohort in comparison with cohorts before and after. It now appears that the major long-term effect of this group will be its sheer numbers, not its value system. The other major demographic event of the seventies was the apparently lasting establishment of work as the norm for women, at least up to age 50 or 55. Periods of nonwork, such as for schooling or for raising children, are now viewed as the exception in all but the uppermost economic classes. The results have been:

- Growth of two-income families, with particular impact on the design of time-off and benefit programs and on the 1981 to 1984 tax-rate reductions
- Uneven success in creating meaningful positions for persons to whom work and organizational discipline are perceived as episodes and in creating bias-free hiring, promotion, and compensation practices with regard to the sexes (which outside forces, as well as government, now seem to require)

Government Regulation   Regulation by government, including two periods of wage and salary controls, became pervasive in the seventies. A major federal benefits regulatory act (ERISA) was passed and a host of significant changes were implemented in the taxation of compensation and benefits. Legislation protecting the employment rights of older workers (ADEA) and women and minorities (EEO) and regulating safety conditions on the job (OSHA) continued to advance at the federal level, as well as at the state and local levels where, unlike the benefits area, federal regulation is not preemptive. As more sophisticated forms of compensating officers and key employees became widespread, the Securities and Exchange Commission (SEC) created new forms of expanded disclosure for these practices, and its "no-action letters" became a way of life for corporate counsel charged with implementing new types of compensation for corporate insiders. Federal legislation regulating corporate activities was passed in a number of areas (e.g., mergers), but several attempts to assert direct federal control over major businesses, by providing federal business corporation charters, failed. The IRS made a number of attempts to extend the taxation of miscellaneous corporate benefits and perquisites but was unsuccessful in getting Congress either to legislate in this area or to allow the IRS to extend taxation to additional forms of noncash compensation by administrative rules. In the important area of "unreasonable compensation," where a specific statutory standard is hard to envision, the courts began to demonstrate a more sophisticated acceptance of logical, preplanned ways of motivating owners through compensation even when the outcome was higher than that for similar positions in large publicly held organizations.

During the seventies, trends in compensation also reflected changing business concerns. Table 1 classifies a number of trends as coming from the business sector.

• *External competitiveness* and *internal equity* have always been the basic objectives in compensation programs, in order to attract and retain the right kinds of employees. It is generally recognized that extreme precision in either one is at the expense of the other. Each organization must find a balance between them, and organizations that fill a higher percentage of their exempt positions each year (whether due to growth or terminations) lean more heavily toward external competitiveness.

• *Long-term planning* has become widespread and has provided a basis for *pay-for-performance* systems which (1) measure progress toward longer-term goals in addition to making the annual plan and (2) extend over a number of years for positions that participate in management over that time frame. This supplements the emerging economic need, already discussed, for performance compensation.

• External business influences also created trends in compensation programs. The growth of the *compensation committee* as an institution reflected a concern with the appropriateness of both the appearance and the reality of management compensation. It also recognized that a strong compensation program under today's conditions requires continuing attention at the board level, rather than an annual session to grant increases and bonuses as had been customary at many companies in the sixties. Frequent changes in *accounting rules*—as the accounting profession sought to keep up with developments in compensation and benefits—required compensation personnel to acquire another type of working know-how and, in some instances, even became a major factor in the adoption and termination of plans. *Mergers* required an additional measure of flexibility in established compensation programs, since in neither large nor small business combinations would compensation and related organizational issues normally be addressed beforehand. *Stockholder initiatives* on compensation issues rarely occurred, but the few that did kept management alert. Although a negative vote by 50 percent of the stockholders actually might be required to defeat a compensation plan proposal, any negative vote over about 5 percent is carefully examined.

Strategic Planning   Throughout most of the seventies, strategic planning (including dimensions beyond a longer-term, financial plan) was really in its infancy in most organizations. Planning of this type is needed before human resources and compensation planning can occur on a much more meaningful basis than straight-line projection.

Total Compensation Planning   In the seventies, total compensation planning was only beginning to be understood. Integrated philosophy and administration are needed in order to direct an organization's programs toward its strategic objectives and to offer reasoned explanations for saying "no" to the multitude of proposals which come along. Surprisingly, many organizations which claim to use total compensation planning actually use it only for static periodic measurements (via external surveys, etc.) of total competitive program value, and they do not employ available tools in the dynamic planning process. This is like taking a transpolar flight over uncharted terrain and settling for a series of instant, still photos instead of looking out the windows!

The success of business organizations in establishing compensation trends in the eighties, therefore, seems to depend on the successful use of *strategic* and *total compensation* planning in ways which reinforce each other. Looking back to the impact of the other trends of the seventies, we might also hope for some reduction in the degree to which economic, demographic, and sociopolitical factors affect the work place.

WHAT WILL HAPPEN TO THESE TRENDS IN THE EIGHTIES?

Two new trends are predicted on the basis of our experience in the early eighties.

Multibusiness Companies   Multibusiness companies, which have existed for a long time, will increase in relative numbers. They will begin to adopt human resource policies, including compensation, based more on the needs of each significant business area and less on a single corporate model. Differences in compensation among industries and geographical regions will continue to be a fact of life, although the industry leaders may change somewhat over the decade. A major impediment to having separate practices for each business unit is the need to transfer employees between units. In the face of more specialized technology, higher relocation costs, and the growth of two-earner families, transfer will be less common.

Personalized Compensation   Personalized compensation will become an objective of leading-edge companies. It already exists in several forms:

- Individual performance evaluation for salary administration.
- Management and sales incentives tailored to specific individual goals.
- Individualized statements of benefits and compensation. Although the individual statements now generally provide only the appearance of individualization, the computer technology which underlies them has led some organizations to explore the possibility of real individualization.
- Specialized career ladders, including alternative ladders in high-technology job families.
- Career-path salary administration looks at employee potential as well as performance in the current job in determining salary. This is akin to the multitrack system used in some schools, where a student goes through the grades by chronological age but the curriculum is adjusted to his or her learning level. Computers can be used to evaluate the employee's progress against a career target which is reassessed periodically.
- Various forms of "flexible" and "cafeteria" benefit plans allow the employee to tailor parts of the benefit program to individual perceived needs—

sometimes to take cash in lieu of certain benefits. The appearance of double coverage when a working couple both receive employer-paid family health coverage, the desire of second-income earners for time off instead of benefits, the changes in the tax law, and the growing concern about the adequacy of retirement income have been major factors in the consideration of these arrangements. The complicated nature of the subject, the need to solicit employee opinion, and the additional administrative work required must be considered.

It seems likely that further manifestations of a trend to make compensation react more personally to individual employee situations will appear in the eighties. Table 2 shows a prediction of the relative future strength of compensation trends. Four qualifications must be kept in mind:

- The purpose of a forecast like this is to stimulate thought and discussion; absolute accuracy cannot be expected.
- The strength shown is relative to past levels of the same trend, not to levels between trends. Internal equity and external competitiveness will remain the most important factors, although their relative strength may be declining.
- The trends interact. The reader may prefer his or her own set of trends as a way of conceptualizing the development of compensation.
- The importance of a trend will not be the same to every organization or industry.

Compensation trends predicted to decline include:

- EEO- and OSHA-type legislation, which seems at this writing to have reached its height.

TABLE 2   Changing Trends in Compensation Programs in the Eighties

Area/trend	More change	About the same	Less change
Internal			
Employee-generated	ADEA Aftertax protection	Due process	EEO Inflation protection
Company-generated	Pay for performance, productivity, incentives Personalized compensation	External competitiveness	Internal equity
External			
Government-generated	SEC disclosure rules IRS taxation of fringes and perks	SEC other IRS unreasonable compensation Corporate law	IRS benefits regulation
Company-generated	Compensation committee involvement Multibusiness companies	Accounting rules Mergers and divestitures	Stockholder involvement

- Inflation protection, which will be less important than other ways of distributing pay dollars (e.g., performance).
- Internal equity, which in the old sense will be partially displaced by multibusiness and personalized compensation concepts.
- IRS benefits regulation, which would require significant new enabling legislation to match the level of the seventies.
- Stockholder involvement in compensation, which (as with other corporate operations) occurs only in the event of real excesses or a vacuum of power. Both are seen as declining possibilities.

Trends in compensation predicted to remain about the same are those that have a continuing validity and/or constituency. They deserve special comment in only two areas:

- Corporate law changes—including federal charters, securities-law revisions, and others—seem to have a special constituency which provides a continued forum for the issues but is not likely to produce major legislation.
- Mergers have increased in response to the lower cost of acquiring assets by buying public companies rather than acquiring equivalent assets by building up an organization. Lower interest rates and higher price earnings multiples—both anticipated sometime in the eighties—will reduce this tendency over the decade as a whole, although it may not happen immediately. A major exception is financial institutions, where frequent mergers will almost certainly continue for some years. Also, divestitures and spin-offs will grow in importance over the decade.

Increasing trends include the new trends toward multibusiness companies and personalized compensation. The role of the compensation committee and the impact of accounting rules on compensation are other increasing trends generated by external business focus. Internally generated business trends include long-term planning and pay for performance. Governmental influence is projected to increase in the areas of SEC disclosure requirements and IRS taxation of fringes and perks, where a systematic statutory basis for defining what is and is not taxable can be expected by the mideighties. ADEA protection for older workers, while implemented through government, is a direct product of employee concerns and will increase as the "baby boom" generation begins to reach the protected age of 40. Aftertax protection, although rarely achieved in the seventies when high inflation combined with tax-bracket creep, will probably be used on the downside by labor-intensive companies. When there are not enough dollars to go around after top performers receive needed levels of increase, marginal performers may have to be content with a tax reduction as the principal form of additional compensation.

Since there are expected to be more increasing trends than stationary or declining trends, the eighties will be a turbulent decade in compensation as well as in worldwide business generally.

THE PUBLIC SECTOR

Compensation trends in the public-employee arena are worthy of their own detailed discussion. (See Chapter 54.) We will merely point out three expected compensation trends which do not have counterparts in the private sector.

- The actions of state and local governments will have greater relative importance as the number of federal employees remains level or declines. Although many compensation programs at the state and local levels have suffered from political interference as well as lack of organization and understanding, there is evidence that this is improving.
- There is a real possibility of severe financial difficulty, tantamount to bankruptcy, in a minority of local governments and also in a number of state and local pension plans. Compensation necessarily will be restricted in such instances, perhaps for years. Ability to pay at all levels of state and local government will be significantly reduced from the levels of the seventies.
- For 15 or 20 years, the absence of either financial or personal-performance "bottom line" measures in most public-sector jobs has actually tended to make it easier to increase compensation. Pay and benefit levels have risen to meet private-sector levels, but no generally applicable yardsticks have been developed to measure (1) whether jobs are needed and (2) whether incumbent performance justifies marketplace pay level.

It seems likely that this outcome will be reversed in the eighties. Unless acceptable yardsticks for performance and productivity are developed and disseminated quickly, reduced ability to pay cannot be translated into an appropriate mix of position reductions and a flattening of the high rates of per capita increase which public-sector compensation experienced in the seventies. Since employment at many levels of government has grown without checks and balances, the existence of performance standards would make the goal of "fewer but better people" a realistic one for public-sector managers. It would also bring into focus an important issue which is gradually emerging: When is it appropriate to pay nonelected officials more than their elected superiors? This is now rarely done; when it does occur, it is chiefly in medical positions. Unless political realities change so that full-time elected officials receive salaries comparable to those of private-sector workers with similar responsibilities, the pay of elected officials in the eighties may also be exceeded by that of professionals in finance, law, employee relations, engineering, and information systems.

chapter 62

Equal Employment Opportunity

Armando M. Rodriguez

COMMISSIONER, EQUAL EMPLOYMENT OPPORTUNITY
COMMISSION, WASHINGTON, D.C.

SCOPE OF THE CHAPTER

The purpose of this chapter on equal employment opportunity (EEO) issues is to describe the administrative processing of an Equal Employment Opportunity Commission (EEOC) charge, beginning at the time an employer receives the first official notification by the commission. Assume there is a private employer, under the jurisdiction of the EEOC, that does not have any contracts with the federal government. Assume also that a presently employed female alleges she was denied a promotion because of her sex and has filed a charge with the EEOC under Title VII of the Civil Rights Act of 1964.

The information this chapter provides has two specific purposes:

1. To alert the employer to the legal issues and responsibilities that result from a charge being filed
2. To suggest that the employer obtain legal assistance in order to avoid additional allegations of violation of the law

The bibliography gives specific resources that can provide additional information and answers to some of the issues raised in the chapter. The resources range from simple nonprofessional explanations to sophisticated legal references. Figure 1 provides a simple overview of the complete process.

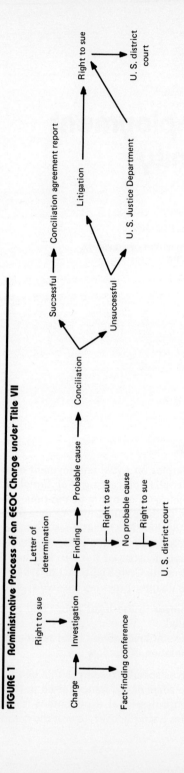

FIGURE 1 Administrative Process of an EEOC Charge under Title VII

EQUAL EMPLOYMENT OPPORTUNITY ISSUES:
WHERE ARE YOU, EMPLOYER?

An employer has an affirmative duty to
maintain a working environment free of bias
and may not engage in employment
discrimination. Employment discrimination is
an expensive business.

On Monday morning you open your mail and find a letter from the EEOC informing you that one of your employees has filed a complaint of discrimination, alleging that she was denied a promotion because of her sex. The EEOC informs you that this allegation, if true, may constitute a violation of Title VII of the Civil Rights Act of 1964, as amended.

Immediately you try to evaluate the situation. You feel you have a good grasp of your business and a good rapport with your employees. This is the first time you have received this kind of complaint. The following questions go through your mind.

> *What should I do? What kind of conduct is prohibited by the Civil Rights Act of 1964? Does this law apply to me? Why did this employee state that I discriminated against her? What kind of investigation are they likely to conduct? What kind of documents should I preserve? Do I keep only the documents that relate to this employee? Would the EEOC's representative ask to see my records? What kind of records do they want? What will happen if I refuse to provide the information they request? If I refuse to cooperate in the investigation or if they conclude that the charge has merit, what kind of sanctions would they impose on me? What should be my next step? Will this affect my business in this town only? Can I call the EEOC office that this letter came from? What kind of questions do I ask? What kind of information do they want from me? Can I talk with my employee—try to explain and to get information from her—without running the risk of inviting a retaliation claim? Can I tell her supervisor about this? How should I instruct the supervisor to treat her in the future? Can I talk about this in public, or is this a confidential investigation?*

The above unanswered questions may suggest that you should retain a lawyer. The lawyer will most likely ask you to bring all the documents that you have received from the EEOC. He or she will explain to you that Title VII prohibits employment discrimination based on color, race, sex, national origin, or religion. The EEOC also has jurisdiction in cases of age and equal-pay discrimination.

Individuals who feel that they have been discriminated against may file a complaint in the nearest EEOC district office. That office will commence an administrative investigation by notifying you that a charge has been filed (EEOC Form 131). In some cases a copy of the charge may be attached to the notice (EEOC Form 131-A), a fact-finding conference may be scheduled (EEOC Form 131-B), or you may be requested to furnish information in response to a questionnaire (EEOC Form 131-C). As part of its preliminary investigation, the commission may ask if you intentionally discriminated against your employee because of her race, color, sex, national origin, religion, or age or if you intentionally are paying her a lower salary than similarly situated male employees simply because she is a female. At the same time the commission will search for any unfair or unequal application of your employment policies.

Your lawyer should ask you if you have a policy which applies to all employees but which may have a particular *impact on females,* blacks, or people of foreign national origins for any specific reason. For example, if you require employees to work Friday, Saturday, and/or Sunday, your schedule may have an adverse impact on employees of certain religions. Similarly, a requirement that all your employees and/or applicants for employment be citizens of the United States may have an adverse impact on residents who are immigrants. In addition, tests or examinations may be culturally biased and have an adverse impact on certain minority groups. Unless the policies that have an adverse impact can be shown to be a business necessity or reasonably predictive of successful job performance, they may constitute evidence of discrimination.

The first recommendation from your lawyer most likely will be not to talk with the employee but to be sure the employee is treated in the same manner as before she filed the charge. Brief the supervisor who works with the employee. The filing of a charge does not prevent an employer from imposing legitimate discipline. However, any disciplinary action taken against this employee in response to filing the charge will constitute *retaliatory* action, a serious violation of the act. A retaliatory action is considered a separate violation, with additional investigations and remedies. For example, the EEOC could take immediate action and request from an appropriate U.S. district court a temporary injunction against further retaliatory conduct. You should call upon the supervisor of the employee to retrieve her personnel files, time and attendance records, appraisal, evaluations, and any other information which relates to her employment.

In preparing a response to the charge of discrimination, your lawyer may ask you to address immediately the following issues:

EEO-1 report.   Do you have more than 100 employees? If so, have you filed an EEO-1 report with the EEOC this year?

The filing of an EEO-1 report is a legal obligation of any employer subject to Title VII with 100 or more employees. The forms and instructions can be obtained free from the EEOC. This report will reveal the total number of employed persons and the ethnic classification of your labor force. It will also show the job classification of all employees in your labor force, professionals as well as nonprofessionals. Failure to file this report will be an element that can be used against you.

Union.   Do your employees belong to a union? Has their union expressed concern about your hiring and promotion policies? Has their union challenged your hiring or promotion policies or procedures? To what extent does the union insist upon rigid adherence to contractual seniority clauses in selecting individuals for hiring and promotion?

As a result of this initial *self-analysis,* you can formulate a general EEO policy that covers all employees. The policy should express your compliance with equal employment laws: that you are an equal opportunity employer; you do not discriminate because of color, race, sex, national origin, religion, or age; and you pay equal wages to men and women for equal work.

If your policies do not appear to satisfy legal requirements, you need to advise your personnel officer that your company does not have a written promotion policy or that the procedures for upward mobility and promotion are not applied equally to all employees. Some practices to review include: Are all your supervisors white males? Has there ever been a female supervisor? Are all your managers white Anglo-Saxon protestant males? Is hiring invariably done from the outside? Are vacancies posted? Do supervisors always select the most qualified employees for promotion? Does a uniform written evaluation system exist? Are females in management positions paid less than males performing the same jobs? Finally, are there EEOC posters in your work place?

Using your answers to the above questions, your lawyer should attempt to narrow this *investigation* to the precise issue raised in the charge—namely, the denial of a single promotion to a female employee. At this time, your lawyer should contact the EEOC office and explore the possibility of reaching a non-fault settlement. Such a negotiated settlement is signed by you, the employee, and the EEOC. The agreement may set forth certain employer obligations intended to ensure that promotion policies are implemented in accordance with Title VII standards. Examples of such obligations might include:

- Develop a new job posting system.
- Eliminate requirements limiting the promotion of female employees.
- Develop training for female employees.
- Review the recruitment and hiring process.
- Evaluate job performance in relation to wages.

As part of the agreement, the commission and the employee would agree not to institute a lawsuit under Title VII of the Civil Rights Act of 1964, as amended.

If there is no settlement and the commission determines after a full investigation that there is reasonable cause to believe you discriminated against the employee, a formal conciliation effort will be undertaken to settle the dispute. It normally takes the commission six months to one year from the beginning of the initial allegation of discrimination to the time of conciliation. This could mean that the amount of *back pay* will increase. Back pay is the difference between the salary the employee is making now and the salary she would have made, plus interest, if she had obtained the promotion. As part of the settlement, it may be required that you promote the employee. If she used a lawyer, her attorney's fees and costs may also be included as part of the settlement.

If the commission finds reasonable cause to believe that discrimination has occurred and conciliation fails, the commission has the authority to file a complaint against you in an appropriate U.S. district court on behalf of the charging party individually or on behalf of the class of female employees who also may have been unlawfully denied promotions. The commission may bring a class action to obtain remedies for females who are members of the class.

The commission may also issue a right-to-sue letter, which entitles the charging party to institute her own lawsuit on either an individual or a class basis. Defending against such a lawsuit can generate costs and attorneys' fees—employment discrimination is expensive. It is also difficult to justify to your shareholders, who will be deprived of part of their profits if the court orders your company to pay substantial damages.

PREVENTING A DISCRIMINATION CHARGE

Conducting a *self-evaluation* of your company's employment policies is the best way to prevent a discrimination charge. Check your employment application form. What kind of information do you ask the applicant? Check the questions provided by the EEOC for what you may or may not ask the applicant. For example, questions to a female applicant about whether she has children or a sitter to care for her children generally are prohibited. Who conducts the interview, what is asked, how the applicants are evaluated, and who makes the final evaluation are all important. Do you have objective criteria for selecting employees and are the subjective elements kept to a minimum? The hiring process and the way you advertise your company's available positions are very important. Do you advertise in minority and female-oriented newspapers?

You need to be aware of population characteristics—the racial composition of the civilian labor force in the area where you recruit. What is the percentage of blacks, Hispanics, females, and other minorities in the qualified civilian labor force in your recruitment area? Some jobs, particularly those at the entry level, do not require that the applicants have a specific license or qualification. You should be sure you have a cross-representation of the community from which you recruit. Obtain information from the Federal Bureau of the Census about the composition of your community. Data by occupation for the civilian labor force are published by the Bureau of Labor Statistics of the Department of Labor. To prevent discrimination, develop a reasonable and appropriate affirmative action program that will eliminate any imbalance in your labor force.

SELECTED BIBLIOGRAPHY

EEOC Publications

EEO legislation

Laws Administered by EEOC (1981). Text of Title VII of the Civil Rights Act of 1964, as amended; Age Discrimination in Employment Act of 1967, as amended; Equal Pay Act; and Section 501 of the Rehabilitation Act of 1973, as amended.

Laws and Rules You Should Know (1979). Major equal employment laws and executive orders prohibiting employment discrimination; regulations and guidelines of the Equal Employment Opportunity Commission.

Guidelines and regulations

Adoption of Additional Questions and Answers on the Uniform Guidelines on Employee Selection Procedures (45 FR 29530, May 2, 1980).

Adoption of Questions and Answers to Clarify and Provide a Common Interpretation of the Union Guidelines on Employee Selection Procedures (44 FR 11986, Mar. 2, 1979).

Affirmative Action Guidelines (29 CFR, Part 1608, 44 FR 4422, Feb. 20, 1979).

Guidelines on Discrimination Because of National Origin (Revised) (29 CFR, Part 1606, 45 FR 85636, Dec. 29, 1980).

Guidelines on Discrimination Because of Religion (Revised) (29 CFR, Part 1605, 45 FR 72610, Oct. 31, 1980).

Guidelines on Discrimination Because of Sex (as Amended) (29 CFR, Part 1604). Includes amendment and questions and answers on Pregnancy Discrimination Act and Amendment on Sexual Harassment.

Uniform Guidelines on Employee Selection Procedures, adoption by four agencies (29 CFR, Part 1607).

Posters

Age Discrimination Is Against the Law. Required to be posted by covered employers.

Equal Employment Opportunity Is the Law. Joint poster of Equal Employment Opportunity Commission and Office of Federal Contract Compliance Programs. Required to be posted by covered employers (English/Spanish).

EEOC reports

15th Annual Report: FY 1980.

14th Annual Report: FY 1979.

12th and 13th Annual Reports: FY 1977–1978.

Affirmative Action and Equal Employment: A Guidebook for Employers, Vols. 1 and 2 (1974). Basic legal principles (as of 1974). Detailed, step-by-step guidance for voluntary affirmative action programs. Available from GPO.

Job Patterns for Minorities and Women in Private Industry: 1979 Report. Occupational employment by industry broken down according to race, ethnic group, and sex. United States, state, and SMSA data for employers who submit annual reports to the Equal Employment Opportunity Commission. Available from GPO.

EEOC pamphlets

Age: Persons 40–70 Note Age Discrimination Is Against the Law (1981). Pamphlet summarizes requirements and protections of Age Discrimination in Employment Act of 1967, as amended, and tells how to file complaints.

The Equal Employment Opportunity Commission (1981). Pamphlet summarizes legal responsibilities, structure, and function of the commission. Lists headquarters and field offices.

Equal Pay: Equal Work Equal Pay, Men and Women (1981). Pamphlet summarizes provisions of Equal Pay Act and tells how to file complaints.

Filing a Charge (1981). Pamphlet describes how to file a charge and procedures for processing charges under Title VII, the Age Discrimination in Employment, and Equal Pay acts. Lists addresses and telephone numbers of the offices.

The Law Today (1980). Brief summary of prohibited discrimination under all legal authorities administered by the Equal Employment Opportunity Commission. Lists addresses and telephone numbers of field offices.

Pre-Employment Inquiries (1981). Questions and answers related to inquiries—on application forms and in interviews—which comply with legal requirements for nondiscrimination.

Religious Discrimination (1980). Brief overview and background of revised guidelines on discrimination because of religion.

Title VII of the Civil Rights Act of 1964 (1981). Pamphlet summarizes provisions of Title VII of the Civil Rights Act of 1964, as amended.

The above publications may be obtained from the Equal Employment Opportunity Commission, Office of Public Affairs, 2401 E St., N.W., Washington, D.C. 20506.

Additional References

Anderson, Howard J.: *Primer of Equal Employment Opportunity,* Bureau of National Affairs, 1978. An overview of the law of equal employment opportunity, federal antidiscrimination statutes and executive orders, and procedures.

Connolly, Walter B., Jr., and Michael J. Connally: *A Practical Guide to Equal Employment Opportunity* (rev. ed., 2 vol.), Law Journal Seminars-Press, Inc., New York, 1979.

EEOC Compliance Manual (3 vol.), EEOC, Washington, D.C. A guide to procedures, interpretations, and conciliations; available through the EEOC district office.

EEOC Compliance Manual (1 vol.), Bureau of National Affairs, Washington, D.C.

EEOC Compliance Manual, Prentice-Hall, Inc., Englewood Cliffs, N.J., 1980. Official procedures, policies, standards, and techniques used by EEOC in its investigations and affirmative action programs.

EEOC Compliance Manual, Commerce Clearing House, Inc., Chicago, 1981. Multivolume report includes *Procedures* (Vol. 1), *Interpretations* (Vol. 2), *Conciliations* (Vol. 3), and *General Counsel Manual.*

EEOC Decisions, Commerce Clearing House, Inc., Chicago. From June 20, 1968–Jan. 19, 1973; subsequent decisions found in *Employment Practice Guide* (Vol. 2), Commerce Clearing House, Chicago.

EEOC Field Notes, Office of Field Services of EEOC Headquarters, Washington, D.C. These notes provide instructions to the EEOC district and area offices.

Employment Practices Decisions—Federal and State Courts, Commerce Clearing House, Inc., Chicago; multivolume.

Fair Employment Practices Cases, Bureau of National Affairs, Washington, D.C. Federal and state court decisions on employment discrimination; multivolume; published weekly.

Fair Employment Practices Manual (4 vol.), Bureau of National Affairs, Washington, D.C. A complete handbook and guide to federal and state regulations of fair employment practices; biweekly publication.

Federal Regulation of Employment Service—Job Discrimination, Lawyers Co-Operative Publishing Co., New York, 1978.

Guidebook to Fair Employment Practices, Commerce Clearing House, Inc., Chicago, 1981. A guide to what is permitted and required under federal and state laws dealing with equal employment opportunity.

Larson, Arthur: *Employment Discrimination* (4 vol.), Matthew Bender, New York, 1980. Covers discrimination on the basis of sex, race, religion, age, national origin, handicap, homosexuality, transexuality, and veteran status.

Philo, Conrad D., and Marlin M. Volz: *West's Federal Practice Manual: Civil Rights and Employment Discrimination* (2d ed.), West Publishing Co., 1980; *Presenting and Defending the Administrative Case* (Vol. 10), "Private Sector Practice," Chapter 176, Sections 16053 et seq., pp. 609–693; *Selection of Remedies* (Vol. 10), Chapter 174, Sections 15911 et seq., pp. 463–562.

Schlei, Barbara Lindeman, and Paul Grossman: *Employment Discrimination Law*, Bureau of National Affairs, 1976. A casebook dealing with Title VII of the Civil Rights Act of 1964, as amended, and other laws that prohibit employment discrimination. (1979 Supplement). See Chapter 26, "EEOC Administrative Process," pp. 768–815.

Table of Cases

Fullilove v. Klutznick, 100 S.Ct. 2758 (1980). Mandatory set-aside programs for minority businesses in public-works contracts.

Griggs v. Duke Power Co., 401 U.S. 424 (1971). Adverse impact theory of employment discrimination.

McDonnell-Douglas Corp. v. Green, 411 U.S. 792 (1973). Disparate treatment theory of employment discrimination.

United Steelworkers of America, AFL-CIO v. Weber, et al., 433 U.S. 193 (1979). Company and union voluntary affirmative action in collective bargaining.

Articles

FitzGerald, D.: "Discriminatory Job Interviewing—How to Avoid It," *Law Institute Journal*, November 1980, pp. 724–729.

Leap, T. L., W. H. Holley, Jr., and H. S. Feld: "Equal Employment Opportunity and Its Implications for Personnel Practices in the 1980's," *Labor Law Journal*, November 1980, pp. 669–682.

Pyburn, K. M., Jr.: "Responding to Charges of Employment Discrimination," *Law Notes*, summer 1978, pp. 63–67.

chapter 63

Notes on the NAS Study of Equal Pay for Jobs of Equal Value

Heidi I. Hartmann

ASSOCIATE EXECUTIVE DIRECTOR, COMMISSION ON
BEHAVIORAL AND SOCIAL SCIENCES AND EDUCATION,
NATIONAL ACADEMY OF SCIENCES, WASHINGTON, D.C.

Donald J. Treiman

PROFESSOR, DEPARTMENT OF SOCIOLOGY, UNIVERSITY
OF CALIFORNIA, LOS ANGELES, CALIFORNIA.

The problem of "comparable worth," or "equal pay for jobs of equal value," or "pay equity," arises because of the large and continuing differential in men's and women's earnings and the persistent segregation of men and women in the labor market. The earnings gap has remained at approximately 40 percent for practically as long as statistics have been kept; that is, women who work full time, year round, earn on average 60 percent of what full-time, year-round male workers earn. Women are increasingly expressing their dissatisfaction with their wage rates and, in particular, claim that it is the traditionally women's jobs that are underpaid. Many of these jobs—e.g., nurse, librarian— require several years of specialized education; to the women holding such jobs, the earnings gap may be especially apparent. More generally, in 1978, among

NOTE: The views expressed herein are those of the authors and not of the National Academy of Sciences.

full-time, year-round workers, black and white women with college educations earned less than white men with eighth-grade educations, giving rise to widespread feelings among women that they are underpaid.

In recent years increasing emphasis has been placed on the prevalence of job segregation as an explanation for the earnings gap. The index of segregation, an overall measure, indicates that almost two-thirds of working women or men would have to change occupations in order for women to have the same occupational distribution as men across the detailed occupations of the census classification,[1] and this has been the case since at least 1900. Further, the more an occupation is dominated by women, the less it pays. In 1970 (the latest year for which comprehensive data are available), occupations that were performed solely by women paid on the average less than half as much as occupations that were performed solely by men. Overall, 35 to 40 percent of the wage gap between men and women can be attributed to the fact that women tend to work in lower-paying occupations than men do. The remainder of the gap is due to the fact that women tend to earn less than men in the same occupation.[2]

It is the existence of low-paid, predominantly female jobs that causes the issue of comparable worth to arise. Are these jobs poorly paid because they are held by women? Would they be paid more if men held them? Should they be paid more? How can one determine what they should be paid? The Committee

---

[1]The index of segregation, or index of dissimilarity, is given as

$$\Delta = \Sigma \frac{|x_i - y_i|}{2}$$

where x_i = the percentage of one population (e.g., men) in the ith category of a classification
y_i = the percentage of the other population (e.g., women) in the ith category.
Δ is then the percentage of either population that would have to shift categories to make its distribution exactly equal to that of the other population.

[2]To clarify this point, it is useful to distinguish between jobs and occupations. Jobs are specific sets of tasks and responsibilities performed in a specific work setting. Occupations are aggregations of jobs on the basis of their similarity. Aggregations of jobs into occupational categories may be more or less gross, depending on the purpose. Examples of jobs are "emergency room nurse at George Washington University Hospital," "psychiatrist at St. Elizabeth's Hospital," "surgeon in private practice in the XYZ medical group." In the 1970 U.S. Census detailed occupational classification, these jobs would fall into two categories: "physicians, medical and osteopathic," and "registered nurses." From this example we can see that part of the earnings gap between men and women can be attributed to occupational segregation, since men are more likely to be physicians and women are more likely to be nurses, and physicians earn more than nurses. But part of the gap is due to *job* segregation within occupations. Among physicians, women are more likely to work in salaried positions and men are more likely to be in private practice; women are more likely to practice low-paying specialties, such as psychiatry, while men are more likely to practice high-paying specialties, such as surgery; and so on. Of course, even within jobs men may earn more than women due to greater experience, productivity, or even overt discrimination, despite the illegality of this situation under the 1963 Equal Pay Act. Still, it is clear that the bulk of the pay differential between men and women is due to the fact that the jobs men perform tend to pay more than the jobs women perform.

on Occupational Classification and Analysis of the National Research Council was formed in 1978,[3] at the request of the Equal Employment Opportunity Commission, to undertake a study of the issues involved in measuring the comparability of jobs: What bases—skill, effort, responsibility, working conditions, etc.—exist for comparing jobs? Can they be adequately measured? Are they appropriate criteria for allocating jobs to pay classes? Can procedures be found for deciding in any particular instance whether and to what extent pay differences between jobs involve discriminatory elements?[4] In addition to these general questions, the Equal Employment Opportunity Commission was particularly interested in whether methods of job classification, analysis, and evaluation currently in use are biased by traditional stereotypes or other factors. Having worked with the Committee on Occupational Classification and Analysis for three years,[5] we offer in this chapter our particular perspective on this issue and on the committee's report "Women, Work and Wages: Equal Pay for Jobs of Equal Value."[6] We begin with a review of the major findings of the committee and follow this with comments expressing our own perceptions regarding the report and its uses.

---

[3]The committee was chaired by Professor Ann R. Miller, Population Studies Center and Department of Sociology, University of Pennsylvania. The remaining members were Dr. David P. Campbell, Vice President of Research and Programs, Center for Creative Leadership; Mary C. Dunlap, Esq., a San Francisco attorney; Professor G. Franklin Edwards, Department of Sociology and Anthropology, Howard University; Professor Richard C. Edwards, Department of Economics, University of Massachusetts; Professor Leon Festinger, Department of Psychology, New School for Social Research; Dr. Gary D. Gottfredson, a psychologist at the Center for the Social Organization of Schools, Johns Hopkins University; Professor John A. Hartigan, Department of Statistics, Yale University; Ms. Doris P. Haywood, Vice President, Human Resources, Metropolitan Life Insurance Company; Mr. Wesley R. Liebtag, Director of Personnel Programs, International Business Machines Corporation; Professor Robert E. B. Lucas, Department of Economics, Boston University; Professor Karen Oppenheim Mason, Department of Sociology and Population Studies Center, University of Michigan; Dr. Ernest J. McCormick, Professor Emeritus, Department of Psychological Sciences, Purdue University; and Mr. Gus Tyler, Assistant President, International Ladies' Garment Workers' Union.

[4]Discrimination, as it is used here, refers to disparate treatment or outcomes based on the social characteristics of workers, e.g., their gender. Clearly, some part of the wage differentials observed between women and men results from legitimate factors, e.g., productivity-related characteristics of workers or the characteristics of their jobs, such as complexity, responsibility, etc. But some part of the wage differentials between jobs may be the result of factors connected to the sex composition of job incumbents; that is, jobs may be paid less because they are done mainly by women, not because they would be paid poorly regardless of who did them. If a job's pay level is linked to the sex composition of its incumbents, the pay level itself is viewed as discriminatory in the committee's report.

[5]Hartmann, an economist, served as research associate to the committee; Treiman, a sociologist, served as study director.

[6]Donald J. Treiman and Heidi I. Hartmann (eds.), "Women, Work, and Wages: Equal Pay for Jobs of Equal Value," *Final Report of the Committee on Occupational Classification and Analysis to the Equal Employment Opportunity Commission*, National Academy Press, Washington, D.C.; 1981. The report is available from the National Academy Press, 2101 Constitution Ave.. N.W., Washington, D.C. 20418.

THE COMMITTEE'S FINDINGS

The concept of comparable, or relative, worth raises many questions about the value of work. Why do movie stars and professional athletes earn such high salaries? What should be the relative pay rates between white-collar and blue-collar occupations? What is the relative worth of manual versus mental effort? At least at the outset, the committee found it difficult to consider the particular problem of the relative worth of men's and women's jobs without considering the general issue of how work should be valued and what it should be paid. Moreover, the committee also grappled with the question of whether or not this was a legitimate problem for study. "Isn't a job worth what it's paid?" has certainly been one reply common among economists. However, even in conventional economic theory, jobs are paid what they are worth only in the absence of discrimination and under conditions of a perfect market for labor. This led the committee to investigate the evidence regarding pay discrimination on the basis of sex. The committee approached the problem by investigating the overall situation of women in the labor market and summarizing and reporting evidence on wage differentials between men and women, on the extent and causes of job segregation by sex in the labor market, and on the operation of labor markets in general.

The committee came to three major conclusions. (1) Wage discrimination is widespread. (2) From this conclusion it follows that existing wage rates cannot be used to measure the relative worth of jobs: jobs are not necessarily paid what they are worth. The committee concluded, moreover, that there is no other universally acceptable standard of job worth. (3) However, once employers (and employees) agree on what should be valued in jobs, measures can be found to determine to what extent various jobs incorporate those values. Such a method is job evaluation, which is widely used for setting pay rates throughout American business and industry and also elsewhere in the advanced industrialized world. Existing job evaluation procedures probably are not appropriate for assessing the relative worth of jobs in a highly sex-segregated work world, but they can be modified to be made appropriate. Let us describe each of these conclusions in somewhat more detail.

Wage Differentials   Chapter 2 of the committee's report, "Evidence Regarding Wage Differentials," begins with a discussion of the human capital model of earnings differentials. In this model, it is assumed that people are paid for their productivity and that if people with the same productivity are paid differently, the difference can be taken as a measure of discrimination. Typically, the model expresses earnings as a function of variables thought to be related to productivity. There are a number of problems with the model. First, wage differentials exist for reasons other than productivity differences—for example, temporary shortages or surpluses of workers in various occupations. Second, human capital is usually taken to be a proxy for productivity, and human capital, that is, one's education, health, etc., may or may not be a good indicator of one's productivity. Third, the indicators of human capital themselves may not be good. A researcher may be interested in job-relevant training on the assumption that such training contributes to productivity, but he or she may have only a measure of general educational attainment (i.e., the years of schooling completed). Fourth, the treatment of any unexplained difference in earnings (i.e., the residual) as an indicator of discrimination requires the strong assumption that all legitimate determinants of wage differences have been measured and have been measured without error. All these potential difficulties notwithstanding, the results of studies utilizing the model have been remarkably consistent over the past 25 years. In recent years the basic model has been expanded to incorporate characteristics of jobs, as well as of workers, that relate to earnings.

Studies that focus only on the characteristics of workers generally explain about one-fourth of the gross earnings differential of 40 percent, and never more than half. Consequently, the remaining gap in earnings, 20 percent or more, is often attributed to the presence of discrimination of one form or another. A second set of studies—those utilizing models incorporating information about the jobs people hold and attempting to use characteristics of jobs in addition to characteristics of people to account for the gross earnings gap—generally explain a greater part of the earnings gap, leaving a smaller residual to be considered the result of discrimination. There is little evidence, however, that particular characteristics of occupations (e.g., measures of skill requirements, effort, responsibility, working conditions, etc.) actually contribute to the explanation of earnings differentials. Rather, it is often the use of occupational classifications as explanatory variables that improves the explanatory power of the models. These findings confirm the importance of job segregation as a determinant of wage differentials. The committee's conclusion, after reviewing findings using both types of models, was that discrimination is likely operating in the labor market with significant effects on women's earnings and the pay rates of women's jobs in particular.

Labor Market Structure   In Chapter 3, the committee reviewed the operation of labor markets, focusing on the institutional model of the labor market, which they found to be a useful one for understanding the persistence of job segregation and earnings differentials. The institutional view is that the labor market is characterized by rigidities and barriers to mobility of various sorts. Consequently, one cannot expect differentials in wages to disappear over time on their own. In fact, differentials that have been established would tend to persist, even for equally productive people. Similarly, job segregation by sex, once established, would tend to persist.

Issues of comparable worth, the committee's report pointed out, emerge most clearly in situations in which a single firm employs a large work force across many different jobs. Such situations are not uncommon in the United States; at least half the work force is employed by large-scale employers. For most workers in large firms, the conditions of employment are determined mainly by administrative rules. Once an employee enters a large-scale establishment, he or she becomes part of an internal labor market in which jobs are usually filled from within and workers are usually deployed in accordance with established rules and procedures rather than in direct competition with workers in the external labor market. Promotion from one job to another, for example, will depend on how the various jobs are organized into job ladders and on various rules, such as the consideration given to seniority in the promotion decision. While theorists do not agree on the causes of the establishment of internal labor markets, most agree that such markets do exist and do limit direct competition with the external market for many employees. If all jobs were open to such direct competition, employers would have little use for extensive compensation analysis except perhaps for area wage surveys to determine the going wage. Many firms do, however, use such analyses, particularly job evaluation.

In the institutional view, earnings are determined not only by the human capital the worker brings to the market but also by the way his or her job is structured. Employers often have several alternatives in how they choose to structure jobs, within the constraints of customs and traditions. For example, a sequence of jobs could be organized into a career ladder, with employees starting at the bottom of the ladder and moving into successively more responsible—and higher-paying—jobs as they gain experience. Typically, the jobs men do are organized into longer career ladders than the jobs women do. But many women's jobs could be structured differently. One could conceive of secretarial work as a skilled craft with apprenticeships, entry-level jobs, and career ladders. Secretarial jobs organized in this way might have higher productivity, reduced job turnover, increased job tenure, and steeper age-earnings profiles.

Clearly, in hiring workers and structuring jobs, there is a complex interaction of factors at play—with employers having control over some factors, but not others. It is certainly the case that most firms in the American economy exhibit job segregation by sex and that much of job segregation is the result of the placement of newly hired individuals. To some extent, placement is determined by supply, which is often beyond the scope or control of the employer—at least in the short run. Still, several within-firm studies show that much of the earnings differential between women and men within firms is due to differential job assignments when individuals first enter; men and women with equal qualifications are assigned to different entry-level jobs with differing implications for their subsequent careers.

Evidence from Comparable Worth Cases   The committee also reviewed several of the more important studies specifically aimed at assessing whether jobs of equal worth are equally paid. In each case, the measure of job worth was derived from a job evaluation study. Two are described here in some detail. The first is a review of the history of wage-setting practices at various Westinghouse and General Electric plants, involving production workers in the electrical manufacturing field. The second, done in the state of Washington, is a study of state civil service employees. Both studies explicitly use job evaluation systems to measure the worth of jobs and then compare jobs of equal worth (according to those systems) with respect to their wage rates. The General Electric and Westinghouse experiences are particularly instructive in that they are probably typical of a large number of companies. In the 1930s, GE and Westinghouse developed job evaluation systems for the purpose of standardizing wage rates throughout their plants. At the time, most production jobs at their plants were entirely segregated by sex and were generally identified as men's or women's jobs, but all jobs were measured with the same job evaluation system. Men's and women's jobs were classified in the same labor grades, each labor grade corresponding to a specified range of job evaluation scores, but were separately identified as male or female. It was customary at that time, however, to pay women less than men. Consequently, even for jobs with the same job-worth scores, the women were paid less, about 18 to 20 percent less by Westinghouse and about 33 percent less by General Electric. In 1963, when the Equal Pay Act was enacted, separate schedules for men's and women's jobs became illegal. At one Westinghouse plant, labor grades 1 to 5 for men were simply renumbered grades 6 to 10 and the higher male grades were given even higher numbers (11 to 15). This resulted in a wage scale that increased linearly from grades 1 to 5, which were female, through grades 6 to 15, which were male. However, female grade 1, which was, of course, now no longer identified as female, had the same job-worth points as male grade 6, which was, of course, no longer identified as male; but grade 1 continued to be paid much less than grade 6.

The Washington study was conducted at the request of women's groups in the state's civil service system and their state AFSCME-affiliated union. A job evaluation consultant, Norman Willis and Associates of Seattle, was brought in specifically to investigate the claim that men's and women's jobs of comparable worth were paid differently. A total of 121 positions, in which at least 70 percent of the incumbents were of the same sex, was chosen for evaluation. Of these positions, 59 were men's jobs and 62 were women's jobs. The study found that the pay rates for jobs held mainly by women averaged about 80 percent of the pay rates for jobs held mainly by men who attained the same scores in the job evaluation.

The review of these studies contributed to the committee's conclusion that there is substantial discrimination in the labor market and, in particular, that wages are higher in some jobs and lower in others than they would be in the absence of job segregation. The existence of job segregation is not in dispute, the causes for it are; but the committee concluded that although there is an element of choice in the jobs women hold, there is also evidence of exclusionary practices by employers and of the systematic underpayment of jobs mainly held by women. That is, the wage rates of jobs held traditionally by women are depressed relative to what they would be if women had equal opportunity in the labor market.

Job Evaluation   An important task of the committee was to evaluate the desirability of using existing job evaluation plans to determine job worth for the purpose of resolving claims of pay discrimination. Job evaluation procedures are used to order jobs hierarchically on the basis of judgments regarding their relative skill, effort, responsibility, working conditions, etc., and on this basis to group them into pay classes. Since these plans reflect what employers value in jobs, they have obvious potential as a standard for determining whether jobs are paid what they are worth to their employer. Such a standard would only be appropriate, however, if the job evaluation plan were applied in a fair and unbiased way. Specifically, the issue is whether there are any features of job evaluation systems that lead to the undervaluation of jobs done mainly by women compared to jobs done mainly by men.

The committee's work on job evaluation is contained in its interim report as well as in the final report. The committee's interim report "Job Evaluation: An Analytic Review," reviewed various types of job evaluation plans and pointed out three major problems resulting from the way these plans are currently designed and implemented.[7] First, judgments about the content of jobs tend to be highly subjective. Second, the way that compensable factors are chosen and weighted tends to perpetuate existing wage disparities between men's jobs and women's jobs. Third, the use of multiple plans within the same firm precludes the comparison of the relative worth of jobs in different sectors of a firm, e.g., shop, office, and executive.

Subjectivity. Various features of jobs (called job factors) are identified and measured by job evaluation plans, and the choice of factors as well as the way they are combined into an overall score can affect the final outcome, that is, the relative ranking of jobs. For example, suppose responsibility is a feature of jobs that is regarded as contributing to their relative worth. If responsibility is measured by the job factor "number of people supervised," and if the available ratings are one or two people, 10 points; three to five people, 20 points; over five, 30 points, such a range may not fully represent all the variation in the job feature. Might there not be significant differences between supervising 6, 20, or 200 people? Moreover, measured factors may not fully reflect the underlying criterion of value. To continue with the same example, the number of people supervised may not be the only indicator of responsibility; to be comprehensive, other features of responsibility would need to be identified as well, such as coordinating and scheduling meetings, managing time, etc. Insofar as women's jobs involve coordinating and scheduling while otherwise comparable men's jobs involve supervision, the use of supervision rather than coordination and scheduling as a measure of responsibility would tend to undervalue women's jobs. Finally, the way that particular jobs are evaluated with respect to particular features may reflect pervasive cultural stereotypes regarding the nature of men's work versus women's work. For example, in one job evaluation plan, "length of time to become fully trained" was used as a measure of skill requirements. In this plan the judgment was made that it takes two months to become fully trained as a typist and 12 months to become fully trained as a truck driver, a judgment that many women (and probably many men, as well) would challenge.

Factor weights. In most job evaluation plans, the scores on the various factors are added up to produce a summary job-worth score. The points assignable to each factor determine the relative importance, or weight, of the various factors for the total score. These points are often assigned in such a way as to produce a hierarchy of job worth that corresponds as closely as possible to the existing wage hierarchy of jobs. This is hardly surprising when it is realized that one of the major motivations for the development of job evaluation systems was to make more rational the existing structures of wage rates within firms.

Many of the job evaluation systems in use today were developed by using a firm's existing pay structure to determine statistically which attributes of jobs

---

[7]Donald J. Treiman, "Job Evaluation: An Analytic Review," *Interim Report of the Committee on Occupational Classification and Analysis to the Equal Employment Opportunity Commission,* National Academy of Sciences, Washington, D.C., 1979. The report is available from the National Academy Press, 2101 Constitution Ave., N.W., Washington, D.C. 20418.

best predict their pay rates. In this approach, a set of factors that is thought likely to be related to existing pay differences among jobs is identified—factors representing differences in skill, effort, responsibility, and working conditions. Each job is scored on each of the factors. These factors are then used to predict existing pay rates (usually via the statistical technique of multiple regression analysis), and those factors contributing substantially to the prediction are included in the job evaluation plan, with weights proportional to their contribution. The factors and factor weights can then be used to assign pay rates to new jobs and to adjust the pay rates of existing jobs that are overpaid or underpaid relative to the predictions of the formula. This method provides an empirically derived underlying structure with which the pay rates of all jobs in a firm can be brought into conformity. This is sometimes called a "policy-capturing" approach—the implicit policy underlying the existing pay system is made explicit. Job evaluation plans developed in this way necessarily produce hierarchies of job worth that are closely related to existing pay hierarchies: this is what they are designed to do.

The difficulty is that this method of choosing and weighting factors to be included in the job evaluation plan necessarily reflects any inequities in the pay rates prevailing at the time the job evaluation plan was developed.[8] Since most currently used job evaluation plans were developed at a time when jobs done mainly by women tended as a matter of policy to be paid less than comparable jobs done mainly or entirely by men, factors that tended to differentiate between men's and women's jobs necessarily were accorded heavy weight. Moreover, even job evaluation plans developed afresh today can incorporate market-wage bias, if men's and women's jobs are rated significantly differently on some factors (e.g., responsibility), because as we have seen, current wage rates often embody discrimination. In short, because existing job evaluation plans tend to replicate existing pay hierarchies, they cannot be used without modification as independent standards for assessing whether jobs are paid according to their worth. Below we review the committee's suggestions for modifying these plans to overcome this difficulty.

Multiple plans.   The third problem identified by the committee in its interim report was the use of multiple plans by many business firms. It is often the case that one plan is used for clerical workers, another plan for managerial level workers, and yet a third plan for manual workers. When multiple plans are used, it is difficult to compare jobs across sectors of the firm. Since a major source of the wage differential between men and women stems from the fact that women tend to be concentrated in clerical jobs, which pay poorly, while men tend to be concentrated in manual and managerial jobs, which tend to pay better than clerical jobs, the inability to compare jobs across sectors makes an assessment of the possibility of wage discrimination very difficult.

---

[8]Job evaluation plans are also developed in other ways. Sometimes the choice of factors and factor weights is made arbitrarily, without explicit reference to market wage rates, in which case the weights could be free of bias from this source. It is likely that even in this case, however, the "arbitrary" choice is in fact affected by knowledge of what is valued in the marketplace.

Modifying Job Evaluation Plans   Despite these problems, the committee concluded that job evaluation plans are potentially useful for the purposes of identifying and correcting wage discrimination. In a plan that has been implemented by the employer, one can assume that the employer accepts the values
of job worth as expressed by the job evaluation plan. Often, of course, the
employer has made no explicit statement of what the firm values. However, the
identification of job factors and the weights given to various job factors are
themselves an implicit expression of what employers value, of what they are
willing to pay for. When a plan is in use, the firm or a consultant or an employee
group might wish to examine it to see how well it is designed and implemented.
Does the plan identify all the job factors that contribute to the job feature being
measured? Does the range of values available for a given factor fully reflect the
range of variation in the factor actually exhibited in the firm's jobs? Are the
weights assigned free from bias? Are the factors measured as objectively as
possible?

In addition to recommending close scrutiny of existing job evaluation plans
to determine whether they appear to treat jobs held mainly by men and jobs
held mainly by women in an equitable manner, the committee's report offers
several suggestions for statistically adjusting these plans to remove any discriminatory effects that are designed into them by their initial reliance on existing
pay rates as a criterion for the selection and weighting of compensable job factors. The typical job evaluation plan utilizes a formula of the following sort:

$$\text{Job worth} = \Sigma J_i^* = \Sigma b_i J_i \tag{1}$$

where J_i^* = the scores on the measured job factors used in the developed plan
$\quad\quad J_i$ = the scores on the job factors as initially measured when developing the plan
$\quad\quad b_i$ = the weights for each factor

As we have noted, the weights typically are derived by estimating a multiple
regression equation of the form

$$\hat{Y} = a + \Sigma b_i J_i \tag{2}$$

where $\hat{Y}$ = the actual pay rate for each job (or the midpoint of a range of pay rates)
$\quad\quad J_i$ = the scores on the job factors as initially measured when developing the plan
$\quad\quad b_i$ = the net regression (slope) coefficients indicating the weight to be accorded
$\quad\quad\quad$ each job factor to maximize predictability of the actual pay rates
$\quad\quad a$ = the intercept, the predicted pay rate for a job with zero points on all the job
$\quad\quad\quad$ factors

One way to correct for bias in the weights resulting from the fact that men's
jobs tend to be paid more than women's jobs is to reestimate the weights, adding to the estimation equation an additional variable, percent female in each
occupation. That is, an existing job evaluation plan could be corrected for bias
by estimating a multiple regression equation of the form

$$\hat{Y} = a' + \Sigma b_i' J_i^* + cF \tag{3}$$

where $\hat{Y}$ = the actual pay rate for each job in the firm
$\quad\quad J_i^*$ = the scores for each job on each of the factors in the job evaluation system
$\quad\quad\quad$ currently in use
$\quad\quad F$ = the percent female among incumbents in each job
$\quad\quad a'$ = the intercept
$\quad\quad b_i'$ = the reestimated weights for the job factors
$\quad\quad c$ = the weight for percent female

Such an equation can be used in two ways. First, if the coefficient c is different from zero, it can be inferred that there is pay discrimination on the basis of gender. Specifically, a negative coefficient c would indicate that if all the other job factors are held constant, the higher the percentage of women among incumbents, the less a job pays. Jobs that are identical in all other respects but that differ by one point in their percent female would be expected to differ by c dollars in their pay rates in this firm. For example, suppose Y is the annual salary and c equals 20. Then if two jobs in a firm had identical job characteristics but 90 percent of the incumbents of one job were men and 50 percent of the incumbents of the other job were women, the two jobs would be expected to differ by $800, or $20(90 - 50)$, in annual salaries. It would then be possible to adjust pay rates for jobs so as to eliminate the effect of gender composition on pay rates net of the effect of the other, legitimate, job factors. For example, by adding $-cF$ dollars to the pay rate for each job, all pay rates could be brought up to the level of jobs with comparable scores on the other job factors but which are performed only by males. Other adjustments are, of course, possible as well.

The second use of such an equation would be to produce bias-free weights for job factors, since the b_i' estimated by equation (3) indicate the effect of each job factor if the sex composition of the jobs is held constant. That is, two jobs with the same percent female and the same scores on all the job factors but one, say, the first one, would be expected to differ by b_1' dollars. Thus a new, unbiased, job evaluation formula could be created:

$$\text{Job worth} = \Sigma b_i' J_i^* \tag{4}$$

If such a formula were used to assign jobs to pay classes, there would be no net effect of gender composition on pay rates. To be sure, there might be a correlation between percent female and pay rates, because the jobs done mainly by men and the jobs done mainly by women may differ in their compensable characteristics. But holding constant such differences, there would be no effect of sex composition. This is the precise sense in which the new weights could be said to be unbiased.

A second way to correct the determination of weights in this type of job evaluation plan is to use in the regression estimation equation only those occupations which are held mainly by white men. In this way weights will not be biased, since there is presumably no discrimination against white men in the labor market. This procedure, however, is reasonable only if men's jobs and women's jobs have similar features, that is, if enough men's jobs have the same features as are found in women's jobs, weights can in fact be determined for those factors by this method.

COMMENTARY

Unresolved Issues and Next Steps   A number of issues were necessarily left unresolved in the committee's report because the research necessary to resolve them has not yet been done. We briefly review some of these issues here.

First, the economic consequences of implementing a policy of comparable worth are unclear. A major argument against comparable worth made by some is that it is unrealistic and impossible to alter the forces of supply and demand.

As the committee argued in the report's chapter on labor markets, however, supply and demand are not God-given economic forces that emerge from nowhere. Rather, they are the *result* of many historical and current events, including discriminatory practices. Laws or regulations can themselves alter supply and demand and can raise or lower prices. In this sense, paying jobs according to their worth is not different from paying a minimum wage or excluding alien labor or providing tax incentives to hire inner-city workers. All are interventions in the market in the interest of particular public policies. Still, employers who are forced, by collective bargaining or the results of litigation, to pay higher wages to women in women's jobs than they are accustomed to paying, might justifiably fear negative economic consequences, particularly if they are operating in a competitive product market. It should be noted, however, that the same fears have been expressed in the past but have been proved groundless. For example, the specter of bankruptcy was widely raised in the south when the wages of blacks were increased after passage of the Civil Rights Act in 1964, but bankruptcies did not ensue. Some percentage of firms, particularly large ones where issues of comparable worth are most likely to be raised, simply do not operate in a competitive environment. Moreover, a comparable-worth policy has been implemented in Australia without disruption of the economy. Most firms there were able to absorb the higher costs without adverse effect on themselves, the employment of women, or the general economy. From this evidence there is reason to believe that a comparable-worth policy could be adopted without disastrous economic results. Nonetheless, much more detailed research, or practical experience, or a combination of both needs to accumulate before we will be in a strong position to evaluate the economic impact of implementing a comparable-worth policy.

Second, job evaluation procedures will become much more useful tools for resolving pay equity disputes if their technical adequacy is improved. While job evaluation practices represented the state of the art of psychometric scaling in the late 1930s, when they were first developed, they have (with a few exceptions) hardly advanced since then. A great deal has been learned in the past 40 years about how to create reliable, valid, and unbiased scales, and this knowledge needs to be applied to current job evaluation practices. In addition, there are a number of specific issues involving job and compensation analysis that need to be resolved. For example, there has been almost no research on the specific question the committee was asked by the Equal Employment Opportunity Commission: Does bias enter into the evaluation of jobs? The committee was able to conclude, first, that bias enters into the weights of job factors because these weights are derived from market wage rates, which in themselves incorporate bias, and second, that bias probably enters the evaluation itself through subjective judgments, since research has shown that many judgmental processes incorporate bias. But no experimental studies of the rating of jobs have been done, even though we do have experimental studies of the rating of individuals (for example, the response of personnel managers to identical résumés, when some are thought to be women's and some are thought to be men's). Because the results of this type of study show that bias does enter judgments, the committee reasonably concluded that bias enters the judgments made about the rating of jobs, but job rating is an area where much fruitful research could be done.

There is also much that we do not know about determining the characteristics of jobs. Do men's and women's jobs have similar characteristics? Can one plan be developed and used across all different types of jobs? We would argue that given the changes in the labor market, men's and women's jobs are becoming more similar and can now be measured on one plan rather more easily than previously. In many ways manual jobs are becoming nonmanual, for example, as they increasingly involve the use and knowledge of computer processing, and nonmanual jobs are becoming more manual, for example, as they increasingly involve the use of more sophisticated technical equipment. Moreover, we have examples of single job evaluation schemes applied to all jobs in several large corporations. And the *Dictionary of Occupational Titles* utilizes one job evaluation scheme for the entire economy. Some 12,000 occupations, purporting to cover all jobs in the economy, are measured on a number of criteria, and the same criteria are used for all occupations.[9] This is an area where the committee did not come to a conclusion and where more research could usefully be done. Our prediction is such research will lead to the conclusion that plans can be developed and used to adequately measure the job attributes of all jobs in a firm. We do not believe that one plan could be developed and used across the entire economy, but rather that any firm could develop a single plan which could be used throughout the firm and which reflects its own values and needs.

In our judgment, the improvement of job evaluation procedures and their adaptation for use in resolving pay equity disputes will occur gradually, as employers, employees, and consultants work together to carefully examine existing systems for inadvertent bias, to redesign them as necessary, and to experiment with new procedures of the sort discussed above for statistically removing the bias that results from incorporating the effects of pay inequities. At one point in the work of the committee, the staff prepared a set of draft guidelines for the development of bias-free job evaluation procedures. But it became clear in the course of committee discussion that the technical basis was lacking which could justify imposing any particular set of procedures on individual enterprises. We concur in the committee judgment and believe that progress will best be made by management and employees of large numbers of individual enterprises (firms, government agencies, etc.) working together to arrive at an equitable pay hierarchy for the enterprise.

How the Report Will Be Used   In our judgment the committee's report will undoubtedly encourage the comparable-worth cause. The report states that claims of comparable worth are in fact reasonable in many cases because discrimination operates in the labor market to depress the wage rates of women's jobs and also to depress the job evaluation scores that some plans have assigned to women's jobs. The report supports the notion that job evaluation systems when designed and used properly can identify instances of discrimination and their results could be used as guidelines to adjust the wage rates of women's jobs. The committee's interim report was cited twice in *Gunther v. County of*

---

[9]Ann R. Miller, Donald J. Treiman, Pamela S. Cain, and Patricia A. Roos (eds.), "Work, Jobs, and Occupations: A Critical Review of the *Dictionary of Occupational Titles*," *Report of the Committee on Occupational Classification and Analysis to the U.S. Department of Labor*, National Academy Press, Washington, D.C., 1980.

Washington; the 1981 Supreme Court decision gave legal standing to claims of pay discrimination based on the concept of comparable worth. (Specifically, the decision held that claims of pay discrimination involving comparisons of *different* jobs can be brought under Title VII of the 1964 Civil Rights Act.) It is likely that the final report will be cited in lawsuits and possibly even in collective-bargaining negotiations in support of the claim that women's jobs are underpaid.

It is interesting to note, however, that there may be one limiting aspect of the committee's report. The committee stresses that there is no strictly scientific basis for determining the standards of job worth. What a job should be worth is not a scientific question, the report states. Rather, once that question has been answered by a process that elicits value decisions, social science measurement techniques can be used to measure the extent to which various jobs incorporate the characteristics valued. This has implications for the legal treatment of consultants' studies of wage discrimination based upon job evaluation plans. A consultant's findings of discrimination could be challenged by management's claim that the consultant's plan does not reflect the firm's values. Management could offer another plan which it claims better reflects its values and which indicates no evidence of discrimination. This might be difficult to do, however. Such a plan would need to account entirely for the observed association between the sex composition of jobs and their pay rates on the basis of a set of measured factors. But the choice of factors would then need to be able to withstand scrutiny. Are they bona fide compensable factors or simply surrogates for sex composition? While the notion of "bona fide compensable factors" has no legal standing, at least as yet, it is evident that gender cannot be one of them. It is unlikely that the courts will allow, nor that employees would accept, measures of job worth that do not bear some plausible relation to the consensually validated overarching set of criteria embodied in the catechism "skill, effort, responsibility, and working conditions."

When a consultant sells a plan, he or she essentially sells a set of values to a firm. When a firm agrees to use a plan, the firm tacitly, if not explicitly, accepts the values embodied in the consultant's plan. The consultant's presentation, however, may also be an occasion for management to consider seriously what it wants to value. In our view, employees should be included in this process as well. When employers and employees can agree on the criteria for establishing pay differences between jobs, all will benefit. To paraphrase the sociologist W. I. Thomas, things that are perceived as fair are fair in their consequences. It is of interest to note that a growing number of job evaluation plans are being developed jointly by management and unions. The Joint Union-Management Occupational Job Evaluation Committee of AT&T and the Communications Workers of America is perhaps the most prominent current example.

We want to emphasize, however, that the lack of a strictly technical basis for establishing criteria of job worth does not mean that job worth cannot be accurately measured once consensus has been achieved as to the criteria of worth appropriate to the jobs in question. We believe, as did the committee, that psychometric and other social science techniques can be used to improve the measurement of job worth.

In our view the comparable-worth strategy is an important addition to the array of equal employment opportunity mechanisms for dealing with the outcomes resulting from discrimination. Comparable worth does not, however, solve all the problems associated with discrimination. Equal access should continue to be emphasized. Most importantly, we know that there are inequalities in wage rates for the same jobs across firms and that women tend to be concentrated in low-wage firms. The comparable-worth strategy, as it has been used thus far, has been limited to comparisons of the pay rates for various jobs within a single firm. It has not been applied across firms. Consequently, to the extent that women work disproportionately in low-wage firms, comparable-worth strategies are irrelevant. Only access to high-wage firms would improve the earnings of women workers. All societies have low-wage jobs by definition, since in no society are all jobs paid the same. Paying jobs according to their worth will not eliminate the low-wage sector, although it may redistribute the burden between men and women and may also reduce the extent of income inequality.

Equal pay for jobs of equal value should not be understood as a substitute for the sexual desegregation of the labor force. Even if comparable-worth strategies succeed in raising the wages of jobs traditionally done mainly by women, some women may still wish to enter traditional male jobs because of their intrinsic interest. Moreover, differences in power, prestige, and prospects for promotion will not necessarily be eliminated simply by reducing the wage gap between jobs, although doing so may in fact provide some impetus in that direction. If employers must pay similar salaries to, say, secretaries and salespeople, they may be encouraged to restructure secretarial jobs in such a way as to reduce turnover and thus exploit the firm-specific skill and knowledge accumulated by secretaries with long tenure. Still, in Australia and Sweden, where the wage gap between male and female workers has been reduced substantially, job segregation continues undiminished. Hence it is necessary to continue vigorously to pursue affirmative action and other policies designed to improve equality of access to occupational opportunities.

A final difficulty with the comparable-worth strategy as it is generally understood today is that it encourages reliance on job evaluation, a technocratic solution to a political and value problem. It is technocratic in two senses.

First, the technology of job evaluation, in which a set of job characteristics is measured and assigned scores that are then combined in some specified way into an overall score, encourages reliance on job characteristics that are relatively easily measured and are common to a large number of jobs. Unique or subtle requirements or other features of jobs that are not easily measured tend to be ignored and hence do not contribute to the measurement of job worth. Moreover, once a job evaluation system is in place, it is difficult to change, even if the nature of work changes. While individual jobs may be reevaluated, the criteria by which jobs are evaluated tend to remain fixed. The use of job evaluation thus tends to introduce a certain rigidity in the wage-setting process.

Second, the use of job evaluation procedures effectively forces management and workers to rely on people with technical expertise in this area to advise both management and labor about what a particular job is worth. In many ways this restricts the bargaining flexibility of managers and workers. Unions, in particular, often object to the imposition of a job evaluation plan because of this restriction. Not only may it restrict flexibility, but it enhances the role of technical experts and may make the people most directly involved in the work, managers and workers, feel a loss of control over the conditions of employment.

Nevertheless, offsetting the negative effects of the technocratic character of job evaluation is a strong positive effect. Properly used, job evaluation plans can be highly effective educational tools. Because these plans make the bases for pay differences explicit, they make it easier to identify specific instances of pay inequity. Moreover, the principles of compensation embodied in a plan can be directly assessed by employers and employees, and if they are perceived to be inequitable or otherwise unsuitable, they can be altered. Finally, scrutiny of these plans can raise people's consciousness about the nature of their jobs and why they are paid what they are paid. Women, in particular, often hold a low opinion of themselves or their work. A job evaluation plan that demonstrates the complexity and skill involved in their jobs can enhance women workers' understanding of the importance and value of their work. It is not surprising that many comparable-worth cases have arisen in the public sector, where pay hierarchies tend to be explicit and openly available. Claims of comparable worth force explicit discussion about relative pay rates. As such, they politicize wage setting in a new, possibly even revolutionary, way.

chapter 64

A Current Business Response to the Equal-Worth Concept

Richard E. Wing

FORMER DIRECTOR, CORPORATE COMPENSATION
DEPARTMENT, EASTMAN KODAK COMPANY,
ROCHESTER, NEW YORK

It is assumed that the reader understands the existing distinction between pay for "equal work" and pay for "equal worth" as standards for identifying pay discrimination. How does the equal-worth concept relate to internal equity? In a broad sense and with important differences in detail, the achievement of internal equity through job measurement and the equal-worth concept are compatible, if not identical, principles.[1] If this is correct, why is there so much opposition to the equal-worth concept as advocated by spokespersons for women's rights?

1. *Force of law.* The primary objection is to intruding the force of law into an intricate process for which there are no reliable economic or social guidelines beyond marketplace data. Opponents of equal worth visualize correctly the potential for the expenditure of huge sums of money in the unjustifiable and frustrating application of a nonquantifiable goal.

Job evaluation is not an exact science. The results of its application, while

---

[1] Compare these thoughts with the final section, "Commentary," of Chapter 63 and with the discussion of "Comparable Worth and Other Legislative and Judicial Initiatives"— relating to employment in the public sector—in Chapter 54.

practical in an environment conducive to negotiation between management and individuals or between union and management on a company by company basis, are not sufficiently reliable or valid as a guide to legally binding decisions by the courts. This conclusion is supported in the interim report of the Committee on Occupational Classification and Analysis of the National Research Council to the Equal Employment Opportunity Commission.

2. *Lack of definition.* The controversy over the introduction of equal worth in place of equal work as the test for pay discrimination is made more acute by the failure of its proponents to define their concept. Job evaluation is but one element of a multielement pay-determining process. Does the equal-worth concept apply to comparisons within one institution or company, or is it intended to apply across society? When arguing for their cause, proponents of the concept frequently illustrate their concerns by relating occupations, such as equating teachers to liquor store clerks or police officers. Extension of the concept to the entire national pay determination process is not a viable alternative.

The moderate voices proposing equal worth believe that evaluation plans can be designed to remove any potential inherent sex bias while being applied to all jobs to achieve a reasonably equal job worth for everyone. Other critics distrust job evaluation, market data, and essentially every current pay administration practice.

False Basis for Action   The existence of pay discrimination caused by occupational segregation and the extent to which it exists cannot be demonstrated by macro analysis of pay data for men and women. It is unfortunate that the theorists have been restricted to the use of aggregate data and have not had access to information on a company-by-company basis. Nevertheless, regardless of the type of analysis used, the extent of *wage* discrimination caused by occupational segregation is really unknown. Professor George T. Milkovich summarizes this problem:

> Thus, existing empirical formulations and methodologies have not adequately modelled the wage determination process and hence do not adequately account for the role of discrimination. This is principally due to: (1) the omission of significant work-related factors in most models; (2) the lack of focus on the employer-union and individual job interaction as the level of job analysis; (3) the absence of adequate measures for the factors; and (4) the lack of micro, publicly available data to perform such analysis.[2]

Harry V. Roberts, professor of statistics at the University of Chicago's Graduate School of Business, illustrates the effect of ignoring work-related factors in a broad occupational category.

> Suppose that in the early 1970s, a statistician is studying possible discrimination among flight personnel of Skyways Airlines. Direct regression is used. After statistical adjustment for a proxy, say years of schooling, the statistician finds

---

[2] George T. Milkovich, *Comparable Worth: Issues and Alternatives*, Equal Employment Advisory Council, Washington, D.C., 1980, p. 46.

that males have mean annual incomes that are $70,000 higher than those of females.

After finishing the study, the statistician learns that all the males are pilots and all the females are flight attendants.[3]

In the illustration chosen, the discriminatory factor may be occupational segregation coupled with lack of mobility for women to advance from flight attendant to pilot jobs. The large difference in average pay may not be pay discrimination; an appropriate analysis of job worth might still justify the pay difference between the two jobs.

Job differences within broad occupational categories of the type illustrated and differing distribution of women compared to men in lower-paying service industries account for a large part of the so-called pay discrimination reportedly calculated from macro occupational data comparing average rates of pay for women with average rates for men. The application of the equal-worth concept should have no direct effect on these reasons for the so-called pay gap.

Market Forces Are Ignored Under present wage-determining processes, employers must react to supply and demand factors in establishing rates of pay. Frequently, for nonexempt jobs, area pay differentials reflect local market conditions. These factors appear to be difficult, if not impossible, to accommodate in an equal-worth approach.

Much of the thrust for a new standard for measuring pay discrimination may be due to the same factors as those the Civil Rights Act of 1964 was designed to correct. Although slow in producing results reflected in average earnings, the affirmative action programs in effect and the upward mobility of women in the job market, coupled with free access to specialized educational preparation, offer a solution that allows corrective action within a relatively free wage-determining process. Such a solution avoids major economic dislocations and also avoids embroiling the courts in litigation for which decision-making standards are either lacking or too vague for quantitative action. There is the strong possibility, indeed the likelihood, that proponents of equal worth will not accept the current interpretations of the Equal Pay Act and Title VII of the Civil Rights Act. With constant pressure, they may well succeed in obtaining, through legislation or further legal interpretations, some form of an equal-worth standard for assessing pay discrimination. If it is assumed that this objective will be accomplished in about five years, the key question is, What can employers do to prepare for such an eventuality?

Listen to the Critics Review the more important writings that advocate the equal-worth standard. Statistical techniques applied to broad macro occupational groups may overstate the amount of pay discrimination based on sex, but some significant amount of sex discrimination must exist, fostered by too much attention to market data that may have perpetuated job relationships not supportable by careful internal analysis of job content.

---

[3] Harry V. Roberts, *Comparable Worth: Issues and Alternatives*, Equal Employment Advisory Council, Washington, D.C., 1980, p. 192.

Assess Your Liabilities   Most employers honestly have no idea of the extent to which pay discrimination on an equal-worth basis exists, or if it exists at all. The problem differs for various institutions. For a manufacturing company, the typical situation is one in which a single evaluation plan applies to factory production, skilled trades, and service jobs; a second plan applies to all nonexempt salaried jobs and covers clerical workers, computer operators, technicians, drafters, and designers; and a third plan applies to most exempt professional, administrative, outside-sales, and executive jobs.

Design a plan, or modify an existing evaluation plan, applicable to all nonexempt jobs. A different plan based on a horizontal distinction should prove acceptable to equal-worth advocates. It is the vertical stratification of plans that fails to satisfy their objectives. Obviously, the design objectives of the new plan include the attempt to avoid any sex bias to the degree that it is possible.

Include in the plan design a careful review of the methods of job analysis and job description now in use. These elements can also be a potential source of sex bias.

Involve about three well-qualified female persons, along with an equal number of males, in the design and testing of the plan. Without actually installing the plan, have the team evaluate the nonexempt jobs in your organization (if a large corporation, evaluate one division and extrapolate the results). You may find, upon analyzing the data, that your results reveal the situation illustrated in Figure 1.

The potential cost of implementing an equal-worth concept is obviously the cost of increasing the rates of clerical and related jobs to equal those of factory and related jobs. It is probable that an overall higher rate line for jobs paid on an incentive (work-measurement) basis will be acceptable providing the difference in pay is attributable to measured output.

There are a number of companies for which such a study will reveal that no cost obligations are necessary to achieve equality between nonexempt subgroups.

Obligations for Application of Equal-Worth Standard   If an equal-worth standard is adopted, there are a number of restrictions that should be placed on its application. Some can be defined, others await definition following the identification of potential problems.

FIGURE 1   An Evaluation of Nonexempt Jobs

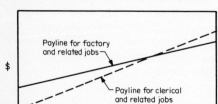

$

Payline for factory and related jobs

Payline for clerical and related jobs

Increasing job value

1. *Time to correct inequities.* A period of several years from the introduction of the new standard should be allowed for correcting inequities. In the case illustrated in Figure 1, equity can be achieved by accelerating annual increases to the lower-paid group and decelerating increases to the higher-paid group. In instances where negotiated rates make up the higher-paid wage structure, negotiating a lower-than-average annual increase for this group may be difficult. However, this latitude must be open to management. It cannot be assumed that all corrective action must be in the direction of immediately equating pay to the highest-paid jobs.

2. *Equal-worth decisions confined to one company or one institution and one geographic area.* No consideration should be given to equal-worth measurements between companies or organization entities. This means teachers' jobs can be viewed only within the framework of a single school district or political subdivision, nursing jobs only within one hospital. Any relationships outside the parent organization could not be litigated on an equal-worth basis. To do so would ignore the economic realities peculiar to each organization.

Area pay differentials in existence are substantial, and equal-worth decisions should avoid any attempt to modify or affect such differences. This poses a problem for legal decision makers. Knowledgeable survey specialists can identify as many as seven different labor markets within the Standard Metropolitan Statistical Area (as defined by the Bureau of Labor Statistics) comprising New York City and upper New Jersey. Other large metropolitan statistical areas also reflect multiple labor markets. The problem is further complicated by the fact that a single company may have three different locations within an area. Currently, rates of pay and the occupational groups may be different at each location. Based on an unbiased job evaluation plan applied to all nonexempt occupations and survey data, a company should be able to demonstrate that pay differences, when measured against an equal-worth standard, were due to area labor markets and not to sex discrimination.

3. *Seniority and performance.* Any equal-worth standard should allow differences in pay under merit pay plans where such differences are attributable to seniority or individual performance.

4. *Unattractive jobs.* Knowledgeable consultants have predicted that over the next decade, management will be forced to pay higher and higher relative rates for jobs that are unattractive to many people. This is a real factor currently being experienced by some organizations. Job prestige is not likely to be an acceptable evaluation factor, yet legal decision makers must cope with this problem using an equal-worth pay standard. Possibly, out-of-line rates can be justified if the offer refusal rate is above some reasonable norm. This is not an easy problem to solve, as the refusal rate for a given job can be artificially inflated by extending offers to individuals who are not qualified or interested in the job being offered.

5. *Supply and demand problems.* Engineers have been in short supply and high demand for approximately 30 of the past 36 years. Certain types of physical scientists and data processing systems personnel are in short supply. Under any standard for measuring pay discrimination, managers must have the right to meet marketplace demands for pay. To refuse this right merely exaggerates the problem. This is one of the most crucial obstacles to overcome if equal worth is to become the new pay standard.

6. Business reasons. There are sound, strategic business reasons for an organization to pay an entire occupation at rates that are out of line with an equal-worth pay determination. As an example, a company may decide that for the coming 10 years it will place special emphasis on its marketing function and seek outside experienced candidates who have demonstrated unusual performance in their fields for sales and advertising staff and executive jobs. The consequences of such a decision may be that the exempt personnel in marketing are paid considerably higher than their counterparts in other company activities. Management needs the right to make such decisions; yet measured by equal-worth standards, an inequity seems to exist. For sound business reasons, a legal approach must accommodate the need to pay some jobs at rates that are out of line with equal-worth considerations.

In summary, if an organization has made a real attempt to achieve equitable internal alignment of jobs and has documented the work, including the evaluation plan design methodology, it should be in a position to defend itself from charges of pay discrimination based on sex or ethnicity. Documentation of all the work undertaken to achieve equity of job values is a must.

It should be assumed that any response to the equal-worth clamor will be prudent and moderate. The economic consequences of any other response are too grave.

chapter 65

Administering Salaries in an Inflation-Prone Economy

Marsh W. Bates

PARTNER, THE HAY GROUP, CHICAGO, ILLINOIS

Inflation has been a key problem in most nations of the world during the 1970s and 1980s. The United States, while enjoying lower rates than many other economies, has nevertheless had uninterrupted inflation for the last 15 or more years. Even during recession periods, ours has proved to be an inflation-prone economy.

Inflation frustrates managements' efforts to allocate available salary dollars in an equitable fashion. The greater the degree of inflation and the more frequent the changes in rate of inflation, the greater the frustration. When inflation is accompanied by an economic slowdown in a commercial or geographic sector (e.g., autos, midwest), the effect is compounded as firms' salary positions in the marketplace erode.

Employee morale and output are threatened as performance-oriented salary programs become inflation-driven and as typical increases in salary lag behind published inflation rates. Employee acquisition and retention becomes an issue as competitive pay position necessarily diminishes in economically affected sectors. *Swings* in inflation, low to high and back again, cause further disruption, as labor contracts, salary actions, bonuses, and other pay measures fall out of step with economic change.

Salaries can be managed in an inflation-prone economy to reduce frustration and threat. This requires:

- Understanding the relationship of inflation and pay as it has existed
- Establishing methods of predicting and tracking inflation and salary movement in appropriate sectors
- Creating a philosophy of salary administration that properly balances response to inflation with pay for performance
- Implementing this philosophy through planned, controlled salary administration
- Communicating economic reality and salary philosophy to employees

Given that salaries are a major expenditure in most firms and are a significant tie between the organization and its only major resource that makes free decisions—people—salary programs must be seen by employees as responsive to economic times, and as fair, to serve the employer well.

UNDERSTANDING INFLATION AND PAY

The inflation indicator most associated with pay is the consumer price index (CPI). This index tracks the price of a market basket of goods and services required by several hypothetical "typical" families. It has come under fire in recent years as not being typical—not reflecting current home-, auto-, and food-purchasing patterns or income patterns emerging from multiple wage earners in a family.

The CPI overstates inflation actually felt by most salaried workers, yet it remains the index discussed by those employees. Its use in many major collective-bargaining agreements to determine cost-of-living adjustments (COLAs) causes further focus on the CPI. A typical cost-of-living adjustment formula is an increase of 1 cent per hour for each 0.3 points of increase in the CPI. Thus for every 10-point increase in the CPI, wages go up 33 cents. The 1979 to 1980 CPI change of 29.6 index points meant an automatic escalation of nearly $1 per hour in wages covered by such a formula. Frequently, adjustments equivalent to COLAs have been accorded salaried workers (on all or part of their salaries) to maintain parity with hourly wage earners. COLAs have provided automatic inflation-related increases to a highly visible segment of the American work force.

A potentially more valid view of inflation is the implicit price deflator (IPD) for the gross national product. This measure is used by the Department of Commerce to restate the gross national product—the value of all goods and services produced in the United States—in constant-dollar terms. Thus the IPD is a broader view of inflation than the CPI. Table 1 shows the difference in inflation for 1976 through 1980 using the two indicies.

Over the five-year period the CPI change was 53.2 percent and the IPD change was 41.1 percent. Adjustment by the former would increase a $20,000 salary to $30,640, while use of the latter would bring it to only $28,220, a total difference of 8.6 percent, largely created in the two high-inflation years. While the IPD does not consider inflation only in regard to wage earners (transfer

TABLE 1   Difference in Inflation, 1976–1980, in %

	1976	1977	1978	1979	1980	Cumulative
CPI change	5.8	6.5	7.7	11.3	13.6	53.2
IPD change	5.1	5.9	7.3	8.5	9.0	41.1
Difference	0.7	0.6	0.4	2.8	4.6	12.1

payments, such as social security, to non-wage earners have increased to nearly 10 percent of gross national product) and does not reflect the impact of imports (e.g., oil), an understanding of inflation from this broader perspective is necessary for salary program determination, implementation, and communication. In high-inflation times the CPI appears to overstate inflation.

The time span shown in Table 1 found salaries (and at higher levels, salaries plus bonuses) in industrial companies increasing, as illustrated in Table 2.

Relative to the CPI change for the same period, salaries fell some 3½ percent behind inflation. Salaries changed over 8 percent more than the IPD over the same period. Thus the story changes depending on the measure used. However, given "bracket creep"—more pay taxed at higher marginal rates—and increases in both the social security wage base and its tax rate, the purchasing power of people who remained in the same job-size category would not have increased. Their take-home pay would have increased by less than the IPD increase rate and by far less than the CPI increase rate.

Salary and bonus figures for the period are presented but afford less valid comparison. Bonuses at job size C were 22 percent in 1976 and 26 percent in 1981. Bonuses paid in 1976 were generally based on corporate performance for 1975—a recession year. It may be argued that 1976 salary plus bonus is low and that the salary-only indicator is more representative. Note that the foregoing compensation information covers industrials. Banks, insurance companies, and nonprofit organizations generally pay less at each job size. Their rate of change over the period was lower than industrial change except for banks at job size C, where the rate of change was faster.

The Hay Group's Compensation Information Center has analyzed each year's movement of cash compensation in industrial companies relative to CPI changes in the prior year. Over the longer term, we find that a reasonable pre-

TABLE 2   Increase in Salaries, 1976–1981

	Job Size		
	A	B	C
5/1/76 salary	$12,400	$30,800	$64,600
5/1/81 salary	$18,500	$46,000	$96,700
Difference	49.2%	49.4%	49.7%
5/1/76 salary and bonus	$12,600	$33,100	$78,400
5/1/81 salary and bonus	$18,500	$49,800	$122,300
Difference	49.2%	50.4%	56.0%

SOURCE: Compensation Information Center, The Hay Group.

diction of base-salary change for the following year can be calculated by adding 2.2 percentage points to 67 percent of the CPI change for the current year.

Next year's salary practice change (%)
= 0.67 × current CPI change (%) + 2.2%

The 20-year relationship (1961 to 1981) of these variables has a 0.88 coefficient of determination, which demonstrates that the formula provides a reasonable measure.

A somewhat less reliable predictor of next year's *total* cash compensation (salary plus bonus) is:

Next year's total compensation change (%)
= 0.60 × current CPI change (%)
+ 0.10 × change in return on equity[1] (%) + 2.6%

This relationship has a .68 coefficient of determination.

Each firm should know its salary-change rate relative to inflation, understand the pressures put on individual purchasing power, and, as necessary, be able to communicate facts about inflation and pay to its employees.

TRACKING AND PREDICTING PAY AND INFLATION

Salaries, as differentiated from wages, are an imperfect reflection of supply and demand for labor. Surveys by Research for Management, a member of The Hay Group, covering over 100,000 salaried employees in hundreds of firms, show that few employees know the competitive level of their firms' pay practices in the marketplace. Dissatisfaction with salary levels appears as frequently in high-paying firms as in lower-paying firms.

Employers have a much clearer view of the marketplace. Competitive information, scarce in the 1960s, became readily available during the 1970s as salary surveys became more common, sophisticated, and used. Company participation in salary surveys, once tentative, is frequent and willing. Some surveys covering management, professional, and technical positions are conducted by one or more of the subject companies; but most authoritative surveys are performed by consulting firms or associations. Surveys covering clerical salaries and hourly wages (more localized in nature, to reflect the relevant labor market) are typically (1) sponsored by a local firm or association, (2) extracted from Bureau of Labor Statistics data or, (3) conducted and maintained by consulting firms.

Criteria for judging the appropriateness of a survey to an individual firm's needs include:

- Relevance of companies and jobs surveyed
- Relevance of the labor market covered (e.g., national versus local)
- Availability of subset information from the survey data base
- Context of the survey—relating to the past and the future
- Assurance that jobs of the same nature and scope are being compared

---

[1]Fortune 500.

- Continuity that allows for consistency of reporting and interpretation
- Format that facilitates management and employee communication
- Cost that is reflective of value received

Many major organizations use more than one survey for each employee population group to assure an accurate view of the marketplace. A firm's current position against survey information and predictions of change in the compensation marketplace are two critical elements in the development of a salary philosophy and a salary administration program. This knowledge and ability to predict are even more crucial in times of rapid inflation or change in the rate of inflation.

Tracking and predicting inflation is necessary, since a large percent of recent salary change has been in response to inflation. The predictive portion of salary surveys includes inflation as a major element, and firms should know the probable rate of change in employee purchasing power in order to prepare a planned response and to articulate this response to employees.

CPI and IPD changes are reported and predicted regularly (as are other indicators). Predictions by the nation's senior economists and by the best econometric models are published regularly in business periodicals. More detailed information should be available through a firm's planning or finance functions or its financial counselors.

SALARY PHILOSOPHY—RESPONSIVE TO PERFORMANCE OR THE ECONOMY?

"Our company will offer salary opportunity equal to the prevailing practices in the communities and markets from which we draw employees." Statements such as this frequently form the totality of a firm's written salary philosophy. While such statements continue to be desirable, in times of high inflation they do not go far enough. Management must think through another substantial issue. Will scarce salary-increase dollars be devoted to inflation fighting, or will the concept of pay for performance continue to prevail? A similar issue exists in periods of reduced inflation accompanied by recession. Will scarce *working-capital* dollars be withheld from the salary program, or will the concept of pay for performance continue to prevail?

The early 1970s found the CPI increasing at an annual rate of about 5 percent. Records of the Compensation Information Center of The Hay Group show that raises for par performers during that period were 7 percent annually, for outstanding performers 12 percent. Similar salary treatment for par and outstanding performers in the 10 percent and over CPI environment of 1980 and 1981 has resulted in average salary practice[2] movement of about 10 percent and average increases to outstanding performers of about 12.5 percent. This represents a change in performance and reward leverage, as shown in Table 3.

---

[2] Hay Compensation Information Center surveys show that actual overall salary movement by participating firms exceeds the planned percentage. This is due in part to a tendency to give average performers more favorable ratings than they deserve.

TABLE 3 *Performance and Reward Leverage, Early 1970s to 1981, in %*

	Early 1970s	1980–1981
1. Annual CPI change (approx.)	5	10
2. Annual salary increase, average performer (approx.)	7	10
3. Line 2 as % of line 1	140	100
4. Annual salary increase, outstanding performer (approx.)	12	12.5
5. Line 4 as % of line 1	240	125
6. Line 4 as % of line 2	170	125

Table 3 shows the following:

■ An increase in inflation was accompanied by an increase in salary adjustments, but almost all was given to the average performer; awards to outstanding employees remained about constant (lines 2 and 4).

■ The premium paid to outstanding (versus average) performers declined from 70 to 25 percent (line 6—each number minus 100 percent).

■ An increase in inflation (productivity also flattened) was accompanied by a reduction in the leverage of the average pay versus inflation increase from 40 percent to zero (line 3—each number minus 100 percent).

■ An increase in inflation was accompanied by a reduction in the leverage of pay versus inflation rate for outstanding performers—from 140 to 25 percent (line 5—each number minus 100 percent).

The prolonged recession beginning in late 1981 put even greater pressure on the performance-reward relationship in firms that were forced to implement pay freezes, where bonuses were reduced or eliminated, and where the unproductive became unemployed. A dramatically lowered inflation rate was accompanied by lower salary-increase budgets. Significant premiums for high performance were, in most companies, unaffordable.

The employee who has experienced both the 1970s and 1980s must recognize the difference in rate of pay change versus rate of inflation. The outstanding performer must recognize that the premium for excellence has diminished.

Each firm must make the hard philosophical choice of whether inflation (or recession) will drive it to relative equality of salary increase for employees or whether it will continue significant differentiation based on individual performance. The latter choice, in turn, offers two options: whether significant differentiation will be financed within existing, tight salary-increase budgets (which requires taking from low performers to give to high performers) or will be financed by the allocation of additional funds for this purpose.

Over the longer term the philosophical choice would appear to impact dramatically on the nature of the salaried work force in an organization and, therefore, on the nature of the organization itself. A pay program that provides little differentiation for high performers (other than through promotion) and that provides little real gain in purchasing power should cause dissatisfaction to high performers and give them impetus to leave. Average performers would be relatively unaffected, while low performers would applaud the egalitarian approach and would stay.

A pay program that provides significant differentiation in awards, based on performance, should have the opposite effect—assuming it is based on a normal-sized salary-increase budget. High performers would get large increases, funded by slightly lower increases to average performers and dramatically lower increases to low performers. Economic encouragement is provided for high performers to stay and for low performers to leave.

This latter approach is less comfortable for management, as it requires the fortitude to appraise performance accurately and to manage salaries, rather than claiming lack of funds or choosing the course of least resistance, increases to all. However, it retains in the organization the talent necessary for growth and change. The philosophy of pay for performance was battered by inflation in the 1970s and early 1980s and further battered by the recession that followed. It is still the philosophy that promotes excellence.

IMPLEMENTING PAY FOR PERFORMANCE DURING ECONOMIC ADVERSITY

How long should it take an outstanding performer to achieve outstanding pay status? How long should it take a par performer to reach an average pay status? Each firm must choose its own answer and manage its pay program to achieve that plan.

The typical salary range employed by commercial organizations for management, technical, and professional jobs has a maximum that is 150 percent of the minimum and a target job rate most frequently called the "range midpoint," as shown in Figure 1. The range is adjusted periodically in response to inflation, labor supply, or a conscious change in market competitiveness of the pay plan. Most major employers have adjusted their ranges annually during the 10 years up to 1982 in response to surging inflation.

To move good performers upward through the range, toward the appropriate performance-related levels, their salary increases must, of course, exceed the range adjustment itself. Thus if a firm adjusts ranges upward by 8 percent, an increase larger than that percent will be required to advance an individual within the job's salary range.

FIGURE 1 Typical Salary Range

Maximum	120%	Target rate for outstanding performers
Midpoint	100%	Target rate for par performers
Minimum	80%	Entry rate for job newcomers

Prior to the late 1970s, with the exception of the period of wage controls in the early 1970s, this was accomplished with vigor. For example, during 1971 and 1972 when the CPI increase was approximately 4 percent per year, Hay compensation comparison data show that firms moved their salary ranges upward by about 4½ percent per year. Further, salary-increase guides in these firms called for a 6 to 7 percent increase for average performers and an increase of 12 percent for outstanding performers whose salaries were low in the range established for their jobs. (Figure 2).

Had this practice continued over time (4½ percent range movement, 6½ percent to average and 12 percent to outstanding performers), average performers would have moved from the range minimum to the midpoint in 10 years and outstanding performers would have been advanced through the entire range in six years. Outstanding performers' pretax earnings were increasing at about double the rate of average performers' and were observably outpacing the change in the CPI.

By the end of the decade the CPI change was in excess of 10 percent per year. Companies were increasing salary range midpoints at the rate of 8 to 9 percent per year (10 percent and over in 1980 to 1981) and salary increases were allocated as shown in Figure 3.

Movement within the salary range for average performers had slowed or stopped, and it would now take an outstanding performer 11 years to move from minimum to maximum. Pretax income advances for the average performer fell below the CPI change but equaled the IPD change. The outstanding performer had lost most of the earlier rate of acceleration of earnings versus the average performer. Lacking promotion, most employees stood still or lost ground.

What was needed to retain true pay for performance in a time of scarce dollars and high inflation (e.g., 10 percent) was a salary range increase of 8 percent, reflecting scarcity of funds, and a salary-increase guide that provided:

- No increase for poor performers (0 percent)
- Range increase plus 2 percent for average performers (10 percent)
- Range increase plus 4½ percent for above-average performers (12½ percent)
- Range increase plus 8 percent for outstanding performers (16 percent)

This would produce the effect shown in Figure 4.

The driving force of salary treatment becomes performance differentiation and movement through range, not inflation-based range adjustment and resul-

---

FIGURE 2   Salary-Increase Guide—1971

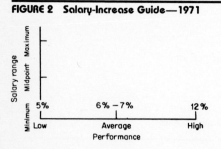

FIGURE 3   Salary-Increase Guide—1979

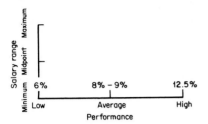

tant uniformity of salary treatment. This can be expressed in terms of compa-ratios (which equal salary as a percent of range midpoint). Table 4 illustrates the proposed recognition of the different levels of performance over a period of years for employees who start out at 80 percent of the range midpoint. The progression within the range, shown in the table, would be in addition to what-ever range movement is adopted.

An inexperienced newcomer would normally start at or near the minimum. A proven individual hired at the midpoint would either have to perform better than average or, if deemed average, would receive range adjustment level increases. An experienced individual hired at 90 percent of the midpoint and providing average performance would reach the midpoint in five years. Below-average performance should not be tolerated or rewarded beyond the normal probationary period.

Table 4 shows the maximum time it should take for in-range movement. Though outstanding performers will frequently be promoted *prior* to full move-ment through the range, the latter possibility must be provided for as an alter-native. Note that the above concept also applies to raises that are given as a percent of midpoint rather than of salary. Basing raises on the midpoint is a less common practice and favors employees low in the salary range.

How does a firm move its ranges 8 percent and provide 10 to 16 percent raises to the majority of its employees? Range movement should be indicative of the amount of new funds management will commit to the employee group. By authorizing an 8 percent range movement, management should be agreeing to

FIGURE 4   Effect of Salary-Increase Guide and 8% Salary Increase Budget

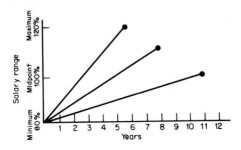

TABLE 4   Planned Compa-Ratios and Performance   (Range Movement Percent = R)

Year	Average, R + 2%	Above average, R + 4½%	Outstanding, R + 8%
0	80.0	80.0	80.0
1	81.6	83.6	86.4
2	83.2	87.4	93.3
3	84.9	91.3	100.8
4	86.6	95.4	108.8
5	88.3	99.7	117.5
6	90.1	104.2	126.9
7	91.9	108.9	
8	93.7	113.7	
9	95.6		
10	97.5		
11	99.5		

a year-end payroll (for the same number of employees in the same jobs) that is 108 percent of the beginning payroll. This is true, of course, with any level of range movement. (See also "Moving Target" in Chapter 20.)

The salary-increase budget should usually exceed the range adjustment amount. This is because funds recovered through personnel shifts should, in large part, be returned to the salary program. Salary recovery (also called "slippage" or "turnover recovery") occurs when higher-paid employees leave the organization and are replaced, through promotion or hiring, by lower-paid employees. In some situations, of course, the recovery will be negative.

The Hay Group's Compensation Information Center surveys amounts and use of recovery. Firms report that salary recovery averages 1.8 percent of exempt salaries. However, only about 20 percent of respondents report a return of recovered funds to the salary program. When funds are not returned to the program, overall salaries fall and the companies' compa-ratios fall.

Salary recovery that occurs while jobs remain unfilled (several days or weeks at lower job levels, frequently months at senior levels) should not be returned to the program, as this would inflate year-end payroll. Rather, these recovered funds should be used to offset recruiting, orientation, and training expenses associated with turnover.

If the recovery that can be returned to the salary program is presumed to be 1½ percent of salaries, the salary-increase budget in an 8 percent range adjustment year will be 9½ percent. This does not mean that the average increase need be 9½ percent, since some employees will not deserve increases (i.e., poor performers or employees higher than appropriate in the job range). The average increase to those getting increases will be higher than 9½ percent.

Table 5 shows how a typical population might be distributed and rewarded. In the example, the average increase to employees receiving adjustments is 10 percent, as 95 percent of the payroll shared a 9.5 percent salary-increase budget. This average increase can itself be raised by a tougher performance assessment, causing more people to be given minimal increases or no increase at all.

The example assumes an 8 percent range movement, although it can be seen

TABLE 5   Salary-Increase Budget—Distribution and Reward of Typical Population.

Category	% of initial payroll	% increase	Increase as % of initial payroll
Outstanding performers below range maximum	5	16	0.8
Above-average employees below appropriate level	15	12.5	1.9
Average employees below range midpoint	50	10.0	5.0
Employees paid at an appropriate level	15	8.0	1.2
Probationary, part-year, or slightly overpaid employees	10	6.0	0.6
Below-average or overpaid employees	5	0.0	0.0
	100		9.5
Less salary recovery			1.5
Annualized net payroll increase			8.0

that the concept works for any degree of range movement. For instance, if the range movement was only 2 percent and the salary recovery was only 1 percent (since salary recovery tends to reduce during recessions), the subtotal in the last column would be 3 percent rather than 9.5 percent. (The salary recovery would be shown as 1 percent, and the annualized net payroll increase as 2 percent). The allocation in the "% increase" column would have to be reduced accordingly and more concentrated among the better performers.

The process can be worked in reverse as a budgeting effort. It can be integrated into most major firms' human resource systems. Best, the process provides high performers with recognition, reward, and encouragement to stay and low performers with recognition and encouragement to change or leave.

COMMUNICATING TO EMPLOYEES

Too much current employee communication about organizations' salary administration is ad hoc. If the employee asks or the manager is willing, some interaction on the salary program may occur. Formal programs of employee communication do exist in many organizations, covering *how* salaries are administered, but too few tell *why*. When an organization mounts a campaign to tell why certain macro decisions are made, it too frequently comes off as propaganda rather than economic education. When the purpose for micro decisions is communicated, the campaign is viewed as cost containment.

Communication about compensation should not be a campaign, but rather an ongoing, expected part of an employee's relationship with the firm. Economic education should express the firm's beliefs about the future and about where its employees will fit in the future. Communicating that your firm's salary program is inflation-driven is not positive to the high achievers who will make the firm different. On the other hand, communicating that pay for performance is still an objective in times of economic change *is* positive. To be able to make this positive communication a firm must:

- Believe that the employee has the right to know the compensation opportunity afforded by the job
- Communicate to the employee the types of performance that will be considered poor, par, and outstanding
- Have a performance planning, appraisal, and communication process that allows differentiation to be made and accepted
- Have a performance-based salary program that produces results which are seen and felt within the organization
- Be willing to manage the work force through valid performance appraisal and responsive salary-increase allocation, creating turnover where it should occur.

The employer should then provide regular information on the state of the economy and the firm's resultant position. This information should be translated into the firm's coming investment in capital goods, technology, material, and people. The firm should take credit for its response—with assurances to average and above-average performers that their rewards will be continuing and appropriate within the company's ability to pay.

part L

Total
Remuneration

chapter 66

Reward Management:

The Integrating Process of Human Resources Strategy

Daniel L. Stix

GENERAL PARTNER, THE HAY GROUP,
PHILADELPHIA, PENNSYLVANIA

The only "right" compensation is that amount and form which an organization is willing and able to pay for required work and which is acceptable to people willing and able to do the work. Reward management techniques and surveys give perspective on the consequences of levels and patterns of pay and benefits but don't yield unique answers. Techniques and surveys of the kind described in this handbook should not create fixed cost patterns and operational constraints. Compensation must be managed as a variable, flowing from the overall strategy and success of the enterprise.

It also must be managed in a way that reflects and is consistent with the culture of the enterprise. Culture is often described as the elements that give unique character to the organization, including its policies and practices, and the priorities and personal styles of key individuals.

The rewards offered to employees, and the occasions for those rewards, are among the most visible and potent manifestations of the organization's culture. They must be designed to drive, reinforce, and sometimes alter the culture in ways that support the organization's goals. Reward management, then, can be defined as the systematic process governing the exchange of all forms of direct and indirect compensation that an organization grants for the results, efforts, qualifications, and capabilities which employees provide, within the context of the organization's culture and overall strategy. By contrast, other processes of human resources management are placement—including recruitment, selection, transfer, and separation; work direction—including communication, training, development, and performance appraisal; and employment relationships—including policy design and control and employment records. The reward process symbolizes and represents all aspects of employer-employee relationships and the results they produce.

Traditionally, the primary sources of corporate direction for the reward process have been personal philosophies of owners and executives. The process has also been shaped by competitive practices and by employment and tax laws. It has been modified by preferences of individual employees and of organized labor. It has been augmented or constrained by current patterns of financial success. However, such forming and modifying forces have not held any *necessary* relationship to strategy. Judgments and actions may have been humane or harsh, wise or foolish, rational or emotional, but the basic question—"To what extent do they support the standards for human performance and cost which are implicit in the enterprise's strategy?"—was rarely asked and almost never answered. A linkage between the strategy of the enterprise and its reward process is needed.

HUMAN RESOURCE RESULTS

To build such a linkage, the areas relating to people which must produce results are:

- *Productivity:* Having results actually produced by individuals in performance of their jobs
- *Capability:* Having enough people with the skills that are appropriate for the required work
- *Cost:* Having expenditures for employees that are consistent with operating economics
- *Welfare:* Having working conditions and contexts that provide acceptable levels of safety, comfort, and security
- *Compliance:* Having employment processes, practices, and relationships that meet appropriate regulatory standards
- *Order:* Having clear patterns for general and individual employer-employee relationships

STRATEGIC HUMAN RESOURCE ISSUES

Specific requirements for human resource results derive from resolutions to critical sets of issues which are inherent within the strategy of each enterprise:

- **Work context.**   Different products and services, markets and technologies require different key occupations. They also require different emphases on individual excellence versus superior teamwork. Additionally, they call for differences in the kinds of input that employees must produce. Some enterprises place greater emphasis on disciplined applications of energy and effort; others place greater emphasis on imagination, judgment, and craftsmanship.

■ **Continuity.** Different types of enterprises have longer or shorter performance cycles for investments and returns. In some cases there are natural events or technical processes (the life of a mine or a plant) that structure the necessary stability or discontinuity of employment and organizational functioning. In other cases, processes of human resource management must be designed in ways that yield the necessary degree of continuity.

■ **Economics.** Some enterprises have patterns of demand that give greater pricing flexibility than others. There are also differences among enterprises in requirements for capital investments to support and improve human productivity. These differences in the inherent economics of the enterprise translate into greater or lesser emphasis on labor costs and broaden or constrict the range of alternative patterns that can be applied for human resource management.

■ **Values.** Different structures are needed for ownership, governance, participation, and support. Differences in obligations to, and expectations for, employees derive from the value systems that are associated with those structures.

REWARD PROCESS CRITERIA

In broad terms, the actions necessary to implement the reward process in order to produce expected results required by the strategy of the enterprise (as detailed in this handbook) are job identification, job measurement, pricing, reward administration, and communications. A wide variety of techniques and practices can be used independently or in combination for each of those actions. Each pattern of techniques and practices has advocates and critics, advantages and disadvantages. In addition to how effectively the reward management process achieves required results, there are other criteria, listed below, which should be considered in the design and execution of the reward process.

■ **Internal equity.** The reward process should provide for differences in compensation in relation to differences in the contributions by individuals to the enterprise. These differences may be associated with job requirements and opportunity or with individual effort, qualifications, proficiency, or loyalty.

■ **External competitiveness.** The reward process should provide for pricing of jobs and performance at levels that are competitive with alternative employment opportunities of desired and prospective employees.

■ **Employee acceptance.** The reward process should reinforce other forms of communication regarding what the enterprise wants employees to do. It also should fit with individual and group concepts of "proper treatment."

■ **Legal acceptance.** The reward process should be acceptable within boundaries or limits set by the societies within which the enterprise functions.

■ **Operating economics.** The reward process should maintain levels and rates of expenditure that conform to funding patterns of the enterprise.

■ **Efficient administration.** The maintenance and application of the reward process should be integrated as much as possible with other forms of necessary work within the organization; the process should be simple enough to be understood fully by users and affected individuals.

There are many different elements within the reward process for each enterprise. Criteria to select individual and combined elements must have a dynamic balance. They cannot usually be applied equally, and they require continual refinement to keep them properly aligned with the emphasis of the organization. However, a reward process that fails to consider most of the preceding criteria is likely to be ineffective.

OPTIONS AND TRADEOFFS

In the reward process the options and tradeoffs that support a human resource strategy driven by the total strategy of the enterprise are defined by continuing responses to the following questions.

Strategic Issues

▪ What job designs and performance standards reflecting the state of relevant technologies, the relative availability of capital and labor, the required time frame for payout, and the probability of success of individuals versus teams must be considered?

▪ What are the labor and talent markets from which employees who meet specifications for the enterprise are likely to be drawn?

▪ In order to attract, retain, and motivate employees with required qualifications to meet performance standards, what level in each market sector should the enterprise attempt to achieve in its reward structures?

▪ If all employees are not to be paid identically, what justifications for differential treatment should be accepted?

▪ What mix of direct and indirect compensation elements should be adopted for each different group of employees?

Tactical Issues

▪ At a given time, relative to historic and projected patterns of success, what can the organization afford to pay and what will employees accept?

▪ What symbolic circumstances relating to the organization or employees may affect the perceived value and acceptability of rewards?

▪ What immediate or projected economic circumstances may alter the level of rewards that the organization can provide and employees will accept?

▪ What supply and demand dynamics relating to quality and qualifications of labor and talent may affect ultimate rewards?

▪ To bridge the gap between *strategically* appropriate compensation practices and current or past practices, what patterns of action are required?

Group or Individual Application Issues

▪ How can general reward patterns be adapted to specific performance, qualifications, characteristics, availability or special leverage of individuals or particular groups?

▪ What patterns of action for compensation are required by the nature and extent of labor organization in the corporation?

▪ What social values or regulatory pressures may affect acceptability of reward actions?

SUMMARY

Each industry and each national or regional economy tends to have characteristic human resource strategies. However, each unique enterprise gains part of its strength by selective variation from the pattern of its industry—in relation to its own positioning and to particular strategic requirements. Therefore, the reward process for an enterprise must include decisions about work design and markets and about selection, design, and implementation of reward elements to be included. The process must be continually tested against criteria of sound reward management. It must integrate other human resources–related management processes to produce human resource results that are required by the general strategy of the enterprise.

There is no singularly "right" pattern or level of compensation. By making creative use of the opportunity for variation and competitive advantage, executives can do more about the effectiveness of the human resources in their enterprise than by dealing with virtually any other set of issues. Rewards, which symbolize the culture of the enterprise, should be designed to link the directional requirements of the organization with the performance of the individuals who must produce its results.

Index